American Literary Scholarship 1995

American Literary Scholarship
An Annual 1995

Edited by Gary Scharnhorst

Essays by David M. Robinson, Leland S. Person,
Kent P. Ljungquist, John Samson, Kenneth M. Price,
Alan Gribben, Greg W. Zacharias, Michael Coyle,
Laura Cowan, Philip Cohen, Albert J. DeFazio III,
William J. Scheick, Robert E. Burkholder, Lawrence J. Oliver,
Jo Ann Middleton, Catherine Calloway, Jerome Klinkowitz,
Timothy Materer, Lorenzo Thomas, James J. Martine,
Gary Lee Stonum, Daniel Royot, Christoph Irmscher,
Algerina Neri, Keiko Beppu, Jan Nordby Gretlund,
Elisabeth Herion-Sarafidis, Hans Skei, and Antonio C. Márquez

Duke University Press   *Durham and London*   *1997*

LC 65-19450   ISBN 0-8223-1952-7

Printed in the United States of America

on acid-free paper ∞

Contents

Foreword

The longevity and unique significance of *American Literary Scholarship*, now in its 33rd annual incarnation, is a tribute to the hundreds of Americanists who have devoted their time to this project over the years, foremost among them its founding editor James Woodress. In the first sentence of his foreword to *ALS 1963*, the first volume in this series, Woodress explained that the "idea for this book originated when I returned from a year in Europe and was overwhelmed by the quantity of scholarship produced in my absence." I am confident that the sheer bulk of published criticism in the field, inclusively defined, continues to justify the project. Whereas the *MLA Bibliography* a third of a century ago listed some 1,500 items in American literary studies, the most recent bibliography lists some 5,000 items. Correspondingly, the annual has more than doubled in length over the years, from 240 pages in 1963 to well over 500 pages today. Of necessity, and the point cannot be emphasized enough, *ALS* is a selective review of this scholarship. For the record, the task of each of the 30 contributors to *ALS* is increasingly complicated by the fluid contours of literary study. While the scholarly trends in 1963, in the heyday of the New Criticism, were simple and straightforward, they are remarkably various and assorted today.

The ongoing reconfiguration of *ALS* chapter coverage is focused this year on the sections formerly entitled "Foreign Scholarship." Now retitled less felicitously but more accurately "Scholarship in Languages Other Than English," chapter 21 now features a section on "Spanish Language Contributions" written by Antonio Márquez of the University of New Mexico; it treats both American literature in the Spanish language and Spanish-language scholarship. Other chapters have changed hands. Kent P. Ljungquist, Worcester Polytechnic Institute, returns to the "Poe" chapter this year, spelling Benjamin F. Fisher; John Samson,

Texas Tech University, contributes "Melville," replacing John Wenke;
Kenneth M. Price, College of William and Mary, takes over "Whitman
and Dickinson" from Martha Nell Smith; Alan Gribben, Auburn University at Montgomery, assumes "Mark Twain" from Tom Quirk; Lawrence J. Oliver, Texas A & M University, contributes the chapter
"Late-19th-Century Literature," replacing Laura E. Skandera-Trombley;
and Keiko Beppu, Kobe College, takes her routine turn with the "Japanese Contributions" section of chapter 21.

As usual, too, the changes will continue. Next year *ALS* will feature
both a pair of new and a pair of returning contributors. Priscilla Wald
and Mark Patterson, University of Washington, will take over the difficult "Themes, Topics, Criticism" chapter from Gary Lee Stonum, Case
Western Reserve University. Benjamin F. Fisher, University of Mississippi, and Richard Hocks, University of Missouri, will each return
after a brief hiatus to "Poe" and "Henry James," respectively. We express
our sincere gratitude to the retiring contributors. Would but we could
award them service ribbons. *ALS* chapters are labors of love, their authors
often sacrificing their summer months for little more tangible reward
than royalties sufficient to dine out once or twice.

Authors and publishers can assist in the production of *ALS* and insure
its comprehensiveness by forwarding offprints and review copies, whatever the year of publication, to Professor David J. Nordloh, Department
of English, Indiana University, Bloomington, IN 47405.

We are grateful, too, for the support, both moral and budgetary, of
many departmental and college-level administrators at the University of
New Mexico and Indiana University. I am also indebted to Andy Smith,
my research assistant; to Terence Ford and his staff in the MLA Center
for Bibliographical Services for a preprint of the annual *MLA Bibliography*; and to the unflappable Bob Mirandon and Pam Morrison of Duke
University Press, who prime the engine and oil the gears. Without their
calm influence and sober advice, the editors and the annual would be
much the poorer.

Gary Scharnhorst
University of New Mexico

Key to Abbreviations

Festschriften, Essay Collections, and Books Discussed in More Than One Chapter

America and the Sea / Haskell S. Springer, ed., *America and the Sea: A Literary History* (Georgia)

American Anatomies / Robyn Wiegman, *American Anatomies: Theorizing Race and Gender* (Duke)

American Diversity, American Identity / John K. Roth, ed., *American Diversity, American Identity: The Lives and Works of 145 Writers Who Define the American Experience* (Holt)

American Poetry: The Modernist Ideal / Clive Bloom and Brian Docherty, eds., *American Poetry: The Modernist Ideal* (St. Martin's)

The American Roman Noir / William Marling, *The American Roman Noir: Hammett, Cain, and Chandler* (Georgia)

The American Trilogy, 1900–1937 / John C. Waldmeir, *The American Trilogy, 1900–1937: Norris, Dreiser, Dos Passos and the History of Mammon* (Locust Hill)

American Women Short Story Writers /

Julie Brown, ed., *American Women Short Story Writers: A Collection of Critical Essays* (Garland)

American Women Writers and the Work of History / Nina Baym, *American Women Writers and the Work of History: 1790–1860* (Rutgers)

Ariadne's Lives / Nina da Vinci, *Ariadne's Lives* (Fairleigh Dickinson)

Becoming Canonical in American Poetry / Timothy Morris, *Becoming Canonical in American Poetry* (Illinois)

Better Red / Constance Coiner, *Better Red: The Writing and Resistance of Tillie Olsen and Meridel Le Sueur* (Oxford)

Beyond the Pleasure Dome / Sue Vice, Matthew Campbell, and Tim Armstrong, eds., *Beyond the Pleasure Dome: Writing and Addiction from the Romantics* (Sheffield, 1994)

Bibliographical Guide to the Study of Western American Literature / Richard W. Etulain and N. Jill Howard, eds., *A Bibliographical Guide to the Study of Western American Literature* (New Mexico)

The Cambridge Companion to Ameri-can Realism and Naturalism / Don-ald Pizer, ed., *The Cambridge Companion to American Realism and Naturalism: From Howells to London* (Cambridge)

"The Changing Same" / Deborah E. McDowell, *"The Changing Same": Black Women's Literature, Criticism, and Theory* (Indiana)

The City in African-American Literature / Yoshinobu Hakutani and Robert Butler, eds., *The City in African-American Literature* (Fair-leigh Dickinson)

Cloak and Dagger Fiction / Myron J. Smith, Jr., and Terry White, eds., *Cloak and Dagger Fiction: An An-notated Guide to Spy Thrillers* (Greenwood)

A Common Life / David Laskin, *A Common Life: Four Generations of American Literary Friendship and Influence* (Simon & Schuster)

Constituting Americans / Priscilla Wald, *Constituting Americans: Cul-tural Anxiety and Narrative Form* (Duke)

Critical Response to H. G. Wells / William J. Scheick, ed., *The Crit-ical Response to H. G. Wells* (Green-wood)

Daughters of the Great Depression / Laura Hapke, *Daughters of the Great Depression: Women, Work, and Fiction in the American 1930s* (Georgia)

The Delegated Intellect / Donald E. Morse, ed., *The Delegated Intellect: Emersonian Essays on Literature, Science, and Art in Honor of Don Gifford* (Peter Lang)

The Disobedient Writer / Nancy A. Walker, *The Disobedient Writer: Women and Narrative Tradition* (Texas)

"Doers of the Word" / Carla L. Peter-son, *"Doers of the Word": African American Women Speakers and Writers in the North (1830–1880)* (Oxford)

Dream Revisionaries / Darby Lewes, *Dream Revisionaries: Gender and Genre in Women's Utopian Fiction, 1870–1920* (Alabama)

Ellen Glasgow: New Perspectives / Dor-othy M. Scura, ed., *Ellen Glasgow: New Perspectives* (Tennessee)

The Environmental Imagination / Lawrence Buell, *The Environmen-tal Imagination: Thoreau, Nature Writing, and the Foundation of American Culture* (Harvard)

The Errant Art of Moby-Dick / William V. Spanos, *The Errant Art of* Moby-Dick: *The Canon, the Cold War, and the Struggle for American Studies* (Duke)

The Ethnography of Manners / Nancy Bentley, *The Ethnography of Man-ners: Hawthorne, James, Wharton* (Cambridge)

Fables of Subversion / Steven Weisen-burger, *Fables of Subversion: Satire and the American Novel, 1930–1980* (Georgia)

Facing Facts / David E. Shi, *Facing Facts: Realism in American Thought and Culture, 1850–1920* (Oxford)

Fathering the Nation / Russ Castro-novo, *Fathering the Nation: Ameri-can Genealogies of Slavery and Freedom* (Calif.)

Forgiving the Boundaries / Terry Caesar, *Forgiving the Boundaries: Home as Abroad in American Travel Writing* (Georgia)

Forked Tongues? / Ann Massa and Alistair Stead, eds., *Forked Tongues? Comparing Twentieth-Century British and American Literature* (Longman, 1994)

From Outlaw to Classic / Alan Golding, *From Outlaw to Classic: Canons in American Poetry* (Wisconsin)

The Grief Taboo / Pamela A. Boker, *The Grief Taboo in American Literature: Loss and Prolonged Adolescence in Twain, Melville, and Hemingway* (NYU)

Having Our Way / Harriet Pollack, ed., *Having Our Way: Women Rewriting Tradition in Twentieth-Century America* (Bucknell)

How We Found America / Magdalena J. Zaborwska, *How We Found America: Reading Gender Through East European Immigrant Narratives* (No. Car.)

Images of Central Europe / Waldemar Zacharasiewicz, ed., *Images of Central Europe in Travelogues and Fiction by North American Writers* (Stauffenburg)

International Women's Writing / Anne E. Brown and Marjanne E. Goozé, eds., *International Women's Writing: New Landscapes of Identity* (Greenwood)

Literature Against Philosophy / Mark Edmundson, *Literature Against Philosophy, Plato to Derrida: A Defence of Poetry* (Cambridge)

The Literature of Labor and the Labors of Literature / Cindy Weinstein,

The Literature of Labor and the Labors of Literature: Allegory in Nineteenth-Century American Fiction (Cambridge)

A Living of Words / Susan Albertine, ed., *A Living of Words: American Women in Print Culture* (Tennessee)

Los Angeles in Fiction / David Fine, ed., *Los Angeles in Fiction: A Collection of Essays, Revised Edition* (New Mexico)

Modern American Short Story Sequences / J. Gerald Kennedy, ed., *Modern American Short Story Sequences: Composite Fictions and Fictive Communities* (Cambridge)

Modernist Alchemy / Timothy Materer, *Modernist Alchemy: Poetry and the Occult* (Cornell)

The Modern Voice in American Poetry / William Doreski, *The Modern Voice in American Poetry* (Florida)

The Music in African-American Fiction / Robert H. Cataliotti, *The Music in African-American Fiction* (Garland)

Narrative Ethics / Adam Z. Newton, *Narrative Ethics* (Harvard)

National Identities and Post-Americanist Narratives / Donald E. Pease, ed., *National Identities and Post-Americanist Narratives* (Duke)

The Naturalistic Inner-City Novel in America / James R. Giles, *The Naturalistic Inner-City Novel in America: Encounters with the Fat Man* (So. Car.)

Nietzsche in American Literature and Thought / Manfred Pütz, ed., *Nietzsche in American Literature and Thought* (Camden House)

Scheming Women: Poetry, Privilege, and the Politics of Subjectivity (SUNY)

Southern Women's Writing, Colonial to Contemporary / Mary Louis Weaks and Carolyn Perry, eds., *Southern Women's Writing, Colonial to Contemporary* (Florida)

Subjects and Citizens / Michael Moon and Cathy N. Davidson, eds., *Subjects and Citizens: Nation, Race, and Gender from* Oroonoko *to Anita Hill* (Duke)

Susan Glaspell: Essays / Linda Ben-Zvi, ed., *Susan Glaspell: Essays* (Michigan)

Swindler, Spy, Rebel / Kathleen De Grave, *Swindler, Spy, Rebel: The Confidence Woman in Nineteenth-Century America* (Missouri)

Telling Travels / Mary Suzanne Schriber, *Telling Travels: Selected Writings by Nineteenth Century American Women Abroad* (No. Ill.)

That Pale Mother Rising / Eva Cherniavsky, *That Pale Mother Rising: Sentimental Discourses and the Imitation of Motherhood in 19th-Century America* (Indiana)

Tradition, Voices, and Dreams / Melvin J. Friedman and Ben Siegel, eds., *Tradition, Voices, and Dreams: The American Novel Since the 1960s* (Delaware)

Violence, Silence, and Anger / Deirdre Lashgari, ed., *Violence, Silence, and Anger: Women's Writing as Transgression* (Virginia)

"Who Set You Flowin'?" / Farah Jamine Griffin, *"Who Set You Flowin'?: The African-American Migration Narrative* (Oxford)

Periodicals, Annuals, and Series

AAR / *African American Review*

ABSt / *A/B: Auto/Biography Studies*

Acoma

Agenda

AHR / *Afro-Hispanic Review*

AICRJ / *American Indian Culture and Research Journal*

AIQ / *American Indian Quarterly*

AJES / *Aligarth Journal of English Studies*

AL / *American Literature*

Albion (Woodbridge, Ont.)

Allegoria

ALR / *American Literary Realism*

AmDram / *American Drama*

AmerHeritage / *American Heritage*

Americana (Univ. de Paris IV)

American Enterprise

AmLH / *American Literary History*

AmPer / *American Periodicals*

Amst / *Amerikastudien*

AmStScan / *American Studies in Scandinavia*

AmTheatre / *American Theatre*

Anglican and Episcopal History

Anglofiles

ANQ: A Quarterly Journal of Short Articles, Notes, and Reviews

APR / *American Poetry Review*

AQ / *American Quarterly*

AR / *Antioch Review*

ArQ / *Arizona Quarterly*

Art press

ASch / *American Scholar*

ASInt / *American Studies International*

Atenea

Atlantis

ATQ / *American Transcendental Quarterly*

BB / *Bulletin of Bibliography*
Bibliographical Society of Australia and New Zealand Review
Biography / *Biography: An Interdisciplinary Quarterly*
Bollettino del C.I.R.V.I.
BoundaryII / *Boundary 2: An International Journal of Literature and Culture*
BSWWS / Boise State University Western Writers Series
ByronJ / *The Byron Journal*
CanL / *Canadian Literature*
CCTEP / *Conference of College Teachers of English Studies*
CEA / *CEA Critic*
CentR / *Centennial Review*
CHA / *Cuadernos Hisopano-americanos*
ChauR / *Chaucer Review*
CHum / *Computers and the Humanities*
CimR / *Cimarron Review*
CL / *Comparative Literature*
CLAJ / *College Language Association Journal*
CLAQ / *Children's Literature Association Quarterly*
CLQ / *Colby Library Quarterly*
Clues: A Journal of Detection
CML / *Classical and Modern Literature*
CollL / *College Literature*
Commentary
Comparatist: A Journal of the Southern Comparative Literature Assn.
ConL / *Contemporary Literature*
CQ / *Cambridge Quarterly*
CRevAS / *Canadian Review of American Studies*
Crit / *Critique: Studies in Modern Fiction*

Criticism: A Quarterly for Literature and the Arts
CritQ / *Critical Quarterly*
CrossRoads / *CrossRoads: A Journal of Southern Culture*
CS / *Concord Saunterer*
CWH / *Civil War History*
Cycnos (Univ. de Nice)
Dioniso
DLB / *Dictionary of Literary Biography*
DQ / *Denver Quarterly*
EA / *Etudes Anglaises*
EAL / *Early American Literature*
EDJ / *Emily Dickinson Journal*
EdL / *Etudes de Lettres*
EGN / *Ellen Glasgow Newsletter*
EigoS / *Eigo Seinen* (Tokyo)
ELH [formerly *Journal of English Literary History*]
ELN / *English Language Notes*
ELWIU / *Essays in Literature* (Western Ill. Univ.)
EONR / *Eugene O'Neill Review*
ES / *English Studies*
ESC / *English Studies in Canada*
ESP / *Emerson Society Papers*
ESQ: A Journal of the American Renaissance
Europe
EuWN / *Eudora Welty Newsletter*
EWhR / *Edith Wharton Review*
Expl / *Explicator*
Extrapolation: A Journal of Science Fiction and Fantasy
Fitzgerald Newsletter
FJ / *Faulkner Journal*
FNS / *Frank Norris Studies*
Frontiers
FT / *First Things* (New York)
Futuro presente
GaR / *Georgia Review*

Genders
GPQ / Great Plains Quarterly
Granta
HC / Hollins Critic
Hemingway Newsletter
Hispanófilia
Historical Journal of Massachusetts
History Workshop Journal
HJR / Henry James Review
HK / Heritage of the Great Plains
HLB / Harvard Library Bulletin
HN / Hemingway Review
HudR / Hudson Review
IFR / International Fiction Review
Il piccolo Hans
Il Ponte
Il verri
Indice
IowaR / Iowa Review
IPQ / International Philosophical Quarterly
JACult / Journal of American Culture
JAF / Journal of American Folklore
JAmS / Journal of American Studies
JASAT / Journal of the American Studies Assn. of Texas
JDN / James Dickey Newsletter
JDTC / Journal of Dramatic Theory and Criticism
JEP / Journal of Evolutionary Psychology
JER / Journal of the Early Republic
JFCSMP / James Fenimore Cooper Society Miscellaneous Papers
JHI / Journal of the History of Ideas
JJQ / James Joyce Quarterly
JML / Journal of Modern Literature
JNT / Journal of Narrative Technique
Journal of Homosexuality
Journal of Military History
Journal of the American Musicological Society

JQ / Journalism Quarterly
JR / Journal of Religion
JSW / Journal of the Southwest
K&K / Kultur og Klasse
KALit / Kansai American Literature
KR / Kenyon Review
KRev / Kentucky Review
L&B / Literature and Belief
L&C / Language and Communication
L&M / Literature and Medicine
L&P / Literature and Psychology
Legacy: A Journal of Nineteenth-Century American Women Writers
Leggere
LFQ / Literature/Film Quarterly
Library of Congress Information Bulletin
Ling&L / Lingua e Literatura: Revista dos Departamentos de Letras de Faculdade de Filosofia, Letras e Ciencas Humanas da Universidade de Sao Paulo
Lingue e letteratura
LIT / Literature Interpretation Theory
L'Ozio
Manuscript Society News
Margaret Fuller Society Newsletter
MD / Modern Drama
MELUS: The Journal of the Society for the Study of Multi-Ethnic Literature of the United States
Menckeniana: A Quarterly Review
MFS / Modern Fiction Studies
Michigan History
MissQ / Mississippi Quarterly
MissR / Missouri Review
MLQ / Modern Language Quarterly
MLS / Modern Language Studies
MMisc / Midwestern Miscellany
Monatshefte
Mosaic: A Journal for the Interdisciplinary Study of Literature

MQ / *Midwest Quarterly: A Journal of Contemporary Thought*
MQR / *Michigan Quarterly Review*
MR / *Massachusetts Review*
MS / *Modern Schoolman*
MSEx / *Melville Society Extracts*
N&Q / *Notes and Queries*
NCF / *Nineteenth-Century Literature*
NCHR / *North Carolina Historical Review*
NConL / *Notes on Contemporary Literature*
NDQ / *North Dakota Quarterly*
NEQ / *New England Quarterly*
NER / *New England Review and Bread Loaf Quarterly*
NewC / *The New Criterion*
New Yorker
NHR / *Nathaniel Hawthorne Review*
NLH / *New Literary History: A Journal of Theory and Interpretation*
Novel: A Forum on Fiction
NR / *Nassau Review*
NRep / *New Republic*
NTQ / *New Theatre Quarterly*
Nuovi Argomenti
NYRB / *New York Review of Books*
NYTBR / *New York Times Book Review*
OUT
OVER here
PAAS / *Proceedings of the American Antiquarian Society*
Paideuma: A Journal Devoted to Ezra Pound Scholarship
P&L / *Philosophy and Literature*
Palimpsestes
PAPA / *Publications of the Arkansas Philological Society*
ParisR / *Paris Review*
Parnassus: Poetry in Review
PennH / *Pennsylvania History*

Playbill: The National Theatre Magazine
PLL / *Papers on Language and Literature*
PMHB / *Pennsylvania Magazine of History and Biography*
PMLA: Publications of the Modern Language Assn.
PNotes / *Pynchon Notes*
PoeS / *Poe Studies*
Poesia
PostS / *Post Script: Essays in Film and the Humanities*
PoT / *Poetics Today*
Prétexte
Prospects: An Annual Journal of American Cultural Studies
Prospero / *Prospero: Rivista di Culture Anglo Germaniche*
Psychological Reports
PUUHS / *Proceedings of the Unitarian Universalist Historical Society*
QWERTY / *QUERTY: Arts, Littératures, & Civilisations du Monde Anglophone*
Quimera
RALS / *Resources for American Literary Study*
RANAM / *Recherches Anglaises et Américaines*
Raritan, A Quarterly Review
RCF / *Review of Contemporary Fiction*
RChL / *Revista Chilena de Literatura*
REALB / *REAL: The Yearbook of Research in English and American Literature*
Reden
Renascence: Essays on Value in Literature
RES / *Review of English Studies*
RFEA / *Revue Francaise d'Etudes Americaines*

RI / *Revista Iberoamericana*

RLMC / *Rivista de Letterature Moderne e Comparate*

RO / *Revista de Occidente*

RSAJ / *RSA Journal: Rivista di Studi Nord-Americani*

RWT / *Readerly/Writerly Texts*

SAF / *Studies in American Fiction*

Sagetrieb: A Journal Devoted to Poets in the Pound–H.D.–Williams Tradition

SAIL / *Studies in American Indian Literature*

SAJL / *Studies in American Jewish Literature*

SAL / *Southwestern American Literature*

SALit / *Chu-Shikoku Studies in American Literature*

Salmagundi: A Quarterly of the Humanities and Social Sciences

SAQ / *South Atlantic Quarterly*

SAR / *Studies in the American Renaissance*

SB / *Studies in Bibliography*

SBN / *Saul Bellow Journal*

SCr / *Strumenti Critici: Rivista Quadrimestrale di Cultura e Critica Letteraria*

SCR / *South Carolina Review*

SDR / *South Dakota Review*

SELit / *Studies in English Literature* (Tokyo)

SELL / *Studies in English Language and Literature*

SFS / *Science-Fiction Studies*

Shenandoah

ShortS / *Short Story*

SHR / *Southern Humanities Review*

Signs: A Journal of Women in Culture and Society

SIR / *Studies in Romanticism*

SLJ / *Southern Literary Journal*

SLSN / *Sinclair Lewis Society Newsletter*

SNNTS / *Studies in the Novel* (Univ. of North Texas)

SoAR / *South Atlantic Review*

SoQ / *Southern Quarterly*

Soundings: An Interdisciplinary Journal

SPAS / *Studies in Puritan American Spirituality*

Spring

SR / *Sewanee Review*

SSF / *Studies in Short Fiction*

StAH / *Studies in American Humor*

StHum / *Studies in the Humanities* (Indiana, Pa.)

StTCL / *Studies in Twentieth-Century Literature*

StWF / *Studies in Weird Fiction*

Style

Sur

SWR / *Southwest Review*

Talisman

TCL / *Twentieth-Century Literature*

TCrit / *Texto Crítico*

TDR / *The Drama Review*

Testo a fronte

Theatre Week

TJ / *Theatre Journal*

TLS / (London) *Times Literary Supplement*

TSB / *Thoreau Society Bulletin*

TSLL / *Texas Studies in Language and Literature*

TSWL / *Tulsa Studies in Women's Literature*

TUSAS / *Twayne's United States Authors Series*

TWN / *Thomas Wolfe Review*

UMSE / *University of Mississippi Studies in English*

Utopian Studies

UTQ / *University of Toronto Quarterly*
VPR / *Victorian Periodicals Review*
VQR / *Virginia Quarterly Review*
W&I / *Word and Image: A Journal of Verbal/Visual Enquiry* (London, England)
WAL / *Western American Literature*
W&Lang / *Women & Language*
WCPMN / *Willa Cather Pioneer Memorial Newsletter*
WL / *Women and Language*
WL&A / *War, Literature, & the Arts*
WMQ / *William and Mary Quarterly*
World & I
WS / *Women's Studies*
WSJour / *Wallace Stevens Journal*
WWR / *Walt Whitman Quarterly Review*
YJC / *The Yale Journal of Criticism: Interpretation in the Humanities*
YR / *Yale Review*

Publishers

Absalon / Lund: Absalon
Actes Sud / Arles: Actes Sud
Alabama / Tuscaloosa: Univ. of Alabama Press
Alianza / Madrid: Alianza Editorial
Almqvist and Wiksell / Stockholm: Almqvist and Wiksell
American Philosophical Society / Philadelphia: American Philosophical Society
Andrea Livi / Fermo: Andrea Liva Editore
Anhinga / Tallahassee: Anhinga
Anthropos / Madrid: Editorial Anthropos
Arcade / New York: Arcade (dist. by Little, Brown)

Arizona / Tucson: Univ. of Arizona Press
Asefi / Milan: Asefi
Associate / Rome: Edizioni Associate
Autonomedia / Brooklyn: Autonomedia
Ballantine / New York: Ballantine Books (div. of Random House)
Beacon / Boston: Beacon Press
Bedford / New York: Bedford Books (dist. by St. Martin's)
Belknap / Cambridge, Mass.: Belknap Press of Harvard Univ. Press
Bergen / Bergen: Univ. of Bergen
Blackwell / Oxford: Basil Blackwell
Blaue Eule / Essen: Die Blaue Eule
Blizzard / Milford, Conn.: Blizzard Publishing (dist. by LPC/InBook)
Bompiani / Milan: Gruppo Editoriale Fabbri, Bompiani, Sonzogno, Etas
Bowling Green / Bowling Green, Ohio: Bowling Green State Univ. Popular Press
Braziller / New York: George Braziller
Bucknell / Lewisburg, Pa.: Bucknell Univ. Press (dist. by Associated Univ. Presses)
Bulzoni / Rome: Bulzoni Editore
Calif. / Berkeley: Univ. of California Press
Cambridge / New York: Cambridge Univ. Press
Camden House / Columbia, S.C.: Camden House
Castalia / Madrid: Castalia
Castelvecchi / Rome: Castelvecchi
Center for Great Plains Studies (Lincoln)
Chadwyck-Healey / Alexandria: Chadwyck-Healey

Chicago / Chicago: Univ. of Chicago Press

Cideb / Rapallo: Cideb

Cierre / Verona: Cierre Edizioni

CIRLEP / Reims: CIRLEP

C.I.R.V.I. / Turin: C.I.R.V.I.

Clarendon / Oxford: Clarendon Press

Columbia / New York: Columbia Univ. Press

Contemporary / Chicago: Contemporary Books

Contemporary Research / Dallas: Contemporary Research Press

Continuum / New York: Continuum Publishing (dist. by Harper & Row Pubs.)

Copper Canyon / Port Townsend, Wash.: Copper Canyon Press

Cornell / Ithaca, N.Y.: Cornell Univ. Press

Corti / Paris: Corti

Costa & Nolan / Genoa: Costa & Nolan

Crown / New York: Crown Publishing Group (affil. of Random House)

December / Highland Park, Ill.: December Press

Delaware / Newark: Univ. of Delaware Press (dist. by Associated Univ. Presses)

Destino / Madrid: Destino

Didier-Erudition / Paris: Didier-Erudition

Duke / Durham, N.C.: Duke Univ. Press

ECW / Milford, Conn.: ECW Press (dist. by LPC/InBook)

Edições Colibri / Lisbon: Edições Colibri

Edisco / Turin: Edisco

Edizioni dell'Orso / Alessandria: Edizioni dell'Orso

Eerdmans / Grand Rapids, Mich.: W. B. Eerdmans

Einaudi / Turin: Einaudi

Empiria / Rome: Empiria

ENS / Fontenay-aux-Roses: ENS editions

Eötvös Loránd / Budapest: Eötvös Loránd University

E.S.I. / Naples: E.S.I.

ETS / Pisa: ETS

Facts on File / New York: Facts on File, Inc.

Fairleigh Dickinson / Teaneck, N.J.: Fairleigh Dickinson Univ. Press (dist. by Associated Univ. Presses)

Farrar / New York: Farrar, Straus & Giroux

Feltrinelli / Milan: Feltrinelli

Florida / Gainesville: Univ. of Florida Press

Fordham / New York: Fordham Univ. Press

Four Walls / New York: Four Walls Eight Windows

Francke / Tübingen: A. Francke Verlag GmbH

Franco Angeli / Milan: Franco Angeli

Franco Muzzio / Padua: Franco Muzzio Editore

Frassinelli / Milan: Frassinelli

Gale / Detroit: Gale Research (subs. of International Thompson Publishing)

Garland / New York: Garland Publishing

Garzanti / Milan: Garzanti

Georgia / Athens: Univ. of Georgia Press

Georg Olms / Hildesheim: Georg Olms Verlag

Giunti / Florence: Giunti

Greenwood / Westport, Conn.: Greenwood Press

Hall / New York: G. K. Hall (div. of Macmillan Publishing)

Harcourt / San Diego, Calif.: Harcourt Brace Jovanovich

Harper / New York: Harper & Row Publishers

HarperCollins / New York: HarperCollins Pubs. (div. of News Corp)

Harvard / Cambridge: Harvard Univ. Press

Holt / New York: Henry Holt (subs. of Verlagsgruppe Georg Von Holszbrinck)

Hopkins / Baltimore: Johns Hopkins Univ. Press

Idaho / Moscow: Univ. of Idaho Press

Illinois / Champaign: Univ. of Illinois Press

Indiana / Bloomington: Indiana Univ. Press

Instar Libri / Turin: Instar Libri

Iowa / Iowa City: Univ. of Iowa Press

Iowa State / Ames: Iowa State Univ. Press

Jewish Publication Society / Philadelphia: Jewish Publication Society

Johnson / London: Samuel Johnson

Kansas / Lawrence: Univ. Press of Kansas

Kent State / Kent, Ohio: Kent State Univ. Press

Kentucky / Lexington: Univ. Press of Kentucky

Knopf / New York: Alfred A. Knopf (subs. of Random House)

Kodansha / New York: Kodansha (dist. by Farrar, Straus & Giroux)

Königshausen / Wurzburg: Verlag Königshausen und Neumann

Library of America / New York: Library of America (dist. by Viking Penguin)

Liguori / Naples: Liguori

Lithos / Rome: Lithos

Little, Brown / Boston: Little, Brown (div. of Time)

Locust Hill / West Cornwall, Conn.: Locust Hill Press

Longman / White Plains, N.Y.: Longman

LSU / Baton Rouge: Louisiana State Univ. Press

McFarland / Jefferson, No. Car.: McFarland

Macmillan / London: Macmillan Publishers

Maison / Bordeaux: Editions de la Maison des Sciences de l'Homme d'Aquitaine

Maison des Pays Ibériques / Bordeaux: Maison des Pays Ibériques

Manchester / Manchester: Manchester Univ. Press (dist. by St. Martin's Press, subs. of Macmillan Publishing)

Marsilio / Venice: Marsilio

Mass. / Amherst: Univ. of Massachusetts Press

Mellen / Lewiston, N.Y.: Edwin Mellen Press

Mentor / New York: Mentor Books (imprint of New American Library, subs. of Pearson)

Methuen / New York: Routledge, Chapman & Hall

Michigan / Ann Arbor: Univ. of Michigan Press

Mich. State / East Lansing: Michigan State Univ. Press

Minimum Fax / Rome: Minimum Fax

Minnesota / Minneapolis: Univ. of Minnesota Press

Miss. / Jackson: Univ. Press of Mississippi

Missouri / Columbia: Univ. of Missouri Press

MLA / New York: Modern Language Assn. of America

Mobydick / Faenza: Mobydick

Mondadori / Milan: Mondadori

National Poetry Foundation / Orono: University of Maine

NCTE / Urbana, Ill.: National Council of Teachers of English

Nebraska / Lincoln: Univ. of Nebraska Press

Neimeyer Verlag (Tübingen)

New England / Hanover, N.H.: Univ. Press of New England

New Mexico / Albuquerque: Univ. of New Mexico Press

Newton Compton / Rome: Newton Compton

No. Car. / Chapel Hill: Univ. of North Carolina Press

No. Ill. / DeKalb: Northern Illinois Univ. Press

Northeastern / Boston: Northeastern Univ. Press

North Texas / Denton: Univ. of North Texas Press

Norton / New York: W. W. Norton

NYU / New York: New York Univ. Press

Odense / Odense Univ. Press

Ohio / Athens: Ohio Univ. Press

Ohio State / Columbus: Ohio State Univ. Press

Okla. / Norman: Univ. of Oklahoma Press

Orchises / Alexandria: Orchises Press

Orígenes / Madrid: Editorial Orígenes

Oxford / New York: Oxford Univ. Press

Pantheon / New York: Pantheon Books (div. of Random House)

Pàtron / Bologna: Pàtron

Penguin / New York: Penguin Books

Península / Barcelona: Ediciones Península

Penn. / Philadelphia: Univ. of Pennsylvania Press

Penn. State / University Park: Pennsylvania State Univ. Press

Per Kofod / Copenhagen: Per Kofod

Peter Lang / New York: Peter Lang Publishing (subs. of Verlag Peter Lang AG [Switzerland])

Pittsburgh / Pittsburgh: Univ. of Pittsburgh Press

Pliegos / Madrid: Pilegos

Potpourri / Prairie Village, Kan.: Potpourri Publications Co.

Princeton / Princeton, N.J.: Princeton Univ. Press

Provence / Aix: Univ. de Provence

PSN / Presses de la Sorbonne Nouvelle

PUB / Presses universitaires de Bordeaux

PUP / Presses de l'Université Paris-Sorbonne

PUPerpignan / Cahiers de l'Université de Perpignan

PUR / Presses universitaires de Reims

PURennes / Presses universitaires de Rennes

Raffaelli / Rimini: Raffaelli Editore

Random House / New York: Random House

Riuniti / Rome: Editori Riuniti

Rodopi / Amsterdam: Editions
Rodopi BV
Rowohlt / Reinbek bei Hamburg:
Rowohlt
Rumeur / La Rochelle: Rumeur de
Ages
Rutgers / New Brunswick, N.J.:
Rutgers Univ. Press
Sage / Thousand Oaks, Calif.: Sage
Publications
Saggiatore / Milan: il Saggiatore
St. Martin's / New York: St. Martin's
Press (subs. of Macmillan Publish-
ing)
Salzburg / University of Salzburg
San Diego / San Diego State Univ.
Press
Scandinavian / Oslo: Scandinavian
Univ. Press
Scarecrow / Lanham, Md.: Scarecrow
Press
Scolar / Aldershot: Scolar (dist. by
Ashgate Pub.)
Scribner's / New York: Charles
Scribner's Sons
Settimo Sigillo / Rome: Settimo
Sigillo
Sheffield / Sheffield: Sheffield Aca-
demic Press
Simon & Schuster / New York: Si-
mon & Schuster (div. of Para-
mount Communications)
So. Car. / Columbia: Univ. of South
Carolina Press
So. Ill. / Carbondale: Southern Il-
linois Univ. Press
Stanford / Stanford, Calif.: Stanford
Univ. Press
Stauffenburg / Tübingen: Stauffen-
burg

Strangers / London and Newport:
Strangers Press
SUNY / Albany: State Univ. of New
York Press
Susquehanna / Selinsgrove, Pa.: Sus-
quehanna Univ. Press (dist. by As-
sociated Univ. Presses)
Syracuse / Syracuse, N.Y.: Syracuse
Univ. Press
Tartaruga / Milan: La Tartaruga
Tennessee / Knoxville: Univ. of Ten-
nessee Press
Texas / Austin: Univ. of Texas Press
Texas A & M / College Station: Texas
A & M Univ. Press
Theoria / Rome: Theoria
Twayne / New York: Twayne Pub-
lishers (imprint of G. K. Hall)
Ultima / Kolding: Ultima
Univ. Editions / Huntington, W.V.:
University Editions
Univ. Press / Lanham, Md.: Univer-
sity Press of America
Uppsala / Uppsala Univ. (dist. by
Almqvist and Wiksell)
Viking / New York: Viking Penguin
Virginia / Charlottesville: Univ. Press
of Virginia
Visor / Madrid: Visor
Wayne State / Detroit: Wayne State
Univ. Press
Winter / Heidelberg: Carl Winter
Wisconsin / Madison: Univ. of
Wisconsin Press
Wissenschaftliche / Darmstadt:
Wissenschaftliche Buchgesellschaft
Wissenschaftlicher / Wissenschaft-
licher Verlag Trier
Yale / New Haven, Conn.: Yale Univ.
Press

American Literary Scholarship 1995

Part I

1 Emerson, Thoreau, Fuller, and Transcendentalism

David M. Robinson

This year's chapter on Transcendentalist scholarship is dedicated to the memory of Walter Harding, Thoreau Society founder and secretary who died 10 April 1996. I encourage everyone to read Harding's charming "A Rambling History of the Thoreau Society" (*CS* 3: 5–81) and Elizabeth Hall Witherell's "A Tribute to Walter Harding" (*TSB* 215 [1996]: 1–3). It has been a remarkable year for Transcendentalist studies, including Robert D. Richardson, Jr.'s epochal biography of Emerson, Len Gougeon and Joel Myerson's edition of *Emerson's Antislavery Writings*, Lawrence Buell's study of Thoreau and American environmental writing, important books on Thoreau by Robert Milder and Laura Dassow Walls, and on Fuller by Christina Zwarg.

i Emerson

a. Biographical and Critical Studies   There have been many excellent books on Emerson over the years, but I have no hesitation in describing Robert D. Richardson, Jr.'s *Emerson: The Mind on Fire* (Calif.) as the best. Comprehensive in its factual detail, penetrating and perceptive in its work of interpretation of both the man and his works, Richardson's book will be the standard of reference for Emerson studies for a very long time. Two characteristics give the work its impact. The first is familiar to readers of Richardson's *Henry David Thoreau: A Life of the Mind* (see *ALS 1986*, pp. 15–16), a thorough command of Emerson's intellectual milieu based on a painstaking assemblage and interpretation of his reading. While source study has been a staple of Emerson criticism, Richardson synthesizes this material with a unique authority, reminding us again and again that Emerson was an active and committed reader, engaging what he read as if his life depended on it. Of particular importance is

Richardson's discussion of Emerson's protracted struggle against "the potential for nihilism in Hume"; he further reconstructs the impact of the Scottish commonsense philosophers in orienting Emerson toward his high-stakes defense of philosophical meaning. "To a great extent Emerson's life and work—indeed, transcendentalism itself—constitutes a refutation of Hume," Richardson argues. While the philosophical texts would change somewhat as Emerson's work continued, Richardson underlines the continuing battle to salvage coherence and moral purpose from the threat of enervating doubt as the key to Emerson's intellectual career. Richardson's second major achievement is to re-create the dynamics of Emerson's emotional life and his social attachments. The Emerson we find here is far different from the cold and detached man that has been widely accepted in Emerson criticism. Much of Richardson's emphasis is placed on Emerson's deep bond with his first wife, Ellen, and his first child, Waldo, and the impact of their respective losses on Emerson's emotional vitality. Richardson persuasively argues that the Emerson who eventually emerged as our great philosopher did so in large part to survive the searing pain of his loss of Ellen. Before her death in 1827 "Emerson was a rationalist who was fascinated but not wholly convinced by the truth of idealism. After this time Emerson believed completely, implicitly, and viscerally in the reality and primacy of the spirit, though he was always aware that the spirit can manifest itself only in the corporeal world." Richardson is also insightful about Emerson's marriage with Lydia Jackson and his close friendships with Thoreau, Fuller, Caroline Sturgis, and others, all of whom profoundly molded his life. Richardson pointedly considers the importance of his friendship with Fuller. "More than any other person—except possibly Ellen—Margaret Fuller got through to Emerson's emotional life," and she deeply influenced him intellectually as well. Richardson reminds us through these portraits of Emerson's relationships that his work was the product of lived experience as well as of reading and rational thinking.

Len Gougeon's *Virtue's Hero* (see *ALS 1990*, pp. 4–5) brought much-needed attention to Emerson's involvement with the antislavery movement; Gougeon and Joel Myerson have now edited *Emerson's Antislavery Writings* (Yale), which furthers our understanding of that involvement. The volume compiles 14 public speeches and four published letters written from 1838 until 1863, including a heretofore unpublished 1855 lecture on slavery, four other speeches available previously only in newspaper accounts, and new versions edited from manuscript sources of

Emerson's important addresses of 1851 and 1854 on the Fugitive Slave Law and his 1863 "Fortune of the Republic." Gougeon describes Emerson's growing acceptance of his ethical responsibility to lend his voice to the antislavery cause and his quickening involvement in it after his 1847–48 trip to England. This gathering of material emphasizes ethical commitment and social action as key categories in Emerson's thinking after the mid-1840s.

George Kateb's *Emerson and Self-Reliance* (Sage) is an important reassessment of Emerson's philosophy of individualism, extending Kateb's earlier analysis of Emerson as a philosopher of "democratic individualism" (see *ALS 1994,* pp. 12–13). Kateb argues that "self-reliance is not one particular substantive or doctrinal principle like other ones," but "an intellectual method, a method of truth," marked principally by "receptivity," a "power of uncommitted sympathy" that is the essential element of democracy. The principal strength of Kateb's study is its determined commitment to present Emerson's work as a usable ethic in the contemporary world. Its weakness is wedded to that strength—a resistance to Emerson's historical context, particularly to what Kateb labels the "religiousness" of Emerson's outlook, a quality that compromises Emerson's ability to grant "intrinsic or self-sufficient value" to things in this world. But Kateb also observes that Emerson's religiousness originates in his craving for "a world that can be honestly understood as morally intended," and he concludes that religiousness "is a good deal less than an insuperable obstacle" in our final judgment of Emerson. Kateb is most persuasive in laying out the ethical and political implications of Emerson's self-reliance, arguing that it implies a life of "restless, unfixed, . . . unceasing creation and abandonment of channels and positions" and a selfless, "unegotistical spirit" of work and endeavor. Such a stance for the individual is the basis of a democratic culture, as "democracy becomes, in its political process, the register of diversity, of *individual* diversity, perhaps even of individual uniqueness."

In *Emerson in His Sermons: A Man-Made Self* (Missouri) Susan L. Roberson traces the autobiographical strand in Emerson's sermons, finding in them a narrative of "exploration of traditional doctrine, crisis, rejection, and creation of a new self." Roberson emphasizes the death of Ellen in 1831 as the crisis point of this narrative, arguing like Richardson that this was a deeply transformative event for him. "Baptized by death and depression, Emerson emerged from his grief with a new insight, in which the primacy of personal vision was declared." Emerson developed an image of a "perfect character" in his journals and later sermons "whose power is proportional to his independence from society." Roberson makes a persuasive case for reading the sermons as indicators of Emerson's inner growth, texts that disclose both the psychological dynamics and the cultural bounds necessary to understand his complex evolution.

I am pleased to welcome the concluding volume 10 of Eleanor Tilton's extension of Ralph L. Rusk's original six-volume edition of *The Letters of Ralph Waldo Emerson* (Columbia). This volume includes correspondence from 1870–81, appendices of related manuscript materials, and comprehensive calendars of the Rusk and Tilton volumes that chronologically arrange all letters printed or recorded in the editions. Every scholar who has worked in this field has reason to be thankful for Tilton's work in this edition. Robert D. Richardson, Jr.'s "Read Only to Start Your Own Team: Emerson on Creative Reading" (*YR* 83, i: 84–91) surveys Emerson's reading tastes and habits, emphasizing the self-directed quality of his reading program and its contribution to his search for stimulus as a writer.

b. Sources, Contexts, Influence   The investigation of Emerson's connections with pragmatism was extended in two important new works. James M. Albrecht's " 'Living Property': Emerson's Ethics" (*ESQ* 41: 177–217) is a thorough and convincing reinterpretation of Emerson in light of his relocation of value "in the act of doing," centering on a careful elaboration of the ways that Emerson's emerging pragmatism complicates "attempts to define him against the ideological poles of capitalism and Marxism." Albrecht presents a trenchant critique of recent portrayals of the political limitations of Emerson's individualism by Myra Jehlen (*ALS 1986*, p. 381) and Sacvan Bercovitch (*ALS 1993*, p. 8), arguing that "Emerson views culture not as a totalizing system of control but as a medium that allows for and requires performance." Emerson's extension to others of the possibility of meaningful action within the culture forms the basis of "a communitarian ethos of pluralism," an ethical and social vision that is much more politically engaged than the narrow individualism with which his work is sometimes associated.

Albrecht's reading of Emerson's political relevance meshes well with that of Kateb and with James Livingston's *Pragmatism and the Political Economy of Cultural Revolution, 1850–1940* (No. Car., 1994), an impressive, intellectually rigorous analysis of the cultural implications of the transition from Transcendentalism to pragmatism. Livingston explains how William James made use of the early attempts of Emerson and Whitman "to reopen if not redraw the space between the order of ideas and the order of events, between thoughts and things." Whitman's inclination "to treat thoughts and things as indissolubly related" was an advance beyond Emerson's initial wrestling with the question in *Nature,* and Whitman's tendency was important to James in the "reconstruction of subjectivity" that was central to pragmatism.

Mark Edmundson provides further perspectives on Emerson's political and ethical viability in *Literature Against Philosophy.* Edmundson uses Emerson, William Blake, and Hannah Arendt to respond to Michel Foucault's analysis of contemporary culture. Finding in Foucault the same hostility to "fixed selfhood" that marks Emerson and Blake, Edmundson is nevertheless troubled by Foucault's refusal "to offer transforming alternatives" to the cultural impasse. Emerson, like Blake and Arendt, is important precisely because "he has a strong conception not just of fate but of potential freedom." The importance of Emerson's struggle against determinism is also emphasized in Stanley Cavell's *Philosophical Passages: Wittgenstein, Emerson, Austin, Derrida* (Blackwell), an extension of Cavell's recent work on Emerson's philosophical stature. Cavell reads "Fate" as "a parable of the struggle against slavery" in its insistence that freedom is "the condition of philosophical thinking." "Emerson's way of confronting fate, his recoil of fate," Cavell argues, "is his writing, in every word." In "Gödel's Theorem and Postmodern Theory" (*PMLA* 110: 248–61) David Wayne Thomas uses Emerson as "an orienting reference" in a well-informed and penetrating discussion of the relation of Kurt Gödel's incompleteness theorem to recent critical theories based on antifoundationalism and indeterminacy. Thomas argues that contemporary theorists have overlooked both Emerson's and Gödel's idealist assumptions, assumptions that are working unacknowledged in accounts of critical agency, even those positing "a non-unified or 'decentered' subject." "The mobile, seeing, vigilant consciousness" that marks both Emersonian discourse and much of postmodern theory, Thomas asserts, "is, wittingly or not, an involvement in idealist logical perception."

Russ Castronovo in *Fathering the Nation* discusses Emerson's role in the creation of a "monumental culture" in 19th-century America, the process of cultural formation through which national identity came to be expressed in the significance of public monuments narrating a version of the national past. Castronovo discusses Melville's skepticism of this process, part of Melville's larger critique of the implications of Emersonian Transcendentalism.

Richard R. O'Keefe's *Mythic Archetypes in Ralph Waldo Emerson: A Blakean Reading* (Kent State) portrays Emerson as a visionary poet in the Blakean mold, focusing on a four-part mythical structure of Creation, Fall, Redemption, and Apocalypse shared by Blake and Emerson. O'Keefe does not argue for a direct Blakean influence on Emerson, but he pursues instead the conceptual analogues of their thinking, noting the long line of Emerson readers who have in one way or another commented that the essays "do not behave like discursive prose." O'Keefe offers extended readings of "Hamatreya," *Nature,* "Circles," the Divinity School *Address,* and the later "Works and Days" in constructing his portrait of the Blakean Emerson. Armida Gilbert's " 'To sing in Horror, to Laugh in Hell': Byron's Influence on Emerson's Poetry" (*Byron J* 23: 50–62) is an astute analysis of Emerson's changing assessments of Byron. Enamored of Byron in his youth, Emerson gradually distanced himself in the 1820s, until his European journey of 1832–33 and Egerton Brydges's 1834 reevaluation of Byron in *Fraser's* helped to renew his appreciation. Gilbert describes Emerson's continuing ambivalence about Byron, which included a consistent admiration for his technical and musical facility, but reservations about his intellectual depth and moral vision, especially in comparison with Wordsworth. Even so, a "Byronic tone" continues in Emerson's poetry, suggesting that "Byron had permanently shaped Emerson's poetics."

Our understanding of the purposes and structure of "Experience" was advanced in two new essays. Richard R. O'Keefe's " 'Experience': Emerson on Death" (*ATQ* 9: 119–29) extends Barbara Packer's and Sharon Cameron's recent interpretations of the essay's treatment of grief. O'Keefe proposes Heidegger's concept of "the death-of-the-other," the "*experience which cannot be experienced,*" as a useful analogue in assessing Emerson's treatment of grief in the essay. He argues convincingly that "Experience" is a philosophical investigation of grief rather than a record or expression of it. In " 'Somewhat Comes Of It All': The Structure of Emerson's 'Experience' " (*ATQ* 9: 21–39) Kyle Norwood finds "a progressive pattern to the lords of life" sections that structure the essay. Norwood calls particular attention to "Surprise" and "Subjectiveness" as crucial sections, describing Emerson's achievement of a complex and fragile affirmation in the essay.

Thomas D. Birch ("Toward a Better Order: The Economic Thought of Ralph Waldo Emerson," *NEQ* 68: 385–401) links the economic ideas of *Nature*, "Wealth," and "Farming" to the theories of Francis Wayland and Henry Carey. Birch argues that Emerson ascribed to the prevailing view that "wealth generated by capitalism [was] primarily and increasingly an intellectual product destined to serve the public good." This view entailed Carey's assumption of "a harmony of interests among different economic classes" and "complex, mutually beneficial and sustaining interdependencies among the different factors of production." P. Eddy Wilson ("Emerson and Dewey on Natural Piety," *Journal of Religion* 75: 329–46) compares Emerson's and Dewey's turn to "natural piety" as a response to nihilism, concluding that Emerson's naturalism involved "a return to a metaphysical commitment," whereas Dewey's focused on "a plan of action that is fundamentally self-affirmative." Some perspectives on Emerson's reputation in the early 20th century can be gained from Edgar C. Reinke's translation of *The Roosevelt Lectures of Paul Shorey (1913–1914)*, ed. Ward W. Briggs and E. Christian Kopff (Georg Olms). Shorey, the great American Platonist and classical scholar, presents his Berlin University audience with a view of American literature centered on Emerson and the New England tradition.

Other work on Emerson included a new edition of Eric W. Carlson's *Emerson's Literary Criticism* (Nebraska), including a new introduction; an edition of *Representative Men* (Marsilio) with an introduction by Pamela Schirmeister; Wesley T. Mott's attribution of an anonymous 1853 essay on Emerson to John Ross Dix (" 'An Etching of Emerson' [1853] and the Problem of Attribution," *ESP* 6, i: 1–4); David Lyttle's exposition of "Emerson's Transcendental Individualism" (*CS* 3: 89–103); Will Stephenson and Mimosa Stephenson's note on the "science-baffling star, without parallax" in "Emerson's 'Self-Reliance' " (*Expl* 53: 81–82); and Ernest Fontana's account of the influence of Emerson's attack on "bibliomaniacs" (*The American Scholar*) on George Eliot's *Romola* (*ELN* 32, iv: 70–75).

ii Thoreau

a. New Monographs Three important books, each of which has a major impact on our sense of Thoreau's development and influence, mark this as an especially rich year in Thoreau studies. Lawrence Buell's *The Environmental Imagination* is the most significant work yet to emerge from the burgeoning field of literature and the environment; it will establish the framework for much of the continuing discourse in this field. Buell recounts the development of an environmental sensibility in American literature, emphasizing the roles of several lesser-known 19th-century nature writers such as Susan Fenimore Cooper, Celia Thaxter, and John Burroughs, and including cogent treatments of contemporary writers such as Leslie Marmon Silko, Wendell Berry, and Gary Snyder. Buell's historical orientation is informed by a deep interest in questions of literary genre and canon formation. Buell also proposes what seems to me a very workable set of criteria for what constitutes an "environmental text."

Buell's study centers on Thoreau's Walden experiment, which included five distinct "environmental projects," each of which "required Thoreau to approach nature through a certain kind of schematic, classifying lens" and forced him toward "a more particularized immersion" in the natural environment. The resulting course of Thoreau's development, Buell argues convincingly, is a halting but nevertheless recognizable evolution from "homocentrism toward biocentrism," suggested by both his increasing commitment to work in natural history and his "almost neopagan sense of the neighborliness of nature." Even though Thoreau has been elevated to environmental sainthood in the late 20th century, Buell recognizes that for both personal and historical reasons he did not "make the abuse and endangerment of nature his main theme," comparing him in this respect to George Perkins Marsh, whose *Man and Nature* (1864) made him "the first American prophet of environmental disaster." In Buell's account of the complex process of Thoreau's canonization as both a literary craftsman and environmental prophet, the articulation of a "reciprocal interchange" between "humankind and nature" in Thoreau's work has achieved a particular resonance with modern readers, bringing environmental thinkers back to him repeatedly in their efforts to formulate a more satisfying and empowering sense of environmental values. Buell's command of the texts and issues of the American tradition of nature writing will make this work an essential point of reference for future studies of environmental writing.

Books by Robert Milder and Laura Dassow Walls bring new attention to the question of Thoreau's later development, each of them offering important accounts of Thoreau's evolution away from Emersonian idealism. In *Reimagining Thoreau* (Cambridge) Milder portrays Thoreau as a restless figure unable to find a satisfactory place in his community and consumed with a need to use his role as an author to ease his sense of maladjustment. "Painfully sensitive to Concord's judgment of him, Thoreau responded by disparaging his townsmen en masse and defining himself by what he was not." Locating the fuel of Thoreau's developing literary accomplishment in this inner drive toward self-justification, Milder also shows how Thoreau could turn his own restlessness on himself in a brilliant reading of *Walden* as an uneasy amalgam of two texts in partial conflict. Using Ronald Clapper's genetic text of *Walden,* Milder establishes two different and in some sense differing strands in the book. The first is the well-known narrative of discovery and renewal established principally in the early versions of the text, one in which the speaker confidently challenges readers and attempts to confirm his own rightness of purpose. The second is an "adaptational" narrative in which a less confident and confrontational narrator attempts to "resolve the anxieties of identity and vocation, more generally of being-in-the-world, and establish the terms for a satisfying relationship to experience." Milder feels that Thoreau underwent a significant personal transformation in 1849–50 while revising the *Walden* manuscript, signaled in the tone of "Walking," and manifesting itself in the later drafts of *Walden* as "a more chastened figure poised physically and spiritually between the purity of nature and the impurity of the human world, to which he, too, belongs." This more modest, factually oriented Thoreau struggles with problems of inspiration and visionary understanding; his presence in the later drafts complicates and destabilizes the text's rhetorical purposefulness and organic unity.

Laura Dassow Walls's *Seeing New Worlds: Henry David Thoreau and Nineteenth-Century Natural Science* (Wisconsin) is an impressive demonstration of how deeply Thoreau was engaged in science and how astutely he understood the varied scientific currents of his day. Walls presents a Thoreau whose scientific assumptions and practices were closest to those of Alexander von Humboldt and who used Humboldt and others to develop an "empirical holism" as a philosophical alternative to the "rational holism" of Coleridge, Emerson, and other romantic naturalists. Such a stance evolved gradually in Thoreau's work, closely linked to his actual experiences as a nature observer and field naturalist. "In his walks, surveys, travels, and reading," Walls argues, "Thoreau was moving away from a grand and abstract transcendentalism toward a detailed observation of the specifics of nature, in its unaccountable diversity." The term "unaccountable diversity" is indicative of Walls's view of Thoreau as an observer of particulars who found wholes increasingly elusive—and increasingly irrelevant. As Walls forcefully argues, this reconstruction of Thoreau's scientific assumptions adds new authority to the growing consensus that the later work should not be read as a declension from *Walden*. Walls's contention that this late work shows Thoreau "happy to relinquish the search for symbolic totality" will surely help to frame the continuing discourse on the shape of Thoreau's career. Walls makes the best case I have seen thus far for a Thoreau whose intellectual vigor and reach continued to expand, and she finds in him a strikingly modern appreciation of "a new world in which cosmos and chaos were not antagonists, but in which cosmos, 'Beauty,' was chaos by another name."

b. *The Cambridge Companion* These three important new monographs are supplemented by *The Cambridge Companion to Henry David Thoreau*, ed. Joel Myerson (Cambridge), 13 impressive new essays by leading scholars that comprehensively address Thoreau's development, works, and reputation. Walter Harding's "Thoreau's Reputation" (pp. 1–11) reminds us that the growth of Thoreau's reputation was not a steady process. The variety of Thoreau's identities "as a nature writer, an economist, a literary artist, an exponent of the simple life, a philosophical anarchist, and an environmentalist," each contributed to what is now his widespread appeal. Harding stresses the importance of H. G. O. Blake's editorial championing of Thoreau as a nature writer, H. S. Salt's appreciation of Thoreau's political radicalism, and F. O. Matthiessen's analysis of Thoreau's achievement in aesthetic form as important turning points in the evolution of three important aspects of Thoreau's appeal. Robert D. Richardson, Jr.'s "Thoreau and Concord" (pp. 12–24) documents the variety of ways in which Thoreau's "attachment to Concord gave his writing a sense of place unsurpassed in American writing." The circle of intellectuals that Emerson cultivated in Concord afforded Thoreau the intellectual range and stimulus that he needed as a writer, and Concord's rivers and fields and ponds provided him with his subject matter and literary forms. "Place is not what matters," Richardson observes; *"caring* about a place is what matters," and he shows with discernment how Thoreau's caring for Concord informed and quickened his work.

Robert Sattelmeyer's "Thoreau and Emerson" (pp. 25–39) is a perceptive account of Thoreau and Emerson's important relationship, emphasizing their struggle "to realize the high and noble friendship that each aspired to but despaired of ever achieving." The early roles of mentor and protégé gradually evolved to a period from 1841 until 1848 when they achieved "their closest association and greatest intimacy" as Thoreau launched his literary career, accepted Emerson's nudge toward natural history writing, and served, in Emerson's words, " 'as private secretary to the President of the Dial.' " The relationship was based in part on "a powerful element of idealization in Thoreau's concept of Emerson," an attitude that could not be sustained after Emerson's return from England, when his disappointment over Thoreau's failure to involve himself more deeply in public life became evident, and Thoreau reacted in injured defensiveness.

Linck C. Johnson's analysis of *"A Week on the Concord and Merrimack Rivers"* (pp. 40–56) demonstrates how Thoreau "transformed what he had originally conceived as an essay mingling travel and natural history into a far more ambitious and complex work." Johnson places Thoreau's grief for his brother at the center of the book, but he emphasizes that Thoreau's grieving is part of a larger philosophical inquiry into questions of impermanence and renewal. Thoreau's observations in the book of the recurrent cycles of natural life provided important emotional and intellectual sustenance for him. In "Thoreau as Poet" (pp. 57–70) Elizabeth Hall Witherell observes that while "Thoreau's poetry is for the most part unremarkable in its subject and its form," it "assumes special interest and importance" when analyzed "in the context of Thoreau's literary ambitions." Thoreau was most keenly interested in poetry in the early stages of his writing career, having received Emerson's praise and encouragement for his poetic efforts. Witherell identifies a cluster of five poems written in 1841—"Independence," "Cock-crowing," "Inspiration," "The Soul's Season," and "The Fall of the Leaf"—that constitute Thoreau's "least known but most significant poetic work," explorations of "the relationship between nature and the conditions of the writer's creative life." Yet these poems also mark the point at which Thoreau turned his energies primarily to prose, using poems thereafter to elaborate particular themes or passages in his prose.

In "Thoreau and His Audience" (pp. 71–91) Steven Fink argues perceptively that Thoreau regarded "any active consideration of audience as adulterating or debasing the work," but he also "actively sought an outlet in both the popular weekly and monthly magazines aimed at a broad, general audience." This tension accounts for Thoreau's "complex, demanding, and often antagonistic rhetorical stance toward his audience," and it made the lecture platform an important alternative form of expression to writing for the periodicals. Richard J. Schneider's *"Walden"* (pp. 92–106) surveys the variety of formal and thematic achievements that have continued to keep *Walden* at the center of American literary studies. Schneider understands that a large part of Thoreau's accomplishment was to sustain seemingly contradictory impulses in *Walden*. The book presents both "linear and circular travel structures" and superimposes other generic forms to achieve its rich and complex texture. This complexity arose in part from the rapid evolution of Thoreau's own thinking as he drafted and revised the text, and it reflects his increasing capacity to think on multiple levels.

In "Thoreau in His Journal" (pp. 107–23) Leonard N. Neufeldt emphasizes the textual variety and multiplicity of goals represented in Thoreau's Journal, proposing the "anthology" as the most useful metaphoric description of it. He offers four useful "mappings" of the Journal that capture its multiple resonances: "(1) the microlinguistic," focused on Thoreau's use of language for self-construction; "(2) the intratextual," in which "recurrent structural properties, themes, and motifs" are the focus; "(3) the multitextual," in which the reader comes to recognize that the Journal is "not only a heterogeneous text but also a nest of texts"; and "(4) the intertextual," in which the reader explores the Journal's relation to its various selves and to "the corpus of Thoreau's works."

Joseph J. Moldenhauer's *"The Maine Woods"* (pp. 124–41) includes a thorough account of each of Thoreau's excursions into Maine, a composition and publication history of each of the resulting narratives, a consideration of the differing philosophical qualities of each essay, and a discussion of the critical reception and stature of each. Moldenhauer describes "The Allegash and East Branch" as "the one most informed by a sense of mystery, myth, blood- or racial knowledge, and the inadequacy of scientific and rational analysis to account for experience." Joe Polis, Thoreau's Penobscot guide on that expedition, fulfilled Thoreau's aspirations for a life occupying a "midway or 'frontier' position between woods and village, radical simplicity and sophisticated culture." In " 'A Wild, Rank Place': Thoreau's *Cape Cod*" (pp. 142–51) Philip F. Gura notes the close relationship between *Cape Cod* and the essays of *The Maine Woods*, and establishes clearly that they "can be read as elaborations—indeed, as further considerations—of the Walden experience." Thoreau's recognition of the power and indifference of the sea is the central experience of the book, one that impresses on him the importance of survival itself as a virtue and that elevates the importance "of knowing the difference between appearance and reality." *Cape Cod* thus provides "further testament to Thoreau's commitment to know himself through nature," a nature, however, that is harsh and resistant to sentimental or anthropomorphic interpretation.

In "Thoreau's Later Natural History Writings" (pp. 152–70) Ronald Wesley Hoag considers the development and thematic significance of eight later nature essays, important texts in the growing critical recognition that Thoreau was "a much more significant naturalist than was previously thought." Hoag believes that these essays establish Thoreau as "a protoecologist, practicing an unborn science that would itself insist on humanity's attitudes as a key to the conservation or degradation of the environment." Lawrence Buell assesses Thoreau from the perspective of modern environmental studies in "Thoreau and the Natural Environment" (pp. 171–93), describing Thoreau's "irregular" or nonlinear movement toward a stance of respect for the "substantial reality" of nature apart from human uses or desires. Buell finds a cluster of interconnected and overlapping purposes that constitute Thoreau's environmental concerns, expanding loci of attention that indicate Thoreau's gradual divergence from Emerson toward a naturism of refined factual observation, a developing sense of the intrinsic worth of the natural world, and an environmental "politics of preservation."

In "Thoreau and Reform" (pp. 194–214) Len Gougeon surveys eight essays collected in *Reform Papers* to trace Thoreau's "unmistakable movement from the passive to the active mode" in social reform. While he possessed an ingrained skepticism of group activities and institutional formation, Thoreau nevertheless became increasingly persuaded by the moral imperative of antislavery. Gougeon describes "Life Without Principle" as Thoreau's "true jeremiad," centering on his attack on the "material corruption" of American society.

c. Other Critical and Biographical Essays   Bradley P. Dean and Ronald Wesley Hoag have compiled a valuable reference tool for Thoreau's early lecture career ("Thoreau's Lectures Before *Walden:* An Annotated Calendar," *SAR,* pp. 127–228). A calendar of the lectures after *Walden* will be published in *SAR 1996.* Dean and Hoag arrange the 43 lectures included in this installment chronologically, and they provide detailed contextual information drawn from a wide range of primary sources and recent scholarship. They note that while Thoreau's aspirations for a career as a lecturer were never fulfilled in terms of financial reward or public influence, much contemporary reaction suggests that he was successful in reaching his audiences and making a positive impression on them. Dean and Hoag have gathered important information for the continuing discussion of Thoreau's relationship with his audience, as discussed above by Milder and Fink.

Dieter Schulz's "Thoreau's House" (*Values in American Society*, ed. Tibor Frank [Eötvös Loránd], pp. 29–39) offers a perceptive reassessment of Thoreau's attitude toward his Walden house, noting the way that his meditation in "House-Warming" on "a larger and more populous house, standing in a golden age" suggests an unsettled preoccupation with the "myth of Paradise and the Fall." Schulz takes account of the pervasive imagery of houses and natural shelters in *Walden* (the ideal house as nest, shell, or burrow), but he also observes that these images suggest a "disproportion" between the human and the natural, making the house the sign of "an estrangement—and a necessary estrangement—from nature." Ning Yu presents a new approach to the structure of "Natural History of Massachusetts" ("'The poem of Concord' and the Structure of Thoreau's 'Natural History of Massachusetts,'" *CLQ* 31: 268–78), emphasizing Thoreau's "meticulous use of spatial organization in the essay" as he moves the narration "from indoors to outdoors and then along the river through the town," encompassing a more "biocentric" vision in the process.

Cultural assumptions about the role of the author were the subject of two essays. In "Healthful Employment: Hawthorne, Thoreau, and Middle-Class Fitness" (*AQ* 47: 681–714) Michael Newbury considers the figuration of authorship in Hawthorne and Thoreau as a manifestation of "cultural anxiety about the expansion of nonmanual work." Newbury notes Hawthorne's struggle with the relationship between physical activity and the work of writing, comparing him with Thoreau, whose "manual labors create an enabling figuration of authorship grounded in bodily labor and material production." In "Doing 'Pioneer Work': The Male Writer in Thoreau's *Week* and *Walden*" (*ESQ* 41: 289–305) Joe Boyd Fulton argues that for Thoreau "the relationship of writer to nature mirrors that of male to female" and that this "dichotomy has some stirring resonances with recent language theory," namely, the concept of "phallogocentrism" in Derrida and *"l'écriture féminine"* in Kristeva. As an author, Thoreau attempted to translate "the mother tongue, speech based in nature, to the written father tongue," coming closest to succeeding in the sandbank passage in *Walden*. In "At Home with Lidian: Henry Thoreau in 1847–1848" (*CS* 3: 35–48) Harmon D. Smith considers Thoreau's life in the Emerson household immediately after he left the pond, shedding light on his relationship with both Lidian and Waldo, and noting how the dynamics of both Lidian's health and of the Emerson marriage profoundly shaped these years.

Two essays concentrated on Thoreau's stance toward political resistance in "Resistance to Civil Government." Morris B. Kaplan's "Civil Disobedience, Conscience, and Community: Thoreau's 'Double Self' and the Problematic of Political Action" (*The Delegated Intellect*, pp. 37–63) describes how "Resistance to Civil Government" "serves to problematize the concept of political action as such and of the self which engages in it." Kaplan believes that Gandhi and Martin Luther King, Jr., translated "Thoreau's politics of conscience into a program of resistance for the oppressed" and that Thoreau's own position is less oriented to mass movements than to the ethical and political situations of individuals "situated in the midst of shifting perspectives and relations through which they must experimentally make their ways." Joan Cooney's "Neither Nonresistance Nor Violence: Thoreau's Consistent Response to Social Evils" (*CS* 3: 133–39) is an analysis of "the principles underlying Thoreau's civil resistance," concluding that he consistently endorsed "pragmatic direct actions guided by moral principle, even when the use of physical force was required."

Other essays on Thoreau include Joseph J. Moldenhauer's "A Supplement to Thoreau's Reading" (*TSB* 209 [1994]: 5–9); Moldenhauer's identification of "A New *Cape Cod* Source" (*TSB* 210: 1–2); Gary Scharnhorst's report of an 1849 report of a Thoreau lecture ("Mary from Western Maine on 'Economy' in Portland, 1849," *TSB* 209 [1994]: 2–3); David Fuller's discussion of Thoreau's knowledge of John Brown's involvement in the 1856 murders at Pottawatomie Creek ("Thoreau and John Brown's Pottawatomie," *TSB* 210: 2–3); Adam Paul Weisman's analysis of the cultural limitations of Thoreau's account of his excursion in French Canada ("Postcolonialism in North America: Imaginative Colonization in Henry David Thoreau's *A Yankee in Canada* and Jacques Polin's *Volkswagen Blues*," *MR* 36: 477–500); Anne LaBastille's "Thoreau and the Woodswoman" (*CS* 3: 21–33) in which the author compares her experience in the woods with Thoreau's; Donna Mendelson's discussion of Annie Dillard's use of Thoreau ("Tinker Creek and the Water of

Walden: Thoreauvian Currents in Annie Dillard's *Pilgrim*," *CS* 3: 51–62); and J. Parker Huber's discussion of John Muir's reading of Thoreau ("John Muir and Thoreau's Maine," *CS* 3: 105–18).

iii Fuller

Over the past several years Christina Zwarg has developed a challenging and illuminating interpretation of Fuller (see *ALS 1989*, p. 10; *ALS 1990*, p. 16; *ALS 1991*, p. 16; and *ALS 1993*, pp. 18–19), keyed to a revaluation of her theories of reading and conversation and a reassessment of the importance of her relationship with Emerson. In *Feminist Conversations: Fuller, Emerson, and the Play of Reading* (Cornell) Zwarg culminates this work, establishing Fuller's importance in contemporary theoretical discourse and providing a clearer picture of her central role in the evolution of Transcendentalism. Zwarg wants us to understand Fuller's feminism in contemporary theoretical terms, seeing in her career "a series of cultural negotiations that constitute the type of resistance—sometimes contradictory in nature—that lends meaning to the word *feminism* today." Zwarg believes Fuller's significance has been overlooked by literary historians and feminist critics who have for different reasons construed her relationship with Emerson in hierarchical terms. Fuller's process of working out her feminism had a profound impact on Emerson, Zwarg argues, and she characterizes their relationship as "complex, mutually empowering, and interactive." Fuller's early commitment to the example of Goethe was supplemented after her 1843 trip to the Midwest by an increasing interest in the political discourse of Fourier, whose importance emerged in part through her conversations with Emerson. Fuller's particular understanding of "Fourier's critique of Western culture" contributed to her growing theory of active, radical reading and was a decisive element, Zwarg argues, in *Summer on the Lakes, Woman in the Nineteenth Century*, and Fuller's articles for the *New York Tribune*. Emerson responded to her advocacy of this form of reading and social critique in *Representative Men*, taking Fuller's lead in moving toward a more "writerly text," open to the reader as an "active agent" in its reading. Zwarg brings a new urgency to our understanding of the mutuality of the Fuller-Emerson friendship and calls us to recognize the political significance of Fuller's theories of writing, reading, and conversation.

Larry J. Reynolds's "From *Dial* Essay to New York Book: The Making of *Woman in the Nineteenth Century*" (pp. 17–34 in *Periodical Literature in Nineteenth-Century America*) is a discerning description of Fuller's conflicted sense of audience in the early 1840s. Reynolds describes "The Great Lawsuit" as the result of "an ongoing, intertextual conversation with a group of like-minded friends," a coterie that Fuller had cultivated through her persistent efforts to promote conversation, journal-sharing, and the circulation of poems and essays. While Fuller's original essay was addressed to this "large circle of ideal friends," her appointment to the *New York Tribune* forced her to expand her sense of audience. The revision of "The Great Lawsuit" into *Woman in the Nineteenth Century* shows the effect of Fuller's need to address an unknown and possibly unsympathetic public and resulted in "a far more feminist work than the essay from which it originated," as Fuller added new material that "addresses women almost exclusively." Sandra M. Gustafson ("Choosing a Medium: Margaret Fuller and the Forms of Sentiment," *AQ* 47: 34–65) describes the "revisionary sentimentalism" of Fuller's work and argues that her intervention into the forms of sentimental discourse had an impact on later feminism that has not been sufficiently recognized. Like Annette Kolodny (see *ALS 1994*, p. 22), Gustafson argues that in *Woman in the Nineteenth Century* Fuller creates "a new feminist discourse" that "alternates between analysis and rhapsody, intimacy and bombast, conversation and oratory." Catherine C. Mitchell's *Margaret Fuller's New York Journalism: A Biographical Essay and Key Writings* (Tennessee) reconstructs the milieu of the *New York Tribune* and reminds us of Fuller's underappreciated role in its early development and of the impact of journalistic work on Fuller's development and reputation. Mitchell includes a large selection of Fuller's *Tribune* articles from 1844–46.

In an illuminating discussion of the decline of Fuller's literary reputation in the 1880s Thomas R. Mitchell ("Julian Hawthorne and the 'Scandal' of Margaret Fuller," *AmLH* 7: 210–33) describes how Julian Hawthorne used his father's derogatory comments on Fuller's marriage to Giovanni Angelo Ossoli as part of a larger strategy to advance his father's literary reputation by positioning him and his wife, Sophia Hawthorne, as exemplars of domesticity and marital happiness, contrasting them with a version of a thwarted and somewhat dangerous Fuller. Controversy attended the publication of *Nathaniel Hawthorne and His Wife* (1884), as Fuller was defended by friends and supporters such as Thomas Wentworth Higginson, James Freeman Clarke, and Christopher Pearse Cranch. Even so, Julian Hawthorne's "vituperative attacks on Fuller clearly damaged her position within the American literary canon," part of a backlash against the emerging "New Woman" in American culture. Mitchell's essay will be an important contribution to our development of a more complete narrative of Fuller's cultural reception. Of related interest is Scott Ash's reinterpretation of the Hawthorne-Fuller relationship ("Rereading Antagonism as Sibling Rivalry: The Hawthorne/Fuller Dynamic," *ATQ* 9: 313–31), one that rejects as oversimplified the "conception of Hawthorne as an anti-Fuller, anti-reform conservative ideologue" and depicts Hawthorne as Fuller's "simultaneously jealous and grieving younger brother," who shared in important respects her desire to develop a dissenting voice against the national culture and who "wants to but fears to follow his more mature sister's footsteps." Finally, I would call attention to the Fall 1995 issue of the *Margaret Fuller Society Newsletter* (3, i), which contains the abstracts of 22 papers presented at the conference on Fuller chaired by Fritz Fleischmann at Babson College, 29–30 April 1995. As these abstracts indicate, there is much new work under way on Fuller.

iv The Transcendentalist Movement

Dean Grodzins's "Theodore Parker's 'Conference with the Boston Association,' January 23, 1843" (*PUUHS* 23: 66–101) is an outstanding contribution that will become a permanent part of our understanding of the Transcendentalist Controversy. Grodzins prints for the first time the complete text of Parker's journal account of his dispute with the Boston Association, and he links this incident with Parker's controversial South Boston sermon and his criticism of the council of Unitarian ministers that had adjudicated a dispute between reform preacher John Pierpont and his Hollis Street congregation. Noting that differences in theology and politics were only part of the reason for the dispute, Grodzins explains how differing conceptions of the minister's role led to the breach between Parker and his colleagues. Grodzins presents a vivid portrait of Parker and has a keen eye for the nuances of opinion and personality among his moderate colleagues such as Nathaniel Langdon Frothingham and Ezra Stiles Gannett. Elisabeth Hurth extended her illuminating series of articles on biblical interpretation among 19th-century Unitarians and Transcendentalists with two related essays. In "'The Last Impiety of Criticism': The Reception of D. F. Strauss's *Leben Jesu* in New England" (*ESQ* 40 [1994]: 319–52) Hurth demonstrates that more liberal

Unitarians and Transcendentalists accepted Strauss's work only with deep reservations. "Beneath the transcendentalist response to Strauss lay the continuing commitment to Jesus as a historical divine personage," Hurth explains, noting that while Parker and others welcomed Strauss's blows to a narrowly empirical evidentialism best represented by Andrews Norton, they were "unwilling to surrender the historical Jesus to a Hegelian Christology" advocated by Strauss, believing it "was not sufficient for the uses of Jesus as an exemplary ideal of humanity's infinite potentialities." Such complexities of reception demonstrate the "difficulty of setting up hard theological boundaries between Unitarianism and transcendentalism." In "That 'Grand Model of Humanity': William Henry Furness and the Problem of the Historical Jesus" (*SAR*, pp. 101–26) Hurth locates Furness's extensive research in Jesus studies within the Unitarian defense of the historical accuracy of the gospel accounts. She describes Furness's contribution to the Transcendentalist construction of Jesus "as a uniquely endowed personality appealing to the spiritual core of human nature."

Ora Frishberg Saloman's *Beethoven's Symphonies and J. S. Dwight: The Birth of American Music Criticism* (Northeastern) is a valuable reconstruction of Dwight's development as a music critic, connecting his championing of Beethoven and instrumental music in general to his Transcendentalist and Fourierist ideals. I have always found Dwight one of the most interesting and appealing of the Transcendentalists, one who clearly illustrates the convergence of aesthetic, spiritual, and political ideals within the movement. While scholars have known in general terms that Dwight became a leading American music critic, Saloman makes the path of his development clear, stressing his gradual absorption of German discourse on Beethoven and the symphonic genre in the 1830s and 1840s. Acquainting himself with Beethoven at first largely through his piano sonatas and piano transcriptions of his symphonies, Dwight was among the earliest reviewers to welcome and comment on the first American symphonic performances. Dwight saw in Beethoven's symphonies, especially the Ninth, a new expression of the struggle toward, and achievement of, human sympathy and harmony, ideals that he had pursued in his involvement with the Brook Farm experiment.

In "A Boston Feminist in the Victorian Public Sphere: The Social Criticism of Caroline Healey Dall" (*NEQ* 68: 429–50) Howard M. Wach offers welcome attention to Dall's intellectual development and her contribution to the discourse on women's rights, emphasizing her struggle to overcome a personal crisis in 1839 brought on by her conflicting needs to "make use of her talents and energies" and to "adhere to the conventions of feminine propriety." Wach stresses Dall's achievement in "combining arguments for women's unique abilities with purely egalitarian claims for admission to the public sphere," thus advancing the feminist cause on two fronts.

In "Racial Nationalism and Its Challengers: Theodore Parker, John Rock, and the Antislavery Movement" (*CWH* 41: 142–60) Paul E. Teed explores Parker's "paradoxical acceptance of both abolitionism and Anglo-Saxon racial nationalism," views that led him to link "Anglo-Saxon racial destiny with American national character" and to promulgate the stereotype of the "childlike, docile, and affectionate" African. Parker's implication in 1858 that "the inherent absence of bravery in black slaves had prevented them from overthrowing their oppressors" was answered by the African American abolitionist leader John S. Rock, whose defense of the courage of the slaves and emphasis on the oppression of slavery brought Parker to modify his views somewhat, but not to abandon his "romantic racialism." Parker's disciple Thomas Wentworth Higginson is the subject of Kent P. Ljungquist and Anthony Conti's "'Near My Heart' After Fifty Years: Thomas Wentworth Higginson's Reminiscence of Worcester" (*CS* 3: 121–31), an essay that sketches Higginson's historical work and reprints a 1903 reminiscence of his decade in Worcester (1852–1863). Alan Brasher's publication of "James Freeman Clarke's Journal Accounts of Ralph Waldo Emerson's Lectures" (*SAR*, pp. 83–100) illustrates Clarke's interest and admiration of Emerson's lectures, primarily the "Human Culture" series of 1837–38.

Three articles focused on aspects of the Fruitlands experiment. Joel Myerson's "A Catalogue of Transcendentalist Materials in the Fruitlands Museums" (*SAR*, pp. 1–60) compiles the printed and manuscript material from "perhaps the least-used collection of Transcendentalist-related materials." The Alcott family is particularly well-represented in these collections. Jacqueline E. M. Latham's "Fruitlands: A Postscript" (*SAR*, pp. 61–67) adds information about the English socialist community Concordium, which had connections with the Fruitlands experiment. Sandra Harbert Petrulionis ("'By the Light of Her Mother's Lamp': Woman's Work Versus Man's Philosophy in Louisa May Alcott's 'Transcendental Wild Oats,'" *SAR*, pp. 69–81) explains Alcott's satirical representation of Transcendental utopian ideals of Fruitlands "as a further perpetuation of the sexual division of labor." Two reminiscences of late-19th-century Concord were brought to light: Janice Milner Lasseter's "'Boston in the Sixties': Rebecca Harding Davis's View of Boston and Concord During the Civil War" (*CS* 3: 65–86) and Joel Myerson's "Concord in 1882: The Journal of Florence Whiting Brown" (*SAR*, pp. 291–344).

Oregon State University

2 Hawthorne

Leland S. Person

Absent any major critical book this year, Hawthorne scholarship was still well-served by several outstanding essays, most of them embedded in thick descriptions of Hawthorne's cultural background: for example, Thomas R. Mitchell on Julian Hawthorne's efforts to promote his father at Margaret Fuller's expense, Michael Newbury on Hawthorne's and Thoreau's views of work, Scott Derrick on homosexuality in *The Scarlet Letter*, Stephen Knadler on the growth of psychiatry and *The House of the Seven Gables*, and Nancy Bentley on race in *The Marble Faun*.

i Editions, Biography, and Bibliography

Since I jumped the gun and reviewed Hawthorne's *Miscellaneous Prose and Verse* (Ohio State) a year early, readers should check *ALS 1994* (pp. 25–26) for my brief assessment of this invaluable volume of the Centenary Edition.

Three interesting essays link Hawthorne and his Concord contemporaries, Fuller and Thoreau. In "Julian Hawthorne and the 'Scandal' of Margaret Fuller" (*AmLH* 7: 210–33) Thomas R. Mitchell argues that Julian deliberately provoked a scandal in 1884 by publishing a carefully edited version of Hawthorne's infamous notebook entry on Fuller's marriage in *Nathaniel Hawthorne and His Wife*, hoping thereby to "realign and strengthen his father's position in literary history even as he destroyed Fuller's." Adroitly linking Julian's project to gender politics, Mitchell notes Julian's calculated contrast between the "domesticated, manly," and happily married Hawthorne and the fallen, feminist "New Woman" (Fuller), who threatened to disrupt the Hawthornes' and other couples' "blissful" marriages. Of particular interest to Hawthorne scholars: Mitchell describes Julian's newsprint feud with Thomas Wentworth

Higginson, Christopher Pease Cranch, Frederick Fuller, and others over the accuracy of Hawthorne's notebook account of Fuller, and he summarizes and quotes some of this interesting primary material. Scott Ash in "Rereading Antagonism as Sibling Rivalry: The Hawthorne/Fuller Dynamic" (*ATQ* 9: 313–31) covers some of the same ground in arguing that Hawthorne actually relied on Fuller as a "metaphoric older sibling" to show him how to achieve a balance between conformity and the dissent he at least partly desired.

Insightfully linking Hawthorne and Thoreau to widespread "cultural anxiety about the expansion of nonmanual work and material nonproductivity," Michael Newbury in "Healthful Employment: Hawthorne, Thoreau, and Middle-Class Fitness" (*AQ* 47: 681–714) insists that Hawthorne's Brook Farm experiences and his writing of "The Custom-House" represent attempts to "reclaim for authorship the virtues and physical health persistently associated with manual labor and production." Newbury establishes a rich background in American social history for this very intelligent "rhetorical history of the relations between white-collar work, the middle-class transformation of physical labor into physical fitness, and the particular occupation of antebellum authorship." Hawthorne's attraction to Brook Farm and his project in "The Custom-House," he suggests, reflect his desire to "situate himself in an economy that would re-establish a noncommercial basis for authorship by grounding it in support provided by labors of the hand."

Buford Jones and John Randolph Miller, Jr., provide a valuable listing of current Hawthorne research, including many hard-to-find book chapters, in *NHR* (21, i: 36–47).

ii Books

Covering some of the same ground as G. R. Thompson (*ALS 1993,* pp. 23–24) and Thomas R. Moore (*ALS 1994,* p. 26), Michael Dunne in *Hawthorne's Narrative Strategies* (Miss.) deliberately ignores the "content" of Hawthorne's fiction, but he also resists employing a rich technical language to analyze and classify the narratological strategies that do interest him. Although references to narrative theorists (especially Gerard Genette) and terms such as metalepsis and diegetic (even metadiegetic and extradiegetic) appear, Dunne has difficulty supporting his repeated claims about the "amazing variety of technical experiment" by which Hawthorne established narrative authority and controlled his readers. He does, however, provide ample evidence of Hawthorne's self-conscious craftsmanship and concern for narrative control. The 1837 *Twice-Told Tales* "abounds in experiments with verb tenses, points of view, authorial interventions, and attributions of authority," Dunne argues, and he goes on to catalog examples by touching briefly on "Sights from a Steeple," "Little Annie's Ramble," "Sunday at Home," "The Minister's Black Veil," "Dr. Heidegger's Experiment," "David Swan," and others. Although Dunne usefully observes that Hawthorne explored "metafictional modes of narrative involving significant elements of authorial intervention and self-referentiality," he does not do for Hawthorne what critics such as John T. Irwin and Michael J. S. Williams have done for Poe. Dunne insightfully links "Alice Doane's Appeal," *The Blithedale Romance,* and *The Marble Faun* in a chapter on "Narrative Levels and Narrative Authority," for example, but he contents himself with rather superficial formal descriptions rather than in-depth analyses. Similarly, when he examines "Narrativity and Historicity" in "Legends of the Province House" and *The House of the Seven Gables,* he observes that Hawthorne's narrator "controls" historical materials. In the immediate context of the many provocative New Historical readings of Hawthorne's fiction, Dunne's formalistic descriptions seem arid.

Historical background and its contexts and intertexts characterize the student casebook *Understanding* The Scarlet Letter (Greenwood) that Claudia Durst Johnson has compiled. From Michael Wigglesworth's diary to Dan Quayle's diatribe against the television character Murphy Brown, from Anne Hutchinson and Cotton Mather to TV evangelists Jim Bakker and Jimmy Swaggart, Johnson provides numerous controlled opportunities for undergraduate research papers. Johnson's general introduction emphasizes Hester's conflict with the Puritan community, especially on sexual grounds. Johnson introduces each set of historical excerpts with a brief essay explaining their connection to the novel, and she includes study questions and suggested topics at the end of each chapter. An intriguing volume from which every Hawthorne scholar can learn something.

iii General Essays

Klaus P. Stich's "Well-Tempered Temperance: Hawthorne's Dionysian Aspect" (*NEQ* 68: 83–105) summarizes epistolary and anecdotal evidence about Hawthorne's drinking. After concluding that for Hawthorne "temperance is life enhancing only if understood as the controlled consumption of rather than abstinence from alcohol," Stich surveys references to alcohol and elixirs in "The Old Manse," the unfinished novels, and *The Blithedale Romance* (confirming Coverdale's resemblance to his creator and deriving Coverdale's conviviality from Hawthorne's admiration for his neighbor, Ephraim Bull, developer of the Concord grape). Hawthorne's fondness for alcohol, Stich reasons, contributed to his "controlled deliberations on the effervescence of life."

Including eight well-chosen illustrations, Randall A. Clack's "The Alchemy of Love: Hawthorne's Hermetic Allegory of the Heart" (*ESQ* 41: 307–38) follows previous scholars in demonstrating Hawthorne's interest in alchemy, but Clack adds an interesting new twist in showing how extensively Hawthorne employed alchemical tropes to represent his ideal of love. Like lead, in Hawthorne's view, the human heart is "base matter" that can be transmuted to "reflect a golden ideal" through the agency of love or sympathy. Clack insightfully traces this pattern in seven tales ("The Man of Adamant," "Ethan Brand," "The Great Carbuncle," "Peter Goldthwaite's Treasure," "Egotism; or, The Bosom-Serpent," "The Birthmark," "The Golden Touch") and in *The Scarlet Letter* and *The House of the Seven Gables*.

Locating *The Scarlet Letter* in Salem rather than Boston and repeatedly referring to Miles Coverdale as "Cloverdale" rob Nina daVinci Nichols (*Ariadne's Lives*, pp. 39–58) of some scholarly authority in her otherwise able archetypal analysis of Hester Prynne, Zenobia, and Miriam. All three heroines, as passionate Ariadnes of "thwarted desires," struggle against Hawthorne's view of Eros as "at once reprehensible and glorious."

iv Essays on the Novels

a. *The Scarlet Letter*   In an especially cogent essay, " 'A Curious Subject of Observation and Inquiry': Homoeroticism, the Body, and Authorship in Hawthorne's *The Scarlet Letter*" (*Novel* 28: 308–26), Scott S. Derrick argues that a "contest between two versions of the body—as subject of rational inquiry and as the site of resistance to reason—informs the representation of homosexuality" in Hawthorne's complexly homophobic novel. Derrick brilliantly and sensitively examines the scene in which Chillingworth accosts the sleeping Dimmesdale, using Sylvester Graham's *A Lecture to Young Men* (1834) and its various sexual phobias to interpret Dimmesdale's and Chillingworth's "symptomology" as victims of sexual disease. Derrick then links sexuality to narrative, arguing that Hawthorne's desire to be a successful male author led him to contain homoeroticism, which surfaces in the novel's center (chaps. 9–12), within a heterosexual plot. The best essay I know on Hawthorne's representation of homoerotic desire in *The Scarlet Letter.*

From a different but equally fruitful point of view, Ken Egan, Jr., in "The Adulteress in the Market-Place: Hawthorne and *The Scarlet Letter*" (*SNNTS* 27: 26–41) also examines the relation between writing and transgressive sexuality. Citing the widely accepted view that Hawthorne identifies artistically with Hester Prynne, Egan wonders in what sense artistic reproduction is an act of adultery and the male author an adulteress. The answer: To be a male writer in Hawthorne's culture was "necessarily to be an 'adulteress,' " or "feminized adulterer of 'the truth.' " Egan insightfully explains how "adultery" and "adulteration" aptly characterize the tensions (empowerment, guilt) Hawthorne felt about his artistry and his novel.

In a deft analysis of structuring principles, "The Power of Generalizations in *The Scarlet Letter*" (*NHR* 21, ii: 1–6), Terence Martin argues that generalizing statements "bring a unique and radical authority to bear on fictional narrative." He goes on to show that Hawthorne's novel "abounds" with generalizations (e.g., the second sentence of the narrative) that predicate the existence of categories and realities outside the fictional world. Implicitly, Martin's analysis challenges previous claims that *The Scarlet Letter* is a self-enclosed metafiction that undermines belief in referentiality. He also shows how using generalizing statements helps Hawthorne reveal the limitations of the Puritans' Ramist, or binary, logic.

Intertextual and comparative studies dominated the year's criticism of *The Scarlet Letter;* each offers a new literary lens through which we can glimpse new facets of Hawthorne's novel. Matthew Gartner in *"The Scarlet Letter* and the Book of Esther: Scriptural Letter and Narrative Life" (*SAF* 23: 131–51) claims that the novel "grew out of an intimate and sympathetic reading of the Book of Esther." In Hawthorne's "updated scripture" Hester figures as a composite of Esther and Vashti, Dimmesdale as Mordechai, and Chillingworth as Haman and Ahasuerus. Gartner goes beyond allegorical parallels—Hester's visit to the Governor's Hall parallels Esther's visit to King Ahasuerus; Dimmesdale's election sermon recalls Mordechai's letter of Purim—to reveal an uncanny connection to the 16th-century Miles Coverdale's "Book of Hester" and its "semiotic instability" (in the Coverdale Bible, published in 1535).

Richard Kopley in "Hawthorne's Transplanting and Transforming 'The Tell-Tale Heart'" (*SAF* 23: 231–41) discovers enough similarities between Poe's tale and chapter 10 of *The Scarlet Letter* ("The Leech and His Patient") to make a convincing case for some influence. Acknowledging the differences enables an interesting contrast between Poe's tale of damnation and what Kopley sees as Hawthorne's account of Dimmesdale's salvation.

Raymond J. Wilson III in "The Possibility of Realism: 'The Figure in the Carpet' and Hawthorne's Intertext" (*HJR* 16: 142–52) claims suggestively that Hawthorne's reference to moonlit figures in the carpet in the "neutral territory" passage from "The Custom-House" inspired James's tale and occasioned a dialogue about the ability of fiction to reveal truth.

In an ambitious essay, "The Ironic Romance of New Historicism: *The Scarlet Letter* and *Beloved* Standing in Side by Side" (*ArQ* 51, i: 33–60), Charles Lewis argues that Morrison's novel "problematizes" New Historicist readings of Hawthorne's romance and that historical romance fiction and New Historicist criticism are "similar discursive modes." By appropriating the conventions of American historical romance, Morrison enables us to see that, *contra* Sacvan Bercovitch and Jonathan Arac, Hawthorne's romantic techniques are "not inherently constituted upon the absence of social conflict and the identities of difference, nor do they necessarily signify a repressed presence of that conflict." Mara L. Dukats's "The Hybrid Terrain of Literary Imagination: Maryse Condé's Black Witch of Salem, Nathaniel Hawthorne's Hester Prynne, and Aimé Césaire's Heroic Poetic Voice" (*CollL* 22, i: 51–61) also puts *The Scarlet Letter* into an interesting intercultural and intergenerational relationship, as she reads Condé's Caribbean novel *I, Tituba* (1986) and its narrator as a "rewriting of Hester Prynne."

Nancy A. Walker (*The Disobedient Writer,* pp. 144–70) analyzes Margaret Atwood's *The Handmaid's Tale* as another "complex revision" of *The Scarlet Letter* that features many "reversals and subversions." Walker creates a fascinating conversation between the two novels, especially on the topic of "fundamentalist repression" of women. By showing how Atwood extends Hawthorne's "quarrel with narrow-minded zealotry into a dystopian vision that calls into question the very notion of social progress," she will help Hawthorne scholars see the latent, feminist, dystopian tendencies of *The Scarlet Letter.*

Matei Calinescu in "Secrecy in Fiction: Textual and Intertextual Secrets in Hawthorne and Updike" (*PoT* 15 [1994]: 443–65) emphasizes Updike's "ironic transposition" of Hawthorne in his *Scarlet Letter* trilogy. Hawthornians will benefit especially from Calinescu's learned treatment of *The Scarlet Letter* as a sophisticated exploration of secrecy and its relation to reader response.

b. *The House of the Seven Gables* Besides reprinting selected early reviews and criticism and essays by Nina Baym, Bruce Michelson, and William J. Scheick, Bernard Rosenthal's *Critical Essays on Hawthorne's* The House of the Seven Gables (Hall) includes four new essays, plus an informative survey of criticism and critical issues by Rosenthal himself. In a convincing influence study Joseph Flibbert (" 'That Look Beneath': Hawthorne's Portrait of Benevolence in *The House of the Seven Gables*," pp. 114–28) concludes that Hawthorne adapted ideas about benevolence and sympathy from Adam Smith, Francis Hutcheson, Thomas Brown, Dugald Stewart, and David Hartley, illustrating his own darker view of the moral sentiment by contrasting Judge Pyncheon's "posture of benevolence" with the other characters' sincere "sentiment of sympathy." Allan Emery's "Salem History and *The House of the Seven Gables*" (pp. 129–49) considers the novel a "deeply serious investigation" of Salem's past, a counterargument to Joseph Felt's halcyon view in the second edition of his *Annals of Salem* (1845, 1849). Emery makes a compelling case for *Gables* as a revisionist history, focused on class conflict, aristocratic ambition, and selfishness keyed to Salem characters and events (including Quaker and witch persecutions). From a more contemporaneous vantage point Thomas Woodson in "Salem in *The House of the Seven Gables*" (pp. 150–66) finds evidence that Hawthorne interpolated his bruised feelings about his Custom-House ouster into the novel. He also surveys Hawthorne's other literary references to Salem for parallels to Hawthorne's observations in *Gables*. David Callaway concludes the volume with a useful "Annotated Select Bibliography of *The House of the Seven Gables*" (pp. 167–94).

The best psychological reading of *Gables* since Frederick Crews's 1966 book, Stephen Knadler's "Hawthorne's Genealogy of Madness: *The House of the Seven Gables* and Disciplinary Individualism" (*AQ* 47: 280–308) ingeniously links the birth of the antebellum asylum, psychiatry, and Hawthorne's representation of the Pyncheons in order to argue that Hawthorne had little faith in moral reform movements. With debts to

Michel Foucault and impressive research into 19th-century sources, Knadler assesses antebellum constructions of subjectivity and "tactical uses" of insanity. Ironically detached from his narrator, Hawthorne disparages the "categorizing imperative" of psychiatric discourse and its collusion with judiciary institutions (represented by Jaffrey Pyncheon) that would redistribute the Pyncheon property on the basis of hereditary insanity. Knadler's research also sheds new light on Phoebe Pyncheon as an agent of "coercive" socialization. Contributing to this fascinating argument is a sharp analysis of mental hygienics and psychological self-regulation in "Egotism; or, the Bosom Serpent."

Whereas previous Morrison-Hawthorne studies have focused on *The Scarlet Letter,* Wesley Britton in "The Puritan Past and Black Gothic: The Haunting of Toni Morrison's *Beloved* in Light of Hawthorne's *The House of the Seven Gables*" (*NHR* 21, ii: 7–23) argues that Hawthorne's second novel "foreshadows much of the content and many of the techniques residing in *Beloved,*" which he regards as a "literary mapping of the 'symbolic geography'" begun by 19th-century white Romantics. Britton examines the "personified houses," similar characters (Phoebe and Paul D) and imagery (especially water) in both novels. He compares *Beloved's* family with the Pyncheons, demonstrating how both novels develop the effect of "guilt and the haunting presence of evil" identified with blackness.

c. *The Blithedale Romance* In a difficult psychoanalytic essay (*That Pale Mother Rising,* pp. 61–91) Eva Cherniavsky negotiates a complex theoretical triangle (Freud, Lacan, Elizabeth Grosz) on her way to analyzing Miles Coverdale as a "masculine fetishist" who invests desire less in Zenobia or Priscilla than in the veil that "(re)covers both women's lack [of the phallus]." While *Blithedale* "gestures toward" an alternative—performative—conception of the maternal, Hawthorne leaves Coverdale "arrested" before the "loss of the archaic maternal body" and thus divided as a "desiring subject."

Good insights sometimes come in small packages. Douglas L. Hollinger's "The Courtship of Miles Coverdale" (*ANQ* 8, iii: 8–11) plausibly discovers Miles Standish and Priscilla Mullins behind Hawthorne's characters and their love story.

d. *The Marble Faun* Nancy Bentley (*The Ethnography of Manners,* pp. 24–67) offers a fascinating account of *The Marble Faun* as an "internal ethnographic drama." Citing the "image of the faun" as "a personal fetish" for Hawthorne that signifies racial ambiguities, Bentley compellingly elaborates connections among the novel, pre-Civil War America, and 19th-century ethnological theory. Especially noteworthy: Bentley's analysis of Donatello as a test case for Reconstruction era questions about racial essentialism and primitivism; her effort to connect the "aesthetic segregation" for which the novel has long been criticized with the issue of racial segregation.

With Marxian historicist questions in mind, Rosemary Mims Fisk in *"The Marble Faun* and the English Copyright: The Smith, Elder Contract" (*SAR,* pp. 263–75) unearths Hawthorne's original contract with his English publishers, who stipulated a three-volume work, in order to explain why Hawthorne padded the novel with so much arguably extraneous background material from his Italian notebooks. Examining the three volumes one at a time, she illuminates Hawthorne's efforts to construct a salable commodity for the English market.

Joseph N. Riddel (*Purloined Letters,* pp. 105–11) briefly examines *The Marble Faun* as an example of "genealogical crisis." Hawthorne problematizes the act of interpretation, Riddel argues, as a vexed relationship between originals (e.g., the Faun of Praxiteles) and the copies or translations (e.g., Donatello) that "always already" supplant them.

Will and Mimosa Stephenson in "Oxymoron in *The Marble Faun*" (*NHR* 21, i: 1–13) posit a "proto-modernist" Hawthorne, and they provide an impressive catalog of examples to evidence his more frequent use of oxymoron as a "dominant rhetorical device" in his last completed novel.

v Essays on the Tales and Sketches

To counter Sacvan Bercovitch's contention (see *ALS 1991,* pp. 22–23) that literary texts remain bound to dominant, liberal discourse, Peter J. Bellis in "Representing Dissent: Hawthorne and the Drama of Revolt" (*ESQ* 41: 97–119) focuses on "My Kinsman, Major Molineux" and "Howe's Masquerade." The former "challenges the progressive historiography that Bercovitch identifies with nineteenth-century liberalism" by critiquing American Revolutionary myths, especially in its depiction of the unruly, Indian-clad mob of colonists. The latter collapses distinctions between aesthetic representation and revolutionary action and so reveals that literature need not be bound to liberal ideology.

Harold K. Bush, Jr., in "Re-Inventing the Puritan Fathers: George Bancroft, Nathaniel Hawthorne, and the Birth of Endicott's Ghost" (*ATQ* 9: 131–52) contributes significantly to the current conversation about Hawthorne's cultural embeddedness. With help from Northrop Frye and James Davison Hunter, Bush depicts Hawthorne as a revisionist historian in "Endicott and the Red Cross" and "The May-Pole of Merry Mount." Specifically, Hawthorne repudiates Bancroft's "happy claims attributing democratic freedoms of religion and conscience to the Puritans" in order to represent his own more "acute sense" of competing liberal and conservative visions of America.

In an equally insightful vein, political scientist Jonathan Mendilow in "Nathaniel Hawthorne and Conservatism's 'Night of Ambiguity' " (*Political Theory* 23: 128–46) examines "My Kinsman, Major Molineux" in the 19th-century political context of Tocqueville's *Democracy in America*. While both writers recognized the increasing egalitarianism of American political life, especially as reflected in the "subjectification of knowledge and morality," Hawthorne emerges as a more pessimistic conservative pragmatist who recognized the irreversibility of democracy and counted only on individual self-restraint to prevent mobocracy.

In contrast to many recent critics, Frederick Newberry in " 'The Artist of the Beautiful': Crossing the Transcendent Divide in Hawthorne's Fiction" (*NCF* 50: 78–96) makes a strong case for Owen Warland's artistic success by referring to Wolfgang Iser's triad of the real, the fictive, and the imaginary and Nelson Goodman's notion of "worldmaking." At the climactic moment, when Owen's butterfly emerges from its ornate box, Hawthorne transgresses the border of mimetic representation and "ushers" characters and readers alike into the "imaginary." In the process Hawthorne instructs us in the possibilities of imaginative worldmaking and thus expresses the "transcendent instant of art." A well-wrought article that challenges us to reconsider the re-creative power of fantasy and imagination.

Like other critics before her, Lynn Shakinovsky in "The Return of the Repressed: Illiteracy and the Death of the Narrative in Hawthorne's 'The Birthmark' " (*ATQ* 9: 269–81) considers "Birthmark" a tale of signification and vexed reading. Her new angle: a thorough look at connections between the female body, writing, and reading. Aylmer's "murderous illiteracy" causes not only Georgiana's death but the death of the narrative itself, because he forecloses woman's power of signification that constitutes the narrative. The most controversial claim in her argument:

the narrator is "contaminated" and linked "firmly" with the murderous Aylmer. Although Shakinovsky ignores some relevant recent scholarship, her essay represents the best feminist reading of "The Birthmark" since Judith Fetterley's in 1978.

Illustrating the many dimensions of New Historical scholarship, Paul R. Petrie's "Hawthorne in Time of Schism: 'The Gentle Boy' and the Second Great Awakening" (*SPAS* 5: 149–78) extends Michael Colacurcio's investigation of contemporaneous contexts for the tale as a refiguration of 19th-century religious conflict. Petrie places more emphasis on Hawthorne's critique of the issues—"emotionalism versus restraint, doctrinal purity versus natural compassion, private spiritual experience versus communal obligation, right thinking versus righteous action"—that situated the Awakening at "centerstage" in 19th-century American life. In Petrie's view, Hawthorne warns against intolerance by both religious camps as he gives the moderate Dorothy Pearson his "unalloyed approval" for her "unformalized yet undeniably ethical brand of Christian sentimentality."

Julie E. Hall in " 'Tracing the Original Design': The Hawthornes in Rappaccini's Garden" (*NHR* 21, i: 26–35) argues provocatively that the putatively pure Sophia Hawthorne not only served as Beatrice Rappaccini's "dark" model but actually shared Beatrice's victimization as a "poisoned maiden," thanks to her own father's scientific administrations. Although Hall does not develop a full-fledged interpretation of the tale, she makes effective use of Sophia's 1829–31 journal in supporting her claim that, like Beatrice, Sophia suffered from poisons (arsenic, mercury, opium, morphine) prescribed by her dentist father and various physicians.

Cindy Weinstein (*The Literature of Labor and the Labors of Literature*, pp. 53–86) expands her earlier essay on "The Birthmark" (see *ALS 1993*, p. 33) by adding an interesting analysis of "The Celestial Railroad," featuring a new "economics of allegory" in which Hawthorne destabilizes name/character relations by making them dependent on market forces. Hawthorne's anonymous narrator, she argues, "instantiates the market-based personhood produced by an economics of allegory, which fully enacts the logic of the market while imagining itself transcendent." In effect, Hawthorne's tale deconstructs the "hermeneutic stability" of Bunyan's text and world.

Benjamin Goluboff in " 'A Virtuoso's Collection': Hawthorne, History, and the Wandering Jew" (*NHR* 21, i: 14–25) argues insightfully that this little-known sketch illustrates Hawthorne's conflicted view of history—as a burden to progress and as useful material for the literary imagination. Usefully citing several appearances of the Wandering Jew legend in Hawthorne's writing, Goluboff argues that Hawthorne "deploys" the figure in "A Virtuoso's Collection" in the service of a progressive, nationalist "agenda," which he ultimately subverts.

vi Essays on the Children's Literature

John Lednicky's "The Myth and the Fall: Hawthorne's Critique of Democratic Literary Reform" (*ESQ* 41: 121–51) focuses on the frames of *A Wonder Book* and *Tanglewood Tales* to argue that Hawthorne critiques contemporary mythological and educational theories represented by Charles Anthon's *Classical Dictionary*, the "Young America" movement of the 1840s, and Bronson Alcott's Temple School experiments. Through his narrator Eustace Bright, who initially models democratic authorship before "falling" into professionalism, Hawthorne "questions the integrity of a literary project based on the principles of democratic idealism."

vii Miscellaneous

Readers may want to compare the text of playwright Douglas Langworthy's theatrical version of *The Scarlet Letter* (*AmTheatre* 12, ii: 21–38, including a one-page interview with Phyllis Nagy) with Roland Joffé's screen adaptation. Langworthy's Hester is a "stunning young seamstress who's a master of irony"; Dimmesdale is "sexy and rather capable" (despite his tendency to ask Hester, "Are we there yet?"); Pearl is the "most unusual child in the world" and "must be played by an actress in her late 20s, who at no time attempts to play her as a child."

Southern Illinois University at Carbondale

3 Poe

Kent P. Ljungquist

The publication this year of *The American Face of Edgar Allan Poe* (Hopkins) and *The German Face of Edgar Allan Poe* (Camden House) allows a revaluation of Poe's contributions and influence both at home and abroad. The former, a collection ed. Shawn Rosenheim and Stephen Rachman, promises more on Poe's engagement with American culture than it actually delivers, especially since seven of its 13 essays are previously published reprints or revisions. Rosenheim and Rachman's introduction establishes the limits of their approach by noting Matthiessen's and Parrington's dismissals of Poe, then jumping quickly to Derrida, Lacan, and Continental critics. They suggest that Poe criticism that intervened between the 1920s and the rise of literary theory was colored by binding myths and illusions. Contributors apparently find little variety or utility in scholarship of this intervening period, and errors occasionally intrude, such as the claim that Poe spoke at the Boston Athenaeum (actually the Boston Lyceum, which met at the Odeon, a converted theater). Fewer problems of this kind occur in *The German Face of Poe*, less ambitious in scope but more carefully attuned to traditions of Poe scholarship. Additional comments on individual studies are found below.

i Biographical Studies

Having waited a half century for an authoritative biography to replace Arthur Hobson Quinn's, scholars continue to digest the implications of Kenneth Silverman's *Edgar A. Poe: Mournful and Never-Ending Remembrance* (see *ALS 1991*, p. 44). Several studies this year, of course, rely on Silverman, but more important, deal with biographical cruxes raised anew by him.

Kevin J. Hayes in "Poe's Earliest Reading" (*ELN* 32, iii: 39–43) takes the straightforward approach of examining several books that Poe read during his boyhood sojourn in England. Poe consulted works on English usage, world geography and history, and an anthology of prose and poetry by British authors. The influence of Murray's *English Grammar* persisted until the mid-1830s when it was cited in Poe's reviews. Although Poe did not document the books he consulted as amply as other figures of the American Renaissance (e.g., Melville, Emerson), Hayes reminds us that much more work can be done on his reading.

According to David Leverenz ("Poe and Gentry Virginia," *American Face*, pp. 210–36) Poe manufactured a posture of gentlemanly, aristocratic leisure imbibed from British models. His pose as a Southern gentleman was essentially a fiction, which masked tensions that existed among merchant, plantation, and yeoman interests in Virginia. His hoaxing and intellectual gamesmanship reflected his ostentatious deployment of cultural capital in the literary marketplace. Within this biographical framework, Leverenz offers brief, witty, and provocative readings of "The Man of the Crowd," "The Purloined Letter," "Cask," and "Hop-Frog"—dramas of subjectivity that suggest the uncertain social status of their main characters.

Challenging conventional biographical treatment of Maria Clemm's relationship to Poe ("Maria Clemm, Poe's Aunt: His Boon or His Bane?" *MissQ* 48: 211–24) Burton R. Pollin questions her overall honesty and probity. In examining the evidence for assigning literary executorship to Rufus Griswold, Pollin lays the blame firmly at Mrs. Clemm's door. Assisted by Stella and Sylvanus Lewis, she overlooked Griswold's animosity toward Poe in favor of his editorial stature and competence. Pollin also addresses the textual history and reception of the Redfield edition, a subject also dealt with in Kent Ljungquist and Buford Jones's "William S. Robinson on Griswold: Poe's 'Literary Executioner'" (*PoeS* 28: 7–8).

The biographical crux addressed by Scott Peeples is the final episode of Poe's life, the murky circumstances attending his death in Baltimore in October 1849 ("Life Writing/Death Writing: Biographical Versions of Poe's Final Hours," *Biography* 18: 328–38). Surveying both 19th-century and modern biographies, Peeples notes how the suspect accounts by Dr. John Moran, the physician who attended Poe at Washington Hospital, have influenced the tone, content, and even the structure of these renderings. Peeples concludes that the biographical genre, exemplified in treatments of Poe, blurs the distinction between fact and fiction since life-writing is a textual construct. Omitted from his survey is N. Bryllion Fagin's *The Histrionic Mr. Poe* (1949), the biography that uncovered the artifice and self-consciousness in Poe's presentation of his life to readers.

This is perhaps the place to mention Louis Renza's " 'Ut Pictura Poe': Poetic Politics in 'The Island of the Fay' and 'Morning on the Wissahiccon' " (*American Face*, pp. 305–29), which extends his previous work on "Poe's Secret Autobiography." After claiming that these landscape sketches both reflect and resist various aesthetic categories, Renza notes how Poe revises or undermines their politically codified meanings. Poe ultimately refers us back, via a series of low-level autobiographical allusions, to an "intangible" scene where Poe is the first and only reader of his texts. Renza's method combines synopsis, recourse to secondary criticism on aesthetics, and strained speculation (e.g., "The Island of the Fay" contains a pun on "Lafayette").

ii Bibliography, Sources, Influences

Kent Ljungquist's "Prospects for the Study of Edgar Allan Poe" (*RALS* 21: 173–88) follows a charge to outline the most promising areas and topics for future study; inevitably, this bibliographic essay surveys previous scholarship as a foundation for future investigations. Among the topics specified for new research are Poe's lecturing career; his response to social movements (Freemasonry, temperance); his role in publishing history; and his reception in popular culture. I attempt to supplement 19th-century bibliography on Poe in two studies. I draw on previously unrecorded reprints from New England newspapers in "Some Unrecorded Reprints of Poe's Works" (*ANQ* 8, i: 20–22). In a more ambitious study I assemble 20 previously unrecorded items from Boston newspapers in "Poe's 'Al Aaraaf' and the Boston Lyceum: Contributions to Primary and Secondary Bibliography" (*VPR* 28: 199–216). These items shed new light on Poe's reception at the Boston Lyceum, including reprints of the lengthy "Al Aaraaf" in the *Boston Daily Star* on three successive days.

Scholars on the track of potential magazine sources for Poe's fiction and poetry will want to consult J. Lasley Dameron's "More Analogues and Resources for Poe's Fiction and Poems" (*UMSE* 11–12 [1993–95]: 460–64). Some fruits of Dameron's source hunting can be found in "Poe's *Pym* and Scoresby on Polar Cataracts" (*RALS* 21: 258–68), which extends his previous research on polar travel accounts to William

Scoresby's *An Account of the Arctic Regions with a History and Description of the Northern Whale-Fishery* (1820), a volume that served to enhance verisimilitude in Pym's startling descriptions of immense cataracts. A favorite target for source hunters, *Blackwood's Magazine,* yields Byron K. Brown's discovery of a review by the critic John Wilson ("John Snart's *Thesaurus of Horror:* An Indirect Source of Poe's 'The Premature Burial,'" *ANQ* 8, iii: 11–14). Wilson's review in an 1819 issue of *Blackwood's* exploits and satirizes Snart's overcharged description of live burial.

One target of Dameron's magazine researches, the *Democratic Review* (see *ALS 1991,* p. 50), yields Terence Whalen's "Poe's 'Diddling' and the Depression: Notes on the Sources of Swindling" (*SAF* 23: 195–201). A story in an 1839 issue refers to the "science of raising the wind," a phrase echoed in the various titles of "Diddling," Poe's humorous essay on swindling. Noting another diddler in the New York *Corsair,* Whalen shows how these magazine sources expand Poe's frame of reference in "Diddling" to encompass the economic marketplace in which counterfeit wares were offered to the public by literary confidence men. Poe's text may be a response to the Panic of 1837, though an earlier version of the piece (entitled "Raising the Wind") may have figured in Poe's Folio Club collection.

Far more than a source or influence study, Thomas Hansen's *The German Face of Edgar Allan Poe* examines the sometimes inflated claims about Poe's knowledge of German language and culture. His monograph (developed with the assistance of Burton R. Pollin) ranges from Poe's reputation for "Germanism" to his training in languages and his treatment of German writers, references, and allusions. He notes how the most notorious German features of Poe's work often derived from English sources. While disagreements with previous critics may be occasionally overstated, the treatment of the subject is thorough and the citation of scholarship wide-ranging. Though Poe's reputation for erudition does not escape unscathed, the reader takes away from this study a firmer understanding of his tactics as a practicing magazinist. An appendix supplies a useful checklist of Poe's German references in poems, tales, and essays.

A less wide-ranging study of influence, Katrina Bachinger's *Edgar Allan Poe's Biographies of Byron* (Mellen, 1994) suggests that Poe's fiction constitutes a series of "Byronographies." In this extension of Bachinger's *The Multi-Man Genre* Poe's tales are distinguished from factual biographies in their intertextual relationship to Byron's image or myths developed by Byron's critics. Few would discount the Byronic influence on Poe, and Bachinger offers cogent arguments for the endurance of that impact even after Poe had given up Byron as an explicit model. Bachinger, however, pursues a Byronic Poe relentlessly and to the exclusion of other sources. She strains credulity when she claims that the "Letter to Mr. B——" is addressed to Byron, that Poe took the title of *Eureka* from *Childe Harold's Pilgrimage,* that "Berenice" is based on Byron's romance with Mary Chaworth. Bachinger's bibliographical survey of the Byron-Poe connection omits significant work by Benjamin F. Fisher, Dennis Pahl, and Kent Ljungquist. Her insight that Ligeia is a siren was anticipated by Daryl E. Jones (see *ALS 1983,* pp. 54–55), and her claim that Poe's pseudonym "Lyttleton Barry" derived from Bulwer was made in 1970 by Burton R. Pollin. A July 1835 review of Irving's *Crayon Miscellany,* appearing in the Harrison edition and cited as an example of Byronic influence, was not Poe's.

Among other influence studies, Richard Kopley in "Hawthorne's Transplanting and Transforming 'The Tell-Tale Heart'" (*SAF* 23: 231–41) argues that Hawthorne's reading in *The Pioneer* and his continuing interest in Poe in the late 1840s caused him to transfer elements of Poe's tale into *The Scarlet Letter.* Kopley focuses on the motif of the "Evil Eye," then carefully examines structural aspects of Poe's tale and its thematic transformation into Hawthorne's fiction. In "Edgar Allan Poe in Edith Wharton's *Old New York*" (*PoeS* 28: 9) David Ketterer examines the context of Poe-esque allusions in Wharton's "False Dawn." In "'Walking to Sleep' and Richard Wilbur's Quest for Rational Imagination" (*TCL* 41: 249–65) Philip White takes up Wilbur's quarrel with the aesthetics of Poe. White opposes values important for Wilbur (balance, order, and engagement with society and nature) to Poe's flight from temporal realities.

iii Poe and Detection

In "Winning the Game: Inductive Reasoning in Poe's 'The Murders in the Rue Morgue'" (*SIR* 33 [1994]: 223–54) Loisa Nygaard asserts the dominance of inductive reasoning in Poe's tales of ratiocination. Examining the game played between Poe and his readers, she detects uncertainty accompanying Dupin's inductive methods as he narrows his field of investigation. Nygaard cites authorities on inductive reasoning that Poe may have consulted (William Whewell, Mill, Macaulay), but her analysis founders when claiming that Poe wrote the so-called "Paulding-Drayton" review, an erroneous attribution also made by Joan Dayan in *The American Face of Poe* (pp. 181–82). This defense of slavery in the 1836 *Southern Literary Messenger* has been conclusively shown to be the work of Judge Beverley Tucker. Nygaard also seems unaware that Poe had a hand in Thomas Wyatt's *A Synopsis of Natural History*.

Whewell's possible influence on Poe also plays a role in Lawrence Frank's " 'The Murders in the Rue Morgue': Edgar Allan Poe's Evolutionary Reverie" (*NCF* 50: 168–88), which approaches Poe's first detective story from the perspective of the history and philosophy of science. Frank situates the tale at a time of historical transformation and crisis when resurgent evangelicism and natural theology were confronted by new developments in science. Among scientific influences, Frank devotes primary attention to the work of J. P. Nichol, who advanced Laplace's nebular hypothesis to American audiences. Frank reads back the influence of Nichol, cited in *Eureka,* to an earlier point in Poe's career. Both Frank and Nygaard would have been well served to draw on Susan Welsh's excellent work on Poe's knowledge of the rhetoric and philosophy of science (see *ALS 1991,* p. 47).

Shawn Rosenheim reapplies his theoretical approach to cryptography in "Detective Fiction, Psychoanalysis, and the Analytic Sublime" (*American Face,* pp. 153–76). Aligning Dupin with disembodied reason (termed the "analytic sublime"), Rosenheim explores the disjunction between linguistic signs and physical bodies in the Rue Morgue. Given his interest in Poe's "elaborate sexual symbolism," an invitation to psychoanalytic critics, it is surprising that Rosenheim fails to cite J. A. Leo Lemay's study of "Murders" (see *ALS 1982,* p. 51).

Building on John Walsh's researches into the historical Mary Rogers, Laura Saltz's elaborate and detailed contribution to *The American Face of Poe* (" 'Horrible to Relate!': Recovering the Body of Marie Rogêt,' " pp. 237–67) examines Marie Rogêt as textual subject. Saltz offers insightful comments on Poe's omissions, evasions, and concealments as he transformed Mary Rogers into Marie Rogêt. Noting how topics related to female sexuality (e.g., abortion) were often driven underground in the periodical milieu of the 1840s, Saltz takes a fresh look at the ways the New York dailies profitably exploited the scandal and disappearance of Mary. Poe's tale, through the contradictory figure of Marie, mirrors the publishing world in which a mutilated female body accrues interest in a system of mass circulation. The tale's irresolution reflects ambiguous attempts to interpret the feminine in antebellum culture, and Saltz shows how Poe's editorial interpolations merit as careful scrutiny as his more overt flourishes.

The only essay this year that treats all three Dupin stories is William Crisman's well-documented "Poe's Dupin as Professional: The Dupin Stories as Serial Text" (*SAF* 23: 215–29). Challenging the general assumption that Dupin is an amateur detective as well as more specific assertions by a range of critics, Crisman treats Dupin as a fee-for-service professional, analogous to a prizefighter who takes on an occasional challenge for a rich purse. He sees persuasive evidence of monetary exchange in the tales, and he finds in Dupin's quest for money a need to alleviate his aristocratic dispossession. As one traces Dupin's evolution from "Murders" and "Marie Rogêt" to "The Purloined Letter," one detects a growing professionalism, but not necessarily a debasement of intellectual detachment or acuity via market forces. Rather, Crisman recalls Poe's attachment to materialist theories of mind, evidenced in "Mesmeric Revelation" and selected satires.

iv   The Narrative of Arthur Gordon Pym

Once an anomaly in the Poe canon, his longest narrative became the subject of a second book-length study, J. Gerald Kennedy's Arthur Gordon Pym *and the Abyss of Interpretation* (Twayne). Dividing critics of *Pym* into two recognizable categories—those who trace Pym's growth toward spirituality and selfhood and those who find a blind movement toward illusion or meaninglessness—Kennedy leaves the reader hanging at the edge of an interpretive abyss. Poe's challenge to coherent readings is previewed in the preface to *Pym,* aimed at hoaxing gullible readers. Kennedy traces whatever limited growth Pym achieves, and he establishes the limits of that development in the episodes at Tsalal. Kennedy may minimize the cogency of visionary readings of *Pym,* especially in his discussion of its enigmatic ending, and I wish he had included in his bibliographical survey the work of J. P. Hussey, Judith Sutherland, Curtis Fukuchi, and William Lenz. Nevertheless, he provides an informative reader's guide to the narrative and the multiple interpretations it has stimulated.

One topic mentioned prominently in Kennedy's overview, *Pym*'s relationship to antebellum debates on slavery and race, is the subject of Sam Worley's *"The Narrative of Arthur Gordon Pym* and the Ideology of

Slavery" (*ESQ* 40 [1994]: 219–50). The Tsalalian episodes seem to be
influenced by proslavery discourse, suggested by Worley's sampling of
writings by Southern apologists, and the portrayal of the natives con-
forms to a commonly held image of blacks as bloodthirsty savages or
compliant children. Worley may exaggerate the extent to which writers
for the *Southern Literary Messenger* reflected purely sectional political
bias, since that magazine aimed to reach a national audience, as evidenced by the positive reception of its early issues in selected Northeastern newspapers. He may also exaggerate the extent to which natural
phenomena in *Pym* (i.e., the penguin rookery) mirror social hierarchies.
Worley concludes that Poe's conservative social vision may, in fact, be
undermined by the competing levels of language in the text.

v Poe as Literary Critic

Stephen Rachman in "'Es lässt sich nicht schreiben': Plagiarism and
'The Man of the Crowd'" (*American Face,* pp. 49–87) provides an
overview of various theories of plagiarism. Rachman, moving the subject
beyond Poe's alleged pilfering from specific authors, examines the theatrical and critical use of borrowed materials in new texts. He examines
the *Marginalia* in terms of Poe's removal of other texts into his own
critical space. With Poe's use of materials from Dickens's *Sketches by Boz*
in "The Man of the Crowd" as a case study, Rachman expands his
discussion to the destabilization of authorship in antebellum culture.
Noting the prominent metaphor of absorption in Poe's comments in the
"Longfellow War," Rachman underscores the connections between the
act of writing and an author's reading of other texts.

James Russell Lowell's call for an "American criticism" is the subject of
Meredith L. McGill's "Poe, Literary Nationalism, and Authorial Identity" (*American Face,* pp. 271–304). The biographical portrait of Poe
supplied by Lowell for *Graham's Magazine* in 1845 marked an important
consolidation of Poe's reputation, especially as its contents were incorporated into the program of the "Young America" movement in New York.
Through a figurative reading of Lowell's essay, McGill examines its praise
for Poe's "independent" (i.e., "self-supporting") critical practice. Within
the context of the essay's reception in New York periodicals, Poe is seen as
a full participant (rather than merely a victim or critic) of antebellum
publishing practices. Like Rachman, McGill addresses the "Longfellow
War," but her interest lies less in Poe's attempt to establish literary

priority over his New England antagonist than in the struggle for authorial distinction in a system that circulated or scattered undifferentiated or anonymous texts. The attack on Longfellow, coupled with his subsequent appearance at the Boston Lyceum, did much to unsettle Poe's tenuous and fleeting ties to Young America. McGill suggests that Lowell's essay may have anticipated William Carlos Williams's treatment of Poe in *In the American Grain.*

Jonathan Elmer's argument in *Reading at the Social Limit: Affect, Mass Culture, and Edgar Allan Poe* (Stanford) defies easy summary, but he too invokes Lowell and Williams to explore Poe's ambivalent attitude toward a culture of mass circulation. For Elmer, Poe's criticism ceaselessly verifies the same world that seems to undermine claims to originality and ownership. In plagiarism controversies Poe asserts his principles relentlessly, since the stakes in these wars are nothing less than character, conscience, the necessary application of self-critical faculties. This claim leads Elmer to an ingenious reading of "William Wilson," a text that calls into question notions of subject and possession. Novel juxtapositions also highlight Elmer's chapter on the fate of Little Eva in *Uncle Tom's Cabin* and the death throes of Poe's Ernest Valdemar (excerpted in *American Face,* pp. 91–120). For Elmer the sentimental and the sensational are complementary modes, since they both communicate across an apparent divide between life and death, defined as a social limit. Interactions at this limit occur as scenes of reading and interpretation, provoking Poe's distortion of sentimental motifs in "Valdemar." If the flow of sensibility (imaged as tears, floods, streams) is contained by didacticism in the sentimental novel, Poe tests and transgresses those limits as M. Valdemar is liquidated on his deathbed. In sections of the book where Poe is not center stage, Elmer's specialized critical vocabulary (relying on Zizek, Lacan, and others) may test the limits of some readers' patience. He offers analyses of "The Man That Was Used Up" and "Autography," which purport to offer access to unique "personalities" only to disclose generic or social figures.

vi Poetry, Poetics

This year marked the 150th anniversary of the publication of "The Raven," *The Raven and Other Poems,* and Poe's reading at the Boston Lyceum (at which he read "The Raven"), but only E. W. Pitcher's note, "Poe's 'The Raven' and the *Anacreonta*" (*N&Q* 42: 188–89), touches on

Poe's most famous poem. If T. O. Mabbott noted how the opening of "The Raven" bore similarities to a passage in Thomas Moore's translation of the *Anacreonta*, Pitcher finds a version with phrasing and diction closer to Poe in the *Pennsylvanian Magazine*. Daniel Hoffman brings his authoritative knowledge of Poe and poetics to bear in "Edgar Allan Poe: The Artist of the Beautiful" (*APR* 24, vi: 11–18). Sensitive to the limits of Poe's aesthetics as well as to his poetic excesses, Hoffman nonetheless praises "The Lake" as a nature poem and the formal properties of the "Sonnet—To Science." He also defends Poe's literary ballads, noting that they were often real aloud and that their metrical and rhythmic effects were more acceptable in Poe's time. Hoffman also reminds us that several of Poe's poems dramatize the psychological states of their speakers. As an elegantly written overview, Hoffman's essay is recommended reading.

If Hoffman also reminds us that Poe was drawn to dramas that contained the seeds of their own destruction, Gillian Brown ("The Poetics of Extinction," *American Face*, pp. 330–44) asserts that signs of intelligence transcend those forces of oblivion. Her general essay notes the survival of mind and consciousness via the narrator in "Usher." Poe eschews the generative power of women in favor of their service to consciousness, evidenced by their survival in memory or as poetic subjects.

vii Individual Tales

In "Harems, Orientalist Subversions, and the Crisis of Nationalism: The Case of Edgar Allan Poe and 'Ligeia'" (*Criticism* 37: 601–23) Malini Johar Schueller begins with the promising premise of approaching "Ligeia" as an Oriental tale. Schueller finds in American Orientalism an identification with Britain as a power that held sway over people of color. Poe in "Ligeia" parodies Orientalist discourse, which intersects with parallel discourses of Southern nationality and womanhood, all of which undergo eventual subversion. By the end of Schueller's study, Poe's tale has been burdened by so much ideological baggage that it may be unrecognizable, except to those partial to politicized readings. Schueller is not alone in naively attributing the "Paulding-Drayton" review to Poe (see section iii, above), and she mistakenly identifies critic Kenneth A. Hovey as Alan Hovey. The subversion of gender relations is also taken up by Eva Cherniavsky ("Revivification and Utopian Time: Poe Versus Stowe," *American Face*, pp. 121–38), who unaccountably claims that "virtually no critics have perceived Ligeia's maternal characteristics."

(John W. Robertson, Joseph Wood Krutch, and other psychoanalytically inclined critics have stressed Poe's quest for a mother figure, and, most notoriously, Marie Bonaparte was nearly apologetic in repeating her Freudian thesis when including "Ligeia" among her "Tales of the Mother.")

In "Painful Erasures: Excising the Wild Eye from 'The Oval Portrait'" (*PoeS* 28: 1–6) Paula Kot examines textual changes in the tale originally titled "Life in Death." The series of gazes in the tale lead her to unmask the power relations implicit in the narrator's masculine perspective and in male-sponsored art. Kot pays specific attention to Poe's elimination of the passage on the "wild eye," which allows the tables to be turned on the narrator. Kot sometimes distinguishes Poe and his narrator, then blurs that distinction when it suits her thesis. She draws on work of Elisabeth Bronfen, whose "Risky Resemblances: On Repetition, Death, and Mourning" (*Death and Representation* [Hopkins, 1993], pp. 103–29) also addresses Poe's attitude toward dying women.

"William Wilson," a tale that invites psychological rather than political readings, is the subject of two studies, both of which can be read alongside the relevant chapter in Jonathan Elmer's *Reading at the Social Limit* (see section iv, above). According to Julia Stern ("Double Talk: The Rhetoric of the Whisper in 'William Wilson,'" *ESQ* 40: 185–218) Poe's tale is grounded in the sectional politics of the 1830s. The rendering of the split self has political suggestiveness, reflecting contemporary debates about secession and abolition. Though her reading is not ultimately convincing, she offers interesting comments on the genre of melodrama, which offers insight into the failed integration of the warring doubles of the story. In "The Common Property of the Mob: Democracy and Identity in Poe's 'William Wilson'" (*MissQ* 48: 197–210) Theron Britt examines the tale within the framework of Poe's dismissals of the democratic rabble. According to Britt, the tale inscribes fear about the threat to the individual brought on by conflicts between Whigs and Democrats in the 1840s. Britt's analysis might have been strengthened by citation of previous discussions by Elizabeth Phillips on Tocqueville and David Long on the American Whigs (see *ALS 1990*, p. 49). If the target of the tale is the American political landscape of the 1830s, moreover, Britt never adequately explains why Poe chose not to address that milieu directly nor to set the story on American soil.

Two short studies address Poe's humor with decidedly different results. In "What if Poe's Humorous Tales Were Funny? Poe's 'X-ing a Paragrab' and Twain's 'Journalism in Tennessee'" (*StAH* 3: 36–48) Tom Quirk essentially uses Poe as a foil to Twain in his comparison of each author's handling of journalistic practices. Quirk's verdict: Twain is much funnier. After "Lifting the Lid on Poe's 'Oblong Box'" (*SAF* 23: 203–14) Bonnie Shannon McMullen detects self-referential and political elements. Her discussion moves beyond the surface story to note its parodic or ironic touches and its send-up of popular fiction. The tale contains puns and low-level allusions, and even its grotesque humor may be one index of Poe's higher artistic motives.

Worcester Polytechnic Institute

4 Melville

John Samson

This was a strong year for Melville studies, with several significant book-length studies published. Among the topics that received particular attention were Melville's influences and his relationship to the visual arts; *Moby-Dick* continued to be the focus of major attention; and "Benito Cereno" was the subject of several good essays.

i General

Three accomplished books address philosophical concerns over the course of Melville's career. The most narrowly focused is *Melville's Art of Democracy* (Georgia), in which Nancy Fredricks applies Kant's concept of the sublime to a reading of *Moby-Dick* and *Pierre* in order "to identify and analyze various theoretical positions represented in Melville's work that bear on the relation between democratic values and artistic-critical practice," particularly "issues of class, popular culture, feminism, and aesthetics." Drawing on historical as well as theoretical contexts, Fredricks sees the two works as a contrasting diptych in which Ahab's fanaticism and Pierre's enthusiasm demonstrate two errors in facing the Kantian sublime. She also ably uses historical materials to discuss typology in *Moby-Dick* and melodrama and the Antirent War in *Pierre*. Fredricks's conclusion develops her thesis further in a discussion of Platonism and the Kantian sublime in Melville's short works, particularly "The Piazza." Focusing on the continuous but shifting "dualistic conflict, both linguistic and philosophical," between head and heart, Clark Davis in *After the Whale: Melville in the Wake of* Moby-Dick (Alabama) traces this central thematic concern from *Moby-Dick* through *Billy Budd, Sailor*. Seeing *Moby-Dick* as involving a Bakhtinian dialogue between mind (Ahab) and body (Ishmael) and the forces of language in which each is rooted, Davis shows—in the "ascetic," "fragmented," and "inverted" fiction that follows—Melville's decreasing faith in the body and in the embodiment of meaning. Davis then presents a notably coherent and persuasive reading of the poetry. In the "political and theological revisions of *Battle-Pieces* and *Clarel*" and through the later poems and *Billy Budd, Sailor,* Davis argues, "Melville pushes always in search of the double voices that offer the potential for reunion, the way toward rebirth and transcendence that Ishmael's experience and the whale's 'live sea' provide." Similar in seeing a dualistic concern pervading Melville's work, yet offering a more scholarly and precise analysis is John Wenke's *Melville's Muse: Literary Creation and the Forms of Philosophical Fiction* (Kent State). Grounding his study in a careful consideration of Melville's reading, Wenke concentrates on "the emerging forms through which 'the moral imagination' achieves expression." He begins with a strong account of Melville's attempt in *Mardi* to develop a literary form adequate to his philosophical quest. Wenke then discusses how "metaphysical ingredients" such as allusion, scenes of reading, and essayistic excursions found in *Redburn* and *White-Jacket* lead to the full and multilayered philosophical discourse of *Moby-Dick*—a particularly powerful reading of the conceptual framework (the conflict between the noumenal and the phenomenal in all its varied and complex articulations) of Melville's masterwork. Finally, Wenke analyzes *Pierre* and *The Confidence-Man* as extensions of Melville's "ontological and epistemological preoccupations": Pierre is "unable to escape the fixed text he has made of his life," but the narrator "records unfolding negotiations between what is knowable and inscrutable"; *The Confidence-Man* reveals Platonic dialogue and performance as means of self-possession and empowerment.

Several shorter studies also cover wide periods in Melville's work. In *America and the Sea* (pp. 127–45) Haskell Springer and Douglas Robillard chart Melville's course as writer of sea literature and thus provide a clear and sound introduction to the importance and meaning of the sea throughout his career. The two authors show that Melville "dove deeply into a nautical world of power and mystery, discovering, inventing, and revealing a sea of meanings stretching far beyond the immediate into psychology, culture, metaphysics, and literary expression itself." David Laskin's section on Melville and Hawthorne in *A Common Life* (pp. 27–94) adds little to previous accounts of their relationship, however. Ruth Blair's "Melville and Hawaii: Reflections on a New

Melville Letter" (*SAR*, pp. 229–50) is an insightful and valuable account of Melville's relationship with Hawaii. Blair's original and painstaking research not only clarifies Melville's ambivalent attitudes but provides evidence of "the 'hybrid' quality" of the missionaries' and others' views of Melville and his works. The incidents Blair describes are, moreover, "glimpses of the ways in which white people who had opted to settle in Polynesia privately confronted the gap of understanding between themselves and the 'other.' " Cindy Weinstein's chapter on "Melville's Operatives" in *The Literature of Labor and the Labors of Literature* (pp. 87–128) develops the thesis that "Melville's allegorical characters foreground the potentially damaging consequences of industrial labor at the same time as they enable him to devise an alternative narrative of literary labor." Weinstein's strong, well-grounded argument discusses Melville's subversive critique of the work ethic in *Mardi*, the "conflicted relations to changes in labor" involving individual accountability in *Moby-Dick*, and the question of interiority in *Billy Budd, Sailor* as related to the Haymarket trials and to legal issues in "Benito Cereno." Lee Clark Mitchell's " 'Another World, Yet One to which We Feel the Tie': Melville's Melodramatic Imagination," pp. 21–31 in *Colóquio Herman Melville*, ed. Teresa Ferreira de Almeida Alves and Teresa Cid (Edições Colibri, 1994), argues that melodrama, the mode which attempts to express totality, characterizes the qualities in Melville's prose that attempt to move beyond nature or realism. As Mitchell concludes, "Melville's art becomes a series of gestures to transcendent truths that never in fact *are* realized." George Monteiro's "Melville's Camoens and the Figure of the Artist," pp. 87–110 in *Colóquio Herman Melville*, reviews Melville's references to the epic poet.

Two book-length reference works should be valuable tools for Melville studies. Robert L. Gale's *A Herman Melville Encyclopedia* (Greenwood) contains entries summarizing Melville's works, characters, places, and references. It aims, Gale says, "to be of special help to readers just beginning to appreciate Melville," but it will also be a convenient aid to more experienced students and teachers. Of more value to Melville scholars is Brian Higgins and Hershel Parker's collection, *Herman Melville: The Contemporary Reviews* (Cambridge); in making these reviews readily available, along with a concise yet thorough introductory summary, Higgins and Parker indeed offer "a substantial sourcebook and . . . a challenge to scholars and general readers alike." Also of assistance to Melville scholars is the expansion and clarification provided by

Merton M. Sealts, Jr., in "A Second Supplementary Note to *Melville's Reading* (1988)" (*MSEx* 100: 2–3). Hershel Parker in "Biography and Responsible Uses of the Imagination: Three Episodes from Melville's Homecoming in 1844" (*RALS* 21: 16–42) previews a short but highly significant series of events from Parker's forthcoming biography and provides interesting insights into the scholarly and imaginative work of the biographer.

Four essays deal with Melville's influence on more recent authors. Martin Wank in "Melville and Wolfe: The Wisdom of Ecclesiastes" (*TWN* 19, ii: 1–19) adds little to our understanding of Melville and the Bible but does make a limited case for his influence on Wolfe. María Irene Ramalho de Sousa Santos in "Plagiarism in Praise: Paul Auster and Melville," pp. 111–22 in *Colóquio Herman Melville,* discusses Auster's *The New York Trilogy* (1987) as an intentionally Melvillean parody of the American Renaissance authors, particularly Thoreau. In the same collection Mário Vitor Bastos's "Herman Melville and the Poetry of W. S. Merwin" (pp. 139–48) discusses the affinities between Melville's and Merwin's sea poetry, while Adelaide Batista's "Herman Melville and Europe: Eugénio de Andrade in 'Plaza del Viento' " (pp. 149–59) focuses on Melville's impact on modern Portuguese writers, especially the poet de Andrade.

ii The Visual Arts

Deepening recent interest in Melville and the visual arts are several studies, the most important of which is clearly Elizabeth A. Schultz's *Unpainted to the Last:* Moby-Dick *and Twentieth-Century American Art* (Kansas). Schultz presents a literally illuminating and comprehensive account of visual artists' engagement with Melville's text—in their illustrated editions, in abstract expressionist paintings and sculptures, in narrative and realistic representations, in objects, popular culture, performance art, architecture, etc. The many artists Schultz analyzes, "in their attempt to embody 'the visible truth' in the novel, . . . deepen the reader's and the viewer's understanding of its many meanings for American culture in particular and for humanity in general." She includes a vast number of illustrations, as well as lively and perceptive discussion of the artistic and literary issues raised by her topic. A beautiful and valuable book, *Unpainted to the Last* will be of great interest to Melville scholars and to anyone involved in American cultural studies. Schultz supplements her book with an essay, "Re-Viewing Melville: The Illustrated Editions" (*MSEx* 103: 1–18), which describes illustrated versions of *Moby-Dick* and other works. She shows that "these illustrators individually and collectively open Melville's works in terms of space, time, and motion and in terms of the possibilities for discovering meaning." John Bryant's "Clifford Ross on Melville and Modern Art: An Interview" (*MSEx* 102: 1–7) reveals the impact of *Moby-Dick* on a contemporary artist and provides interesting insights into both of its title's topics. Two essays by Robert K. Wallace identify the connection of Melville to the art of his day and ours. "Melville's Prints: The Ambrose Group" (*HLB* 6, i: 13–50) deepens our awareness of Melville's interest in art, his interest in Hazlitt, and the relation of the prints and his reading to his poetry; "Frank Stella Under the Sign of Melville, Encore" (*Art press* 200: 18–25) relates Stella's works *Hooloomooloo, Loohooloo,* and *Ohonoo* to Melville's locations in *Omoo* and *Mardi.*

iii Typee to *White-Jacket*

Elizabeth Renker's "Melville's Spell in *Typee*" (*ArQ* 51, ii: 1–31) is a clever argument for "Melville's anxiety about the scene of writing," largely because of his "copying" large amounts of material from his sources. The anxiety, Renker attempts to show, is evident primarily in his orthography—his spelling problems and his bad handwriting—and in the theme of tattooing. Tightly if dubiously argued, the essay might be more convincing with a more concerted consideration of those sources that Renker rightly claims are important to Melville's composition of the novel. Less striking is John Carlos Rowe's "Melville's *Typee:* U.S. Imperialism at Home and Abroad," pp. 255–78 in *National Identities and Post-Americanist Narratives;* Rowe reviews issues of race and empire but adds little to previous discussions, which he selectively cites. In Paul Lyon's sophisticated psychoanalytical reading, "From Man-Eaters to Spam-Eaters: Literary Tourism and the Discourse of Cannibalism from Herman Melville to Paul Theroux" (*ArQ* 51, ii: 33–62), *Typee* is a "founding text" in the tradition he discusses: its perspective "embodies the tastes, fantasies, and even internal critiques or self-divisions of a dominant culture." Boris Vejdovsky's *"Typee,* or Melville as Apprentice Seaman and Freshman Writer" (*EdL* 3 [1993]: 87–103) ignores virtually all criticism of the novel since D. H. Lawrence and is little more than a commonplace, freshman account. Drawing on the theories of Foucault and de Certeau

but on little historical or critical research, Cesare Casarino in "Gomor-
rahs of the Deep or, Melville, Foucault, and the Question of Hetero-
topia" (*ArQ* 51, iv: 1–25) analyzes the semiotics of space mainly in *White-
Jacket;* its tropes and representations are "directed toward producing a
radically heterogenous space" characteristic of the crisis of modernity in
Western cultural discourse over the last two centuries, particularly the
discourse of homosexuality.

iv Moby-Dick

Three shorter essays deal with Melville's sources. Collamer M. Abbott in
"Melville and the Panoramas" (*MSEx* 101: 1–14) discusses the likelihood
that Melville had seen several panoramas, a popular exhibition form in
the late 1840s; Abbott also argues that this form may have had an
influence on Melville's "panoramic style" in the novel. Douglas Robillard
in "Lorenz Oken and *Moby-Dick*" (*MSEx* 100: 8–9) briefly indicates
how concepts from Oken's *Elements of Physiophilosophy* figure in Melville's novel. James C. Keil's "Melville's 'American Goldsmith': *Moby-
Dick* and Irving's *A History of New York*" (*MSEx* 102: 13–16) finds that
"Melville made frequent use of the words, ideas, tone, narrative technique, and structure of Irving's *History.*" Examining *Moby-Dick* as influence are two essays in *C. L. R. James: His Intellectual Legacies* (Mass.,
1994), ed. Selwyn R. Cudjoe and William E. Cain. Cedric J. Robinson in
"C. L. R. James and the World System" (pp. 244–59) asserts the continuing power of James's reading of *Moby-Dick* in *Mariners, Renegades,
and Castaways,* while Cain in "The Triumph of the Will and the Failure
of Resistance: C. L. R. James' Reading of *Moby-Dick* and *Othello*"
(pp. 260–73) sees the reading as "extremely provocative" yet "inaccurate,
an enlightening distortion" that says more about James than Melville.

   Among the studies interpreting aspects of the novel is Lyle Glazier's
"Melville's 'Feminine Air' and 'Masculine Sea'." (*AJES* 16 [1994]: 138–56).
Glazier rates the characters in *Moby-Dick* on a scale of "masculine
strength and feminine sympathy," with Ishmael striking the balance
between the two; more interesting is his suggestion, not fully developed,
that Melville is counterposing Platonic and Aristotelian systems of
thought. Rod Phillips's "Melville's *Moby-Dick*" (*Expl* 53: 92–95) points
out the obvious racial issues in the "Stubb's Supper" chapter. Using the
deconstructive formulations of metaphor and the body, Doran Larson in
"Of Blood and Words: Ahab's Rhetorical Body" (*MLS* 25, ii: 18–33)

shows Ahab involved in a figural "struggle between materialism and deconstruction" that also exposes a text struggling with "the problem of analogy" central to Western philosophy. A more concerted study of the novel, Pamela A. Boker's "'Circle-Sailing': The Eternal Return of Tabooed Grief in Melville's *Moby-Dick*" in *The Grief Taboo* (pp. 38–67) presents a psychoanalytical reading that focuses on the characters' and Melville's experience of maternal abandonment. Thus, Ahab's repressed grief over this loss is channeled into an aggression against the image of the "bad mother"—nature, the sea, and "the white-whale breast of Moby Dick"—while Ishmael demonstrates "the regressive lure toward unconscious, egoless merging with the lost 'good mother'"—ambivalence, utopian fantasy, and Queequeg. Whether or not one agrees with her model, one can credit Boker for seeing the novel as "Melville's perilous voyage into the depths of the unconscious."

For those who are able to navigate his formidable theoretical vocabulary and complex syntax, William V. Spanos's *The Errant Art of* Moby-Dick is extraordinarily rewarding. Using primarily Heidegger and Foucault, Spanos demonstrates that Melville's novel is deliberately "errant," "an indissolubly multisituated, negatively capable or de-structive project that escapes—indeed, exists to undermine—the totalizing, hegemonic American discourse" that reaches from the Puritans to the Vietnam War. In showing how Melville undermines this "American episteme"—in its ontological, anthropological, economic, political, and literary aspects—Spanos testifies to the full range of Melville's genius and situates the novel firmly in its time but also presciently in ours. Situating his own reading in opposition to the cold war ideology of past Melville critics and in response to more recent New Americanists, Spanos provides considerable insight into the development of *Moby-Dick* criticism and its relation to larger political and intellectual issues. *The Errant Art of* Moby-Dick should find its decentered place among the finest studies of Melville's novel.

v *Pierre* through *The Confidence-Man*

Hershel Parker's controversial "Kraken Edition" (HarperCollins) of what Parker argues in his extensive "Introduction" (pp. xi–xlvi) is "the original *Pierre*" omits all passages on Pierre-as-author but includes marvelous illustrations by Maurice Sendak. With no direct evidence for his editorial choice but with a full and detailed biographical account of the novel's

creation and publication, Parker may not convince everyone that this is
indeed the ur-*Pierre*. This edition, "intended to supplement (not to
rival) the text Harper published," does, however, offer a provocative
challenge to our conception of Melville as novelist. Priscilla Wald's " 'As
From a Faithful Mirror': *Pierre, Our Nig,* and Literary Nationalism,"
pp. 106–71 in *Constituting Americans,* places *Pierre* in the context, fully
and insightfully presented, of the Young America movement and "the
narrative of Manifest Destiny." Seeing "Hawthorne and His Mosses" as
Melville's initial critique of "Young America's paradigm of authorship,"
Wald shows Pierre unknowingly confronting this paradigm and the
larger cultural discourse it represents. His is "a culturally unauthorized
story" in which Pierre's internalization of cultural conventions, evident
in the Gothic and in Young America, limits his authorship and structures
his sense of self even as he futilely and conflictedly attempts to assert
his independence. John Bryant in *"Israel Potter* Old and New: The
Discourse between Facsimile and Critical Edition" (*RALS* 21: 261–
73) develops the dialogue between Hennig Cohen's facsimile and the
Northwestern-Newberry editions of the novel, demonstrating the value
to Melville scholars in the textual differences and in Cohen's considerable
back matter. Bryant's analysis ultimately aims "to argue for more deeply
historical ways of approaching Melville."

Among the essays dealing with Melville's short fiction, Maurice Lee's
"Melville's 'Mistakes': Correcting the Politics of 'Poor Man's Pudding
and Rich Man's Crumbs' " (*ESQ* 41: 153–75) is likely the best. In his
scholarly and persuasive study Lee shows how Melville's supposed "mistakes" are, when read in light of considerable historical research, tactical:
Lee's careful examination of references to Napoleonism, exchange rates,
and the morality of sugar production reveals Melville's tale to be an
intricate and powerful "commentary on class oppression" in 1854 and its
relation to racial and national issues. It is, like Melville's other tales, "a
calculated satire of antebellum political rhetoric." David Harley Serlin in
"The Dialogue of Gender in Melville's 'The Paradise of Bachelors and
the Tartarus of Maids' " (*MLS* 25, ii: 80–87) concentrates on Melville's
"fluid" narrator and conceives of the tale as "set within a liminal space in
which the privileging of sexuality, or gender, or power is never absolutely
maintained." Less originally, Teresa F. A. Alves's "A Glimpse of the
Enchanted Isles from Melville's Royal Box," pp. 51–59 in *Colóquio
Herman Melville,* relates *The Piazza Tales,* particularly "The Encan-
tadas," to Spenserian scenarios. Marvin Hunt in " '*That's* the Word':

Turning Tongues and Heads in 'Bartleby, the Scrivener' " (*ESQ* 40 [1994]: 275–92) focuses on the linguistic and intellectual changes Melville's narrator undergoes as a result of his experiences with the scrivener. "Foiling the language of rational inquiry," Hunt says, "Bartleby draws the narrator from an Enlightenment methodology . . . toward a more capacious way of speaking—and thus of knowing—based in suprarational linguistic devices" such as metaphor, a final position that Hunt believes parallels Emerson's "The Poet." Thomas Bulger's " 'Bartleby,' Burton, and the Artistic Temperament" (*MSEx* 101: 14–17) examines Melville's subtle use of Burton's categories in his characterizations, with Bartleby as "radically melancholy" and the narrator as "the sanguine melancholy of the creative consciousness."

Among the short fiction, "Benito Cereno" received the most concerted and successful attention. Sheila Post-Lauria's "Editorial Politics in Herman Melville's 'Benito Cereno' " (*AmPer* 5: 1–13) locates Melville's tale in the context of the editorial policies of *Putnam's Monthly*, showing that Melville's engagement with the issues of nationalism and race reflects similar positions voiced in numerous political articles in the magazine. Recognizing this link between text and context, Post-Lauria argues, may "help to clarify a narrative structure and voice that some have seen as ambiguous at best." Gavin Jones's "Dusky Comments of Silence: Language, Race, and Herman Melville's 'Benito Cereno' " (*SSF* 32: 39–50) is a careful discussion of the issue of language, demonstrating that Delano, as representative of racist linguistic tendencies in the 1850s, "is blinded by an African community capable of manipulating various levels of communication (writing, masquerade, song), and capable of a competence in the Spanish tongue that flatly contradicts the type of European (or 'Indo-European') linguistic absolutism that attempted to create hierarchies of language to justify its colonial and cultural aims." Adam Zachary Newton's *Narrative Ethics* includes a reading of "Benito Cereno" (pp. 207–22) that centers on the ethical impact of facial and other visual imagery. Newton concludes that "one of *Benito Cereno*'s two logics (or ethics) of monstration—the de-facing of a black man—can't help undercutting the other—the 'showing forth' of an America tormented by and through slavery." In a close reading of Delano and Melville's "lawyerly" narrator, Richard V. McLamore in "Narrative Self-Justification: Melville and Amasa Delano" (*SAF* 23: 35–53) argues that "*Benito Cereno*'s textual strategies hinge upon an imposition of the nascent, predominantly Northern form of grasping, exploitive, and prejudicial self-definitions masked and often confused by the idealist, religiously-colored nationalistic sentiment that is narratively attributed to Delano's character." Dennis Pahl in "The Gaze of History in 'Benito Cereno'" (*SSF* 32: 171–83) insightfully uses Foucault's Nietzschean genealogy to approach the issue of historiography in Melville's tale. Recognizing the violence inherent in such totalizing accounts of history as Delano's, Pahl sees Melville's view of history as "one that, in revealing history's imposing gaps, its eloquent silences, and its counter-discourses, finally makes it possible for the Other (otherwise kept silent) to speak." Less successfully applying a poststructuralist perspective is Reinhold J. Dooley's "Fixing Meaning: Babo as Sign in 'Benito Cereno'" (*ATQ* 9: 41–50). Dooley's textbook deconstruction presents Babo as an embodiment of the sign that subverts Delano's logocentric drive to fixity. Finally, Earl Rovit's "Melville and the Discovery of America," pp. 7–19 in *Colóquio Herman Melville,* generalizes about the presence of "the discovery paradigm" in "Benito Cereno" and other Melville works.

vi The Poetry and Later Works

In a qualitatively and quantitatively weak year for criticism dealing with this period, Juana Celia Djelal's "All in All: Melville's Poetics of Unity" (*ESQ* 41: 219–37) is an exception. In a striking reading of the rhetorical qualities, the dialectical harmony, of *"The Portent"* and "Billy in the Darbies" Djelal shows Melville confronting issues of divisiveness and fragmentation, with John Brown and Billy Budd as figures who represent Melville's own "agonistic" career in fiction as well as his encounter with his nation's fragmentations. "Melville's poetry," she concludes, "emerges from the sense of oneness he recognizes in disparate engagements between individuals, between individuals and institutions, between self and soul." Worth little attention is Laurence Stapleton's chapter "About Melville and the Angel" in *Some Poets and Their Resources: The Future Agenda* (Univ. Press); oddly cast in the form of a dialogue, it offers at best an introductory glimpse at Melville's poetry. Massimo Bacigalupo's "Reading the Melville Macrotext," pp. 33–45 in *Colóquio Herman Melville,* notes that "one of the fundamental situations in Melville is indeed that of reading and interpreting the signs of the world," an issue he examines in *John Marr and Other Sailors.* Margaret Seligman Cook in "Fatal Traps, Fatal Consequences: John White Webster and *Billy Budd*" (*MSEx* 103: 19–21) argues that the Webster case may offer more parallels to Melville's novel than previously recognized. Even though John F. Birk's *Herman Melville's* Billy Budd *and the Cybernetic Imagination* (Mellen) provides much material concerning the scientific and technological contexts of Melville's work, its main contention—that Billy is an android—remains absurd.

Texas Tech University

5 Whitman and Dickinson

Kenneth M. Price

This year was exceptional for Whitman studies. Scholars can welcome a major new biography by David Reynolds, several important new works documenting Whitman's international appeal, and a valuable collection of essays which highlights current approaches to the poet, Ezra Greenspan's *Cambridge Companion to Walt Whitman*. Moreover, much fanfare attended the return after 50 years of four of the "lost" notebooks (another six remain missing) to the Library of Congress. Sadly, the year also saw the death of Gay Wilson Allen, the most influential Whitman scholar of this century.

Scholarship on Dickinson was less extensive, though it certainly possesses energy based on exciting new projects dedicated, as it were, to the *un*editing of her work. A host of scholars are finding inadequacies— not to say distortions—in print versions of Dickinson. Most of the strongest scholarship on the poet is now returning to manuscript sources and considering with great care and ingenuity what Jeanne Holland has called the poet's "domestic technologies of publication."

i Walt Whitman

a. Bibliography, Editing   On a regular basis Ed Folsom continues to produce remarkably thorough and judicious annotated bibliographies of Whitman criticism (*WWR* 12: 192–96, 268–73). Folsom and Gay Wilson Allen also contributed numerous selected bibliographies listing translations and the "most important critical statements about Whitman from various cultures" in *Walt Whitman and the World* (Iowa).

A handful of new discoveries add to the store of factual information. Paul Berman's delightful essay, "Walt Whitman's Ghost" (*New Yorker*, 12 June, pp. 98–104), records how he located, with help from Elias and

Sean Wilentz, the house in Brooklyn (still occupied by working people) where Whitman put the final touches on the 1855 *Leaves of Grass*. Jerome Loving's " 'Broadway, The Magnificent!': A Newly Discovered Whitman Essay" (*WWR* 12: 209–16) reprints an editorial Whitman published in *Life Illustrated,* 8 November 1856, extending by more than two months Whitman's relationship with a magazine published by Fowler and Wells, the phrenologists involved in publishing the first two editions of *Leaves of Grass*. William Baker's " 'I feel much possessed with the wounded & sick soldiers': An Unpublished Walt Whitman Letter" (*N&Q* 42: 195–96) prints the full text of Whitman's thanks to Dr. Le Baron Russell for a contribution to the poet's effort to assist the suffering and dying soldiers. Equally intriguing is the uncollected Whitman letter located by Arthur Sherbo. "Last Gleanings from the *Critic:* Clemens, Whitman, Hardy, Thackeray, and Others" (*SB* 47 [1994]: 212–21) records Whitman's response to Edmund Gosse's essay "Has America Produced a Poet?"; Whitman's answer in the 24 November 1888 number is that Bryant, Emerson, Whittier, and Longfellow and perhaps others deserve rank equal to the best English writers, Shakespeare excepted. In "Four Letters About Whitman in the Angeli-Dennis Papers" (*WWR* 12: 246–52) Roger Peattie provides two letters by both Joseph B. Marvin and Charles Rowley (one by Marvin contains extracts from an unlocated Whitman letter). Interestingly, Rowley claims that followers of Henry George and the "Knights-of-Labour are putting Whitman's ideas" to direct political use. In *Walt Whitman and Sir William Osler: A Poet and His Physician* (ECW) Philip W. Leon studies exhaustively—and somewhat repetitively—Osler's draft of his fragmentary lecture (never delivered) "Walt Whitman: An Anniversary Address with Personal Reminiscences."

The year's great find was not a discovery but a recovery. Alice Birney's "Missing Whitman Notebooks Returned to Library of Congress" (*WWR* 12: 217–29) describes the fascinating series of transactions that led to the return of four crucially important Whitman notebooks after an absence of 50 years. She also discusses the decision to make digital images of material that the Rare Book Conservator has placed in the "Handle Only Once" category. The digitized material can be found at http://LCWEB.LOC.GOV[.] Gail Fineberg's "Whitman on the Web: Four Recovered Notebooks to Be Digitized" (*Library of Congress Information Bulletin* 54: 139–44) is noteworthy for its excellent illustrations and its intriguing account of the technical process involved in deacidifying paper and other aspects of the preservation process.

Ed Folsom and I also initiated work on the "Walt Whitman Hypertext Archive," a project undertaken with the support of the Institute for Advanced Technology in the Humanities at the University of Virginia as well as our home institutions, the University of Iowa and the College of William & Mary. Work has begun on "Song of Myself," the first step in the building of a larger structure that aims to collect, digitize, encode, and present in a hypertextual environment all aspects of Whitman's work, including correspondence, notebooks, prose works, etc. The Walt Whitman Hypertext Archive will be able to distribute, in digital form, large amounts of material at low cost, thus making rare Whitman items available to a broad audience. Parts of the Archive are now accessible at http://jefferson.village.virginia.edu/whitman[.]

b. Translations: Intercultural Studies   This was a banner year for studies of Whitman's international impact. Leading the way was *Walt Whitman and the World,* ed. Gay Wilson Allen and Ed Folsom; the book is dedicated to Allen, who died while it was in press. In 18 informative chapters it traces how Whitman has been absorbed—in wildly various ways and more extensively than any poet since Shakespeare—into cultures around the world. To illustrate the book's achievement, I will point to some especially enlightening chapters in a work that is strong throughout. Guiyou Huang's chapter on Whitman and China (pp. 406–28) shows a sharp eye for the political and poetic uses of Whitman in a Chinese context. His work illuminates both *Leaves of Grass* and Chinese culture, allowing us to think of both in fresh ways. M. Wynn Thomas's section on the British Isles (pp. 11–70) combines an informative introduction with a judicious selection of primary documents. Roger Asselineau contributes three illuminating chapters on Whitman in Italy, in Portugal, and in France and Belgium (pp. 268–81, 147–59, 233–67). In his chapter on the German-speaking countries (pp. 160–230) Walter Grünzweig prints a rich assortment of translated documents; he asserts in his introductory section that our understanding of "reception processes" will be "incomplete if we dogmatically apply a bilateral and unidirectional model of cultural transfer." Grünzweig works out this idea in more detail in *Constructing the German Walt Whitman* (Iowa), a study of Whitman's reception history in Germany and the give-and-take of intercultural dialogue. In eye-opening detail, he demonstrates how Whitman became a vital force in German culture between 1890 and 1933, contributing to the development of German naturalism, German expressionism, and even—in one bizarre case—to the rhetoric of a prominent National Socialist poet, Heinrich Lersch. Although Whitman has been somewhat less important in German culture in the post–World War II era, Grünzweig notes that he continues to have cultural resonance, even becoming critical to one political campaign in the 1960s.

A special double issue of *WWR*, also dedicated to Allen, focuses on translation. The lead piece, "Whitman in Translation" (13: 1–58), transcribes a roundtable discussion held during the Whitman centennial celebration of 1992. The 12 participants describe the poetic balancing act required if one is to be faithful to the original while being creative in one's own tongue. This informative discussion is followed by my own interview with Zhao Luorui, the gifted Chinese translator of *Leaves of Grass*, and Ken McCullough's interview with U Sam Oeur, a Cambodian poet and political figure (13: 59–63, 64–67). Also shedding light on issues of translation is "Borges's 'Song of Myself' " by Fernando Alegría (*Cambridge Companion to Walt Whitman*, pp. 208–19). He points out that Borges, in his intriguing "Note on Whitman," thinks of Whitman as a double, in fact in a way uncannily similar to Borges's own conception of himself as two, notably illustrated in "Borges y yo." Through a process of double translation—Alegría translates Borges's translations of Whitman back into English—the emphases of Borges's rendition are highlighted.

c. Biography   The year's most dramatic accomplishment is David Reynolds's *Walt Whitman's America: A Cultural Biography* (Knopf). This study successfully integrates biographical insights with broader cultural history in a "life and times of America's most representative poet." In thoroughgoing fashion Reynolds reconstructs the years before *Leaves,* though he also takes the greatest risks in this section, hinging interpretation on the questionable story that Whitman was tarred and feathered in Southold because of sexual activity with a male student. This story first surfaced in the 1960s and has been given little credence by previous scholars; Reynolds's work will no doubt prompt further inquiries. Although he has interest in the psychosexual origins of Whitman's poetry, Reynolds's real concern is with more public or external forces. Thus, he notes that the "seeds of *Leaves of Grass* were sown in the political crisis of 1850," the year in which Daniel Webster threw his support behind the Fugitive Slave Law. Reynolds discusses Whitman's own vacillation about slavery *and* his "sympathetic portraits of blacks in *Leaves of Grass.*" He turns to contextual forces in seeking to understand Whitman's longtime ambivalence about slavery: "colonization took hold strongly in Brooklyn, and abolitionism was generally opposed as divisive and disruptive." Although fairly critical of Whitman's postwar career, Reynolds contributes to our understanding of the poet's ability late in life to work the magazine market to good effect, all the while protesting his treatment in such publications. Reynolds's book is a remarkable accomplishment, an invaluable guide to understanding Whitman's life in its cultural context.

d. Criticism: General *Whitman Between Impressionism and Expressionism: Language of the Body, Language of the Soul* (Bucknell) attempts a "comprehensive, full-length analysis of [Whitman's] language as such." This highly technical study by Erik Ingvar Thurin offers not readings of poems but instead analysis of such matters as nominalization, inversion, coordination, and ellipses of the predicate. Thurin displays an admirable knowledge of European languages and literature and a good grounding in translations of Whitman. Still, scholars will probably find more useful C. Carroll Hollis's *Language and Style in* Leaves of Grass (see *ALS 1983*, pp. 80–81) and James Perrin Warren's *Walt Whitman's Language Experiment* (*ALS 1990*, p. 78), works which are less technical in their approach and more compelling in their critical insights.

In "Some Remarks on the Poetics of 'Participle-Loving Whitman'" (*Cambridge Companion to Walt Whitman*, pp. 92–109) Ezra Greenspan explores Whitman's fondness for the present participle. This essay notes that the poet's reliance on the present participle first becomes apparent in "Pictures," once again confirming the pivotal nature of that early work. As he moved toward his mature poetry, Whitman grasped the significance of the present participle as a grammatical form that could help him realize his "kinetic vision." Also in this volume Stephen Railton's "'As If I were With You'—The Performance of Whitman's Poetry" (pp. 7–26) explores "I" and "you" as part of Whitman's commitment "to a performance that will transform the reader." He usefully studies how Whitman modulates his voice from oratory to seduction in part by exploiting a distinctive ambiguity of English (that the pronoun *you* can be used for either singular or plural).

A range of questions—regarding the development of Whitman's style, the evolution of his politics, and the movement from popular culture norms to the experimentation of *Leaves of Grass*—are addressed in David S. Reynolds's "From Periodical Writer to Poet: Whitman's Journey Through Popular Culture." This essay in *Periodical Literature in Nineteenth-Century America* (pp. 35–50) categorizes Whitman's early works and places them in the context of popular culture. Some themes of *Leaves of Grass* were present in the "foreground," and some emerged directly out of the changed social and political climate of the 1850s. In another contribution, "Politics and Poetry: *Leaves of Grass* and the Social Crisis of the 1850s" (*Cambridge Companion to Walt Whitman*, pp. 66–92), Reynolds turns his attention to tracing the relationship between Whitman's "shifting political loyalties [1846–55], his maturation as a poet, and the larger national audience." Reynolds's helpful overall statement on Whitman and race strikes me as an excellent brief description of a very complicated issue: "Whitman followed a kind of arc around the center in his racial attitudes, starting fairly conservative, then becoming quite progressive (it was in this middle phase that the broadly democratic first edition of *Leaves of Grass* appeared), and finally settling into a deepened conservatism during and after the Civil War." On the other hand, some readings are thin: his remarks on the black drayman in "Song of Myself" imply that this is an unambiguously positive statement, though the staging of the black body and the swift movement of Whitman's description from man to beast indicate that this passage has problematic features as well.

Like Reynolds, Martin Klammer is interested in understanding how Whitman's development was linked to the crisis over slavery. In *Whitman, Slavery, and the Emergence of* Leaves of Grass (Penn. State) Klammer relies heavily—perhaps too heavily—on *Franklin Evans* when he draws the conclusion that the early Whitman was a "pro-slavery apologist." This novel—which sold better than any of Whitman's other books—contains his most extended treatment of African Americans, and Klammer is right to stress its importance. Still, he overstates the case when he finds a proslavery Whitman behind the novel. After all, the plantation Whitman describes has an alcoholic serving as master, a lust-crazed overseer, and a mulatto Margaret serving as pitiable victim. This is hardly the rosy stuff of plantation fiction. Klammer is on better footing when he argues that Whitman's primary allegiance was to the interests of white laborers; he also offers detailed analyses of the politics of the 1850s in relation to Whitman's new experiment in poetry.

Christopher Beach's " 'Now Lucifer was not dead': Slavery, Intertextuality, and Subjectivity in *Leaves of Grass*" (*CRevAS* 25, ii: 27–48) usefully contrasts Whitman's efforts to convey black subjectivity to the "exteriorizing and conventionalizing poetic discourse of Whittier and Longfellow." Whitman's notebooks reveal that he once planned to draft a "Poem of the black person." Beach observes that to plan a poem dedicated to portraying a sense of "black subjectivity," instead of the more common goal of forwarding abolitionist views, must be credited as a radical approach. Like others before him, Beach finds the "Black Lucifer" passage in "Sleepers" to be Whitman's most searing indictment of slavery and most successful attempt to enter the consciousness of a slave. And, like Klammer, he finds the Whitman of 1855 to have gone as far as he could—and ever would—in "entering into black experience." Reynolds, Klammer, and Beach all hold that Whitman's development was linked to the crisis over race and slavery. Robert Adolph, however, takes the curious view that Whitman pays "little attention" to the issue of race. This assessment aside, Adolph's comparison of Whitman and de Tocqueville—"Whitman, Tocqueville, and the Language of Democracy" in *The Delegated Intellect* (pp. 65–88)—is reliable, if predictable.

The cultural work of *Leaves of Grass* may have been to "testify to the cultural naturalization" of a white European male immigrant settler population. That at least is one of the conclusions of Robert Olsen in "Whitman's *Leaves of Grass:* Poetry and the Founding of a 'New World' Culture" (*UTQ* 64: 305–23). For Olsen, *Leaves* remains vital because the reader is required to play an essential role, to complete and realize the undertaking. He holds that the "inclusive democratic poetic voice [of *Leaves of Grass*] challenges the necessary formal distinctiveness that would make it a form of literary discourse." Whitman's poetic mode of production is "journalistic" (in Benedict Anderson's sense): his juxtaposition of texts loosely (if at all) related encourages readers to find similarity in diversity. According to Olsen, "the liberty to express individual identity and difference becomes the basis for community and communal poetry." He sees that Whitman's *Leaves* "ultimately reflects the ambiguity of liberalism, which wants to make individual liberty into the basis for a stable community."

In "Singing America: From Walt Whitman to Adrienne Rich" (*KR* 17, i: 103–19) Peter Erickson questions Whitman's status as a type of multicultural hero. Erickson holds that Whitman "displaces and even negates the distinctive identities of those to whom he extends his overweening sympathy" because his acts of sympathy are too often acts of appropriation. He applauds, instead, Adrienne Rich's self-aware practice of "identity politics" as a corrective to the difficulties "inherent in Whitman's limitless capacity for sympathetic identification." If Erickson rightly highlights difficulties in Whitman's outlook, he also leaves a crucial question unanswered: *why* do so many ethnic writers nonetheless define their roles and projects through specific reference to Whitman's example? James T. F. Tanner explores one such instance in "Walt Whitman's Presence in Maxine Hong Kingston's *Tripmaster Monkey: His Fake Book*" (*MELUS* 20, iv: 61–74), showing just how liberating her *constructed* version of "Whitman" could be for her own enterprise. Her zany protagonist is a Chinese-American playwright (mis)named for the poet, Wittman Ah Sing.

In complicated ways Whitman welcomed association with outcasts of all stripes. Joann P. Krieg's "Walt Whitman and the Prostitutes" (*L&M* 14: 36–52) studies Whitman's conflicted attitude that shows both compassion for prostitutes and concern for health of individuals and the body politic. She considers his treatment of prostitutes in both journalism and poetry, especially in "To a Common Prostitute" and "The City Dead House." She wonders, too, whether Whitman himself might have frequented prostitutes (she notes his reference in a letter to a "frenchy" who left him in a "deplorable" state) but then concludes that "recent scholarship establishing the poet's homosexuality would seem to discredit even the suggestion." The working assumption here about the polar nature of sexuality—that one is always and unwaveringly homosexual or heterosexual—seems especially odd when applied to a poet whose work explores various eroticisms.

In " 'A Strong and Sweet Female Race': Cultural Discourse and Gender in Whitman's *Leaves of Grass*" (*ATQ* 9: 283–98) Christopher Beach tries to position himself between what he mistakenly calls the "recent consensus" that Whitman's works are conservative or misogynistic and an earlier view that saw a "progressively feminist Whitman." Critics such as Harold Aspiz, he contends, erred when they argued that Whitman's rhetoric "harmonizes with the avant-garde feminist opinion of his era." However, in " 'Being a Woman . . . I Wish to Give My Own View': Some Nineteenth-Century Women's Responses to the 1860 *Leaves of Grass*" (*Cambridge Companion to Walt Whitman*, pp. 110–34) Sherry Ceniza forcefully counters this claim. Viewing Whitman from the perspective of some of the "most socially involved woman's rights activists of the time," Ceniza concludes that it is difficult to read Whitman's sexual politics as "reductive for women, problematic though specific passages may be." She provides fascinating information on Mary A. Chilton, free love advocate and author of important articles in *The Social Revolutionist,* and on Juliette Beach and C.C.P., two women who reviewed the 1860 edition.

In " 'I Sing the Body Electric': Isadora Duncan, Whitman, and the Dance" (*Cambridge Companion to Walt Whitman,* pp. 166–93) Ruth L. Bohan notes that Duncan proclaimed Whitman one of her three "dance masters" and credited his poetry with having instilled in her "my great spiritual realization of life." This excellent chapter provides an overarching analysis of the importance of Whitman to Duncan. He "conferred poetic authority on Duncan's pioneering resolve to represent her body openly and without shame." Drawing from Whitman, Duncan based her movement in the solar plexus, the part of the body commonly linked to feeling and emotion.

The solar plexus, rather than the head, was of course at the center of Whitman's frontispiece of 1855. Ed Folsom's "Appearing in Print: Illustrations of the Self in *Leaves of Grass*" (*Cambridge Companion to Walt Whitman,* pp. 135–65) explores what the late C. Carroll Hollis called "the most successful metonymic trick in poetic history," Whitman's insistence on the book as a man. Folsom's informative discussion of the frontispiece portrait of Whitman from the 1855 *Leaves of Grass* includes a comparison with Frederick Douglass. For Douglass, the escape was from coarse to refined clothes; for Whitman, "the escape was in the opposite direction." Some sense of the care Whitman invested in his self-presentation is suggested by his selection of only eight out of more than 125 photographs to illustrate his books.

Two treatments of Whitman and the Civil War appeared this year. M. Wynn Thomas's "Fratricide and Brotherly Love: Whitman and the Civil War" (*Cambridge Companion to Walt Whitman,* pp. 27–44) develops a compelling analysis of the importance of George Washington Whitman to the poet's experience and understanding of the war. The Whitman family's need to hear from George through letters prompted Walt, the professional writer, to adopt his own "wartime vocation as amateur amanuensis," writing letters home for soldiers or conveying to families news of injuries, recoveries, and deaths. As Thomas notes, "Whitman's genius for doing this was inseparable from the humility of spirit with which he sought to adapt himself to the situation of the men." John M. Picker's "The Union of Music and Text in Whitman's *Drum-Taps* and Higginson's *Army Life in a Black Regiment*" (*WWR* 12: 230–45) challenges Scott Giantvalley's view that T. W. Higginson experienced a gradual "unbending" to Whitman and instead stresses a relationship marked by "fierce animosity." Nonetheless, he argues that the Civil War writings of Higginson and Whitman "reveal a significant resemblance" through their opposite movements: "While the poet transforms his text into a musical collection, the Colonel records the sounds he hears in ways which emphasize their textuality."

Whitman's connections to music are also explored in two essays. Carla Verdino-Süllwold and Thomas Hampson's " 'The Frailest Leaves of Me': A Study of the Text and Music for Whitman's 'To What You Said' " (*WWR* 12: 133–49) focuses on a nine-line poem, unpublished by Whitman, that was found among the scraps of papers constituting the manuscript of "Democratic Vistas." They persuasively date "To What You Said," previously thought to be from around 1860, as being from the mid-1870s, with Anne Gilchrist the implicit addressee. Hampson, a renowned baritone, also notes that Leonard Bernstein was intrigued by the questions surrounding this lost poem and selected it to represent Whitman in his 1976 cycle *Songfest*. Even more intriguing is David Metzer's account of how one particular musician appropriated, and at times extended, the poet's work in "Reclaiming Walt: Marc Blitzstein's Whitman Settings" (*Journal of the American Musicological Society* 48: 240–71). From 1925 until 1928 Blitzstein composed nine songs to texts by Whitman. Although left unpublished, the songs constitute, in Metzer's view, "one of the boldest celebrations of Whitman's homoeroticism by an American artist, a remarkable distinction given the oppressive environment in which they were written."

This year was noteworthy for several fresh analyses of Whitman's late poetry. Willard Spiegelman makes good use of Whitman's neglected poetry from the Annexes, especially "Unseen Buds." Spiegelman's "Our American Cousins" in *Majestic Indolence: English Romantic Poetry and the Work of Art* (Oxford, pp. 142–50) includes one section on Whitman and Frost in a book that examines pastoral poetry and the phenomenon of indolence. He sees Whitman as confirming and transforming a legacy inherited from the English Romantics and holds that he outdoes all of them in employing "passiveness" to augment identity in "unprecedented ways."

The most effective section of Arthur Golden's "Whitman's 'Respondez!,' 'A Rounded Catalogue Divine Complete,' and Emerson" (*EA* 48: 319–27) is concerned with Whitman's late works. Golden's essay begins with a consideration of how Emerson was at the center of the 1856 edition of *Leaves* and of the poem "Respondez!," which in the "abrasive-ness of its satiric thrust [differs] from anything else in *Leaves of Grass.*" Golden claims that everywhere else in this edition Whitman "assidu-ously courted Emerson," though this ignores the extraordinary mixture of attitudes expressed in the 1856 open letter. More persuasive is Golden's analysis of the late poem "The Rounded Catalogue Divine Complete," which he connects with Whitman's old age efforts to distance himself from the "master."

Although a number of critics make passing use of Whitman's late poetry, only James Perrin Warren considers directly the problem of eval-uating this long-neglected body of work. In "Reading Whitman's Post-war Poetry" (*Cambridge Companion to Walt Whitman*, pp. 45–65) War-ren provides a useful critical context for assessing Whitman's late poetry. He questions the widely held view that Whitman's best poetry was re-stricted to the first decade of his career. Taking "Passage to India" as a test case, he challenges Arthur Golden's influential reading, "Passage to Less Than India: Structure and Meaning in Whitman's 'Passage to India'" (see *ALS 1973*, p. 91).

Several scholars pursued fundamental questions relating to the origins of poetry. In "Whitman's 'Poem of the Road'" (*WWR* 12: 170–85) Harold Aspiz reads the poem ultimately called "Song of the Open Road" as a journey into both the world and a visionary realm: the road thus becomes the ultimate source of poetry "antecedent to the poet's own utterance." The optimistic vision put forth in "Poem of the Road" is a reaction to the debased and homely and limited lives that Whitman knew well. In "Representing the Kosmos: The 'Lyric Turn' in Whitman" (*WWR* 12: 150–69) Onno Oerlemans notes how recent criticism has identified lyric as "solipsistic" and has devalued the desire for a mode of "pure subjectivity." Oerlemans, however, contends that in Whitman and Wordsworth lyric is a mode that seeks "origins of meaning" and is thus apolitical, or prepolitical. He argues that one finds in "Song of Myself" a yearning (as in section 11) to obliterate the self so as to inscribe the identity not of the individual "Walt Whitman" but of a "kosmos" gener-ally, an aim best illustrated in accounts of sexual encounter. Like Oerle-mans, Robert J. Scholnick confronts the enigma of originality in his insightful essay, "'The Original Eye': Whitman, Schelling, and the Re-turn to Origins" (*WWR* 11 [1994]: 174–199). Exploring what others have called the American need for beginnings, Scholnick shows how Schel-ling's work *On the Relation of the Fine Arts to Nature* prefigures essential aspects of Whitman's practice. He clarifies the paradox of "originality": the original is the "underived," yet its link to "origins" points to "parentage, ancestry, and derivation."

If Whitman became a key figure for the modernists, it was only after an intriguing early reception history. Timothy Morris's "Whitman as the American Homer" in *Becoming Canonical in American Poetry* (pp. 27–53) considers even Whitman's "prereception," particularly early 19th-century beliefs in a "poetics of presence," beliefs that held that a poem is most successful when it gives voice to a writer's distinct personhood. Morris believes that such ideas were so powerful that if Whitman had not existed, he would have been invented. This ambitious piece moves easily between well-known and obscure writers, using deftly theoretical perspectives, and drawing on English, American, and African texts. Regrettably, the chapter occasionally falls into inconsistency: for example, he says that Whitman and Poe struck their contemporaries as being "original but hardly as stunningly remarkable as they now seem," yet he also claims that Whitman caused Josiah Gilbert Holland bewilderment on account of his "overoriginality." Morris contends that the model of Whitmanian presence has fundamentally affected how Dickinson, Moore, and Bishop have been read, evaluated, and canonized. A less complex view of reception history underlies John Simon's "Edward Carpenter, Whitman and the Radical Aesthetic," an essay in Christopher Parker's collection *Gender Roles and Sexuality in Victorian Literature* (Scolar, pp. 115–27). Simon's essay, though uneven, will be valuable to scholars for its insights into the biography of Carpenter.

In "The Culture of Pre-Modernism: Whitman, Morris, and the American Arts and Crafts Movement" (*ATQ* 9: 103–18) John F. Roche argues that for the North American arts and crafts movement Whitman is the "most celebrated native inspiration." Whitman and Morris are linked because of their status as oppositional artists and because of their "preoccupation with book design." The affinities between these artists are real, but the article fails to live up to its promise because key points it raises are left unpursued. If Whitman was a guiding light of premodernism, he was equally central to the development of American modernism itself, as Alan Trachtenberg demonstrates in "Walt Whitman: Precipitant of the Modern" (*Cambridge Companion to Walt Whitman*, pp. 194–207), an eloquent and wide-ranging study that breaks from the standard practice of finding the vital sources of modernism in Europe or Africa. As Trachtenberg notes, to list Whitmanian modernists is to give a roll call of the key innovators who changed the shape and sound, the look and texture, of architecture, painting, dance, poetry, and fiction.

ii Dickinson

a. Bibliography, Editing   Joel Myerson's "Supplement to *Emily Dickinson: A Descriptive Bibliography*" (*EDJ* 4, ii: 87–128) updates and corrects his earlier superb bibliographical work.

In the most significant Dickinson publication of the year, *Emily Dickinson's Open Folios: Scenes of Readings, Surfaces of Writing* (Michigan), Marta L. Werner explains her project as an editorial undoing. She seeks to lay bare the condition of texts obscured by earlier editorial work which gave little sense of the poet's compositional process. Werner's focus is on 40 manuscripts located at the Amherst College Library, almost all of which are linked (sometimes circuitously) to the name "Judge Otis P. Lord." She provides photographic facsimiles of these late manuscripts accompanied by typed transcriptions. The effect of Werner's work is to constellate these works "not as still points of meaning or as incorruptible texts but, rather, as *events* and phenomena of freedom." She is interested in the aesthetics of the page, in the way Dickinson through her "bright Orthography" produced simultaneously pictures and writing.

Werner's enthusiasm at times becomes excessive: "on surfaces still strange to us, we would encounter a writer who both fully assented to the exigencies of touch while also freely accepting, even enlisting, every crease of the paper, every slash and blow of the pencil, as a singular fortune." Yet we need to appreciate the nature of her critical intervention: her commentary operates in opposition to a genre (the introduction to the scholarly edition) that is often dry, at times pedantic. Her introduction is lyrical in the best sense, personal, moving, suggestive, even while at times cryptic. She is aware of how Dickinson biographies and editions have been shaped to fit particular critical biases. And she shows how Dickinson "did not stop writing in 1864; she stopped writing *books.*" Dickinson began to seek and to discover something beyond the book's purview.

In a contribution to a special issue of *EDJ* (4, i) on "Editing and the Letters" Ellen Louise Hart joins Werner in calling into fundamental question Thomas H. Johnson's editorial practices. In "The Elizabeth Whitney Putnam Manuscripts and New Strategies for Editing Emily Dickinson's Letters" (pp. 44–74) she observes that Johnson initiated the practice of separating texts by genre instead of respecting Dickinson's manuscript groupings. Hart notes that the acquisition by Harvard's Houghton Library of the Putnam documents shows Dickinson linking herself with Maria Whitney—a young woman so close to the married Samuel Bowles as to raise eyebrows—in what Judith Farr has called a "widowed sisterhood."

In "Emily Dickinson to Abiah Root: Ten Reconstructed Letters" (pp. 1–43) Ralph W. Franklin presents an important group of letters from 1845 until 1854. He reconstructs the 10 letters to Abiah Root, whose holographs are still missing, by matching fragments at Amherst to transcripts at Yale, returning clipped passages to the appropriate locations in the letters. The process validates the rough accuracy of Johnson's editing: he was correct in every instance in assigning clippings to individual letters, though he omitted two clippings and some postscripts by other hands. Franklin's work, including editorial apparatus, is meticulous; one only wishes that this extensive labor yielded more surprises.

In an illuminating essay, "The Importance of a Hypermedia Archive of Dickinson's Creative Work" (pp. 75–85), Martha Nell Smith articulates the aims of the Emily Dickinson Editing Collective. With interests congruent with Werner's, she notes that a hypermedia archive can take into account Dickinson's "method of publication and more fully disseminate the range of her manuscript art and poetic experimentation." As in *Rowing in Eden,* Smith underlines her view that Susan Gilbert Huntington Dickinson played an immensely important role as a "participatory reader and sometimes coauthor of Dickinson's works."

b. Publication History and Copyright Questions   This was a strong year for essays treating issues of publication and copyright. The hard realities of property and piracy are treated in Elizabeth Horan's "Mabel Loomis Todd, Martha Dickinson Bianchi, and the Spoils of the Dickinson Legacy" in *A Living of Words* (pp. 65–93). Horan's careful study of the publication correspondence reveals a neglected aspect of the Dickinson business: "publishers avoided court by building coalitions among themselves and with academics. These coalitions turned the losses of individual claimants into corporate gains by undermining all attempts to maintain the poet's legacy as an exclusive familial preserve." The shift from manuscript to book (and from gifts to sales) had the kind of debasing effect Dickinson associated with publication, reducing the lives of several women to legal wrangling over the ownership of manuscripts.

Robert J. Scholnick contributed " 'Don't Tell! They'd Advertise': Emily Dickinson in the *Round Table*" to *Periodical Literature in Nineteenth-Century America* (pp. 166–82). Scholnick notes that "Some keep the Sabbath going to Church" appeared first in the 12 March 1864 issue of the New York weekly magazine under the title "My Sabbath." As he demonstrates, the *Round Table* was just then "mounting an attack on the corrupting conditions of publishing and literary reviewing." How this magazine came to possess "My Sabbath" remains mysterious, but it seems likely that Dickinson's family ties to the editors—Henry Edward Sweetser and Charles Humphreys Sweetser—were important. (Henry's mother was Emily Dickinson's aunt Catherine, her father's sister; Henry's cousin Charles was class poet at Amherst College in 1862.)

Another strong article is "Dickinson's 'Alone and in a Circumstance' and the Theft of Intellectual Property" (*ESQ* 41: 65–95). Jerrald Ranta reproduces the manuscript of poem 1167, the work written around a stamp and two attached strips of paper bearing the names "George Sand" and "Mauprat," the leading male character in Sand's novel of that name. Focusing on the names-stamp construction, Ranta probes Dickinson's reading, her homespun publishing techniques, and her cognizance of copyright issues. He finds in Dickinson's poem a thorough awareness of the controversy over international copyright law. Ranta has versed himself in those periodicals treating this matter that Dickinson is likely to have read. Interestingly, he finds that "Alone and in a Circumstance" contains echoes of Higginson's analysis of the copyright problem in "Americanism in Literature" and holds that the poem's "spider" may be an "expanded acronym of the initial letters (Sp D R)" of the *Springfield Daily Republican,* a paper that had appropriated Dickinson's own intellectual property.

c. Criticism: General   In a biographical study, "Measuring the Sun: Emily Dickinson's Interpretation of Her Optical Illness" (*ESQ* 41: 239–55), James R. Guthrie provides yet another (following Sewall, Wolff, Barker, and others) informed yet ultimately speculative interpretation of Dickinson's eye problem and her responses to it. He notes that some poems suggest that she interpreted her illness as a "series of direct encounters with divinity" that left her with conflicting emotions but also with an increased awareness of her own creative power. He suggests that her illness may have triggered her most productive period as a poet.

Sylvia Henneberg's "Neither Lesbian nor Straight: Multiple *Eroticisms* in Emily Dickinson's Love Poetry" (*EDJ* 4, ii: 1–19) follows queer theory in finding "models of binary opposition" extremely limiting and no longer tenable. She agrees with Judith Butler that the "very act of revealing and defining 'sexuality' immediately and invariably makes the term subject to deconstruction." Taking issue with such critics as Paula Bennett and Martha Nell Smith, Henneberg makes a persuasive case for Dickinson's emotional and erotic mobility.

Several essays concern themselves with questions of silence and "presence" in Dickinson's work. Suzanne Juhasz's "Adventures in the World of the Symbolic: Emily Dickinson and Metaphor" questions the recent emphasis on silence, the claim that "woman and language are dichotomous concepts." This essay, appearing in Lynn Keller and Cristanne Miller's *Feminist Measures: Soundings in Poetry and Theory* (Michigan [1994], pp. 139–62), makes a powerful argument for a theory "that grants women access to all dimensions of language, including the symbolic." Symbolic language is not opposed to "women's gendered identity," but it has more than one idiom or dialect (which we might associate with masculine and feminine) that battle for dominance. Cynthia Hogue's theoretically oriented "'I Did'nt Be—Myself': Emily Dickinson's Semiotics of Presence" in *Scheming Women* (pp. 31–72) argues that Dickinson "posits strategies of self-dislocation" to counter the objectification of the feminine she finds to be characteristic of Romantic literature. She elaborates ideas first presented by Joanne Feit Diehl about how Dickinson was paradoxically both aided and hindered by the "self-difference that the Romantics imaginatively resolved in the face of the awesome and unrepresentable aspects of nature that characterize the poetry of the sublime." In a less sophisticated essay, "'Near, but remote': Emily Dickinson's Epistolary Voice" (*EDJ* 4, i: 86–107), Erika Scheurer argues that recent scholarship focuses on Dickinson's "Derridean silence," her emphasis on writing rather than the logocentrism of speech. She, on the other hand, contends that Dickinson also valued the "presence of voice in text" and actively weighed the relative strengths of written and oral discourse.

Timothy Morris's "Dickinson: Reading the 'Supposed Person'" in *Becoming Canonical in American Poetry* (pp. 54–80) holds that Dickinson achieved canonical status despite a critical field shaped by the "Whitmanic American Homer." He charts what he calls the "largely male project of . . . narratizing Dickinson, from 1890 to 1945." If Whitman fulfills a "poetics of presence," Dickinson enacts a "poetics of reticence," and if he is monologic, she is dialogic. Such schematic formulations, familiar in this much-worked comparison, have dangers (as Morris himself notes, it is impossible for any writer truly to be monologic). He argues that Dickinson became canonical because of her "availability as the ultimate virginal site for criticism"; critical assumptions about authorial presence provoked male curiosity about the female characteristics supposedly revealed in her gendered poems.

In "Illuminating the Eclipse: Dickinson's 'Representative' and the Marriage Narrative" (*EDJ* 4, ii: 44–61) Susan Harris examines the "Representative," approaching this "supposed person" mentioned in a letter to Higginson not as a conveyor of Dickinson's personal presence but as a poetic construct. She tracks the speaker's development from apprenticeship to mastery through the progress of the marriage poems. Acknowledging the difficulty of seeing these poems as forming a single narrative, Harris nonetheless finds an internal coherence in those concerned with *entitlement*. She argues that Dickinson's persona must "earn her title by creating through her own poetry a concept of wifehood that will displace the cultural ideal that the word 'Wife' is assumed to represent." Ide Hejlskov Larsen also notes how Dickinson refused to accept social constructs as natural or inevitable. In "Emily Dickinson Challenges American Myths: The Ritual Power of Words—to Re-create, Kill, and Make Sex" (*EDJ* 4, ii: 62–86) she sees Dickinson as engaged in "ongoing civil war" with myths that once energized American Studies—the pastoral garden threatened by the machine, the errand into the wilderness, the American Adam and Eve. She gives close readings of "I tie my Hat—I crease my Shawl—" (443) and "My Life had stood—a Loaded Gun" (754), arguing against those critics who have seen the "little girl" persona as crucial for Dickinson, the role that has her "begging the father figure for recognition." She finds instead that "Dickinson and her persona are . . . conscious of the structures of domination in society and the self."

Katharine Rodier's " 'What is Inspiration?': Emily Dickinson, T. W. Higginson, and Maria White Lowell" (*EDJ* 4, ii: 20–43) notes that Dickinson questioned Higginson in two separate letters about Maria White Lowell, the first wife of James Russell Lowell and a talented poet in her own right. Noting that Dickinson's question about inspiration may be "coy, defiant, or inscrutable," Rodier credits Higginson with more sensitivity in his reading of the poet and in his response to her than have many critics. She also considers Higginson's assessment of and response to Maria White Lowell.

Although a 1995 publication, *Emily Dickinson's Fascicles* (Penn. State)

received commentary in *ALS* last year, and I concur with Martha Nell
Smith's assessment of this work focusing on fascicle 40. Dorothy Huff
Oberhaus finds (or constructs) a unity through tracing the fascicle's
allusions to the Bible and the echoes of the Christian meditative tradition. Even readers unpersuaded by her religiously oriented conclusions
will be impressed with the depth of her research, the self-consistency
of her argument, and the ingenuity of her interpretations. If Marta
Werner's book (celebrating Dickinson's "wild and beautiful irresolution") opens up possibilities and resists closure, Oberhaus moves to limit
or channel interpretations, and rarely alludes to—much less addresses—
other viable readings.

Where is scholarship on Dickinson and Whitman heading? Both
fields are strong, and both (like the profession at large) are preoccupied
with concerns about gender and sexuality. Whitman criticism also shows
a marked concern with questions about race. But beneath this ongoing
cultural reading of the two poets, significant textual problems and concerns persist. Work now being undertaken on electronic editions of both
poets should add to the vitality of these already dynamic fields.

College of William & Mary

6 Mark Twain

Alan Gribben

As the century in which Mark Twain died approaches its end, the majority of his works have been reissued in scholarly editions, hundreds upon hundreds of critical studies have dissected his writings, and one might presume that few surprises could be left in store where this eminent author is concerned. Yet this year brought more than its share of the exciting developments that have characterized Mark Twain scholarship over the years—including published access to the first half of his *Huckleberry Finn* manuscript, lost for more than a century, and another disturbing clue about his racial attitudes as a young man. In the area of critical approaches the momentum clearly lies with "cutting-edge" methods focusing on Twain's involvement with his culture rather than on his individual talent and literary achievements. Such critical trendsetters as Forrest G. Robinson, Susan Gillman, and Shelley Fisher Fishkin, building on the ideas of James M. Cox, showed the way for a dozen other commentators inclined to see Twain in the context of his society rather than as a transcendent genius. Though tending to be exclusionary and self-referential, these examinations of Twain's cultural and historical context in sum confirm that Twain studies have come of age on the critical scene. For that matter, this year Samuel Clemens the man underwent in print a belated, posthumous "outing" as an alleged practicing homosexual both preceding and following his marriage. Mark Twain continues, in other words, to keep company with the dozen major authors routinely subjected to the hottest critical trends in American academe.

i Editions

Every two or three years since 1988 the Mark Twain Project at Berkeley has brought out a thick collection of Clemens's letters. So prolific was his correspondence and so assiduous are the Project's annotation and description procedures that volume 3, for example, gathered only the letters from a single year—1869. The latest volume requires 792 pages and takes readers up to 31 December 1871. By this point Clemens's lecture schedule was in high gear and his letter-writing had assumed the effortless pace he would maintain throughout his life. On 6 February 1870, for instance, he wrote to six different people. One of these half-dozen letters became famous; it was addressed to his boyhood chum Will Bowen and ran through a dense and fecund catalog of their youthful antics in Hannibal, some of which turned up in *Tom Sawyer* and later works. On the same day Clemens also penned a boastful letter to his former pilot-mentor, Horace Bixby, informing him that *The Innocents Abroad* "has met with a greater sale than any book ever published except Uncle Tom's Cabin," but conceding nonetheless that "I would rather be a pilot than anything I ever tried." The rich variety of *Mark Twain's Letters, Volume 4, 1870–1871,* ed. Victor Fischer and Michael B. Frank (Calif.), will bedazzle even those scholars who think they are already familiar with virtually all details of Twain's biography.

In " 'Assaying in Nevada': Twain's Wrong Turn in the Right Direction" (*ALR* 27, iii: 64–79) Lawrence I. Berkove publishes and deftly explains an undated, incomplete, 19-page manuscript now at Vassar College that parallels material in chapter 36 of *Roughing It* (1872). Around 1868, as it proves, Twain registered in these preliminary notes a sympathetic attitude toward Conrad Wiegand, a victim of the corruption, lawlessness, and brutality associated with the Comstock mines, but by 1871 Twain— apparently beset by a mixture of motives and concerns—joined Joe Goodman and others in scoffing at Wiegand's claims, justifiable as they were. Twain's recollections of Comstock mining operations revealed an awareness of the less civilized side of Nevada life that he chose not to portray in *Roughing It.* "He stood to lose a great deal from pressing his criticisms," explains Berkove. "If Westerners resented them he would lose sales, incur incalculable hostility from wealthy and influential men, and possibly lose his money-making reputation as a humorist." As a result, *Roughing It* became a "less honest" book than it might have been. (Forrest G. Robinson refers to the figure of Conrad Wiegand for different purposes in "An 'Unconscious and Profitable Cerebration': Mark Twain and Literary Intentionality" [*NCF* 50: 357–80].)

An ingenious gleaning of more than 40 of Mark Twain's most amusing stories and sketches about the pranks, foibles, and lessons of childhood, fictional as well as autobiographical, results in *Mark Twain's Book for Bad*

Boys and Girls, ed. R. Kent Rasmussen (Contemporary). Drawn from various sources, including Twain's novels and collected sketches, the contents (for example, "Advice to Youth," "Tom Sawyer Slaughters the Innocents," and "Edward Mills and George Benton: A Tale") are obviously aimed at trade-book sales, but the editor is sufficiently scrupulous about textual citations to make the volume usable and diverting for scholars as well.

A second edition of John Y. Simon's *General Grant by Matthew Arnold with a Rejoinder by Mark Twain* (Kent State), originally published in 1966 by So. Ill. University Press, couples Arnold's comments about the war hero-president's *Personal Memoirs* with Twain's indignant defense of his personal idol in an 1887 speech. Actually Arnold only passingly criticized Grant's English grammar and even complimented his "straightforward" language for "saying clearly in the fewest possible words what had to be said, . . . frequently, with shrewd and unexpected turns of expression." But in Twain's eyes, Arnold had besmirched a "unique and unapproachable literary masterpiece" whose "flawless" style "no man can improve upon."

Jerry Thomason and Tom Quirk's edition of Mark Twain's *Colonel Sellers: A Drama in Five Acts,* published in *MissR* (18, iii: 109–51) and based on a text of 1874 prepared for Thomason's doctoral dissertation, fills in a gap in the documentation of Twain's sporadic efforts to score as a dramatist. Though Twain wrote or collaborated in writing more than 20 plays, it was only the redoubtable *Colonel Sellers,* "now published for the first time," that remained on the stage for 12 years and earned Twain over $100,000.

An award for editorial imagination should go to Howard G. Baetzhold and Joseph B. McCullough, whose *The Bible According to Mark Twain: Writings on Heaven, Eden, and the Flood* (Georgia) pulls together fictional works about "the biblical account of creation and its aftermath," along with Twain's "efforts to revise the traditional portrait of Heaven and the afterlife." In large part supplanting Ray B. Browne's valuable *Mark Twain's Quarrel with Heaven* (1970), *The Bible According to Mark Twain* collects "Eve's Diary," "Passages from Shem's Diary," "Adam's Soliloquy," "Captain Stormfield's Visit to Heaven," "Captain Simon Wheeler's Dream Visit to Heaven," "Letters from the Earth," and nearly a dozen other stories and sketches. Especially hilarious is "Etiquette for the Afterlife," with advice such as "if you get in—don't tip him. That is, publicly." And "above all things, avoid *over-*dressing. A pair of spurs and a fig-leaf is a plenty." Baetzhold and McCullough carefully stipulate the copy-text, and they supply background information (and often Twain's notes and drafts) for each selection. Few volumes outside the Mark Twain Project series match this level of thoroughness, erudition, and sheer attractiveness.

The editorial event of the year, however, had to be the publication of the first modern version of Mark Twain's *Adventures of Huckleberry Finn* directly deriving from the long-missing first half of the holograph manuscript, which surfaced in 1990 and became the subject of lengthy legal negotiations over its owership. Walter Blair, the acknowledged dean of scholarship devoted to Twain's masterpiece, lived long enough to learn of the discovery of this fabled literary manuscript, but to his heir apparent, Victor A. Doyno, author of *Writing Huck Finn: Mark Twain's Creative Process* (see *ALS 1991*, pp. 94–95), fell the privilege of preparing the most comprehensive edition of the manuscript released in the 20th century. In *Adventures of Huckleberry Finn,* intro. by Justin Kaplan, foreword and addendum by Victor Doyno (Random House), Doyno tells the complicated story of its discovery in Los Angeles (and eventual return to Buffalo, New York, where Twain had sent the 665 sheets in 1887), and he promises that the revisions and discarded pages thus recovered will reveal "an even darker, more satirical, and more provocative work than the first published edition turned out to be." Justin Kaplan's introduction defends the book against charges of racism (now a routinely obligatory task) and argues that "the newly found manuscript shows Mark Twain working . . . to develop a voice, idiom, and dramatic persona that were to enter American letters with the force of nature and revelation." Doyno's textual addendum describes major changes that Twain made in the manuscript. Particularly noteworthy is the evidence that it required *three* attempts for Twain to capture Huck's authentic colloquial voice in the famous first sentence of the novel. Doyno chooses to reinsert the raftsmen's passage as well as a previously unknown episode involving Jim and cadavers, a more elaborate camp meeting scene, and other material deleted from the first edition in 1885. Thirty sheets from the handwritten manuscript are reproduced in facsimile, including several involving Pap Finn's treatment of his son. The volume invites us into Mark Twain's octagonal study to watch him at work, and although Random House designed the edition for trade sales as well as the academic market, it belongs in every scholar's library. Even the original E. W. Kemble illustrations are retained. A preview of the previously unpublished portion known as "Jim and the Dead Man" appeared in the *New Yorker* (26 June 1995, pp. 128–33), along with brief commentaries on *Huckleberry Finn* by Bobbie Ann Mason, Roger Angell, E. L. Doctorow, William Styron, and David Bradley. Doctorow, for one, lamented that in Twain's conclusion "the greatest picaresque since Cervantes and Diderot is thrown away in doddering shtick. . . . The same thing that made Twain blow his greatest work generates its troublesome moral conundrum—the depiction of Jim."

ii Biography

A damning episode in Samuel Clemens's young adulthood surfaces in Robert Sattelmeyer's "Did Sam Clemens Take the Abolitionists for a Ride?" (*NEQ* 68: 294–99). It seems that a September 1854 entry in the account book of the Boston Vigilance Committee, a radical abolitionist group, recorded a payment of $25.50 to one "Samuel Clemens," purportedly to provide him with "passage from Missouri Penitentiary to Boston—he having been imprisoned there two years for aiding Fugitives to escape." Sattelmeyer makes a persuasive case that "Clemens perpetrated a hoax on the Boston Vigilance Committee, representing himself as an abused abolitionist to secure the price of a railroad ticket between Missouri and the East Coast." During the turmoil of the decade leading up to the Civil War, what Sattelmeyer delicately calls Clemens's "unexamined assumptions" and "financial stress" combined to inspire the 19-year-old printer to take advantage of the national uproar over slave "rescues" and procure free transportation. Viewed in conjunction with Clemens's casually demeaning references to African Americans during his travels of this period, this new piece of evidence will be cited in future studies as a fresh indication of just how large a turn Clemens made in his thinking about slavery, New England, practical jokes, harmless lies, and personal integrity.

Sattelmeyer's find was not the most sensational development in Mark Twain biography in 1995, however. That distinction went to Andrew J. Hoffman's "Mark Twain and Homosexuality" (*AL* 67: 23–49). Hoffman rather bravely tried out these speculations in a trial run at an Elmira College conference in August 1993, which generated articles and op-ed pieces in *The Chronicle of Higher Education* (8 September 1993) and numerous newspapers and magazines. Without hesitation Hoffman admits the paucity of evidence concerning Clemens's sexual background and inclinations. Merely from "odd notes, letters, newspaper squibs, and coincidences," Hoffman draws "evidence—circumstantial, but incontestable; inconclusive, but suggestive—that Clemens had a series of strong, loving, and romantic relationships with other men. This was a shocking, perhaps transforming, revelation." Confessing that "I myself remain only partially convinced; I see room for doubt," Hoffman remarks that "merely suggesting the possibility of Clemens's homosexual experience has provoked debate and, in some cases, personal attack." Certain people erroneously construed "my hypothesis about his sexuality as though it were an attack on his character." Hoffman deduces that Clemens slept with Clement T. Rice, Dan DeQuille, Artemus Ward, and perhaps other men amid the bohemian atmosphere of Virginia City and San Francisco. Charles Warren Stoddard may have been another conquest in England in 1873, even after Clemens's marriage in 1870. Though conceding that "none of these incidents necessitates the conclusion that Samuel L. Clemens loved men," Hoffman points out that "among the gentry and educated prior to the Civil War, same-sex relationships were the norm before marriage." He cites as examples Thoreau, Melville, and "even the Reverend Henry Ward Beecher."

The result of Hoffman's interpretations is a "web of circumstantial evidence" that "indicates a preoccupation with a special sort of bond between men in Samuel Clemens's life and Mark Twain's work." However, "I don't believe . . . that proof will ever surface. Instead, I claim only to have destabilized this one aspect of Clemens's biography." Once such a disturbing question has been raised, Hoffman wonders if scholars will not wonder "how romantic were his other celebrated friendships, with William Dean Howells and the Reverend Joseph Twichell?" Hoffman ponders whether this secret life might have encouraged the division between Mark Twain and Samuel L. Clemens, which "allowed him to hide—perhaps from himself—his romantic interests in other men." Whatever one's reaction to Hoffman's often equivocal but ultimately assertive opinions, they need to be taken into account by those currently writing on Twain's friendships, literary characterizations, and self-image. This is too racy and potentially earthshaking a topic to dismiss. Mark Twain scholars should get accustomed to dealing with the issue that Hoffman has cogently introduced, unsupported as it may seem to many commentators.

Far less incendiary is Harold K. Bush, Jr.'s contention—in "The Mythic Struggle Between East and West: Mark Twain's Speech at Whittier's 70th Birthday Celebration and W. D. Howells' *A Chance Acquaintance*" (*ALR* 27, ii: 53–73)—that Twain's performance in front of the Fireside Poets on 17 December 1877 was not as immediately controversial as teachers and scholars usually assume. But it is true that Twain's talk "lampoons the highly romantic and didactic verse of these nearly sainted poets by having it vulgarized by the imposters who recite it." Over the ensuing weeks "gossipy renditions aided in multiplying the belief that Twain's speech should be regarded as outrageous behavior and irreverent effrontery." In the end, "Twain and Howells can each be said to have internalized within themselves a conflict that was then regnant in the culture as a whole." A useful revisiting of an embarrassing episode in Clemens's life and a signal event in the American literary chronicle, Bush's essay is the most informative article on the subject since Henry Nash Smith's classic "That Hideous Mistake of Poor Clemens's" (1955).

Gary Scharnhorst condenses Clemens's California years into a riveting synopsis in "Mark Twain, Bret Harte, and the Literary Construction of San Francisco," an effective (if abruptly truncated) chapter in *San Francisco in Fiction* (pp. 21–34). Looking back at his days on the West Coast, Mark Twain "fictionalized himself. . . . From the distance of Quarry Farm and Hartford, San Francisco seemed a far country and his own experiences there the riotous living of a prodigal." Penetrating these deceptions, Scharnhorst tells of the intertwining of Mark Twain's aspirations and Bret Harte's massive successes. Their play *Ah Sin* (1877) "was arguably the most disastrous collaboration in American literary history." Among other consequences, "it led directly and immediately to the end of their friendship."

iii General Interpretations

The Cambridge Companion to Mark Twain, ed. Forrest G. Robinson (Cambridge), self-consciously confronts topics that earlier generations of Mark Twain scholars purportedly glossed over. Race, slavery, class, and gender are prominent, although the essays also involve the effects of religion, travel, and popularity on Twain's writing. "How is it," asks the editor Robinson, "that we have overlooked so much for so long? How has it served our cultural and ideological agendas to settle for such partial and incomplete readings?" One of the surprises in the collection is the number of times that Henry Nash Smith's legacy is invoked; Robinson and others take seriously a scholarly critic whose name has been relatively ignored for a decade and a half. Louis J. Budd (pp. 1–26) provides a lighthearted but comprehensive analysis of Mark Twain's functions and tenacity as an American icon. Robinson in "The Innocent at Large: Mark Twain's Travel Writing" (pp. 27–51) credits Twain for being "a radical . . . in his critique of Euro-American imperialism and in his implied advocacy of reform," but he also writes that "on the conservative side was his belief that fallen human nature is irretrievably mired in illusions." Shelley Fisher Fishkin (pp. 52–73) poses and answers questions of the type that Laura Skandera-Trombley and others have recently been asking about Twain's relationships with women. In "Banned in Concord: *Adventures of Huckleberry Finn* and Classic American Literature" (pp. 93–115) Myra Jehlen is severe in condemning elements in the novel: "There is little to dispute . . . over the political offensiveness of Jim's reenslavement on the Phelps farm" and "his humiliation at the hands of the increasingly idiotic Tom"; "the ending is disturbing because it is . . . a cheat, a defeat, and an affirmation." To her mind, Twain "appropriated" black Jimmy's dialect, but failed to "imagine" an African American narrator—consequently "Jimmy's idiom only extends Huck's cultural power" and the book is therefore *not* "multicultural." In "Black Critics and Mark Twain" (pp. 116–28) David Lionel Smith credibly extends his earlier landmark essay on "Huck, Jim, and American Racial Discourse." John Carlos Rowe (pp. 175–92) provides a political analysis of *A Connecticut Yankee*. In "Mark Twain's Travels in the Racial Occult" (pp. 193–219) Susan Gillman looks at "the protean nature of stereotypes, the tendency of such major categories of difference as race, sexuality, and pathology to become associated, to stand in for one another," in Twain's late writings. The late Stanley Brodwin in "Mark Twain's Theology: The Gods of a Brevet Presbyterian" (pp. 220–48) adds a rich coda to his substantial cluster of essays about the theological and philosophical dimensions of Twain's fiction.

Despite the laudable ambitions of *The Cambridge Companion,* the compass of its vision is strikingly smaller than its title would imply. Two of its 11 contributors are from the same university, two more from another. Their essays repeatedly cite each other's work for authority and reinforcement. The list of recommended "Further Reading" hints at the exclusivity of this club of commentators. Aside from entries for six of the volume's contributors, only a sum total of a dozen critical studies of Mark Twain, culled from the hundreds and hundreds of possibilities, are deemed worthy of inclusion in the *Cambridge Companion's* list of approved readings. And yet, for all of Robinson's promise of a "sobering . . . reassessment of our leading author," the essayists rather unexpectedly pull their punches, seldom identifying or castigating the preceding scholars who failed to face the implications of Twain's writings unflinchingly.

Mark Twain's admiration for the theater and for "performance" in every sense, though well-accepted, has never been explored in full, and Randall Knoper's *Acting Naturally: Mark Twain in the Culture of Performance* (Calif.) attempts to remedy this deficiency. Paying tribute to Cox, Robinson, Gillman, and Fishkin, Knoper asks "to what extent is Mark Twain America's fool because America made him thus, providing the conditions of celebrity and entertainment, spectacle and spectatorship, of which he is both epiphenomenon and epitome?" Above all, Knoper sets out to determine "the ways in which he was a theorist of representation and a careful critic and analyst of cultural performance." Representations of "gender, race, and class" particularly interest Knoper, and in a chronological treatment of Twain's absorption with the theatrical he investigates the "rowdy masculinity" of Twain's early days as well as allusions to homosexuality, transvestism, mental telepathy, minstrel shows, mesmerism, spiritual mediums, theatrical burlesque, and various other manifestations of "authentic" performance. Lawrence Levine's ideas provide distinctions between lowbrow and highbrow tastes. The responses of Twain and his newspaper friends to Ada Isaacs Menken's bohemian reputation and near-nude role in *Mazeppa*, for example, receive several pages of analysis. Knoper unduly protracts the dissection of a neglected sketch Sam Clemens published in 1852, imposes forced readings on some of Twain's other least-remembered early sketches and reviews, and allows repetitiveness to creep in too often. Nonetheless, *Acting Naturally* is a welcome reminder of the centrality of the theater in 19th-century culture and in Twain's life and works. Portions of Knoper's book will redefine our responses to Twain's performative instincts and ventures.

Terry Caesar's *Forgiving the Boundaries* combines the latest trends in ideological and postcolonial criticism with examples from two centuries of guidebooks, journals, memoirs, and fiction. Mark Twain is quoted to the effect that "travel is fatal to prejudice, bigotry, and narrow-mindedness," and Twain's name and writings illustrate many of Caesar's points. Such 19th-century tourist-writers as Henry James and Edith

Wharton alternate with Paul Theroux and P. J. O'Rourke, and cultural critics such as Clifford Geertz, Sacvan Bercovitch, and Terry Eagleton provide vocabularies for discussing the phenomenon of travel. In "postmodern" terms, declares Caesar, travel writing amounts to "a revalued example of *writing* only nominally motivated by the 'transcendent signified' of travel, and enticingly heedless to its fatefully commercial presentation as somehow a *work*." The shortcomings of Caesar's thesis received a rebuke ("not really illustrated, demonstrated, or elaborated") by Peter Carafiol in *SoAR* 61, i: 135–40.

Don Florence's *Persona and Humor in Mark Twain's Early Writings* (Missouri) endeavors to sidestep the perceived "duality or conflict between 'Clemens' and 'Twain'" that so many commentators have detected. "This study is concerned . . . with Twain as the controller of his works. . . . a literary personality that is both in and behind a given work and normally includes a narrative voice, though it goes beyond any particular narrator. . . . To adopt the terminology of the Geneva School of phenomenological criticism, Mark Twain is the mind that we sense both governing a work and expressing itself through that work—the literary mode of thought, if you will, that Samuel Clemens entered into whenever he sat down to write." Rather than a donned mask, "Mark Twain" more nearly represents "an aspect, mode of thought, or 'fact' of Samuel Clemens that has been fictionalized. . . . Perhaps Mark Twain is a birth-mark, or rather a 'thought-mark' of Samuel Clemens, essential to his expression." Twain's western literary hoaxes have seldom received such a thorough examination as Florence provides. In these jests Twain "implies that it's all justified by gains in freedom and humor—the tone of such pieces is almost always buoyant." Disagreeing with Pascal Covici, Jr., Florence proposes that "the world intrinsically resists interpretation and rational explanation, in which case the hoax mirrors a complex and relativistic world, a world where there may be no final objectivity or absolute truth." Twain's humorous versatility in *Roughing It* suggests that "monotony is death. *Roughing It,* with its play of adventure, perspective, and comic technique, is life."

A somewhat similar approach is taken by Bruce Michelson in *Mark Twain on the Loose: A Comic Writer and the American Self* (Mass.), which arrives at the conclusion that "a drive for absolute liberation, from a host of social, psychological, artistic, and even biological confinements, energizes and informs Mark Twain's work." Critics have "preferred to discuss boundedness, domesticity, and affirmations" rather than "Mark Twain's

penchant for anarchic humor and *detournement* for the hell of it."
Indeed, "the habit of insisting on Mark Twain's moral steadiness and
artistic shapeliness is an interesting cultural phenomenon in itself, a
long-term and many-handed project to tame a cultural hero." Essentially, Twain grew more and more opposed to "whatever seemed rigid
and regulating to mind and identity: any confining orthodoxy, whether
political, religious, aesthetic, imaginative, or even biological." Michelson
argues that "temples will not crash down on us if as readers we pay more
respect to this penchant for anarchy in Mark Twain's comic art." Citing
varied traditional and breakaway interpretations of Twain's literary comedy, Michelson shrugs off the conflict of competing critical explanations:
"I see no reason why such views of Mark Twain's humor have to be
reconciled, or why one reading should be privileged over others. There is
no reason why the comic outbreak must have a single or consistent effect
upon an individual mind, or upon a given culture."

One of the substantial collections of Mark Twain scholarship this year
is also one of the most difficult to obtain in the United States—the
combined Summer and Winter issue of the British journal *OVER here*,
whose first 78 pages contain essays by Louis J. Budd defending Hank
Morgan and *A Connecticut Yankee*, John Cooley sorting out the female
protagonists in Twain's late period, Everett Emerson responding to
Budd's points about *A Connecticut Yankee*, Peter Messent reviewing
books by Gregg Camfield and Laura Skandera-Trombley, Jennifer L.
Rafferty analyzing labor and technology in *A Connecticut Yankee* and
"No. 44, The Mysterious Stranger," Skandera-Trombley discussing
cross-dressing, gender-switching, and female characters in Twain's fic-
tion, and Jim Zwick rehearsing Twain's views on imperialism. Budd's and
Skandera-Trombley's articles in particular introduce fresh perspectives.

Cindy Weinstein's *Literature of Labor and the Labors of Literature* presents a challenging if rather stiff and humorless exposition of the "allegory
of labor in Twain . . . through examining Twain's vexed allegiances to the
construction of persons as constituted in the market and literary economies." Her chapter of more than 40 pages looks at the engineers in *Life on
the Mississippi* ("the narrator articulates an ideology of efficiency which he
both deplores and celebrates"), the Man-factory in *A Connecticut Yankee*
("a kind of homoerotic economy that substitutes mechanical reproduction for biological reproduction"), and the "duplicate" characters in "No.
44, The Mysterious Stranger," which "stages the conflict between labor
and management in late-nineteenth-century America."

Worth mentioning is one of Louis J. Budd's valedictory addresses to Mark Twain scholars delivered as a keynote lecture at a conference honoring him in 1993 and subsequently published as Number Six in the Quarry Farm Papers series issued by the Elmira College Center for Mark Twain Studies. Titled "Mark Twain: The Ecstasy of Humor," Budd's wide-ranging glance at sources and patterns accounting for Twain's comic artistry catalogs Twain's successes in liberating himself and his readers "from ordinary realities," attaining "escapes into deep time or space," transmitting "a sense of engaged empowerment," and achieving "irrepressible ecstasy."

iv Individual Works to 1885

In "Tom Sawyer's Games of Death" (*SNNTS* 27: 141–53) Harold Aspiz demonstrates that even a short novel everyone knows by heart harbors complex patterns of "games of death and games of resurrection." Tom Sawyer's childhood is "a bright world set off by the shadowy terrors of danger, death and conformity." Aspiz recites so many often-forgotten incidents that most readers must rethink several premises. But he also ignores an antecedent article with vital affinities to his reasoning, Judith Fetterley's "The Sanctioned Rebel" (1971), published in the same journal. Even so, Aspiz gives us a savvy analysis of a book whose contents too many take for granted. "Never again in Mark Twain's major writings will death games be played with such *élan*, joy, and lightheartedness," Aspiz concludes.

Tom Sawyer's name also comes up repeatedly in Lynne Vallone's discerning comparison and contrast of juvenile fiction for boys and girls in *Disciplines of Virtue: Girls' Culture in the Eighteenth and Nineteenth Centuries* (Yale). "Adolescent or preadolescent boys and girls historically were not encouraged to share reading material," a reflection of "the 'segregation' they would experience in later life through the separate-sphere economies of the domestic and the commercial." In *Tom Sawyer*, Vallone notes, "only Tom actually comes out ahead because he knows, as does the reader, that in a youthful fantasy, work is worthless." Likewise, *Huckleberry Finn* demonstrates that, "in spite of the dangers, the comic vision is unrelenting in Twain, whereas comedy is mitigated and finally undercut by social convention in the girls' books." The literary characters created by Louisa May Alcott, Susan Coolidge, and Elizabeth Stuart Phelps, for example, have plots in common in which "each girl grows up in the course of her novel, whereas Tom Sawyer and Huck Finn remain eternal boys."

How many articles of any consequence have taken up Mark Twain's best-known burlesque of detective stories? Peter Messent injects complexity into Twain's tale in "Keeping Both Eyes Open: 'The Stolen White Elephant' and Mark Twain's Humor" (*StAH* 3: 62–84).

One of Twain's less-studied books receives a suggestive reading in Earl F. Briden's "Through a Glass Eye, Darkly: The Skeptic Design of *Life on the Mississippi*" (*MissQ* 48: 225–37), which recounts the ways in which "Twain's 1882 return to the river . . . activated a skepticism about the nature and grounds of knowledge." Gradually, Twain discovered the unreliability of "society's various discourses—romantic, scientific, legal, historical—knowledge of which both constitutes authority and establishes a person's epistemological horizons." Whether as a cub pilot or the author of a "standard work" on the river, Twain learns that "the real is escaping him even as he sets it down. . . . We occupy worlds fashioned from words, images, dreams, and memories—the static, opaque signs that define experience." Briden's analysis needs a fuller unfolding, and he oddly avoids any contact with Horst H. Kruse's *Mark Twain and* Life on the Mississippi (*ALS 1981*, p. 467), the only book entirely devoted to the composition and reception of the work Briden studies. Even so, Briden's article moves onto the list of helpful insights about a trip that unlocked Twain's memories of the Mississippi River region.

v Adventures of Huckleberry Finn

This year yielded yet another reprint of the 1885 first edition of *Huckleberry Finn,* hardly a notable event in itself. Indeed, this Bedford/St. Martin's Press version disappointingly omits the so-called raftsmen's passage and many of the Kemble illustrations, which the editions issued by the Iowa-California Mark Twain Project, Random House, and other publishers have gratifyingly begun to include. But in this instance the text of Twain's novel is simply mandatory for college classroom adoption; editors Gerald Graff and James Phelan are far more committed to presenting the accompanying "eighteen readings on three critical controversies," consisting of "traditional literary analysis and more recent approaches such as feminism and gay studies." In an introductory essay, "Why Study Critical Controversies?," Graff and Phelan rehearse Graff's by now familiar arguments about the benefits of teaching rather than hiding professional controversies; citing Robert Scholes's *Textual Power*, the editors inform students that "heated debates about multicultural, feminist, postcolonial, and other 'ideological' approaches to literature and the humanities often overlap with the battles erupting on many campuses, including perhaps your own," and invite them to join the fray over "controversies about authority and pedagogy." Interestingly, Graff and Phelan come down in favor of teaching *Huckleberry Finn* in the classroom, despite "the pain Twain's book may inflict," but for the sake of fairness they also devote eight pages to Julius Lester's claims about "Twain's contempt for blacks" and Lester's contention that "my children's education will be enhanced by not reading *Huckleberry Finn*." Five brief essays debate the merit of the ending that Twain devised, including a new and spirited defense of the conclusion by Richard Hill. Seven other essays take up the heated topic of racism, centered on an excerpt from Fishkin's *Was Huck Black?* (1993). Six additional pieces struggle with a proclaimed "Controversy Over Gender and Sexuality" in the novel, in the process tiring out poor Judith Loftus and her lamentably limited role by an incessant analyzing of her every word and action. Leslie Fiedler's insinuations about homoerotic overtones make a reappearance from 1948, and the casebook ends with Christopher Looby's praise for the risk Fiedler took "in publishing such an essay when he did" and Looby's strained effort to imply that Twain had reasons to associate antebellum Hannibal with interracial male homosexual wish-fantasies along with actual acts of male sexual intercourse. Students may or may not be engaged and enlightened by such attempts to make a 19th-century literary work "relevant" (Looby cites "the beating of Rodney King and the arrest of O. J. Simpson" as current examples of similarly "charged representations" of race and sex), but the mature scholar-critic is apt to be left with the feeling that there is *so much more* to the novel than these three thematic approaches, however voguish, can possibly convey. Still, the Graff-Phelan volume should be given credit for its earnestness in attempting to reach "students who remain silent, bored, and alienated" in the presence of a classic work.

In an overlooked article Gary P. Henrickson objects to deconstructive readings of *Huckleberry Finn* that discuss Huck as an "author" and thus "historical," rather than assuming he is a character in a novel created by Mark Twain. Henrickson's salutary "How Many Children Had Huckleberry Finn?" (*NDQ* 61, iv [1993]: 72–80) merits notice.

An admirable chapter from Tom Quirk's *Coming to Grips with* Huckleberry Finn (*ALS 1993*, p. 75)—"The Realism of *Adventures of Huckle-berry Finn*"—finds a place in *The Cambridge Companion to American Realism and Naturalism* (pp. 138–53).

vi Individual Works After 1885

According to Jason G. Horn's "Mark Twain, William James, and the Funding of Freedom in *Joan of Arc*" (*SAF* 23: 173–94), Twain's Joan is the "image of reconciled thought and action, an exemplary marriage of human genius and divine intellect, bold in spirit, pure, good, and true. . . . Few would expect Mark Twain to engage in such a style. But he did." Horn senses that "*Joan of Arc* continues the fictional theorizing upon consciousness begun as early as *Huckleberry Finn*. The question of whether being in reality is free or determined, or a complex nature of the two, and related tensions of the apparent divisions of the mind . . . are still the problems compelling Mark Twain's attention." Twain's attempt to deliver Joan by liberating free thought into effective action can be better understood through the works of "one of Twain's contemporaries and acquaintances: William James." James's "somewhat idiosyncratic theory of truth" illustrates "the way in which Twain deflated historical literary authority in his effort to clear the way for fresh discourse con-cerning Joan's life." Although not all the pairings of James's ideas and Twain's narrative appear as relevant as Horn would wish, he makes an intriguing guess as to why Mark Twain cited a fictional Jean François Alden as the translator of the nonexistent Joan of Arc text—possibly to nettle Henry Alden, a Harper's editor who had refused to publish Twain's satire of Samuel Royston's *The Enemy Conquered; or, Love Triumphant.*

One of Mark Twain's sojourns abroad forms the subject of an article by Carl Dolmetsch, who continues his revelatory investigations of Twain's connections with Europe in "'It Was Still the Middle Ages in Austria': Mark Twain's *Mysterious Stranger* as a Critique of Habsburg Austria" (*Images of Central Europe*, pp. 94–103). Dolmetsch persuasively insists that Twain's late novella "can only be fully understood against the background of the writer's Austrian experiences" and that "Twain in-tended Eseldorf as an Austrian microcosm. It was not the Austria of 1702 but that of 1898."

Cynthia Ozick in "Mark Twain and the Jews" (*Commentary* 99, v: 56–62) presents a different take on the same stay in fin de siècle Vienna, a city "notoriously, stingingly, passionately anti-Semitic." Partly because of the Dreyfus Affair, 1898 became "the year of a vast European poisoning, by insidious sloganeering and hideous posters and caricatures." She links this "noisome" atmosphere to Mark Twain's writing of "The Man That Corrupted Hadleyburg" and other pieces of that period. But Twain's "Concerning the Jews," though "remembered . . . as charmingly philo-Semitic," is instead "part self-contradictory panegyric . . . honorably motivated but ultimately obtuse and harmful."

vii Reference Books

After spectacular gains in reference works in recent years—including James D. Wilson's *A Reader's Guide to the Short Stories of Mark Twain* (1987) and most notably J. R. LeMaster and James D. Wilson's *The Mark Twain Encyclopedia* (1993)—yet another formidable addition now shoulders its way to the fore: R. Kent Rasmussen's aptly titled *Mark Twain A to Z: The Essential Reference to His Life and Writings,* foreword by Thomas A. Tenney (Facts on File). The comprehensiveness of this 552-page volume is simply incredible. Staggering in its scope, yet remarkably reliable about details, *Mark Twain A to Z* ought to be on the shelves of every library containing two or more volumes of Mark Twain's writings. Surprisingly, it manages to go beyond reference facts and supplies critical asides with refreshing perspectives. This book makes possible an entirely new era in Mark Twain studies—what was formerly time-consuming to find before (like a description of the Paige typesetter, the story of Clemens's relationship with Albert Bigelow Paine, or the publishing history of the San Francisco *Alta California*) is now conveniently packaged within two covers. There is even a lavish episode-by-episode synopsis of each of Twain's works, from "The Dandy Frightening the Squatter" to *A Tramp Abroad* to "The Stolen White Elephant" to *Tom Sawyer Abroad* to *1601*. It would be impossible to overpraise this magnificent literary resource.

viii Miscellaneous

A descriptive note by Mark Woodhouse in the *Dear Friends* newsletter (Autumn, pp. 2–3) of the Elmira College Center for Mark Twain Studies announces the donation to the Center, in installments, of nearly 90 books (many of them annotated) from the personal library of Samuel Clemens and his family. Robert and Katharine Antenne of Rice Lake,

Wisconsin, made this gift; Mrs. Antenne had inherited the volumes from her great aunt, Katy Leary, a native of Elmira, New York, and a member of the Clemens household for 30 years.

The Mark Twain Forum, founded in 1992 by Taylor Roberts as a discussion group conducted via electronic mail, continues a growth keeping pace with the burgeoning use of the Internet in general. Now serving more than 400 subscribers with instantaneous announcements and queries, the Forum offers a book review department (started in 1993) that makes it possible to read an informed review only weeks after a title has appeared in print. To subscribe without charge, send a message to LISTSERV@YORKU.CA with the one-line message: SUBSCRIBE TWAIN-L and your full name. One can visit the Forum on the World Wide Web at URL (http://web.mit.edu/troberts/www/twain/twain.html). The information being exchanged can vary widely in quality and levels of research, but the advantages of overcoming the scholar's habitual sense of isolation and enjoying an ability promptly to get in touch with others with similar interests easily outweigh occasional and minor irritations. Mark Twain would have been elated with all the gadgetry enabling this breakthrough and soon would have posted a suitable quip.

Auburn University at Montgomery

7 Henry James

Greg W. Zacharias

It is fitting to open this year's James chapter with a gesture of gratitude to Daniel Mark Fogel, who, after serving as editor of the *Henry James Review* for all of its 16 years, has stepped down from that post. Dan Fogel not only managed the *HJR* to its present status as one of the best single-author journals in English, but his editorial policy, which reached out to all Jamesians to help them develop as scholars and to feel welcome and comfortable as colleagues, extended the importance of the *HJR* far beyond its readers. I believe that I represent Jamesians everywhere in saying that we are deeply grateful for all of Dan Fogel's work to improve the quality of James scholarship and his generosity in nurturing the James community.

The scholarship published this year continued to change our impression of James the man from one who lived apart from the world to one who was immersed in it. One part of that world receiving special attention was James's family. The last part of his career also continued to be an area of close investigation and analysis. While the number of "influences and parallels" essays declined, which I attribute to a change in the nature of James scholarship, the year saw new efforts to reevaluate approaches that had become standard in the 1970s and 1980s. An apparent effort to avoid ideologically fixed positions for their own sake distinguishes these efforts (see below, Zwinger; Horne; Foss). If it is true, as some commentators have written, that the quality of public discourse is in decline, perhaps James scholarship offers a model for its recovery. For, as John Carlos Rowe writes in his foreword to *Henry James's New York Edition: The Construction of Authorship,* "If James is valued because his hopes and worries still speak to us, then let us celebrate his masterful adaptability, even changeable qualities, rather than his testament to some dubious universal truth."

i Biographical Studies, Bibliography, Editions

Carol Holly argues in *Intensely Family: The Inheritance of Family Shame and the Autobiographies of Henry James* (Wisconsin) that personal relationships in the James family were shaped and sustained over several generations by the emotional and psychological dynamics of shame. Holly finds those dynamics represented in Henry James's own "autobiographical project and the biographical experience to which it is intimately related." Both that project and experience reveal a recurrent pattern of "control, perfectionism, blame and denial," which "inhibits or defeats the development of authentic intimate relationships, promotes secrets and vague personal boundaries, unconsciously instills shame in the family members, as well as chaos in their lives, and binds them to perpetuate shame in themselves and their kin." Having been trapped between the desire to know the truth about his family and to turn away from it, James in *A Small Boy and Others* performs "an act of self-assertion" in which he "at last achieves what he always sought—mastery over his family." One of the more interesting aspects of *Intensely Family* elaborates the role of illness in the family, including James's own eating disorder, as a strategy for gaining power.

James the lover of gardens, though ignorant of gardening, is the subject of Cynthia Reavell's "Lamb House Garden" (*HJR* 16: 222–26). One year, for example, "he won no fewer than thirteen prizes [at flower shows], mostly firsts—even though George Gammon, the gardener, had done all the work."

In "A Bibliographic Note: A Copy of William James's *A Pluralistic Universe,* with Markings by Henry James" (*HJR* 16: 191–94) Adeline R. Tintner describes passages in his copy of his brother's book that James highlighted with ink dots, pencil dots, and pen notations. These particular markings offer insight into his view of his brother's thinking, and they gain significance when we recall Henry's words to William on 18 July 1909: "I'm *with* you, all along the line. . . . As an artist and a 'creator' I can catch on, hold on, to pragmatism, & can work in the light of it and apply it. . . ."

Arthur Sherbo added to his work updating the bibliography of secondary material on James in "Henry James in the *Dial* (And Elsewhere)" (*HJR* 16: 93–114). Among the items Sherbo brings to light are articles, from which he quotes extensively, by Henry McBride and Gilbert Seldes from the *Dial,* an anonymous *Dial* review of "A Landscape Painter," and an *Albany Review* piece by Desmond MacCarthy on *The American Scene.* Sherbo also notes essays from the *New English Weekly* on James's fiction and the *Washington Square*-inspired play *The Heiress,* two reviews of shorter fiction from the *Dublin Review,* a review of *Henry James: The Painter's Eye* from the *London Magazine,* and one brief eyewitness account of James in Rye.

Dorothy B. Holton's "Henry James's *The Princess Casamassima:* A Bibliography of Primary Material and Annotated Criticism" (*HJR* 16: 321–29) is helpful. But users should be aware that the bibliography is not complete. For example, the 1886 one-volume Macmillan edition is omitted, as is the 1888 Macmillan edition. Edel, Laurence, and Rambeau's *A Bibliography of Henry James* is missing from Holton's "Principal Sources." While the *MLA International Bibliography* up to this year is cited as a source, the most recent critical work on the novel I saw in Holton's section on "Books, Essays and Articles" is 1991, with omissions to be found for publications in 1991 and earlier.

A new edition of *The Turn of the Screw,* ed. Peter G. Beidler, was published as a part of the Bedford Books Case Studies in Contemporary Criticism series. This *Turn of the Screw* relies on the New York Edition and includes "relevant portions" of James's Preface. A series of essays, which follow the text of the short novel, orients students to the work's critical history. A biographical and historical contexts section (pp. 3–19) overviews, among other items, "Modern Spiritualism and the Ghost Story" and the "Composition of the Story." Beidler's own "A Critical History of *The Turn of the Screw*" (pp. 127–51) is a comprehensive introduction to the scholarly debate that has kept the nouvelle at or near the center of interest for Jamesians since its first publication. The following examples of some critical approaches to *The Turn of the Screw* are included, with each approach preceded by a short introductory essay and a selected bibliography on that particular method. "A Reader-Response Perspective" is represented by Wayne C. Booth's " 'He began to read to our hushed little circle': Are We Blessed or Cursed by Our Life with *The Turn of the Screw?*" (pp. 163–78). "A Deconstructionist Perspective" is exemplified by Shoshana Felman's " 'The grasp with which I recovered him': A Child Is Killed in *The Turn of the Screw*" (pp. 193–206). "A Psychoanalytic Perspective" is shown with Stanley Renner's " 'Red hair, very red, close-curling': Sexual Hysteria, Physiognomical Bogeymen, and the 'Ghosts' in *The Turn of the Screw*" (pp. 223–41). "A Feminist Perspective" is conveyed by " 'What then on earth was I?': Feminine

Subjectivity and *The Turn of the Screw*" by Priscilla L. Walton (pp. 253–67). Bruce Robbins offers "A Marxist Perspective" in " 'They don't much count, do they?': The Unfinished History of *The Turn of the Screw*" (pp. 283–96). The Bedford edition, which is available in both paper and hardcover, should be welcome and useful in the classroom.

ii Parallels and Influences

In "The Romance of Old Clothes in a Fatal Chest" (*HJR* 16: 315–20) Mary Y. Hallab reasons that the source of "The Romance of Old Clothes" could be a popular contemporary melodrama, *The Mistletoe Bough: or, The Fatal Chest,* or perhaps the story of Cinderella in Briggs and Tongue's *Folktales of England.*

The suicide of Grace Mavis is a "mysterious act," which supplies the key with which Adeline R. Tintner unlocks the relation of "The Patagonia" to a Trollope story ("James's 'The Patagonia': A Critique of Trollope's 'The Journey to Panama,' " *SSF* 32: 59–66). Tintner shows not only that the plots of the two stories "are very close," but that the differences, which turn "Trollope's rather chatty tale about the plight of a young girl . . . into the tale of the tragic trap a young woman of sensibility finds herself in," are important because they represent James's "conscious, critical act."

Finding that James's "The Beast in the Jungle" "echoes," "explores," and "appropriates" Maupassant's "Promenade," Ileana Alexandra Orlich ("Tracking the Missing Link: Maupassant's 'Promenade' and James's *The Beast in the Jungle,*" *Comparatist* 18 [1994]: 71–89) surveys similarities and differences between the two works in terms of narrative style, central characters, and the "theme of unlived life." One key point is that by "sharpening and expanding the thematics of Maupassant's story, James produced a subtle new architecture, a work of great psychological density and emotional poignancy."

Vivienne Rundle's "Defining Frames: The Prefaces of Henry James and Joseph Conrad" (*HJR* 16: 66–92) uses the two sets of prefaces as a way to investigate "the nature of each writer's relation to his readership" and "the relationships between writing and responsibility" and between "narrative structure and narrative performance." Rundle contends that the prefaces "*displace*" the novel by "substituting *James's* writing and *James's* reading for the reader's own experience of the text."

iii Critical Books and Collections

In *The Rhetorical Logic of Henry James* (LSU) Sheila Teahan details how principles of James's narrative or rhetorical logic determine all aspects of the fiction, even those which James might not have anticipated and which lead to narrative "collapses" when "James's representational praxis is at odds with its own theory" or when "both theory and praxis are internally incoherent." An awareness that "the Jamesian reflector . . . [is] radically performative: it produces the material it claims only to represent" enables Teahan to map and explain the operation of James's narrative logic exactly where Jamesian theory meets literary language—at the center of consciousness. For "both a representational strategy and an implicit theory of narrative, the center of consciousness furnishes the formal principle of a large body of James's novels, as well as the focus of many of his speculative essays on writing and representation." Teahan explains the way politically charged language conditions Hyacinth Robinson to (mis)understand his world in *The Princess Casamassima.* Teahan also examines in *What Maisie Knew* whether "in giving terms to Maisie's knowledge, James's narrator merely expresses an existing preverbal consciousness or actually creates it." Her analysis of *Roderick Hudson* details the way "Roderick's artistic impasse is precisely that of a disjunction between image and word, between allegorical vehicle and tenor." She notices that it is "Strether's fundamental unaccountability" that brings *The Ambassadors* "to a representational impasse." Teahan studies Milly Theale's illness and consciousness in *The Wings of the Dove* because "on the one hand, Milly's illness is the basis of her narrative authority. . . . On the other, her death is virtually caused by her status as center of consciousness, for her illness quickens her receptive consciousness to an ultimately fatal degree. . . ." She discovers in *The Awkward Age* a point of conflict where the "rhetorical logic of the reflector" is disrupted by the scenic method, which "abandons the discursive representation of consciousness." In all, Teahan's is a conceptually rich book.

Like Teahan, Evelyne Ender in *Sexing the Mind: Nineteenth-Century Fictions of Hysteria* (Cornell) describes and explains James's narrative collapses. At the same time, like Pierre A. Walker (below), Ender places James in a French context. Yet where Teahan reads the breaks in the narrative as a function of James's rhetorical logic, Ender reads them as a function of James's and his culture's understanding of gender, which produces a kind of "fiction of hysteria." And where Walker places the James texts in a French literary-cultural context, Ender places them in the context of her reading of James's readings of George Sand and Flaubert. Ender's method combines "a thematic approach to hysteria" with "a narratological and rhetorical analysis." She bases her method on the principle that "gender, as the meaning imposed upon sexual differ-ence and as the translation into the mental domain of a bodily fact, must necessarily be understood as a textual effect." Thus, the James texts enable her "to highlight how reading and writing intervene in the process of gendering." Tracing the shift in French medical literature of the location of hysteria from the body to the "psychological sphere," and demonstrating that James's "critical texts . . . provide extraordinary insight into the literary figurations of sexual identity," Ender explains that "hysteria" is used here not for its historical or clinical value, but as "a heuristic model that produces a number of theoretical insights." For Ender, then, James gives evidence of "the complex association, in nineteenth-century representations of subjectivity, between aesthetic or moral stakes and questions of sexual identity or gender." James's critical essays on Sand show "that the attempt to master sexual difference, in other words to ground the representations of subjectivity on the delinea-tions and possible legislation of a 'sexual identity,' inevitably leads to an aporia." Representations of gender similar to the ones expressed by James's Sand are found in the descriptions of Verena Tarrant and Olive Chancellor in *The Bostonians*. In both the novel and his last essays on Sand, "James writes in the guise of a historian of gender, and his project shows the main concerns expressed in his critical texts on the French writer; the questions of woman, of sexual difference, and of feminism." In the face of such crisis-provoking questions, Ender explains the narra-tive collapse of the last pages of *The Bostonians*: "To speak of James's hysteria in his novel is then to address the fantasies of gender that are produced in the work of representation. Such fantasies are the product of a hysteria that is both private and collective."

Making a strong case for reading James in a "pan-Western" or "trina-tional" (English, French, American) context, Pierre A. Walker concen-trates on one of them in *Reading Henry James in French Cultural Contexts* (No. Ill.). Through close reasoning and careful scholarship, he extends previous studies of James's use of the French language and French settings in his fiction to examine the way James "incorporated conven-tions and stereotypes of French culture along with explicit and implicit references to French literary texts." Knowledge of those conventions and stereotypes enables readers to begin to regain a contemporary understanding of James's texts and to resolve "interpretive cruxes" in them. Walker discusses the significance of Geneva in "Daisy Miller" in terms of that city's French stereotypes in Victor Cherbuliez, especially *Paule Méré*. James's references in *The Princess Casamassima* to the work of Octave Feuillet and Balzac inform the reading of Hyacinth's and the Princess's friendship, of the Princess's capricious personality, of Hyacinth's suicide, and of the way that James makes ironic the convention of "the young man from the provinces." A complex of references to the Virgin Mary and to Mary, Queen of Scots, the legend of Origen's self-castration, *The Vicar of Wakefield, Pendennis, The Newcomes, Notre Dame de Paris, Louis Lambert,* and the importance of Strether's comparison of himself to the Bern *Zeitglockenthurm* ground Walker's reading of *The Ambassadors.* James's references in *The Awkward Age* to "quintessential literary characterizations of innocence (Goethe's Margaret and Hugo's Esmerelda), to the obvious associations within a French context of the name Fernanda, and to similarities in James's representation of the 'problem' of the 'modern girl' and the marriage market to the representation of the same problem in the fiction of Gyp," according to Walker, resolve a number of critical issues in the novel. Allusions to Zola, Molière, the younger Dumas, Sardou, and Diderot provide additional intertextual keys. Literary allusions in *The Tragic Muse* are significant because "it is the foregrounding in texts such as *La Cousine Bette, Mademoiselle de la Seiglière, Il ne faut jurer de rien, L'Aventurière,* and *Le Lionees pauvres* of deceitful, dissimulating characters that leads us to pay attention to deceit, pretending, falseness, acting, humbuggery, and dissimulation in all the walks of life James's novel represents."

In *The Politics of Exile,* his study of James Baldwin's ideological relation to his predecessors, especially James, Bryan R. Washington seeks to explain how black readers confront "white texts." Washington's questions generate fresh readings of "Daisy Miller" especially, but also "The Beast in the Jungle" and *The American Scene.*

Henry James's New York Edition: The Construction of Authorship, ed. David McWhirter (Stanford), contains excellent essays on the New York Edition and the later part of James's career. Only the essays by McWhirter, Jerome McGann, J. Hillis Miller, and Eve Kosofsky Sedgwick have appeared elsewhere. The following, from John Carlos Rowe's foreword, characterizes the collection overall: "These new Henry

Jameses are . . . full of life and interest, not only in their times but for our
time, which as we begin to understand it continues to wind its way back
to its early modern origins as it unfurls into our own new century." In
" 'The Whole Chain of Relation and Responsibility': Henry James and
the New York Edition" (pp. 1–19) McWhirter introduces the collection:
"The essays gathered in this volume constitute a collective attempt to
apprehend the full complexity of Henry James's self-performance. . . .
Taken together, they suggest how the Edition might serve as a locus for
considering not only the question of Henry James but also the problematics and permutations of modern literary authority." Ross Posnock in
"Breaking the Aura of Henry James" (pp. 23–38) argues for recognition
of "the incongruities that mark the texture of James's genius" and explores how "James in 1904 . . . stages his own spectacle of public
vulnerability." In "Ozymandias and the Mastery of Ruins: The Design of
the New York Edition" (pp. 39–57) Stuart Culver contends that "the
New York Edition is . . . yet another performance of the artist in his later
manner, one that exploits the limits of the ready-made format of the
deluxe edition in its effort to make the sea of Jamesian fiction itself
emerge, and to redefine its author as a presence that always exceeds
efforts to enclose or commemorate its achievements." Sara Blair in "In
the House of Fiction: Henry James and the Engendering of Literary
Mastery" (pp. 58–73) discusses the figures of domestic architecture, with
which James imagines his literary authority, in the context of his representations of women "and the long-standing ambivalence of feminist
readers of his master texts." Thus, Blair reads "domesticity as the autho-
rizing ground of James's performance." In "Ambiguous Allegiances:
Conflicts of Culture and Ideology in the Making of the New York
Edition" (pp. 77–89) Michael Anesko offers a review of the difficulties of
publishing the Edition in England, of the cultural significance of its
design and construction, of contemporary evidence that belies the notion that James was seen more as an English novelist than an American
one, and of the surprising popularity in England of seven-penny editions
of the novels. Ira B. Nadel explains in "Visual Culture: The Photo
Frontispieces to the New York Edition" (pp. 90–108) that the frontispieces gave James a way to use photography to validate his fictional world
and to renew his place in American literary culture. Paul B. Armstrong
argues in "Reading James's Prefaces and Reading James" (pp. 125–37)
that some of the particular features of the Prefaces, such as James's display
of the "reader's future . . . through the author's past," indicate that the

Prefaces function as "introductory texts [which] help provide the reader with a hermeneutic education that simulates modes of understanding appropriate for construing his fiction." In "Doctoring the Text: Henry James and Revision" (pp. 142–63) Julie Rivkin conducts an analysis of the Preface to *The Golden Bowl* and of "The Middle Years" as a way to "explore James's own representations of revision." In "The Emotional Aftermath of the New York Edition" (pp. 167–84) Carol Holly exposes the importance of James's Fletcherizing dietary habit from 1908 until 1910, when he seems to have tried to manage his feelings of failure and loss by controlling his eating, which led to anorexia nervosa. Pointing out instances of James's paradoxical stance toward readers of the Prefaces, which calls into question his frankness or at least his attitude toward frankness, Alfred Habegger emphasizes in "New York Monumentalism and Hidden Family Corpses" (pp. 185–205) that "The New York Edition is an artful structure erected on a place where something closely resembling a fatal family curse had worked itself out." That curse had to do with James's confusion and shame about what he did and did not know about family ghosts, especially about his father and about his uncle, John Barber James. Habegger then reads the autobiographical volumes as "monuments," which are a consequence of James's "belated . . . effort to look all that wasted life square in the face without turning to stone." Finally, Martha Banta in "The Excluded Seven: Practice of Omission, Aesthetics of Refusal" (pp. 240–60) speculates what readers "would have confronted if the seven novels left out of the New York Edition [*Watch and Ward, Confidence, Washington Square, The Europeans, The Bostonians, The Other House, The Sacred Fount*] had been incorporated within its sanctioning imprint as well as what manner of author we are offered as the consequence of these excisions." Banta shows that the "ruling principle" for including and excluding works was simply "winnowing the perpetually weak from the potentially strong."

In *The Ethnography of Manners* Nancy Bentley investigates the "high literary authorship for American novelists . . . organized around a specialized practice of writing about manners" in the late 19th and early 20th centuries. Moreover, she articulates the concept of culture, itself represented and reinforced in the novels she discusses, "as a problematic but enabling myth, a literal pretext for the work of writing manners and the site at which fiction both feeds and is nourished by other nonfictional genres." Bentley's closest study of James centers on *The Sacred Fount*. In that analysis she makes at least five points: (1) that the novel redefines the

Victorian middle-class family in terms of "the relations linking art, property, and women through the exchange medium of marriage," all of which is understood as a community based on the bonds of taste, not kinship; (2) that it redefines the novel form, in which James's analysis of taste and manners "was matched . . . by contemporary social theorists"; (3) that totemism, desire, culture, and their relations inform James's "exquisite economy" of style and define the fetishistic bonds of the "community of taste"; (4) that James, like contemporary ethnographers, explored "the gendered nature of power"; and (5) that the destruction of Poynton is to be read in terms of an "authorial gesture or act."

The Fall 1995 issue of *HJR* (16, iii) contains a special section titled "Race Forum" (pp. 247–303), which consists of an introduction by the new editor, Susan M. Griffin, and nine short essays, several of which work in direct dialogue with others. While some readers may be disappointed by the brevity of the essays on this important issue in James studies, all will find that the "Forum" raises key questions from a range of methodological approaches. In "The Person Sitting in Darkness: James in the American South" (pp. 249–56) Eric Haralson examines James's "paradoxical formula" in *The American Scene,* which "testifies to the powerfully present absence (or absent presence) of African Americans, [and] situates itself within the long line of colonial perspectives on the ontology and subjectivity of exotic, abject beings." In "The Return of the Alien: Henry James in New York, 1904" (pp. 257–63) Beverly Haviland argues that *The American Scene* contains James's complex and non-normative idea of ethnic identity and sense of his own cultural dispossession, which itself "creates a bond of solidarity with all those who have been dispossessed of their heritage, including the people whom we now call Native Americans." Sara Blair in "Documenting America: Racial Theater in *The American Scene*" (pp. 264–72) finds, unlike Haviland, that "James's text vividly rehearses the racial logic of America's distinctive nation-building idiom, in which the character of whiteness, in its 'inveterate bourgeois form,' is being forged." Blair's method depends on the contextualization of James's language in his chapters on Richmond and the Lower East Side and the stereographic documentation of black cotton workers and of a Lower East Side street scene. Ross Posnock responds to the Blair essay in "Henry James and the Limits of Historicism" (pp. 273–77), to which Blair then rejoins (pp. 278–81). Posnock takes James's "self-confessed marginality" as a central reason why he, unlike other canonical authors, is not seen by those who work in cultural studies as a figure of "repression, of ideological containment." Posnock also questions the comprehensiveness of Blair's investigation of James's "relation to African Americans as they are depicted in *The American Scene*." Answering Posnock and Blair, Kenneth Warren points out that our very investigations of James's meaning and thus of his value "are never simply a repudiation of the past but rather a critical engagement with it" ("Still Reading Henry James?" pp. 282–85). Walter Benn Michaels responds to Toni Morrison's remark that James scholarship of *What Maisie Knew* has ignored the key role of the Countess because Jamesians refuse to recognize the "Africanist presence" in *Maisie* just as literary scholars in general refuse to recognize that presence in American literature overall ("Jim Crow Henry James?" pp. 286–91). Michaels thus explains the meaning of the Countess in terms of turn-of-the-century Jim Crow culture as represented in "writers like Thomas Dixon." Leland S. Person's "In the Closet with Frederick Douglass: Reconstructing Masculinity in *The Bostonians*" (pp. 292–98) discusses the novel's transposition of race and gender "through a complex process of subject positioning" in which, for Douglass and James's Basil Ransom, "Racial subordination can be reinscribed as gender superiority."

iv Criticism: General Essays

Richard A. Hocks in "Henry James's Incipient Poetics of the Short Story Sequence: *The Finer Grain* (1910)" (*Modern American Short Story Sequences,* pp. 1–18) explains why James's late collection, *The Finer Grain,* unlike earlier published short story collections, "presents us with a short story sequence proper." Hocks bases his determination of the "sequence proper" on the compositional circumstances of the stories, their narrative style and "significant language," the narrative integrity of the sequence, recurrent elements of characterization and plot, recurrence of "'predicaments,'" especially "the lethal combination of hyperconsciousness with loneliness," the sequence of geographic settings, and "the problematized 'sexual relation' between the heroes." Hocks finds the sequence "modernist in resonance" and concludes that "the difficulty attending these last tales arises not from their artistic integrity but from their anticipation of the tangential, fragmentary nature of modernity itself."

By comparing the narrative of "The Pupil" with that of the U.S. buddy film *The Last Boy Scout* (1991), Lynda Zwinger ("Bodies That Don't Matter: The Queering of 'Henry James,'" *MFS* 41: 657–80) questions why a "readerly certitude about what is there is conditioned by a confident statement of what is not." Zwinger thus reexamines what has become the dominant scholarly view that "Henry James was queer (but had no sex)." But in her reexamination of what has nearly come to be accepted without question, Zwinger, like Philip Horne (below), seeks to preserve the vitality of the range of discussion by which, as James wrote in "The Art of Fiction," "art lives." Zwinger thus reminds us that "The Pupil," "like most of the rest of James's fiction, is an *investigation* of sexuality—of its roots, gnarled and gnarly as they are."

Two essays by Richard Henke concerning performativity and masculinity deserve mention. In "The Embarrassment of Melodrama: Masculinity in the Early James" (*Novel* 28: 257–83) Henke surveys James's passive male characters as a way to understand his "most radical insights into the construction of masculine identity." *Watch and Ward* is useful for such an examination because its "very simplicity helps reveal more purely James's concerns about the problematics of masculinity as an uneasy opposition of action and passivity which he more intricately pursues later." More, Henke investigates the reasons why *Watch and Ward* is "for James and his critics . . . such an embarrassing novel." Henke concludes that the source of the embarrassment is the novel's origin in popular melodrama, which "depicts a world that simultaneously demands that manhood be attained through action and yet enforces 'the frame of respectability' to limit any 'strong action' which might establish this gendered identity." Henke also traces the problem of masculinity in *Roderick Hudson, The American,* and *The Ambassadors.* Henke concludes that James moved "away from pure melodrama" in order to critique the "fixed position of masculinity in the genre." In "The Man of Action: Henry James and the Performance of Gender" (*HJR* 16: 227–41) Henke demonstrates that gender was a central issue, especially for F. O. Matthiessen, in "the rise of James's literary fortunes" during the 1930s and 1940s. Henke also surveys James's use of the rhetoric of economic masculinity ("language . . . that is rife with aggressive and assertive images"), which appears in the context of the language of "surrender, submission, languishing . . . about something traditionally perceived as 'feminine.'"

"It is the fascination of truth, of a reality mysteriously hidden behind the world's materiality, that makes certain characters of James epitomize the emblematic search of modern mind for a perpetually elusive knowledge," writes Christian Moraru in " 'Real' and 'Right' Things: Mimetic

Rivalry and Epistemological Project in Henry James's Short Stories" (*StHum* 21 [1994]: 147–64). Moraru relates several James texts, especially "The Real Thing," to James's belief "in art's and the artist's capacity to generate an individual, unique type of truth." In "Contagious Appearances: Nietzsche, Henry James, and the Critique of Fiction" (*Nietzsche in American Literature and Thought,* pp. 79–95) Daniel T. O'Hara investigates the way James associated the act of writing with what he "envisions as 'the whole chain of relation and responsibility' constituting society." O'Hara explains that James created such a link in the later novels, at least, by a "contagious emanation of creativity," a function of "restricted point of view," by the way characters respond creatively to the genius of other characters or the way James responded imaginatively to his own characters. O'Hara argues that readers also respond creatively to James's novels "so that they, too, become authorial." Such a chain of creative contagion suggests "a democratically aesthetic sovereignty."

Noting that the years 1892–96 were among those during which James sought most vigorously and failed most desperately to gain recognition and income from the popular book market, which he had "frequently characterized as feminine and infantile," Kristin King (" 'Lost Among the Genders': Male Narrators and Female Writers in James's Literary Tales, 1892–1896," *HJR* 16: 18–35) investigates four tales from the 1890s ("Greville Fane," "The Death of the Lion," "The Next Time," and "The Figure in the Carpet"), in which "male narrators' supervision of women's influence over male authors attempts to discount the threat of feminine literary authority." In light of her examination of gender, authority, and James's career, King finds that themes of "vulgar commodification of fiction associated with unlicensed feminine authority underscore James's anxiety about eroded male privilege" and his certainty about the continued success of women writers in the modern marketplace.

Although James's use of portraits is an established area of scholarly and critical interest, Frederick Wegener points out in " 'Looking as If She Were Alive': The 'Duchess Effect,' the Representation of Women, and Henry James's Use of Portraits" (*CentR* 38 [1994]: 539–77) that the early "The Story of a Masterpiece" has been little studied. An allusion in the story to Browning's "My Last Duchess" provides Wegener with an example of what he terms "The Duchess effect," a "process of artistic creation [which] somehow thrives cannibalistically, subsisting on the human materials out of which images are made, as the model surrenders its reality to a painting, and a living being appears metaphorically transformed into a motionless image." While James's apparent attention to the problems of women has generated interest by a range of feminist scholars who have noted a progressive deepening of James's sensitivity to those problems from *Portrait* to *Maisie*, Chris Foss denies that advance. Instead, Foss asks us to understand that feminist recuperations of James "serve to repress the persistency of the texts' masculinist vision" ("Female Innocence as Other in *The Portrait of a Lady* and *What Maisie Knew:* Reassessing the Feminist Recuperation of Henry James," *ELWIU* 22: 253–68).

v Criticism: Individual Novels

In " 'I Trust You Will Detect My Intention': The Strange Case of *Watch and Ward*" (*JAmS* 29: 365–78) Lindsay Traub locates James's embarrassment in the novel's form, which inadequately conveyed his parody of a popular genre. Although today we have difficulty explaining the presence of the novel's "overtones of incest and paedophilia" and its particular eroticism, Traub explains that during the 1860s a range of popular novels like *Watch and Ward* exploited the relationships of "orphans, guardians, wards, young girls and older men." But James, Traub argues, treated these popular and conventional literary situations parodically in order to point out the danger and immorality of "the mutation of a quasi-parental relationship into a marital one," a thematic element Traub finds "throughout James's work."

Donald Weber uses James's characterization of Newman in France as a way to understand Cahan's Levinsky in the United States ("Outsiders and Greenhorns: Christopher Newman in the Old World, David Levinsky in the New," *AL* 67: 725–45). Weber's analysis of the two novels reveals that James's descriptions of "Americans abroad straining to mask, seeking to repress their rough native/New-World style anticipates in uncanny ways *the* overarching subject of early-twentieth-century immigrant writers in America: the comedy and, more often, pathos of innocent 'greenhorns' caught in the process of what came to be termed 'Americanization.' "

Two articles focus on *The Portrait of a Lady*. John W. Crowley in "*The Portrait of a Lady* and *The Rise of Silas Lapham:* The Company They Kept" (*The Cambridge Companion to American Realism and Naturalism*, pp. 117–37) works to situate James and Howells as both producers and products of realism. Crowley chooses the 1881 edition of *Portrait* because it represents "the highest degree of James's . . . commitment to the idea that realism embodies 'the true principles of literary art.' " In addition to his survey of James's reviews of Howells and of Howells's criticism of James, Crowley notes that in his novels Howells tended to rely more on external signs such as speech and action to represent character while James's "portrait of Isabel Archer emerges not only through the dramatic method, but also through direct commentary on her inner life and indirect narrative access to her consciousness." Elaborating the economic dimension of Jamesian realism, Crowley follows Wai-Chee Dimock in saying that both James and Howells recognize that economics is "a vital instrument in moral arbitration." Bonnie Herron compares the 1880 *Macmillan's* serial of *Portrait* with the 1908 New York Edition version in "Substantive Sexuality: Henry James Constructs Isabel Archer as a Complete Woman in His Revised Version of *The Portrait of a Lady*" (*HJR* 16: 131–41). Through an examination of changes in the free indirect discourse, Herron shows that the New York Edition *Portrait* maintains interest in the action of Isabel's mind but also reveals a maturer and "more sexually aware" character.

Caroline Field Levander writes in "Bawdy Talk: The Politics of Women's Public Speech in *The Lecturess* and *The Bostonians*" (*AL* 67: 467–85) that 19th-century linguists, as well as male novelists such as James, defined the nature of female speech in terms of tone rather than content, which for them characterized male speech. With tone being a function of the body rather than the intellect, contemporary linguistic theory supplied American culture with a "polic[ing]" function that encouraged the exclusion of women from the public arena. Levander shows that James critiques such a gendered understanding of speech, though he "eventually capitulate[s]" to it in *The Bostonians* through Basil Ransom's relation to Verena Tarrant.

In "Satire in *The Tragic Muse*" (*SAF* 23: 3–18) Chris Brown reads Gabriel Nash as the novel's "satirist in mufti" and thus locates not only the satiric component of the novel, but the way that component operates within a Swiftian comic tradition. Placing Nash in the context of similar Jamesian characters, including Mark Ambient of "The Author of Beltraffio," and in the tradition of "the professional, not the 'natural,' fool," Brown resists the "Paterian" definition of Nash's character and aesthetic at the same time he shows how "aestheticism gives the vantage for his satire. . . . Nash vents his creator's spleen, particularly on the British theater." Finally, however, James follows his typical pattern by allowing the satire "to modulate into sympathy" as he "becomes engaged with the characters."

By accounting for what James called the novel's "screens" and for its "*two* red herrings" Adeline R. Tintner works to solve the puzzle of the identities of the actual pairs of lovers in *The Sacred Fount* ("A Gay *Sacred Fount:* The Reader as Detective," *TCL* 41: 224–40). Tintner reveals that the pairs of lovers are actually two men, Gilbert Long and Guy Brissenden, on the one hand, and two women, May Server and Grace Brissenden, on the other. James's remarks about the novel in his letters, events in James's life, and his literary representation of homosexuality elsewhere supply Tintner with an interpretive context.

Claire Oberon Garcia shows in "The Shopper and the Shopper's Friend: Lambert Strether and Maria Gostrey's Consumer Consciousness" (*HJR* 16: 153–71) that the prevalence of economic language and imagery in *The Ambassadors* is significant because it suggests that "the novel is more historically engaged than it appears" and thus represents the way commercialism and aesthetics were intertwined at the turn of the century in the United States.

Contending that feminist readings of *The Wings of the Dove* "do not go far enough," and in contrast to Foss's article (above), Doran Larson reads the novel as a story of "mothers, friends, sisters, and daughters," a work of "female-homosocial exchanges" which depends on the "originary ethos of the mother" ("Milly's Bargain: The Homosocial Economy in *The Wings of the Dove*," *ArQ* 51, i: 81–110). Such an ethos redefines the meaning of value from use value, which is typical of male homosociality, to the reciprocal giving of exchange value, which typifies female homosocial relationships and defines "an entirely new narrative economy of signification—an economy in which an aesthetic of the signifier, and of supplementarity, *is* the signified." Larson's analysis is exceptional for its acuity and suggestiveness.

Two of the year's best articles concern *The Golden Bowl.* In "The Poetics of Cultural Decline: Degeneracy, Assimilation, and the Jew in James's *The Golden Bowl*" (*AmLH* 7: 477–99) Jonathan Freedman uses two Jewish characters, Gutterman-Suess and the antique dealer, and another racially "other" character, Prince Amerigo, to investigate the "racial drama of that book." Holding simultaneously central and marginal roles in the novel, the Jewish characters, writes Freedman, are positioned to raise the issue of "the status of cultures past in the capitalist imperium of the present. . . ." They function as "the benchmark against which the assimilation of Amerigo is measured." In addition to her sharp-edged investigation of James as author and narrator, Irena Auerbuch Smith's "The Golden Goal: Toward a Dialogic Imagination in Henry James's Last Completed Novel" (*HJR* 16: 172–90) is unusually balanced between the exposition of her reading and a discourse with relevant scholarship. Recognizing that James's narrative stance allows him to incarnate "himself as a character in his own text" and also to engage "in a dialogue with his characters rather than dictate to them 'the words of truth,'" Smith shows how James stands at once within and outside his text. In addition, his characters work to issue and to determine the "words of truth." The result of James's examination of truth and fiction (or truth through art) is that "authorial discourse . . . holds value in the novel only when that value is placed there through the voice of another . . . not the author."

vi Criticism: Shorter Fiction

Philip Horne asks fundamental and necessary questions regarding the effect of gender studies, especially Sedgwick's *The Epistemology of the Closet,* on the state of James scholarship. Among Horne's excellent points in "Henry James: The Master and the 'Queer Affair' of 'The Pupil'" (*CritQ* 37, iii: 75–92) is his caveat that readers should remain cautious about "the assumption reflected in much current criticism . . . that the sexual is the basic or underlying or 'deep' realm of meaning. . . . The risk is that all motivation can become inappropriately, a-prioristically, sexualised." Also Horne questions James's meaning of the term "queer," which he points out is not as clear as queer theorists understand it to be and for Horne stands as an example of "the abuse of speculation." Horne then seeks to place "a homoerotic reading . . . into serious and interesting tension with the complex balance of other more explicit strains in the story, about duty and sacrifice, money and honour, education and experience," and even "moral traditions of the James family," without excluding any reading, including a homoerotic one.

Sam Whitsitt works to expose both what is the "lesson" James refers to in his *Notebook* entry on "The Real Thing" and to whom James directs it ("A Lesson in Reading: Henry James's 'The Real Thing,'" *HJR* 16: 304–14). Whitsitt approaches his analysis not by searching for "some parable about art" but by examining the way memory or "pastness" "fractures the present moment." Such an approach allows Whitsitt to make an analogy between "the artist's relation to Miss Churm—a relation wherein the artist establishes his own identity by effacing the other—and the reader's relation to the text wherein the reader gains identity by identifying the essence of the text and effacing in the process the narrative 'face' itself."

Raymond J. Wilson III reads "The Figure in the Carpet" as a response to Hawthorne's implicit argument about the shortcomings of fiction in revealing "truth about reality—with James arguing on the side of the truth-telling ability of fiction" ("The Possibility of Realism: 'The Figure in the Carpet' and Hawthorne's Intertext," *HJR* 16: 142–52). David Liss argues in "The Fixation of Belief in 'The Figure in the Carpet': Henry James and Peircean Semiotics" (*HJR* 16: 36–47) that a Peircean concept of meaning, which depends on the conditions under which a particular meaning is produced, is central to reading the story. For Liss, "the 'figure' is not a quantifiable thing, it is not an identifiable object, but a process." In "'The Harmless Pleasure of Knowing': Privacy in the Telegraph Office and Henry James's 'In the Cage'" (*HJR* 16: 53–65) Andrew J. Moody demonstrates how knowledge of the social, gender, and class conditions of newly professionalized telegraph workers informs a reading of the story. The contemporary security of messages having been outlined, Moody concludes that there "is little evidence" that the unethical sale of secretive information by telegraph officials "was a common problem in Great Britain." Thus "James constructs a fictional cage built of honor and nobility."

vii Criticism: Nonfiction

In "Travel Writing and the Metropolis: James, London, and *English Hours*" (*AL* 67: 201–32) Brigitte Bailey investigates "the role of aesthetic language and pictorial conventions and their ideological implications." Those implications depend on the relation of James's essay "London," which opens *English Hours,* to the overall narrative of the collection and thus to its overall meaning. The placement of "London" "makes the subsequent pieces appear to be excursions from London . . . , provides the defining context for other essays on London, and implicitly enmeshes the rest of the collection in what is now the focal project of the whole text: developing ways of seeing the modern imperial city." Those "ways of seeing" are related to the effects of power "emanating from and shaped by the unimaginable center," which itself "constructs the margins." Bailey's analysis of James's urban aesthetic extends to Pennell's etchings for the 1905 edition of *English Hours.*

Relying on Theodora Bosanquet's unpublished "Diary" and James's correspondence with Scribner's as evidence of the chronology of changes to the plan for the New York Edition, Priscilla Gibson Hicks in "A Turn in the Formation of James's New York Edition: Criticism, the Historical Record, and the Siting of *The Awkward Age*" (*HJR* 16: 195–221) determines which of the changes in the ordonnance of the Edition were James's own and which, if any, were pressed onto him by his publisher. Such changes are important because the consequent juxtapositions created by the reordering suggest James's understanding not only of *The Awkward Age,* but of the New York Edition's design. For Hicks, the changes signal a plan that stresses classification and juxtaposition and gives *The Awkward Age,* rather than *The Tragic Muse,* an important place in binding, not just dividing, the earlier run of long novels with the successive run of shorter fictions.

Finally, Allan Burns ("Henry James's Journalists as Synecdoche for the American Scene," *HJR* 16: 1–17) finds that James's characterizations of journalists Henrietta Stackpole from *The Portrait of a Lady,* Matthias Pardon of *The Bostonians,* and George Flack of *The Reverberator* function as a synecdoche for "James's evolving conception of the United States," which James articulates most forcefully in *The American Scene.* When Burns confronts the inevitable question of whether James was anti-democratic, he answers that James's conservatism is in the realm of art, not in "the actual institutions of aristocracy."

Creighton University

8 Pound and Eliot

Michael Coyle and Laura Cowan

Once again this year no single methodology or topic dominated either Pound or Eliot studies, despite the publication of important and sometimes controversial work. Perhaps the single most fundamental trend has been the continuing reconfiguration of the very field of modernism and, consequently, of Pound's and Eliot's places in it. For a change, Eliot studies felt the heat of ideological combat more than did Pound studies. But the pressure of gender studies, and of the relation of what used to be called "high modernism" to "the occult," or to things Victorian, or to developments outside literature in English, continue to reform our opinions about what modernism was, and is. Michael Coyle is responsible for the Pound commentary here, Laura Cowan for the Eliot.

i Pound

a. Text, Biography, and Bibliography   The most important edition of new material by Pound is undoubtedly E. P. Walkiewicz and Hugh Witemeyer's edition of *Ezra Pound and Senator Bronson Cutting: A Political Correspondence, 1930–35* (New Mexico). The editors have reproduced all surviving material exchanged between the poet and the senator, including not only letters but Pound's "Ez Sez" editorials in Cutting's newspaper, the *Santa Fe New Mexican;* Pound's distressed obituary on Cutting's death in a plane crash and his subsequent letter to the editor of the Santa Fe paper; and finally a syndicated caricature of the period that "reflects the popular conception of Cutting as an intellectual leader." The editors' purpose is more than archival. They argue that "viewed in the context of his correspondences with Cutting and others, Pound's politics look far less eccentric, unpatriotic, and uniformed than they can seem when viewed in isolation." Cutting was, of course, not a random correspondent; he was an outspoken opponent of the New Deal and a public advocate for Social Credit economics. His exchanges with Pound not only help to establish the valency of Pound's Americanness—a much-discussed topic in 1995—but also bring a new perspective to our understanding of his mixture of poetry and politics. Walkiewicz and Witemeyer have produced a thoughtfully and responsibly designed volume. The first and last chapters frame the whole in a thematic chiasmus and function as contextualizing essays. All letters and editorials are followed by explanatory notes, and the three middle chapters of Pound's and Cutting's writings are carefully introduced; individual letters are followed by explanatory notes.

Interest in Robert Spoo's publication of 20 previously unknown letters by Pound to James Joyce, Nora Barnacle Joyce, and Stanislaus Joyce (*JJQ* 32: 533–81) hardly needs explanation. Spoo's annotation is expansive and helpful. He submits that "some annotators conceive of their job in terms of rudimentary catechism, as if their role were to provide simple answers to simple questions. But historical documents rarely ask simple questions; rather, they hold out to us a palimpsest of partially erased, elliptical, overlapping contexts. As a note grows, it leaves behind simple problem-solving and approaches the condition of biography."

b. General Studies and Pound's Relation to Other Writers   Three general guides to Pound were published this year, all by English scholars. The first of these, Ian F. A. Bell's "Ezra Pound," appears in *American Poetry: The Modernist Ideal* (pp. 28–46); the second guide, more comprehensive in scope, is Peter Nicholls's *Modernisms: A Literary Guide* (Macmillan). Interestingly enough, Bell situates his study squarely in the context of an American literary tradition, while Nicholls insists that Anglo-American modernism, although arguably the hegemonic model, was nevertheless but one modernism among several.

Bell asks readers to see Pound through the lens of Melville's *Pierre,* whose protagonist " 'immaturely' attempts a 'mature work.' " The largest effect of Bell's gesture is to displace the preemptive claims of "the Men of 1914" to have first articulated the modern; his more immediate purpose is to *re*present *Mauberley*'s famous challenge to romantic "notions of a unified or integral self." Bell surrounds his subject with a rich welter of other voices: Henry Adams, Dora Marsden, Emerson, Wilde, and Alexander Kaun—as well as theorists of 19th-century French painting. But ultimately what makes his historicist context so American is its emphasis on consumption. Having followed Kaun's 1916 review of the Ravenna edition of Wilde's works, a review that iterates how thoroughly Wilde's theories and paradoxes had been absorbed by others in the decade after his death, Bell moves to explain the enduring controversy surrounding Pound's "Medallion"; its artifice, Bell affirms, "is what simultaneously questions and falls prey to the habits of consumption."

By contrast with Bell's essay or Nicholls's book (see below), a third guide, Roland John's *A Beginner's Guide to the Cantos of Ezra Pound* (Salzburg), "makes no claim to originality" and is less a work of criticism than of appreciation. John unapologetically declares the *Cantos* to be "the most important poem of the century," and he identifies its "outstanding facet" as Pound's "consistency of vision." John's book grew from an article originally written for *Agenda* and is self-consciously "meant for the general reader." It is a digest of other books on the *Cantos,* many of which, like Christine Brooke-Rose's *A ZBC of Ezra Pound* (see *ALS 1971,* pp. 279–80), were themselves designed as primers.

Nicholls's book also demonstrates a knowledge of earlier scholarship, but *Modernisms* not only represents a magisterial consolidation of 20 years of publication in the field since Malcolm Bradbury and James Walter McFarlane's *Modernism: 1890–1930* (1976), but also inflects that historical sense with a supple response to poststructuralist theory. It is hard to know where to begin with a book that accomplishes so much and wears its vast learning so lightly. It is not just the plural of Nicholls's title—his ability to relate so many European "tangents" to Anglo-American modernism (Ian Bell has called this volume a "Baedeker to a continent")—that makes it so valuable. Nicholls also demonstrates how the complexity of modernist praxis resists the attempts of *post*modern criticism to simplify it; in other words, he never loses sight of the power of criticism in shaping its subject. As Nicholls explains, *Modernisms* attempts no documentary survey; instead it strives "to provide a conceptual map of the different modernist tendencies." He sees his main subject as the "translation of politics into style, and the tensions it reflects between the social and the aesthetic," tensions that remain indelibly inscribed in the language of postmodern theory.

Nicholls has a good deal to say about Pound, particularly in his chapter "Modernity and the 'Men of 1914,'" where he articulates the difference between Pound's attitude toward tradition and the more agonistic relations to it of such Continental writers as Filippo Tommaso Marinetti. Like Bell, Nicholls makes special account of "Medallion," but Nicholls is particularly interested in identifying the woman who, along with the soprano Raymonde Collignon, appears in the poem. Quoting from Pound's account of her performance, Nicholls concludes that the "verbal manifestation" of the poem "signifies not a retreat into aestheticism but a form of 'armour' against 'utter consternation' and the 'drift' towards sensual indulgence." Nicholls returns to Pound in a later chapter, "The Narratives of High Modernism." Submitting that Pound's allusions characteristically perform what they refer to, Nicholls describes how the *Cantos* "develops the implications of Imagism, using allusion and citation to create a collision of time schemes that yields (to borrow Derrida's formulation) 'a series of temporal differences without any central present, without a present of which the past and the future would be but modifications.'" There is not only matter but model here for future work. Although Nicholls's "main subject" is political, his arguments rest on careful attention to formal detail. *Modernisms* will serve new students of its subject, and it also should help all of us recover our bearings on a rapidly changing field.

Among the most imaginative studies of the past several years, Daniel Tiffany's *Radio Corpse: Imagism and the Cryptaesthetic of Ezra Pound* (Harvard) opens by theorizing how—by "contesting or simulating the visible"—images "often reinvent visuality." Insofar as they withhold from the eye the visualization that they seem to promise, images present what Tiffany calls "negativity"; similarly, he argues, since "writing about images can bring to light only what resists the observant eye," to write about images "is to write about nothing." This move would seem to risk readers for a book on imagism, but Tiffany presses still further. Another approach is to call the image "cryptic." Parleying with Marx and Blanchot, Tiffany connects this "nothing" with fetishism and, ultimately, with Blanchot's discussion of the cadaver: something that is "neither the same as the one who was alive, nor another, nor another thing." In this way Tiffany argues for what he calls Pound's "cryptaesthetic." Later in his opening chapter Tiffany protests that "the proper subject of my book is not a general theory of the image or of vision, but a specific historical instance of what Martin Jay calls the 'scopic regimes of modernity.'" This book's strength is that its discussion of this "scopic regime" never for a moment assumes that we have moved beyond the historical blindnesses of Pound himself. Tiffany sees the issues of imagism not so much as a matter for history as for our own (impossible) self-examination. The book closes with an acknowledgment that it, too, is a kind of negation, "the very tombstone of the illicit," a crypt that conceals the very thing it attempts to represent but that is nevertheless also a "monument—to artifice, to meaning, and, most surprisingly, to tradition."

Michael Alexander and James McGonigal's collection of essays, tributes, and testimonials, *Sons of Ezra: British Poets and Ezra Pound* (Rodopi), may not on the whole break new scholarly ground, but it serves an important purpose—particularly for U.S. readers. These essays remind us that the story of Pound's reception followed a much different course in Britain than it did in the United States. Most of the Englishmen who helped establish Pound's postwar academic reputation are here: William Cookson, Donald Davie, Charles Fisher, and Charles Tomlinson, to name a few, and of course all speak more in their capacities as poets than as critics. Davie, for example, considers how "whenever I tried to write in a Poundian style (and I tried often), I didn't like what I came up with . . . . Perhaps my British sensibility rejected a graft from what was after all American." Nevertheless, Davie declares himself to be "a son of Ezra." The editors observe that all of their contributors are really "grandsons" of Ezra—none is from Basil Bunting's generation—and consider the absence in this volume of "daughters." There are, they find, no British equivalents of Mary Barnard, and they waited too long to get in touch with younger possibilities like Christine Brooke-Rose or Denise Levertov. No British publisher would touch the book, and by the time the volume was accepted by the Dutch house of Rodopi, the editors felt it improper to keep their initial contributors waiting any longer. The gendered nature of this tribute volume, then, raises in and of itself fundamental questions about the construction of modernism as a field.

Alexander and McGonigal speculate that Pound's somewhat "male" fixation on economic questions might explain his failure to attract the attention of younger female poets. This same fixation did not deter him from making contact with several young American women, but it very much informs Robert Luongo's *The Gold Thread: Ezra Pound's Principles of Good Government and Sound Money* (Strangers). In fact, Luongo begins by describing Pound as "a warrior poet of the twentieth century, not unlike the ancient heroes of his Odyssean epic, *The Cantos.*" If Alexander and McGonigal's volume reminds us that Pound's reception proceeded differently in England than it did here, Luongo's book (like John's) reminds us that after, and perhaps in spite of, a half-century of academic criticism, Pound's vision still attracts true believers. Luongo's dismissal of recent criticism of Pound as the "insipid" work of "tepid snifflers" speaks for itself.

The other principal study this year of "Pound's economics" is Salah el Moncef's "Gold, Representation, and the Reversible Dynamic of Symptomatic Return in Ezra Pound" (*Boundary 2*, 22, i: 117–42). Moncef cites most work on the topic published since Peter Nicholls's *Ezra Pound: Politics, Economics and Writing* (see *ALS 1984*, p. 137); his own book proves a well-researched and theorized study. Generally, Moncef contests that gold in Pound's writings does not emerge as either an "exclusively 'good' or 'evil' agency." Rather, gold retains throughout Pound's career an "extremely ambivalent and far-reaching meaning." Gold, "as a condensed signifier," becomes "emblematic of the poet's and society's impotence only insofar as its supplementing power is withheld from the 'right' poet or the 'right' politician who suffers from its demonic otherness—that is, its alienation and misappropriation by the subverters of concrete monetary and discursive representation." Like others who address the question, Moncef accepts the fundamental analogy between Pound's economies of money and of language, but his sense of a reversible dynamic submits fiscal economies to textual ones.

The phrase "reversible dynamic" might also apply to the explorations of Anglo-American cultural differences in *Forked Tongues?* The volume deliberately pursues its comparison by exploring less-often discussed writers and texts. Nevertheless, Pound figures in two interesting pieces: Mark Jarman's "Brer Rabbit and Brer Possum: The Americanness of Ezra Pound and T. S. Eliot" (pp. 21–37), which returns only in its title to the material treated so brilliantly last year by Michael North; and Keith Tuma's "Is There a British Modernism?" (pp. 232–52). Jarman turns a poet's ear to Pound's and Eliot's language, and he considers why their "Americanness" is harder to locate than, say, Williams's or Moore's. Tuma's excellent piece questions and historicizes Donald Hall's announcement in *Parnassus* in 1979 "that the poetries of England and the United States have become discontinuous." "If," Tuma asserts, "we want to contest C. H. Sisson's almost archaic idea of a single tradition of English-language poetry transcending national boundaries, it is essential to consider not just individual poets and poems but also the institutions which have differently shaped the reception of poems in Britain and America." Tuma's essay constitutes an important and overdue contribution to our understanding of the relation of modern poetry to the academy, as well as to our historical sense of how things came to such a pass.

The range of Kathryne V. Lindberg's interests means that some of her strongest work often appears in places beyond the traditional pale of

Pound scholarship. "In the Name of Nietzsche: Ezra Pound Becomes Himself and Others" in *Nietzsche in American Literature and Thought* (pp. 155–77) is a case in point. The essay returns to the topos she treated so powerfully in *Reading Pound Reading: Modernism after Nietzsche* (see *ALS 1987*, p. 113), but Lindberg's position has developed a good deal in the decade since. This is an essay that no one interested in Pound's changing relation to academic discourses should miss. Lindberg's lightness of tone is a refreshing break from the stern sobriety of so many theoretically informed studies, but this lightness is not so much comic as it is Nietzschean. As the title of Lindberg's essay suggests, she is interested in period appropriations of Nietzsche more than—as in her first study— Pound's distinct debts. She observes, in fact, that it is not possible to "fix or isolate a strain of Nietzscheanism that might be cultured or killed in order to yield a politically correct or fully Fascist Pound." In establishing that impossibility, Lindberg names the lesson that we might have learned from Nietzsche long ago—and so have saved ourselves much of the past half-century of bitter contest over whether Pound *is* or *is not* a fascist: Pound presents "a peculiar problem for (American?) readers of poetry, who persist in believing that good and evil can be separated absolutely— even as they might be made to correspond with the beautiful and the ugly." Shortly thereafter, she joins to this warning a further "injunction to avoid over-psychologizing the motives of the writers we want to admire." Finally, Lindberg submits that Pound assimilated Nietzsche through the active mediation of A. R. Orage and the *New Age*. She rightly characterizes that magazine as "roughly Nietzschean and deeply contradictory, if intellectually shallow," a mélange whose very lack of "homogenous doctrine or unified theory" can help us understand that, during the first quarter of the 20th century, " 'Nietzsche' meant more a style of thought than a particular methodological rigor or definite position."

As Lindberg discusses Orage's generally unsuccessful attempts to "police" Pound's "incursions into 'theory,' " she notes that Pound often put Orage on edge by dint of his "invasion of Orage's own turf—promotional editing." What Lindberg notes so succinctly figures among the central concerns of Michael Coyle's *Ezra Pound, Popular Genres, and the Discourse of Culture* (Penn. State). Indeed, Coyle's book opens by reflecting on Pound's fondness for excerpting from the popular press and then *re*presenting those excerpts in less flattering contexts: a practice he learned from Orage. In general, however, Coyle is interested less in how

Orage mediated Pound's reception of Nietzsche than in how he mediated Pound's reception of Ruskin, which reception is not only the topic of his chapter " 'A Profounder Didacticism': Ruskin, Orage, and Pound's Vision of Cultural Totality," but also informs the rest of the book. Coyle frames his study with an examination of T. S. Eliot's edition of *Literary Essays of Ezra Pound* (1954), where Eliot overtly endeavors to redact Pound's critical activity. As with Pound's press-cuttings, this *re*presentation works on the basis of contextual changes and generic transformation. Both in its conception as *literary* essays and in its individual selections from Pound's work, Eliot's edition responds to the controversy that followed Pound's receipt of the Bollingen Prize for Poetry in 1948. The redactive *Literary Essays of Ezra Pound* was among the final maneuvers of a more general New Critical retrenchment—the success of which is evident from the critical and public acceptance of Eliot's edition.

From this definitive moment in the institutionalization of modernism Coyle moves backward to unpack its implications for our sense of Pound. Conceiving his subject as Pound's writing in relation to the changing features of critical discourse, Coyle demonstrates how, in so many of the places where Pound has struck postwar readers as radical or idiosyncratic, he was in fact at his most conservative. Fundamentally, and without understanding himself as doing any such thing, Pound was almost wholly immersed in the Ruskinian discourse of organicist and totalizing cultural critique. Pound's mediated access to this tradition is initially explored in terms of period figures like A. R. Orage, but subsequent chapters pursue his relations with other contemporaneous questions, such as the Victorian contest between translation and paraphrase; the late-century popular fascination with the troubadors; the popularizing primers in economics that paradoxically marked the growing specialization of knowledge on the subject; modernist arguments about music and poetry; even the popularizing of narrative history.

The most general implication of all of these particular intersections in Pound's work is that his experiments in both poetry and prose were deeply inscribed in the Victorian discourse of culture—"culture" not as an idea or even an ideal, but as a way of representing human experience—particularly our collective relation to history. More generally still, Coyle's thesis portends Pound's enduring ties to the taste of the Victorian world. That topic is taken up as well by Mary Ellis Gibson's carefully researched and sharply focused *Epic Reinvented: Ezra Pound and the Victorians* (Cornell). Gibson has written a broadly important book. Whereas Coyle focuses on "culture" as a discourse and sees Pound's historicism as symptomatic of that discourse, Gibson homes in on Pound's historicism—and finds in it the means of resolving the apparent contradiction between his aestheticist and activist, or reformist, impulses. Drawing on Fredric Jameson's *Marxism and Historicism* (1988), Gibson demonstrates the extent to which aestheticism shadowed even the earliest expressions of historicist sensibility. Pound's course was, she establishes, "anti-aestheticist at the outset," and Gibson explains how Pound's very way of thinking about history informed the most fundamental, and morally reprehensible, contradictions of his career.

As Gibson develops her larger thesis, and so reveals the immediate pertinence of an issue largely neglected in scholarly discussions of Pound, she manages along the way to make a number of nearly stale topoi come to life. Her discussion of Pound's relationship with Ford Madox Ford is the best we yet have had, largely because she is able to situate Ford within a resonantly Victorian context. Similarly, whereas most earlier studies that have treated Pound's debt to Pater have had to emphasize Pater's contributions to Pound's aestheticism, Gibson is able to establish Pater's importance to Pound's *anti*-aestheticist impulses.

Of course, Gibson's primary focus is on Pound's reinvention of the epic. Her comments here are grounded in her discussion of historicism, but, crucially, she resists any temptation to reach for one grand conclusion. Moreover, unlike many studies of recent years more aggressively grounded in poststructuralist theory, Gibson declines to "look for a generic stability in *The Pisan Cantos*" or elsewhere in Pound's new epic. Like Coyle, she is comfortable with generic heterogeneity, and she considers different sections of the poem in terms of distinct generic intersections. *Pisan Cantos,* for instance, she presents "as a section of the poem in which epic and elegy are brought most clearly into tension." In sum, this book's pursuit of literary history reflects sustained engagement with theoretical discourse, yet remains focused on the text and its relation to history—or historical discourses.

William Doreski's "Eliot and Pound: Political Discourse and the Voicing of Difference," pp. 83–114 in his *The Modern Voice in American Poetry,* is more overtly concerned with questions of discourse, even though he is exploring traditional notions of poetic voice. Doreski's discussion of Pound focuses on *Hugh Selwyn Mauberley,* and he frames his treatment of its "dialogic voices" by situating the poem in the context of those "English poets in the 1890s who resisted Browning and the dramatic monologue by attempting to reinvent a 'pure poetry' of un-alloyed lyric." The tension Doreski sets up, in other words, is precisely the one so vividly deconstructed by Gibson; one cannot help but wonder how his analysis might have differed had he had the advantage of her work. Nevertheless, there is much of interest here, and Doreski himself is generally self-conscious of the pitfalls of binary oppositions. In *Mauberley*, Pound retains "Browning's grip on history but turns the dramatic monologue around. Instead of writing a narrative monologue infused with lyric moments, Pound writes a sequence of lyrics knitted together with a single monologic voice interrupted by the brief interjections of other characters." Evidently, Doreski would describe the writing of the *Cantos* in much the same way. Another familiar binary that has long attended discussions of *Mauberley* would have it that *Mauberley* "rejects poetic modes and poetic voices developed by Pound in London while the *Cantos* look forward to his life on the continent and to new modes of poetic and aesthetic experience." Doreski thankfully puts this conve-nient opposition to rest and considers what it means that Pound was already at work on the *Cantos* when composing *Mauberley*. Ultimately, Doreski suggests that *Mauberley* is far less conventional than it looks and that it is composed according to principles essentially consonant with those familiar in the *Cantos*. *Mauberley* is, he writes, "an open-ended sequence and postulates any number of reiterations of its pluralistic structure. Further reiteration would not change that loose structure, only further confirm its continuity." As for the voice of the poem, it is not, Doreski explains, "a conventional Browning monologue voice, not two or more such voices. It is a voice beyond omniscience," the kind of voice Hugh Kenner has described in *Ulysses:* a voice that is clearly self-reflexive and "represents a mind that 'arranges' the work *as a literary work."* In *Mauberley* this voice speaks not "as a witness to events as such but to the literary event in question, the formation or recovery of aesthetics from the rubble of the second decade of this century and the third and fourth of Pound's life." This voice is, Doreski perceives, the voice of the *Cantos*. *Mauberley* in this sense is not merely a farewell to Pound's old aesthetic, but is already possessed of Pound's mature voice.

Notions of "difference" also inform Jean-Michel Rabaté's *The Ghosts of Modernity* (Florida). This is Rabaté's best work yet, and the chapter "Uncoupling Modernism" (pp. 188–215) rightly figures as the final one. Although Rabaté is not the only author this year to disclaim historical narrative, he manages great clarity of purpose: "not a history of modernity but an archaeology of modernism." " 'Modernism' was used for the first time, with its full meaning, by Verlaine in reaction to Rimbaud's writings," Rabaté explains, as he then develops "the concept of the literary couple." In the event, he focuses on four literary couples, because his group of four "seems to exhaust the possibilities of sexual permuta-tion": besides Rimbaud and Verlaine, Gertrude Stein and Alice Toklas, Robert Graves and Laura Riding, and Pound and Eliot ("whose sexuality may be questionable but who were, for better or worse, both married"). Rabaté emphasizes the "disjunctive nature" of Pound and Eliot's collab-oration (pity that Rabaté examines only their collaboration on *The Waste Land*, which was neither their first nor their last), and views it as an attempt to "provide a justification for the 'modern movement.' "

The year saw two other studies of Pound's work as collaborator and, in particular, his work as "foreign editor" for one of the small magazines edited by women. Paul Vanderham's "Ezra Pound's Censorship of *Ulys-ses*" (*JJQ* 32: 583–95) tries to get at the "ethical, political, philosophical, or religious convictions" that stiffened Pound's objections to certain passages in *Ulysses*. Vanderham is fascinated by the fact that "the first censor of *Ulysses* was also its first prominent champion," and he finds in this irony far-reaching implications not only for the reception of *Ulysses* but also for our understanding of modernist poetics. Jayne E. Marek's *Women Editing Modernism: "Little" Magazines and Literary History* (Ken-tucky) makes no mention of K. K. Ruthven's work on Pound and female editors, but Marek otherwise gives credit where credit has long been overdue. She aims to recognize the contributions of such influential editors of modernist writing as Harriet Monroe and Alice Corbin Hen-derson at *Poetry*, Margaret Anderson and Jane Heap at the *Little Review*, or Marianne Moore at the *Dial*. (Marek has less to say about Dora Marsden and the *New Freewoman* or *The Egoist*; readers interested in Marsden will, however, find a discussion of her in Ian F. A. Bell's essay, noted above.) Marek's work is not itself particularly theorized—her approach is predominantly empirical—but her conclusions invite noth-ing less than the re-theorization of modernist activity. Having discussed the accomplishments of female editors, she turns in a final chapter to Pound. Significantly, she calls this chapter "A Distorting Lens," and in it she directs attention to the characteristic tendency of literary historians to view the activity of these editors through Pound's often condescending and manipulative writings to and about them. Much of this material is familiar, but Marek draws two general conclusions. First, she contrasts

"Pound's didacticism" with Monroe's "open door" policy and with Heap and Anderson's "love for 'conversation.'" Second, Marek observes that "Pound's expressions of derision for women are couched in the same language that he used about the United States of America—a language often utilizing gendered imagery in censorious terms." Like other writers this year, Marek is concerned with demonstrating that modernism was and is more plural and more complex than it often has been taken to be.

William Pratt's *Singing the Chaos: Madness and Wisdom in Modern Poetry* (Missouri) might serve as a reminder of that "often has been taken to be"; the book, although "it does not set out to be a complete history," attempts to thematize modernist activity. The poems at the end of Pasternak's *Dr. Zhivago* (1957) are offered as "the last coherent group of modern poems"—never mind, for example, the brilliance a decade later of African American poet Melvin Tolson's *Harlem Gallery* (1965). H.D. gets three pages as "a further imagist" who wrote of "feminine subjects" in a "rather masculine" way, and Laura Riding gets nine pages ("Fugitive, Witch or Goddess?"); otherwise, no women are found among the nearly 40 poets whom the author hears "singing the chaos."

Timothy Materer's *Modernist Alchemy* is the latest contribution to a rapidly developing area of modernist study. Taking its place alongside books published by Leon Surette, Demetres Tryphonopoulos, Akiko Miyake, and James Longenbach, Materer's makes it increasingly difficult for skeptics to deny the occult's configurative role in the formation of early modernism. If Surette's *The Birth of Modernism* (see *ALS 1993*, pp. 103–04) demonstrated the pervasiveness of occult interests in 19th-century intellectual life, connecting it through Nietzsche with Pound, Eliot, and Yeats, Materer's new book charts the course of the occult beyond that modernist triumvirate and across the variegated forms and careers of modernist poetry. In fact, Materer's first chapter essentially picks up where Surette leaves off; it studies the course of "Daemonic Images" from Yeats to Pound and finds in them a springboard for further investigations. Subsequent chapters treat Eliot as Magus, H.D.'s Hermeticism (an important contact, as H.D. scholars have long known), Robert Duncan, Sylvia Plath, Ted Hughes, and James Merrill. In other words, what has struck many readers (like me) as an odd hangover from late-Victorian drawing rooms emerges as an enduring presence—something that well into our own time continues to spark the writing of serious poetry.

Where Surette implicated Nietzsche in occult discourse, Materer blurs the lines between period understandings of psychology and "psychical research." Materer traces the influence of such research on *Guide to Kulchur* (1938) and beyond, suggesting that it is responsible for much of the often-noted obscurity of *Rock-Drill* (1955) or *Thrones* (1959). Although Materer concludes his treatment of Pound by noting that Pound was not a "true occultist," he does so not to insist on some purity that Pound was too corrupt to meet, but to explain the failure of Pound's "frequent stridency" of tone. It is, Materer finds, the very "brashness" of Pound's writing, the energy that separates him from so many merely period occultists, that makes the "gnomic utterances in the late *Cantos*" sound pretentious: "true occultists, such as Yeats and H.D., seem to avoid this portentousness through their evident sincerity." The value of this work is that "the occult" enables Materer to focus on particular *kinds* of writing rather than falling into the trap of an ideas-based treatment of poetry; by informing an explanation of Pound's nagging problem of tone, this study should interest a much wider readership than its topic might suggest.

This year also witnessed the collection and republication of two bodies of work that have been influential in shaping Pound's critical reception. First, Hayden Carruth's *Selected Essays and Reviews* (Cooper Canyon) gathers work written over nearly 50 years. Carruth's role in the Bollingen controversy of the late '40s has yet to be fully acknowledged, and though his contributions to that fracas do not show up here, Pound figures throughout *Selected Essays*. No surprise, given how ready Carruth could be to take on the question of poetry and politics, as in the essay of 1963, "Poets without Prophecy." The essay "Ezra Pound and the Great Style" (1966) contains an interesting anecdote in which was foreshadowed the appearance of the poem that now concludes the *Cantos:* "Fragment (1966)": "That her acts / Olga's acts / of beauty / be remembered."

The University of Georgia Press has now brought out two new collections of Hugh Kenner's essays and reviews. *Mazes,* the first, collects essays written from 1961 until 1988, and *Historical Fictions,* the more literary half of the diptych, collects pieces published from 1970 through 1990. The presentation of both volumes is modest, almost breezy, and readers will encounter here a fair representation of Kenner's impressive range and enduring curiosity.

c. Shorter Poems and Translations   Peter Nicholls remarks how early Pound's practice of translation "developed from a conventional idea of rendering the immanent meaning of the original to a much more complex sense of *interaction* between the translator's language and that of the text upon which he works" (*Modernisms*, p. 168). Nicholls's insight, among other things, underscores the centrality of translation to Pound's poetics. In different ways most of the year's new studies of Pound's translations proceed on that same precept.

Peter Davidson's *Ezra Pound and Roman Poetry: A Preliminary Survey* (Rodopi) stands out from other recent scholarship primarily for its profession not to stand out. Davidson's presentation is modest almost to a fault, for he has written a careful study that does much more than its title leads one to expect. In fact, he probably has written the most important study of Pound's engagement with the classics since J. P. Sullivan's *Ezra Pound and Sextus Propertius* (1964). Unlike last year's study by classicist Niall Rudd, for example, which proposes that much of the controversy surrounding Pound's *Homage to Sextus Propertius* "had to do with post-war cultural changes, and with the general decline of Latin in the educational system," but then dropped that premise to take up the old classicist niggling, Davidson's study of Pound's borrowings from and translations of Roman poetry has lots to say about his relations with Victorian and Edwardian cultural orthodoxies. More precisely, Davidson considers the extent that Pound's understanding of "the conduct proper to a poet" owed to period ideas about the classics. But while "Pound's readings of the Latin poets" was "coloured by a complex scale of priorities," no other single factor played so great a role as what Davidson calls "the neoteric epic of the nineteenth century, the *Latin Dictionary* of Lewis and Short." In a sense, Davidson's explanation returns to Hugh Kenner's familiar trope of "words set free." As Davidson explains, Pound was "free of the constraints of the career Classicist: he has a lack of set, consensus ideas about the meanings of words. He is in some ways a tentative Latinist, free in his use of the dictionary to generate meanings."

This account of Pound's translations from Latin should remind experienced Pound readers of his Fenollosa-influenced negotiations with Chinese poetry. Davidson's study opens up its subject to many of the broadest historical questions facing contemporary modernist scholarship. It does so, however, through carefully focused attention on a series of Poundian negotiations. The first chapter treats "Pound and the *Pervigilium Veneris*"; the second "Pound and Horace"; subsequent chapters focus on Catullus, Sextus Propertius, Ovid, and Vergil. One appendix lists all references to Roman poetry in the *Cantos;* a second discusses the relation of Pound's metric to classical meters; the third lists the sources in Propertius for Pound's controversial *Homage.*

Pound's Fenollosan negotiations figure importantly in Zhaoming Qian's impressive *Orientalism and Modernism.* Qian's purpose is "to assert the place of the Orient in the Modernist movement," and although he recognizes that "a comprehensive work on Orientalism and Modernism would cover at least two or three more prominent Modernist figures," he maintains that "the Pound-Williams dichotomy appears to stand at center." That Qian is working with dichotomies, or that he can see "the Pound and Williams dichotomy" as standing "at center," indicates his distance from poststructuralist considerations. Generally, despite Qian's initial positioning of his work against Edward Said's (Said's "Orient" is the Muslim world, Qian's "the Far East, particularly China"), this is not a book much alert to theoretical issues. It succeeds, nevertheless, in reframing Pound's often-studied work of the 1910s. Qian's work with epistolary and manuscript evidence is painstaking, and when joined to a thorough reading of earlier critical treatments of Pound's interest in China it can produce surprising results. For example, Qian's detective work on the actual compilation of *Des Imagistes* enables him to conclude that the manuscript actually reached New York by early November 1913—not, as critics have long believed, the previous summer. That Pound compiled the volume in October and early November means that he was working on it in the flush of his first excitement over Ernest Fenollosa's manuscripts (Mary Fenollosa first met with Pound on 29 September 1913).

Qian is at his best presenting the force of archival research, and his work here should inform subsequent accounts not only of *Cathay* but of the early *Cantos.* In his broadest argument Qian proposes that Pound, like other modernists, was interested in the other because it "mirrors the self." Scholars previously have suggested that "Pound's China" is really more about Pound than China, and for this reason his having based his work on erroneous premises is irrelevant. However, it is by no means clear that Qian wishes to invite any such dismissal. In fact, he goes out of his way at various points to show how Pound, even with little knowledge of his originals, was all the same able to intensify their emotion. We still lack, in other words, a way of understanding the relations between Pound's praxis and the theories on which it was based.

In concluding his discussion of Pound, Qian demonstrates the want of further theorizing, begging perhaps the largest single question we might ask about Pound's reliance on Fenollosa: "we must understand that [Fenollosa's] admiration for the alleged pictorial qualities of the Chinese written language is absurd and misleading." That this question of Fenollosa's "absurd and misleading" theory ought not to wait longer is evident from its emerging as well in Melita Schaum's "The Grammar of the Visual: Alvin Langdon Coburn, Ezra Pound, and the Eastern Aesthetic in Early Modernist Photography and Poetry" (*Paideuma* 24: 79–106). Schaum finds in "the Oriental influence" generally, and in Pound's response to Fenollosa more particularly, an important link between modernist poetry and photography: "the Oriental study of form, then, is clearly not just an experimentation with static design . . . but includes an animation of the elements."

d. *The Cantos* Although most of Terri Brint Joseph's *Ezra Pound's Epic Variations: The* Cantos *and Major Long Poems* (National Poetry Foundation) treats Pound's early movement from short to longer poems, with whole chapters focused on "Near Perigord," *Homage to Sextus Propertius,* and *Hugh Selwyn Mauberley,* the trajectory of her work moves, as did Pound's, to the *Cantos.* This is a quietly perceptive book. Making little fuss over her own methodology, Joseph respects and frequently acknowledges the contributions of poststructuralist work on Pound, while nevertheless insisting that Pound always remained "preeminently a poet of presence." In this insistence, she seems most immediately to respond to the work of the late Joseph Riddel; her point is well-taken, although one wants to add that ultimately the point is not whether or not Pound understood his own project in antifoundationalist terms, but whether critics understand that *their* own work can secure no foundation—in their subject-texts or anywhere else. Generally, however, Joseph draws strength among the critical differences surrounding Pound's work, and she observes that the persistent controversies in Pound studies "may ultimately work in favor of a central aspect of his project for modern poetry: neither the general public nor literary critics have been willing to treat Pound's politics as a 'merely aesthetic concern.' "

Joseph covers much ground in a short space. Like Coyle, she makes a great deal of Donald Davie's perception of "how 'strikingly old fashioned' [Pound] remained even at his most innovative." She is good on

Pound's differences from T. E. Hulme; like Bell, Doreski, and Nicholls, she brings new clarity to our understanding of *Mauberley*. A book for scholars already conversant with Pound criticism, perhaps, *Pound's Epic Variations* is nevertheless one that can help model how we might bring both sympathy and criticism to the study of Pound's work.

e. Creative Responses to Pound   One mark of how deeply felt questions of Pound's political affiliations are is that they continue, more than a half-century after his last radio broadcast, to stir controversy. Another mark, perhaps more telling still, is that responses continue to take artistic as well as critical form. Two such responses were published this year. In a volume that poet Donald Justice has praised for its "moral earnestness," *Unspeakable Strangers: Descents into the Dark Self, Ascent into the Light* (Anhinga), its author, Van K. Brock, addresses a poem to Pound. Brock's very title enacts the ambivalent legacy of cultural history. Calling his poem "Hang It All, Ezra Pound: The Hero as Biography of the Age" and placing it in a section of poems entitled "Fathers and Brothers," Brock frames his response to Pound within Pound's famous ambivalence toward Browning—and Browning's implicitly ambivalent respect for Thomas Carlyle (the hero as biography of the age). Brock's poem turns on the asking of several decidedly *un*-rhetorical questions: "Ez, where / *were* the pure villains you ranted / when you raved war?" The poem plays not only with some of Pound's phrases but also with the sometimes biblical language of *Pisan Cantos*.

   Timothy Findley's *The Trials of Ezra Pound* (Blizzard) is based on the preliminary hearings for what was to have been Pound's trial for treason. The setting moves among Rapallo, Gallinger Hospital, the courtroom, and St. Elizabeths, and so moves as well among different periods in Pound's life. The cast of characters is perhaps larger than what one would expect, and it includes important figures besides the inevitable Dr. Muncie, Dr. Overholser, Chief Justice Bolitha Laws, or Julian Cornell. Findley also represents Dorothy Pound, William Carlos Williams, reporter Albert Deutsch, and Sheri Martinelli. The plural of Findley's title—"Trial*s*," not just "Trial"—bespeaks the playwright's purpose in doing justice to the moral complexity of Pound's situation. All said and done, Findley's new play invites comparison with Ronald Harwood's dramatic treatment of the postwar controversy surrounding the career of German conductor Wilhelm Furtwängler, "Taking Sides" (1995).

ii Eliot

a. Text, Biography, and Bibliography   A *Concordance to the Complete Poems and Plays of T. S. Eliot,* ed. J. L. Dawson, P. D. Holland, and D. J. McKitterick (Cornell), will be a valuable resource for Eliot scholars. Based on the 1969 *Complete Poems and Plays of T. S. Eliot,* published in England by Faber and Faber, the editing appears scrupulous, and the text is clear and easy to use. A useful preface and lucid technical introduction guide the reader. The preface describes instances of the "serendipity of scholarship" that the concordance will provide. For example, the editors decided on a word-frequency cutoff point of 200 and thus reduced the concordance by more than half. The high-frequency words, which could not in good conscience be omitted, highlight Eliot's preoccupations. *Know,* for example, occurs 677 times, more frequently than *if* or *never.*

"Eleven Reviews by T. S. Eliot, Hitherto Unnoted, from the *Times Literary Supplement:* A Conspectus" (*N&Q* 42: 212–15) by David Bradshaw describes unsigned reviews written from 1927 through 1930. The subjects, which include Dante, Elizabethan and Jacobean literature, and Charles Maurras, all figure importantly in this year's criticism.

b. General Studies   The front-page article in the arts section of the *New York Times* for 1 January 1995, "Between the Art and the Artist Lies the Shadow," draws attention to Eliot's anti-Semitism and strikes the year's prevailing note for scholarship and the popular press. Citing "Gerontion" and "Sweeney Among the Nightingales," Diana Jean Schemo maintains that "to learn that Eliot was an anti-Semite becomes a betrayal, as if we were taken in by fine phrases alone." Whereas a generation of scholars and readers dismissed or discounted Eliot's politics, today's most compelling scholarship addresses the politics of his poetry and prose.

Anthony Julius's *T. S. Eliot, Anti-Semitism, and Literary Form* (Cambridge) is the most thorough of any examination of Eliot's anti-Semitism yet published. A painstaking study of both the poetry and prose, Julius contrasts Eliot's treatment of Jews in different genres. They appear as "destructive sceptics" and "free-thinking Jews" in the prose and as "uncomprehending philistines" in the poetry and drama. Julius's carefully constructed argument considers the defenses that have been advanced to account for or excuse Eliot's undisputed prejudice and methodically dismantles them all. Christopher Ricks's *T. S. Eliot and Prejudice* (see

ALS 1988, pp. 125–26) and Jeffrey Perl's *Skepticism and Modern Enmity* (*ALS 1989*, pp. 128–29) receive particular scorn. Julius's last chapter refutes the contention that Eliot repudiated or regretted his anti-Semitism in later life.

Julius's book is more than a study of Eliot; its careful elaboration of different types of anti-Semitism and numerous treatments of Jews in literature include discussions of Shakespeare, Marlowe, and Dickens as well as modernists such as Pound and Williams and critics like de Man or Heidegger. The shape of Julius's arguments sometimes risks condemning Eliot for others' crimes. For example, he quotes a particularly noxious passage from Huysmans or de Man to explain Eliot, and Eliot's guilt is intensified by association.

Julius disagrees with those who discount Eliot's anti-Semitism by arguing that it was never clearly thought out or that it was an incidental feature of a brief phase (poems of *Ara Vos Prec*). He insists that it is central to Eliot's work—indeed, that anti-Semitism "invigorates" his poetry. Eliot's "inventive" use of anti-Semitic tropes proves his point; Eliot's work "comprises a virtuoso display of what anti-Semitism can bring to the making of poems." Julius repeatedly compares "quotidian anti-Semitism" or uninspired, derivative anti-Semitism with Eliot's "imaginative," "creative" anti-Semitism. I am not sure that I agree with or see the value in such distinctions.

Kenneth Asher offers a more tempered discussion of Eliot's political failings in *T. S. Eliot and Ideology* (Cambridge). Asher counters the "divide" theorists who contend that Eliot's philosophy shifted on his conversion (or for any other reason). He maintains that a coherent philosophy based on Eliot's commitment to a French reactionary tradition and especially the writings of Charles Maurras informed his entire oeuvre. Maurras's vision was described by *Nouvelle Revue Française* in 1913 as "classique, catholique, monarchique." (Even Eliot's self-definitions, it appears, are borrowed.) Eliot's attraction to Maurras's elevation of the "classical" and his broader political campaign was based, among other reasons, on their mutual belief in original sin, a distrust of romantic individualism, a desire for community, and a regret over the crass materialism, mechanization, and artificiality of industrialism and capitalism.

All of Eliot's poetry and prose, according to Asher, is politically motivated and historically conceived. Eliot's criticism of the modern "dissociation of sensibility," for example, is a lament for the loss of monarchy and the English Revolution. The anti-Semitism of "Burbank with a Baedeker and Bleistein with a Cigar" results from Maurras's view that Jews are alien to the classical, Latin tradition. The cyclical view of time in *Four Quartets* is commonly interpreted as religious. Asher points out, however, that the Christian view of time is not cyclical but linear, and that *Quartet's* cyclical view is political.

Asher's study proceeds chronologically and analyzes both the poetry and prose. He portrays a conservative Eliot—a portrait consistent with accepted views, but at odds with recent postmodern reconsiderations of the poet. (Perhaps that difference arises because his emphasis is political and not philosophical.) Asher concludes with a chapter on Eliot's ambiguous and ambivalent relationship with the New Critics. The New Critics' attempt to espouse Eliot's aesthetics in purely literary terms without Eliot's political and historical underpinnings results in grandiose religious claims for poetry that the critics cannot substantiate. Even if Asher's broader thesis that Maurrasian politics colors every nuance of Eliot's works seems overstated, his discussion of Eliot's career, his politics, and the individual works is undeniably valuable.

New Criticism takes the lead in John Harwood's *Eliot to Derrida: The Poverty of Interpretation* (St. Martin's), a broad-based condemnation of institutionalized American scholarship since the 1930s. This work is one of many this year to evaluate the term "modernism." Using a history of the interpretation of Eliot's poetry as a point of departure, Harwood describes the reification of "modernism" and the systematic institutionalization of Eliot and Eliot criticism. He credits Pound for *The Waste Land* and feels that Eliot's guilt about Pound's role in its composition explains his lifelong ambivalence toward his masterpiece. Harwood's history of the reception of *The Waste Land* and his account of the many attempts to define modernism and the circular arguments that have ensued are cogent and informed. The authority of his judgments is in some cases undermined by his querulous disdain for Eliot's bad taste and the virulence of his descriptions, like "sheer dreadfulness" and "loose, inferior verse." Harwood believes that modernism and the academic criticism—specifically New Criticism—that grew out of it set the stage for the emergence of radical theory that (like modernism) claims to break absolutely from the "mystified past." He represents all postmodern theory, and deconstruction in particular, as "a displaced religious quest." He also argues that the hero worship of Eliot enabled the personality cults that characterize contemporary theory.

William Pratt is part of the New Critical legacy that Harwood describes. Pratt's *Singing the Chaos,* a collection of essays about more than 30 modernist poets, also tackles the definition of "modernism." An apologist for modernist poetry, Pratt celebrates its ability to "sing the chaos" and the far-reaching effects of its stylistic innovations. His definition of modernism as the "Age of Irony" reveals his debt to the New Critics, yet his attention to the "supratemporal," the visionary, and the supernatural places him in the 1990s. Although his essays tend to oversimplify the modernists' relationship to the past, the ones on Eliot contain useful historical and biographical information that is of value for the general reader.

Like Pratt, Timothy Materer is interested in the spiritual dimension of modernism. His *Modernist Alchemy* continues Leon Surette's enterprise in *The Birth of Modernism:* the revision of the critical tradition that has neglected modernism's debt to the occult and Symbolism. A comprehensive study of the occult's influence on modernist poets from W. B. Yeats to Ted Hughes, Materer's book emphasizes the compatibility between skepticism and belief. Eliot is the only "dissenter" among the fold. The chapter on Eliot, hence, seems to fit uneasily. Materer maintains that Eliot was fascinated by occultism in spite of his rejection of it. However, Eliot resists his attraction to the occult because of occultists' "restless desire for the absolute" and their inadequate connection with normal experience. This book will be an important reference for future scholars.

Several articles also highlight the spiritual. These include Tatsuo Murata in "Buddhism in T. S. Eliot" (*MS* 73: 17–45) and J. Bottum's "What T. S. Eliot Almost Believed" (*FT* 55: 25–30). Murata, who argues that Buddhism structures Eliot's whole career, traces Buddhism throughout his work. Bottum maintains that Eliot's intellect blocks his achievement of the selfless self-consciousness required of true spirituality.

c. Relation to Other Writers   Michael Coyle devotes a chapter of his book *Ezra Pound, Popular Genres, and the Discourse of Culture* to Eliot's selective editing of Pound's *Literary Essays.* Coyle's precise attention to questions of genre and the definition of modernism makes this book essential reading for all students of modernism. Like Harwood, Coyle highlights Eliot's exploitation of the institutionalization of literary criticism. His approach is more even-handed, however. His sophisticated sense of the history of modernism and contemporary literary theory brings a new perspective to this issue. Coyle is original in isolating a "brief but distinct period" in Eliot's writing during which "The Frontiers of Criticism" dominated his philosophy and his focus was on the nature of "purely aesthetic experience." Both Eliot's selection and organization of Pound's essays were highly circumscribed. Driven partly by a desire to save Pound's reputation by separating the political man from the artist and partly by a desire to conform to contemporary formalistic approaches, Eliot chose essays that presented a unity and coherence of literary vision that were Eliot's goal, but not Pound's. Coyle astutely argues that Eliot's resulting collection gives a false sense of the "literariness" and "aestheticism" of Pound's essays. Coyle himself stresses the inclusive nature of Pound's poetry and criticism.

Also of note, Sumanyu Sapathy attributes the first review of *The Waste Land* in *TLS* to J. W. N. Sullivan in "Eliot and J. W. N. Sullivan" (*N&Q* 42: 216). Sapathy credits Sullivan with introducing Eliot to contemporary scientific theories and to Thomism.

d. Poems and Plays   Politics and the definition of modernism also dominate some of the most provocative discussions of Eliot's poetry and plays. Michael Tratner's *Modernism and Mass Politics: Joyce, Woolf, Eliot and Yeats* (Stanford) attempts to unsettle some of our most reified commonplaces about modernism. In his attempt to align literary and political history, Tratner contends that modernism is a reaction against 19th-century individualism and an "effort to produce a mass culture." A detailed examination of the "surprising similarities between modernist literature and contemporary theories of the crowd," Tratner's analysis of Eliot's politics supports Asher's interpretation of Eliot, if not his thesis. Two chapters treat Eliot: " 'The Mob Part of the Mind': Sexuality and Immigrant Politics in the Early Poems of T. S. Eliot" and "Movements Unconscious of their Destiny: The Culture of the Masses in 'The Waste Land.' " His discussions underline Eliot's desire to create a unified mass culture. Tratner repeatedly moves back and forth between individual and mass psychology: "The humanist ideal of creating individuals who can transcend their culture leads not just to mobs in the streets, but to a mob inside each individual, a horde of impulses released from any control by the cultural part of the psyche." Eliot feared the "mob part" of his own mind—which had lost touch with a coherent culture—as much as he feared it in society. Tratner turns the anti-Semitism of the early poetry into "outgrowths of Eliot's self-hatred." Bleistein, for example, is a "midwestern American of mixed heritage traveling around Europe, like

Eliot." *The Waste Land,* on the other hand, attempts to construct a community by creating a myth that can communicate in different ways with radically estranged social hierarchies.

William Doreski also insists on the political nature of modernism in *The Modern Voice in American Poetry,* which includes chapters on Robert Frost, Wallace Stevens, William Carlos Williams, Marianne Moore, Eliot, Pound, and Robert Lowell. He describes modernist poets' use of the rhetorical devices of prose fiction, drama, and extraliterary sources to move beyond "the stifling desire for lyric purity" and to address historical, social, and political issues. Doreski demonstrates Eliot's political engagement through a close examination of the manipulations of different rhetorics and different perspectives in "Portrait of a Lady." By shifting authority and power between the speaker, the lady, and the reader, Eliot moves his poem outside the usual boundaries of poetry and narrative to dramatize the politics of a community. Doreski's descriptions of Eliot's manipulation of his audience are particularly incisive.

"Modernism" also preoccupies Rainer Emig, whose *Modernism in Poetry* (Longman) searches for an "internal" definition of the term that goes beyond "external" descriptions of modernist poetry's stylistic features or its social and economical circumstances. He charts the development of his modernist poetics by isolating its crucial features in the poetry of Gerard Manley Hopkins, W. B. Yeats, Eliot, and Pound. The problematic relation between subject and external reality in modernist poetry drives his discussion. He blames many modernists' "drift towards fascism" on the dubious autonomy of the modernist poem. His discussion of Eliot—which is brilliant in its marriage of technical observations with general theory—focuses on Eliot's move from metaphor to metonymy. Emig emphasizes metaphor's creative capacity—a synthesis, rather than a substitution—and argues that metonymy replaces metaphor as the operative trope in Eliot's poetry—and in modernist poetry in general. His final chapters give a psychoanalytic, economic, and linguistic context to his discussion of the specific poets. Emig draws on and synthesizes a prodigious range of critics and theorists. The greatest value in his work probably is found in this synthesis.

Alistair Davies also studies the definition of modernism and its relation to our critical tradition in "Deconstructing the High Modernist Lyric," pp. 94–107 in *British Poetry, 1900–50: Aspects of Tradition,* ed. Gary Day and Brian Docherty (St. Martin's). Davies analyzes "the radical transposition of the lyric . . . from centre to margin" in literary criticism. He challenges Marjorie Perloff's delineation of two modernist traditions, the Symbolist and the anti-Symbolist, and her contention that the Symbolist tradition—which includes Yeats and Eliot—"depend(s) upon an unquestioned and hierarchical set of dualisms inherited from the romantic lyric." Using specific analyses of "Prufrock," *The Waste Land,* and *Four Quartets,* Davies argues that the poetry of both Eliot and Yeats works to undo the dualisms that structure them. He demonstrates "a double practice of writing, at once closed and open, determinate and indeterminate, symbolic and allegorical." He goes on to analyze the high-modernist lyric in the context of the critical practices of Geoffrey Hartman and Paul de Man.

Several authors turn to *Four Quartets* for a look at Eliot's spiritual or religious concerns. "Perplexity in the Edgeware Road: *Four Quartets* Revisited Yet Again" (pp. 164–75) by Thomas T. Howard is one of many essays in *Permanent Things: Toward the Recovery of a More Human Scale at the End of the Twentieth Century,* ed. Andrew A. Tadie and Michael H. Macdonald (Eerdmans), that examine the spiritual concerns of modern writers. Howard argues that an "excruciating awareness of the ambiguities of our condition" gives force and credibility to *Four Quartets.*

In *Language Mysticism: The Negative Way of Language in Eliot, Beckett, and Celan* (Stanford) Shira Wolosky examines the topos of literary inexpressibility in the context of theological traditions exemplified by her authors. Her chapter on Eliot, which focuses on the negative asceticism in *Four Quartets'* drive for unity, reveals a tension between a positive ambition for transcendence and its negative route. Wolosky enumerates the strategies that Eliot uses, but her discussion is sometimes disappointing in its lack of detailed attention to rhetorical ploys or linguistic techniques.

John Gordon's attention is rigorously technical. His "T. S. Eliot's Head and Heart" (*ELH* 62: 979–1000) contrasts medical tropes based on the heart and on the brain in literature in general and, in particular, in Eliot. Drawing on medical history since the 18th century, he argues that medical science has moved from a heart-centered anatomy to a brain-centered one and that literary tropes have followed in kind. Eliot, according to Gordon, regretted the "modern age of nerves" and lauded "an older, nobler age of blood." His article throws new light on ambiguous conceits throughout the poems, on Eliot's criticism of modern medicine, and on what E. M. Forster has called Eliot's "homage to pain."

e. Criticism Several treatments of Eliot's criticism echo Asher's concerns in *T. S. Eliot and Ideology*. David Bradshaw's "Lonely Royalists: T. S. Eliot and Sir Robert Filmer" (*RES* 46: 375–79) examines a recently uncovered 1928 *TLS* article by Eliot, "Augustan Age Tories." Bradshaw links Eliot's royalism, not to Maurras, but to the influence of the 17th-century Royalist, Sir Robert Filmer. "T. S. Eliot, Jacques Maritain, and Neo-Thomism" (*MS* 73:71–90) by Shun'ichi Takayangi, S.J., connects Eliot's interest in Maurras and *L'Action Française* with his neo-Thomism.

Ronald Schuchard also links religion and politics. "Eliot and Ignatius: Discovery and Abandonment in Donne" (*MS* 73: 1–16) charts Eliot's different attitudes toward John Donne and the influence of Ignatius of Loyola on both Donne and Eliot's changing views of him.

Schuchard's article grows out of his studies of *The Varieties of Metaphysical Poetry* (see *ALS 1993*, pp. 107–08)—a book that overshadows much of this year's work. David Gervais argues in "T. S. Eliot: The Metaphysical and the Spiritual" (*CQ* 24: 243–62) that *The Varieties* will change the way we read Eliot's work. He views the Clark Lectures as religious criticism that dramatizes Eliot's search for spirituality in a secular world. In "Civilization and Its Discontents: Eliot, Descartes, and the Mind of Europe" (*MS* 73: 59–69) Jewel Spears Brooker uses *The Varieties of Metaphysical Poetry* to explain the anti-Cartesian thrust of Eliot's analysis of our modern condition, a subject she has treated thoroughly in other works.

"Modernism" is implicit in Brooker's work, and revaluations of our definition of the elusive term absorb several of the best interpretations of Eliot's criticism. David Chinitz echoes Tratner's concern in "T. S. Eliot and the Cultural Divide" (*PMLA* 110: 236–47). Chinitz's examination of the essays demonstrates Eliot's interest in popular culture and challenges our conventional notions of high modernism as "a pristine and sacralized high art" defending against the "threatening pollution of 'lower levels' of culture."

Sanford Schwartz also turns to the definition of modernism in "Post-Modernizing Eliot: The Approach from Philosophy" (*MS* 73: 115–27). A look at various attempts to examine Eliot through a postmodern lens, Schwartz's study concentrates on three revaluations of Eliot: Stanley Scott's *Frontiers of Consciousness: Interdisciplinary Studies in American Philosophy of Poetry* (1991), Richard Shusterman's *T. S. Eliot and the Philosophy of Criticism* (1988), and Jeffrey Perl's *Skepticism and Modern Enmity: Before and After Eliot* (1989). Schwartz brings an encyclopedic knowledge of philosophy and a thorough grasp of Eliot's oeuvre to his task. All three works again prove that our traditional interpretations of Eliot "obscure the more radical elements of his work." Schwartz queries several presumptions implicit in all three analyses, which impose a developmental narrative on Eliot's career that Schwartz unravels. These presumptions also belie the structural complexity of Eliot's work in their "evitable propensity to transmit structural complexity into temporal sequence."

Kristian Smidt's analysis depends on the kind of developmental narrative that Schwartz questions. "T. S. Eliot's Criticism of Modern Prose Fiction" (*ES* 76: 64–80) argues that Eliot's interests were always social, but Smidt sees a shift in Eliot's theories after his conversion, which accounts, for example, for the change in his attitude toward Henry James. Smidt's insistence that Eliot's greatest and most sustained enthusiasm was for detective stories lends credence to critics like Chinitz and Tratner, who emphasize Eliot's interest in popular genres and the masses.

Colgate University
University of Maine

9 Faulkner

Philip Cohen

It is a standard rhetorical trope in these *ALS* essays to bemoan the current deluge of scholarship and criticism. The professionalization of literary studies in the academy and the need to publish or perish seems to have resulted in an emphasis on quantity over quality. Putting aside the issue of the difficulty of insulating the humanities and the academy from the evaluative criteria of the capitalist and positivist culture in which we find ourselves, however, most of the scholars reviewed in *ALS* would not even have gone to college or graduate school, let alone taught in a university not too long ago. Thus, I am content to keep the floodgates open and hope that the good work rises to the surface. Some of this year's good work on Faulkner includes Richard Gray's *The Life of William Faulkner*, Donald Kartiganer and Ann Abadie's collection *Faulkner and Ideology*, Philip Weinstein's collection *The Cambridge Companion to William Faulkner*, and Thomas Inge's *William Faulkner: The Contemporary Reviews*.

i Bibliography, Editions, and Manuscripts

Patricia C. Willis's transcription of Faulkner's early short story "Christmas Tree" from a Rosenbach Museum and Library typescript appears in *YR* (83, i: 26–30). Faulkner claimed to have rewritten this story from memory as "Two Dollar Wife" in 1936 for *College Literature*. Cheryl Minnick's very helpful "Faulkner and Gender: An Annotated Select Bibliography (1982–1994)" (*MissQ* 48: 523–53) offers nonevaluative summaries of the subject matter and theoretical approaches of its entries and illustrates how varied and fertile critical inquiry on this subject has become in the past two decades.

ii Biography

Writing a new and useful biography of Faulkner at this stage of the game poses difficult challenges for even the most seasoned scholar. For example, Joel Williamson's *William Faulkner and Southern History* (see *ALS 1993*, pp. 113–14) offered much outdated literary criticism with fascinating but circumstantial speculation on miscegenation and white-collar crime in Faulkner's family background, the results of research into previously unexamined archival material. Given Blotner's and Williamson's works, interpretive, critical biographies of Faulkner will probably be preferred to noncritical ones. Richard Gray's biography, *The Life of William Faulkner* (Blackwell, 1994), which arrived too late for last year's chapter, is an example of the critical, interpretive approach. Primarily influenced by Bakhtin's dialogic notions of self, language, and writing and by theoretical work on ideology by Louis Althusser, Raymond Williams, and Fredric Jameson; by Roland Barthes's meditations on writing; by Lacanian and Kristevan psychology; and by feminist theory, this postmodernist biography occasionally reveals vestiges of formalism in that it views as flawed novels that are riven by irresolvable conflicts. Gray's Faulkner is not the apolitical modernist of yesteryear. Rather, Gray seeks to perform a delicate balancing act by reinserting Faulkner into his region's history and culture without rendering his individuality invisible. We need not deny Faulkner's individuality, he argues, but "acknowledge that this individuality was the product of a series of intersecting, social and cultural, forces." Gray reads each of Faulkner's books as it "attends to the problems and opportunities, the animating impulses, the determining movements of the writer's consciousness and culture." (Unfortunately, he deals only with those short stories that are textually connected to the novels.) The volume offers little new biographical information. Indeed, it seems to be more a critical work than a biography with its long insightful discussions of novels bracketed by brief expository passages of biography. On the positive side, Gray is all at once sympathetic, critical, and analytic as biographer, refusing to cast Faulkner's contradictory and constantly changing attitudes and beliefs about race, gender, and class in the most positive or negative lights possible.

An introductory three-part chapter lays out Gray's approach: "On Privacy: William Faulkner and the Human Subject," "History as Autobiography: The World of Faulkner," and "Autobiography as History: The Life of Faulkner." Here, Gray sets forth the long social, historical, racial, economic, cultural, and familial foreground that preceded Faulkner's birth. The first part contains a shrewd discussion of Faulkner's penchant for adopting different personae and reinventing his past as a means of simultaneously concealing and revealing aspects of his personality. Gray articulates a Bakhtinian approach to Faulkner as a creator of polyphonic novels in which various voices, idioms, and characters are private and autonomous and at the same time part of a larger social group. This Faulkner is a postmodern writer whose characters are "irrevocably private and yet implicated in history, a complex web of *social* relations." This Faulkner hewed to a homegrown version of Bakhtin's socialized conception of language, whereas earlier biographers portrayed Faulkner as a modernist magician orchestrating the illusion of objectivity and detachment in his novels, all the while seeking to control every detail of an overall design that admittedly features openness, ambiguity, and contradiction.

In "History as Autobiography" Gray rightly contends that the early 20th-century South's agricultural monopoly of cotton, economic poverty, defeat in the Civil War and subsequent occupation, patriarchal familial and social structures, and history of slavery and segregation deeply shaped Faulkner's life and writing. Faulkner sought to commemorate and criticize his region and its antebellum myths and postbellum realities as it lurched from a rural, agrarian society to an urban, industrial one. Represented neither as an autonomous individual nor a victim of a totalizing society or culture, Faulkner inserted "himself in the space between conflicting interests and practices" and dramatized in his fiction the contradictions such conflicts engendered. Thus, inventing and elaborating Yoknapatawpha County became for Faulkner a way of understanding the South and its history. Gray's Faulkner is clearly one for our time, but not all will agree that he was as consciously a social and historical a novelist as Gray contends. Still, I admire the attempt here to work out notions of the self and the artist that negotiate a middle ground between liberalism and poststructuralism. In "Autobiography as History" Gray treads familiar biographical ground, arguing that the story of Faulkner and his clan is inseparable from that of his region. He is especially good on how Faulkner's "vexed and lifelong love affair with his mother" repeatedly compelled him as a person and as an artist to try to recover "a lost [pre-Oedipal] wholeness, the absent figure of the mother" and his fictional males to ardently pursue women who remain elusive, shadowy, and marginalized. If the artist for Faulkner was usually a male seeking to compensate for or appropriate the female ability to give birth, the muses he sought inspiration from and the world he sought to capture in art were usually feminine. Faulkner often followed his culture in marginalizing women, Gray points out, but he also made that same marginalization an object of analysis. Gray is especially interesting on how aesthetic and sexual, especially incestuous, pursuits are linked in the fiction, with both pursuits acting "as forms of restitution and/or replacement for a lost wholeness."

Bakhtin's influence on this volume is everywhere apparent in its emphasis on voice, on the dialogic exchange between inner and outer voices and between individual and communal voices. For example, Gray has much to say about how *The Sound and the Fury* "issues from Faulkner's recognition that we make our identities, personal and communal, out of a process of speech that is continuous and open-ended." And he is enlightening on how the disjunctions of tone and genre in *As I Lay Dying* render the book a form of Bakhtinian carnival with its "rituals of subversion" and "barely organized riot and release" and resistance to closure. Gray does not feel compelled to praise all of Faulkner's novels equally. While he admires *The Sound and the Fury* and *Absalom, Absalom!,* he feels free to discuss the problems as well as the virtues of *Sanctuary* and *The Unvanquished.* And he is equally instructive on problems in *Go Down, Moses* that may have resulted from Faulkner's repudiation and revision of the formulaic depictions of comic blacks that characterized some of the stories in their original appearance in national magazines. There is also an interesting discussion of Faulkner's conservative representation of Lucas Beauchamp in *Intruder in the Dust* as more a patriarchal Southern male than a black man, although it is worthwhile to point out that portraying a black man in these terms in the 1940s was, nevertheless, a subversive gesture. Gray repeatedly stresses the relevance of American writers such as Mark Twain, Joel Chandler Harris, and Augustus Baldwin Longstreet to the young Faulkner's artistic development at the expense of European writers such as Joyce, Balzac, and Flaubert, who were arguably much more important to him at the time as his letters and essays from the period reveal. Gray stresses the influence of American folk/populist traditions on Faulkner and his fiction over that of the European art novel, even though Faulkner's genius, for me, lies in synthesizing those two traditions.

The Life of William Faulkner easily strikes me as the most theoretically sophisticated addition to the shelf of Faulkner biographies. More concise and focused than Frederick Karl's biography, its value lies less in uncovering new biographical information or in offering up new interpretations of the novels and stories than in synthesizing the best postmodern theory, critical work on Faulkner, and our preoccupations with issues of race, class, and gender and connecting them to the biography. Like Williamson, Gray stresses Southern history, culture, society, economics, and race relations and how they shaped Faulkner and his novels. On the other hand, Gray frequently engages in psychobiographical readings of the fiction and Faulkner's artistic decisions but offers scant biographical support for his assertions. The book is simply much more speculative than he admits.

It is good to have Frederick L. Gwynn and Joseph L. Blotner's *Faulkner in the University* (Virginia) back in print as an affordable paperback with a new introduction by Douglas Day. This indispensable collection of formal and informal talks and question-and-answer sessions at the University of Virginia in 1957 and 1958 first appeared in 1959. The volume is essential reading for all Faulknerians as long as we remember that Faulkner was a celebrated public figure. His changed circumstances and his audiences for these sessions when he was a writer-in-residence at Virginia should contextualize these pronouncements on fiction he had written years earlier. Seeing *Faulkner in the University* back in print prompts me to wonder when Random House will publish a much-needed reprint of *Selected Letters of William Faulkner* (1977). Better yet, when will an expanded and enlarged edition of the letters appear?

Tom Dardis's " 'Oh Those Awful Pressures!': Faulkner's Controlled Drinking" in *Beyond the Pleasure Dome: Writing and Addiction from the Romantics,* ed. Sue Vice, Matthew Campbell, and Tim Armstrong (Sheffield Academy, 1994, pp. 192–99) is a brief but persuasive rejoinder to the myth of controlled drinking that some of Faulkner's biographers have promulgated: that is, Faulkner was not an alcoholic but an extraordinary writer who went on controlled binges when the pressures in his life became too intense. Dardis's response: Faulkner was an extraordinary writer who was also an alcoholic who drank all the time whether he was experiencing extreme pressure or not.

iii General Criticism

All students of Faulkner are indebted to M. Thomas Inge for his essential *William Faulkner: The Contemporary Reviews* (Cambridge), a much-needed collection of reviews in primarily American newspapers and journals that replaces John Bassett's long out-of-print *William Faulkner: The Critical Heritage* (1975). From *The Marble Faun* to *The Reivers*— posthumously published works are not included—a selection of reviews of each volume is followed by a checklist of additional reviews. Reviews of the *Portable Faulkner* with the Compson appendix are included, but I wish reviews of the Modern Library dual edition of *The Sound and the Fury* and *As I Lay Dying* were as well. Simply put, however, Inge's book is now the starting point for anyone interested in the reception of Faulkner's fiction. Now if only Cambridge would publish a paperback for classroom use.

The essays in Philip Weinstein's valuable *The Cambridge Companion to William Faulkner* generally draw on postmodern cultural theory to connect the private act of reading Faulkner to broader ideological, social, and cultural activities in the 20th century, especially those involving race, gender, and subject formation. The essays aim at and, in most cases, achieve the difficult goal of appealing to both students new to Faulkner and experienced Faulkner scholars. After Weinstein's helpful introduction, which glosses the essays, the volume is divided into two sections: "The Texts in the World" and "The World in the Texts." In the first part, Richard Moreland discusses "Faulkner and Modernism" with an emphasis on *Light in August* (pp. 17–30), Patrick O'Donnell examines "Faulkner and Postmodernism" with an emphasis on *Go Down, Moses* (pp. 31–50), John T. Matthews connects Faulkner's modernist practices to the production of 20th-century mass culture in "Faulkner and the Culture Industry" (pp. 51–74), André Bleikasten addresses Faulkner and modernist European novelists in "Faulkner from a European Perspective" (pp. 75–95), and Ramón Saldívar discusses the colonial and postcolonial subject in *Absalom* and in Américo Paredes's *George Washington Gómez* in "Looking for a Master Plan: Faulkner, Paredes, and the Colonial and Postcolonial Subject" (pp. 96–120). In the second section, Cheryl Lester writes about "Racial Awareness and Arrested Development: *The Sound and the Fury* and the Great Migration (1918–1928)" (pp. 123–45), Judith Bryant Wittenberg examines race as a social and especially linguistic construction in "Race in *Light in August*: Word-symbols and Obverse Reflections" (pp. 146–67), and Carolyn Porter discusses fatherhood and patriarchy in *"Absalom, Absalom!*: (Un)Making the Father" (pp. 168–96). Warwick Wadlington's "Conclusion: The Stakes of Reading Faulkner—Discerning Reading" (pp. 197–220) traces out the connections "between the private, subjective state of reading . . . and the status of Faulkner as a major literary figure" and literary institution, with an emphasis on *Go Down, Moses.*

I found the essays by Moreland, O'Donnell, Bleikasten, and Porter especially instructive. Moreland describes Faulkner as a writer who occupied different novelistic stances: readerly or realist, writerly or modernist, and participatory or postmodernist. For O'Donnell, *Go Down, Moses* is a postmodern transitional book in Faulkner's career. In it, he replaces his earlier modernist urge to escape the world of history by creating a formal replacement for it that never completely expunges that historical reality with an attempt to represent "the contradictory iterability and singularity of a nontranscendent version of history." As skeptical of current critical trends as he is in his contribution to *Faulkner and Ideology* (see below), Bleikasten argues not that Faulkner's social and cultural milieu but his aesthetic power explains his greatness as a writer. The essay refreshingly treats Faulkner as "a novelist of European descent," reminding us that he was influenced by European writers as much if not more than by American writers. Finally, Porter performs a feminist Lacanian close reading of *Absalom* as a "concerned interrogation of fatherhood as the enigmatic source and vehicle of social identity and political sovereignty." She reads the young Sutpen's traumatic affront by a black butler at the door of a plantation big house and its aftermath as a representation and critique of how patriarchy maintains its authority by inscribing the patriarchal ideal in young males during the process of subject formation. The collection is ideal for undergraduate and graduate courses on Faulkner precisely because it reflects no single approach to Faulkner; the contributors are all self-conscious about their critical procedures; and the pieces are all written in accessible prose and often comment on each other.

This year's volume from the annual Faulkner conference at the University of Mississippi is *Faulkner and Ideology: Faulkner and Yoknapatawpha, 1992* (Miss.). Ed. Donald M. Kartiganer and Ann J. Abadie, the collection's best essays comprise a broad spectrum of conceptual and methodological positions from liberal humanist to postmodernist. Some contributors share a liberal understanding of ideology as a set of beliefs and values more or less consciously chosen by individual subjects. In these essays a complex liberal notion of subject formation is also espoused in which ideological supervision of both our social arrangements and inner lives is never total. Others focus on the relationship between consciousness, the conditions of material reality, and our everyday practices, along with the various ways by which our experience is unconsciously shaped by broadly social ideological discursive and nondiscursive formations. There is little conformity in these essays, but there is an occasioned tendency to articulate one's views in a critical vacuum and to lose sight of the relevance of one's argument to Faulkner studies.

André Bleikasten's "Faulkner and the New Ideologues" (pp. 3–21), a scathing assault on current left-oriented cultural and ideological work on Faulkner, leads off the volume. He casts himself as one who called for more ideologically inflected writing on Faulkner only to be bitterly disappointed by the reductive sermonizing, moral absolutism, and excessive emphasis on content over form that answered his call. Bleikasten accuses a number of Faulkner critics of condescending commentary on the work of earlier scholars, of lockstep obeisance to current poststructuralist orthodoxies, and of reducing Faulkner's oeuvre to one design, a critical representation of the South. His assault on the poststructuralist emphasis on the contextual determinants of textual content and significance reflects his belief that "paying close attention to a text's immanent formal properties is . . . a prerequisite for a valid analysis of its ideology." Bleikasten's charges are both sweeping and strong, especially his allegation that current work on Faulkner is glibly reductive in its disparaging representations of Western civilization, culture, and literature and of modernity and modernism. The critics he chastises would no doubt rebut his charges by arguing that all cultural activities are intrinsically political. Louis D. Rubin, Jr.'s "William Faulkner: Why, the Very *Idea!*" (pp. 329–52), a less persuasive companion piece to Bleikasten's salvo, casts a cold eye on current practices in Faulkner studies. As an unrepentant advocate of the elitist modernist category of "Literature" with its privileging of complex imaginative literature over other forms of discourse, Rubin inveighs against the reductive and simplifying tendencies of ideological critics. He rejects not a particular way of reading Faulkner but the very notion of interpretive context as though we were actually capable of confronting the text itself. What Rubin takes as unalterable central features of a text that precede interpretation, however, may actually follow them. And whether or not a novel has an integrity that precedes context or interpretive orientation that can or ought to be violated is a proposition much in debate.

Richard Gray's "On Privacy: William Faulkner and the Human Subject" (pp. 45–69), an earlier version of part of his biography, does not bear out Bleikasten's and Rubin's charges. He examines the tension between Faulkner's near-obsessive need for privacy and the complex social milieu in which he placed his alienated characters, and he links the author's own desire for privacy to his detached, objective attitude toward his characters' autonomy. The bulk of the essay lucidly articulates Gray's Bakhtinian approach to Faulkner. A conservative postmodernist, Gray writes that language was a field of contention for Faulkner and that "the human subject still has a chance to alter the terms of his or her own culture" in his work. He illustrates this paradox with a brief, overly optimistic reading of *Light in August* that stresses Joe Christmas's use of his indeterminate racial status to challenge and subvert the linguistic practices of his society that marginalize blacks by denying them definition and substance. Joe's hideous death by castration at the hands of Percy Grimm, Gray claims, is burned into the minds of the onlookers, undermining their racist views of blacks and the words used to label them.

Anne Goodwyn Jones's "Desire and Dismemberment: Faulkner and the Ideology of Penetration" (pp. 129–71) is a masterful poststructuralist attempt to knit together several discourses in Faulkner under the heading of an ideological metanarrative of sexual penetration. This metanarrative, she argues, is a significant agent in the construction and regulation of male and female desire and sexuality that privileges active penetration over being passively penetrated and reserves sexual and social dominance for heterosexual males. Goodwyn Jones examines the emphasis on "companionate marriage" and an ambivalent attitude toward sexual relations in popular progressive sex manuals like Theodore H. Van de Velde's *Ideal Marriage* (1926) and in *Flags in the Dust, The Sound and the Fury, Light in August,* and "Barn Burning" in order to argue that they legitimize female desire but also seek to subordinate it to masculine control. One paradoxical aspect of the paradigm she sketches is that the ideology of penetration "marshals the organization of a single directed subject," which seeks to disseminate the object during male orgasm "at the very moment of the most risk to its coherence," and that dismemberment in this ideology and in Faulkner's work represents the feminine, "the origin, goal, and risk of penetration." Some readers may feel that too much theoretical scaffolding, too much Van de Velde and not enough Faulkner, is present in this lengthy essay, but it is a fascinating piece that is, I hope, the start of a larger study on the construction of desire and sexuality in Faulkner. I found it suggestive at every turn of how we might read sexuality in

Faulkner's life and work. Goodwyn Jones's reading of "Faulkner's work as located within (and at times resisting) this ideological position" is also exemplary.

Martha Banta's "The Razor, the Pistol, and the Ideology of Race Etiquette" (pp. 172–216) treats the formation from 1897 to 1907 of manners to govern white-black relations, especially "codes of violence predicated upon keeping people in their 'place.' " Drawing on a welter of cartoons, editorials, and essays from *Life,* a New York City weekly, Banta charts the shift in white Northerners' attitude toward blacks. Because of a rising tide of immigration from eastern and southern Europe and Asia, America's imperialist moves in the Caribbean and the Pacific, and a growing fear that inferior races might dilute the purity of the Anglo-Saxon race through miscegenation, Northerners abandoned sympathy for blacks for Southern fear that blood would deluge white civilization and culture. Banta briefly brings her analysis to bear on three scenes of interracial violence in Faulkner: Christmas's murder of Joanna Burden, Grimm's murder and mutilation of Christmas in *Light in August,* and Lucas Beauchamp and Zack Edmonds's brutal face-off in *Go Down, Moses.* All three scenes dramatize "the way social identity is linked to one's choice of weapons of violence which, in turn, have acquired their cultural accreditation through their complicity with ideologies of race etiquette."

An intelligent example of liberal ideology critique is Richard H. King's "Faulkner, Ideology, and Narrative" (pp. 22–44), which focuses on the ideological dimensions of Faulkner's founding narratives. Likening ideology to the stories we tell ourselves to explain who we are and justify our actions, King goes on to distinguish between two founding narratives in Faulkner: the sublime mode of obsessive, violent, and ruthless self-assertion found in *Absalom, Absalom!* and "The Bear"; and the pastoral, even comic, mode of detached, ironic, and bemused narration found in the appendix to *The Sound and the Fury,* "Mississippi," and the historical introductions to *Requiem for a Nun.* In exploring the ideological implications of these two modes, King notes that the sublime narrative is a form of radical critique, whereas the pastoral form is a conservative one. Furthermore, Faulkner practiced the first before World War II and the second after it. In effect, King is proposing a new way of characterizing the post–World War II shift in Faulkner's fiction and in the way it was read.

In "Faulkner and the Democratic Crisis" (pp. 70–94) Robert H.

Brinkmeyer, Jr., contends that the debate in the United States over the meaning of democratic ideology and the origins of fascism during the 1930s and 1940s had a profound effect on Faulkner's fiction. Brinkmeyer lays out the particular debate between leftist and traditionalist Southern intellectuals and writers over whether fascism might be more likely to issue from the agrarian, conservative South or the industrialized, democratic North. After glancing at the relatively uncomplicated traditionalism of "The Tall Men," "Two Soldiers," and "Shall Not Perish," Brinkmeyer argues that *Go Down, Moses* and especially "Delta Autumn" were shaped by this debate. Less persuasively, he discusses *The Hamlet* and *Absalom* as oblique illustrations of how American dictators might come to power, although other Faulknerians have more plausibly read Flem Snopes as the quintessential American entrepreneurial capitalist who rises from rags to riches in a satirical version of the American Dream. Brinkmeyer's Faulkner is a complicated and thoughtful Southern traditionalist who often challenged extreme regionalist thinking and who was sympathetic to the lot of the downtrodden except when they rose up angrily to demand redress.

Pursuing a decidedly nonpostmodernist critique of consumer culture, Ted Ownby's "The Snopes Trilogy and the Emergence of Consumer Culture" (pp. 95–128) addresses Faulkner's ambivalent fictional responses to America's burgeoning consumer culture with its emphasis on excitement and novelty. If Faulkner was sympathetic to the liberation from grinding poverty and reactionary tradition that consumer goods offered the working classes, he was also critical of the self-indulgence and acquisitive materialism that mere consumption engendered. Ownby ranges insightfully over Faulkner's representations of consumerism in *The Town, Intruder in the Dust, Light in August, As I Lay Dying,* and *The Reivers* to demonstrate this ambivalence. The heart of the essay is a discussion of Ab, Mink, Montgomery Ward, Flem, and Linda Snopes Kohl in the Snopes trilogy and their relation to the ideology of consumerism. Purveyor of French postcards, Montgomery Ward embarks on "the commodification of immediate pleasure," while Flem, who possesses neither traditional nor modern attitudes to material goods, tragically "never finds enjoyment in the benefits of the economic system he helps bring to Yoknapatawpha" (p. 117).

Faulkner's obsessive need for privacy is revisited in Noel Polk's lively yet sobering " 'Polysyllabic and Verbless Patriotic Nonsense': Faulkner at Midcentury—His and Ours" (pp. 297–328). Polk ranges widely and expertly over Faulkner's biography, letters, interviews, nonfiction, and fiction of the 1950s, especially *A Fable*, to address the troubling contradictions between the intensely private man who protected that privacy zealously and the Nobel laureate who increasingly courted, even relished the role of public spokesman, between the optimistic content of his public comments and the painfully unhappy facts of his private life. Along the way, Polk has useful things to say about our tendency to project the opinions of the hopeful, even genial canonized public author of the 1950s into the tortured dark work of the 1920s, 1930s, and 1940s. Polk traces "Faulkner's willingness to engage political and ideological issues publicly" to a midlife crisis he was experiencing and to a subsequent rejection of alienation. The essay focuses on the theme of ideology, primarily mankind's desperate need for its illusory comforts, in Faulkner's late work and concludes with a consideration of *A Fable*, which is about "the established forces that perpetuate and maintain . . . myths, those who benefit by them, and those who know not only how to manipulate them to their own advantage but how to keep the . . . masses believing that those myths operate in their own best interests."

The evidence of this volume suggests that ideological criticism does not necessarily have to be left-oriented or reductive, and that different types of ideology critique are not only desirable but possible. Whether growing out of New Criticism, traditional American Studies, or poststructuralist practice, much of the work in this collection is sensitive to the nuances of a writer's language and form, even as it explores how subjects are formed, how power is distributed in the social, economic, political, and cultural arrangements of the past and present, and how such distributions are maintained. I have discussed this collection at greater length in "Faulkner Studies and Ideology Critique in the 1990s" (*MissQ* 49, iii [Summer 1996]).

First published in 1993 in the Netherlands, Ineke Bockting's *Character and Personality in the Novels of William Faulkner* (Univ. Press) gives "an inside view of the textual process of characterization" in *The Sound and the Fury, As I Lay Dying, Light in August,* and *Absalom, Absalom!* Bockting combines stylistics and psychoanalysis to argue that while initially Faulknerian characters create and sustain selves through texts, these texts become more and more openly texts created by family, society, and history. To explore "the layeredness, complexity, and conflictual nature of personality" in Faulkner, she supplements the classical Freudian personality construct with post-Freudian contributions such as

Klein's and Kristeva's emphasis on the pre-Oedipal phase of personality development as well as neo-Freudian projects like Karen Horney's work on the neurotic defensive strategies that impede the individual's drive toward self-fulfillment. Using linguist Roger Fowler's notion of "mind-style," the distinctive linguistic presentation of an individual mental self, Bockting explores how phonology, morphology, lexicalization, syntax, and viewpoint shift work to convey the characters' different conceptualizations of reality. Curiously, the book contains no references to Lacan's linguistic revision of psychoanalysis that has become so central to the field of Faulkner studies or to the work of such Lacanian Faulknerians as Deborah Clarke, Doreen Fowler, James M. Mellard, Carolyn Porter, Jay Watson, and Philip Weinstein. Neither does Bockting show an awareness of work in recent years by Noel Polk and Michael Zeitlin, two of the more sophisticated practitioners of Freudian-influenced Faulkner criticism.

Tanya T. Fayen's *In Search of the Latin American Faulkner* (Univ. Press) employs Jauss's reception aesthetic and Itamar Even-Zohar's polysystem theory of translation to examine Faulkner's critical reception. To determine which of Faulkner's narrative innovations were first resisted and then adopted by Latin American writers, Fayen compares Faulkner's critical reception in the United States to his reception in Latin America from the 1930s on; she also studies many of the translations and retranslations of Faulkner's work into Spanish and Portuguese. While her discussion of Faulkner's reception throughout the Americas breaks little new ground, the book's originality lies in her analysis of "the conflicts and compromises translators made with Faulkner's deviance from conventional modes of expression." She usefully treats translations of Faulkner as critical readings that challenge traditional, culturally established logic.

Susan Donaldson has guest-edited an impressive issue of the *Faulkner Journal* (9, i–ii [1993–94]) on Faulkner and sexuality. To discuss Faulkner, his fiction, and sexuality, most of the contributors draw on postmodern scholarship on sexuality with its interest in "the cultural construction of desire, with the crucial link to be perceived between sexuality and subjectivity, and with the distribution of power to be detected in the most intimate of human relations." Many contributors contend that Faulkner's art serves "as a testing ground of sorts for alternative gender and sexual roles." For example, Evelyn Jaffe Schreiber's occasionally dense "What's Love Got to Do with It? Desire and Subjectivity in Faulkner's Snopes Trilogy" (pp. 83–98) draws on the cultural theories of

Raymond Williams and Gloria Anzaldúa and Slavoj Žižek's reading of Lacan to analyze evolving definitions of gender roles and sexual desire and the dynamics of societal change in the trilogy and to lay bare the "powerful combination of cultural and psychic patterns" that "creates the behavior that defines both the women and men." Specifically, she focuses on how Eula Varner's and Linda Snopes Kohl's positions move from being marginalized object to becoming central subject, auguring an emergent culture in contrast to the patriarchal residual and dominant cultures of Yoknapatawpha County. For Schreiber, Eula's character development reflects these conflicting aspects of her culture; circumscribed by the pretenses of the patriarchy, she is, nevertheless, able "to subvert the system through her ability to completely immobilize men." After arguing provocatively against the critical view that Eula is a victim of the patriarchy because she becomes a subject by committing suicide, Schreiber turns her attention to Linda whose arrangement of Flem's murder becomes a blow against the dominant culture. I remain skeptical that Eula's suicide is a positive act of empowerment and that Linda's new Jaguar is "a deliberate symbol of her subject role because she ordered it in anticipation of Flem's murder," but Schreiber's comments on how "Eula weakens Gavin's subject identity with her suicide, and Linda crushes it with her revenge tactics," are well worth reading. (I discuss the other essays from this special issue below.)

Minrose C. Gwin has gathered some excellent pieces for this year's special issue on Faulkner for *MissQ,* one of which is James M. Mellard's "Something New and Hard and Bright: Faulkner, Ideology, and the Construction of Modernism" (48: 459–74), which unfortunately has a Shandian blank page at a crucial part of the argument. This piece, which ought to be read in conjunction with Mellard's "Realism, Naturalism, Modernism: Residual, Dominant, and Emergent Ideologies in *As I Lay Dying*" in *Faulkner and Ideology* (see below), treats the roles of Faulkner and Southern Agrarian Robert Penn Warren in the early 1930s and Marxist radical Georg Lukács in the mid-1950s in the retroactive construction of modernism as an aesthetic ideology in fiction. Sensitive to the differences between the two critics, Mellard nevertheless finds fascinating affinities between them which suggest the beginning and end of "that moment when modernism *has become the subject it will have been.*" Both rejected sociological realism as the fictional documentation of preconceived theses, championing instead the value of objectivity. In praising Faulkner's objectivity and poetic form, Warren participated in the construction of modernism out of naturalism, although he did not yet stress form over content. Lukács also stressed objectivity, technical refinement, and the reduction of content. Mellard identifies the novel as "an unpredictable exemplar of modernist aesthetics" in the making because it clearly reflects realism and naturalism as it constitutes itself as a subject. Thus, *As I Lay Dying* embodies the residual ideology of realism, the dominant ideology of naturalism, and the emergent ideology of modernism in its yoking of traditional folk materials to modernist techniques.

In the same issue of *MissQ* David Newman's " 'the vehicle itself is unaware': New Criticism on the Limits of Reading Faulkner" (48: 481–99) attempts a postmodern recuperation of New Criticism. After briefly examining some of the harsher charges that the New Critics advocated an apolitical, ahistorical formalism which masked an underlying conservative political agenda, Newman analyzes some of Allen Tate's criticism and then at more length Cleanth Brooks's discussions of *Light in August* and *As I Lay Dying* in *William Faulkner: The Yoknapatawpha Country*. He reasonably argues that "under the monolithic label of New Critic a great deal of diversity and complexity is reduced to a single, isolable, purely literary position." Moreover, Faulkner shared an ambivalence about notions of aesthetic purity with the New Critics and their critics that masks other shared needs: "a need to judge, to make decisive pronouncements that are necessarily less complicated than the entanglement of needs they emerge from and gratify." I applaud Newman's desire to reverse the current tendency to reduce the New Critics to a caricature. I especially found persuasive his contention that Brooks's well-known thesis about the individual and the community in Faulkner is no more circular and overlooks no more gaps in the novels than does our own contemporary reversal of his position.

Two important reissues in paperback deserve to be noted. Olga W. Vickery's *The Novels of William Faulkner: A Critical Interpretation* (LSU) first appeared in 1959 (rev. 1964) and still serves as an example of what the New Criticism, at its best, was capable of saying about Faulkner. Vickery sought to respond to charges that Faulkner's novels were not well-constructed by analyzing point of view and structure in individual works. John T. Irwin's classic psychoanalytic study *Doubling and Incest/Repetition and Revenge: A Speculative Reading of Faulkner* originally appeared in 1975. Hopkins has published an expanded edition, which consists of the original book and two essays that have appeared elsewhere: "*Knight's Gambit:* Poe, Faulkner, and the Tradition of the Detective Story" and "Horace Benbow and the Myth of Narcissa."

William E. H. Meyer, Jr.'s "Faulkner's Aural Evangelism: An Essay in Religious Aestheticism" (*CLAJ* 39: 104–15) discusses Faulkner as "a rhetorical evangelist" who preaches a "genuine Southern religion, an aesthetic theism or auro-evangelism which has as its center the god of folk-traditions, legends, tales, and the rhetoric of 'the thunder and music of prose.'" Specifically, he is interested in how Faulkner drew on "the rhetorical power of the homiletical/Biblical tradition" to transform traditional Christianity into a Southern religious aestheticism. Meyer compares passages of Faulkner's prose with passages mostly culled from a 1960 collection entitled *The World's Great Sermons* without explaining his rationale for selecting this volume. Nor does he draw on earlier studies of Southern oratory, whether from the pulpit or otherwise, or on previous discussions of Faulkner's prose style, or on voice in his fiction such as Stephen M. Ross's *Fiction's Inexhaustible Voice* (see *ALS 1989,* p. 141). Meyer comments intelligently on how the aural dominates the other senses in Faulkner, but his broad unsupported generalizations seem to owe more to the oratory under examination than to scholarly argument.

In a second piece, "Culture Wars/Gender-Scars: Faulkner's South vs. America" (*CrossRoads* 3, i [1994]: 112–26), Meyer writes that Faulkner's "creation of gender is preeminently the more general *cultural* problem of simply being a proud but defeated Southerner under the aegis of Yankee power." Refusing to acknowledge let alone argue with the growing body of postmodern Faulkner scholarship that portrays him as a critic of the South from the left, Meyer ranges through Faulkner's novels to argue that the war between the sexes therein is not a biological desire for domination and surrender but "the profound acting-out of the all-embracing cultural war with America itself." Again, he stresses Faulkner's emphasis on Southern rhetoric and oratory, here as a means of uniting Southern men and women and Southern whites and blacks and enabling them to resist Northern hypervisual culture. In my opinion, the essay suffers from the same flaws as "Faulkner's Aural Evangelism": it simply ignores relevant contemporary scholarship and seems excessively sympathetic to Faulkner's Southern chauvinism. Moreover, Meyer has a tendency to treat uncritically the many voices in Faulkner's fiction as expressions of the author's opinions and beliefs.

Montserrat Ginés's "Don Quixote in Yoknapatawpha: Faulkner's

Champion of Dames" (*SLJ* 28, ii: 23–42) explores parallels of character and situation between Cervantes and Faulkner. More importantly, his discussion of the knightly function of Quentin Compson in *The Sound and the Fury*, Gavin Stevens in *The Town* and *The Mansion*, Byron Bunch in *Light in August*, and Julius Priest in *The Reivers* seeks to rehabilitate Faulkner's failed idealists as quixotic characters who are "illusion-ridden, impractical, unheroic or self-defeated" but also "dignified in their quest for virtue." Ginés inexplicably omits Horace Benbow from his discussion, fails to mention that Quentin has repressed incestuous desires for Caddy, and uncritically uses Faulkner's later public statements to interpret the earlier works. Gustavo Pellón's "Ideology and Structure in Giardinelli's *Santo Oficio de la memoria*" (*StTCL* 19: 81–99) discusses the similarities between *As I Lay Dying*, *The Sound and the Fury*, and Mempo Giardinelli's 1991 novel in terms of structure and point of view and argues for a clear case of influence.

In "Faulkner's Anti-*Bildungsromane*" (*JASAT* 25 [1994]: 50–58) David L. Vanderwerken examines Faulkner's depiction of the failed initiation of children into adulthood in *The Sound and the Fury*, *Light in August*, *Absalom, Absalom!*, and *Go Down, Moses*. In ironically and satirically manipulating the conventions of the bildungsroman genre, Faulkner creates a scathing series of anti-bildungsroman novels in which boys from dysfunctional families seek surrogate parents and undergo disastrous sexual educations only to become failed adults whose development has been arrested both psychologically and emotionally.

One last note: *Teaching Faulkner*, the newsletter put out by the Center for Faulkner Studies at Southeast Missouri State University under the editorship of Robert W. Hamblin, continues to publish helpful pedagogical suggestions.

iv Individual Works to 1929

This year saw the publication of three good essays on Faulkner's second novel, *Mosquitoes*, in *FJ* (9, ii). Lisa Rado's " 'A Perversion that Builds Chartres and Invents Lear Is a Pretty Good Thing': *Mosquitoes* and Faulkner's Androgynous Imagination" (pp. 13–30) looks briefly at *Mayday* and *Soldiers' Pay* before arguing that Faulkner's second novel was influenced by "new cultural constructions of femininity and sexuality." In particular, Rado contends that sexual indeterminacy is linked in Faulkner's work to the artist and to creativity. In response to the blurring of gender divisions, Faulkner envisioned his creative imagination, "his own process of poetic production," as generated "from a double-sexed imagination." This strategy both empowers him sexually and artistically but threatens him with fears concerning feminization, homoeroticism, and the female body. *Mosquitoes* foregrounds these anxieties. In *"Mosquitoes'* Missing Bite: The Four Deletions" (pp. 31–41) Minrose C. Gwin helpfully prints for the first time the complete text of the four passages dealing with implicit and explicit homoeroticism, male homoeroticism, and lesbianism that editors at Boni & Liveright cut from the novel. While her essay concentrates on the deletions in relation to the textual history of *Mosquitoes* and their placement in the novel, Gwin comments on how the homoerotic content of the excised material "further disrupted the normativity of heterosexuality" and naturalized heterosexual practice. Finally, Meryl Altman's rather rambling but interesting "The Bug That Dare Not Speak Its Name: Sex, Art, Faulkner's Worst Novel, and the Critics" (pp. 42–68) muses on why "aesthetic metadiscourse, lesbianism, and women's writing, occur here together, and never again in Faulkner's work." Altman discusses how the male high-modernist division between masculine artistic creation and feminine artistic failure in the novel plays itself out linguistically in the distinction between male dysphemism and female euphemism but is ultimately challenged by the text. I especially appreciated her contention that Faulkner critics, early and late, have uncritically associated gender reversal and gendernonconforming behavior with homosexuality and thus have been as quick as a Freudian psychoanalyst to spot latent homosexuality throughout Yoknapatawpha County. For Altman, Faulkner, especially in *Mosquitoes*, is "the poet of non-standard sexuality, of masculinities and femininities regressing toward and away from the 'norm.' "

In "One Goal Is Still Lacking: The Influence of Friedrich Nietzsche's Philosophy on William Faulkner's *The Sound and the Fury*" (*SoAR* 60, iv: 35–52) Marco Abel submits that nihilism in the novel remains a subject of debate that may be resolved by using Nietzsche's philosophy and that "such debate and resolution offers a richer and more complex interpretation than most previous commentators of the novel have allowed." Abel's new spin is that the Christian elements in the novel are paradoxically nihilistic in Nietzschean terms since Christianity is "a system that does not assert *life* as its primary value" and because it "seeks meaning by meaningless prayer to a non-existent deity." Abel makes some interesting observations about the Compsons' entrapment in their own memories and the meaninglessness of their lives as a form of Nietzschean nihilism. The essay's title, however, is a misnomer: after briefly discussing Nietzsche's influence on modernist writing in general, Abel proceeds to a Nietzschean reading of the novel, especially of Quentin's section, and to Nietzsche's solution to the problem of nihilism rather than to any biographical connections between the philosopher and the novelist. Still, his assertions that the novel's "formal skeleton dominated by apparent confusion, disintegration, and dissolution" is the fictional equivalent of Nietzsche's primary argumentative technique of the paradox is a valid one, as is his observation that the novel transforms the reader into a kind of Nietzschean superman by making him or her an active participant in the search for meaning.

Arthur Brown's dense "Benjy, the Reader, and Death: At the Fence in *The Sound and the Fury*" (*MissQ* 48: 407–20) proposes that the narrators of the novel's four sections "reproduce the reader's dubious position inside and outside of the story, and thus implicate the reader in the 'real life' of the novel and put the reader's own 'right to death' in question." Viewing death as the novel's generating principle enables us to see that the death-in-life existence of the Compson brothers is reproduced in the act of narration that "places them in contact with us, with our mortal lives, and thus resurrects the possibility of their death . . . their humanness."

In "Quentin Compson's Scouting Expedition on June 2, 1910" (*EL-WIU* 22: 113–22) Charles Chappell exhaustively and persuasively argues that critics have been misled by Faulkner's assertion in the appendix that Quentin jumped to his watery death from a bridge in Cambridge. Rather, the 1929 novel shows Quentin carefully hunting for a remote bridge out in the countryside so as to avoid any unwanted interference with his plans to commit suicide. In "Faulkner's Fiction Makes Addicts of Us All" (*Beyond the Pleasure Dome*, pp. 291–98) Marcy Lassota Bauman argues that the novel is an accurate portrayal of a family with alcoholism, although Faulkner has cloaked the work "in a tapestry of guilt and denial." Peggy Bach's "A Serious Damn: William Faulkner and Evelyn Scott" (*SLJ* 28, i: 128–43) discusses the relationship between novelist Evelyn Scott and Faulkner, the origins of Scott's laudable review of *The Sound and the Fury,* and some parallels between the two writers. The essay helpfully reprints in full Scott's "On William Faulkner's 'The Sound and the Fury.' "

Terrell L. Tebbetts's "Dilsey and the Compsons: A Jungian Reading of

Faith and Fragmentation" (*PAPA* 21, i: 78–98) concerns itself with how Jung's theory of individuation "richly explains much of what becomes of all the trapped Compson children and relates their condition . . . to Dilsey and her Easter sermon." Tebbetts argues that Dilsey's Christianity provides "the nurture and the psychological wholeness that the Compson family fails to provide." While the Compson siblings have difficulties with individuation because of ego-self problems that result from the parenting failures of their parents, Dilsey's ego, animus, and shadow are perfectly harmonized.

In "Time, Death, and Gender: The Quentin Section in *The Sound and the Fury*" (*CCTEP* 59 [1994]: 53–59) Bing Shao offers a close reading of the book's second interior monologue in terms of the increasing struggle between linear, rational, patriarchal time and cyclical, monumental, and semiotic women's time. The monologue's increasingly extended illogical or irrational passages reveal an acceleration of the "feminine undermining of the 'Law of the Father.'" After identifying these passages as feminine rather than symptomatic of psychic disintegration, Shao argues that Quentin's suicide stems from his inability to escape binary ways of thinking as he finally rejects Mrs. Compson for Mr. Compson and women's time for patriarchal time. The essay breaks little new ground, in part because it seems unaware of much of the recent significant work on gendered notions of time in Faulkner and refuses to connect its insights to the rest of the novel.

v Individual Works, 1930–1939

Amy Louise Wood's "Feminine Rebellion and Mimicry in Faulkner's *As I Lay Dying*" (*FJ* 9, i–ii [1993–94]: 99–112) applies the French feminist thought of Irigaray, Cixous, and Kristeva to Addie Bundren's posthumous monologue. Woods argues that Addie uses her body to rebel against her patriarchal culture, "establishing meaning through the physical pains and pleasures of her nurturing motherhood and selfish sexuality." Engaging in what Irigaray terms "mimicry," Addie manipulates and distorts the roles and meanings of mother and adulteress to create an independent, powerful self. For example, Addie's beatings of her students are a powerful subversion of patriarchal "feminine and bodily meaning" because she turns feminine masochist suffering outward into sadism and carries out "a feminine merging of self and other . . . in a violent and unnurturing way." Personally, I felt sorry for the children. Wood also argues that Dewey Dell repeats this same struggle for self-definition but remains isolated and disconnected because "she cannot resolve the notion that she is pregnant by the man she desires."

James M. Mellard's instructive "Realism, Naturalism, Modernism: Residual, Dominant, and Emergent Ideologies in *As I Lay Dying*" (*Faulkner and Ideology,* pp. 217–37) ought to be read in tandem with his "Something New and Hard and Bright" (see above). Here, he examines how realism, naturalism, and modernism and their supporting ideologies contend with one another in the conflicted sites of Faulkner's novel and his critical reception. Drawing on Raymond Williams's distinctions between residual, dominant, and emergent ideologies, Mellard demonstrates that most reviewers and critics of early Faulkner valorized features of residual realism and dominant naturalism while attacking the "formalism, objectivity, [and] interiority" of emergent modernism. He argues that Faulkner deploys "traditional realist or naturalist devices . . . of objectivity and descriptive representation" in *As I Lay Dying* in order to subvert them "by virtue of their extremity or their subtle (or sometimes blatant) violations of the representational norms of realism and naturalism." This defamiliarization of the narrative techniques of the residual and dominant aesthetic ideologies of realism and naturalism functions as an emergent, oppositional modernism in the novel. In an insightful analysis of how Faulkner's incipient modernist use of the similes of oral storytelling in Tull's monologues underscores language's inability to represent reality, Mellard is especially attentive to how Faulkner's language subverts the ideology of traditional mimesis. I wish he had extended his analysis to the figurative language employed by the novel's other characters. Possessed of a complex notion of ideology and how it operates in literary texts, the essay is chock-full of insights about the conflicted aesthetic and ideological site that is *As I Lay Dying.* Although he frequently refers to traditional oral storytelling in the novel, it is unclear how Mellard connects the genre to the three primary aesthetic ideologies he examines. More importantly, while Mellard might be the first to object to formalist critical practices that valorize unity and coherence, his notion of Faulkner's incipient modernism seems to rest on just such a privileging; that is, *As I Lay Dying* is presented as neatly unified in its subversive use of modernist practices.

In "Floyd Collins and the Sand Cave Tragedy: A Possible Source for Faulkner's *As I Lay Dying*" (*KRev* 12, iii: 3–18) Lucas Carpenter notes some plausible parallels of character, action, and theme between the particulars of Collins's entrapment and eventual death in Sand Cave and Faulkner's novel. Although Faulkner wrote several poetic versions of the event and Collins's corpse underwent some bizarre travels of its own, Carpenter falls into the pitfall of some influence studies when his language shifts quickly from "probably" to "must," "surely," and "certainly."

The critical rehabilitation of Temple Drake proceeds apace in Amy Lovell Strong's unpersuasive "Machines and Machinations: Controlling Desires in Faulkner's *Sanctuary*" (*FJ* 9, i–ii [1993–94]: 69–81). Part of the book's "thematic of controlled and controlling desires," Strong contends, is that "Popeye functions as a technology, faceless, but able to exert [psychological] power with his penetrating gaze." Although she does not run away after her rape, Temple "never gives up trying to access power over her situation and power over her own body." I found unconvincing Strong's argument that Temple refuses to recognize the erotic self that Popeye constructs for her by lashing back at him "in language that challenges his power over her." Strong's solution to the Faulknerian parlor game of figuring out why Temple commits perjury at Goodwin's trial is that the male principals in the courtroom extract her perjured testimony to serve ends other than Temple's, specifically "to define, construct, and consequently circumscribe women's sexuality." Strong neglects to address, however, the contradiction between her assertion that Temple reclaims agency from Popeye and her portrayal of Temple as a lifeless victim of the patriarchy, first in the courtroom and then in the Luxembourg Gardens.

In "'Dont Think I'm Afraid to Tell': Talking and Taboo in William Faulkner's *Sanctuary*" (*QWERTY* 5: 267–75) Ineke Bockting maintains that taboo terms in the novel represented by ellipses and euphemisms are a fictional re-creation of the "ambivalence of the American South with respect to social relations [primarily between men and women] during the first decennia of this century." Although unaware of John Matthews's seminal "The Elliptical Nature of *Sanctuary*" (*ALS 1984*, p. 170), Bockting makes some interesting observations about Southern prohibition and segregation's origins in a Freudian "primitive touching phobia" that radiates outward "toward relations between the sexes, classes, and races in a way that is characteristic" of Faulkner's time and place.

Many of Cathy Peppers's observations in "What Does Faulkner Want? *Light in August* as a Hysterical Male Text" (*FJ* 9, i–ii [1993–94]: 125–37) have been made before, but she has interesting things to say about the novel's modernist concern with the construction of male subjectivity.

Applying Freud's definition of female hysteria in the Dora case to the masculine text, Peppers conceives of the "hysterical male text as marked by a narrative of excessive rechanneling and deferral, and a representation of male subjectivity constructed of a plurality of coding/uncoding." In particular, she analyzes the conflict between Joe Christmas's hypermasculine, even fascistic characterization, and a contradictory set of masochistic codes that undermine the unity of his identity. This "hysterical coding/uncoding of Joe's masculine identity" creates a heterogeneous subjectivity "that entangles the hypermasculine with the emasculated but in no way redeems the feminine."

Peter L. Hays's well-researched "Racial Predestination: The Elect and the Damned in *Light in August*" (*ELN* 33, ii: 62–69) cites the references to Presbyterianism and predestination in the novel to argue that Faulkner used Presbyterianism's "emphasis on predestined selection of the elect and the damned, on the gifts of God's grace without regard for one's acts" as "a metaphor for racial relations in this country." Since Joe Christmas believes he is partly black and thus damned by social, legal, and moral conventions, he acts accordingly. Hays might have strengthened his argument by seeing if the many references to predestination and inevitability in Faulkner's other novels support his claim.

Doreen Fowler's " 'I Am Dying: Faulkner's Hightower and the Oedipal Moment" (*FJ* 9, i–ii [1993–94]: 139–48), the most recent of her Lacanian readings of Faulkner's fiction, explicates Hightower's vision in the penultimate chapter of the novel as a series of reflections leading him to pass, belatedly, through a Lacanian Oedipal stage that allows him to become a complete self and to join the social order. Fowler argues that Hightower has heretofore refused to submit to the Law of the Father and accept the symbolic castration or the Oedipal law of "alienation into language." A subject in the process of constitution, Hightower has instead substituted his veneration of his grandfather's fatal Civil War exploit for the phallic father and his adopted mother, the church, for the phallic mother. His climactic vision, however, enacts his passage into full subjectivity and the Symbolic Order.

Jay Watson's "Overdoing Masculinity in *Light in August;* or, Joe Christmas and the Gender Guard" (*FJ* 9, i–ii [1993–94]: 148–77) is a thoughtful, highly readable discussion of the novel as centering "on the ultimately unsuccessful effort of a radically unstable masculinity to police itself and the tremendous ambivalence and strain this effort produces in the Southern community." Drawing on Marilyn Butler's notion of "gender trouble" or culturally unintelligible behavior that reminds us of the constructed nature of gender identity and French feminist theory, Watson contends that all of the novel's major characters are victims of and participants in the policing activities of Jefferson's gender guard. He focuses on Joe Christmas's hypermasculinity as "an uncanny extension of masculine sexual desire and opportunity that seems to the nervous populace of Yoknapatawpha to acknowledge neither law nor limit." Watson's sophisticated close reading of the novel argues that Christmas inspires panic and violence precisely because he represents "an uncanny, contradictory, consummatory incarnation of masculinity, an aggressive, predatory desire." Indeed, he transgresses the incest taboo, inspires homosexual panic and miscegenation fears, and practices conventional masculine heterosexuality out of wedlock. Watson thus reads Percy Grimm's vigilantism as attempts to establish his own masculine identity and to remasculinize Jefferson, which has been threatened with encroaching feminization. His castration of Christmas thus seeks to delimit Joe's identity by fixing his gender by means of fixing his sex.

In her overly long "Knowing and Remembering: *Light in August* as Readerly/Writerly Text" (*RWT* 1: 35–65) Irene Visser contends that Faulkner's novel is a text that meets both of Barthes's terms. Far from being a flaw as some have pointed out, the book's multiple and disparate plotlines are a "structural device" that prompts "the reader to construct coherence and, in so doing, to co-create the novel." While indebted to reader-response theory, Visser's methodology deliberately eschews a socialized or historicized notion of readers for an abstract "overarching intersubjective construct without chance aspects of individual dispositions." Essentially, she believes that the reader must assimilate the novel's many disruptive reversals of narrative time and action, its apparently incomplete and unresolved conclusion, and its frequent repetitions of key words and phrases into "a consistent and coherent vision of Joe Christmas' character and tragedy." In particular, Visser demonstrates that the often critically observed "link between darkness, despair, revulsion and the smell of women and negroes remains a strong emotive factor in [Christmas's] subconscious" and that Christmas learns a stoic masculinity that stresses inflexible resistance in order to maintain one's integrity. Some may bristle at her insistence that the prostitute Bobby and Joanna Burden might have released him from the circle of rejection and violence that has ensnared him since childhood but that they fail to do so. More importantly, the essay's emphasis on seeking consistency and coherence in the narrative, despite its reader-response theoretical foundation, seems haunted by formalism.

J. Hillis Miller's "Ideology and Topography in Faulkner's *Absalom, Absalom!*" (*Faulkner and Ideology*, pp. 253–76) draws on Marx, Althusser, and de Man's notions of ideology to examine how the novel's characters "come to be what they are as the result of the impingement on them of various ideological forces." He argues that the ideological errors about the real material conditions of characters' existence are passed down the generations in the novel by means of storytelling. In the most stimulating part of the essay Miller asks whether any escape from this ideological domination is possible in the novel and in our reading of it. In effect, he sets forth an ethics of reading in which the reader is morally responsible for the interpretation he or she actively constructs from reading the entire text and the actions that may result from that interpretation. Part of such an ethical reading must pay attention to how ideology and subjectivity are "embodied . . . in all the material changes men and women have made" to the landscape in the novel. Curiously, Miller has little to say in the essay on the different topographies of *Absalom* and their ideological implications. The essay also seems seriously flawed by a lack of interest in anything that earlier readers have said on the subject. The predictable result is that Miller often repeats in compelling prose what has been said before.

The late Jim Hinkle's *Reading Faulkner: "The Unvanquished"* (Miss.) has been completed by Robert McCoy and forms one of the year's entries in the series of glossaries and commentaries on Faulkner's fiction that Hinkle himself originally conceived. It explains, identifies, and comments on elements of the novel that readers may find unfamiliar or difficult, and it includes a chronology of the book.

vi Individual Works, 1940–1949

In "Faulkner's Real Estate: Land and Literary Speculation in *The Hamlet*" (*MissQ* 48: 443–57) Joseph Urgo delivers yet another imaginative, wholly original, and highly readable essay. This one takes as its starting point the transformation of the worthless Old Frenchman place into a valuable piece of real estate by means of Flem's machinations, and it argues that "*The Hamlet* embodies a form of landed-capitalist aesthetics" and that Faulkner here "articulates a sense that literary value might be

understood in terms of property, as real estate." Throughout the essay
Urgo draws parallels between Flem's role as a structural speculator who
turns land into property by concentrating on what the land might mean
to others and Faulkner's literary program for northern Mississippi: "the
transformation of a piece of property . . . into something mapped, divided into narrative lots, and yielding literary exchange value." Though
speculative, the essay's attention to Faulkner's role as a literary entrepre-
neur sketches in some of the less visible connections between capitalism
and modernism, thus providing a much-needed counterweight to critical representations of Faulkner as an ardently subversive detractor of
capitalism.

Neil Watson's "The 'Incredibly Loud . . . Miss-fire': A Sexual Reading
of *Go Down, Moses*" (*FJ* 9, i–ii [1993–94]: 113–23) explores frustrated
and consummated human sexuality as the source of "much of the novel's
dramatic and symbolic force." Watson connects the book's failed male/
female relationships, both black and white, to its devaluation of procreation and marginalization of women. Although he says next to nothing
about critics who have dealt with this subject, Watson intriguingly
explores the book's "subtext of homoerotic desire that underlies a male-
dominated cultural exchange." In a world where both taboo male/male
and "normal" heterosexual pairings fail to occur and where prescribed
male bonding clashes with proscribed homosexuality, a celibate bach-
elorhood becomes the only alternative.

Louise Westling asserts in her useful "Women, Landscape, and the
Legacy of Gilgamesh in *Absalom, Absalom!* and *Go Down, Moses*" (*MissQ*
48: 501–21) that the archaic masculinist "equation of woman and landscape is a premise that lies behind all of Faulkner's writing about Yoknapatawpha County"; she explores the revulsion from women and blacks
expressed by Faulkner's men and occasionally by him in relation to his
representation of the "historical and ethical relation of human beings to
the earth and its life." For Westling, the demonizing of women by
Faulkner's men reflects their attempt to disguise and evade their own
complicity in "the displacement of another people on the land and the
ravishing of an existing ecosystem for their own gain." After some
remarks about Quentin's masculinized retelling of Miss Rosa's story in
Absalom and Sutpen's biography as a collective sympathetic masculine
effort, Westling turns to a penetrating discussion of Faulkner's dramati-
zation of "the hysterical extremes of masculine revulsion, the ruthlessness
and violence of male aggression against land and women and dark-

skinned peoples, [and] the devastation caused by masculine 'heroism' "
in *Go Down, Moses*. Specifically, she argues that Faulkner demonstrates
"the bankruptcy of Isaac McCaslin's code of renunciation and [reveals]
its complicity with those who have destroyed the land and degraded its
inhabitants." Like other critics in recent years, Westling thus reverses the
earlier critical tendency to idealize Ike. Westling is at her best when
discussing *Go Down, Moses* and "the deep, submerged history of masculine identity defined through active antagonism" to women and land,
but the connections she traces in her essay between the Gilgamesh epic
and Faulkner's work strike me as too general. A more important problem, perhaps, is that Westling treats not *Go Down, Moses* but only "The
Old People," "The Bear," and "Delta Autumn," a kind of *Go Down,
Moses* lite, without offering a rationale for this limited selection. After all,
other stories in the work also explore masculine interactions with women
and land.

In "Molly's Vision: Lost Cause Ideology and Genesis in Faulkner's *Go
Down, Moses*" (*Faulkner and Ideology*, pp. 277–96) Glen Meeter intriguingly focuses on Molly Beauchamp as a prophetic visionary who
conflates several Old Testament stories. In a typological reading of the
biblical allusions in the novel, Meeter teases out the significance of
Molly's chant concerning her executed grandson Butch Beauchamp; she
and Lucas and Butch "represent the line of birthright" to the McCaslin
land figured as Canaan, while Roth Edmonds's "claim to the promised
land . . . comes to him through her, his foster mother." Ike's repudiation
of his inheritance, on the other hand, is founded on a competing story,
that of the Fall with man's original sin as one of "trying to own and tame
the land." But this repudiation is tainted by its association with the
moribund exclusionary ritual of the hunt and his fear of miscegenation
as divine retribution. For Meeter, the book's meaning arises from the
tension between these two visions: Ike is allowed to make his case
powerfully, but Molly is given the last word. Therein lies the problematic
nature of Meeter's argument; to find it persuasive, one has to accept that
Faulkner would place a dialectic at the heart of the book that stresses the
primacy of Molly's vision for the McCaslin land over Ike's and yet fail so
completely to give Molly anything remotely approaching equal time,
space, or dialogue.

Unlike recent work by Susan Donaldson and Dawn Trouard that
characterizes Faulkner's appendix to *The Sound and the Fury*, written for
inclusion in Malcolm Cowley's *Portable Faulkner*, as a progressive rewrit-

ing of the novel in terms of gender, Thadious M. Davis's "Reading Faulkner's Compson Appendix: Writing History from the Margins" (*Faulkner and Ideology*, pp. 238–52) describes the piece as a conservative revision that emphasizes the Compson patriarchal line at the expense of women and blacks whose roles are diminished. She mounts a complex biographical argument that Faulkner's valorizing of masculinity and of masculine activities such as ownership, property, warfare, and enterprises of competitive exchange in the appendix reflects his response to his sense of himself as a middle-aged, marginalized Southern writer. His appendix is thus "a white masculinist construction of history." Curiously, Davis makes no mention of Faulkner's entries on Quentin or Benjy Compson that might undermine her emphasis on exaggerated masculinity in the appendix. This is clearly an ambitious, speculative essay, but Davis overlooks the numerous ways in which the genealogy critiques the rise and fall of the House of Compson and by extension the white male South and perhaps white America. Philip Dubuisson Castille also treats the appendix in "Compson and Sternwood: William Faulkner's 'Appendix' and *The Big Sleep*" (*PostS* 13, iii [1994]: 54–61). Despite its title, the essay treats equally the influence of *The Sound and the Fury* on Faulkner's screenplay for *The Big Sleep* and of the screenplay on the appendix. Castille provides an excellent specific illustration of how Faulkner drew on his fiction for his work in Hollywood when he argues that Faulkner drew on Jason Compson's misogyny and "mixed emotions of arousal and hatred" of Miss Quentin for particulars of the relationship between Philip Marlowe and Carmen Sternwood. His contention that Faulkner's screenwriting skills in the 1940s influenced the cinematic technique of the appendix seems less persuasive, given the critical consensus that Faulkner's genealogy rather than a purely visual technique foregrounds his later, more discursive prose style.

vii Individual Works, 1950–1962

Judith Bryant Wittenberg's suggestive "Temple Drake and *La parole pleine*" (*MissQ* 48: 421–41) is an intertextual, even dialectical reading of *Requiem for a Nun* and Lacan's "Function and Field of Speech and Language in Psychoanalysis," both published in the early 1950s. In *Requiem*, Temple undergoes a Faulknerian "talking cure" and moves toward self-understanding, subjectivity, and a fully individualized speech in which the events of one's past become ordered rather than contingent.

But this movement "is ultimately constricted by the codes and conventions of *langue* as well as by the deficiencies of her interlocutor-analyst," Gavin Stevens. Thus, a patriarchal society and a flawed talking cure take their toll on Temple's rhetorical versatility and ability to narrate lucidly, which instead give way to a personal speech that is "limited, fragmentary, and inconclusive." Because of *Requiem's* explicit references to *Sanctuary,* Wittenberg examines Faulkner's treatment of these issues in the earlier novel in which Temple's "partial and qualified accession to the realm of linguistic conventions and her relative lack of individualized speech" show that she has yet to "complete the acquisition of *langue* and pass through to *parole* to arrive at a state of integrated psycho-linguistic selfhood." Wittenberg is very good on the empty speech and arrested linguistic development of Temple and on Horace Benbow as Temple's failed interlocutor-analyst whose understanding of Temple is compromised by his own problems. An argument against reading these two works separated by more than 20 years as intimately connected aesthetically, intellectually, and biographically, however, might see this approach as ahistorical, with a whiff of the totalizing impulse behind it. Given Faulkner's frequently hazy memory of the specifics of his earlier novels, it seems more likely that *Sanctuary* played a minor role in the genesis of *Requiem.* Such a criticism might have been disabled had Wittenberg pointed out and accounted for the many differences between the two novels. While she is right to reject earlier uncritical approval of Horace and Gavin, she disposes of Faulkner's ambivalent attitudes about them too easily for my taste since there are times when it seems uncomfortably difficult to separate their opinions from those of the implied and biographical authors. Nevertheless, this readable essay has much of interest.

David C. Cody's "Faulkner, Wells, and the 'End of Man'" (*JML* 18 [1993]: 465–74) tells us far more about H. G. Wells and turn-of-the-century pessimism about entropy and evolution than about Faulkner, but Cody does make a persuasive argument that Faulkner's Nobel Prize speech is indebted to, perhaps even an optimistic response to, the despairing penultimate chapter of Wells's *The Time Machine.*

viii The Stories

Less a critical work than a useful resource, Diane Brown Jones's thorough *A Reader's Guide to the Short Stories of William Faulkner* (Hall, 1994) covers 31 of the 42 stories in *Collected Stories*. Because Faulkner carefully arranged the stories into the various sections of the volume, Jones has decided to maintain the integrity of the sections by including the stories in "The Country," "The Village," "The Wilderness," and "The Middle Ground." Space considerations lead her to exclude the stories in "The Wasteland" and "Beyond," even though this meant omitting important pieces like "Carcassonne." This format also means that important published and unpublished short stories that Faulkner eventually incorporated into his novels have been excluded. Still, this strategy enables her to discuss the remaining stories more extensively; for example, she devotes 55 pages to "A Rose for Emily." With the exception of most initial reviews, each chapter summarizes everything substantial published in English on a short story under the headings of publication history; circumstances of composition; sources and influences; relation to other Faulkner works; interpretation and criticism; and works cited. I especially appreciated Jones's attention to the critical significance of the extant textual evidence concerning the composition and revision of the stories.

Lawrence R. Rodgers's "'We all said, "she will kill herself'": The Narrator/Detective in William Faulkner's 'A Rose for Emily'" (*Clues* 16: 117–29) examines "Emily" as an early example of the detective figure in Faulkner's fiction and of his "lifelong interest in shaping his fiction around the theme of detection." Rodgers's argument that the unnamed narrator functions as a detective figure who represents the community, all of whom are unaware of their own complicity in Miss Emily's murder of Homer Barron, is vitiated by a selective awareness of scholarship on the subject, an uncritical acceptance of Faulkner's own comments on his work, and unsubstantiated generalizations about Faulkner's short story composition habits.

University of Texas at Arlington

10 Fitzgerald and Hemingway

Albert J. DeFazio III

Several works of lasting significance grace a year where quality prevails over quantity and serious academic studies, especially, distinguish themselves from the usual fare. Signal contributions include Miriam B. Mandel's annotations of Hemingway's novels; James L. W. West III's critical edition of *This Side of Paradise;* Robert and Helen H. Roulston's survey of Fitzgerald's short fiction; James Nagel's handy anthology of criticism on *The Sun Also Rises;* and Frederic J. Svoboda and Joseph J. Waldmeir's published proceedings of an especially productive conference. Editor Susan F. Beegel's *Hemingway Review* continues admirably in its professional and innovative vein, offering a dozen articles, as many notes and reviews, and lively correspondence. Newsletters for each author not only provide notes and notices but substantial commentary. Charles M. Oliver, editor of the *Hemingway Newsletter,* excerpts pertinent discussion from Jack Jobst's electronic discussion group; and Ruth Prigozy and the other editors of the *Fitzgerald Newsletter* include detailed reviews of recent publications. Solid studies of themes and techniques are joined by provocative examinations which test the psychological politics and ideology of *The Great Gatsby* and which assess *The Sun Also Rises* for its treatment of nihilism. The critical scope for both authors dilates a bit to include several of Fitzgerald's underrepresented short stories, Hemingway's *Across the River and into the Trees,* "Today Is Friday," the "Jimmy Breen" manuscript, and the excised coda from *The Sun Also Rises.*

i Text, Letters, the Archives, and Bibliography

"Going . . . going . . ." are the exclusive rights to publish writing from the 1920s. Fitzgeraldians continue to meet the challenge of producing critical

editions; this year's accomplishment is *This Side of Paradise*, ed. James
L. W. West III. Though new to the Cambridge Edition of the Works of
F. Scott Fitzgerald, West has been at this task, in a sense, for nearly 20
years: his dissertation collated the seven "significant textual witnesses"
and his *The Making of* This Side of Paradise documents its composition
process (see *ALS 1983*, pp. 173–74). The fruits of his long association with
the text reveal themselves in the notes, the apparatus, and his editorial
policy, which discovers authorial intention by privileging "editorial judgment and historical imagination" over genealogy. West's ambition is to
produce "the book that Fitzgerald meant to write"; such a "text is
eclectic—not the text of a single document but rather a construction,
influenced by editorial judgment, of a text that never existed before."
West reifies the abstraction by establishing the text according to the
principles advanced by W. W. Greg and Fredson Bowers and extended by
G. Thomas Tanselle; specifically, the text reflects Fitzgerald's "*active*
intentions" and incorporates his "*horizontal* extension of those intentions between MS and first print, and beyond." Because the "extant
witnesses" share authority, the Cambridge edition has no copy-text.
Even the manuscript bears 156 proposed alterations, made by Katherine
Tighe at Fitzgerald's request: the author accepted all but 10; West rejects
another eight "as not reflecting Fitzgerald's *active* intentions." West's
introduction includes examples of emendations and refusals; his thorough apparatus inscribes the choices he encountered. In the end, the
Cambridge text is "purged of the misspellings and other errors that
disfigured the original edition," a sensible approach that may one
day have us reading about Eckleburg's *irises* rather than his *retinas*.
Matthew J. Bruccoli has established a text of *Tender is the Night: A
Romance* (Johnson) that "reproduces the editor's marked copy of the first
printing" of the novel, "providing the emendations required for a critical
edition" and is intended to be used with his forthcoming *Reader's Companion to F. Scott Fitzgerald's* Tender is the Night (So. Car.); appendices
include a statement of editorial policy as well as an explanation of the
novel's time scheme. The *Manuscript Society News* (16: 63–66) reminds
us that the University of South Carolina's Thomas Cooper Library has
become the repository for Matthew J. Bruccoli's extraordinary collection
of Fitzgerald.

Peter Carroll's "Ernest Hemingway, Screenwriter: New Letters on *For
Whom the Bell Tolls*" (*AR* 53: 261–83) publishes five "new" letters from
1942 that were seen but not directly quoted by biographer Carlos Baker.

These letters address Hemingway's concern that "fatal ignorance, bad writing and bad construction" mar the screenplay of *Bell*. Addressed to his Hollywood agent, Donald Friede, but intended for screenwriter Dudley Nichols, these lively epistles insist on numerous revisions to the Cooper-Bergman film so that it, like the novel, would "show what men and women would die for" and perhaps be "extremely valuable in our fight against Fascism."

"News from the Hemingway Collection" (*HN* 14, ii: 142–43; 15, i: 129–30) by Stephen Plotkin of the John F. Kennedy Library details openings, acquisitions, and grants; this year's celebrated feature is 15 linear feet of "The Mary Hemingway Papers," which "record Mary's life after Hemingway's death in 1961" and include the manuscript of *How It Was*. Plotkin also provides an archivist's perspective on Hemingway's Finca Vigía in "Library Curator Attends Hemingway Conference in Cuba" (*Kennedy Library Newsletter* no. 5). In "[Carlos] Baker Materials Now Available" (*Hemingway Newsletter* 30: 3) Barbara Volz announces additional openings of "biographical files and working papers" at Princeton, though some restrictions apply. A useful tool that compiles more than 1,500 Hemingway items and reviews the author's critical reputation in France is Geneviève Hily-Mane's *Ernest Hemingway in France: 1926–1994: A Comprehensive Bibliography* (CIRLEP), which includes French translations, articles, and treatments of reputation. I contribute bibliographies to *HN* (14, ii: 136–41; 15, i: 117–28) and the *Fitzgerald Newsletter* (5: 17–22).

ii Biography

With the exception of Frances Kroll Ring's "The Resurrection of F. Scott Fitzgerald" (*Fitzgerald Newsletter* 5: 1–4) this year's biographies are more "around" than "about" Fitzgerald. As a means of hanging on and of retelling a tale, progeny of minicelebrities Scottie Fitzgerald Smith and Sheilah Graham heave their hearts into their mouths and produce a pair of hefty biographies. Robert Westbrook's *Intimate Lies: F. Scott Fitzgerald and Sheilah Graham: Her Son's Story* (Harper) focuses on the "anatomy of a love affair," so his task is finite, his tale dramatic, pace quick. Graham's association with Scott sadly ended at "an inconclusive moment"; nonetheless, Westbrook reports, he left her with two cherished gifts—"self-confidence" and "a lingering sense of poetry." Eleanor Lanahan's *Scottie: The Daughter of . . .* (Harper) casts a cradle-to-grave biographical net.

The sea of information from which she draws—including 64 boxes of her mother's papers, a diary written for the children, her own experience, and various published and unpublished sources—yields up plenty of raw material, including generous snatches of Scottie's own writing. Her mother's life filled with conventions and candidates and compositions and celebrations, Lanahan depicts Scottie as the consummate "giver." Scottie and Sheila, who became dear friends, shared much, including a challenging childhood and a turbulent adulthood; in the end, they reveal themselves to be "survivors," no mean feat, all things considered. Author of *Against the Current: As I Remember F. Scott Fitzgerald* (see *ALS 1986*, p. 161), Ring, weary of biographies that emphasize alcohol and yoke Scott with responsibility for Zelda's illness, recalls with admiration Fitzgerald's passion for reading, writing, and growing as well as his communications with Zelda even after prospects for her recovery or their reuniting had waned.

In "Gone Fishin'" Jack Jobst details Hemingway's acquaintance with Kalaska, the setting of "The Light of the World" and "The Battler," by revisiting the sites, interviewing residents, and drawing on Hemingway's journal of his fishing trip with Lewis Clarahan in the summer of 1916 (*Michigan History* 79, vi: 45–49). Peter Hays corrects the notion advanced by Bernard Drabeck and Helen Ellis in *Archibald MacLeish: Reflections* (1986) that Dr. Carl Weiss treated Hemingway's skylight-induced head wound in March 1928; Weiss did not arrive in Paris until June 1929 ("Huey Long's Assassin and Hemingway," *Hemingway Newsletter* 29: 4).

Two personal reminiscences testify to the physical and spiritual diminishment of the aging Hemingway; two others speculate about the demons that drove him. Wallace Paul Conklin's "My Day with Hemingway" (*AmerHeritage* 46, viii: 38–40) describes Conklin's visit to Cuba in early 1955 and remembers the author as lonely but eager for companionship, worried about finances but due $4,000 in Nobel Prize money, and so pained by injuries sustained in the plane crashes in Africa that he stood up but once during a visit of several hours. In December 1957 Norman Lewis pocketed a letter of introduction from Jonathan Cape, Hemingway's English publisher, and at the behest of Ian Fleming sojourned to Cuba to see if Hemingway was somehow connected to the Cuban revolutionaries. In "Hemingway in Cuba" (*Granta* 50: 209–24) Lewis quotes his report to Fleming: the man "no longer cares to hold opinions, because his life has lost its taste . . ." and "to meet him was a shattering experience of the kind likely to sabotage ambition. . . . ." Scott Donaldson pieces together the causes of the author's physical and psychological travails in "Hemingway and Suicide" (*SR* 103, ii: 287–95): genetic inheritance, accumulated injuries, and, finally, his inability to enjoy his "ultimate reason to live"—which was to write. But even when he was writing well and often, notes Peter L. Hays in "Hemingway's Clinical Depression: A Speculation" (*HN* 14, ii: 50–63), photographs and correspondence from the 1920s suggest that fluctuations in his weight are symptomatic of the onset of his bipolar (manic-depressive) mood disorder. Surely a gauge of our interest in psychoanalytic inquiry is Robert J. Craig's review-article ("Hemingway 'Analyzed,' " *Psychological Reports* 76: 1059–79), which assesses seven published analyses by Lawrence Kubie, Philip Young, Richard Drinnon, Irvin Yalom, Jacqueline Tavernier-Courbin, Gerry Brenner, and Philip Scharfer, providing a brief summary and commentary that illuminates points of contention; Young's views are described as "most correct," although he "places too heavy an emphasis on Posttraumatic Stress Disorder symptoms." Craig finds "general agreement" that there exists "incomplete but reasonable speculative evidence that Hemingway may have been manic-depressive."

iii Sources, Influences, Parallels

Barbara Hochman's rich reading of Nick/Fitzgerald's "self-conscious examinations of the illusion-making process" in "Disembodied Voices and Narrating Bodies in *The Great Gatsby*" (*Style* 28 [1994]: 95–118) proposes to do for *Gatsby* what Peter Brooks has done for Walter Benjamin's "The Storyteller," which is to view the novel "as an expression of discomfort with 'the decontextualization of discourse' and attempt 'to rediscover certain contextual coordinates of narrative in narrative voice. . . .' " Focusing on the hidden-and-conspicuous seams between the narrating bodies, she discovers "Fitzgerald's uncertainty about the extent to which the time-bound process of 'excretion'—the signs of a writer's craft—are hidden or accessible within the finished narrative." W. L. Godshalk's "*The Great Gatsby* and Edward Thomas's 'Rain' " (*ELN* 32, iv: 75–78) posits Thomas's line "Blessed are the dead that the rain rains upon" as the source of the anonymous murmurer's quip "Blessed are the dead that the rain falls on" and speculates about the deviation. Dalton and Maryjean Gross in "Fitzgerald's *The Great Gatsby*" (*Expl* 53: 230–31) dub the same line "folk wisdom," most likely uttered by the postman who is "almost certainly an allusion" to *The Vegetable*'s "best postman in the world." Addressing mutual admiration and influence, Susan Wanlass's "An Easy Commerce: Specific Similarities Between the Writings of T. S. Eliot and F. Scott Fitzgerald" (*ELN* 32, iii: 58–69) identifies numerous lines and passages that suggest each author's indebtedness to the other.

Hemingway, too, saw modest advances in this category. Exploring a parallel is Ben Stoltzfus's "In Another Time: Proust, Hemingway and the Fourth Dimension" (*IFR* 22: 15–20), which examines "time" in relation to Proust's thematic treatment of "meaning" and Hemingway's "love." Michael Szalay's "Inviolate Modernism: Hemingway, Stein, and Tzara" (*MLQ* 56: 457–85) considers how the three create "textual" and "personal" identity, suggesting that for Hemingway "textual identity," which can be absolute, "represents an escape from human vulnerability," suggested by Harry Morgan's missing arm or Jake's unfortunate wound. Robert Paul Lamb's meandering "Observations on Hemingway, Suggestiveness, and the Modern Short Story" (*MQ* 37: 11–26) actually surveys the techniques of several writers (among them Flaubert, Chekhov, Nabokov, James, and Flannery O'Connor) and discusses compression, diction, and the rendering of emotion in "Indian Camp." Comparing two works that contain representations of the female body in pain, *A Farewell to Arms* and *None Turn Back,* Bonnie Wilde Cunningham's "Autobiography and Anaesthesia: Ernest Hemingway, Storm Jameson, and Me" (*WS* 24: 615–29) argues that Hemingway "confuses life and art by transferring, gendering, and denying the pain that flows from his life to his art" whereas Jameson "intertwines life and art, locating, validating, and affirming her own pain in her art."

Among the source or influence studies, Dennis Ryan's "Dating Hemingway's Early Style/Parsing Gertrude Stein's Modernism" (*JAmS* 29: 229–40) conducts a stylistic analysis of "Up in Michigan" and concludes that its debt to Stein is "enormous." Christoph Kuhn's "Hemingway and Nietzsche: The Context of Ideas" (*Nietzsche in American Literature and Thought,* pp. 223–38) is an influence study that also addresses the complex unity of *In Our Time.* Kuhn recognizes the "pervasive Nietzschean attitudes and ideas" in Hemingway's collection, seeing the tension between the interchapters and the stories as a reflection of the contradictory Apollonian and Dionysian forces discussed in Nietzsche's *The Birth of Tragedy,* "a book whose insights anticipated if not shaped the modern mind." Lisa Tyler's "Passion and Grief in *A Farewell to Arms:* Ernest

Hemingway's Retelling of *Wuthering Heights*" (*HN* 14, ii: 79–96) is a solid source study which "makes Catherine sound less like a geisha girl and more like a Romantic heroine." Tyler's analysis "places the novel squarely in the Romantic tradition" and "suggests that Hemingway was more open to the writing of women writers (and indeed feminist women writers) than might be expected." In "*A Farewell to Arms* and Hemingway's Protest Stance: To Tell the Truth Without Screaming" (*HN* 15, i: 72–86) William Dow offers that "Hemingway appropriated in *A Farewell to Arms* [Henri] Barbusse's method of '*constater*,' his technique of suspending protest in 'poetry,' and his creation of a distinctly modern antiwar consciousness"; analyzing the literary, biographical, and intertextual links between *Farewell* and *Le feu,* Dow concludes that both works "demand that the reader move to an intuitive, atemporal mode of inquiry in order to understand the protest patterns and language of his world."

Examining Hemingway's influence is Paul Eisenstein's "Finding Lost Generations: Recovering Omitted History in *Winter in the Blood*" (*MELUS* 19, iii [1994]: 3–16), which notices James Welch's practice of omission—presumably learned from Hemingway, whom he studied and admired—and suggests how both authors use the technique for thematic purposes. With reference to *A Farewell to Arms,* Kurt Fickert's "Two Characters in Search of an Author: [Uwe] Johnson's *Zwei Ansichten*" (*Monatshefte* 87: 187–202) remarks the novels' technical and thematic similarities that allow the star-crossed protagonists to gain validity and the narrators to win trust.

iv Criticism

a. Full-Length Studies: Fitzgerald　A decade ago this chapter could lament with cause that "Fitzgerald's short stories have never received the attention they deserve"; since then, Alice Hall Petry (see *ALS 1989,* pp. 160–61), Bryant Magnum and John Kuehl (*ALS 1991,* pp. 156–57), and Stephen Potts (*ALS 1993,* pp. 133–34) have contributed to the enterprise begun by John A. Higgins's book-length treatment of a quarter-century ago (*ALS 1971,* pp. 128–29) and sustained by Jackson R. Bryer's collection of essays (*ALS 1982,* p. 169). This year boasts another full-length treatment by Robert Roulston and Helen H. Roulston, *The Winding Road to West Egg: The Artistic Development of F. Scott Fitzgerald* (Bucknell), whose ambition is to read all of the stories written before

Gatsby and, explicating their themes and techniques, articulate their relationship to the novel. This plan works for Fitzgerald, tireless worker and reworker of his published and unpublished lines, although—despite a very brief epilogue which acknowledges that life and writing existed for Fitzgerald after *Gatsby*—the novice reader might be left with the impression that it was Fitzgerald, and not Gatsby, who met his demise at the novel's conclusion. The Roulstons' text, eminently readable and sensible, measures the stories against one another and *Gatsby*, demonstrating that "growth" for Fitzgerald "was more a process of accretion than of displacement." As they trace advances in his narrative skills, they foray into biography and pursue sources and influences; likewise they engage in an intelligent dialogue with existing scholarship. Their contribution is not to take us deep into the great eight stories (Kuehl) or to pursue a thesis (Magnum and Potts) or to stimulate interest in the neglected (Bryer) so much as it is to show us the accuracy of Fitzgerald's assessment of himself as a "plugger" rather than "a natural writer like Ernest Hemingway." We have had for some time the example of *This Side of Paradise* to reveal Fitzgerald's cut-and-paste composition process; *Winding Road* illustrates how again and again Fitzgerald experimented with favorite themes and techniques, winnowing and sharpening his perceptions—even mining his own past (to wit: "music drifting into my window from the Katsbys' house") to produce the "opulent synthesis" that is *Gatsby*. While the Roulstons certainly achieve their purpose, their study needs to be joined by others with diverse ambitions and methodologies. Assessing *The International Theme in F. Scott Fitzgerald's Literature* (Peter Lang) Elizabeth A. Weston stretches a useful essay into a tenuous monograph. Her placement of Fitzgerald's work in light of texts by James, Twain, Hawthorne, Hemingway, and Wharton will prove useful to undergraduates, but a lengthy chapter given to biography and reticence in lieu of analysis limits the usefulness of this study.

b. Full-Length Studies: Hemingway Admirable and indispensable, Miriam B. Mandel's *Reading Hemingway: The Facts in the Fictions* (Scarecrow) annotates the people/characters, animals, and cultural constructs in the nine novels. A user-friendly reference tool, it arranges entries alphabetically by novel and backs them with thorough notes and an index. The service that Mandel has provided for students and researchers—especially in light of the absence of scholarly editions—is immeasurable. In contrast to Mandel's massive effort—450 pages of annotations, 65 pages of explanatory notes, and 30 pages of works cited—this next item comes to us without notes or a bibliography. Frank Kyle's slim volume, *Hemingway and the Post-Narrative Condition: An Unauthorized Commentary of* The Sun Also Rises (Univ. Editions) claims that the novel is a response to "the post-Narrative condition," which was brought about by the death of the Grand Narratives in World War I. In a chapter-by-chapter reading, Kyle explains how the novel models techniques for "surviv[ing] meaningfully" while bathed in the post-Narrative condition, which is nihilism. This commentary began as a conference paper and the casualness of its conversational tone is amplified by the author's parenthetical dilations throughout the text. While the study enjoys a few refreshing moments, it is essentially a monologue, written with reference to a single secondary text on Hemingway.

c. Collections   Introduced by Frederic J. Svoboda and coedited with Joseph J. Waldmeir, *Hemingway: Up in Michigan Perspectives* (Mich. State) gathers two dozen essays from the 1991 "Up in Michigan II" conference, most of them splendid, all of them worthwhile. The first gathering explores connections to Michigan, commencing with Waring Jones's "A Moveable Michigan" (pp. 7–14), a warm welcoming that reminds us of how Michigan echoes through Hemingway's canon. Svoboda's "False Wilderness: Northern Michigan as Created in the Nick Adams Stories" (pp. 15–22) tells us that it is the "*memory* of the frontier," both physical and moral—and not the actual/historical thing—that Hemingway celebrates. In "Hemingway Bids Goodbye to Youth: Childhood's End in Seney" (pp. 23–28) Jack Jobst demonstrates how "Big Two-Hearted River" expresses the end of young Hemingway's "unattached bachelor youth." Paul Strong's "The First Nick Adams Stories" (pp. 29–36) discusses the "pretty good unity" of *In Our Time*. William Braasch Watson's "The Doctor and the Doctor's Son: Immortalities in 'Indian Camp'" (pp. 37–45) pits physician father against artistic son, whose art helps him to achieve a kind of immortality. Larry E. Grimes's "William James and 'The Doctor and the Doctor's Wife'" (pp. 47–57) articulates the philosopher's dichotomy between "healthy-minded" religion (linked to Grace and the doctor's wife) and the "sick soul" (represented by Clarence and the doctor) and suggests that the doctor finds comfort in a third option—"life without grace or guts seems possible" as Nick invites his father to observe the squirrels at story's end. With characteristic wit, H. R. Stoneback's "'Nothing Was Ever Lost': Another

Look at 'That Marge Business' " (pp. 59–76) regrades the rocky biocritical road of Bump's depiction. Frank Scafella's " 'Nothing' in 'Big Two-Hearted River' " (pp. 77–90) confronts the double significance of "nothing," which is simultaneously an "absence and a presence in Nick's thinking" and which is essential to mending a heart and restoring a memory devastated by war. And in "The Fantasies of Omnipotence and Powerlessness: Commemoration in Hemingway's 'Fathers and Sons' " (pp. 91–101) Erik Nakjavani brings Freud and Sartre to bear on Nick's tribute to his father as well as his growth as a man and an artist. The anthology's second part, "Leaving Michigan Behind," contains a single tantalizing conversation about the content and quality of the "Jimmy Breen" manuscript, entitled "Hemingway and the Limits of Biography: An Exchange on the 'Jimmy Breen' Manuscript Between Michael Reynolds and Linda Wagner-Martin, with Audience Comment" (pp. 105–26). The final section, "Hemingway in the World," addresses a half-dozen Hemingway texts. In "Narrational Values and Robert Cohn in *The Sun Also Rises*" (pp. 129–36) James Nagel argues that Cohn's "destruction of Jake's therapeutic construct," rather than Cohn's religion, prompts his harsh treatment. Not so, claims Wolfgang E. H. Rudat, whose "Anti-Semitism in *The Sun Also Rises:* Traumas, Jealousies, and the Genesis of Cohn" (pp. 137–47) repeats the charge, attributing it to "a combination of unresolved inner conflicts." Linda Wagner-Martin's "The Secrecies of the Public Hemingway" (pp. 149–56) reviews evidence suggesting Hemingway's indebtedness to Vicente Blasco Ibánez, the Spanish author. Robert W. Lewis's "Manners and Morals in *A Farewell to Arms*" (pp. 157–65) illustrates how Catherine "epitomizes the transformation of what may at first glance appear to be merely superficial forms of social intercourse into radical behavior that demonstrates how one may live and die well and rightly." In "Hemingway's *A Farewell to Arms:* The World Beyond Oak Park and Idealism" (pp. 167–75) Robert A. Martin equates the loss of this idealism with Henry's appreciation of a nihilistic perspective. Bickford Sylvester's "The Sexual Impasse to Romantic Order in Hemingway's Fiction: *A Farewell to Arms, Othello,* 'Orpen,' and the Hemingway Canon" (pp. 177–87) considers the tension between romance and sexuality. Questioning her sympathy for Margot and the lion, Mark Spilka's "Nina Baym's Benevolent Reading of the Macomber Story: An Epistolary Response" (pp. 189–201) challenges the logic of Baym's reading in her article "Actually, I Felt Sorry for the Lion" (see *ALS 1990*, p. 177). In a rare treatment of "Hemingway's 'Today Is

Friday' as Ballad of the Goodly Fere" (pp. 203–11) Warren Bennett links Hemingway's intentions to Ezra Pound's in composing "Ballad of the Goodly Fere": both seek "the masculinization of Jesus of Nazareth," which "contributes to an understanding of Hemingway's code hero or exemplar figure." Paul Smith's "Love and Death in Hemingway's Spanish Novel" (pp. 213–20) argues that the thematic center of the novel "rests somewhere within a complex analogy between the ways of death and the ways of love" and discovers "a pattern in which the ways of dying—suicide, sacrifice, killing—are associated with, and may initiate, a way of loving, as a way of loving will finally initiate a way of dying." Allen Josephs pursues echoes of T. S. Eliot's "Burnt Norton" in "Love in *For Whom the Bell Tolls:* Hemingway's Undiscovered Country" (pp. 221–28), which details four aspects of the undiscovered country—Spain, the novelized war, death, and love—the last of which is Hemingway's principal interest. Linda Patterson Miller's "Something in It for You: Role Models in *For Whom the Bell Tolls*" (pp. 229–39) considers Sara and Gerald Murphy as sources for Pilar and Pablo. Thomas Gould's " 'Anti-War Correspondence': Reshaping Death in the *For Whom the Bell Tolls* Manuscript" (pp. 241–48) uses several illustrations to demonstrate that the revision of scenes involving violent death, whether they are external narrative or internal monologue, typically involve expansive insertions which create a more "vivid, brutal, and realistic picture of war," reminding readers not only of the horrors of the Spanish Civil War but also of the prospective terror of Hitler's newly begun war in Europe. In "Reconsidering the Travesty of Himself: Another Look at *Across the River and into the Trees*" (pp. 249–64) Michael Seefeldt argues that readers have failed to appreciate the novel's allegory, character, and structure—starting points for a well-deserved revaluation. Robert E. Gajdusek's "The Suspended Woman in the Work of Ernest Hemingway" (pp. 265–74) observes the charged meaning of frozen or suspended women removed from the process of decay or rot who may be a sacrifice to art or mythically protected from fatal cycles of life. Providing closure to the volume is Kelli Larson's "Stepping into the Labyrinth: Fifteen Years of Hemingway Scholarship" (pp. 275–81), which discusses the critical canon of 1974–1989, praising recent innovations and fresh methodologies, damning repetitive and derivative studies.

James Nagel's introduction (pp. 1–31) to his *Critical Essays on Ernest Hemingway's* The Sun Also Rises (Hall) provides a staccato-paced overview of the initial reception and subsequent criticism of the novel that

"changed everything." Addressing 80 years of scholarship, Nagel's overview gives the new student an extraordinarily convenient starting point,
the wizened veteran a succinct review. A handy addition to the more
than 30 collections of criticism on Hemingway, the anthology selects
eight contemporary reviews—no need for more, given book-length collections of reviews by Robert O. Stephens (see *ALS 1977*, p. 168) and
Jeffrey Meyers (see *ALS 1982*, p. 167); and it settles on a dozen articles—
nine reprinted and three commissioned. All but three of the articles were
published since 1980 and represent growing interest in gender, cultural,
and manuscript studies, and by virtue of his conspicuous absence, a
waning preoccupation with the "code hero." The new essays include
Robert E. Fleming's "Second Thoughts: Hemingway's Postscript to *The
Sun Also Rises*" (pp. 163–69), which considers the newly discovered coda
to the novel and suggests that Hemingway "decided, at least for a time,
that the use of one's acquaintances did not do them any lasting harm";
Linda Patterson Miller's "Brett Ashley: The Beauty of It All" (pp. 170–
84), which places Brett at the center of the novel and observes that Jake
"uses parallel structures and mirroring devices that reveal Brett within a
larger emotional framework and emphasize the fact that appearances can
both deceive and destroy"; and Jane E. Wilson's "Good Old Harris in
The Sun Also Rises" (pp. 185–90), which argues that Harris is a "positive
force," "an affirmation of humane, natural values in contrast to the
degeneration that follows."

d. General Essays   In the lone Fitzgerald item, Charles R. Hearn's
"F. Scott Fitzgerald and the Popular Magazine Formula Story of the
Twenties" (*JACult* 18, iii: 33–40) surveys about 100 stories of the decade,
identifies their formulae, and considers how Fitzgerald worked within
and strained against the requirements of commercial fiction, succeeding
admirably on occasion but failing eventually to sustain his extraordinary
pace. Exciting to read but daunting to contemplate is Michael Reynolds's
"Prospects for the Study of Ernest Hemingway" (*RALS* 21: 1–15). Reynolds recognizes the substantial achievements in Hemingway studies
since—and in large part because of—the opening of the John F. Kennedy
Library in 1980: these include more than 30 scholarly books, a dozen
essay collections, and hundreds of articles. But the work of lifetimes
remains ahead, and to accomplish it Reynolds would arrange a quick
marriage between the scholarly imagination and the electronic mate that
we all must court if we are to accelerate the pace of our contributions. A

sampling of his proposed endeavors includes better bibliographies in hypertext; publishing Hemingway's canon on-line or on CD-ROM; nurturing our interest in textual studies so as to produce standard and variorum editions that are long overdue—Reynolds even fingers James L. W. West III for the task of grouping the "first generation of editors to work out the parameters of the problem"; and, perhaps most importantly, he extols the virtues of collaboration, imagination, and dedication. In a second general study, "Hemingway's *In Our Time:* The Biography of a Book" (*Modern American Short Story Sequences,* pp. 35–51), Reynolds identifies two non-narrative elements that lend coherence to *In Our Time;* it is both "a literary biography of an American male learning to write in the postwar period" and "a visual scrapbook of the age that spawned it."

e. Essays on Specific Works: Fitzgerald A pair of innovative book chapters and two notes on a single story merit brief notice. Lois Tyson's "The Romance of the Commodity: The Cancellation of Identity in F. Scott Fitzgerald's *Great Gatsby*" in her *Psychological Politics of the American Dream* (pp. 42–62) argues that "the American dream itself is a source of corruption"; that sympathy for Gatsby stems from readers' desires "to protect their own ideological investment and the American dream of their own"; and that the "seductive appeal with which the commodity is portrayed" is behind much of Gatsby's "emotional seduction of narrator Nick Carraway and of the many readers who rally to his cause." The American dream's "ideological power" seems extraordinary "in terms of its ability to seduce authors and critics" because *Gatsby* simultaneously critiques commodity psychology, by having Gatsby fail, and "repackages and markets that dream anew," by having many readers "continue to invest in Gatsby's dream." In "Corinthian Crooks Are Not Like You and Me: Mystery, Detection, and Crime in *The Great Gatsby*" (*Clues* 16: 35–45) W. Russel Gray examines the popular elements of mystery, detection, and crime and claims that the novel transcends them, becoming a "tragedy of manners."

In *The Politics of Exile,* whose thesis is that James and Fitzgerald must be reread in light of James Baldwin, Bryan R. Washington focuses first on Fitzgerald's co-opting or recontextualizing of James's primary preoccupations in "The Daisy Chain: *The Great Gatsby* and *Daisy Miller* or The Politics of Privacy" (pp. 35–54). Washington reads *Gatsby* as a revision of "Daisy Miller," focusing on thematic concerns that the authors shared: the extent to which the American female can civilize the American male; the notion that the United States is a land of innocents in need of experience available only in Europe; the paradoxical reverence for capital and dismissal of capitalism; and, most importantly, "the coming obliteration of the Anglo-Saxon." Just as James lamented "emancipation of the slaves" and "despaired at the ubiquitous presence in America of Jews," so too did Fitzgerald declare "war not only on white 'ethnics' but also on African Americans." A second chapter, " 'Communities' of Exiles: *Tender is the Night*" (pp. 55–69), views that novel as a narrative of "outrage and accusation" which suggests that white women and black men are "the hungriest predators" in a pack seeking to devour traditional America.

Peter L. Hays's "A Note on Moral Wavering in 'Babylon Revisited' " (*Fitzgerald Newsletter* 5: 9) observes "Charlie's wavering morality with his equally wavering itinerary in the opening paragraph of the story." Cecil D. Eby's "Fitzgerald's 'Babylon Revisited' " (*Expl* 53: 176–77) contrasts Paul's economic appreciation of "the crash" with Charlie's emotional assessment of it. Following Scott Donaldson's lead, Craig Monk's "The Political F. Scott Fitzgerald: Liberal Illusion and Disillusion in *This Side of Paradise* and *The Beautiful and Damned*" (*ASInt* 33, ii: 60–70) focuses on the author's political thought, noting that *Paradise*'s vindication of "liberal ideals prevalent at the time of America's involvement in World War I" is replaced by a "more pessimistic outlook" spawned by the "spiraling mood of liberal disillusionment" as the Republicans rose to power following the war.

f. Essays on Specific Works: Hemingway   A pair of biocritical studies shed light on the author's process of turning facts to fiction. Judy Jo Small and Michael Reynolds's "Hemingway v. Anderson: The Final Rounds" (*HN* 14, ii: 1–17) both expands and subtilizes our appreciation of the Anderson/Hemingway feud, prompted by *The Torrents of Spring,* by delving into the manuscripts, correspondence, and biography, arguing that each author's parting shot was delivered fictionally—Hemingway's in "The Killers," which they read as an "oblique confession" of the author's fear of aging and vulnerability; and Anderson's in "The Fight," which characterizes the conflict as "silly." Marisa Anne Pagnattarro's " 'Che Ti Dice La Patria?': Shadows of Meaning" (*HN* 14, ii: 37–49) demonstrates that "several autobiographical omissions and manuscript deletions" elucidate the tale's "shadow meaning," which implies that "nothing redeeming is to be found in duplicity"; while the surface offers a political critique of fascism, its shadow is "deeply rooted in auto-biographical concerns," and the "self-serving behavior of the Italian fascists [is] disturbingly parallel to Hemingway's own renunciation of his first marriage for personal motives."

Gender issues remain a vital concern in Hemingway studies, and continuing the dialogue most recently addressed by Lisa Tyler (see *ALS 1994*, p. 182) Marylyn A. Lupton's "The Seduction of Jim Gilmore" (*HN* 15, i: 1–9) "looks beyond contemporary ideas to the history of the story" and concludes that Liz was "up" for her encounter with Jim. Stanley Renner's "Moving to the Girl's Side of 'Hills Like White Elephants' " (*HN* 15, i: 27–41) finds that the woman in the story "effectively distances herself from the influence of her male companion and enables herself, evidently for the first time, to realize what is in her own mind," specifically that she does not want to abort the child. Ira Elliott's "Performance Art: Jake Barnes and 'Masculine' Signification in *The Sun Also Rises*" (*AL* 67: 77–94) considers Jake's male identity in terms of his wound and his encounter with the homosexuals at the *bal musette*. Determining (with Judith Butler of *Gender Trouble*) that gender is a cultural construct, Elliott suggests that if there is hope for Jake, it may be found in the image of the homosexual man, who integrates both masculine and feminine and may signal the onset of new kinds of relationships. Peter F. Cohen's " 'I Won't Kiss You . . . I'll Send Your English Girl': Homoerotic Desire in *A Farewell to Arms*" (*HN* 15, i: 42–53) considers the theories of Eve Sedgwick and Gayle Rubin in arguing that Rinaldi attempts "to transfer *his* beloved—Catherine—to Frederic in order to eroticize his relationship with his American friend." Charles J. Nolan, Jr.'s less-satisfying "Hemingway's Complicated 'Enquiry' in *Men Without Women*" (*SSF* 32: 217–22) covers old ground about the story's ambiguity en route to concluding that the complex motives of the characters suggest life's complications.

Exploring metafictive elements, Don Summerhayes's "Fish Story: Ways of Telling in 'Big Two-Hearted River' " (*HN* 15, i: 10–26) offers "a series of ruminations on passages . . . which seem to invite a freer play of association than usual and to attract attention to the self-consciousness of writing as writing"; for example, he observes a vacillating mimetic code when, midstory, the narrator suddenly wishes he were reading something; or when the third-person narrator slips into first person, initially describing a trout as the biggest "[h]e [Nick] had ever seen," but later in the same paragraph commenting that it was "the biggest trout that I had ever heard of." James H. Meredith in "The Eyewitness Narrator in Hemingway's *Collier's* Dispatches and 'Black Ass at the Cross Roads'" (*WL&A* 7, i: 43–59) concentrates on the complex narrative personae who are both writers and participants and notes that the dispatches and story focus on "the exact moment a hero is being changed by his experiences of war" rather than the author's typical concern, the lasting psychological affects of war.

Robert Paul Lamb focuses on the protagonist's culture in "The Love Song of Harold Krebs: Form, Argument, and Meaning in Hemingway's 'Soldier's Home'" (*HN* 14, ii: 18–36) and agrees that the story is "about a disillusioned war veteran and a conflicted mother-son relationship" but adds that it is also about "the way in which fundamental social constructs," such as conventions of dress and conduct and the American family, "seemed to be everywhere disintegrating in the mid-1920s." Lyall Bush's "Consuming Hemingway: 'The Snows of Kilimanjaro' in the Post-modern Classroom" (*JNT* 25: 23–46) proposes that "the story might be read as an allegory of debilitating sickness of a consumer culture that renders all things—women, experiences and words—as objects to be voraciously devoured on the way to others, from America, to Europe, to Africa."

Milton Birnbaum's "The Aging Process: A Literary Perspective" (*World & I* 10: 426–39) focuses on the waiters in "A Clean, Well-Lighted Place" in determining that a sense of "caring community" fosters a healthy outlook toward the aging, but with "no such sense of direction or caring community, the individual feels hopeless." Matts Djos, examining "Alcoholism in Ernest Hemingway's *The Sun Also Rises:* A Wine and Roses Perspective on the Lost Generation" (*HN* 14, ii: 64–78), calls the novel "a remarkable portrait of the pathology of the disease of alcoholism" and "a portrait of degeneration without solutions."

Pamela A. Boker's "Negotiating the Heroic Paternal Ideal: Historical Fiction as Transference in Hemingway's *For Whom the Bell Tolls*" (*L&P* 41, i–ii: 85–112) finds the novel to be Hemingway's "generally successful attempt to work through his hero's separation-individuation process" and concludes that the novel is psychologically, if not artistically, integrated; "by the strength of its coherent psychological narrative, we are given new reason to judge the novel as a serious fictional enterprise." Carl

Eby's " 'Come Back to the Beach Ag'in, David Honey!': Hemingway's Fetishization of Race in *The Garden of Eden* Manuscripts" (*HN* 14, ii: 98–117) explains the anecdote (reported in A. E. Hotchner's *Papa Hemingway*) in which Hemingway claims to have danced with Josephine Baker as a "day dream" that collapsed his favorite fetishes into a single icon. Craig Kleinman's "Dirty Tricks and Wordy Jokes: The Politics of Recollection in *A Farewell to Arms*" (*HN* 15, i: 54–71) claims that "the politics of Henry's retrospective narration emerge in the form of jokes and their relation to his unconscious (and subconscious)" and that "joke structures and displacement devices" are employed "to resist Western notions of progress and negotiate the present toward a more livable future."

Have you heard the one about Harold Bloom and George Plimpton? It seems as though the participatory journalist interviewed the learned academician in "The Canon of Western Humor: A Conversation with Harold Bloom" (*ParisR* 37: 38–72) and the scholar alleged that the "closest thing to humor in Hemingway" would be "God Rest You Merry, Gentlemen." The road to hell is paved with un-got jokes and curious dismissals of the hilarious "stuffed-dog" episode between Jake and Bill in *The Sun Also Rises*.

Scott Donaldson's informative note, "Protecting the Troops from Hemingway: An Episode in Censorship" (*HN* 15, i: 87–93), details a failed attempt to eliminate Armed Services Editions of Hemingway's *To Have and Have Not* and *Selected Short Stories* because of their "extremely deleterious effect on our personnel." S. A. Cowan's "Amateur Boxing in Hemingway's *The Sun Also Rises*" (*ELN* 33, i: 58–61) sees that "the main importance of boxing in the novel is the way it is used to portray and satirize . . . Cohn, whose status as a boxer and romantic lover is strictly amateur." Miriam B. Mandel's "Headgear and Horses: Authorial Presence in *A Farewell to Arms*" (*IFR* 22: 61–66) reveals how seemingly small details combine to deflate our sympathy for Frederic Henry; Mandel's "A Reader's Guide to Pilar's Bullfighters: Untold Histories in *For Whom the Bell Tolls*" (*HN* 15, i: 94–104) provides short biographies of several bullfighters mentioned by Pilar in the novel and broadens our appreciation of Hemingway's ability to work "local culture" into his narratives; and her "Note on Jordan's Sleeping Bag" (*Hemingway Newsletter* 29: 4) discovers that its model was likely Hemingway's own, purchased at Abercrombie & Fitch.

g. Miscellaneous   Pack Gerhard Köpf's *Papa's Suitcase: A Novel,* trans.
A. Leslie Willson (Braziller), for light reading about the mysterious valise
stolen from Hadley in 1922; the bibliophile will appreciate the afterword
that lists the two dozen German texts, primary and secondary, which
serve as sources. Or settle into Michael Palin's *Hemingway's Chair* (Methuen) for another tale about the consequences of reading a little too
much about Papa.

Part II

11 Literature to 1800

William J. Scheick

This year early American literature received less scholarly attention than usual. The most significant publications include several substantial editing projects and a few investigations into the nature of reputation-making. How the current status of a colonial event or an author was generated, especially in terms of the various interests of later times, has recently become a site of inquiry that has yielded surprising disclosures.

i Native Americans and the Colonial Imagination

The appropriation of the Americas by European intellectuals who elucidated chauvinistic concerns is documented in Karen Ordahl Kupperman's *America in European Consciousness, 1493–1750* (No. Car.). Of special note in this superb collection of 13 essays are Sabine MacCormack's differentiation between emphases on the past dispersal of revealed religion and on the natural development of religious principles in colonial explanations of Amerindian paganism (pp. 79–129); Roland Greene's focus on a Petrarchan authorial desire for an unknown Other as the characteristic mode of early descriptions of America (pp. 130–65); John M. Headley's documentation of how, in response to New World discoveries, the Roman Catholic and the Protestant perception of space and time was infused with eschatological predictions (pp. 243–71); Henry Lowood's report on the catalog of nature as a demonstration of how American artifacts were decontextualized in favor of European interest or value (pp. 295–323); and Richard Simmons's discussion of books, set in America, in which the colonial experience served European authors and readers as exercises of the imagination (pp. 361–87). Although the English colonial mind was millennial rather than apocalyptic concerning nature, Lawrence Buell observes in *The Environmental Imag-*

ination (pp. 53–62), this attitude nonetheless prepared for the New World myth of the ideal landscape as unspoiled; it also prepared for the current paradoxical situation in which we maintain such a myth from within an antipathetic technological culture.

Dane Morrison's *A Praying People: Massachusett Acculturation and the Failure of the Puritan Mission, 1600–1690* (Peter Lang) details the tragic rise and fall of Natick, including John Eliot's performance as de facto lawyer on behalf of the settlement. Changes related to the factors that injured Natick are assessed in "'A Melancholy People': Anglo-Indian Relations in Early Warwick, Rhode Island, 1642–1675" (*NEQ* 68: 402–28), in which Joshua Micah Marshall attributes King Philip's War to Native American resistance to an economic transition from trade to agriculture. Michael M. Pomedli studies 13 documents (1736–62) collected by Benjamin Franklin and concludes in "Eighteenth-Century Treaties: Amended Iroquois Condolence Rituals" (*AIQ* 19: 319–39) that the form and content of these works, at once legal and spiritual in mode, were influenced by Native American religious rituals.

William M. Hamlin's *The Image of America in Montaigne, Spenser, and Shakespeare: Renaissance Ethnography and Literary Reflection* (St. Martin's) argues that in European responses to the indigenous peoples of the New World such polarities as savagery and civility, equality and difference, were informed less by facts than by ethnocentric beliefs, including notions of cultural identity and continuity. The New World interracial marriage in *Persiles* challenges the customary distinction between barbarity and civilization; and, Diana de Armas Wilson also notes, a revisionary reciprocity emerges as characters who confront otherness finally assess themselves: "'The Matter of America': Cervantes Romances Inca Garcilaso de la Vega," *Cultural Authority in Golden Age Spain,* ed. Marina S. Brownlee and Hans Ulrich Gumbrecht (Hopkins, pp. 234–59). Appeal to self-interest, specifically financial profit, is the focus of Susan Schmidt Horning's "The Power of Image: Promotional Literature and Its Changing Role in the Settlement of North Carolina" (*NCHR* 40 [1993]: 365–400), which concludes that many New World advertisements were aimed less at potential settlers than at wealthy individuals who could facilitate colonization.

How John Smith managed cultural signs for his own and his colony's benefit, and how his subsequent efforts to narrate his experiences compensated for the loss of Jamestown are considered in *Voyages in Print: English Travel to America, 1576–1624* (Cambridge, pp. 85–140), Mary C.

Fuller's entertaining study of colonial travelogues as less about New World exploration than about a conception of selfhood authorized by a rhetoric of personal deprivation. Readings of North and South American ethnic encounters are included in *Implicit Understandings: Observing, Reporting, and Reflecting on the Encounters between Europeans and Other Peoples in the Early Modern Era,* ed. Stuart B. Schwartz (Cambridge, 1994), an anthology of 20 essays. "Columbian Encounters: 1992–1995" (*WMQ* 52: 649–96) presents James Axtell's daunting review of recent assessments of Columbus's cultural and intellectual milieu, and of the global consequences of his journeys. And *The World Turned Upside Down: Indian Voices from Early America,* ed. Colin G. Calloway (St. Martin's, 1994), usefully provides pertinent documents from 1609 to 1793.

ii Early Colonial Prose

In *Literal Figures: Puritan Allegory and the Reformation Crisis in Representation* (Chicago) Thomas H. Luxon scrutinizes a cryptic attachment to allegory beneath the surface of the professed literalism of Puritanism. He finds evidence in the Puritan valuation of bodily experiences as representations of the divine—an interpretative mode reinforced by the Reformed displacement of Christ's literal bodily presence in the tabernacle to the discursive body of the scriptural text. He also finds evidence in Puritan typology of an attempt to substitute historical for imaginary figures; this attempt barely masks an allegorical pattern of thought in the reading of history as a symbolic expression of divine will. In short, such characteristic Puritan binaries as body and soul, flesh and spirit, earth and heaven, time and eternity are fundamentally representational because they encode the relationship between the figurative and the literal. Had Luxon also considered the place of the Canticles in Puritan eschatological thought, his claims concerning the Puritan attraction to allegory would have been deepened, even as his claims concerning the underground nature of this attraction would have necessarily been modified.

Allegory is also featured in Reiner Smolinski's introduction to *The Threefold Paradise of Cotton Mather: An Edition of "Triparadisus"* (Georgia), an exemplary editorial feat and a substantial contribution to Mather studies. Late in his life, Smolinski explains, Mather abandoned his previous premillennial belief in the literal conversion of the Jewish nation as a prerequisite for the Second Coming and interpreted this Pauline prophecy as an allegory that applied to the Christian church. But if this modification revised the ideas of Cotton's father, it did not reform Increase's concept of a hierarchized heaven literally situated in the clouds above the site of ancient Israel. Also pertinent to an understanding of Mather's eschatology is Jeffrey Scott Mares's "Cotton Mather's 'Problema Theologicum': An Authoritative Edition" (*PAAS* 104 [1994]: 333–440). The views of both Mathers on drinking customs and tavern usage are included in David W. Conroy's *In Public Houses: Drink and the Revolution of Authority in Colonial Massachusetts* (No. Car.).

In "Authority and Witchery: Cotton Mather's *Ornaments* and Mary English's Acrostic" (*ArQ* 51, i: 1–32) I detail how Mather's anxious attempt to enhance women's province and to reclaim, at least to some degree, his own seemingly diminished voice results in a book which fissures in various places as a result of its underground seismic problem with authorization; these unnegotiated and unredeemed bifurcations are similar to those in the conflicted search for authorized voice evident in Mary English's poem. Records of last statements, Erik R. Seeman discloses in " 'She Died Like Good Old Jacob': Deathbed Scenes and Inversions of Power in New England, 1675–1775" (*PAAS* 104 [1994]: 285–314), place the marginalized speech of women and laymen at the center of the reader's attention; these records invert the traditional pattern of power, especially sometimes when they report unconventional opinions.

Colonial ambivalence toward marriage is of interest to Richard Godbeer, whose " 'Love Raptures': Marital, Romantic, and Erotic Images of Jesus Christ in Puritan New England, 1670–1730" (*NEQ* 68: 355–84) overlooks highly pertinent discussions by Karl Keller and especially Ivy Schweitzer. Extending Emory Elliott's findings, Godbeer concludes that in Puritan culture, where gender identities were not exclusively rigid, optimistic invocations of spousal imagery by ministers provided a counterforce to the pessimistic threats of their jeremiads. In " 'The Cry of Sodom': Discourse, Intercourse, and Desire in Colonial New England" (*WMQ* 52: 259–86) Godbeer reports less flexibility and balance in the Puritan response to homosexuality; in contrast to official discourse, the informal and inchoate argot of the colonists, such as the word *molly,* suggests their emphasis on the identity, rather than the acts, of specific groups within the community.

The complex personal, familial, religious, strategic, and commercial motives behind Native American assaults on and alliances with the frontier settlement made famous in John Williams's 1707 narrative are cogently detailed in "Revisiting *The Redeemed Captive:* New Perspectives on the 1704 Attack on Deerfield" (*WMQ* 52: 3–46) by Evan Haefeli and Kevin Sweeney. Various relationships and differences between Indian captivity accounts and Muslim captivity reports interest Paul Baepler, whose "The Barbary Captivity Narrative in Early America" (*EAL* 30: 95–120) features Joshua Gee's hapless experiences in 17th-century Algeria.

By assuming the pose of a popular figure in 18th-century fiction, as Susan Stabile explains in "*A Circumstantial Account;* or, *The Rake's Design:* Robert Bolling's Epistolary Novel" (*AL* 67: 1–22), one Southern author artistically shaped his letter-journal to distance himself from a personal defeat, align himself with his compatriots, and enjoy the last word in his otherwise unsuccessful four-part scheme to seduce a woman.

iii Bradstreet and Early Colonial Poetry

During the colonial period the sea provided a metaphor for individual and cultural pilgrimage or transformation, Donald P. Wharton indicates in a chapter of *America and the Sea* (pp. 32–63). During the Revolutionary era, however, appreciation of the sea was influenced more by maritime commerce and technology, and by an aesthetic valuation of order, unity, and proportion. Raymond A. Craig in "Polishing God's Altar: Puritan Poetics in John Cotton's *Singing of Psalms*" (*SPAS* 5: 1–33) urges the reassessment of Puritan verse in terms of a contrast between divine and artificial elegance, spiritual and natural endowments, proper (psalm-like) and profane uses of song, and public and private devotions.

Scriptural precedent also interests Eileen Razzari Elrod, whose "'Mouth Put in the Dust': Personal Authority and Biblical Resonance in Anne Bradstreet's Grief Poems" (*SPAS* 5: 35–62) contends that Old Testament female personae and models of anger, as well as the patterns of contradiction and contrition, enabled the poet to resist Puritan misogyny, particularly the restrictions placed on female speech. Silence, rather than disclosure, interests Carol R. Mehler, whose "Anne Bradstreet's House Fire: The Careless Maid and Careful God" (*SPAS* 5: 63–71) speculates that the poet attributed the destruction of her home to the design of divine will rather than the careless act of a servant because finding, keeping, and managing servants were prevalent sources of frustration.

T. Gregory Garvey's "To Fill Christ's Coach: The Poet and the Pastor in Edward Taylor's *Gods Determinations*" (*SPAS* 5: 73–93) observes that in the poem's first part Taylor attempts the objective viewpoint of the epic poet, whereas in the second part he records the subjective viewpoint of the anxious laity; by stressing the kinship between these two perspectives, Taylor suggests a continuity between his ministerial and artistic vocations.

iv Edwards, the Great Awakening, and the New Divinity

In "From Edwards to Emerson: A Study of the Teleology of Nature" (*SPAS* 5: 123–47) Dewey W. Hall contends that unauthorized and antithetical tendencies lurk beneath Edwards's celebration of divine truth in his typological interpretations of creation; subjective exegesis, especially a shift to an iconographic linking of meaning and image, supplants scriptural typology. Typology also interests Stephen H. Daniel, whose *The Philosophy of Jonathan Edwards: A Study in Divine Semiotics* (Indiana, 1994) argues that Edwards's method of reasoning *implies* his rejection of classical, medieval, and modern notions of transcendent objective perception and human subjectivity; his method implies that meaning and being mutually abide within signs (communication). Edwards's notion of "consent to Being" is featured in Elisa New's "Beyond the Romance Theory of American Vision: Beauty and the Qualified Will in Edwards, Jefferson, and Audubon" (*AmLH* 7: 381–414), which identifies a tradition in which the human experience of nature is itself a part of nature; in this tradition natural beauty is not understood to be a projective representation of human desire but is instead perceived as an experienced force greater than and inclusive of human desire.

In *Jonathan Edwards, Religious Tradition, and American Culture* (No. Car.) Joseph A. Conforti discloses the changing nature of the "text" of Edwards's reputation from 1790 to 1903 and convincingly concludes that Edwardsian traditions were variously and ambiguously constructed as interpretive responses to controversies during religious revivals, the rise of seminaries, and changes in religious beliefs after the Civil War. How the theological heirs of Edwards problematically interpreted slavery as a divinely designed opportunity for the conversion of Africa is unfolded in John Saillant's "Slavery and Divine Providence in New England Calvinism: The New Divinity and a Black Protest, 1775–1805" (*NEQ* 68: 584–608), which includes Lemuel Haynes's egalitarian emphasis on liberty, education, and community as a revision of this interpretation. How one of Edwards's heirs used individual features of Calvinism in his various responses to local events and thereby gave an impression of inconsistency is a chief consideration in *Law and Providence in Joseph Bellamy's New England: The Origins of the New Divinity in Revolutionary America* (Oxford, 1994) by Mark Valeri.

A late 18th-century attack on Edwards's ideas, especially the notion that salvation was apparently not available in any practical sense, is reviewed in "From Calvinist Metaphysics to Republican Theory: Jonathan Edwards and James Dana on the Freedom of the Will" (*JHI* 56: 397–418), Allen C. Guelzo's demonstration of the ways politics and metaphysics mutually contributed to early national discussions of political liberty. In *"Gracious Affection" and "True Virtue" According to Jonathan Edwards and John Wesley* (Scarecrow, 1994) Richard B. Steele identifies several similarities in the attitudes of these two men concerning religious feeling and moral behavior. How the man reproved by Edwards on the subject of "immediate revelations" made use of such commercial techniques as publicized preaching tours, self-promotion in newspapers, the publication of personal journals, the printing of religious periodicals, and the invention of controversies is documented in Frank Lambert's *"Pedlar in Divinity": George Whitefield and the Transatlantic Revivals, 1737–1770* (Princeton, 1994). And in "Friendship and Idolatry in Esther Edwards Burr's Letters" (*UMSE* 11–12 [1993–95]: 138–50) I focus on the failure of Jonathan Edwards's minimalist version of Puritanism in the instance of his daughter's unauthorized attraction to human companionship as a surrogate religion that verged on a violation of the second commandment.

v Franklin, Jefferson, Wheatley, and the Revolution

That Madison's writings advocate authority over liberty, including property rights over human rights, is a main, if controversial, finding in Richard K. Mathews's *If Men Were Angels: James Madison and the Heartless Empire of Reason* (Kansas). The difficulty of identifying cultural authority, specifically how the dichotomous language of a preface to the 1764 reprint of William Wood's *New England's Prospect* reveals a tension between a colonial periphery clinging to a 17th-century view of trade and an emergent colonial metropolitanism evolving an 18th-century view of commerce, is investigated by Phillip H. Round in "The Discursive Origins of the American Revolution: The Case of Nathaniel Rogers, Merchant of Boston" (*EAL* 30: 233–63).

Relatedly, Thomas Paine, among others in Richard Striner's "Political Newtonianism: The Cosmic Model of Politics in Europe and America" (*WMQ* 52: 583–608), found ambiguity—uncertainty as well as assurance—when relying upon the Newtonian paradigm (harmony, order, balance, mechanism) as a political and social model. Paine's negating logic, designed to discard the old to make way for the new (see *ALS 1985*, pp. 199–200), is included in *Parables of Possibility*, Terence Martin's study of the positive negative as a cultural strategy. Paine is also the subject of two new biographies: *Thomas Paine: Apostle of Freedom* (Four Walls, 1994) by Jack Fruchtman and *Tom Paine: A Political Life* (Little, Brown) by John Keane.

Not biography, but an explication of the Declaration of Independence, informs *Notes on the State of Virginia*, which Alexander O. Boulton's "The American Paradox: Jefferson, Equality and Racial Science" (*AQ* 47: 467–92) interprets in terms of the 18th-century conflict between the science of racial discrimination and the theory of "equal creation." The cultural conflicts of the new nation also interest Joanne B. Freeman, whose "Slander, Poison, Whispers, and Fame: Jefferson's 'Anas' and Political Gossip in the Early Republic" (*JER* 15: 25–57) contends that Jefferson's work reveals a dark inside story of suspicions, conspiracies, secret societies, and selfish motives. The influence of other cultures on Jefferson comprises the subject of George Green Shackelford's *Thomas Jefferson's Travels in Europe, 1784–1789* (Hopkins).

Examining the implausible consistency of accounts of Franklin's early years, David M. Larson's "Benjamin Franklin's Youth, His Biographers, and the *Autobiography*" (*PMHB* 119: 201–23) concludes that the young patriot's rebelliousness and unhappiness have been underestimated. Franklin's reputation during the course of American culture is the focus of Nian-Sheng Huang's disappointing *Benjamin Franklin in American Thought* (American Philosophical Society, 1994). A source for Franklin's conception of the immortality of words and deeds is identified by Michele Valerie Ronnick in "Benjamin Franklin's Almanac of 1738 and Pliny the Younger's Letter 6.16.3 to Tacitus" (*ELN* 32, iv: 48–50). In "Who Named Franklin's Autobiography" (*ANQ* 8, ii: 17–19) John G. Cawelti, with Eric Atherton, points to the 19th-century editor Jared Sparks. And in "A Samuel Johnson Allusion in a Letter to Benjamin Franklin Explained and Amplified" (*ANQ* 8, i: 13–16) Neill R. Joy delves into a patronage missive recording the earliest reference to differences between the two men.

An issue of *PennH* (62: 273–387) devoted to Pennsylvania Loyalists includes a discussion of disaffected women in revolutionary Philadelphia. More than 100 writings by a well-educated Federalist woman are collected by Carla Mulford in *Only for the Eye of a Friend: The Poems of Annis Boudinot Stockton* (Virginia), a valuable edition that includes previously published and manuscript works on political, social, and personal occasions; as a Federalist, Stockton was especially concerned with both potential social disorder and the failure of representational government. Authorial representations of fiction as a literary form interest Catherine Gallagher in *Nobody's Story: The Vanishing Acts of Women Writers in the Marketplace, 1670–1820* (Calif., 1994). Gallagher (pp. 145–202) emphasizes Charlotte Lennox's equivocal intimation that *The Female Quixote* is an originative act also indebted to the romance form; like female identity during the 18th century, the novel as a literary form is most itself when paradoxically it is related to nothing because when it is related to historical antecedents it is dispossessed of signification.

Literary ancestry is also featured in Carla Willard's "Wheatley's Turns of Praise: Heroic Entrapment and the Paradox of Revolution" (*AL* 67: 233–56), which claims that Phillis Wheatley strategically employed the Pope tradition of using epistolary praise either to glorify or to satirize; in the poet's work this convention motivates each reader to acquiesce to her abolitionist position in order to receive acclaim rather than ironic correction. In "Subjection and Prophecy in Phillis Wheatley's Verse Paraphrases of Scripture" (*CollL* 22, iii: 122–30) I suggest that the poet arrogates ministerial privilege and voice when she extrapolates an innovative racial admonition from her poetic treatments of several biblical passages. The problematic appropriation of an African subject's voice to validate white West Indian identity is the topic of Thomas W. Krise's "True Novel, False History: Robert Robertson's Ventriloquized Ex-Slave in *The Speech of Mr John Talbot Campo-Bell* (1736)" (*EAL* 30: 152–64). And *Black Atlantic Writers of the 18th Century,* ed. Adam Potkay and Sandra Burr (St. Martin's), includes selections by Ukawsaw Gronniosaw, John Marrant, Ottobah Cugoano, and Olaudah Equiano.

vi The Early National Period

More Letters from the American Farmer: An Edition of the Essays in English Left Unpublished by Crèvecoeur, ed. Dennis D. Moore (Georgia), includes five heretofore unavailable essays and more complete versions of previously edited manuscript material; these writings represent Crèvecoeur's Loyalist phase, when he was skeptical of the Revolutionary undertaking, and (as the editor explains) their narrative voices indicate a distinct difference between "James" and his creator. The difference between a progressive commitment to Federalism and a contrary conservative commitment to Calvinism informs Richard J. Moss's disappointing psychological portrait in *The Life of Jedidiah Morse: A Station of Peculiar Exposure* (Tennessee); Morse's ambiguous attempt to reconcile his fantasy of communal New England values and his experience of individualistic capitalism is especially evident in his jeremiad *The American Geography.*

A useful and reliable account, based on important manuscript evidence, of the religious and political themes of the author who referred to Phillis Wheatley as a "barbarian girl . . . entitled to the claim of original genius" is provided by Jeffrey H. Richards in *Mercy Otis Warren* (Twayne). Warren's *The Group* is included in *Plays by Early American Women*. In such plays as Rowson's *Slaves in Algiers,* which also appears in this anthology, women contributed to the new nation's foreign policy; Faye E. Dudden makes this claim in *Women in the American Theatre: Actresses and Audiences, 1790–1870* (Yale, 1994), which argues more generally that a desire to participate in public debate, and be paid well at the same time, led some late 18th-century American women to the profession of acting.

During the first decades of the new nation, Philip Gould documents in "New England Witch-Hunting and the Politics of Reason in the Early Republic" (*NEQ* 68: 58–82), historical and literary treatments of the Salem episode ambiguously reflected an anxious concern with the tug-of-war between the debilitating passion of the people and the stabilizing rationality of elite political authorities. Shifting perspectives, as represented in three overlapping and concurrent early-national modes of political rhetoric (the communal, the civic forum, and the marketplace), are examined in Christopher Grasso's "Print, Poetry, and Politics: John Trumbull and the Transformation of Public Discourse in Revolutionary America" (*EAL* 30: 5–31). The perspective of another member of the Connecticut Wits interests Ralph Bauer, whose "Colonial Discourse and Early American Literary History: Ercilla, the Inca Garcilaso, and Joel Barlow's Conception of a New World Epic" (*EAL* 30: 203–32) identifies countercolonial rhetorical strategies borrowed from earlier New World authors; these strategies, as exhibited in Barlow's Creole New World epic, reconfigure the European tradition of colonial discourse by supplanting providential history with a progressive view of America within a hemispheric perspective.

The post-Revolutionary uncertainty over truth and falsehood, legitimacy and illegitimacy in religion, law, and government interests Christopher W. Jones, whose "Praying upon Truth: *The Memoirs of Stephen Burroughs* and the Picaresque" (*EAL* 30: 32–50) focuses on the skepticism toward institutional powers shared by the author of this subversive book and his cultural milieu. Skepticism toward the political and aesthetic homogenization that results from democratic print culture—especially the mass production and distribution of chivalric romances, historical narratives, and didactic genres—is discussed in Grantland S. Rice's "*Modern Chivalry* and the Resistance to Textual Authority" (*AL* 67: 257–81).

vii Brown, Rowson, and Contemporaries

When they turned to national history to record personal insights, cultural episodes, and cultural conflicts, women thought of themselves as participating in the circulation of knowledge. So concludes Sharon M. Harris in "Whose Past Is It? Women Writers in Early America" (*EAL* 30: 175–81), a reinforcement of Nina Baym's earlier study of the special relationship between women and history as a genre. Baym's new book, *American Women Writers and the Work of History,* suggests that early-national female suspicion of fiction likely derived from a concern over the isolation of women; such writers as Susanna Rowson and Judith Sargent Murray emphasized the study of history as a discipline that included women in the ongoing development of the new republic. Evidence for this conclusion emerges as well in *Selected Writings of Judith Sargent Murray* (Oxford), in which editor Sharon M. Harris argues that *Story of Margaretta* is especially noteworthy because its protagonist expresses Murray's philosophy of education, its intellectual interests foreground the issue of gender, and its reader-oriented narrative manner complexly mingles fact and fiction. In "The Scribblings of a Plain Man and the Temerity of a Woman: Gender and Genre in Judith Sargent Murray's *The Gleaner*" (*EAL* 30: 121–44) Kirstin Wilcox relatedly identifies a variety of gendered voices that blur the distinction between the genres of fiction and serial essays; this effect draws attention to Murray's managed acts of literary concealment.

Sharon M. Harris has also edited *Redefining the Political Novel,* which includes her "Hannah Webster Foster's *The Coquette:* Critiquing Franklin's America" (pp. 1–22). Harris argues that Foster's use of the epistolary mode of fiction evades explicit didacticism and thereby counters the tradition of the sentimental novel otherwise evident in her plot; the letters of this novel, moreover, resist patriarchal maxims, such as Franklin's, and intimate a possible communalistic future society in which women can enjoy friendship. In the same volume Christopher Castiglia ("Susanna Rowson's *Reuben and Rachel:* Captivity, Colonization, and the Domestication of Columbus," pp. 23–42) focuses on the use of theme and structure to invert the new nation's version of conquest and to suggest both Native American and female resilience in challenging colonization and captivity at home. At several points Rowson's *Charlotte Temple* acknowledges the cultural representation of white middle-class women as irrelevant to the general interest of the new nation; in opposition to this pattern, Eva Cherniavsky further explains in *That Pale Mother Rising* (pp. 24–40), Rowson's novel suggests a female communal mourning over the loss of maternal identity, a grief that in effect implies an alternative to the status quo.

Contrary and inaccurate early-national representations of Native Americans, as Eve Kornfeld discloses in "Encountering 'the Other': American Intellectuals and Indians in the 1790s" (*WMQ* 52: 287–314), account not only for the rupture of Rowson's *Reuben and Rachel* into two incongruous parts but also for the difference between Philip Freneau's and Charles Brockden Brown's depiction of them. According to Elizabeth Jane Wall Hinds in "Charles Brockden Brown's Revenge Tragedy: *Edgar Huntly* and the Uses of Property" (*EAL* 30: 51–70), Brown's romance dramatizes his resistance to early-national economic change; by valorizing the dispossession of property as a legitimate cause for revenge, Brown defends the declining landed class against the emergent and eventually dominant entrepreneurial class. Commerce and freedom are likewise the main concerns of a verse epistle edited by John R. Holmes in "Charles Brockden Brown's Earliest Letter" (*EAL* 30: 71–77). And construing savior Sophia as Demeter and victimized Constantia as Persephone, Marietta Patrick's "Mythic Images in Charles Brockden Brown's *Ormond*" (*UMSE* 11–12 [1993–95]: 294–302) indicates that the mother-daughter relationship between these two women is not as unhealthy as several past critics have claimed.

An exemplary human role, defined in terms of an ideal of patriotic republican selflessness, is the subject of "Writing a Federalist Self: Alexander Graydon's *Memoirs of a Life*" (*WMQ* 52: 415–32), Stephen Carl Arch's convincing analysis of one man's effort to demythologize the democratic individualism represented by Franklin. And the erotic argument of a 1795 work satirizing doctors and pastors is detailed in "Verse Condoning of Clerical Concupiscence" (*NEQ* 68: 451–57) by A. Owen Aldridge.

I take my leave with the words of William Wood, "As I have observed what I have seen and written what I have observed, so do I desire . . . it may be beneficial to posterity."

University of Texas at Austin

Robert E. Burkholder

This year was the year of the woman, at least insofar as scholarship on early-19th-century American literature is concerned. That is not to say that previous openings in cultural studies or studies of antebellum rhetoric were not pursued this year, but only to acknowledge that those works that seem to have the most potential for a lasting impact on the field—Nina Baym's fascinating study of antebellum women as writers of history, Catherine Hobbs's collection of essays on women's literacy, Patricia Okker's study of Sarah J. Hale and the culture of antebellum women editors, Kimberly Rae Connor's and Anne Dalke's works on the importance of conversion narrative and spiritual autobiography to the African American women's literary tradition—all focus on women's culture and contributions.

In this space last year I complained about the facile, and therefore reductive, treatments of issues related to race, especially in scholarship on Cooper. While this year certainly saw the publication of plenty of not-so-veiled indictments of the troglodytic views of antebellum white men (and even middle-class women), there were more instances of truly balanced approaches that at least invite us to attempt to understand those troglodytic views within the complex framework of their own time. In is, in fact, the apparent revival of interest in a woman writer, Sarah J. Hale, whose conservative views have not made her a popular subject of recent scholarship, that seems to point to an increasing willingness among scholars to devote time and attention to the writings of those with whom they may have little sympathy because the work of such writers may have been important to the time and place that scholars are attempting to understand. As Susan M. Ryan says at the close of her essay on Hale's pro-colonization novel, *Liberia*, "The coexistence of [the] good intentions [of writers like Hale] and their nonetheless damaging representations is a legacy that, however disquieting, we cannot afford to ignore."

i General Studies

In its scope and lucidity Nina Baym's *American Women Writers and the Work of History* is a landmark study. Baym herself indicates as much when she claims that "to the extent that this book substantially reconfigures the overall picture of women's writing between 1790 and the Civil War, it implicitly rewrites all of early American women's literary history and also invites a different approach to the writing of modern women." While most scholars make large claims for the importance of their work, Baym's study, in both concept and execution, seems up to the claims she makes for it. Baym accomplishes this by first reconfiguring the idea that women's influence was limited to the private sphere to include the *public* function of educating children as citizens. Because of this public role, women were advised from the early years of the republic to read history. History reading for many women led to history writing for some of them, and what is stunning is the number of women writers of history that Baym was able to recover. After an introduction that outlines both her scope and methodology, chapter 2 establishes the pervasiveness of history as a discipline for women in the early national and antebellum periods. Chapter 3 discusses those social and cultural conditions that contributed to so many women becoming writers of history in that era. Chapter 4 outlines the master narrative of most of these histories—"a divine narrative progressing inexorably toward a known end, the millennium that would mark history's closure"—and discusses divergences from that narrative. Chapters 5 through 9 treat "poetry, eyewitness contemporary history, travel accounts, novels, and drama (closet and performed), correlating historical writing in these genres with their leading themes and tropes." A final chapter deals with history that focused on women as subjects. The appendix, "Biographical Notes on American Women Writers of History," compiled by Eric Gardner, contains information on more than 150 writers discussed by Baym and reinforces her point that these writers were not scarce, even if some were hard to find.

Another landmark work is *The Oxford Companion to Women's Writing in the United States*. While the scope represented by the volume's 771 entries goes far beyond the concerns of this chapter, its publication is a watershed event that both aids in defining the field of women's writing in the United States and points to the immense potential for future scholarship on writing by and about women. The paired volume, *The Oxford*

Book of Women's Writing in the United States, ed. Linda Wagner-Martin and Cathy N. Davidson, is less satisfying, perhaps because when faced with the daunting task of creating an anthology that mirrors the comprehensiveness and obvious importance of its sister volume, the editors chose instead to create a thematically organized collection of writings that "readers could simply enjoy." While the goal of entertaining readers is certainly admirable, it seems oddly unassuming when juxtaposed with the implicit argument for the cultural importance of women's writing represented by the weighty *Companion.* Another sort of reference work, *Facts on File Bibliography of American Fiction Through 1865,* ed. Kent P. Ljungquist (Facts on File, 1994), is a useful compilation of 106 entries, each devoted to an individual writer and many treating marginalized writers, "designed to provide an accurate record of essential primary and secondary bibliographical information for students."

Even with the sort of acceptance of canon expansion represented in Baym's work and Davidson and Wagner-Martin's *Companion to Women's Writing,* there is still considerable anger in the profession. Proof positive of just that is Susan Danielson's "Domestic Strains: The Woman Question, Free Love, and Nineteenth-Century American Fiction," pp. 73–92 in *The Canon and the Classroom: The Pedagogical Implications of Canon Revision in American Literature,* ed. John Alberti (Garland), a needlessly confrontational presentation of what from Danielson's own description seems to be a well-conceived course on "the debate surrounding the 'woman question' as presented in several nineteenth-century texts." Apparently dismayed that "the bourgeois maternal body has been left intact in/by current academic feminist discourses," Eva Cherniavsky in *That Pale Mother Rising* sets out to undo this affront to the postmodern sensibility by examining motherhood as a political construction in various 19th-century texts. As Cherniavsky describes her task: "we need a feminist history that seeks to deauthenticate rather than (re)mythologize [the bourgeois] conception of motherhood. *That Pale Mother Rising* aims to model this kind of revisionist approach to motherhood." Unfortunately, Cherniavsky's discussions of motherhood in *Uncle Tom's Cabin,* Cummins's *The Lamplighter,* and Jacobs's *Incidents in the Life of a Slave Girl* eschew historical detail for an elaborate postmodern feminist scaffolding, with the result that her study seems oddly ahistorical and finally less successful than Stephanie A. Smith's *Conceived by Liberty* (see *ALS 1994,* pp. 203–04), which aims at similar results but provides a more detailed historical context for interpretive readings of 19th-century texts. Altogether more effective than *That Pale Mother Rising* is Paula Bennett's " 'The Descent of the Angel': Interrogating Domestic Ideology in American Women's Poetry, 1858–1890" (*AmLH* 7: 591–610), an analysis of poems by Elizabeth Stoddard, Elizabeth Stuart Phelps, and Sarah Piatt intended to show how the post-Civil War poetry of these women rejects the "high sentimentalism" (defined as the acceptance of "sensibility as a trustworthy guide to moral and spiritual truth") that had been the standard mode of antebellum poets like Lydia Sigourney, Elizabeth Oakes Smith, and Frances Sargent Osgood.

Shirley Foster and Judy Simons's *What Katy Read: Feminist Re-Readings of "Classic" Stories for Girls* (Iowa) is a generally successful attempt both to define and legitimize the genre of "girl's fiction" for serious study. One important reason for the generic distinctiveness that Foster and Simons note is the sharp differentiation of stories for boys and girls that developed in the early 19th century and resulted in a gender-based didacticism and stories for girls that explored "the possibilities of female self-expression and fulfillment in a male-dominated world." The "prioritization of heroic femininity and the ideologies of girlhood that children's literature encodes" thus becomes the focus of their readings of *The Wide-Wide World, Little Women,* and *The Secret Garden.* A related work is Gillian Avery's lavishly produced *Behold the Child: American Children and Their Books, 1621–1922* (Hopkins), a detailed and comprehensive history of children's literature in the United States. In showing the emergence of a distinctively American style of children's literature in the early 19th century, and in demonstrating how this style emerged from American cultural concerns, Avery's is a work of importance for cultural, intellectual, and literary historians.

This year saw a number of significant books that adopt a cultural studies methodology. Russ Castronovo's *Fathering the Nation* is an ambitious study that offers a reading of American culture through the Foucauldian prism of what Castronovo calls a "genealogical account," which is meant to suggest both the father-son metaphor that is pervasive in antebellum American culture and a methodology which reads America as "a patchwork of stories" that reveals disjunctions in the unity and coherence of the national narrative as imagined by the Founding Fathers. Castronovo announces his purpose as being "to read and dismantle the architecture of national narrative and examine how fragmentation and unity as formal principles have been inextricably wrapped up in the most significant political issues." Chapter 1 uses Cooper's *The Spy* and a number of juvenile biographies of George Washington to gauge the narrative authority of the nation's founders. Later chapters examine William Wells Brown's *Clotel* as an exposé of discrepancies of the national narrative of freedom, and slave narratives as "miscegenated histories" in which narrators author themselves with the legacy of the Founding Fathers, making freedom itself a product of racial interbreeding and casting doubt on the coherence of the national narrative. Another contribution from cultural studies is Cindy Weinstein's *The Literature of Labor and the Labors of Literature.* Weinstein argues "that allegory, as understood, practiced, and received during [the antebellum] period, was the literary mode that foregrounded its relation to labor." Although her principal focus is work by Hawthorne, Melville, Twain, and Henry Adams, anyone interested in early-19th-century American culture will benefit from Weinstein's first chapter, "The Problem with Labor and the Promise of Leisure," which not only provides a useful analysis of attitudes toward labor in antebellum America, but is an interesting reading of Mt. Auburn Cemetery as a cultural signifier concerned with labor on several levels, and a comparative reading of the authorial intrusions in *White-Jacket* and *Uncle Tom's Cabin* to demonstrate how Melville foregrounded the labor of authorship and Stowe, who apparently accepted the bourgeois ideology of the work ethic, hid such labor.

In its concern with the so-called national narrative Terence Martin's *Parables of Possibility*—a wide-ranging study of "the protean importance of a sense of beginning in American literature and culture"—shares some of the same concerns as Castronovo's *Fathering the Nation.* In his six topically arranged chapters Martin first looks at attempts to fix a beginning to serve the nation as a whole and the subsequent rhetorical negation of phenomena so that American beginnings came to seem both radical and atemporal. Martin next turns to an examination of the function of beginnings in American fiction and discusses the effect of the concept of beginnings on fictional characterization, description, and organization. Finally, Martin concerns himself with "the phenomenon and fate of inexhaustible limits" as that theme is treated in a variety of 19th-century texts. Within this framework Martin includes extended readings of the treatment of national origins in Irving's *A History of New York;* of Natty Bumppo as a negative hero, with particular attention to *The Deerslayer;* and of Cooper's representation of radical beginning in *The Crater.* "Creating a National Audience: Jacksonian America, 1828–

1860," the first chapter of Andrew W. Robertson's comparative history, *The Language of Democracy: Political Rhetoric in the United States and Britain, 1790–1900* (Cornell), is a useful study of the emergence of the mass-circulation press and its appeal to a growing audience of readers through a "familiar" rhetorical style. Robertson uses this background for an analysis of the source of power in Lincoln's rhetoric as a fortuitous blending of "the oral speaking tradition with print culture."

Culture is not only a product of such concerns as labor, literature, and rhetoric; it also emerges from a sense of place, and this year there were studies devoted to the cultural significance of both the land and the sea. Steven Olson's *The Prairie in Nineteenth-Century American Poetry* (Okla., 1994) is a work intended to establish a link between the prairie as subject and the concept of Manifest Destiny. For example, in "Exploring the Prairies" Olson writes of how *The History of the Lewis and Clark Expedition* and Irving's *A Tour of the Prairies* create a metaphor of the prairie based on the vast openness of its landscape and of how this metaphor was in turn used to suggest the cultural, political, and ideological openness of America itself. In "Breaking the Sod: The Illinois Prairies and the Public Voice of William Cullen Bryant" Olson argues that Bryant reshaped the experiences of his 1832 visit to Illinois into poetry intended both "to generate an American diction" and to create "a unique mythology of the New World." Other chapters touch on the use of the prairie as metaphor in poems by Alice and Phoebe Cary, Holmes, Lowell, Lydia Sigourney, and John Greenleaf Whittier. In a related study Diana Dufva Quantic's *The Nature of the Place: A Study of Great Plains Fiction* (Nebraska), the focus is on mythic readings of the Great Plains in such works as Cooper's *The Prairie* and Irving's *A Tour of the Prairies* and how such readings continue to affect the ways in which we see that region.

The sea is more than amply represented in *America and the Sea,* a survey that attempts to establish an identity for American literature of the sea, which editor Haskell Springer argues has been relatively ignored compared to interest devoted to the vanished western frontier. Of its 14 chapters covering American writing about the sea "from the days of New World exploration and settlement to 1990," those of most interest are Hugh Egan's survey of "Cooper and His Contemporaries" (pp. 64–82) and Joseph Flibbert's examination of "Poetry in the Mainstream" (pp. 109–26). Egan sees Cooper's career as a writer of sea fiction as something of a bifurcated affair that has him reshaping in his work of the 1820s the tradition of sea fiction established by Smollett and Scott and then refining the genre through a reexamination of the romantic bases of his early work in eight novels of the 1840s. While Cooper is his principal concern, Egan also deals briefly with Irving and Richard Henry Dana, Jr. Flibbert's examination of antebellum poetry of the sea looks at poems by Bryant, Longfellow, Epes Sargent, Simms, and Whittier, among others, to illustrate the idea that this poetry represents three different uses of the sea as trope: as a place of enchantment, as metaphor for death, and as metaphor for life. Other chapters of interest are John Samson's survey of 19th-century journals, narratives, and diaries dealing with sea experiences; Robert Madison's examination of hymns, chanteys, and sea songs; and Elizabeth Schultz's treatment of African American literature and the sea. William E. Lenz's *The Poetics of the Antarctic: A Study in Nineteenth-Century American Cultural Perceptions* (Garland) is also about the sea, specifically about the U.S. Exploring Expedition to the Antarctic from 1838 until 1842. Lenz is interested in the significance of Antarctic exploration in the age of Manifest Destiny as well as the various genres used by writers for accounts of and stories inspired by exploration; however, he gives most of his attention to the 1843 narrative poem *Thulia: A Tale of the Antarctic* by James Croxall Palmer and Palmer's revision of his poem as *Antarctic Mariner's Song* in 1868. While all of this may seem so much arcana, Lenz's argument regarding the important cultural and political functions served by Antarctic explorations cannot be overlooked.

ii Cooper, Irving, and Contemporaries

This year race and racism continued to be the predominant focus in work on Cooper, although, encouraging evidence indicates that scholars are becoming more willing to deal with the complexity of Cooper's treatment of those subjects. For example, John McWilliams's The Last of the Mohicans: *Civil Savagery and Savage Civility* (Twayne) begins with an attempt to contemporize the novel by suggesting that Cooper was puzzled by the same social and political questions that baffle us and that the novel itself "engages us in exactly the same 'identity politics' currently in academic and cultural fashion." McWilliams reads *The Last of the Mohicans* as a generic and stylistic hybrid, argues for Cooper's position on race as that of a "cultural relativist," and asserts that his position on gender is best represented by his depiction of failures of the frontier patriarchy. Although McWilliams's treatment seems pitched to the student looking for an introduction, he also includes discussions—such as a comparison of the handling of racial issues by Cooper, Child, and Sedgwick—that seem to indicate his desire to engage the current politics of the profession. Child and Sedgwick, along with Cooper, are the concern of Domhnall Mitchell in "Acts of Intercourse: 'Miscegenation' in Three 19th-Century American Novels" (*AmStScan* 27: 126–41). Mitchell takes as her model the concept of intercourse in its various meanings—conversation, sexual liaison, and a word associated with a series of laws regulating the exchange of land and goods between Europeans and Native Americans—and examines these forms of intercourse as they appear in *The Wept of Wish-ton-Wish,* Child's *Hobomok,* and Sedgwick's *Hope Leslie.* She finds that all three writers, faced with the novelistic imperative of the correct marriage and the historical imperative of Manifest Destiny, treat the Indians' erasure from history in similar ways that not only reflect the Indian Removal Policies of the 1820s and 1830s, but what Mitchell calls "the condescension of retrospect," a fictionalized version of colonialism in which the forest is claimed imaginatively by the Euroamerican writer and the disappearance of the native is depicted as inevitable.

The complexity of Cooper's handling of race is also the subject of James D. Wallace's "Race and Captivity in Cooper's *The Wept of Wish-ton-Wish*" (*AmLH* 7: 189–209), an argument that Cooper's novel is not about the horrors of miscegenation but the glories of amalgamation. Wallace attempts to demonstrate, like McWilliams, that Cooper was a cultural relativist who viewed racial categories, like class categories, as fluid. He then uses a sensible reading of the popular 1824 captivity account, *A Narrative of the Life of Mrs. Mary Jemison,* as the basis for an interpretation of the tragic deaths of Narra-mattah and Conachet in *The Wept of Wish-ton-Wish* as inevitable within the context of the complex relationships of a Native American family and not as the product of their mixed-race marriage. It is worth noting that Karen Oakes in "'We Planted, Tended and Harvested Our Corn': Gender, Ethnicity, and Transculturation in *A Narrative of Mrs. Mary Jemison*" (*W&Lang* 18, ii: 45–51) argues that Jemison's story is not a captivity narrative at all, but Native American autobiography. Oakes shows how a reading of Jemison's narrative that locates those moments at which perspectives and agendas seem most at odds reveals not only an ethnic voice, but a gendered one.

Cooper's putative cultural relativism is also the focus of Scott Michaelson's "The Color Line, Beavers, and the Destructuring of White

Identity in Cooper's *The Last of the Mohicans*" (*JFCSMP* 5 [1994]: 11–17). Michaelson examines several instances in the novel when race is depicted as mutable, and "whiteness" as a racial signifier is shown to rest on a foundation that includes "redness." What is confusing about Michaelson's argument is that he first posits a need for "destructuring" race, shows us how Cooper himself did so, but then seems uncomfortable with his own argument because, as he says, "Cooper is not a multiculturalist." In "The Beaver and His Cousin in Cooper's *The Last of the Mohicans*" (*ANQ* 8, ii: 11–16) Edward W. Pitcher traces the sources for Duncan Heyward's comparison of beaver villages and Huron villages to 18th-century natural history and, specifically, to *The Contemplative Philosopher,* a work attributed to Richard Lobb. But despite locating a cultural context for Heyward's comments on the relative levels of civilization attained by beavers and Native Americans, Pitcher claims that the context Cooper creates for those comments leaves his own attitudes toward such superstition and racism ambiguous. Christina Starobin's "Reading Cooper" (*JFCSMP* 6: 10–12) expresses her belief that public misconceptions of Cooper are the product of the latest film version of *The Last of the Mohicans* and Twain's famous send-up of his literary offenses. Her suggested remedy—to offer Cooper as a proto-environmentalist and enlightened supporter of interracial marriage—is clearly that of an enthusiastic reader and defender of Cooper's work. It is a short step from Starobin's environmentalist Cooper to George F. Bagby's "Kindred Spirits: Cooper and Thoreau" (*JFCSMP* 5 [1994]: 2–10), which unites this odd couple on the basis of shared views of nature.

Among those commenting on aspects of Cooper's work other than his handling of race is Brian Quinn, whose "James Fenimore Cooper's Social Views as Portrayed in *The American Democrat*" (*SELL* 45: 17–30) is a general introduction to Cooper's thoughts on politics and democracy as they are revealed in his 1838 essay; however, Quinn uses Cooper's views in a rather odd way to criticize contemporary democratic practices in the United States and Japan. In "'A Bold Stroke against the Wilderness': *Wyandotté* and Cooper's Critique of the Jeffersonian Ideology of Domestic Production" (*JFCSMP* 6: 4–9) James J. Shramer discusses *The Pioneers* as an expression of Cooper's apparent support for Jeffersonian agrarianism and opposition to the Hamiltonian vision of America as an industrial power. However, Shramer argues that *Wyandotté* reveals Cooper's rejection of both positions in favor of a "post-Jacksonian hybrid" that would emerge from the conflicting visions of Jefferson and

Hamilton. Cooper's work as a naval historian is David Curtis Skaggs's subject in "Aiming at the Truth: James Fenimore Cooper and the Battle of Lake Erie" (*Journal of Military History* 59: 237–55), which shows how despite Cooper's attempts to be truthful in his treatment of the Battle of Lake Erie in *The History of the Navy of the United States of America*, he was drawn into a controversy over the competence of the command of Oliver Hazard Perry during the battle. Robert D. Madison in "Cooper, Bancroft, and the Voorhees Court Martial" (*JFCSMP* 6: 1–4) speculates on the possibility that an 1845 letter from Cooper to Bancroft, who was then secretary of the navy, may have influenced Bancroft's concurrent attempts to establish a naval academy. In "Cooper and New York's Dutch Heritage" (*JFCSMP* 5 [1994]: 18–24) Wayne Franklin discusses how Cooper used the often incorrect stereotype of Dutch architecture in New York employed by Knickerbocker writers and how he diverged from it. Franklin believes that Cooper may have used descriptions of unpretentious Dutch architecture in his novels as a sort of implicit criticism of Yankee architecture and, by extension, the basic values of Yankee society.

While Irving has remained less controversial than Cooper, the year saw the publication of several substantial revisionist essays on various aspects of his work. M. Thomas Inge's *Washington Irving's Agrarian Fable* (Odense American Studies International Series, No. 14) is a brief monograph that explores the possibility that "The Legend of Sleepy Hollow" is actually an allegory of the competition between agrarianism and progress. As part of his argument regarding Irving's mastery of several languages in "A Chink in the Armor of Stanley Williams's Washington Irving: Irving's Modern Language Skills and His Use of Quevedo's *El Buscón*" (*SoAR* 60, i: 17–28) James C. Keil speculates that Quevedo's 1626 text in its original Spanish version may have been Irving's source for the character of Ichabod Crane. In "Recovering 'Rip Van Winkle': A Corrective Reading" (*ESQ* 40: 251–73) Hugh J. Dawson tries to rescue Irving's story from feminist and political misreadings by arguing that it can be understood only as a complement to "The Wife," the story that precedes it in *The Sketch-Book*. In this context, according to Dawson, "Rip Van Winkle" becomes "a gothic tale of a journey into a night world without pleasure" where a fulfilling marriage is impossible because women essentially do not exist. Peter G. Beidler's "William Cartwright, Washington Irving, and the 'Truth': A Shadow Allusion to Chaucer's *Canon's Yeoman's Tale*" (*ChauR* 29: 434–39) comments on the ironic use of the term "truth" in Irving's tale; Cartwright's *The Ordinary*, the play from which Irving took his epigraph; and Chaucer's tale, which may be alluded to in that epigraph. According to Jonathan A. Cook's "'Prodigious Poop': Comic Context and Psychological Subtext in Irving's *Knickerbocker History*" (*NCL* 49: 483–512), Irving's *A History of New York, From the Beginning of the World to the End of the Dutch Dynasty* is also an elaborate comic allegory in which the "peopling" of North America is meant to suggest human reproduction, and the "infant history of New York" is a parallel to the Freudian model of childhood psychological development. Cook's reading is lively and even convincing, despite his failing to account for Irving's familiarity with Freud. Finally, Daniel E. Williams's "Authoring the Author: Heroes and Greeks" (*EAL* 30: 264–74) projects Irving's concept of authorship into the future by using Diedrich Knickerbocker's romantic reconceptualization of the author as originary and heroic as an entrée to speculate about the ways in which the brave new world of computers and the Worldwide Web will result in newly defining authorship to be something like "collective critical exchange."

Of those in Irving's Knickerbocker circle, only James Kirke Paulding and Fitz-James O'Brien received attention this year. In Paulding's case that attention took the form of an edition of five of his *Stories of St. Nicholas* (Syracuse), which will interest scholars less as holiday fare and more for the anti-Catholic and anti-British sentiment that identify these 1830s tales as political statements inspired by Paulding's association with the patriotic cult of St. Nicholas. Neil Cornwell's "Gothic and Its Origins in East and West: Vladimir Odoevsky and Fitz-James O'Brien," pp. 117–28 in *Exhibited by Candlelight: Sources and Developments in the Gothic Tradition*, ed. Valeria Tinkler-Villani et al. (Rodopi), explores similarities in the use of alchemy in O'Brien's stories "The Diamond Lens" (1858) and "The Sylph" (1837) and several stories by Odoevsky, the leading figure of Russian high romanticism. Cornwell argues that his comparative reading and search for possible shared sources results in the "inescapable conclusion that O'Brien's use of the alchemical tradition . . . lays him open to a charge . . . of plagiarism."

Among work on Bryant and the Schoolroom Poets is Carl Ostrowski's "'I Stand Upon Their Ashes in Thy Beam': The Indian Question and William Cullen Bryant's Literary Removals" (*ATQ* 9: 299–312), which, rejecting as oversimplification the conventional interpretation that Bryant depicted Native Americans as noble savages, examines Bryant's poetic treatment of Indians in poems written between 1821 and 1832 to demonstrate that his depictions embody the cultural tensions inherent in the debate over Indian Removal as well as Bryant's own evolving thoughts on the issue. In "Intellectual Authority and Gender Ideology in Nineteenth-Century Boston: The Life and Letters of Oliver Wendell Holmes, Sr." (*Historical Journal of Massachusetts* 22: 1–16) Tim Duffy does a solid job of exploring how Holmes's approach to medicine and his views on such matters as friendship and conversation demonstrate his own negotiations of masculine and feminine spheres, although it is never apparent how Holmes's example can be generalized to all of 19th-century Boston. Michael J. Bell's " 'The Only True Folk Songs We Have in English': James Russell Lowell and the Politics of the Nation" (*JAF* 108: 131–55) interprets Lowell's 1855 Lowell Institute lecture as an attempt "to write a new idiom through which his fragmented society might define itself" by using the English ballad as a model. Frederick J. Blue in "The Poet and the Reformer: Longfellow, Sumner, and the Bonds of Male Friendship" (*JER* 15: 273–97) aims to correct interpretations of Charles Sumner as a man incapable of personal warmth through his exploration of the long and loving relationship of Longfellow and Sumner, "the Massachusetts odd couple," based largely on published sources. In "Wind and Fire: St. Catherine of Sienna and the North Wind in John Greenleaf Whittier's *Snow-Bound*" (*ANQ* 8, i: 18–20) Gregory E. Jordan asserts that for his poem Whittier drew on both St. Catherine of Sienna's designation as the patroness of extinguishing others' fires and the North Wind's folkloric association with aging and death. All of the poets discussed above, and 27 more, are represented in *Poetry of the American Renaissance: A Diverse Anthology from the Romantic Period,* ed. Paul Kane (Braziller), which contains Kane's informative and useful introductions and notes to selections from the works of poets whom Kane characterizes as representing "both the canon and . . . the apocrypha."

The general subject matter, focus, and quality of research in Susan J. Tracy's *In the Master's Eye: Representations of Women, Blacks, and Poor Whites in Antebellum Southern Literature* (Mass.) give it the earmarks of an important study of writing by George Tucker, John Pendleton Kennedy, William Alexander Caruthers, Nathaniel Beverly Tucker, William Gilmore Simms, and James Ewell Heath. However, one cannot help but wonder how much richer the findings of such a study might have been had Tracy allowed herself to escape from the confines of a "feminist marxist" ideology that clearly inhibits her from locating the "complexity of the human spirit" that she claims is totally absent from every one of the antebellum Southern novels she read. It may finally be too reductive to lump all of this work together as "a testament to the failure of an earlier conservatism." One who would undoubtedly disagree with Tracy, particularly in the case of Simms, is John Mayfield, who begins his " 'The Soul of a Man!': William Gilmore Simms and the Myths of Southern Manhood" (*JER* 15: 477–500) by questioning Simms's commitment to the Southern, patrician paradigm of manliness. Through readings of *Richard Hurdis* and *Woodcraft*, works that he believes feature shifting images of manliness and not representations of a stable patriarchy, Mayfield argues that Simms's imaginative efforts to come to grips with changing social patterns were similar to those of Hawthorne and Melville.

One of the studies of antebellum historiography to appear this year is Eric Wertheimer's "Noctography: Representing Race in William Prescott's *History of the Conquest of Mexico*" (*AL* 67: 303–27). Wertheimer's study is a complication of John Ernest's "Reading the Romantic Past: William H. Prescott's *History of the Conquest of Mexico*" (see *ALS 1993*, pp. 176–77) that takes the reader on a labyrinthine journey through romantic historiography, 19th-century language theory, and an elaborate reading of the neglected first chapter of the *History* to demonstrate that what Ernest characterizes as a "metahistorical commentary" on reading the past as text is actually "the agonistic conflict and ambivalences inherent in the self-conscious mode of representing otherness." In "Re-Inventing the Puritan Fathers: George Bancroft, Nathaniel Hawthorne, and the Birth of Endicott's Ghost" (*ATQ* 9: 131–52) Harold K. Bush also explores Bancroft's use of the Puritans in his *History of the United States* as the basis for a "transcendental view of American history" based on viewing the nation as moving toward millennial fulfillment of ideals established by and represented in the Puritan legacy. Bush positions Hawthorne as explicitly challenging Bancroft's romanticized historiography in stories such as "Endicott and the Red Cross" and "The May-Pole of Merry Mount."

Those interested in antebellum "dark reform" fiction will be glad to note the appearance of a new edition of George Lippard's *The Quaker City; or, The Monks of Monk Hall* (Mass.), ed. by the foremost authority on Lippard's work and his best-known contemporary champion, David S. Reynolds. Those familiar with Reynolds's previous work will find little new in his copious introduction to this edition, but for the uninitiated it is an excellent summary of Lippard's life, career, and importance. Lippard is also the subject of Gary Ashwill's "The Mysteries of Capitalism in George Lippard's City Novels" (*ESQ* 40: 293–317), which is an attempt to redeem Lippard from the charge that his reform message is compromised by the pornographic appeal of his work by reading both *The Quaker City* and *New York: Its Upper Ten and Lower Million* as fictions that internalize the dominant values of capitalism in sensationalism and readers' responses to it. To Ashwill, then, Lippard's work is "a massive deconstruction of industrial capitalism" that works so well because it does not work in a traditional aesthetic sense. As clever as such a reading assuredly is, I tend to balk at an argument that asserts that those things that have always seemed bad are somehow suddenly not bad at all. In "The Peculiar Birthright of Every American: George Watterston's *The Lawyer*" (*SAF* 23: 55–71) Edward Watts disagrees with Reynolds's assertion in *Beneath the American Renaissance* that in the 1820s and 1830s Lippard and George Thompson wrote "dark reform" fiction to subvert a unified "culture of morality" that had controlled literary culture in the United States from 1770 to 1820, and he offers a reading of Watterston's 1808 novel to demonstrate that it was indeed a subversive novel, produced at a time when the literary atmosphere purportedly was homogeneously moral in its support of social and political institutions.

Christoph Irmscher's fascinating "Violence and Artistic Representation in John James Audubon" (*Raritan* 15, ii: 1–34) is one of two studies of Audubon to appear this year. In it Irmscher reads a number of plates for *The Birds of America* against passages from *Ornithological Biography* in order to argue that violence is not only a key component of Audubon's method of composition—he sketched many of his avian subjects by killing them and then re-creating their live appearance using boards and wire frame—but it is also a thematic continuity in a work that has been most often characterized as organizationally chaotic. The other essay that treats Audubon is Elisa New's "Beyond the Romance Theory of American Vision: Beauty and the Qualified Will in Edwards, Jefferson, and Audubon" (*AmLH* 7: 381–414), which is as fine a tracing of intellectual genealogy as one is likely to encounter. Dissatisfied with ideologically oriented analyses of American texts, New asserts that "such criticism drastically underestimates the capacity of an ocular poetics to know the difference between perceptual power, deployed by an ego, and the firm, amplitudinous element of nature's force that gives the ego its very footing, its gravity." The key to New's "ocular poetics" is Jonathan Edwards's delineation of a qualified will, which conceives of limited human freedom being exercised through immersion in and experience of the dynamism of creation. She finds a similar emphasis on the importance of firsthand experience and oneness with nature in Jefferson's *Notes on the State of Virginia,* and she makes a case for Audubon's plates to *The Birds of America* as a significant contribution to the development of American philosophy in their stylized merging of the eye and the world in the visual event that Audubon called a "sighting." The result of New's important essay is a demonstration of how rich criticism can be when it frees itself from the narrowness of reading only ideology into texts that have their genesis in a matrix of personal, cultural, philosophic, and, yes, aesthetic concerns.

Among other studies worth noting is Thomas M. Kitts's *The Theatrical Life of George Henry Boker* (Peter Lang, 1994), which is a slim but well-researched introduction to the life and work of an important antebellum playwright. Barbara F. Luebke's "Elias Boudinot and 'Indian Removal,'" pp. 115–44 in *Outsiders in 19th-Century Press History: Multicultural Perspectives,* ed. Frankie Hutton and Barbara Straus Reed (Bowling Green), is a chronological study of Boudinot's opposition to removal, and his change of heart on that issue, based on his reporting and editorializing in the pages of the *Cherokee Phoenix, and Indians Advocate.* In "Davy Crockett" (*History Workshop Journal* 40: 184–89) Mandy Merck recounts her fascination with Davy Crockett in the 1950s and links her own opposition to the Vietnam War to Crockett's unpopular stand against the Cherokee Removal, which Merck calls "Crockett's most strikingly conscientious act."

iii Women Writers and Others at Mid-Century

I have already characterized this year as one that produced a substantial amount of significant studies of women writers; now I want to pick up that thread to examine several works that expand our understanding of the writing of early-19th-century American women. Catherine Hobbs's *Nineteenth-Century Women Learn to Write* is an important study of the broad range of ways that women in 19th-century America achieved what Hobbs calls "effective literacy," that is, "a level of literacy that enables the user to act to effect change." Since paths to education and empowerment open to men were closed to women, the essays in this collection focus on those sometimes extraordinary means and institutions through which women could pursue literacy. Part 1 is devoted to social and cultural contexts for women's literacy, and it includes Jane Rose's "Conduct Books for Women, 1830–1860: A Rationale for Women's Conduct and Role in America" (pp. 37–58), which examines 20 conduct books to expose the conflicting ideologies presented in them and their possible effect on women's education; June Hadden Hobbs's exploration of the practice of women's hymn text writing in "His Religion and Hers in Nineteenth-Century Hymnody" (pp. 120–44); and Nicole Tonkovich's "Writing Circles: Harriet Beecher Stowe, the Semi-Colon Club, and the Construction of Authorship" (pp. 145–75), which provides valuable information on the Cincinnati literary club that taught men and women to read and may have aided in the reconceptualization of individual authorship for those who participated. Part 2, which focuses on various practices that promoted women's literacy, includes Shirley Wilson Logan's "Literacy as a Tool for Social Action among Nineteenth-Century African American Women" (pp. 179–96), an examination of how mentors and literary study clubs aided African American lecturers such as Sojourner Truth, Frances E. W. Harper, and Ida Wells; Judy Nolte Temple and Suzanne L. Bunkers's "Mothers, Daughters, Diaries: Literacy, Relationship, and Cultural Context" (pp. 197–216), an exploration of how diary-keeping became a practice that extended female literacy; and a cluster of three essays that examine how women were taught rhetoric in several Eastern and Southeastern schools (pp. 230–92).

Telling Travels is an anthology that broadens our understanding of travel writing by American women by providing selections from such little-known writers as Emma Hart Willard, Abby Jane Morrell, and Sarah Rogers Haight alongside the more familiar work of Fuller, Sedgwick, and Stowe. A related study, Linda S. Bergmann's "A Troubled Marriage of Discourses: Science Writing and Travel Narrative in Louis and Elizabeth Agassiz's *A Journey in Brazil*" (*JACult* 18, ii: 83–88), asserts that Elizabeth Agassiz's personal journal offers more information on Brazil than her husband's record of his scientific observations of that country. Like *Telling Travels, Southern Women's Writing: Colonial to Contemporary* and *Plays by Early American Women* are significant anthologies not only for reintroducing a number of previously marginalized writers and works but for making this little-known work available for use in the classroom. Darby Lewes in *Dream Revisionaries* explores a neglected genre and gives some attention to Frances Wright's radically egalitarian Nashoba community and her 1822 novel, *A Few Days in Athens*. In *Swindler, Spy, Rebel* Kathleen De Grave draws on a variety of texts by antebellum women writers—including Alcott, Sedgwick, Stowe, and Southworth—to establish a context for her treatment of the representation of the confidence woman in both fiction and autobiography as one who managed "to step outside her restrictive role as commodity to achieve a personal sense of selfhood, no matter how socially unacceptable that self might be."

A work of note that I neglected to mention last year is Bruce Mills's *Cultural Reformations: Lydia Maria Child and the Literature of Reform* (Georgia, 1994), which presents an interpretation of Child at odds with that of Carolyn Karcher in her *The First Woman of the Republic* (see *ALS 1994*, p. 213). Mills's nuanced readings of Child's major work support his central assertion that Child's success as a reformer is best understood in terms of her ability to moderate in her writing the stridency of more radical voices. Child is also the subject of Tom Petitjean's "Child's *Hobomok*" (*Expl* 53: 145–47), which suggests that Child had to use the supernatural and the concept of preordination to justify interracial marriage to her audience, but that this technique, paradoxically, allowed her to introduce ideas that seem to anticipate feminism and multiculturalism. Of course, Stowe was also the subject of a major new biography in 1994, Joan Hedrick's *Harriet Beecher Stowe,* which is the focus of Robert S. Levine's "In and Out of the Parlor" (*AmLH* 7: 669–80). Levine argues that because of Hedrick's "commitment to a critical orthodoxy of the identity politics of the 1990s," her work is just as hamstrung by its social and cultural milieu as Forrest Wilson's *Crusader in Crinoline* is by the cultural assumptions of the 1940s. In " 'Woe Unto You That Desire the Day of the Lord': Harriet Beecher Stowe and the Corruption of Christianity in *Dred, A Tale of the Great Dismal Swamp*" (*Anglican and Episcopal History* 64: 280–99) Sarah D. Hartshorne writes of *Dred* as Stowe's Book of Revelation, full of the pessimism, dark humor, and biting irony that grew from her understanding of the degree to which Christianity was implicated in the crimes of slavery. Peter A. Dorsey's interesting "De-Authorizing Slavery: Realism in Stowe's *Uncle Tom's Cabin* and Brown's *Clotel*" (*ESQ* 41: 257–88) suggests that because both of these works aimed at doing the cultural work of abolition, they eschewed the aesthetics of fiction for a protorealistic aesthetic that lent authenticity to their depictions of the abuses of slavery. According to Dorsey, this protorealism may have had an effect on realistic fiction after the Civil War, but it also created a straitjacket of authenticity that hampered the work of African American novelists from Frederick Douglass and Harriet Wilson to Richard Wright. Perhaps the most important work on Stowe published this year is Cynthia Griffin Wolff's " 'Masculinity' in *Uncle Tom's Cabin*" (*AQ* 47: 595–618), a brilliant revisionist reading of Stowe's novel against shifting 19th-century notions of masculinity and the contentious factions within the abolitionist movement; Wolff's study authorizes a reconceptualization of the character of Tom.

Work on Louisa May Alcott published this year indicates a scholarly interest in broadening the perspective on Alcott's career beyond a focus on *Little Women*. In fact, only Beverly Lyon Clark comes close to *Little Women* by discussing the first of its sequels in "Domesticating the School Story, Regendering a Genre: Alcott's *Little Men*" (*NLH* 26: 323–42). Clark reads Alcott's novel as a school story in the genre of Thomas Hughes's *Tom Brown's School Days* but with differences that Clark believes regenerated the genre, including Alcott's introduction of females into a type of narrative where they had rarely appeared before and her attempt to bridge gender and generational gaps by using Jo March Bhaer as the moral center of her story. Madeleine Stern's edition, *Louisa May Alcott Unmasked: Collected Thrillers* (Northeastern), prints the texts of all 29 of the rediscovered blood-and-thunder tales that Alcott wrote between 1863 and 1870 and that were previously available only in five separate volumes, beginning with 1975's *Behind a Mask,* ed. Stern and Leona Rostenberg. Stern and Kent Bicknell are responsible for "Louisa May Alcott Had Her Head Examined" (*SAR*, pp. 277–89), a reprinting, with lighthearted commentary, of a report of an 1875 phrenological reading. In Mary Rigsby's " 'So Like Women!': Louisa May Alcott's *Work* and the Ideology of Relations," pp. 109–27 in *Redefining the Political Novel,* Christie Devon, Alcott's protagonist whose character is based on Margaret Fuller's "gendered transcendentalism," is discussed as "a foil for traditional heroics." To Rigsby, instead of the male "rhetoric of strength," *Work* demonstrates the inclination of women writers to use an alternative that resisted heroic individualism and offered in its place a model of transcendent cooperation. In "By the Light of Her Mother's Lamp: Woman's Work Versus Man's Philosophy in Louisa May Alcott's 'Transcendental Wild Oats' " (*SAR*, pp. 69–81) Sandra Harbert Petrulionis discusses Alcott's 1873 parody of Transcendental utopianism as a radical "woman-centered narrative" that inverts (and subverts) the sentimental form "by supplanting the father's with the mother's story, effectively silencing the would-be hero."

Perhaps no work in recent memory will do more to dispel the notion of the monolith of 19th-century American feminism than Patricia Okker's *Our Sister Editors: Sarah J. Hale and the Tradition of Nineteenth-Century Editors* (Georgia). Okker's initial research on Hale helped her discover a sizable culture of female editors in mid-19th-century America (an appendix lists more than 600), and that culture is presented as the context from which Hale emerged. Okker focuses on Hale's theories of the author, the reader, and the text as well as her flexible approach to concepts of sexual difference and separate spheres to show how Hale "manipulated the idea of a woman's culture to argue for a separate public space for woman—a space, not coincidentally, occupied by women's periodicals." Barbara A. Bardes and Suzanne Gossett arrive at a similar conclusion in "Sarah J. Hale: Selective Promoter of Her Sex," pp. 18–34 in *A Living of Words*. They believe that Hale, who has been the target of criticism for her antifeminist views, "must be seen in a context more nuanced than feminist or antifeminist," and they claim that Hale was a selective promoter of women who supported women writers and editors like herself, especially if those women also happened to exemplify Hale's own beliefs in Christianity and the virtues of domesticity. Another rap against Hale has been her support of colonization as an answer to slavery; that is the subject of Susan M. Ryan's "Errand Into Africa: Colonization and Nation Building in Sarah J. Hale's *Liberia*" (*NEQ* 68: 558–83). After a detailed reading of Hale's text, Ryan concludes that Hale's novel is a sort of "wishful distortion" aimed at a white audience. It is, in fact, a story that exonerates whites for their participation in slavery at the same time that it credits them for fashioning, in colonization, the best remedy for slavery. Ryan's treatment of the many moral and aesthetic difficulties of *Liberia* is superb in itself, but it is done for the more important purpose of arguing for an expanded vision that would allow works like Hale's to be considered along with those of Stowe and Child, whose positions on slavery are more acceptable today. Caroline Field Levander's comparison of novels by Hale and Henry James in "Bawdy Talk: The Politics of Women's Public Speech in *The Lecturess* and *The Bostonians*" (*AL* 67: 467–85) demonstrates, according to Levander, how women have been excluded from public arenas by males who defined women's public oratory through their bodies, thus enabling the silencing of women and the consolidation of "the exclusive masculinity of the public arena."

In "Anger in the House: Fanny Fern's *Ruth Hall* and the Redrawing of Emotional Boundaries in Mid-Nineteenth-Century America" (*SAR*, pp. 251–61) Linda Grasso uses the debate following the publication of

Ruth Hall in 1855 to show how "the proliferation of slave narratives, domestic novels, and woman's rights literature made anger in and at the familial, marital, and national house more imaginable than it had been earlier in the century." Like Grasso, Kristie Hamilton in "The Politics of Survival: Sara Parton's *Ruth Hall* and the Literature of Labor," pp. 86–108 in *Redefining the Political Novel,* makes use of Elizabeth Cady Stanton's 1855 review of *Ruth Hall,* and specifically Stanton's description of the novel as "a slave narrative." Stanton's characterization, suggesting that Parton's work is an advocacy novel, is very much in keeping with Hamilton's desire to show that *Ruth Hall* is not only a political novel, but one that represents mid-19th-century, middle-class "woman's fiction" shifting away from narratives that were constrained by dominant cultural assumptions regarding the sphere and duties of women to a sharper political representation of women's oppression.

The work of a number of other women writers was the subject of revisionist interpretations this year. For example, in "Mothering a Female Saint: Susan Warner's Dialogic Role in *The Wide, Wide World*" (*ELWIU* 22: 59–74) Veronica Stewart provides an interesting and complex Bakhtinian reading of Warner's novel that rejects attempts to interpret it "as strictly a socio-religious rather than a literary project"; Stewart views it not as an analogue to *The Pilgrim's Progress* but as a work that carries on an intricate dialogue with Bunyan's text, focusing specifically on the traditional concept of Christian conversion. Dawn Henwood's "First-Person Storytelling in Elizabeth Stoddard's *Morgesons*: Realism, Romance, and the Psychology of the Narrating Self" (*ESQ* 41: 41–63) convincingly asserts that it is the liminal status of Stoddard's novel as a work of romantic realism or realistic romance that accounts for the rejection of *The Morgesons* by Stoddard's contemporary audience. To Henwood, Stoddard's harmonizing of the "contrapuntal strains of romance and realism" is most evident in the blending of "a sharp eye for realistic detail" with the "highly interiorized narrative" of an unconventional first-person narrator. In "The Coded Language of *Female Quixotism*" (*StAH* 3: 23–35) Sevda Çaliskan is similarly concerned with the romance, specifically the ways in which Tabitha Tenney employs the "exclusively male" genre of adventure romance as the basis of her 1801 novel while simultaneously presenting metamessages that undermine the authority of both the romance and the dominant ideology.

Amy Hudock's goal in "Challenging the Definition of Heroism in E. D. E. N. Southworth's *The Hidden Hand*" (*ATQ* 9: 5–20) is to rehabilitate the sentimental by proving its subversive nature. To that end, Hudock reads Capitola Black, the protagonist of Southworth's 1859 novel, as neither the traditional American hero, identified by D. H. Lawrence as "hard, isolate, stoic, and a killer," nor as a conventional sentimental heroine who sacrifices for others to fulfill the demands of the cult of true womanhood, but as a new sort of *female* hero who wins her own way in the world without being a victim or a murderer. In a comparable manner Tracy McCabe in "Avenging Angel: Tragedy and Womanhood in Julia Ward Howe's *The World's Own*" (*Legacy* 12: 98–111) reads Lenora, the central female character in Howe's 1857 verse drama, as a complexly " 'mixed' tragic character" who resists the traditional binary categorizing of women as demons or angels, making the play "a sub-textual feminist exposure of the constructedness of the category of 'woman.' " Dawn E. Keetley's concern in "Unsettling the Frontier: Gender and Racial Identity in Caroline Kirkland's *A New Home, Who'll Follow?* and *Forest Life*" (*Legacy* 12: 17–37) is not how her subject succeeds in subverting the dominant culture, but how she fails. In the two works she examines, Keetley finds that white women succeed at pioneer life because they move fluidly among gender roles, while Native American characters are imprisoned within their rigid primitivism to the point that white pioneers can mimic their primitive freedom and thereby supersede them. In Keetley's view, Kirkland's "*in*ability to move along and test boundaries of race" results in part from her tacit acceptance of rigid racial categories; her failure to question these in her work compromises her challenge to gendered identity in her culture.

Jeffrey D. Groves's "Maria Gowen Brooks (c. 1795–1845)" (*Legacy* 12: 38–46) and Paola Gemme's "Anna Sophia Winterbotham Stephens, 1810–1886" (*Legacy* 12: 47–55) each supply useful introductory biographical sketches of their subjects, as does Victoria Clements in her introduction to a new classroom edition of Catharine Maria Sedgwick's *A New England Tale; or, Sketches of New England Character and Manners* (Oxford). The most notable aspect of *Principles and Privilege: Two Women's Lives on a Georgia Plantation* (Michigan), besides the reprinting of Frances Kemble's 1863 *Journal of a Residence on a Georgia Plantation* and the 1883 *Ten Years on a Georgia Plantation* by Kemble's daughter, Frances Butler Leigh, is Dana D. Nelson's copious introduction. Nelson astutely demonstrates not only that well-to-do women in Victorian America could strongly assert their awareness, ambition, and abilities, but that a "pronounced difference in political sympathy between mother and

daughter . . . exists alongside the many congruences in their personalities and literary styles."

iv African American Writers and the Literature of Abolition

Notable among general studies of antebellum African American writing
are books by Kimberly Rae Connor and John Ernest, each of which
approaches interpretations of these texts from the perspective of religion.
In *Resistance and Reformation in Nineteenth-Century African-American
Literature* (Miss.), his study of work by William Wells Brown, Harriet Wilson, Harriet Jacobs, Martin Delaney, Frederick Douglass, and
Frances E. W. Harper, Ernest states explicitly that understanding the
cultural work of these writers "requires that one take seriously the
dynamics of belief." Specifically, Ernest reads these various writers' works
as similar attempts to influence the reader's understanding of history and
progress through a reliance on what Paul Ricoeur has called "a Christian
interpretation of the mystery of history," a technique that basically tries
to expose and capitalize on discrepancies between secular and providential history. Connor's *Conversions and Visions in the Writings of African
American Women* (Tennessee, 1994) treats Harriet Jacobs's *Incidents in the
Life of a Slave Girl*, Rebecca Jackson's *Gifts of Power*, and *The Narrative of
Sojourner Truth* as dramas of conversion into selfhood that present "a
powerful vision of women in the process of changing and developing
their full human potential." According to Connor, "Religion is inextricably bound to the African-American woman's literary tradition." Carla L.
Peterson's *"Doers of the Word"* necessarily covers some of the same ground
as Connor's study. However, Peterson's examination of the social, political, and cultural work performed by such black women activists as
Sojourner Truth, Maria Stewart, Jarena Lee, Nancy Price, Mary Ann
Shadd Cary, Frances E. W. Harper, Sarah Parker Remond, Harriet
Jacobs, Harriet Wilson, and Charlotte Forten has the very different goal
of enlarging "our historical understanding of nineteenth-century black
resistance movements by supplementing the existing scholarship on
Frederick Douglass, David Walker, Henry Highland Garnet, Martin
Delaney, and other male figures with an examination of the role of black
women in these movements." In "Democratic Idealism in the Black
Press," pp. 5–20 in *Outsiders in 19th-Century Press History: Multicultural
Perspectives,* Hutton demonstrates that unlike the politically partisan and

often mean-spirited mainstream press, the black press, both before and after the Civil War, was consistently optimistic about democratic ideals and their applicability to African Americans.

Two notable explorations of the genre of the slave narrative are those by Richard Hardack and Lindon Barrett. Hardack's "Water Pollution and Motion Sickness: Rites of Passage in Nineteenth-Century Slave and Travel Narratives" (*ESQ* 41: 1–40) examines how "Inverted representations of water and liminal travel in slave and travel narratives are closely linked indices of how the two genres become mutually defining and intertextual." However, Hardack's choice to concentrate on Poe's *The Narrative of Arthur Gordon Pym* and Douglass's *Narrative,* with briefer attention given to Melville's "Benito Cereno" and Jacobs's *Incidents in the Life of a Slave Girl,* finally does more to convince one of the expected— that the narratives of Douglass and Jacobs, while employing similar reliance on water imagery, have a tenuous relationship at best to works like those of Poe and Melville. In "African-American Slave Narratives: Literacy, the Body, Authority" (*AmLH* 7: 415–42) Barrett points out that representations of the body in slave narratives are so closely linked to issues of literacy that the two concerns must be taken as one. Arguing that negotiations of the issues of literacy in these texts is a relatively uniform and stable endeavor, while negotiations of representations of the African American body are highly unstable, Barrett offers a theory of four patterns found in slave narratives for representing the body. He effectively illustrates his theory with readings of a variety of narratives, and he concludes that the four patterns described "account for the primary ways in which ex-slave narrators struggle with the exigencies of long-standing U.S. beliefs and customs positing that African-American bodies betoken a social presence curiously marked by a *visible* absence of mind."

In "Spirit Matters: Re-Possessing the African American Woman's Tradition" (*Legacy* 12: 1–16) Anne Dalke finds the convention of locating the starting point for an African American women's literary tradition in slave narratives to be too restrictive because of the narratives' reliance on modes of realism and naturalism that eschew "the transcendent and ideal to document the verifiable—often the violent" and thereby fail to grant a sense of independent agency to their characters. Instead she proposes, much like Kimberly Rae Connor, an alternative point of origin in spiritual autobiography, claiming that if we could conceive of a tradition emerging from a dialogue between the two genres, we would get a "more complete, and a more complex, sense of the aims and achievements of the African-American women's literary tradition." To prove her point, Dalke contrasts Rebecca Jackson's *Gifts of Power* with Jacobs's *Incidents in the Life of a Slave Girl* to demonstrate how Jackson's Shaker-based approach to experience is more empowering than Jacobs's realism. In a related reading of Harriet Wilson's *Our Nig,* Julia Stern finds an "overarching atmosphere of maternal violence and filial terror," which in turn motivates her argument in "Excavating Genre in *Our Nig*" (*AL* 67: 439– 66) that it is more appropriate to read Wilson's novel through the generic lens of gothic fiction than as a sentimental novel like *Uncle Tom's Cabin.*

Most notable among the wealth of work this year devoted to the writings of Frederick Douglass is a special issue of *ATQ* (9, iii) ed. and introduced by Philip G. Auger. Included in this collection of essays intended to demonstrate "the need for and the richness of reinterpretation of Douglass's life, writing, and cultural influence" is Frank Towers's "African-American Baltimore in the Era of Frederick Douglass" (pp. 165–80), an exploration of various anomalies of African American life in Baltimore from 1790 to 1860; James A. Wohlpart's "Privatized Sentiment and the Institution of Christianity: Douglass's Ethical Stance in the *Narrative*" (pp. 181–94), an examination of the unique ethical stance which Douglass developed in his *Narrative* that allows him to operate "both inside and outside the boundaries of American Christianity"; Lisa Sisco's rich " 'Writing in the Spaces Left': Literacy as a Process of Becoming in the Narratives of Frederick Douglass" (pp. 195– 227), which shows how "Douglass achieves the ability to write in a state of fluidity, of acknowledged heteroglossia, always maneuvering himself into 'the spaces left' by his white enslavers"; T. Gregory Garvey's detailed account of Douglass's transition from the Garrisonian faction of moral abolitionism to the political abolitionism of Gerrit Smith, "Frederick Douglass's Change of Opinion on the U.S. Constitution: Abolition and the 'Elements of Power' " (pp. 229–43); and Russ Castronovo's " 'As to Nation, I Belong to None': Ambivalence, Diaspora, and Frederick Douglass" (pp. 245–60), a reading of three texts which span Douglass's career from 1853 until 1893 that show how he consistently undermined the notion of America as a cultural and racial monolith by arguing for the nation's intercultural foundations and racial and ethnic hybridity. Taken altogether, these essays make a substantial contribution to scholarship on Douglass, but none of them may have the impact of Maggie Sale's superb examination of the national debate over the Creole rebellion, the basis of Douglass's only novel, *The Heroic Slave,* in "To Make the Past Useful: Frederick Douglass's Politics of Solidarity" (*ArQ* 51, iii: 25–60). Sale intends her study to show "the extraordinary power of slaveholders and their advocates to affect policy within the federal government" and "the cultural logic of masculine white supremacy that made the representation of the heroic slave-rebels [of the Creole] nonsensical to most Americans." The establishment of this historical context is excellent foreground for the second part of Sale's essay, a reading of the novel which convincingly demonstrates that Douglass's aim went beyond legally ending slavery "to assert the inherent equality of enslaved African-American men with the patriots of the U.S. Revolution." One might compare the clarity of Sale's argument with the confusion at the heart of Henry Louis Gates, Jr.'s "A Dangerous Literacy: The Legacy of Frederick Douglass" (*NYTBR*, 28 May 1995, pp. 3, 16), a curious report about the research of Maria Diedrich of the University of Münster into the previously lost papers of Ottilie Assing, with whom Douglass apparently had a passionate affair from 1856 until 1881. Gates's account is made all the more curious by his apparent difficulty in coming to terms with one or more of the following: (1) that Douglass is thought of as the first great black American, (2) that Douglass is thought of as the world's greatest black intellectual, (3) that Douglass had affairs, and/or (4) that Douglass in his various acts of "self-creation" never once wrote about his affairs. It is enough to make one's head spin or, at least, to wish that Professor Diedrich was reporting her own research.

In "The City as Liberating Space in *Life and Times of Frederick Douglass,*" pp. 21–36 in *The City in African-American Literature,* Robert Butler notes that after describing his escape from slavery in *Life and Times,* Douglass moves "through increasingly more liberating forms of urban space" at the same time that he three times rejects the pastoral impulse. Butler believes that Douglass helped establish the tradition that "black literature in America is strongly urban in character" through a vision of American life that values the possibilities of city life and runs counter to the mainstream vision, represented by white writers from 1840 to 1890, that venerated the pastoral. For those interested in the intersection of concerns of race and gender as it is represented in Douglass's work, two studies are of note: Robyn Wiegman's meditation on *The Heroic Slave* in *American Anatomies* and Maurice Wallace's "Constructing the Black Masculine: Frederick Douglass, Booker T. Washington, and the Sublimits of African American Autobiography," pp. 245–70 in *Subjects and Citizens*.

Donna Dunbar-Odom focuses on the key issue of literacy in " 'Mastering' Representation: Rhetorical Constructions of the Life of Frederick Douglass" (*CCTEP* 55: 26–32), contrasting representations of literacy by Douglass in his autobiographies with passages in two Reconstruction era biographical sketches of Douglass taken from Lydia Maria Child's *The Freedmen's Book* (1865) and the American Tract Society's *The Freedmen's Third Reader* (1865–66). Not surprisingly, Dunbar-Odom discovers that while Douglass emphasizes the power of literacy to liberate, the textbook sketches emphasize "lessons designed to teach 19th-century Protestant standards of behavior" and dilute the power of Douglass's own "liberatory discourse." Luis A. Jiménez is also interested in comparison in "Nineteenth-Century Autobiography in the Afro-Americas: Frederick Douglass and Juan Francisco Manzano" (*AHR* 14, ii: 47–52). Curiously, though, Jiménez actually seems to find more real differences than similarities in comparing Douglass's *Narrative* with the Afro-Cuban Manzano's *Autobiography*; his discovery, however, does not inhibit him from attempting to locate, with the help of Derrida and Lacan, what he identifies as a "hidden unity." In "Performativity, Autobiographical Practice, Resistance" (*ABSt* 10: 17–33) Sidonie Smith compares Douglass's account of his first antislavery speaking appearance in Nantucket in 1841 from *My Bondage and My Freedom* with William Lloyd Garrison's account of the same speech in his prefatory remarks to Douglass's *Narrative* in order to show that Douglass's later account "challenges the white man's account" and "the way in which Garrison rewrote him as a 'text.' " It might be noted, however, that the type of resistance that Smith goes to such lengths to theorize has been more concretely established by John Sekora (see *ALS 1994*, pp. 217–18) simply by studying the degree of editorial control Douglass exerted over the first and second versions of his autobiography.

Finally, for anyone seeking a broad and generous sampling of Douglass's writings for classroom use, *The Oxford Frederick Douglass Reader*, ed. William L. Andrews (Oxford), would certainly have to be the text of choice. Besides the complete text of the 1845 *Narrative* and substantial selections from the second and third autobiographies, this collection includes reliable texts of *The Heroic Slave, The Lessons of the Hour,* and other important miscellaneous writings. In many ways the very best work in early-19th-century American literature this year springs from the same impulse that surely informed Andrews's selection of texts for this collection—a purposeful open-mindedness that not only represents the subject of the scholarship fairly but aims at extending and enriching the reader's understanding.

The Pennsylvania State University

13 Late-19th-Century Literature

Lawrence J. Oliver

The general contour of the scholarship surveyed below follows patterns established during the past few years. The feminist project of rediscovering or interpreting women writers continues unabated, usually with exciting results; and the boundaries of that project are extending beyond the "literary" into "literacy." The race-class-gender paradigm continues to dominate the critical methodologies; and New Historicism, however one defines it, is pervasive. It is rare to encounter critical studies in which the author does *not* announce that he/she will embed the work(s) under discussion in their historical/cultural contexts; in some cases the construction of the context is more interesting and enlightening than the literary analysis that follows. Such relatively young fields as utopian studies and history of the book (and its offshoot, periodicals studies) continue to mature; while those aged categories, realism and naturalism, refuse to perish, though they are of course constantly being reconceived and reconstructed. The large volume of scholarship on post–Civil War literature reconfirms the wisdom of dividing coverage of the 19th century into two chapters.

i General Studies

That the debate surrounding the terms "realism" and "naturalism" can, after more than a century, still generate vigorous scholarship and criticism is demonstrated by *The Cambridge Companion to American Realism and Naturalism,* a collection of 11 new essays by distinguished scholars. As Donald Pizer observes in his introduction, however much baggage the two terms now carry, they are too firmly rooted in American literary history to be dismissed or ignored, and they constitute a critical response to late 19th-century American culture that warrants continued study.

Louis J. Budd and Richard Lehan, respectively, provide expert introductions to "The American Background" (pp. 21–46) and "The European Background" (pp. 47–73) of American realism/naturalism. Michael Anesko's survey of "Recent Critical Approaches" (pp. 77–94) expresses impatience with contemporary criticism that too readily ignores or depreciates art and experience and their interrelationships. Elizabeth Ammons develops a compelling argument for "Expanding the Canon of American Realism" (pp. 95–114). The remaining seven essays ("case studies") in the volume focus on individual authors. John W. Crowley in *"The Portrait of a Lady* and *The Rise of Silas Lapham"* (pp. 117–37) contends that for James and Howells realism was primarily an exploration of "character," which they (like William James) construed as an accretion of moral choices. Tom Quirk's "The Realism of *Adventures of Huckleberry Finn"* (pp. 138–53) finds the source of the novel's realism in the interplay between Huck's developing consciousness and the palpable events (i.e., the narrative) that impinge on it. Using Crane and Norris's only meeting (in 1898) as his point of departure, J. C. Levenson in *"The Red Badge of Courage* and *McTeague:* Passage to Modernity" (pp. 154–77) considers how both writers moved beyond Howellsian realism (which Levenson rather unfairly labels "provincial") toward darker psychological realms that would be explored by 20th-century modernists. Barbara Hochmann's *"The Awakening* and *The House of Mirth:* Plotting Experience and Experiencing Plot" (pp. 211–35) illuminates how the images of immersion and separation in Kate Chopin's and Edith Wharton's novels are related to the novels' mutual theme that the only safe fusion of individuals occurs imaginatively through art, which allows the artist to "represent otherness" while yet remaining herself. Edna and Lily, both "failed artists," are destroyed because of their inability to accomplish what their creators did so brilliantly: to transform experience into a well-plotted story. The three remaining essays in the volume center on 20th-century figures (Blanche H. Gelfant on Theodore Dreiser; Jacqueline Tavernier-Corbin on Upton Sinclair and Jack London; and Kenneth W. Warren on W. E. B. Du Bois and James Weldon Johnson).

Literary realism is only one of the realisms that David E. Shi explores in his interdisciplinary *Facing Facts,* the central aim of which is to provide a "synthetic overview of the major events, ideas, and individuals that combined to generate the various types of 'realistic' expression and determine their fate in the marketplace of taste." Since the overview is thorough, detailed, and accurate, the book will be of great value to graduate students and to scholars who are unfamiliar with American literature and culture during the period. Specialists in the "Age of Realism," however, will concur with Shi's own assessment that the book does not offer any new theories about realism as a conceptual or aesthetic category. *Facing Facts* supplements, but does not supplant, earlier interdisciplinary studies by Peter Conn, T. J. Jackson Lears, and others. *Periodical Literature in Nineteenth-Century America* is a major contribution to the relatively new but rapidly developing field of periodicals scholarship. Several of the book's 14 essays fall within the boundaries of this chapter. Kathleen Diffley in "Home from the Theatre of War: The *Southern Magazine* and Recollections of the Civil War" (pp. 183–201) examines the important role played by Southern periodicals in advancing the social and political interests of the defeated Confederacy. In "Not Just Filler and Not Just Sentimental: Women's Poetry in American Victorian Periodicals, 1860–1900" (pp. 202–19) Paula Bennett argues that 19th-century periodicals opened a space for a cohort of professional women poets who paved the way for the next—and more revolutionary—generation of women writers. Ambrose Bierce's macabre fiction, as well as his journalistic pieces on the genre, is the subject of Gary Hoppenstand's "Ambrose Bierce and the Transformation of the Gothic Tale in the Nineteenth-Century American Periodical" (pp. 220–38). During the 1880s *Century Illustrated Magazine* launched a successful Civil War fiction series intended to help reconcile North and South; in "The North-South Reconciliation Theme and the 'Shadow of the Negro' in *Century Illustrated Magazine*" (pp. 239–56) Janet Gabler-Hover documents how the series editors pursued their goal of reconciliation by printing fiction and essays by white authors who stereotyped African Americans and portrayed a New South in which racism was a relic of the past. In the collection's final article, "Charles Chesnutt, the *Atlantic Monthly,* and the Intersection of African-American Fiction and Elite Culture" (pp. 257–74), Kenneth M. Price writes astutely of Charles Chesnutt's complex relationship with the *Atlantic Monthly,* publisher of several of his early stories. To make his fiction acceptable to the elite Anglo literary establishment that the *Atlantic* represented, Chesnutt created a dualistic form in his tales that allowed racially prejudiced whites (such as *Atlantic* editor Thomas Bailey Aldrich) to miss the irony evident to more perceptive readers.

As Haskell Springer maintains in his preface to *America and the Sea,* though the sea has been a key "source, scene, and symbol" for numerous

American writers, it has received far less attention from literary historians than has the western frontier. Two of the book's 14 essays, by different authors, concentrate on the late 19th century: Roger B. Stein's "Realism and Beyond" (pp. 190–208) and Bert Bender's "Fiction by Seamen after Melville" (pp. 209–23). Both Stein and Bender emphasize that American sea literature of the post–Civil War decades differed significantly from that of the "golden age" of Cooper, Dana, Melville, and their contemporaries; the heroic vision of these writers was replaced by the more skeptical and ironic perspectives of those who sailed across, or looked toward, the sea during the age of steamships, industrial expansion, and Charles Darwin. Arguing that writers need not possess extensive knowledge of the sea to create compelling writings about it, Stein interprets "sea literature" broadly. His survey of the "metaphysical seascapes" of a wide variety of poets and fiction writers, begins, somewhat surprisingly, with Emily Dickinson. The skeptical and ambivalent attitude toward the ocean projected in her poetry defines, for Stein, the transformation that would be further developed in the works of Howells, Crane ("the imaginative son of Emily Dickinson"), Twain, Jewett, and Kate Chopin. In contrast to Stein's, Bender's analysis of fiction by sea*men* after Melville (1880s to 1930s) is male-centered and restricted to works that deal directly with experience at sea. In the briny fiction of Jack London, Thornton Jenkins Hains, Morgan Robertson, Lincoln Ross Colcord, Hemingway, Peter Matthiessen, and others, the characters voyage through turbulent spiritual waters stirred up by Darwin's theory.

Bender turns his attention from the sea to the shore, but remains focused on Darwinian thought, in a superb article, "Darwin and 'The Natural History of Doctresses': The Sex War Between Howells, Phelps, Jewett, and James" (*Prospects* 18 [1993]: 81–120). With painstaking care, Bender demonstrates how the four writers appropriated those aspects of *The Descent of Man* and other of Darwin's writings to support their own gendered positions in the war over sexual difference, as played out in their respective novels about the ability or inability of women to be medical doctors (*Dr. Breen's Practice, Dr. Zay, A Country Doctor,* and *The Bostonians*). Though Darwin's influence on late 19th-century literature has often been discussed, Bender's article is unique in its detailed analysis of the Darwinian concepts operating above and below the surface of these novels. On the basis of this article, Bender's *The Descent of Love: Darwin and the Theory of Sexual Selection in American Fiction, 1871–1926* will be among the most important books discussed in next year's chapter.

ii The Howells Generation

Interest in Howells subsided somewhat this year, and the recent surge in Chesnutt studies waned. Focusing on Basil March's strolls through the immigrant enclaves in *A Hazard of New Fortunes,* Timothy L. Parrish ("Howells Untethered: The Dean and 'Diversity,'" *SAF* 23: 101–17) argues that March's discovery of his Otherness reflects Howells's feelings of alienation from his audience in the wake of his role in the controversy surrounding the Haymarket riot. Parrish attaches great significance to March's failure to finish his written sketches of the ethnically diverse American scene that he observes during his wanderings. March yields to, rather than forces coherence on, the flux of experience; thus his strolls— representing the "liberal conscience untethered"—deconstruct the concept of "America." Parrish's article is rich in insights and cogently argued. Equally illuminating is Henry B. Wonham's "Writing Realism, Policing Consciousness: Howells and the Black Body" (*AL* 67: 701–24). Merging the line of psychoanalytic criticism of Howells established by John W. Crowley and others with the more recent one focusing on the cultural construction of both "blackness" and "whiteness," Wonham contends that African American characters in Howells's fiction serve as vehicles for representing "insurgent" emotional and psychological states that Howells believed were beyond the realm of the realist aesthetic.

Lawrence Berkove in "'A Difficult Case': W. D. Howells's Impressions of Mark Twain" (*SSF* 31 [1994]: 607–15) suggests that the character Ransom Hilbrook of a "A Difficult Case," a man of severe integrity, is modeled on Mark Twain. Berkove further maintains that the story indicates that Twain had more influence on Howells's thought and art than generally recognized. A less significant study of the Twain-Howells connection is Harold K. Bush, Jr.'s "The Mythic Struggle between East and West: Mark Twain's Speech at Whittier's Birthday Celebration and W. D. Howells' *A Chance Acquaintance*" (*ALR* 27, ii: 53–73), which covers much familiar ground in arguing that Twain's well-known speech, and his and Howells's anxiousness over its reception, reflect the tensions (especially between East and West) in American culture of the day. Also disappointing is Jon-K Adams's "Moral Opposition in Nietzsche and Howells" (*Nietzsche in American Literature and Thought,* pp. 65–78). Adams's analysis of the two men's views on morality and mankind offers no new insights into Howells, and Adams seems unaware of Howells scholarship of the past two decades.

Aside from Price's chapter in *Periodical Literature in Nineteenth-Century America*, the only significant contribution to Chesnutt scholarship this year is Robert C. Nowatzki's " 'Passing' in a White Genre: Charles W. Chesnutt's Negotiations of the Plantation Tradition in *The Conjure Woman*" (*ALR* 27, ii: 20–36), which develops a line of argument similar to Price's. Discussing *The Conjure Woman* in the context of the plantation fiction tradition as represented by Thomas Nelson Page's *In Ole Virginia* and Joel Chandler Harris's *Uncle Remus*, Nowatzki contends that Chesnutt employed the frame narrative device used by his white peers to subvert subtly the ideology of Anglo superiority inscribed in their fictions.

Edward Bellamy's name surfaces often in the works on utopian/science fiction literature by women (see below), but little attention was directed exclusively to his work. Daniel H. Borus's introduction to the Bedford Books edition of *Looking Backward: 2000–1887* firmly situates that novel in its historical context, while contending that the social and economic problems Bellamy addresses are as pressing today as in 1888. Wilfred M. McClay in "Edward Bellamy and the Politics of Meaning" (*ASch* 64: 264–71) likewise suggests that the vision of social solidarity at the heart of *Looking Backward* speaks to a deep yearning for community in our own turbulent times. But McClay warns against the kind of blurring of the religious and political lines that occurs in Bellamy's utopia.

Robert M. Myers rectifies a puzzling injustice of American literary scholarship by giving us the first critical biography of Harold Frederic, *Reluctant Expatriate* (Greenwood). Frederic's critical heyday occurred during the 1960s and 1970s, after which interest in him dropped off sharply. Myers's central thesis is that Frederic's life and writings project the tensions that mark fin de siècle American culture. Given his interest in Frederic's conflicted psyche and his "ideology" (i.e., the ideas he explores in his writings), Myers might have drawn profitably on Peter Conn's *The Divided Mind: Ideology and Imagination in America, 1898–1917* (1983), which Myers never mentions. Still, this well-researched and able biography may rekindle interest in Frederic, perhaps in time for the centenary of the publication of *The Damnation of Theron Ware* (1896).

iii Stephen Crane and Frank Norris

Despite the absence of a book on either Crane or Norris, the harvest of scholarship and criticism was bountiful. Crane scholarship was enriched this year by a five-article *ALR* special issue on the writer, ed. Stanley Wertheim. The opening essay, James Colvert's "Stephen Crane and Postmodern Theory" (*ALR* 28, i: 4–22), is a balanced survey of the major work on Crane by practitioners of deconstructive and other "postmodernist" (Colvert uses that term loosely) theoretical paradigms. Colvert concisely and accurately summarizes the often contentious debate between traditional and "postmodernist" critics. He concludes that Crane studies have benefited from the best work emerging from both the old and new critical approaches. Colvert's essay is followed by John Clendenning's "Stephen Crane and His Biographers: Beer, Berryman, Schoberlin, and Stallman" (*ALR* 28, i: 23–57), a thoroughly researched and fascinating study of how the four biographers in question projected their unconscious fears and desires into their scholarly constructions of their elusive subject. Clendenning provides compelling evidence for his assertion that each of the biographies contains elements of a "hidden autobiography"; his psychoanalytic dissection of the biographers and their works is a major contribution to biography theory as well as to Crane studies. Donald Pizer adds a short essay, "*Maggie* and the Naturalistic Aesthetic of Length" (*ALR* 28, i: 58–65), to his extensive work on American literary naturalism. Whereas most naturalistic novels are densely detailed and expansive, Pizer notes that *Maggie* achieves a naturalistic effect through compression, thus demonstrating that a "naturalistic aesthetic of brevity" is as possible as an aesthetic of length. George Monteiro in "After the *Red Badge:* Mysteries of Heroism, Death, and Burial in Stephen Crane's Fiction" (*ALR* 28, i: 66–79) attempts to decipher Crane's attitude toward heroism by analyzing the motif in several of Crane's later stories, but Monteiro is forced to conclude that the longer Crane peered into the matter, the more mysterious it became for him. The issue of heroism in, not after, *The Red Badge of Courage* is the focus of Melissa Green's "Fleming's 'Escape' in *The Red Badge of Courage:* A Jungian Analysis" (*ALR* 28, i: 80–91). Her essay, however, falls victim to the kind of reductive analysis that Monteiro's resists. Siding with those critics who argue that Henry Fleming's character has undergone little change by the end of the novel, Green attributes his lack of development and confusion to his failure to distinguish between the antagonistic Jungian archetypes of initiation (acting unselfishly for the good of the group) and heroism (elevating oneself above the group).

Bill Brown's "American Childhood and Stephen Crane's Toys" (*AmLH* 7: 443–76) situates Crane's story "The Stove" in the context of the late

19th-century conflict between the genre of "American boyhood" (which Brown argues was integral to the project of preserving a national identity) and the new materialism of the child (the mass production of toys) that destabilized that identity. Brown's critique of that conflict, which is impressive in its scope and detail, will be of more interest to those working in cultural studies than to Crane specialists, since Crane's text ("The Stove") at times all but disappears into its context. Far narrower in scope, and less significant, is Peter Miles's note, "Ernest Skinner, Henry James, and the Death of Stephen Crane: A Cora Crane Inscription" (*ANQ* 8, ii: 19–26), which centers on a copy of *Wounds in the Rain* that Cora inscribed and gave to Stephen's physician, Ernest Skinner, shortly after its author died. To Miles, the gift proves that Cora never blamed Skinner for her husband's death. In "A 'Gorgeous Neutrality': Stephen Crane's Documentary Anaesthetics" (*ELH* 62: 663–89) Mary Esteve draws illuminating connections between William James's conception of the "anaesthetic" or hypnotic state as one of pure being and the condition of "gorgeous neutrality" exemplified in the corpses and insentient characters (e.g., drunks, babies, crowds) that recur in Crane's fiction. By converting lived experience back into sheer data or "anaesthetic experience," Crane, Esteve argues, in effect sabotages the literary realists' project of making sense of phenomena. Esteve grounds her thesis in close readings of several Crane short stories and sketches; her analysis of "When Man Falls, a Crowd Gathers" is exceptionally good.

A section of Adam Zachary Newton's *Narrative Ethics* (pp. 185–207) focuses on *The Monster*. Grounding his ambitious enterprise in the theories of Bakhtin, Cavell, and, most importantly, Emmanuel Levinas, Newton probes the interrelationship between narrative and "ethics," which he defines as "a binding claim exercised upon the self by a concrete and singular other whose moral appeal precedes both decision and understanding." For Levinas, the encounter with the Other's *face* is paramount. For obvious reasons, *The Monster* lends itself well to a Levinasian analysis. However, since Henry Johnson's race in effect renders his face invisible to Whilomville's (America's) whites even before the fire, Newton argues that the novella denies the possibility of any positive ethical relationship as conceived by Levinas.

The long-standing and often rancorous debate over which editions of *Maggie* and *The Red Badge of Courage* are authoritative flared anew this year. In a curiosity of American literary scholarship, Hershel Parker and Brian Higgins's "The Virginia Edition of Stephen Crane's *Maggie:* A

Mirror for Textual Scholars" (*Bibliographical Society of Australia and New Zealand Bulletin* 19: 131–66) has, after a 20-year delay, finally been published in its entirety. (A portion of the essay appeared in *Studies in the Novel* in 1978.) Parker and Higgins are sharply critical of the CEAA-approved, or Virginia, edition of *Maggie* prepared by the late Fredson Bowers, who, they allege, prevented their essay from being printed after he read the typescript in 1975. The Virginia edition's only value, they contend, is the lessons it teaches about how *not* to go about editing a literary manuscript. Parker and Higgins have added a preface in which they accuse Bowers of abusing his immense influence, and they defend the "old-fashioned biographical and bibliographical scholar" in the era of New Historicism. Though the text at issue is *The Red Badge of Courage* rather than *Maggie,* Michael Guemple's "A Case for the Appleton *Red Badge of Courage*" (*RALS* 21: 43–57) is in effect a rebuttal of Parker and Higgins's textual editing principles. Arguing against Henry Binder's 1979 edition of the novel, which is based on the Barrett manuscript, and in favor of the first published edition by Appleton, Guemple applies the theoretical model presented by Jerome McGann in *A Critique of Modern Textual Criticism* (what Parker would deem a "New Historicist" approach, I presume). Wedded to a "Romantic model of the autonomous author," Binder (and those such as Parker who have endorsed his edition) ignored Crane's stated intentions about *Red Badge,* the novel's reception, and the context of its composition. As Binder himself acknowledged, his claim that editor Ripley Hitchcock forced Crane to make emendations is conjectural; indeed, as Guemple demonstrates, correspondence between Crane and Hitchcock indicates that author and editor acted in a spirit of cooperation. Following McGann, Guemple insists that textual scholars must take into account such author-editor cooperation when attempting to establish an authoritative text. Needless to say, it is highly unlikely that a truce in the Crane textual editing wars will be struck anytime soon.

A new biography of Crane by Linda H. Davis is scheduled for publication in 1996. Those interested in the new book and the author's reasons for writing it will want to read "The Red Room: Stephen Crane and Me" (*ASch* 64: 207–20), a deeply personal essay in which Davis—whose father was burned to death when she was a child—probes the roots of both her own and Crane's obsession with death and disfigurement.

Not surprisingly, the bulk of the new scholarship on Norris centered on *McTeague.* Jonathan S. Cullick in "Configuration of Events in the

Narrative Structure of *McTeague*" (*ALR* 27, iii: 37–47) defends the closing chapters of *McTeague* against the charge that they weaken the novel's
structure. McTeague's flight to the desert and his death there, Cullick
argues, are the culmination of one of the novel's central conflicts: the
"tension between the repetition of routine events and the disruption of
unexpected events." Though he approaches *McTeague* from a perspective
different from Cullick's, Thomas K. Dean in "Domestic Horizons: Gender, Genre, Narrative Structure and the Anti-Western of Frank Norris"
(*ALR* 27, iii: 48–63) also drives to the conclusion that the Death Valley
sections of *McTeague* are organically connected to preceding events and
themes in the narrative. Reading *McTeague* and other of Norris's fictions
in the context of the middle-class Westerns such as Wister's *The Virginian*
that captivated the American imagination at the turn of the century,
Dean maintains that Norris disrupts the genre's static generic codes and
critiques its dominant ideology of domesticity. Middle-class western novels typically develop toward what Dean terms a "domestic horizon," a
point of narrative closure at which the male hero is "civilized" by
a woman in a western locale that represents a balance of wildness
and civilization. Norris reverses this structural pattern in *McTeague*, as
McTeague moves away from domestic harmony toward annihilation in
the savage western desert. *McTeague* is thus an "anti-Western," its titular
character "an inverse portrait of the idealized cowboy." Domestic violence in *McTeague* and also in "Fantaisie Printaniere," an 1897 short story
that centers on wife-beating and female masochism, is the subject of
Mary Beth Werner's note, "'A Vast and Terrible Drama': Frank Norris's
Domestic Violence Fantasy in *McTeague*" (*FNS* 19 [1994]: 1–4). Werner
correctly maintains that no hard evidence exists that Norris himself
sanctioned spouse abuse; but her argument that the deaths of the abusive
Zerkow and McTeague undercut scenes which imply that women need,
and often welcome, male discipline rests more on faith than textual
evidence. Finally, Jerome Loving's introduction to the Oxford World
Classics edition of *McTeague* ranges widely over Norris's other works and
emphasizes the class bias at the heart of Norris's naturalistic vision.

In "Frank Norris: The Crisis of Representation" (*ALR* 27, ii: 74–83)
Allan Lloyd Smith explains the apparent incoherences and stylistic
excesses of *Vandover and the Brute* as displacements of repressed homosexual desire onto the body of the text. The crisis of representation in the
novel—that is, its shattering into "incoherent visual suggestiveness"—
stems from Norris's attempt to "speak with clarity the various 'unspeak-

ables' of the *fin de siècle.*" Joseph R. McElrath, Jr., adds "Beyond San Francisco: Frank Norris's Invention of Northern California" (*San Francisco in Fiction,* pp. 35–55) to his substantial corpus of Norris scholarship. McElrath details how the sublime natural landscape of northern California and the strange, unpredictable, and hybrid culture of San Francisco furnished the ideal raw materials for the author of "A Plea for Romantic Fiction," from his 1895 *Wave* essay "A California Vintage" onward. Norris's unfinished Wheat Trilogy receives a full chapter's attention in John C. Waldmeir's *The American Trilogy, 1900–1937* (pp. 43–81). Examining *The Octopus* and *The Pit* from a "larger frame of reference"—that is, the myth of eternal return inscribed in the structures of the trilogies he examines—Waldmeir contends that an "eschatological motive" underlies both novels. This "larger view," however, leads Waldmeir to reductiveness; as in Emerson's *Nature,* the Transcendental frame of reference causes disagreeables to vanish. Nonetheless, even those who will remain unconvinced by Waldmeir's essentially Christian interpretation of Norris's fiction will profit from his illuminating analysis of how Norris learned from his experience as a photojournalist to coordinate in his fiction a series of individual pictures into a dialectical panorama. In a similar vein David Teague in "Frank Norris and the Visual Arts" (*FNS* 19 [1994]: 4–8) suggests that Norris's early training as an empirical artist served him well in his later career as a verbal painter of scenes from everyday life. The 20th anniversary issue of *FNS* reprints Norris's "Miracle Joyeux"; not reprinted since its original publication in *The Wave* in 1897, the short tale is an ironic parable on the oral tradition's construction of Jesus Christ ("a dreamer with unspeakable pretensions").

iv Women Writers: General

Feminist scholars continue to illuminate the intersections between politics and literature, with the focus of some studies shifting from literature to literacy. And this was a big year for the field of women's utopian and science fiction literature.

As the title indicates, *Redefining the Political Novel: American Women Writers, 1797–1901* reconceptualizes the political novel from a feminist perspective, its nine contributors exploring the ways in which 19th-century women writers "exposed, satirized, addressed, and challenged unspoken political ideologies" of their times. The final three essays focus on late 19th-century literature, with uneven results. Dorothy Berkson's

"'A Goddess Behind a Sordid Veil': The Domestic Heroine Meets the Labor Novel in Mary E. Wilkins Freeman's *The Portion of Labor*" (pp. 149–68) is one of the best essays in the volume. Analyzing the dialogic tension between class and gender in Wilkins's 1901 novel, Berkson demonstrates that though Ellen Brewster, the novel's central character, embraces socialist ideals, she remains a traditional Victorian heroine in that she succeeds in reforming, through moral suasion, an individual capitalist but does not alter the economic system that exploits the working class. Claire Pamplin's "'Race' and Identity in Pauline Hopkins's *Hagar's Daughter*" (pp. 169–83) is less impressive than Berkson's piece, for it is largely a synthesis of information about Hopkins's novel and its historical context that is readily available in other studies of Hopkins and/or African American literary history. Duangrudi Suksang in "A World of Their Own: The Separatist Utopian Vision of Mary E. Bradley Lane's *Mizora*" (pp. 128–48) argues that Lane's little-known novel deserves more attention than it has received, not only because it is the first American novel to envision a self-sufficient matriarchal utopia, but also because of its incisive critique of 19th-century patriarchal culture. Suksang also suggests that *Mizora* may have been an important influence on Charlotte Perkins Gilman's *Herland*. *Mizora* is among a host of neglected utopian fictions surveyed in Darby Lewes's *Dream Revisionaries*. Lewes examines how not only gender but race, class, and nationality—especially nationality—shaped the ideological message of the works under discussion. The book's appendix contains a valuable chronological, annotated bibliography of women's utopian fiction from 1621 through 1920.

As Susan Albertine observes in the introduction to *A Living in Words,* although a large and growing body of scholarship exists on women authors and their books, relatively little attention has been paid to women's broader contribution to American print culture. This gendered gap in scholarship is narrowed not only by *A Living in Words* but by a collection of essays with similar objectives, *Nineteenth-Century Women Learn to Write.* Ranging from the colonial through the modernist periods, the dozen contributors to *A Living in Words* seek to lay the groundwork for a more comprehensive study of female professionalism in American "literate," as opposed to exclusively "literary," culture. Two of the essays—Rodger Streitmatter's on Josephine St. Pierre Ruffin (pp. 49–64) and Barbara Diggs-Brown's on Ida B. Wells-Barnett (pp. 132–50)—fall within the scope of this chapter. Though virtually unknown today, the wealthy socialite Josephine St. Pierre Ruffin (whose husband George Lewis Ruffin was the first African American graduate of Harvard Law School and the first African American judge in the North) was founder and editor of *Woman's Era* (1890–97), the first newspaper established by and for African American women. Ida Wells-Barnett, whose *A Red Record: Tabulated Statistics and Alleged Causes of Lynchings in the United States, 1892–1893–1894* (1895) was a major weapon in the antilynching crusade of the 1890s, is (or should be) familiar to scholars of late 19th-century American literary history. Both Streitmatter and Diggs-Brown portray their subjects as strong-willed and astute businesswomen who made substantial contributions to African American journalism. Like *A Living in Words, Nineteenth-Century Women Learn to Write,* a new addition to Virginia's series Feminist Issues: Practice, Politics, Theory, explores women's literate rather than literary cultures; indeed, the dozen contributors to the volume join in a common effort to begin the task of constructing a history of American women's struggle for *literacy* and for the social and political empowerment that stems from the ability to understand and produce verbal texts. Divided into two parts ("Cultures and Contexts of Literacy" and "Practices and 'Voices' of Literacy"), the individual chapters collectively chart the complex courses by which increasing numbers of women during the 19th century, especially the latter half, learned not only to read and write, but to practice what Catherine Hobbs calls "effective literacy," writing and speaking to bring about social change. For example, in "'In an Atmosphere of Peril': College Women and Their Writing" (pp. 59–83) Vickie Ricks analyzes the rhetorical educations of women at Mount Holyoke, Vassar, and Radcliffe. Shirley Wilson Logan's "Literacy as a Tool for Social Action among Nineteenth-Century African American Women" (pp. 179–96) relates how Maria Stewart, Sojourner Truth, Frances E. W. Harper, Ida Wells, and Anna Cooper used words as weapons against slavery, lynching, and racial discrimination. Maryan Wherry in "Women and the Western Military Frontier: Elizabeth Bacon Custer" (pp. 217–29) recounts the fascinating *her*story of Elizabeth Bacon Custer, whose three books and several articles detailing her experiences as a military wife on the Western frontier (all written after her husband George's death) are, not unexpectedly, sharply at odds with most male writers' (and filmmakers') representations of "the West."

Paula Bennett's "'The Descent of the Angel': Interrogating Domestic Ideology in American Women's Poetry, 1858–1890" (*AmLH* 7: 591–610) is a groundbreaking study of women's poetry during the late 19th century. (This essay overlaps slightly with Bennett's chapter in *Periodical Literature in Nineteenth-Century America* discussed above.) Seeking to rescue from obscurity Elizabeth Drew Stoddard, Elizabeth Stuart Phelps, and Sarah Morgan Bryan Piatt, Bennett argues that their poetry projects a determined countervoice to the sentimental verse of their predecessors. Though traditional in form, their poems—especially Piatt's, whom Bennett deems the most accomplished and transgressive of the group—critiqued the ideology of True Womanhood, and in doing so looked forward to the modernist movement that would soon follow.

Two collections of women's writing deserve mention here. *Southern Women's Writing: Colonial to Contemporary* brings together an ample selection of Southern women's writing from the early settlement period to the present. The section on the postbellum South (1866–1917) includes short fiction and poetry by Kate Chopin, Alice Dunbar-Nelson, Mary Noailles Murfree, and others. *Telling Travels* contains travel accounts by Helen Hunt Jackson, Constance Fenimore Woolson, and other late 19th-century figures. Editor Mary Suzanne Schriber's informative introduction highlights how the writers in question used the "travel genre to forward a gender agenda."

v Charlotte Perkins Gilman, Kate Chopin, Sarah Orne Jewett, and Post–Civil War Women Writers

Studies of Gilman and Chopin, and to a lesser extent of Jewett, continue to proliferate. The major event in Gilman scholarship this year was the publication of Mary A. Hill's *A Journey from Within: The Love Letters of Charlotte Perkins Gilman, 1897–1900* (Bucknell), an annotated edition of Gilman's private letters to her second husband, Houghton Gilman. During the four years before her marriage to "Ho," Charlotte regularly wrote long letters to him in which she expressed her most private thoughts and emotions. Since Ann J. Lane's chapter in *To Herland and Beyond* (see *ALS 1990*, p. 229) on Gilman's relationship with Ho quotes extensively from the letters, Gilman scholars will not be surprised by the disquieting images of Gilman that emerge from Hill's edition. Gilman repeatedly confesses feelings of insecurity, self-doubt, shame, and weakness; she is torn between her conflicting desires to be an independent woman and a good wife. The letters in effect document Gilman's internal struggle between the "True Woman" and the "New Woman." However, as Hill emphasizes in her introductory essay, Gilman did not merely pour out what she called her "monster" feelings to Ho; she used her letters as a source of psychological healing and empowerment.

Hill's (at the time unpublished) edition proved to be a major resource for Carol Farley Kessler's explorations of the connections between Gilman's life and utopian writings in *Charlotte Perkins Gilman: Her Progress Toward Utopia with Selected Writings* (Syracuse). Kessler's focus is broader than the book's title suggests, for she does not restrict herself to *Herland* and other of Gilman's works that fall clearly within the category of "utopian literature." In four chapters Kessler probes the interconnections between Gilman's life and the cultural work of her writings. The fifth and final chapter—which occupies more than half the book—contains 14 of Gilman's utopian works (including chapters from *Herland* and *With Her in Ourland*), with introductory notes to each. Like Hill, Kessler contends that writing served a therapeutic purpose for Gilman.

Two articles apply gay/lesbian theory to Gilman's works. The more provocative and theoretically sophisticated one is Jonathan Crewe's "Queering *The Yellow Wallpaper?* Charlotte Perkins Gilman and the Politics of Form" (*TSWL* 14: 273–93). The title may raise eyebrows, since, as Crewe acknowledges, the word "queer" did not become associated with "homosexual" in dictionaries until around 1920. However, skeptics should not be too quick to dismiss Crewe's thesis that the narrator's "queer" behavior is a projection of suppressed lesbian desire, for Crewe's arguments are carefully and thoughtfully developed. Val Gough explores the "lesbian narrative space" of *Herland* in "Lesbians and Virgins: The New Motherhood in *Herland,*" in *Anticipations: Essays on Early Science Fiction and Its Precursors,* ed. David Seed (Syracuse, pp. 195–215). At the end of her utopian novel, Gough argues, Gilman rejected both the resolution of "lesbian-separatism" and of heterosexual marriage, and instead left the Herlanders poised on the brink of achieving the ideal that Gilman desired but could not attain in her own life: to become, in Marilyn Frye's coinage, "willful virgins"—completely independent, yet heterosexual, women. Gilman's utopian fiction is also the focus of Ruth Levitas's " 'Who Holds the Hose?' Domestic Labour in the Work of Bellamy, Gilman, and Morris" (*Utopian Studies* 6: 65–84). Reading *Herland* against Edward Bellamy's *Looking Backward* and William Morris's *News from Nowhere,* Levitas finds fault with Gilman's utopian ideal. Gilman and Bellamy abolished domestic labor from their futuristic novels, she argues, because they considered housework and child-rearing to be demeaning labor that required no skill to perform, a view to which Levitas takes strong exception.

Finally, *The Yellow Wallpaper and Other Stories,* ed. Robert Shulman (Oxford), joins the Oxford World Classics list. The book makes available for classroom use a large selection of Gilman's short fiction that was originally published in the *Impress* and the *Forerunner.* In light of the controversy over the textual history of "The Yellow Wallpaper" generated by Julia Bates Dock's article in the January 1996 issue of *PMLA* (to be discussed in next year's chapter), I should note that Shulman chose to reprint the text of "The Yellow Wall-Paper" that was first published in the *New England Magazine* in 1892, and that he retained the inconsistent spellings of wallpaper. Shulman's introduction to the collection is lucid, thorough, and insightful.

As in Gilman's case, the continuing reassessment of Kate Chopin's writings complicates her position within the feminist tradition. Examining Chopin's portraits of women writers in three works written at different stages of her career ("Miss Witherwell's Mistake," *The Awakening,* and "Elizabeth Stock's One Story"), Heather Kirk Thomas in "Kate Chopin's Scribbling Women and the American Literary Marketplace" (*SAF* 23: 19–34) contends that Chopin not only disassociated herself from her literary foremothers but that her fiction perpetuated the stereotype of them embodied in Nathaniel Hawthorne's spiteful "scribbling women" remark. Chopin, Thomas shows, was deeply conflicted over her desire to reach a wide reading audience while remaining a serious artist. Chopin was also conflicted about race relations, as Sandra Gunning illustrates in "Kate Chopin's Local Color Fiction and the Politics of White Supremacy" (*ArQ* 51, iii: 61–86). Reminding us that Chopin was a daughter of the Old South and wife of a white supremacist, Gunning finds that in *At Fault* and several of her local-color stories Chopin questions the violence with which white racists attempted to control blacks in the late 19th century but does not reject the ideology of white supremacism or endorse full civil rights for blacks. Thus, Chopin's feminism "worked in tandem with her investment in turn-of-the-century racist discourses." The influence of German Idealist philosophy, especially of Arthur Schopenhauer's aesthetic of renunciation, on Chopin and *The Awakening* is the subject of Gregg Camfield's "Kate Chopin-hauer: or Can Metaphysics Be Feminized?" (*SLJ* 27, ii: 3–22). Camfield marshals convincing evidence to support his idea that Chopin, who was introduced to the German Idealists by her trusted physician,

Dr. Frederick Kohlbenheyer, was initially attracted to Schopenhauer's view of art as offering an avenue of transcendence of human suffering and that his metaphysics of sexual love is inscribed in Chopin's first published story. However, by the time she wrote *The Awakening* Chopin had begun to question Schopenhauer's ideal of withdrawal from the world; her ambivalence between renunciation of and immersion in the passionate life lies at the center of her novel. Pamela Glenn Menke's "Chopin's Sensual Sea and Cable's Ravished Land: Sexts, Signs, and Gender Narrative" (*CrossRoads* 3, i: 78–102) is an estimable comparative study of water and land motifs in Chopin's and George Washington Cable's novels. While the two writers attach the same figurative significance to land and water imagery, Menke demonstrates that their use of the imagery is distinctively gendered. In Cable's *The Grandissimes* and *John March, Southerner* the white males must avoid or contain turbulent waters in order to subjugate the land and "Others" and to reconstruct Southern culture, whereas in Chopin's radical "sexts" (Hélène Cixous's term) water figuratively disrupts patriarchal culture and is an enabling force for women like Edna who yearn to escape the constraints of social conventions and gender roles. Roger Platizky in "Chopin's *The Awakening*" (*Expl* 53: 99–102) speculates that Edna, like the mythical Philomela, may be the victim of sexual violation. However, while Edna does exhibit certain behaviors associated with women suffering "post-traumatic conflict," there is—as Platizky admits—no firm textual evidence that Edna was sexually abused as a child.

Two essays extend the feminist re-visioning of *The Country of the Pointed Firs*. In "Visions of Time in *The Country of the Pointed Firs*" (*SSF* 32: 29–37) Margaret Baker Graham applies Julia Kristeva's theory of "women's time" to illuminate both the structure and theme of Jewett's masterpiece. According to Graham, Jewett projects three distinct visions of time in the work: linear, cyclical, and monumental. The monumental vision, represented by the narrator, reaches beyond temporal experience into the mythical and eternal realm. Marilyn C. Wesley in "The Genteel Picara: The Ethical Imperative in Sarah Orne Jewett's *The Country of the Pointed Firs*" (*CLQ* 31: 279–91) takes issue with critics who view the stories' aging mothers as "preoedipal projections." Drawing on the work of Nancy Chodorow, Wesley argues that the women are "postoedipal partners" whose travel experiences have developed in them a strong sense of ethical commitment and communal cooperation. Combining the virtues of home and travel, Mrs. Fosdick is the "emblematic genteel picara." In her note "Sarah Orne Jewett's White Heron: An Imported Metaphor" (*ALR* 27, iii: 81–84) Sheri Joseph relies on ornithological detective work in demonstrating that Jewett's famous bird did not exist in New England at the time the story is set. Jewett "imported" the white heron (snowy egret) from the South to make a political statement about the plume trade's careless predation of the beautiful creature, which was driven to the brink of extinction during Jewett's time.

The experimental and diverse nature of Mary Wilkins Freeman's short fiction is the focus of Shirley Marchalonis's essay "Another Mary Wilkins Freeman: *Understudies* and *Six Trees*" (*ATQ* 9: 89–101). Marchalonis provides illuminating readings of the tales in these lesser-known collections by Freeman as she develops her argument that Freeman's central concern is the individual's conflicting desires to establish an autonomous identity while remaining part of a community. As Freeman explores this tension in her fiction, the characters "win, lose, rebel, triumph, compromise, or reject; the conflict makes the story."

Admirers of Rebecca Harding Davis will celebrate the publication of *A Rebecca Harding Davis Reader*, ed. Jean Pfaelzer (Pittsburgh), which contains 15 of Davis's stories and 16 of her essays. Pfaelzer provides an extensive introduction as well as helpful explanatory notes to the selections. In "Framing a 'Life in the Iron Mills'" (*SAF* 23: 73–84) Richard A. Hood maintains that the narrative structure of Davis's best-known story is even more complex than critics have recognized, especially the "dialogic" outer frame. However, Hood's claim that the narrator may be Deborah looking back at her earlier years in poverty is dubious.

Despite efforts by Cheryl Torsney and others during recent years to stimulate scholarly interest in Constance Fenimore Woolson, she has remained largely in the shadows of the women writers listed above. Sharon L. Dean's announced purpose in *Constance Fenimore Woolson: Homeward Bound* (Tennessee) is to "inch forward" Woolson toward the recognition she deserves. Dean's fine study should move Woolson more than a few inches from the margins; it should in fact be a major boost to the Woolson reclamation project. Dean's central thesis is that in her fiction as in her life, the nomadic Woolson envisioned women's escape from comfortable but stifling homes or communities toward more cosmopolitan—but also conflict-ridden—ones. Like so many other American writers, however, her quest for a home was futile, for she never felt completely rooted to any place or culture. Elizabeth B. Stoddard criticism inches forward with Dawn Henwood's "First-Person Storytelling in Elizabeth Stoddard's *The Morgesons:* Realism, Romance, and the Psychology of the Narrating Self" (*ESQ* 41: 41–63). Henwood argues that Stoddard's most significant innovation is in the area of narrative technique, for she refused to be constrained either by the romantic-sentimental narrative tradition or the newly developed realist one. Stoddard (along with Elizabeth Stuart Phelps, John W. DeForest, and Thomas Nelson Page) also figures in Timothy Morris's " 'A Glorious Solution': Gender, Families, Relationships, and the Civil War Story" (*ArQ* 51, i: 61–79). The several stories that Morris discusses link the male desire for military violence with fear or hatred of women. The article is engaging, but Morris hyperbolizes when he asserts that the Civil War "was fought because some men feared, desired, and hated some women."

Scholars interested in the Jewish-American poet and social activist Emma Lazarus should not fail to read Bette Roth-Young's *Emma Lazarus: In Her World* (Jewish Publication Society). The bulk of the volume is composed of more than 100 of Lazarus's previously unpublished letters to Helena Gilder (wife of Richard Watson Gilder) and several other friends, along with eight letters to Lazarus from Henry James. The texts of the letters and their annotations are preceded by Young's relatively short but valuable study of Lazarus's life and literary work. Previous biographies and biographical sketches of Lazarus have perpetuated the caricature of the "tragic Jewish priestess" that emerged from an essay published by Lazarus's sister Josephine in 1888. Drawing on the letters in the volume and other evidence, Young dispels many myths that have passed as facts about Lazarus and gives us a much more complex portrait.

vi Westerners: Bierce, Harte, Wister, and Others

Ambrose Bierce's critical stock rallied this year. San Francisco's acid-pen satirist is the subject of a new, and much needed, biography: *Ambrose Bierce: Alone in Bad Company* (Crown) by Roy Morris, Jr. Though he respects and admires the controversial writer, Morris does not idolize the man nor overstate his literary accomplishments (as Bierce no doubt would be happy to hear). Morris's book is the product of painstaking research, and the writing style is engaging. His chapters on Bierce's experiences during the Civil War—which occupy about one-third of the book—and of his various journalistic activities are especially informative. To Morris, Bierce's importance to American literary history lies primarily in his realistic stories and journalistic comments on the horror and

banality of modern warfare. However, Morris's analyses of the stories
themselves are often cursory, and he ignores Bierce's poetry. Yet, as Bierce
expert M. E. Grenander reminds us in her introduction to *Poems of
Ambrose Bierce* (Nebraska), Bierce was a productive and versatile poet
who expressed in verse deep-felt feelings that he suppressed in his prose.
Grenander's assertion that Bierce is a much more talented poet than has
been acknowledged is, however, arguable. Nonetheless, this edition,
which brings together all of Bierce's poetry, along with several of his
essays on poets and the art of poetry, will be welcomed by Bierce scholars,
despite the unfortunate fact that the poems are not annotated.

In an essay that Bierce might have relished, Gary Scharnhorst in
"Mark Twain, Bret Harte, and the Literary Construction of San Francisco" (*San Francisco in Fiction*, pp. 21–34) demonstrates that market
forces drove both of these noted local colorists to abandon the realistic
accounts of San Francisco life that one finds in their early journalism and
to construct instead romanticized fictions of the city that appealed to
their middle-brow readers after they went East. Harte receives more
favorable treatment in David Wyatt's introduction to the Oxford World
Classics edition of Harte's *Selected Stories and Sketches*. Wyatt's Harte is a
pioneering writer who employed the sentimental style to explore conflicts stemming from the American West's racial, gender, and economic
differences.

In marked contrast to 1994, Owen Wister drew almost no attention
this year. In "Transatlantic Twins: Rudyard Kipling and Owen Wister"
(*ASch* 64: 599–606) J. C. Furnas's comparisons of Wister's and his
English counterpart's fiction add little to our knowledge of either writer;
further, Furnas's contention that Wister's short stories have been neglected because they are politically incorrect is glib. More enlightening
are two studies of writers who, though relatively unknown today, contributed in important ways to the rhetorical construction of the imagined Southwest: Martin Padget's "Travel, Exoticism, and the Writing of
Region: Charles Fletcher Lummis and the 'Creation' of the Southwest"
(*JSW* 37: 421–49) and Randall C. Davis's " 'The Path toward Civilization': Sociocultural Evolution and *The Delight Makers*" (*ALR* 27, ii: 37–
52). In his influential magazine *Land of Sunshine* (later retitled *Out West*)
and in many books, Lummis popularized the Southwest as an exotic
refuge from the "overcivilized" East, but he did so with a clear Anglo
bias. Similarly, in his 1890 novel *The Delight Makers*, the ethnographer

and historian Adolph Bandelier aimed for an "authentic" portrait of 12th-century Keres (Pueblo) culture in what is now New Mexico. However, Davis reveals how Bandelier's embrace of the "scientific" theory of sociocultural evolution (as promulgated by Lewis Henry Morgan) undermined his realist agenda. The Boise State University Western Writers Series adds Peter Wild's *Theodore Strong Van Dyke* to its list of titles. Wild (also author of an earlier BSWWS pamphlet on Theodore's younger and better-known brother, John) argues that Theodore Van Dyke's satiric historical novel *Millionaires of a Day: An Inside History of the Great Southern California "Boom"* (1890) stands as a classic treatment of its subject and is more artful and satisfying than Mark Twain and Charles Dudley Warner's *The Gilded Age*.

vii Science and Philosophy: Henry Adams, William James, and Others

The major scholarly event in this category is Paul Jerome Croce's *Science and Religion in the Era of William James: Eclipse of Certainty, 1820–1880* (No. Car.), first of a planned two-volume study of James's and his circle's responses to mounting uncertainties in both the scientific and religious realms during the 19th century. Since this volume is concerned primarily with the various personal and cultural influences on James's intellectual development, James himself is on the margins of the study; individual chapters, for example, focus on the elder Henry James, the "shock of Darwin," and the Metaphysical Club, especially members Chauncey Wright and Charles Sanders Peirce. (James and his writings will take center stage in the second volume.) As Croce acknowledges, his "cultural biography" of James is largely restricted to only one stratum of American culture of the period—elite New England culture. But the scientific and religious issues with which James and his peers grappled were, of course, not restricted to any one region, gender, or class. In "The Permanence of William James," the first of three essays comprising *Pragmatism: An Open Question* (Blackwell), Hilary Putnam explores James's conceptions of "holism" and "realism" and his insistence on the interdependence of fact, theory, value, and interpretation. Turning to Wittgenstein in the second essay, "Was Wittgenstein a Pragmatist?," Putnam argues that the German philosopher shared with James a commitment to a Kantian "primacy of practical reason." The continued attraction of James and his

fellow pragmatists in our postmodern age, Putnam argues, is their pluralistic temperament and their philosophical engagement with the "real"
world. What James meant by "the facts," and the power of the will or
faith to create them, are the central concerns of Robert J. O'Connell's "Faith and Facts in James's 'Will to Believe'" (*IPQ* 35: 283–99).
O'Connell determines that James held fast to his view that all "weltan-
schaulich" propositions (e.g., the existence of God) are ultimately settled
by one's faith or will, rather than by empirical evidence. However,
O'Connell leaves for another day the crucial question of whether James
furnished criteria for differentiating between "legitimate" and "illegitimate" grounds for a belief.

In "The Manikin, the Machine, and the Virgin Mary," the final
chapter of her *The Literature of Labor and the Labors of Literature*
(pp. 173–206), Cindy Weinstein approaches *The Education of Henry
Adams* from a literature-and-the-body perspective, exhaustively dissecting the manikin and other images of lifeless bodies in the work. Unable
to cure his manikin-like helplessness, Adams "reproduces his melancholy
in the allegorical bodies of his text," making technology his scapegoat in
the process. Julika Griem's "The Poetics of History and Science in
Nietzsche and Henry Adams" (*Nietzsche in American Literature and
Thought*, pp. 41–64) teases out the similarities and differences between
the two writers, concentrating on their attempts to come to terms with
scientific discoveries of their day, especially Darwin's theory of evolution
and the first and second laws of thermodynamics. Adams, Griem concludes, sought refuge from destabilizing historical change by retreating
to the "interior republic of gentlemen of letters," whereas Nietzsche
"cultivated a philosophy of excess that virtually blew him to pieces."

In 1868 Louis Agassiz, a determined opponent of Darwin, and his
wife, Elizabeth Cary Agassiz, published *A Journey in Brazil,* in which the
eminent scientist engaged in his futile defense of a "creationist" explanation of life, while his wife offered her more personal and subjective
observations about their journey into the South American jungles. According to Linda S. Bergmann, "A Troubled Marriage of Discourses:
Science Writing and Travel Narrative in Louis and Elizabeth Agassiz's *A
Journey in Brazil*" (*JACult* 18, ii: 83–88), Elizabeth Agassiz's account,
which often emphasizes the common humanity of the Brazilian natives
and the white travelers, subverts her husband's scientific theories, especially his insistence on distinct racial species.

***viii* Miscellaneous**

My annotated edition of *The Letters of Theodore Roosevelt and Brander Matthews* (Tennessee) brings together for the first time 271 letters exchanged by Roosevelt and Matthews, a flamboyant professor of dramatic literature at Columbia University and an influential literary critic. The correspondence, running from 1888 through 1919, chronicles Roosevelt's life as a "literary feller" and offers instructive glimpses into the interrelations of politics and literature during the period. Roosevelt's fellow conservationist John Muir is the subject of a new biography: Thurman Wilkins's *John Muir: Apostle of Nature* (Okla.). The book is essentially a chronological summary of Muir's lifelong campaign to protect and preserve American wilderness. Brad Leithauser's *Penchants and Places: Essays and Criticism* (Knopf) includes "Alone and Extremely Alone: Lafcadio Hearn" (pp. 201–09), a reprint of his largely negative book-review essay (*New Yorker*, 22 April 1991) on Jonathan Cott's biography of the eccentric Japanologist. In " 'Ticknor-and-Fields-ism of All Kinds': Thomas Starr King, Literary Promotion, and Canon Formation" (*NEQ* 68: 206–22) Jeffrey D. Groves adds a chapter to the history of the American book and of the formation of the "genteel" literary canon. A Unitarian minister and close friend of *Atlantic Monthly* editor James T. Fields (and also an early supporter of Bret Harte), King (1824–64) left Boston for San Francisco in 1860, where he delivered a popular series of six lectures, "The Chief Poets of America." King sought to instill New England literary, religious, and nationalistic values in Californians, in large part by promoting the *Atlantic Monthly* and other literary productions of the Ticknor and Fields publishing firm.

Texas A&M University

14 · Fiction: 1900 to the 1930s

Jo Ann Middleton

New alignments among the writers in this chapter mark this year's work as scholars cross disciplinary lines to find new insights in new juxtapositions. Late-century struggles to define national identity make the political, cultural, and literary turmoil surrounding the early 20th-century assimilation movement—and resistance to it—particularly cogent. Formerly marginalized women and ethnic writers have continued the move to center stage, sparking new scholarship on the presence of the "other" in canonized writers. Redefinitions of realism and naturalism have kept Jack London studies at the forefront and produced renewed interest in Theodore Dreiser and John Dos Passos; revisions of genre invigorated work on Sherwood Anderson. Willa Cather and Edith Wharton remain the major figures.

i Willa Cather

Something for everyone is available in book-length studies of Cather this year. Philip Gerber's *Willa Cather, Revised Edition* (Twayne) not only updates his seminal introduction (1975) to Cather's life and work, but it serves as an example of scholarship in evolution as Gerber expands and synthesizes his earlier insights with those of scholars who have followed him. Gerber arranges his material chronologically by genre, emphasizes the short stories as "a major literary accomplishment," evenhandedly and thoughtfully considers the "question of Cather biography," summarizes the critical response to Cather in a masterful chapter that reminds veteran Catherites of how far we have come, identifies "the best of the new work," and suggests rich possibilities that Cather offers for future study. Joan Acocella's "Cather and the Academy" (*New Yorker*, 27 Nov., pp. 56–71) takes a less sanguine view of Cather criticism.

Willa Cather and the Myth of American Migration (Illinois), Joseph R. Urgo's study of Cather's "aesthetics of migration," splendidly confirms

Gerber's optimism. Reminding us that Cather kept her suitcases under her bed, Urgo locates transience at the center of American culture, identity, and global empire, then brilliantly redefines Cather as the first major writer whose body of work provides a comprehensive resource for the centrality of cosmic homelessness. His fresh and perceptive readings of the novels support his thesis that the vision of American culture which Cather projects is one "of continuous movement, of spatial and temporal migrations, of intellectual transmission and physical uprooting."

Mildred R. Bennett's groundbreaking work *The World of Willa Cather* (Nebraska) has been reprinted, making accessible material on Cather's family, her friends, and the Red Cloud that formed her sensibilities. *Willa Cather's University Days: The University of Nebraska, 1890–1895* (Center for Great Plains Studies), ed. Kari Ronning and Elizabeth Turner, opens the door to yet another avenue of scholarship with six essays on Cather's undergraduate experience, a chronology of her university days, 14 photographs, and the speech (printed here for the first time) that she gave at a reunion of the class of 1895. Guy Reynolds traces Cather's "networks of friendship" and convincingly explicates affinities and reciprocities among Cather's themes of immigration, cultural transmission, and the development of an American folk culture and her college friend Louise Pound's work in philology, folklore, and literary criticism in "Louise Pound and Willa Cather: An Intellectual Network?" (*WCPMN* 39: 69–72). Susan J. Rosowski's "Willa Cather's Ecology of Place" (*WAL* 30: 37–51) links Cather's close attention to nature with "the ecological model" of her Nebraska professor Charles E. Bessey and the work of her college friends, botanists Edith and Fred Clements, to show how *O Pioneers!* illuminates her understanding of place as "a matter of consciousness." Peter M. Sullivan documents Cather's friendship with two socially prominent New Yorkers (Harriet Boas and Charlotte Stanfield) in "Willa Cather's New York German Friends and Her Novels: A Biographical Note" (*NR* 6, v: 95–100).

Several essays pair Cather with others. Øyunn Hestetun argues that Cooper's *The Prairie* and *O Pioneers!* tell the entire story of the transformation of the land between the Louisiana Purchase of 1803 and the official closing of the frontier in 1890 in "Pioneers on the Prairie: From Desert to Garden," pp. 85–105 in *Performances in American Literature and Culture.* In *A Certain Slant of Light* David Marion Holman cites works of Cather and Ellen Glasgow to demonstrate a common artistic goal: bringing the past and present together into a meaningful, understandable relation; Cather's "nineteenth-century romantic view handled with the techniques of the modern world" manifests her reaction against the realism of her peers as "indictment without instruction," and Holman concludes that she was "a lecturer, a moralist, and a social critic."

John J. Murphy's thoughtful essay "*Shadows on the Rock, Maria Chapdelaine,* and the Old Nationalism" (*WCPMN* 39: 1–6) puts Cather's and Louis Hemon's novels next to Marcel Chaput's 1961 polemic on French-Canadian separatism; these works inform the current debate on nationalism, but they part company with contemporary attitudes by defining a traditional rather than new nationalism. In "Saying '*Goodnight*' to 'Lost' Ladies: An Inter-textual Interpretation of Allusions to *Hamlet*'s Ophelia in Cather's *A Lost Lady* and Eliot's 'The Waste Land' " (*WCPMN* 39: 33–37) Scott L. Newstrom reads a Cather novel with texts by Eliot and Shakespeare. All three texts examine the sexuality, suppression, and social roles of women in a patriarchal world. Daniel J. Holtz links Cather's treatment of "aesthetically unimaginative, narrow-minded money-grubbers" in *O Pioneers!*, "Neighbour Rosicky," and "The Sculptor's Funeral" to Bess Streeter Aldrich's treatment of similar characters in *The Rim of the Prairie* and *A Lantern in Her Hand* in "Willa Cather and Bess Streeter Aldrich: Contrasting Portrayals of Money-Grubbers and "Olafarians'" (*HK* 28, i: 5–10). Carol Miles Petersen should revive interest in Aldrich by aligning her with the realists as well as the romantics in her thoroughly researched biography, *Bess Streeter Aldrich* (Nebraska), and a new edition of 26 of Aldrich's early stories in *The Collected Short Works, 1907–1919* (Nebraska).

In "Words and Music Made Flesh in Cather's 'Eric Hermannson's Soul' " (*SSF* 32: 209–16) John Flannigan expertly explores how the sexual jealousies, violence, and religious tensions of Mascagni's opera *Cavalleria Rusticana* form an integral part of the thematic fabric in Cather's story. Artistic sensibility—or lack thereof—is the subject of Merrill Skaggs's astute and ingenious pairing of Thea Kronborg and Clement Sebastian, "*artists* who are . . . counterpointed in polyphonic lines," in "Key Modulations in Cather's Novels about Music" (*WCPMN* 39: 25–30).

The Song of the Lark inspired three fine essays this year. In "The 'Wonderfulness' of Thea Kronborg's Voice" (*WAL* 30: 257–74) Sharon Hoover relies on Carol Gilligan's paradigms of male and female development to read Thea's character according to a pattern that values integration of commitment to social/community obligations and to individual obligations. Thea represents a whole and healthy woman, linked to her own mother and to the ancient mothers of Panther Canyon, who is able to interpret Fricka as a strong, loving, and responsible woman/goddess. Following the pattern of woman-centered imagery through which Cather shows Mrs. Archie's distorted womanhood, sterility, and death, Evelyn I. Funda contrasts Mrs. Archie's sexual repression and distorted passion with Thea's femininity and artistic passion in "Womanhood Distorted: Mrs. Archie as Thea's Foil in *The Song of the Lark*" (*WCPMN* 39: 30–33). Cather's appropriation of the ideas, words, and images of the Christian Eucharist undergirds Steven B. Shively's compelling thesis that *The Song of the Lark* heralds Cather's rejection of Old Testament rigidity in favor of a decidedly Christian and traditionally ritualistic sacramental view, enabling her to open the Kingdom of Art to women, in " 'A Full, Perfect, and Sufficient Sacrifice': Eucharistic Imagery in Cather's *Song of the Lark*" (*L&B* 14 [1994]: 73–86). Asad Al-Ghalith in "Willa Cather: Light and Mystical Journey" (*IFR* 22: 31–36) contends that Thea Kronborg, Lucy Gayheart, and Jim Burden go through the stages of the mystic on the quest for ultimate knowledge and union with the Divine; Cather reveals elements of her own "mystic consciousness" when she is most concerned with artistic temperament, using light imagery to signify moments of awakening and illumination.

In her superb essay "A New World Symphony: Cultural Pluralism in *The Song of the Lark* and *My Ántonia*" (*WCPMN* 39: 1, 7–12) Ann Moseley counters critics who label Cather "racist" with a clearly reasoned and timely explanation of the context in which Cather created her ethnic characters. Like Antonín Dvořák's *New World Symphony,* Cather's *Song of the Lark* and *My Ántonia* reflect sociologist Horace M. Kallen's metaphor of the United States as "a symphony of cultures." Calling Cather's characters " 'peculiar Americans' rather then 'peculiarly American,' " Hermione Lee suggests that Cather's lifework can be seen as a continuing study of American identity in "Cather's Bridge: Anglo-American Crossings in Willa Cather," pp. 38–56 in *Forked Tongues?* For Karen M. Hindhede, *Death Comes for the Archbishop* works as a site of interplay among Mexican, Indian, and Anglo myths, particularly those emphasizing feminine power; Hindhede explores Cather's use of such Native American and Mexican myths as those of Yellow Corn Girl, Salt Woman, and Grandmother Spider as they intersect with Anglo-Christian spirituality in "Allusions and Echoes: Multi-Cultural Blending and Feminine Spirituality in *Death Comes for the Archbishop*" (*HK*

28, i: 11–19). Terence Martin in *Parables of Possibility: The American Need for Beginnings* (pp. 142–57) proposes that *Death Comes for the Archbishop* puts "Cather-the-artist in a primary position of completing the Creator's work" by engaging the imaginative possibilities of the Southwest to encompass character, event, and history "in a harmony of place and spirit." Latour's initial sense of human diminishment and disorientation in the face of a boundless land is ultimately transformed by surrender to the landscape in a series of new beginnings that culminate in a state of mind to which "nothing has been lost, nothing has been outgrown."

Ann Romines breaks new ground in "Willa Cather and the Coming of Old Age" (*TSLL* 37: 394–413) with astute and reflective readings of *Death Comes for the Archbishop, Shadows on the Rock,* and "Old Mrs. Harris" as explorations of the process and progress of aging. Latour's, Frontenac's, and Mrs. Harris's last days suggest compelling differences: *Death Comes for the Archbishop* concerns a life in which old age brings dignity, value, and "a good death"; *Shadows on the Rock,* an obviously modernist view of the complexities of aging, shifts the focus to the process of aging and dying; "Old Mrs. Harris" reports an old woman's unobtrusive, dignified, resonant death, in spite of physical decline, lack of money, and the partial neglect of her family.

Shadows on the Rock garnered the lion's share of attention given to individual novels this year. In "Historicism and the Sentimental: Sources of Power in Willa Cather's *Shadows on the Rock*" (*WCPMN* 39: 63–67) Elaine E. Limbaugh points out how Cather's blending of the historical and the sentimental allows her to shape the novel's mood and message. My own "Historical Space in *Shadows on the Rock*" (*WCPMN* 39: 49–53) investigates Cather's modernist inquiry into the intricate complexities and subtle relationships among memory, human consciousness, and imagination and suggests the consequences of such interaction for human understanding of time and history. Janis Stout speculates that in her emotionally weighted use of great rocks as images of strength and security, Cather alluded to the hymn "Rock of Ages" in "Cather's Firm Foundations and the Rock of Ages: A Note" (*WCPMN* 39: 59). Heather Stewart's discerning "*Shadows on the Rock:* The Outsider, the Disfigured, the Disadvantaged, and the Community" (*WCPMN* 39: 54–58) draws on Emmanuel Levinas's understanding of "the other" to elucidate the value to the community and the formative influence on Cécile's life of disadvantaged Jacques, disfigured Blinker, Bishop Laval, and Madame Pommier, and such outsiders as Jeanne Le Ber, Pierre Charron, Father Hector, and Noel Chabanel.

In "Language, Gender, and Ethnicity in Three Fictions by Willa Cather" (*WL* 18, i: 52–56) Helen Wussow identifies Alexandra Bergson, Thea Kronborg, and Ántonia Shimerda as outsiders, marginalized and denied access to power. Caught between patriarchies and between languages, all of them preserve their language and creative alternative communities of others who are likewise marginalized because of gender, class, ethnic, or linguistic background.

Unlike those who see clear differences between Alexandra and her father, Neil Gustafson convincingly demonstrates that Alexandra develops her love for the land as she begins to understand and make her father's vision her own in "Getting Back to Cather's Text: The Shared Dream in *O Pioneers!*" (*WAL* 30: 151–62). Calling Paul the "saddest of all," a "New Man" of the "New Age," Patricia Ellen Martin Daly includes "Paul's Case" in *Envisioning the New Adam: Emphatic Portraits of Men by American Women Writers* (Greenwood), an anthology aimed at the "peaceful affiliation and the dissolution of armed gender camps."

Ernest Hemingway's famous dismissal of *One of Ours* continues to irritate Cather scholars and to prompt splendid readings of the novel, such as D. A. Boxwell's "In Formation: Male Homosocial Desire in Willa Cather's *One of Ours*" (*Genders* 20 [1994]: 285–310). Boxwell takes issue with appraisals of *One of Ours* as "an inauthentic, male-identified glorification of war" and argues that Cather's deconstruction of gender and sexual identities in the novel was acute enough to throw Hemingway into "a fit of defensive contempt." Amy Kort identifies Claude as "an unmistakable Nietzschean hero" and pairs him with another, Myra Henshawe, in "Coming Home from Troy: Cather's Journey into Pessimism in *My Mortal Enemy*" (*WCPMN* 39: 38–41) to illustrate what happens when that hero lives to experience inevitable disillusionment. Claude, perhaps the last of Cather's true individualistic heroes, cannot survive; Myra surrenders individuality, finally achieving "Schopenhauer's happiness of release." Blanche H. Gelfant in her *Cross-Cultural Reckonings: A Triptych of Russian, American, and Canadian Texts* (Cambridge) skillfully interpets "murky" clues to show how *My Mortal Enemy* struggles—in vain—to deny, affirm, or reconcile the truth of Driscoll's legacy to Myra: "A poor man stinks, and God hates him."

Alistair Stead explicates Cather's adaptation of the medieval myth of

Sherwood Forest in *A Lost Lady* in "Pastoral Sexuality in British and American Fiction" (pp. 295–314 in *Forked Tongues*). Captain Forrester's vision, courtesy, and selfless generosity grant him Robin's mythic status; Marian (Maidy, Maid Marian, Lady Forrester) finds herself unable to keep to the script. Cao Jinghua attributes Marian's ambiguity, contradictions, discontinuity, and indeterminacy to her essential nature and "disparate self-parts" in "Marian Forrester, Cather's Fictional Portrayal of the Modernist Self" (*WCPMN* 39: 12–16).

In "The Subversive Language of Flowers in *Sapphira and the Slave Girl*" (*WCPMN* 39: 41–44) Françoise Palleau-Papin adds to the work on Cather's flower imagery and demonstrates how, through a discourse on slavery, flowers become a means of expression for the slave woman as well as the narrator. Diane Roberts in *The Myth of Aunt Jemima* (Routledge, 1994, pp. 167–71) finds echoes of the classic fugitive slave narrative and the old-fashioned abolitionist novel in *Sapphira* and suggests that, for different reasons, Henry and Sapphira both seek to rid their world of disruptive bodies.

Finally, three unrelated items deserve mention. Susan Rosowski, Charles Mignon, Kari Ronning, and Frederick M. Link's "Editing Cather" (*SNNTS* 27: 387–400) gives us an insider's look at the monumental task, the occasional surprises, and the delights involved in preparing and publishing the Cather Scholarly Edition. Moving personal essays on the meaning of Cather scholarship in their lives by Rosowski (pp. 29–38) and Ann Fisher-Wirth (pp. 11–18) appear in *Private Voices, Public Lives*.

ii Edith Wharton and Ellen Glasgow

In addition to a sheaf of thoughtful essays, Wharton scholarship is enriched this year with three book-length studies and three new volumes of her work. *Wharton's New England* (New England) contains seven stories, *Ethan Frome,* and editor Barbara A. White's excellent introduction; less socially dense than Wharton's other fiction, these stories probe psyches and souls, projecting onto New England aspects of Wharton "that she most feared: repression, coldness, inarticulateness, mental starvation, and even lack of high culture." The paperback edition of *A Son at the Front* (No. Ill.) makes Wharton's World War I novel readily accessible, particularly to feminist scholars exploring women's engagement in that war, as Shari Benstock points out in her fine introduction. Julie

Olin-Ammentorp in "'Not Precisely War Stories': Edith Wharton's Short Fiction from the Great War" (*SAF* 23: 153–72) suggests that both the content and style of Wharton's fiction and nonfiction changed after the war; "Coming Home," "The Refugees," "Writing a War Story," and *Fighting France* illustrate her attempt to come to terms with the war and the "after-war world." Frederick Wegener draws on Wharton's correspondence with Scribner's to reveal the rigorous effort and perseverance that kept her working on *The Writing of Fiction* during the five years following the war in "Edith Wharton and the Difficult Writing of *The Writing of Fiction*" (*MLS* 25, ii: 60–79).

Edith Wharton Abroad: Selected Travel Writings, 1888–1920, ed. Sarah Bird Wright (St. Martin's), contains excerpts from all seven of Wharton's travel works that reveal her "incurable passion for the road," her love of landscape and architecture, and her wide-ranging cultural inquisitiveness. This fascinating volume also has the advantage of Wright's astute introduction, a preface by Shari Benstock, 21 illustrations, and a handy glossary of foreign words and phrases used by Wharton in her texts. Terry Caesar adds to the discourse on Wharton's travel writing with his discussion of *A Motor-Flight Through France* as a protest against a modern concept of tourism that dissolves national identity in the mass in *Forgiving the Boundaries*.

The Cambridge Companion to Edith Wharton (Cambridge) includes Millicent Bell's superb introductory essay and summary of Wharton criticism (pp. 1–19), a recently discovered contemporary review of *The Valley of Decision* (pp. 199–202) by Vernon Lee (aka Violet Paget), and nine essays. In "Forms of Disembodiment: The Social Subject in *The Age of Innocence*" (pp. 20–46) Pamela Knights proposes that *The Age of Innocence* radically suggests that "without the shape, the social mold, there may be no self at all," and in "'Hunting for the Real': Wharton and the Science of Manners" (pp. 47–67) Nancy Bentley adopts Marcel Mauss's phrase "science of manners" to describe Wharton's exploration of cultural questions raised by early anthropology. The erasure of race and the inescapable presence of race as a category in Wharton's work are the concerns of Elizabeth Ammons's important "Edith Wharton and the Issue of Race" (pp. 68–86). Elaine Showalter cleverly compares Elmer Moffatt to Donald Trump in her analysis of *The Custom of the Country* as "a book about the peculiar art of the American deal, from dilettantish aestheticism to blunt acquisitiveness" in "Spragg: The Art of the Deal" (pp. 87–97). Gloria C. Erlich traces Wharton's tyrannical female consciences to the internalized voice of her mother in "The Female Consciousness in Edith Wharton's Shorter Fiction: Domestic Angel or Inner Demon?" (pp. 98–116); Rhonda Skillern draws on French feminism and Jacques Lacan to examine Charity's character and behavior in "Becoming a 'Good Girl': Law, Language, and Ritual in Edith Wharton's *Summer*" (pp. 117–36); and Maureen Howard finds echoes of *Emma* and *Sister Carrie* in *The House of Mirth* in "The Bachelor and the Baby: *The House of Mirth*" (pp. 137–56). In "Justine: or, the Perils of Abstract Idealism" (pp. 157–68) James W. Tuttleton examines the little-read *The Fruit of the Tree* to locate the reason for its failure (lack of a coherent vision); and in "Edith Wharton's Italian Mask: *The Valley of Decision*" (pp. 169–98) William Vance discusses the text as "an Italian romance" in the tradition of George Eliot's *Romola*.

Kathy A. Fedorko's *Gender and the Gothic in the Fiction of Edith Wharton* (Alabama), the first book-length study of Wharton's extensive use and adaptation of gothic elements, is impressive, innovative, and persuasive. Fedorko considers 16 gothic stories in juxtaposition with the major realistic novels that reflect and revise them (*The House of Mirth, Ethan Frome, Summer, The Age of Innocence, Hudson River Bracketed,* and *The Gods Arrive*) in a series of thoughtful and thought-provoking analyses that draw on Jungian concepts, feminist archetypal theory, and recent work on the female gothic. Fedorko explores Wharton's "evolutionary rendering" of the tension between masculine and feminine limitations, the process of individuation in both men and women, and the potential for gender integration in "fe/maleness." Equally substantial and groundbreaking is Carol J. Singley's *Edith Wharton: Matters of Mind and Spirit* (Cambridge), a major study that is the first to explore the depth and breadth of Wharton's religious, spiritual, and philosophical search and to place her work in the context of American intellectual thought and religious history. Singley details Wharton's interest in Calvinism, Transcendentalism, Anglicanism, Catholicism, Darwinism, and Platonism in clearly written prose and traces difficult philosophical and intellectual themes through Wharton's life and work by focusing on the short fiction and seven novels (*The House of Mirth, Ethan Frome, The Reef, Summer, The Age of Innocence, Hudson River Bracketed,* and *The Gods Arrive*). Monika Elbert in "The Transcendental Economy of Wharton's Gothic Mansions" (*ATQ* 9: 51–67) finds that, in her ghost stories, Wharton allows spiritual concerns to triumph over economic circumstances to affirm an American Transcendental vision, recalling Emerson's ambivalence toward Europe and Thoreau's sabotage of capitalism.

Nancy Bentley takes a philosophical, historically focused approach to the workings of anthropological theory and ethnographic practice in the fiction of Hawthorne, James, and Wharton in her exhaustively researched and provocative *The Ethnography of Manners*. Wharton's motif of "metaphorical primitivism" can be traced to her fascination with contemporary anthropological discourse and can be seen in Lily Bart's ritualized social sacrifice and Undine Spragg's atavistic voracity. *The Custom of the Country*, "an ethnography of modern marriage" in which commercial and social relations are finally indistinguishable, reveals that "the exchange of wives is at the heart of the tribal economy," which has as its definitive figure the divorcée "who not only directs her own marital exchange but has proven her power to repeat and extend it." Wharton shares a chapter with Henry James (pp. 103–88) in *A Common Life*, David Laskin's charming study of four great American literary friendships.

The Custom of the Country is the most provocative Wharton novel this year—and Undine Spragg has become almost respectable! In "The Remarrying Woman as Symptom: Exchange, Male Hysteria, and *The Custom of the Country*" (*ALR* 27, ii: 1–19) Phillip J. Barrish sees Undine as a symptom of "repressed trauma" to premodern patriarchal systems that cannot sustain an awareness of "the forms of exchange that underlie . . . family traditions, national histories, and aesthetic standards." Undine functions *as* a symptom, but she does not *suffer* symptoms; standing for a means of exchange that makes possible the identities of those around her, she achieves a power and security that commands respect. In *Swindler, Spy, Rebel* Kathleen De Grave demonstrates that Undine is clearly a "new confidence woman" by comparing her to Lillie Ellis in Harriet Beecher Stowe's *Pink and White Tyranny;* although she is "seriously flawed," Undine never sees herself as anything but a commodity, and she consistently demands the right to speak. In "What Does **** Want? Desire and Consumerism in Edith Wharton's *The Custom of the Country*" (*ALR* 27, iii: 19–36) Ariel Balter contends that the novel is not only about consumerism, but it is "conspicuously consumptive" since both Wharton's and her characters' desire for consumer goods is mediated by a capitalist commodity culture. Undine wants material goods and social approval; Ralph wants Undine and

Undine's objects; Elmer wants social status; and Wharton, who wants identity as a writer, creates a consumer product (the text) and achieves material success in the business and literary worlds. In *Notes from the Periphery* (pp. 93–112) Susan P. Castillo locates expatriate female characters who "challenge existing cultural norms and live to tell the tale" in *The Custom of the Country, Madame de Treymes,* and *The Reef,* and Stephen Orgel edits and introduces the new World's Classics edition of *The Custom of the Country* (Oxford).

Four critics this year discussed *The House of Mirth.* In her chapter on Wharton in *The Feminine Sublime: Gender and Excess in Women's Fiction* (Calif.) Barbara Claire Freeman argues that Lily's changing relation to contingency and chance imply a counterpart to Edmund Burke's idealist account of the sublime. *The House of Mirth* emphasizes the very notions of risk and speculation that Burke prefers to suppress, and Lily enacts a version of the sublime "in which ethics and aesthetics, risk and art, have become inseparable." For Lois Tyson, *The House of Mirth* dramatizes the psychological contradictions to which some women are liable; Tyson asserts that Lily's death is the consummation of her and Seldon's shared desire for abstract perfection (*Psychological Politics of the American Dream: The Commodification of Subjectivity in Twentieth-Century American Literature* [Ohio State, 1994, pp. 17–39]). Barbara Hochman reflects on *The House of Mirth* and *The Awakening* as texts that divulge a tension between the figure of a defeated female protagonist who fails to find her voice and a writer who achieves pleasure, control, and distance in the act of writing in *"The Awakening* and *The House of Mirth:* Plotting Experience and Experiencing Plot," pp. 211–35 in *The Cambridge Companion to American Realism and Naturalism.*

In "The Naturalism of Edith Wharton's *The House of Mirth*" (*TCL* 41: 241–48) Donald Pizer cogently differentiates the naturalism of that novel from Wharton's principal naturalist contemporaries (Crane, Norris, Dreiser), contesting assumptions that the novel is an unqualified representation of social determinism. With Nettie Struther and the final "union" of Lily and Seldon, Wharton adds "the American codicil that the premise is not the entire story" to the assumptions of naturalism by positing a transcendent strength, which can defeat forces of victimization, and a transcendent faith, which holds that some values exist despite their seeming defeat in life. Helge Normann Nilsen argues strenuously that Wharton was a classic naturalist in "Naturalism in Edith Wharton's 'Ethan Frome'" (pp. 179–88 in *Performances in American Literature and*

Culture); in *Ethan Frome,* according to Nilsen, Wharton takes mechanistic determinism as her starting point.

Stacey Margolis's erudite and informative essay, "The Public Life: The Discourse of Privacy in the Age of Celebrity" (*ArQ* 51, ii: 81–101), examines the intersection of legal and literary representations of privacy and celebrity at the turn of the century, when issues of "privacy" and "publicity" became something of a public crisis, and he notes not only important changes in legal discourse on privacy, but he explicates the ways in which Wharton represents the transition.

John Updike submits "Archer's Way," the lone, very fine, essay on *The Age of Innocence* (*NYRB* 30 Nov., pp. 16–18), in which he finds ties to *Anna Karenina, The Princess of Clèves, The Scarlet Letter, The Ambassadors,* and *A Farewell to Arms,* then lucidly links Wharton's "enchanted caricature of her own tribe" to Proust's "simultaneously telescopic and microscopic view; his recognition that grandeur and absurdity coexist; his sense of society's apparent rigidity and actual fragility."

Summer and *The Buccaneers* are each the subject of one essay. In "Degradation and Forbidden Love in Edith Wharton's *Summer*" (*TCL* 41: 350–66) Kathy Grafton draws on Freud to show why the relationship between Charity Royall and Lucius Harney is "profoundly original in literature." Though Harney needs Charity's degradation before finding her sexually accessible, and though Charity can experience her sexuality only if forbidden, Wharton's characters part from the Freudian model in Harney's sincere tenderness and Charity's eventual acceptance of her sexuality. Lee Sigelman demonstrates that the chapters written by Marion Mainwaring to complete *The Buccaneers* break decisively with Wharton's prose style in "By Their (New) Words Shall Ye Know Them: Edith Wharton, Marion Mainwaring, and *The Buccaneers*" (*CHum* 29: 271–83).

Of note are four solid essays in the Spring 1995 number of *EWhR* (12, i): Jean Frantz Blackall's "The Absent Children in Edith Wharton's Fiction" (pp. 3–6); Gianfranca Balestra's "What the Children Knew: The Manuscript of *Disintegration,* an Unfinished Novel" (pp. 7–11); Elsa Nettels's "Children and Readers in Wharton's Fiction" (pp. 12–14); and Julie Olin-Ammentorp's "Martin Boyne and the 'Warm Animal Life' of *The Children*" (pp. 15–19). Finally, Stephanie Branson calls our attention to the "fantastic stories" of Wharton ("Bewitched"), Eudora Welty ("Moon Lake"), and Ellen Glasgow ("Whispering Leaves") as visionary tales that run contrary to the dominant discourses of masculine realistic and modern fiction in "Ripe Fruit: Fantastic Elements on the Short Fiction of Ellen Glasgow, Edith Wharton, and Eudora Welty" (*American Women Short Story Writers,* pp. 61–71).

Branson expands her exploration of Glasgow's "fantastic" tales with a discussion of "Dare's Gift," "The Past," and "The Shadowy Third" as "feminist fictions" in " 'Experience Illuminated': Veristic Representation in Glasgow's Short Stories" (pp. 74–86), one of the 15 essays collected in *Ellen Glasgow: New Perspectives.* Martha E. Cook shares her discovery of a new Glasgow story, reprinted here with her essay connecting its heroine to Virginia Pendleton Treadwell and Dorinda Oakley and linking it to the work of Kate Chopin and Sylvia Plath ("Ellen Glasgow's 'Ideals': A 'New' Story from the 1920s," pp. 3–30). Two essays, "The Romance of Self-Representation: Glasgow and *The Woman Within*" by Nancy A. Walker (pp. 33–41) and "Composed Selves: Ellen Glasgow's *The Woman Within* and Edith Wharton's *A Backward Glance*" by Susan Goodman (pp. 42–55), draw on recent scholarship on autobiography. Walker suggests that Glasgow's autobiography depicts the process of an artist fashioning a self as "romantic exile," and Goodman's comparison of Glasgow and Wharton shows that, though they share many characteristics, they had different responses to Freudian ideas.

Glasgow's poetry has received little attention, but Terence Allan Hoagwood breaks new ground with "The Poetry of Ellen Glasgow: *The Freeman and Other Poems*" (pp. 59–73), his study of the ironized point of view and poetic artifice in Glasgow's "impressively unified poetic volume." In a second essay, "A Feminist Intertext for Ellen Glasgow's Poetry" (*EGN* 34, i: 3–4) Hoagwood explores the intertextual relationships between *The Freeman and Other Poems* and Ella Wheeler Wilcox's *Poems of Passion.*

The 10 remaining essays focus on Glasgow's novels. In "Restoring Order: Matriarchal Design in *The Battle-Ground* and *Vein of Iron*" (pp. 89–105) Lucinda MacKethan examines the imaginative process by which Glasgow based relationships "on sharing rather than competitiveness, on negotiation rather than self-assertion, and on integration rather than exclusion." Beginning with eight previously unpublished letters, Pamela R. Matthews discusses the women-centered plot of *The Wheel of Life* and the narrative implications of women's friendships in "Between Ellen and Louise: Female Friendship, Glasgow's Letters to Louise Chandler Moulton, and *The Wheel of Life*" (pp. 106–23). In "The Framing of Glasgow's *Virginia*" (pp. 124–31) Phillip D. Atteberry calls our attention to the book's narrative structure, which provides "tonal contrasts and structural counterparts that qualify every presentation and question every assertion," and in "'The Problem of the South': Economic Determination, Gender Determination, and Genre in Glasgow's *Virginia*" (pp. 132–45) Francesca Sawaya explicates the novel as a naturalistic text that questions the naturalist project's relation to race and sex. Julius Rowen Raper acknowledges the psychological complexity of modernism in Glasgow's characters of the 1920s, thoroughly analyzing the often contradictory interpretations of Dorinda as either victim or victor in "*Barren Ground* and the Transition to Southern Modernism" (pp. 146–61). In "'Put Your Heart in the Land': An Intertextual Reading of *Barren Ground* and *Gone With the Wind*" (pp. 162–82) Margaret D. Bauer finds a surprising number of parallels between Glasgow's and Mitchell's texts, concluding that the ambiguous ending of *Gone With the Wind* represents triumph for Scarlett when it is read beside the ending of *Barren Ground*.

Caroline King Barnard Hall in "'Telling the Truth about Themselves': Women, Form and Idea in *The Romantic Comedians*" (pp. 183–95) finds intertextualities with T. S. Eliot's *The Waste Land*, analyzes Judge Honeywell and the female characters, and finds in Glasgow's novel "a wistful longing for pre-World War I values and clear understanding of their present irrelevance." In "Glasgow's Time in *The Sheltered Life*" (pp. 196–203) Linda Wagner-Martin uses Julia Kristeva's concepts of women's worlds and time to expertly illuminate Glasgow's indictment of patriarchy and love of linear time. Catherine Rainwater's fine "Consciousness, Gender, and Animal Signs in *Barren Ground* and *Vein of Iron*" (pp. 204–19) locates "a semiotic network of animal references" in nearly all of Glasgow's novels and reads these signs in *Barren Ground* and *Vein of Iron* to reveal Glasgow's engagement with philosophical, religious, scientific, and evolutionary theories. Finally, in "Coming Home: Glasgow's Last Two Novels" (pp. 220–34) Helen Fiddyment Levy focuses on the female-centered "visionary pastoral home place" in *In This Our Life* and *Beyond Defeat*.

David Marion Holman chooses *The Battle-Ground* and *Barren Ground* to illustrate Glasgow's move from historical romance to the realistic social novel (*A Certain Slant of Light*, pp. 86–96). The mythologies of the Old South in *The Battle-Ground* tie its downfall to romantic chauvinism; in *Barren Ground* Dorinda, an archetypal female martyr of the New South, brings the past into a dynamically creative, not destructive, relationship with the present. Catherine Rainwater's second substantial essay, "Ellen Glasgow's Outline of History in *The Shadowy Third and Other Stories*" (pp. 125–38 in *The Critical Response to H. G. Wells*) attributes the change in Glasgow's attitudes toward the future, seen in stories written from 1916 until 1923, to her exchange of the fearful vision of "a dystopian, devolutionary world" inspired by Poe for "a typically Wellsian, tentative faith in a better possible future."

Three unrelated items suggest possibilities for further work. Diane Roberts includes Glasgow in a Southern revisionist project "aimed at recovering and celebrating female sexuality" (*The Myth of Aunt Jemima*, pp. 165–67), but she faults Glasgow for the traditional representations of black women in *The Sheltered Life* since Memoria, a shadow of Eva, is "a reminder of the split between white women, absolved from sexuality, and black women, sexual before all. William J. Scheick's explication of Glasgow's allusion to a lightweight popular novel ("Chambered Intimations: *The King in Yellow* and *The Descendant*," *EGN* 34, i: 8–9) highlights her self-conscious artistry and points to new ways of understanding the complexity of her work. Third, the first of three installments of Rebe Glasgow's 1899 travel journal detailing her seven-month trip to Egypt and Europe with her sisters Ellen and Cary appears in the Fall 1995 number (35) of *EGN*.

iii Gertrude Stein and H. L. Mencken

Two fine books on Stein begin this section. Linda Wagner-Martin's impressively researched, thoroughly engrossing, and sometimes surprising biography, *"Favored Strangers": Gertrude Stein and Her Family* (Rutgers), is a major contribution to our perception of the familial relationships that shaped Stein's humanity as well as her genius. Wagner-Martin provides a lucidly written history of "The Stein Corporation," new insights into the influence of Alice B. Toklas, the story of the Steins' relationships with Matisse, Picasso, Gris, and other painters, as well as the many modernist writers and composers in the rue de Fleurus salon, including Hemingway, Fitzgerald, Virgil Thomson, Thornton Wilder, Janet Flanner, and Mabel Dodge Luhan. The book also contains 16 pages of photographs showing Stein in—and out of—the bosom of her family. The complete extant correspondence between Luhan and Stein can be found in Patricia R. Everett's *A History of Having a Great Many Times Not Continued to Be Friends: The Correspondence between Mabel Dodge and*

Gertrude Stein, 1911–1934 (New Mexico). Everett's superb introduction sets the context for the 104 letters collected here, valuable not only for what we learn about the progression and cooling of the friendship between the two women, but for the glimpses that they offer into the world of the avant-garde. Of tangential interest is *A Living of Words*, which includes Holly Baggett's "The Trials of Margaret Anderson and Jane Heap" (pp. 169–88), Noel Riley Fitch's "Sylvia Beach: Commerce, Sanctification, and Art on the Left Bank" (pp. 189–206), and Mary Lynn Broe's "'Yes, no, peut-être': Caresse Crosby after the Black Sun Set" (pp. 207–27).

In *Women Artists and Writers: Modernist (Im)positionings* (Routledge, 1994, pp. 90–121) Bridget Elliott and Jo-Ann Wallace examine the friendship between Stein and Marie Laurencin, "an important and neglected case study of modernist women's cultural patronage" and a friendship that has been overshadowed by an almost exclusive critical focus on Stein's relationship with Toklas. At different ends of a creative spectrum, Stein insisted on her own "genius," while Laurencin refused to be measured by prevailing male models of success. Michael North devotes a chapter of his splendid study of linguistic mimicry and racial masquerade, *The Dialect of Modernism: Race, Language, and Twentieth-Century Literature* (Oxford, 1994, pp. 59–76), to the role of Africa in the relationship between Stein and Picasso. The writer and the artist took the first steps into cubism and literary modernism by donning the African mask: Picasso transformed the figure of Gertrude Stein by painting a mask on her portrait; Stein rewrote her own story for black characters behind the literary mask of dialect.

Christopher J. Knight links the Stein of *Tender Buttons* to the Monet of the later canvases and locates Stein's work in the tradition of the innocent eye aesthetic in *The Patient Particulars: American Modernism and the Technique of Originality* (Bucknell, pp. 80–116). *Three Lives* and *The Making of Americans* experiment with listening and talking; *Tender Buttons* begins as a quest for the thing-in-itself, but it is undermined by Stein's growing interest in the pleasure of living and in the joy of sensuous words. Stein's hedonism also intrigues Patricia Meyer Spacks, who contends that Stein decided to help the cause of women "by committing herself to her chosen form of pleasure, by sharing that pleasure with others, by justifying in a new kind of narrative the responsiveness and attentiveness long associated with women" in *Boredom: The Literary History of a State of Mind* (Chicago, pp. 243–47).

The pleasures of reading Stein occupy Wayne Koestenbaum in "Stein Is Nice" (*Parnassus* 20: 297–319), a wide-reaching meditation on the ways in which Stein's work demonstrates that "writing and reading are vehicles for exploring the vastness that lies outside a civilization's regular patterns of commerce and conversation." Alison Tate reads Stein to locate the reason for the limitations of Julia Kristeva's approach to modernist language in "A Semblance of Sense: Kristeva's and Gertrude Stein's Analysis of Language" (*L&C* 15: 329–42). Kristeva draws primarily on a structural model of language and the unconscious, while Stein engages in a systematic revolt against both syntactic and textual linguistic constraints to probe "the ways in which language serves to identify, frame, organize and impose its own 'sense' in the rendering of experience."

In "Writing Psychology Over: Gertrude Stein and William James" (*YJC* 8, i: 133–63) Steven Meyer counters critics who have maintained that Stein accepted a "mechanistic conception of life" with a convincing, well-substantiated argument that, not only was she much more critical of mechanistic science than has generally been proposed, but that her constructive and deconstructive criticism emerges in her experimental literary compositions. Stein moved from the precise mechanisms of human personality seen in *The Making of Americans* to the non-mechanistic outlook of *Tender Buttons* as she freed herself from James's "beneficent influence."

Sidonie Smith offers *The Autobiography of Alice B. Toklas* as an example of the performative nature of the entire autobiographical enterprise in "Performativity, Autobiographical Practice, Resistance" (*ABSt* 10: 17–33); Stein undermines the notion of autobiography as expressive of a gendered "self," emphasizing the performative nature of identity, disrupting the stability of "feminine" and "masculine" narratives, and re-siting heterosexual coupling in "the camped-up performance and the 'compelled' performativity of heterosexual norms." Michele Valerie Ronnick's "*Fernhurst*: Gertrude Stein's Little *Iliad*" (*CML* 15: 377–79) follows Stein's textual clues and cogently argues that, overlooking gender roles, Martha Carey Thomas, Mamie Gwinn, and Mr. and Mrs. Alfred Hodder mirror the gods Paris, Aphrodite, and Hera, all involved in a struggle for dominion that shows such emotions "not only cut across boundaries of time and space, but that they belong to all human beings regardless of their sexual orientation."

In one of two articles on the Stein-Hemingway connection Dennis

Ryan reviews the critical field on questions of Stein's influence on
Hemingway, then traces Hemingway's practice of the Joycean "Uncle
Charles Principle" in "Up In Michigan" to Stein's *Three Lives* in "Dating
Hemingway's Early Style/Parsing Gertrude Stein's Modernism" (*JAmS*
29: 229–40). In the other essay Michael Szalay proposes that both Stein
and Hemingway have a crucial investment in textual identity that resists
Tristan Tzara's rigid opposition between physical particularity and "the
undifferentiated soup [that] identity supposedly becomes when it loses
physical form" in "Inviolate Modernism: Hemingway, Stein, Tzara"
(*MLQ* 56: 457–85).

Even in years with no major publication, Mencken scholars keep busy.
Two noteworthy essays take Nietzsche as their starting point. Manfred
Stassen proposes that Mencken selectively chose bits and pieces from
Nietzsche's doctrines to create an "American 'Ersatz' Nietzsche" in his
own person in "Nietzsky vs. The Booboisie: H. L. Mencken's Uses and
Abuses of Nietzsche" in *Nietzsche in American Literature and Thought*
(pp. 97–113). Mencken was drawn to Nietzsche's ideas about the rela-
tivity of truth and values, the preeminence of the individual over the
collective, and the superiority of an "aristocracy of efficiency" over
democracy. In "H. L. Mencken and American Cultural Masculinism"
(*JAmS* 29: 379–98) Melita Schaum convincingly links Mencken's views
on women to Nietzschean heroic vitalism, securely locates his work
within a long history of cultural misogyny, and exquisitely argues that
these views were not only consistent with his own cultural philosophy,
but that they joined a paradigm of masculinism underlying the definition of American culture during the early years of the 20th century. On
another note, Louis D. Rubin, Jr., in "H. L. Mencken of the *Baltimore
Sunpapers*" (*VQR* 71: 189–209) distinguishes Mencken, who remained a
newspaperman all his working life, from his contemporaries who abandoned journalism.

This year's *Menckeniana* includes S. L. Harrison's account of Menck-
en's detailed fiscal records (133: 1–10) and his appraisal of the import of
Mencken's detailed reports from the Scopes trial (135: 1–6); George
Weigel's thoughtful examination of Mencken's religious views (134: 1–
12); reflections on Mencken from C. Vann Woodward (136: 1–6) and
Anthony Frewin (136: 7–12); Jenny Pearson's reassessment of Sara Haardt
Mencken as "one of the women who built the foundations for what is
now a respected writing style" (133: 10–14); a note on Mencken's friend

Albert Jay Nock by Robert M. Thornton (135: 7–8); and Vincent Fitz-patrick's ongoing "Bibliographic Check List" (133: 15–16, 134: 15–16, 135: 10–16, 136: 13–16).

iv Sherwood Anderson, Sinclair Lewis, and Jack London

Anderson has claimed a central role in the current discourse on the short story cycle. J. Gerald Kennedy sees the genre as a provocative analogy to the basic social structure of community, which begins with *Winesburg*'s local emphasis, panoramic view of the collective life, mixed voices, and multiple perspectives, in "From Anderson's *Winesburg* to Carver's *Cathedral*: The Short Story Sequence and the Semblance of Community," in *Modern American Short Story Sequences* (pp. 194–215). *Winesburg*, set in the late 1890s, portrays the end of the collective experience in the United States, inferring that the debasement of language works against the idea of community by blocking communication through vacuous talk and by supplanting shared beliefs with absurd notions disseminated through pulp magazines and tabloids. *Cathedral* also exposes the absence of community, but Carver's stories suggest the possibility of fellowship and communication in the late 20th century if "we attend to each other's narratives and affirm the communal desire of storytelling." Maggie Dunn and Ann Morris propose renaming the genre in *The Composite Novel: The Short Story Cycle in Transition* (Twayne), and they contend that *Winesburg* is "just one representative text in a long-developing genre," examining a wide array of works by Jewett, Stein, Hemingway, Toomer, Faulkner, Welty, Barth, Maxine Hong Kingston, and Louise Erdrich, in addition to *Winesburg*, to explore the wide spectrum of experimentation and genre blending. In *Narrative Ethics* Adam Zachary Newton pairs *Winesburg* with Conrad's *Lord Jim* as antirealist texts that "chart a course" for modernist fiction by turning inward to explore constitutive features of storytelling itself and "the iconic relationship between the novel and the everyday narrating of lives." *Winesburg*'s topic, form, and closeness to Anderson's own personal circumstances herald a shift toward American modernism, toward "an aesthetic of the fragment . . . a kind of anti-Romantic Romanticism."

Two essays consider Anderson's troubled friendships. In "Hemingway v. Anderson: The Final Rounds" (*HN* 14, ii: 1–17) Judy Jo Small and Michael Reynolds persuasively argue that Hemingway's "The Killers" and Anderson's "The Fight" use boxing terms to show how differently they represented their literary battle. Hemingway understood it in terms of youth and age and imminent death for the old ex-champion, while Anderson perceived it as a tale of kinship rivalry fueled by petty vanity, ending in trivial wounds for both. Hilbert H. Campbell tells the poignant tale of the brief but important relationship between Anderson and Thomas Wolfe found in previously unpublished letters, manuscripts, and several entries from Eleanor Anderson's diaries in "Sherwood Anderson and Thomas Wolfe" (*RALS* 21: 58–67); their association was "more important to both, more revealing of their respective personalities, and, finally, more subject to bad luck and misunderstanding than has . . . been recognized."

MMisc contains five solid essays. Philip Greasley offers a close reading of *Kit Brandon* through the lens of oral literary theory in "Sherwood Anderson's Oral Tradition" (22: 9–16); Clarence B. Lindsay proposes that Anderson's fictive treatment of the city in his first two novels both obscured and delayed his emerging aesthetic in "The Unrealized City in Sherwood Anderson's *Windy McPherson's Son* and *Marching Men*" (22: 17–27); Douglas Wixson points out Anderson's appeal to the "untutored Midwestern story tellers" of the literary left who drew upon indigenous traditions of protest and progressive reform to respond to the depression in "Sherwood Anderson and Midwestern Literary Radicalism in the 1930s" (22: 28–39); Paul W. Miller rectifies false assumptions about Stella Anderson Hill's religious fanaticism and attributes Anderson's portrayal of his sister to "the severe limitations of his art as a record of everyday reality" in "Sherwood Anderson's Creative Distortion of his Sister Stella's Character in *The Memoirs*" (22: 40–50); and, finally, David D. Anderson brings this year's scholarship full circle with "The Durability of *Winesburg, Ohio*" (22: 51–58), which details Anderson's accomplishment in *Winesburg*: "he reconstructed the form of the short story, he rewrote the language of literature, he defined the nature of the human experience in our time" to create a work that remains central to this century's literary heritage "in whole as well as in each of its twenty-six parts."

Only two items deal with Sinclair Lewis this year, but the publication next year of James Hutchisson's much-anticipated *The Rise of Sinclair Lewis, 1920–1930* (Penn. State) should rejuvenate Lewis criticism. Rejecting the casual connection between Lewis's alcoholism and his sudden fame, Roger Forseth reads *Mantrap*, Lewis's "least accomplished" novel, as the work of "a self-destructive, self-loathing alcoholic"; Forseth further draws on Grace Hegger Lewis's *Half A Loaf, With Love from Gracie,* and unpublished correspondence to draw a compassionate picture of their codependence and Lewis's personal deterioration in "That First Infirmity of Noble Mind: Sinclair Lewis, Fame—and Drink" in *Beyond the Pleasure Dome* (pp. 216–23). Lewis's compulsion to write, regardless of quality, was as "furious and indiscriminate" as his compulsion to drink; one obliterated his feelings, the other his art. Of the three novels on fascism in the United States written in the 1930s by American novelists, Edward Dahlberg's *Those Who Perish,* Nathanael West's *A Cool Million,* and Lewis's *It Can't Happen Here,* only Lewis's reached a wide audience, and in "The Historical Context of Sinclair Lewis' *It Can't Happen Here*" (*SHR* 29: 221–37) Axel Knoenagel surveys the circumstances out of which Lewis's dystopia arose and skillfully illustrates the interaction of the text with its historical context. The autumn number (4, i) of *SLSN* contains abstracts of papers presented at the 1995 ALA session which point Lewis studies in new directions: Jon W. Brooks suggests evaluating *Main Street* through anthropologist Victor Turner's theories of rites of passage (1); David J. Knauer finds Lévi-Strauss helpful in locating Lewis's critique of monoculture in *Babbitt* (2); and Jay Williams locates the sources for Sam Dodsworth's landscaped suburbs in Edith Wharton and Frank Lloyd Wright.

Jack London continues to garner a lion's (or wolf's?) share of critics' attention, and even his little-known works are surfacing in unexpected places. London's 1910 futurist story "The Unparalleled Invasion: Excerpt from Walt Nervin's 'Certain Essays in History'" can be found in *The Tale of the Next Great War, 1871–1914: Fictions of Future Warfare and of Battles Still-to-Come,* ed. I. F. Clarke (Syracuse, pp. 257–70). *The Critical Response to Jack London,* ed. Susan M. Nuernberg (Greenwood), is designed specifically to document London's critical reception in the United States from a historical perspective. This valuable book contains Nuernberg's fine introduction to London's work; individual sections focus on "To Build a Fire," *A Daughter of the Snows, The Call of the Wild, The Sea-Wolf, The Iron Heel,* and *The Valley of the Moon,* all milestones in London's career; and a selection of general essays represent the variety of critical approaches used to analyze London's fiction. More narrowly focused, but equally impressive and useful, is the Oklahoma edition of *The Call of the Wild,* ed. Daniel Dyer; here are photographs, illustrations, and maps from the Gold Rush era, relevant passages from London's other North-land stories and events from his own life that figure in the novel, information on place-names, personal names, public transportation, flora and fauna, dog breeds, behavior and travel, slang, and a treasure trove of miscellaneous data.

The Call of the Wild, The People of the Abyss, The Sea-Wolf, and The Iron Heel each inspire two essays this year. In " 'Congested Mails': Buck and Jack's 'Call' " (AL 67: 51–76) Jonathan Auerbach maintains that London manages to address issues of vocational training, the quest for social approval by means of diligent work, the material conditions of literary production, and the meaning of fame in The Call of the Wild. Jacqueline Tavernier-Courbin in "The Call of the Wild and The Jungle: Jack London's and Upton Sinclair's Animal and Human Jungles" (The Cambridge Companion to American Realism and Naturalism, pp. 236–62) observes that both London and Sinclair, influenced by Zola, share a belief in survival skills, endurance, and the ability to overcome, as well as an intolerance for error and weakness. Whereas London depicts natural instincts and animal nature in harmony with a beautiful (though cruel) environment, Sinclair creates a revolting and illogical man-made world in which these instincts, pitted against "the powerful industrial machin-ery of the stockyards," are self-destructive. The only other item on Sinclair this year is Scott Derrick's "What a Beating Feels Like: Author-ship, Dissolution, and Masculinity in Sinclair's The Jungle" (SAF 23: 85–100); Sinclair's naturalist, misogynist novel depicts the threat posed by feminine fertility to traditional masculine authority.

In The Naturalistic Inner-City in America (pp. 34–45) James R. Giles explores the merging of ocean, jungle, and primordial metaphors used by London in The People of the Abyss to express the dehumanization of the lower classes; Giles compares the novel to the works of Jacob Riis and Stephen Crane, and he points out the book's dual intent to provide the respectable middle-class reader with a tour of the lower depths of society and to explore the repressed and forbidden areas of the civilized human psyche. Leonard Cassuto's close examination of The People of the Abyss, "The Apostate," and "Koolau the Leper" in "Jack London's Class-Based Grotesque," pp. 113–28 in Literature and the Grotesque, ed. Michael J. Meyer (Rodopi, 1994), provides abundant evidence of how London makes the grotesque into an emblem of social liminality. By depicting the breach of fundamental categories surrounding the definition of what is human, London creates the naturalist brute: not simply an animal, but a human-become-animal who embodies the distinctive and uneasy tension of the grotesque.

In "Modernist Prose and Its Antecedents" (*America and the Sea,* pp. 289–306) Joseph Defalco points out London's blend of biological determinism and romantic hopefulness in Wolf Larsen's journey over a symbolic sea of existence in a Darwinian universe, and he credits London with almost single-handedly preserving sea romance elements. Charles L. Crow finds the formal conventions of the gothic romance and of literary naturalism behind the doubleness running through *The Sea-Wolf* in "Jack London's *The Sea-Wolf* as Gothic Romance" in *Gothick Origins and Innovations,* ed. Allan Lloyd Smith and Victor Sage (Rodopi, 1994, pp. 123–31), and he asserts that the interaction of these traditions produces an open-ended and inconclusive dialogue about class and gender reflecting the author's own uncertainties.

Tony Barley's "Prediction, Programme and Fantasy in Jack London's *The Iron Heel*" in *Anticipations: Essays on Early Science Fiction and Its Precursors,* ed. David Seed (Syracuse, pp. 153–71), is a close reading of the "compulsively intertextual" novel that alludes to a wide variety of utopian/dystopian fantasies. Gerd Hurm's densely philosophical "Of Wolves and Lambs: Jack London's and Nietzsche's Discourses of Nature" (*Nietzsche in American Literature and Thought,* pp. 115–38) seeks to revise the perception that London did not understand the complexities and subtleties of Nietzsche's thought by assessing the affinities and differences between the two men.

In "Jack London's Optimistic View of the Law: A Reading of *The Son of the Wolf*" (*SSF* 32: 67–74) Peter Kratzke lucidly explains how *The Son of the Wolf,* an essentially optimistic book, presents a variety of ways in which the law may sustain the process of competition, dividing the stories according to the three ways that individuals may respond to the law. "The Men of Forty-Mile," "The Wife of a King," and "In a Far Country" demonstrate obedience to rules, whether legal or otherwise; "The White Silence," "The Son of the Wolf," "To the Man on Trail," and "The Wisdom of the Trail" illustrate the implications of disobedience to the law; and "The Priestly Prerogative" and "An Odyssey of the North" show how the law must adapt to changing social needs. David Fine contends that *Burning Daylight, The Valley of the Moon,* and *The Little Lady of the Big House* represent London's most sustained portrayal of *"the* California theme, the search for new beginnings in a new West," marking a shift from his earlier advocacy of socialism as a solution to the inequalities of urban capitalism to a vision of agrarianism as salvation in "Jack London's Sonoma Valley: Finding the Way Home" (*San Francisco in Fiction,* pp. 56–72).

v   Theodore Dreiser, John Dos Passos, and James M. Cain

This year Dreiser inspired two substantial essay collections, three chapters, a third of a book, and Yvette Szekely Eastman's *Dearest Wilding: A Memoir with Love Letters from Theodore Dreiser* (Penn.), which is likely to be the last document we will get from this era. Primarily of interest to Dreiser scholars as a candid account of her 16-year relationship with him (which began with a love affair when she was 16 and he 58), Eastman's memoir is also her attempt to understand her bond with the aging Dreiser, a complex, troubled, jealous, duplicitous, and supportive man. Editor Thomas P. Riggio has annotated the 115 (of 229) letters which Dreiser wrote to Yvette Szekely from 1929 until 1945 that appear here; also printed are 12 photographs and Eastman's comments on other figures in New York intellectual and artistic circles, including her husband, Max Eastman.

Dreiser's Jennie Gerhardt: *New Essays on the Restored Text,* ed. James L. W. West III (Penn.), brings together three generations of Dreiser scholars and critics in a rich interchange of ideas, information, and interpretations. In addition to a checklist of criticism of the 1911 text, this important collection contains West's informative introduction, and 19 essays—18 previously unpublished—that include general assessments by Robert H. Elias (pp. 3–8), Richard Lingeman (pp. 9–16), Judith Kucharski (pp. 17–26), and Valerie Ross (pp. 27–42); analyses of the main characters and the autobiographical roots of the novel by Lawrence E. Hussman (pp. 43–50), Leonard Cassuto (pp. 51–62), and Susan Albertine (pp. 63–74); and a wide array of essays that investigate the literary traditions and historical contexts informing the novel by Philip Gerber (*"Jennie Gerhardt:* A Spencerian Tragedy," pp. 77–90); Clare Virginia Eby ("Jennie Through the Eyes of Thorstein Veblen," pp. 91–102); Christopher P. Wilson ("Labor and Capital in *Jennie Gerhardt,"* pp. 103–14); Daniel H. Borus ("Dreiser and the Genteel Tradition," pp. 115–26); Nancy Warner Barrineau ("'Housework Is Never Done': Domestic Labor in *Jennie Gerhardt,* pp. 127–35); Miriam

Gogol ("Self-Sacrifice and Shame in *Jennie Gerhardt*," pp. 136–46); Yoshinobu Hakutani ("Jennie, Maggie, and the City," pp. 147–56); John B. Humma ("*Jennie Gerhardt* and the Dream of the Pastoral," pp. 157–66); Arthur D. Casciato ("How German Is *Jennie Gerhardt?*," pp. 167–82); Emily Clark ("Samuel E. [G]ross: Dreiser's Real Estate Magnate," pp. 183–93); West ("The Hotel World in *Jennie Gerhardt*," pp. 194–207); and James M. Hutchisson ("Death and Dying in *Jennie Gerhardt*," pp. 208–17).

The 10 new essays in *Theodore Dreiser: Beyond Naturalism,* ed. Miriam Gogol (NYU), raise questions about the whole of Dreiser's work from a variety of critical perspectives, including New Historicism, poststructuralism, psychoanalysis, feminism, and film studies. Barrineau analyzes the radical and truthful picture of working-class women at the turn of the century in *Jennie Gerhardt* (pp. 55–76), and Gogol investigates emotional poles of shame and pride in several of Dreiser's works (pp. 95–111). Shelley Fisher Fishkin (pp. 1–30) and Irene Gammel (pp. 31–54) explore Dreiser's attitude toward women and sexual liberation in his battle against American Puritanism; Scott Zaluda focuses on Dreiser's uneasiness with the dominant male ethos and men's social power (pp. 77–94). Leonard Cassuto applies Lacan's psychological theories to Dreiser's characters (pp. 112–33); Paul Orlov reviews Dreiser's similarities to Heidegger (pp. 134–75); and Lawrence E. Hussman ponders why the films made from Dreiser's novels never match the complexity of their sources (pp. 176–200). Two essays on *Sister Carrie* place the novel "beyond naturalism": M. H. Dunlop focuses on an essential contradiction in references to popular novels in two different editions of the novel (pp. 201–15), and James Livingston explores aspects of modern American consumerism in Dreiser's paradoxical use of "a realist style within the apparently archaic form of romance" (pp. 216–46).

Three Dreiser essays appeared in other collections. Blanche H. Gelfant links desire to determinism as a doctrine of causation common to consumerism, literary naturalism, behavioral psychology, and modern advertising in "What More Can Carrie Want? Naturalistic Ways of Consuming Women" (pp. 178–210 in *The Cambridge Companion to American Realism and Naturalism*). Gelfant suggests that "the ways of consuming women in naturalistic fiction appear to be static, impervious to the historical changes effected by a seemingly radical change of setting, of time and place." In "Addiction, Electricity and Desire" (*Beyond the Pleasure Dome*, pp. 132–42) Tim Armstrong calls attention to the play of electrical energies, electrical pleasures, and electrical addictions in *Sister Carrie,* then postulates that this flux of energies is linked with a new way of figuring the body and the body's relation to consumption. Joseph C. Schöpp points out that Nietzsche's concept of power helped Dreiser bridge the chasm between the spheres of "art-intellect-philosophy" and the realm of finance to "transvalue" the traditional notion of power with its largely political and financial connotations in "Cowperwood's Will to Power: Dreiser's *Trilogy of Desire* in the Light of Nietzsche" (pp. 138–54 in *Nietzsche in American Literature and Thought*). Cowperwood's Will to Power produces a transformation consistently described in Nietzschean terms as a process of infinite self-becoming.

In *The American Trilogy, 1900–1937* (pp. 83–116) John C. Waldmeir offers an archetypal reading of Norris's "Epic of the Wheat," Dreiser's "Trilogy of Desire," and Dos Passos's *U.S.A.* Waldmeir's formidable study argues that the authors used certain discourses within the secular life of the period, such as corporate capitalism and the emerging art of photography, to provide "a religious, transhistorical, and unifying perspective on an otherwise fragmented world." Waldmeir shows how, through repetition, Dreiser's Cowperwood novels expose and mediate primary dialectics (good/evil, material/spiritual, freedom/determinism) in carefully constructed moments of insight, all of which inhere within social situations.

Turning to Dos Passos, Waldmeir finds that compression of time in the biographies, interruptions of chronology in the series of fictional narratives, and attention to seasonal changes in the Camera Eye sections are crucial to the integrity of *U.S.A.,* in which, as Dos Passos says, "personal adventures" of characters "illustrate the development of a society." Cyclic patterns in *U.S.A.* provide a backdrop for chronological change in the trilogy, thereby transforming its otherwise pessimistic conclusion into an affirmation of life's primary sources. Chuck Etheridge focuses on the pattern of doubling in *U.S.A.* to argue that Dos Passos represents society as profoundly corrupt and individuals as either hunters or victims in "Doubling in Dos Passos' *U.S.A.* Trilogy" (*CCTEP* 55: 69–75). In "Historicizing the Female in *U.S.A.*: Re-Visions of Dos Passos's Trilogy" (*TCL* 41: 249–64) Janet Galligani Casey suggests that reading the Newsreels, Biographies, and Camera Eye sections of *U.S.A.* with an eye toward the presentation of women and women's issues reveals that the peripheral modes render "objective female history," whereas the women in the fictional narratives refashion female history into an alternative discourse in which women become speaking subjects rather than silent objects. William Dow suggests Blaise Cendrars as an influence on Dos Passos in "John Dos Passos, Blaise Cendrars, and a 'Squirrel Cage of the Meridians'" (*NConL* 25, ii: 4–5).

After years of relative obscurity, James M. Cain has resurfaced. In his superb study *The American Roman Noir* William Marling elucidates Cain's understanding of the implications of desire in an economy based on consumption and his perception of technology, law, and government as "statistical games played by inhuman sportsmen." Marling analyzes the sources for *The Postman Always Rings Twice* and *Double Indemnity,* enumerates the techniques Cain perfected, and contrasts Cain's journalism with his novels to suggest that California, the first postindustrial economy, became the favored setting of the roman noir because it seemed to preview the future. In "Beginning in the Thirties: The Los Angeles Fiction of James M. Cain and Horace McCoy" (*Los Angeles in Fiction,* pp. 43–66) David Fine claims that dissolution and collapse have been the essential themes of the Los Angeles novel ever since the publication of *The Postman Always Rings Twice* and Horace McCoy's *They Shoot Horses, Don't They?* Both Cain and McCoy saw California as a place of disastrous finishes, not new beginnings, and their novels mark the beginning of "a regional fiction obsessively concerned with puncturing the bloated image of Southern California as the golden land of opportunity and the fresh start."

Peter J. Rabinowitz argues that, if treated seriously, Cain's novels can offer valuable insights into the relationship between music and ethics in "'Three Out of Five Something Happens': James M. Cain and the Ethics of Music," pp. 167–86 in *Rhetoric and Pluralism: Legacies of Wayne Booth,* ed. Frederick J. Antczak (Ohio State). According to Rabinowitz, Cain's novels illustrate the process of listening, provide highly charged examples of how attributive screens and synthetic strategies work, give us a sharpened vision of how listening is intertwined with ethics, and offer an alternative way of listening. Greg Garrett states that, despite what the director said, Cain was not happy with the filmed version of *Mildred Pierce;* he objected to the murder idea and he continued to think of the novel as a book with serious aspirations whose key was Veda's immense talent ("The Many Faces of Mildred Pierce: A Case of Studio Adaptation and the Studio System," *LFQ* 23: 287–92).

vi W. E. B. Du Bois, James Weldon Johnson, Nella Larsen, Jessie Fauset, and Others

Shamoon Zamir's incisive *Dark Voices: W. E. B. Du Bois and American Thought, 1888–1903* (Chicago), the first sustained examination of Du Bois's intellectual formation in the context of American and European history, draws on fresh archival work to trace the influence of William James and George Santayana, and it examines how post-Reconstruction racism moved Du Bois from metaphysical speculation to an instrumentalist knowledge of history, to the new discipline of sociology. Zamir's brilliant comparison of *The Souls of Black Folk* to Hegel's *Phenomenology of Mind* counters critics that place Du Bois in the pragmatist tradition of Emerson and James or represent him as a Hegelian idealist, offering instead a portrait of a man deeply ambivalent about his commitment to heroic vitalism and to positivism, closely linked to Henry Adams in his experience of doubt and historical and personal disaster. Ross Posnock keeps Du Bois in both pragmatist and elitist camps with "The Distinction of Du Bois: Aesthetics, Pragmatism, Politics" (*AmLH* 7: 500–524), clarifying the ways in which pragmatism mediates between the aesthetic and the political with a close reading of "Criteria of Negro Art."

Political issues figure in two additional essays about Du Bois. Lily Wiatrowski Phillips examines *The Black Flame* in the context of social realism to reveal Du Bois's challenge to notions of patriotism, national identity, and social responsibility in "Du Bois and Soviet Communism: *The Black Flame* as Socialist Realism" (*SAQ* 94: 837–64). In this novel, which embodies the quintessential American desire to question authority and puncture complacency, Du Bois radically links capitalism and race, "equating the system that led to the Russian Revolution with a system of racial oppression that threatened to provoke violence." According to Dennis Loy Johnson's thoroughly engaging essay "In the Hush of Great Barrington: One Writer's Search for W. E. B. Du Bois" (*GaR* 49: 581–606), Du Bois's radicalism might be the reason that he is still a controversial figure in his hometown of Great Barrington, where he learned the possibilities of harmonious racial relationships in his youth. *Dark Princess* (Miss.), Du Bois's favorite work, is now available with a fine introduction by Claudia Tate, as is *W. E. B. Du Bois: A Reader,* ed. David Levering Lewis (Holt), which groups selections from Du Bois's extensive writings chronologically under 15 topics, including race concepts, civil rights, women's rights, labor, and imperialism.

In *Living Our Stories, Telling Our Truths* (Scribner's) V. P. Franklin examines the African American intellectual tradition by discussing the autobiographies of Du Bois and James Weldon Johnson, among others. *Darkwater* explores Du Bois's personal background and experiences to illuminate and clarify important matters of principle; *Dust of Dawn* examines the meaning of the African American experience in the United States; *Soliloquy,* published posthumously, expresses profound disillusionment with democratic processes and makes clear his support for the Communist Party. Franklin reminds us that *The Autobiography of an Ex-Colored Man* is *not* an autobiographical work, then shows how Johnson used the story of his own "full and fortunate life" to interpret the significance of black folk traditions to American and Western culture in *Along This Way.* Kenneth W. Warren reflects on the intensifying resistance to racial democracy in the post-Emancipation era and charts the "expansion and contraction of human personality during this nation's first profound assault on the color line" in "Troubled Black Humanity in *The Souls of Black Folk* and *The Autobiography of an Ex-Colored Man*" (*The Cambridge Companion to American Realism and Naturalism,* pp. 262–77). Ironically reversing *Souls,* Johnson makes Booker T. Washington a role model for black Americans, softening Du Bois's harsh critique in favor of romanticizing black enterprise.

Johnson scholars will welcome the important two-volume *Selected Writings of James Weldon Johnson,* ed. and introduced by Sondra Kathryn Wilson (Oxford), which should go far toward rectifying what Wilson regards as Johnson's critical neglect. The first volume collects Johnson's *New York Age* editorials, focusing on his role as "mass educator" and architect of the early civil rights movement in the United States; the second volume contains selections from his social and political writings, his discussion of international questions, writings from his college years, and literary works, including the complete text of *The Autobiography of an Ex-Colored Man.*

Johnson's novel is the topic of three additional items. Aldon L. Nielsen calls the book one of the most profound texts in America's racial history because it exists at "the very hinge point of America's most contradictory and paradoxical racial constructions" (*Writing Between the Lines: Race and Intertextuality* [Georgia, 1994], pp. 172–84). Neil Brooks brings a model of postmodern irony to bear on the text in "On Becoming an Ex-Man: Postmodern Irony and the Extinguishing of Certainties in *The Autobiography of an Ex-Colored Man*" (*CollL* 22, iii: 17–29); despite his

assertion of control as modernist narrator, the Ex-Colored Man cannot
resolve his own postmodern suspensiveness, and the text he seeks to
control betrays the failure of such strategies to tell the story of the
passer—his life remains a blank in the text. In "Race, Homosocial Desire
and 'Mammon' in *Autobiography of an Ex-Colored Man*" (*Professions of
Desire*, pp. 84–97) Cheryl Clarke argues that the novel revises and
ironizes all tropes of knowledge and freedom that characterize 19th-
century black narratives to tell a modernist story of "unknowing, alienation, and the inability to see within the 'veil.'" Perhaps the first anti-
heroic narrator in African American literature, the Ex-Colored Man
articulates some of the most profound, prophetic, and profane musings
on the color line.

Robert H. Cataliotti rates *The Autobiography of an Ex-Colored Man* a
pivotal work in which music is "a touchstone for racial price and a vehicle
through which representative individuals can advance the status of the
black race in American culture" (*The Music in African American Fiction*,
pp. 58–73). His astute discussion of *Home to Harlem* and *Banjo* (pp. 86–
99) demonstrates that Claude McKay's representation of Harlem is
permeated by music and informed exclusively by modern expressions of
folk culture in the context of the rapidly expanding urban community;
McKay, in looking beyond his concentration on contemporary forms of
music in *Home to Harlem* to examine the roots of cultural tradition as
artistic models in *Banjo*, shows that music provides a vital link among
the peoples of the African Diaspora. Elizabeth Schultz (*America and the
Sea*, pp. 233–59) uses the contrast of sea and land in *Home to Harlem*,
Banjo, and works by Langston Hughes and Zora Neale Hurston to illustrate black writers' realization that racial tensions ashore were frequently
transferred to ships, where owners and authorities were always white and
where close quarters intensified hostilities. In "Claude McKay's 'If We
Must Die,' *Home to Harlem*, and the Hog Trope" (*ANQ* 8, iii: 22–25)
Charles J. Heglar proposes that readers have missed the irony in the
conclusion of *Home to Harlem* by not attending carefully enough to the
foreshadowing that skillfully develops McKay's poetic trope of blacks as
"hogs" trapped in the city. In *Ten Is the Age of Darkness: The Black
Bildungsroman* (Missouri, pp. 152–65) Geta LeSeur reads McKay's *Banana Bottom* in light of George Lamming's *Season of Adventure* and
Merle Hodge's *Crick Crack, Monkey;* the strong female protagonists in all
three books contrast with those created by West Indian women, and

their actions and initiations are different from those of their African American sisters.

Michael North focuses on *Songs of Jamaica, Home to Harlem,* and *Banana Boat* to clarify McKay's position as a colonial writer in *The Dialect of Modernism* (Oxford, 1994). North also recalls Alain Locke's disappointed hope that white modernists and the Harlem movement would meet in a common effort to make a new national art that would free all writers from inhibiting standards and traditions; instead of growing into a truly multicultural modernism, the Americanist avant-garde demonstrated "a persistent inability to understand how race fits into its conception of modern America." North's comparison of Jean Toomer's *Cane* and William Carlos Williams's *Spring and All* reveals a good deal in common: both are a mixture of prose and poetry, pastoralism and urbanism, political fears and cultural hopes; both depend on the same organic metaphor for their hopes; nothing could be less organic than the organization of the two works; both are even more difficult to read than *The Waste Land;* and both languished in obscurity for decades.

Before his death in 1993 Robert B. Jones compiled "Jean Toomer: An Annotated Checklist of Criticism, 1923–1993" (*RALS* 21: 68–121), which lists critical essays, anthologies, reviews, and unpublished dissertations. Charles Scruggs announces that not all of Toomer's pre-*Cane* writings were lost; he contextualizes and reprints the texts of three newspaper articles that Toomer wrote in 1919 and 1920 for the *New York Call* ("Ghouls," "Reflections on the Race Riots," and "Americans and Mary Austin") in " 'My Chosen World': Jean Toomer's Articles in *The New York Call*" (*ArQ* 51, ii: 103–26).

Cane is, as ever, a challenge. Linda Wagner-Martin's incisive analysis of the text as a "modernist tour de force" reveals a wide array of literary sources, argues that Toomer regarded genre distinctions as artificial, illustrates Toomer's responsiveness to both female and male characters, and elucidates the thematic complexities of the work ("Jean Toomer's Cane as Narrative Sequence" *Modern American Short Story Sequences,* pp. 19–34). Although students of *Cane* are aware that the "Sempter" of the text is Sparta, Georgia, Barbara Foley in "Jean Toomer's Sparta" (*AL* 67: 747–73) suggests that critics have not recognized the significance of this setting, thereby dehistoricizing the category of "identity" and downplaying the nature and extent of *Cane's* specific historical reference. In *"Who Set You Flowin'?"* (pp. 44–87) Farah Jamine Griffin contends that

Toomer portrays both the beauty and the horror of the South in *Cain*, ultimately concluding that a return to the South is necessary for black redemption.

Turning to Nella Larsen (pp. 154–60), Griffin finds a picture of the South as a stifling hell in *Quicksand*. Sexuality and religion prove brutal for Helga, whose return to the South marks her demise in a "black woman's hell" that focuses on the curse of race. Claudia Tate in "Desire and Death in *Quicksand* by Nella Larsen" (*AmLH* 7: 234–60) draws on Lacan's construct of psyche to assert that "the enigmatic causality of Helga's decisions can be traced to deep conflicts in her subjectivity, specifically between her reticent conscious speaking self and her much more communicative narcissistic ego." The novel's repetitions make implicit a structure that imitates the dynamic structure of the psyche, as Helga learns that patriarchal law, racial attitudes, and sexist convention are also "master plots of hegemonic desire that have formed her social identity."

In his intriguing study *The Wayward Preacher in the Literature of African American Women* (McFarland) James Robert Saunders notes that one of the striking things about *Quicksand* is how tentative Larsen is in suggesting the possibility that the Reverend Pleasant Green is a philanderer. Later novelists, such as Zora Neale Hurston, Paule Marshall, Gloria Naylor, and Terry McMillan, were not so shy. Marilyn Elkins proposes that *Quicksand*, Toni Morrison's *Tar Baby*, and Andrea Lee's *Sarah Phillips* all portray black women's expatriatism as a form of narcissism that conflates exoticism and exploitation rather than as affirmation in "Expatriate Afro-American Women as Exotics," pp. 264–73 in *International Women's Writing*. The later novels use *Quicksand* as an intertextual reference and depend on Larsen's ideological premises. Usha Bande compares Helga to the heroine of Anita Desai's *Where Shall We Go This Summer* to find that their quests for self-definition and urge to flee are remarkably similar, though separated by time and culture in " 'Only Connect' and the Failure to Connect: A Comparative Study of Anita Desai's Sita and Nella Larsen's Helga" (*NConL* 25, ii: 5–7).

Two additional essays consider Larsen's protagonists. In " 'My Picture of You Is, After All, the True Helga Crane': Portraiture and Identity in Nella Larsen's *Quicksand*" (*Signs* 20: 575–600) Pamela E. Barnett reads the description of Helga in terms of visual art and the positioning of the reader as spectator as assertions of the always mediated nature of representation; by focusing on the elaborate process by which Helga becomes an object of art, Larsen critiques a tradition of representation that claims to be mimetic as it actually reproduces stereotypes of the black female. Deborah R. Grayson in "Fooling White Folks, or, How I Stole the Show: The Body Politics of Nella Larsen's *Passing*" (*Having Our Way*, pp. 27–38) extends Foucault's notion of "the gaze" and its power to create and control "the other" to unmask "political strategies working obscurely within and upon the text." In the complexity and occasionally subversive comedy of overlapping gazes turned on Clare, Gertrude, Bellew, and Irene, Larsen provides an opportunity to explore how our uses of language and its binary oppositions silence "the complexity of ourselves and of our text." Corinne E. Blackmer reads *Passing* in light of the legal and cultural assumptions informing its production in "The Veils of the Law: Race and Sexuality in Nella Larsen's *Passing*" (*CollL* 22, iii: 50–67). The novel is an original reconfiguration of and commentary on more conventional plots of racial passing by stressing interpretive anxieties and sexual paranoias that "make convention-bound people reluctant to travel through the many worlds, identities, and sexualities of American society."

Although the endings of *Quicksand* and *Passing* appear to be concessions to the dominant ideology of romance, Deborah E. McDowell points out in *"The Changing Same"* (pp. 78–97) that they become much more radical and original efforts to acknowledge female sexual experience when viewed from a feminist perspective. Both novels struggle with the dialectic between pleasure and danger that defines women's sexual experience in patriarchal societies. In her chapter on Jessie Fauset (pp. 61–77) McDowell contends that critics have consistently ignored the subtle function of class, race, and color and missed the ambivalent stance toward racial uplift in her work. Inherently self-reflexive, *Plum Bun* "passes for just another story of passing and for the age-old fairy tale and romance," baiting the reader with a range of familiar expectations of women and blacks that conform to the culturally coded constructions of gender and race, and then refusing to fulfill them. In "Alternative Afrocentrisms: Three Paths Not Taken Yet" (*American Enterprise* 65, v: 55–65) Elizabeth Wright ("Booker T. Washington"), Bill Kauffman ("Jessie Fauset"), and David T. Beito ("Zora Neale Hurston") suggest how to reconsider the ways in which Washington, Fauset, and Hurston were able to "celebrate the world of blackness without vandalizing historical fact or the self-regard of their non-black fellow citizens."

Two superb studies conclude this section. Jacquelyn Y. McLendon's

The Politics of Color in the Fiction of Jessie Fauset and Nella Larsen (Virginia) breaks new ground, going beyond recent feminist criticism to focus on Fauset's and Larsen's works rather than their lives. In perceptive readings of *Plum Bun, Comedy: American Style, Quicksand,* and *Passing* McLendon demonstrates how the stereotype of the tragic mulatto, invented by white writers, became a political tool and an artistic device in their fiction; Fauset and Larsen show that blacks were despised not for lack of education, money, or manners, but because they were black. Although Cheryl A. Wall focuses on the works of Fauset, Larsen, and Hurston in *Women of the Harlem Renaissance* (Indiana), she adroitly covers the struggles, successes, and failures of a wide range of women, including Marita Bonner, Anne Spencer, Georgia Johnson, Elise Johnson McDougald, Bessie Smith, and Helene Johnson, to clarify and differentiate black female experience and expression during the Harlem Renaissance. A major contribution, Wall's clearly written and thoughtful analysis puts these writers and artists and their works within American literary traditions in general and African American writing in particular. To further study in this area, 10 volumes of the projected 30-volume series of facsimile reprints, *African American Women Writers, 1910–1940,* ed. Henry Louis Gates, Jr. (Hall), appeared this year. Among them: Maud Cuney Hare's *Norris Wright Cuney: A Tribune of the Black People;* Sarah Lee Brown Fleming's *Hope's Highway* and *Clouds and Sunshine;* and Frances Joseph-Gaudet's *"He Leadeth Me."*

vii Westerners, Immigrants, and Exiles

Mary Austin's star continues to rise. *Beyond Borders: The Selected Essays of Mary Austin* (So. Ill.), the first collection of her nonfiction journalism, contains 17 essays on a variety of topics. Reuben J. Ellis provides an introduction, prefaces to each essay, and a selected primary bibliography. Newly available, too, is Jean Toomer's 1910 *New York Call* editorial "Americans and Mary Austin" (*ArQ* 51, ii: 122–26), in which he reviews Austin's protest against one-sided development of American intellectualism, faults her for fostering racial stereotypes, and proposes that she "serves the cause of disunion" by seeking a community of cultural differences.

Tracing Austin's "imaginative self-mythology" as an expert on Native American life, Karen S. Langlois calls her "something of a charlatan" in "Marketing the American Indian: Mary Austin and the Business of

Writing" (*A Living of Words,* pp. 151–68). Langlois also acknowledges that Austin fostered sympathy for Native Americans in a middle-class mass market and helped legitimize a part of Western life that was largely neglected and unknown. In "Storytellers, Story-Sellers: Artists, Muses, and Exploitation in the Work of Mary Austin" (*SAL* 20, ii: 21–33) Betsy Klimasmith looks at the dynamics between storytellers and "story-sellers" like Austin.

Mark T. Hoyer contributes two essays on Austin. In "Weaving the Story: Northern Paiute Myth and Mary Austin's *The Basket Woman*" (*AICRJ* 19: 133–51) he shows that some of the stories in *The Basket Woman: A Book of Indian Tales for Children* adapt myths from the Paiute. The figures of the native basket weaver and the preadolescent boy play a key role in Austin's writing, creating a dual identity by moving across borders of race, gender, and ideology. Hoyer's "Prophecy in a New West: Mary Austin and the Ghost Dance Religion" (*WAL* 30: 235–55) examines Austin's attempts to meld together Native American and biblical stories in new syncretic forms and finds that the Ghost Dance and its prophets hover in the background of her work.

Linda K. Karell chides critics who dismiss Austin in "*Lost Borders* and Blurred Boundaries: Mary Austin as Storyteller" (*American Women Short Story Writers,* pp. 153–66). Karell points out that, by drawing on Native American spiritual beliefs, Austin challenges the ethno- and intellectual centrism that constructs the boundaries of much contemporary feminist theorizing. Austin claims a spiritually authorized power for marginalized characters, insists that spirituality is an *essential* component of female subjectivity, and authorizes female agency by privileging the female storyteller who narrates and unifies the collection. Paradoxically, Austin's essentialism reintroduces the troubling conflation of femininity, spirituality, and nature that has historically authorized attempts to master the female. Charlotte S. McClure describes in "From Impersonators to Persons" (*Private Voices, Public Lives,* pp. 225–37) how Austin, Kate Chopin, and Gertrude Atherton confronted the pressure to accept the values of the patriarchal mainstream of business and competition. Mc-Clure contributes "Gertrude Atherton and Her San Francisco: A Wayward Writer and a Wayward City in a Wayward Paradise" to *San Francisco in Fiction* (pp. 73–95), tracing in it the realistic and symbolic responses of Atherton's characters to the illusion of ease and purposelessness offered by the Californian "fool's paradise."

Four articles on Mourning Dove were published this year. The text of a previously unpublished 16-page story and Alanna K. Brown's introduction to it appear in "Mourning Dove's *The House of Little Men*" (*CanL* 144: 49–60); the story is important because it preserves a part of the long, rich oral tradition of the Okongans, because it illustrates how the tale incorporates commentary on and reactions against assimilation, and because Mourning Dove's rendition of the story depicts her storytelling skills and her command of English. In "The Autobiographings of Mourning Dove" (*CanL* 144: 29–40) George Bowering proposes that *Cogewea, Coyote Stories,* and *Mourning Dove: A Salishan Autobiography* advanced Mourning Dove's principal social and political goals: to make certain that her people's stories and the story of their way of life would be preserved in print and to construct a bridge between Native Americans and the whites on their land. Jay Miller's eloquent defense of his editing of Mourning Dove's work in accordance with the wishes of her family and the Colville Confederated Tribes of Washington State can be found in "Mourning Dove: Editing in All Directions to 'Get Real'" (*SAIL* 7, ii: 65–72). According to Susan K. Bernardin in "Mixed Messages: Authority and Authorship in Mourning Dove's *Cogewea, The Half-Blood: A Depiction of the Great Montana Cattle Range*" (*AL* 67: 487–509), Mourning Dove's and editor Lucullus McWhorter's competing visions of narrative authority and Native authenticity culminate in a novel that formally and thematically enacts the conditions of early Native American literary production. Mourning Dove self-consciously adopted elements of 19th-century sentimental romance plot and appropriated the conventions of the popular western in order to reshape the discourse surrounding Indians in the early 20th century, ironizing the conventional endings dictated by western and women's plots and drawing attention to the ultimate inability of Euro-American literary forms to express the experiences of marginalized peoples. Of interest here is Norris Yates's study of women-authored westerns, *Gender and Genre: An Introduction to Women Writers of Formula Westerns, 1900–1950* (New Mexico), which defines the subgenre, explores connections between these novels and domestic novels, and proposes that these authors "manage the difficult task of achieving true female literary authority by simultaneously conforming to and subverting patriarchal literary standards."

Owen Wister is perennially interesting. In *Trickster in the Land of Dreams* (Nebraska, pp. 73–90) Zeese Papanikolas examines the Western myth of the expert, the lone Westerner with the gun, created in *The Virginian,* and he locates the countermyth of the Western worker that matched and opposed it in the ideology, propaganda, and style of the radical Industrial Workers of the World. Native and immigrant workers, so absent in the cowboy novel and so present in the real West, are perceived by the gap they leave in the western text. James C. Work shares his surprise that the prototypical gunfight in *The Virginian* does not translate well to the short story form in "Variations on the Gunfight in Western Short Stories" (*HK* 28, i: 21–29); the standard gunfight is inevitably a weak climax, so "good gunfight short stories" generally feature unique variations on the scenario that Wister popularized. In "The Only Good Alien Is a Dead Alien: Science Fiction and the Metaphysics of Indian-Hating on the High Frontier" (*JACult* 18, i: 51–67) Gregory M. Pfitzer testifies to the ubiquitous presence of Wister's myth in our culture by tracing popular representations of "aliens" from space to *The Virginian*. J. C. Furnas reminds us that Theodore Roosevelt introduced Wister and Rudyard Kipling in "Transatlantic Twins: Rudyard Kipling and Owen Wister" (*ASch* 64: 599–607), and he argues that the bulk of Wister's best work can be found in the "several score" of neglected stories that precede and follow *The Virginian,* most of which show the influence of Kipling. Both Wister and Kipling, as well as a host of other writers and politicians including Mark Twain, William Dean Howells, James Weldon Johnson, Agnes Repplier, Henry Cabot Lodge, and Woodrow Wilson figure in *The Letters of Theodore Roosevelt and Brander Matthews,* ed. Lawrence J. Oliver (Tennessee). Oliver also provides an astute introduction and thoroughly annotates the 271 letters collected here.

After the bounty of 1994's work, Sui Sin Far is represented by only one essay this year. Annette White-Parks in "A Reversal of American Concepts of 'Other-ness' in the Fiction of Sui Sin Far" (*MELUS,* 20, i: 17–34) explains how in her stories, in radical reversal of readers' expectations, Chinese Americans take on the role of insiders while Anglo Americans shift to the periphery, becoming outsiders. In "Outsiders and Greenhorns: Christopher Newman in the Old World, David Levinsky in the New" (*AL* 67: 725–45) Donald Weber juxtaposes Henry James's Christopher Newman, "the American pilgrim/greenhorn who cannot decode the archaic ways of the Old World," and Abraham Cahan's David Levinsky, "the Talmudic scholar industrialist" who can find no happiness in the bewildering ways of the New.

Scholars will welcome Roberta Simone's handy and timely resource, *The Immigrant Experience in American Fiction: An Annotated Bibliogra-*

phy (Scarecrow), which lists books alphabetically by immigrant group. Magdalena J. Zaborowska's important study, *How We Found America,* explores novels by East European women immigrants that reflect the play between the host country's interpretive powers and the marginalized newcomer's desire to belong. Writers relevant to this chapter who are covered in Zaborowska's volume include Mary Antin, whose *The Promised Land* tells how the new language is simultaneously a key to freedom and an inevitable instrument of repression (pp. 39–77); Elizabeth Stern, whose *My Mother and I* both elicits and rejects the cultural split imposed on the immigrant woman who claims the United States as her birthright but rejects acculturation (pp. 77–112); and Anzia Yezierska, whose feminist texts end in Hollywood clichés that subvert "the restrictive official narrative of female Americanization" (pp. 113–64). Yezierska's *Salome of the Tenements* (Illinois), based on the romance between Jewish immigrant Rose Pastor and millionaire socialist Graham Stokes as well as on her own with John Dewey, exposes the hypocrisy of the privileged class and sardonically criticizes the American melting pot.

For Ole Rølvaag, resisting assimilation is imperative. In "Breaking the Silence: Hymns and Folk Songs in O. E. Rølvaag's Immigrant Trilogy" (*GPQ* 15: 105–15) Philip R. Coleman-Hull carefully and cogently traces Rølvaag's use of Norwegian folk songs and hymns through his immigrant trilogy. In *Giants in the Earth* Rølvaag associates Beret with hymns and Per with folk music to signify the chasm in their relationship; in *Peder Victorious* he suggests Peder's alienation from his roots by his use of mixed traditional songs and American music; a more profound and lyrical blending of the two traditions in *Their Father's God* signals Peder's recovery of his heritage. Øyvind T. Gulliksen notes the difference between Rølvaag's fight to retain the Norwegian language and promote a lasting Norwegian-American culture and his fellow Norwegian-American Thorstein Veblen's focus on a wider scope of cultural criticism in "Ole E. Rølvaag, Thorstein Veblen, and the Independent Farmer" (*Performances in American Literature and Culture,* pp. 74–84).

John E. Miller studies Wilder's *Little House* novels in the context of the history of De Smet, South Dakota, in *Laura Ingalls Wilder's Little Town: Where History and Literature Meet* (Kansas, 1994). Miller establishes an environmental context for the novels, explores the fictional practices, narrative, rules, and storytelling procedures that Wilder developed in collaboration with Rose, her daughter, contrasts textbook history with lived history, and compares Wilder's literary rendition of the prairie to the prairie paintings of Harvey Dunn. Ann Romines produced two very different and equally compelling essays on Wilder this year. In "Preempting the Patriarch: The Problem of Pa's Stories in *Little House in the Big Woods*" (*CLAQ* 20: 15–18) Romines offers a splendid scholarly analysis of the critical gender questions raised by the foregrounding of men's tales in *Big Woods;* in "The Voices from the Little House" (*Private Voices, Public Lives,* pp. 19–28) she offers more personal, perhaps more daring, comment on the help and support that sustain writing women.

After 12 years of "bringing together, organizing, annotating, and publishing Goldman's correspondence, writings, and government and legal documents," Candace Falk announces the publication of the documentary microfilm edition of *The Emma Goldman Papers* and its companion volume *Emma Goldman: A Guide to Her Life and Documentary Sources* (Chadwyck-Healey). The initial part contains Falk's introduction, Stephen Cole's bibliographical essay, a chronology, and several pages of illustrations; the second part contains the reel list and introductory essays to the reels. This monumental work is an invaluable and rich resource for scholars from many disciplines. Blanche H. Gelfant sees similarities between Goldman's autobiography, Dreiser's *Sister Carrie,* and Nikolai Chernyshevsky's *What Is to Be Done?* in *Cross-Cultural Reckonings* (pp. 69–96). Unlike Dreiser's novel, which ends with a vision of life as a tangle, *Living My Life* concludes with the vision of a happy ending, expressing the naïveté and hopefulness of Chernyshevsky's novel.

viii General Studies and Additional Authors

Walter Benn Michaels begins his splendid and provocative study of American modernism, *Our America,* with Calvin Coolidge's observation that "we have a great desire to be supremely American." Michaels brilliantly reinterprets the intersection of the aesthetic movement of modernism and the social movement of nativism in the 1920s as an effort to resolve the meaning of linguistic, national, cultural, and racial identity. He also provides fresh, insightful readings of major works by writers such as Sherwood Anderson, Cather, Faulkner, Hurston, and William Carlos Williams, as well as popular and noncanonical texts, to offer new ways of understanding our current debates over the meaning of multiculturalism and pluralism. David E. Shi begins earlier, but he ends up in the 1920s, in *Facing Facts: Realism in American Thought and Culture,*

1850–1920 (Oxford), which traces the development of the "realistic consciousness" and "modernist sensibility" from antebellum idealism to the Ashcan School, discussing works by Cather, Dreiser, Wharton, and others along the way.

The Harlem Renaissance in Black and White (Belknap), George Hutchinson's important study of the interaction between American cultural nationalism and Harlem Renaissance modernism, investigates the intellectual frameworks and interracial and interethnic networks that produced the movement and subsequently institutionalized black literary modernism. Concentrating on "intentionally egalitarian interracial efforts, intimacies, and commitments," Hutchinson shifts the critical focus to "previously marginalized factors," writing an intelligent, engrossing "new story of the contexts, crosscurrents, and effectiveness of the Harlem Renaissance." In *Constituting Americans* Priscilla Wald carefully attends to disruptions in literary narratives caused by unexpected words, awkward grammatical constructions, rhetorical or thematic dissonances that mark the pressure of untold stories in works by Douglass, Melville, Harriet Wilson, Du Bois, and Stein to show how the evidence of their own authorial struggles reflects on the relationship between literary production and cultural identity. All five demonstrate risky, complicated, and engaging strategies through which they were able to confront cultural anxiety.

American Diversity, American Identity contains short biographies and critical assessments of 145 American writers representing "the particularity and diversity of the American experience"; *Native American Writing in the Southeast: An Anthology, 1875–1935,* ed. Daniel F. Littlefield, Jr., and James W. Parins (Miss.), collects representative works from 28 Native American writers in a variety of forms. And in *The Nature of the Place: A Study of Great Plains Fiction* (Nebraska) Diane Dufva Quantic draws on the work of cultural geographers, historians, and literary critics to elucidate the ways in which a remarkable number of writers, including Cather, Rølvaag, Wilder, Bess Streeter Aldrich, Wright Morris, and Wallace Stegner, depict "the interrelated influences of the various westering myths, the land itself, and the establishment of society."

Focusing on New York as the capital of American literature, music, and language in the 1920s, Ann Douglas has written a fascinating, strikingly original, and thoroughly researched account of the transformation of American culture in *Terrible Honesty: Mongrel Manhattan in the 1920s* (Farrar). Breaking with the "feminine" culture of their predecessors, a number of literary figures germane to this chapter fused high and low art with the new mass media to create a "new ethos of modernity" marked by a boldly masculinized outspokenness that remains a major component of American popular culture today. Shaun O'Connell's *Remarkable, Unspeakable New York: A Literary History* (Beacon) is a less scholarly, chatty, and engaging account of many of the same cultural and literary figures. In "The Three New Yorks: Topographical Narratives and Cultural Texts" (*AmLH* 7: 28–54) Martha Banta asserts that no single "New York" text exists, but she identifies traits that dominate Manhattan street narratives. *Brotherman: The Odyssey of Black Men in America,* ed. Herb Boyd and Robert L. Allen (Ballantine), contains narratives from 11 of this chapter's writers, including Du Bois, Toomer, McKay, Walter White, and Countee Cullen.

Two books on Ring Lardner appeared this year. *The Annotated Baseball Stories of Ring W. Lardner, 1914–1919,* ed. George W. Hilton (Stanford), contains 12 Jack Keefe stories and 12 others, Hilton's informative critical introduction, and extensive notes. Clifford M. Caruthers has edited an expanded edition of *Letters of Ring Lardner* (Orchises), with substantial commentary, useful footnotes, and 16 pages of photographs. Lardner makes an appearance in Edward Robb Ellis's monumental *A Diary of the Century: Tales from America's Greatest Diarist* (Kodansha), as do Sherwood Anderson, Romare Brerden, Fanny Butcher, Alfred A. Knopf, and Sinclair Lewis. In addition, *Floyd Dell: Essays from the* Friday Literary Review, *1909–1913,* ed. R. Craig Sautter (December), contains 57 engaging pieces.

Carl Van Vechten attracts passing attention. In "Partygoing: The Jazz Age Novels of Evelyn Waugh, Wyndham Lewis, F. Scott Fitzgerald and Carl Van Vechten" (*Forked Tongues,* pp. 117–34) David Seed compares party scenes from Van Vechten's *Parties,* Fitzgerald's *Gatsby,* Waugh's *Vile Bodies,* and Lewis's *The Apes of God.* Although all four novels end with images of death, Waugh and Lewis vigorously satirize their partygoers, Fitzgerald finds his partygoers pathetic, and Van Vechten distances himself as observer, chronicling an age that has ended. Jonathan Weinberg begins with Van Vechten's partygoing as celebrity-collecting, then proceeds to a discussion of the collection of 20 "essentially homemade sex books" that Van Vechten left among his papers at Yale in " 'Boy Crazy': Carl Van Vechten's Queer Collection" (*YJC* 7, ii: 25–49). Van Vechten pasted together a history of gay life that comments on the role of advertising in our culture by combining articles, headlines, photographs, and postcards in collages, 15 of which are reproduced. In *Dayneford's Library: American Homosexual Writing, 1900–1913* (Mass.) James Gifford examines six models of homosexuality by close readings of representative literary texts, including works by Sherwood Anderson, Cather, O. Henry, London, Van Vechten, Wharton, and Wister.

Sherrie Inness investigates the cultural dictates prescribing limits to cross-dressing that she finds clearly inscribed in college texts for both men and women in "Girls Will Be Boys and Boys Will Be Girls: Cross-Dressing in Popular Turn-of-the-Century College Fiction" (*JACult* 18, ii: 15–23); the paradoxical nature of cross-dressing reaffirms the very gender boundaries that it seems to contest. In *Intimate Communities: Representation and Social Transformation in Women's College Fiction, 1895–1910* (Bowling Green) Inness examines the common narrative structures in women's college fiction to explore the cultural significance of subjects such as women's sports, social life at college, and homoaffectionate crushes, demonstrating how these texts both challenged the social limitations on college-educated women and quieted their fears. For effectively allaying masculine fears, Martha Patterson chooses the Gibson Girl, who co-opted New Woman ideology while tempering her independence, ambition, and intellectual prowess in "'Survival of the Best Fitted': Selling the American New Woman as Gibson Girl, 1895–1910" (*ATQ* 9: 73–85). Shirley Marchalonis draws on short stories, novels, and juveniles to trace the changing perceptions of educated women, their "green world," and their expectations in *College Girls: A Century in Fiction* (Rutgers).

Laura Hapke's *Daughters of the Great Depression,* a comprehensive, well-written, revisionist study of the "working girl" novels of the thirties, makes a wonderful companion to her earlier book, *Tales of the Working Girl* (see *ALS 1992,* p. 245). Hapke draws on articles and books of the thirties, U.S. Labor Department Women's Bureau statistics, "true romance" stories and "fallen women" films, as well as the fiction of such writers as Claude McKay, Sinclair Lewis, Dorothy Thompson, Agnes Smedley, and Meridel Le Sueur, to explore one of the decade's central conflicts: whether to include women in the workplace or relegate them to a literal or figurative home sphere. Constance Coiner's *Better Red,* the first book-length exploration of Meridel Le Sueur's and Tillie Olsen's relationships to the Communist Party, U.S.A., and the effect of those ties in their writing, is a solid contribution to the effort to promote working-class writing as a legitimate category of literary analysis. Coiner's treatment of Le Sueur focuses on *The Girl,* "Our Fathers," "Annunciation," and "Corn Village." Blanche Gelfant observes in *Cross-Cultural Reckonings* (pp. 25–32) that Le Sueur and Lydia Chukovskaya wrote their texts (*The Girl* and *Sofia Petrovna*) from a desire to tell the "true history" of their times. Both saw writing as an act of indictment and juxtaposed the truth of fiction to "the lies, distortions, and deceptive omissions of newspapers."

In *Women Writers and the Great War* (Twayne) Dorothy Goldman, Jane Gledhill, and Judith Hattaway resurrect the experiences of women in the home sphere and at the front by examining the memoirs, novels, and stories about World War I written by Cather, Wharton, Stein, Atherton, and Dorothy Canfield Fisher, among others. The first book-length collection of Fisher's short fiction, *The Bedquilt and Other Stories,* ed. Mark J. Madigan (Missouri), contains 11 stories, two essays, a chronology, and Madigan's knowledgeable introduction and afterword.

Susan Glaspell: Essays contains 16 essays. Editor Linda Ben-Zvi also provides details about the actual murder case on which *Trifles* was based (pp. 19–48); Elaine Hedges considers *Trifles* and "A Jury of Her Peers" in terms of the lives of prairie women and the solace they found in quilting (pp. 49–69), and Karen Alkalay-Gut questions readings of *Trifles* based on essentialist concepts of women and gender (pp. 71–81). Liza Maeve Nelligan proposes that *The Verge* is the highpoint of Glaspell's feminist aesthetic (pp. 85–104); Barbara Ozieblo discusses the Freudianism in the play (pp. 105–22); Karen Malpede compares Claire Archer with Hedda Gabler (pp. 123–27). Marcia Noe explicates Glaspell's radical destruction of language and form (pp. 129–42); Jackie Czerepinski explores the device of the absent female figure (pp. 145–54); Sharon Friedman locates *Bernice* between "the feminist awakening in *Trifles* and the modernist revolt in *The Verge*" (pp. 155–63); J. Ellen Gainor studies *Chains of Dew,* daring in its treatment of birth control (pp. 165–93); Katherine Rodier discusses Glaspell, Emily Dickinson, and *Alison's House* (pp. 195–218); Karen Laughlin makes a case for that play as a "powerful transgressive study of the dilemma of the female artist" (pp. 219–35); Gerhard Bach argues that Glaspell's plays reshape long-held notions of dramatic invention and form (pp. 239–58); Judith E. Barlow discusses the plays of other women who wrote for the Provincetown Players (pp. 259–300); Colette Lindroth concentrates on Glaspell's first collection of short stories (pp. 303–15); and Veronica Makowsky explicates *Fidelity, Fugitive's Return,* and *Norma Ashe* (pp. 317–30). Sherri Hallgren in " 'The Law Is the

Law—and a Bad Stove Is a Bad Stove': Subversive Justice and Layers of Collusion in 'A Jury of Her Peers' " (*Violence, Silence, and Anger,* pp. 203–18) calls Glaspell's story "an in-joke among women," radically subversive in its exploration of a parallel system of justice by which women are judged according to context by their true peers, enacting between the narrator Glaspell and her readers the same collusion she depicts among her characters. Peggy Bach reviews the particulars surrounding the Provincetown Players' production of Evelyn Scott's *Love: A Drama in Three Acts* and her affair with William Carlos Williams in "Evelyn Scott: From Tennessee to Greenwich Village" (*SoQ* 33, ii–iii: 57–63).

Finally, *Early Stories from the Land: Short-Story Fiction from American Rural Magazines,* ed. Robert G. Hays (Iowa State), contains 30 stories gathered from 11 farm and rural magazines.

Drew University

Catherine Calloway

Twenty-three writers covered in this chapter are featured in book-length studies this year, with John Steinbeck, Flannery O'Connor, Vladimir Nabokov, and Raymond Chandler the subjects of two books each and Harriette Arnow, O'Connor, Peter Taylor, and Chandler each claiming individual essay collections. In addition, Robert Penn Warren, Saul Bellow, and Bernard Malamud are the subjects of special issues of *MissQ, Salmagundi,* and *SAJL.* Welty scholarship decreases, but O'Connor, Hurston, and Wolfe continue to hold their own. Westerners remain sparse in contrast to Easterners who attract a plethora of critical attention.

i Proletarians

a. General A significant contribution to proletarian literature is Laura Hapke's *Daughters of the Great Depression,* which explores the impact of the depression on domestic women who worked within the home and those who worked elsewhere for wages. Much of the literature of this period advocates that women, for the sake of societal morale, should remain in domestic roles rather than in more independent ones. Hapke studies texts by such proletarian writers as John Steinbeck, Meridel Le Sueur, Mike Gold, and Richard Wright as well as some by occasional figures such as Erskine Caldwell, Zora Neale Hurston, and Margaret Mitchell.

b. John Steinbeck Steinbeck scholars will be pleased with Charlotte Cook Hadella's *Of Mice and Men: A Kinship of Powerlessness* (Twayne). Focusing extensively on one text, Hadella examines Steinbeck's work from a number of angles: his own agricultural background; his use of the play-novelette form; the work's critical response; its pastoral Garden of Eden motif; its parallels with two earlier stories, "The Pastures of Heaven" and "Fingers of Cloud"; its Jungian approach; and its stage and film history. Hadella uses these angles of vision to demonstrate Steinbeck's view that regardless of how illusory the American dream may be, it can either "empower or destroy those who seek to attain it." In *Parallel Expeditions: Charles Darwin and the Art of John Steinbeck* (Idaho) Brian E. Railsback explores an overlooked aspect of Steinbeck's work—the Darwinian connections and the "biological perspective" that make Steinbeck unique in American literature. Railsback also applies Darwinian philosophies to individual Steinbeck works, concluding that both Darwin and Steinbeck ultimately view humankind as animalistic. John L. Marsden in "California Dreamin': The Significance of 'A Coupla Acres' in Steinbeck's *Of Mice and Men*" (*WAL* 29: 291–97) argues that when George kills Lennie he is not merely committing an act of mercy; rather, he is destroying the dream of owning land and acknowledging "the triumph of capitalist authority."

c. James Agee and Others Two articles of note appear on Agee. In "Snapshots of the Absolute: Mediamachia in *Let Us Now Praise Famous Men*" (*AL* 67: 329–57) Peter Cosgrove discusses the tension between Agee and Walker Evans that resulted from the "aesthetic envy" between the two. As a writer who believed strongly in the artistry of the written word and who felt threatened by another form of art, in this case photography, Agee had difficulty accepting the technological advancements that a camera represents. Christoph Irmscher studies the use of landscape in *Let Us Now Praise Famous Men* in " 'Muscles of Clay': James Agee's Southern Landscapes" (*Soundings* 78: 383–97). Agee's landscapes "*resist* simplification" and reflect an artistic labor that corresponds to the labor of the tenants he writes about; therefore, Irmscher argues, the writer's aesthetic is not surpassed by Evans's photographs.

Rita Barnard in *The Great Depression and the Culture of Abundance* (Cambridge) contends that societal consumption instead of production resulted from the 1929 stock market crash and the ensuing depression. Barnard examines this emergence of mass culture in the works of Kenneth Fearing and Nathanael West, showing how each writer uses "the fragmentation of experience" and the tenets of postmodernism to reflect his concern about the influence of mass culture on society.

In "Encountering the Urban Grotesque: Nelson Algren's Man with the Golden Arm," pp. 96–118 in *The Naturalistic Inner-City Novel in America,* James R. Giles focuses on the absence of the "ethnic protest formula" in Algren's novel. Unlike the characters in Mike Gold's *Jews*

Without Money or Sherwood Anderson's *Winesburg, Ohio,* the protagonist of Algren's work is not internally "good"; instead, he is sordid and incapable of reform.

A main addition to the O'Hara canon is the paperback expanded version of Matthew J. Bruccoli's *The O'Hara Concern: A Biography of John O'Hara* (Pittsburgh), which provides an in-depth critical study of O'Hara's life and career, written for both the lay reader and the scholar. Bruccoli relies heavily on O'Hara's letters, which add credibility to the volume. Chapters are devoted to O'Hara's upbringing, the influence of New York City on his writing, his success as a writer, his marriage to Belle Wylie, and his later marriage to Katherine Barnes "Sister" Bryan after Belle's death. Especially useful are Bruccoli's extensive bibliographies, one on O'Hara's own literary contributions and another of critical reactions to O'Hara's works. O'Hara's life and work are thoroughly covered, except for the 1924–26 issues of the *Pottsville Journal,* which remain unlocated. The volume concludes with an appendix concerning stories that O'Hara submitted to the *New Yorker,* which reveals that the total number of stories submitted to and rejected by that publication has been understated.

Meridel Le Sueur finally receives overdue attention in Constance Coiner's *Better Red.* Coiner breaks literary ground by examining in depth Tillie Olsen's and Le Sueur's associations with the American Communist Party. Coiner devotes two chapters to Le Sueur, the first focusing on her biography and several of her 1930s essays, the second on her novel *The Girl* and several short stories. Coiner also examines the problematic nature of such boundaries as "canonical literature versus proletarian writing; male canonical literature versus women's writing; belles-lettres versus reportage; and manly proletarian literature versus writing about working-class women's experiences" that divide literary from nonliterary discourse.

d. Richard Wright, Ralph Ellison, and James Baldwin Wright is well represented this year. Yoshinobu Hakutani in "The City and Richard Wright's Quest for Freedom," pp. 50–63 in *The City in African-American Literature,* focuses on Wright's view of the city as a dehumanized, alienated environment. Hakutani points out that even though Bigger in *Native Son* and Cross in *The Outsider* have not shared the same urban experiences, they both manage to retain their humanity. The cities of Africa are the subject of Jack B. Moore's " 'No Street Numbers in Accra':

Richard Wright's African Cities," pp. 64–78 in *The City in African-American Literature*. According to Moore, Wright's account of his journey to the Gold Coast is more than traditional travel literature; it is "a highly subjective account of an exile's journey to the land of his long gone ancestors, a quest of the self in search of itself." This quest succeeds only because Wright does not succumb to any of the cities he visits. Eugene E. Miller in "Richard Wright, Community, and the French Connection" (*TCL* 41: 265–80) examines the European influence of French writers on Wright's work. While evidence indicates that Jean Richard Bloch's "— & Co." could have influenced Wright's *Native Son,* even more obvious parallels in structure, theme, imagery, and tone are apparent between Henri Barbusse's *The Inferno* and Wright's *The Man Who Lived Underground*. Michel Fabre in "Richard Wright's Paris," pp. 96–109 in *The City in African-American Literature,* persuasively argues that while Paris was important to Wright, both for its beauty and its acceptance of African American culture, he did not use Paris as a setting for his fiction as often as other African American writers of his time did. The exception is "Island of Hallucination," which, had it been published, would stand out among the work of Wright and his contemporaries because of its examination of "the debates, intrigues, and rivalries which agitated the [expatriate] group at the café Tournon." James R. Giles's "The Fat Man Finds His Voice, Part 2: Richard Wright's *Native Son,*" pp. 71–95 in *The Naturalistic Inner-City Novel in America,* devotes one chapter to *Native Son*. Giles finds *Native Son* a better work than Gold's *Jews Without Money,* with which it has been compared, and finds the original unpublished version of *Native Son* better than the revised version that was published first. Kimberly Drake in "Rape and Resignation: Silencing the Victim in the Novels of Morrison and Wright" (*LIT* 6: 63–72) criticizes Wright and Morrison for not permitting the female characters who are raped in *Native Son* and *The Bluest Eye* to tell their own stories. This approach cancels each author's "opportunity to develop a more complete account of African American experiences of sexual violence." In "Wright Writing Reading: Narrative Strategies in *Uncle Tom's Children,*" pp. 52–75 in *Modern American Short Story Sequences,* John Lowe focuses on the intertextual aspects of the five stories in Wright's collection, viewing them as "a 'family' of narratives" related by three narrative strategies: "the rehistoricizing, through fiction, of the black experience; the use of biblical narrative patterns in the service of Communism; and . . . Wright's compelling appropriation of the structure and language of torture rituals." H. Nigel Thomas's interest is the exploitation of the African American in "The Bad Nigger Figure in Selected Works of Richard Wright, William Melvin Kelley, and Ernest Gaines" (*CLAJ* 39: 143–64). Thomas notes these authors' concern with the protagonists' reaction to oppression and the violation of their civil rights, concluding that Wright especially demonstrates that the Bad Nigger figure could not exist without white oppression.

Conversations with Ralph Ellison, ed. Maryemma Graham and Amritjit Singh (Miss.), collects 24 interviews with and essays on Ellison dating from 1952 through 1994. The selections offer insight into Ellison's views on the role of the African American writer, his use of black folklore, the influence of other writers on his work, the relationship of history to fiction, his disinterest in Africa, his writing of *Invisible Man,* his love of Negro idioms, the future of the American novel, his family background, and his experiences with jazz. Robert Butler in "The City as Psychological Frontier in Ralph Ellison's *Invisible Man* and Charles Johnson's *Faith and the Good Thing,*" pp. 123–37 in *The City in African-American Literature,* draws parallels between Ellison's and Johnson's novels, noting that in each work characters take journeys from the rural South to Northern urban environments that offer the potential for unlimited individual growth, provided that the urban milieu is looked on as "a psychological and social frontier" and not as "a deterministic environment." Ellison's many accomplishments are noted in James W. Tuttleton's "The Achievement of Ralph Ellison" (*NewC* 14, iv: 5–10). Tuttleton considers *Invisible Man* the best African American novel as well as the best fiction to emerge in the post–World War II era, perhaps even surpassing the works of Kurt Vonnegut, Thomas Pynchon, Bernard Malamud, and John Updike, among others. In " 'Pages to Ripple Beneath My Thumb': The Visible Books of Ellison's *Invisible Man*" (*NConL* 25, iii: 2–3) Michael Powell discusses the appreciation of books by Ellison's protagonist, which strengthens the protagonist's writing of his own book. Caffilene Allen in "The World as Possibility: The Significance of Freud's *Totem and Taboo* in Ellison's *Invisible Man*" (*L&P* 41, i–ii: 1–18) views Ellison's novel from the point of view of Freudian psychology. According to Allen, by metaphorically murdering and eating his two father figures—the founder of the college and his own grandfather—the narrator of *Invisible Man* restructures his world so that for the first time it holds "infinite possibilities" and embraces both love and hate. Timothy L. Parrish in "Ralph Ellison, Kenneth Burke, and the Form of

Democracy" (*ArQ* 51, iii: 117–48) thoroughly examines the influence of Kenneth Burke on Ellison's writing of *Invisible Man*. Parrish contends that readers of the novel must note "the history of the progress of democracy," for Ellison's book is more than the story of the protagonist. Instead, it relates the tale "of an entire culture invisible to itself," including Ellison's readers who are also underground. Ellison had no choice but to make the book's conclusion ambiguous, Parrish argues; in order for democratic vision to exist, there must be "mutual recognition of artist and audience."

Bryan R. Washington's *The Politics of Exile* pays tribute to James Baldwin and others this year. In his study of exile writers Washington looks at two Baldwin novels, *Another Country* and *Giovanni's Room*, in regard to the work of two of Baldwin's predecessors, Fitzgerald and James. According to Washington, while Baldwin tries to go beyond the writing of those authors, he "inevitably falls within it—is indeed, in some senses, its captive." In "If the Street Could Talk: James Baldwin's Search for Love and Understanding," pp. 150–67 in *The City in African-American Literature,* Yoshinobu Hakutani discusses Baldwin's view of love as a necessary ingredient for fruitful relationships. Unlike Wright, whose works are well known for their anger, violence, and alienation, Baldwin endues his works, especially *If Beale Street Could Talk,* with the possibility of love, understanding, hope, and meaningful human relationships. Raymond-Jean Frontain in "James Baldwin's *Giovanni's Room* and the Biblical Myth of David" (*CEA* 57, ii: 41–58) reads Baldwin's novel as an extended elegy in which the biblical-like David mourns the death of Jonathan-Giovanni. As Frontain points out, the pattern of a man mourning a man recurs frequently in Baldwin's fiction, as in *Go Tell It on the Mountain, Tell Me How Long the Train's Been Gone,* and "The Outing." Thorell Tsomondo in "No Other Tale to Tell: 'Sonny's Blues' and *Waiting for the Rain*" (*Crit* 36: 195–209) examines the way that Baldwin and Charles Mungoshi, a Zimbabwean author, create protagonists who fulfill the role of "artist-historians"; they are "poet-prophet[s] committed simultaneously to solitary and communal experience, bound at once to tradition and to change."

ii Southerners

a. Robert Penn Warren   Warren is represented this year by one book, Robert S. Koppelman's *Robert Penn Warren's Modernist Spirituality* (Missouri). Koppelman demonstrates how, despite Warren's claim that he was an agnostic, the spiritual is certainly evident in his works. *A Place to Come To* and *All the King's Men* serve as fictional examples of the religious redemption that can be found in the communion of literature and life. In "A Combat with the Past: Robert Penn Warren on Race and Slavery" (*AL* 67: 511–30) Forrest G. Robinson studies Warren's treatment of race. Like Clemens in *The Adventures of Huckleberry Finn,* Warren sees, yet does not want to see, the evils of slavery. Warren best embodies this tension for and against the issue of race slavery in *All the King's Men,* where Jack Burden shares Warren's own ambivalence toward racial injustice. *MissQ* devotes one issue (48, i) to Warren's work; seven essays deal with fiction. Victor Strandberg in "Robert Penn Warren and the Classical Tradition" (pp. 17–28) discusses Warren's role as a Christian writer, who frequently uses the mythic Fall as the main conflict in his work. However, since many of Warren's biblical allusions are taken from the Old Testament and since Warren has been influenced by writers or admirers of classical texts and was taught Greek by his father, his writing possesses a mainly "quasi-classicist ethos." In "Robert Penn Warren and Regionalism" (pp. 29–38) Joseph R. Millichap demonstrates that Warren's regionalism moves beyond the South. By using the West in *Night Rider* and both the West and New England in *Altitudes and Extensions,* for instance, Warren makes his regionalism more "universal." Koppelman in "*All the King's Men,* Spiritual Aesthetics, and the Reader" (pp. 105–14) probes the "reader-redemption" way of reading *All the King's Men* in which the reader becomes an active spiritual participant in Warren's book as a result of the juxtaposition of "images of God and of literary texts." In "Warren's *Wilderness* and the Defining 'If' " (pp. 115–31) Randy J. Hendricks discusses the significance of the " 'if'-clause motif" that Warren applies to Adam Rosenzweig. By pondering whether he had done this or that, Rosenzweig achieves self-knowledge and the realization that he cannot reshape his experiences. It is "the idealist's heart" that "must be reshaped." James H. Justus in "Warren's *Terra*" (pp. 133–46) focuses on the role of the word "terra" in *A Place to Come,* whose protagonist, Jed Tewksbury, is trying to find his identity and the place where he belongs. "Terra" comes to mean "Not homeland, birthplace, or region, but *company,* fellowship, and intimacy with one's fellows." Lucy Ferriss in "Sleeping with the Boss: Female Subjectivity in Robert Penn Warren's Fiction" (pp. 147–67) applies feminist criticism to Warren's work, examining four aspects: "Women as Plot Device," "Belle

Power," "Narrative Distance and the Unreliable Narrator," and "Warren's Female Persona." Jonathan R. Eller and C. Jason Smith in "Robert Penn Warren: A Bibliographical Survey 1986–1993" (pp. 169–94) offer a thorough overview of Warren's main works and a survey of critical literature on him as well as a "Checklist of Criticism 1986–1993," including books, book chapters, individual essays, bibliographies, dissertations, book reviews, and "Reminiscences and Memorial Tributes."

b. Flannery O'Connor, Eudora Welty, and Katherine Anne Porter

Two books and a number of critical articles attest to O'Connor's continued popularity. Margaret Earley Whitt in *Understanding Flannery O'Connor* (So. Car.) includes 14 essays primarily on writing, the teaching of literature, and *The Habit of Being*, letters to people outside O'Connor's family, and short stories from O'Connor's graduate thesis. Whitt views O'Connor's works in light of two forces behind her writing: her Roman Catholic faith and her Southern background. *New Essays on Wise Blood*, ed. Michael Kreyling (Cambridge), seeks to find and address the source of dissent in O'Connor scholarship in the hope that critics will consider carefully and remain open to new approaches to *Wise Blood*. In the introduction (pp. 1–24) Kreyling perceptively surveys O'Connor's life and writing and sums up previous critical responses to her work. Jon Lance Bacon in "A Fondness for Supermarkets: *Wise Blood* and Consumer Culture" (pp. 25–49) examines how O'Connor's use of popular culture and consumerism demonstrates the detrimental effects of capitalism on American society. The Catholic Church, a beacon of integrity in a capitalistic world, is placed in opposition to the consumer culture to show that another avenue is open to society, one that allows people to remain individuals, not mass-market consumers. In "Framed in the Gaze: Haze, *Wise Blood,* and Lacanian Reading" (pp. 51–69) James M. Mellard views O'Connor's novel as both modern and postmodern, the former reading showing how characters can achieve a redemption that an audience can accept and the latter providing a darker reading of the novel by including a form of desire that belongs to the world of the gothic and nightmare. Hazel Motes represents this darker primal desire, that "of sex *itself.*" Robert H. Brinkmeyer, Jr., in " 'Jesus, Stab Me in the Heart!': *Wise Blood,* Wounding, and Sacramental Aesthetics" (pp. 71–89) argues that *Wise Blood* differs from other O'Connor works in "its [rare] final affirmation of faith. . . . Hazel's self-mutilations . . . echo Christ's Incarnation, and Mrs. Flood's witnessing of Haze signals her spiritual revolution." Christ is seen as one who heals, rather than one who punishes. Patricia Smith Yaeger in "The Woman Without Any Bones: Anti-Angel Aggression in *Wise Blood*" (pp. 91–116) explores O'Connor's use of a fictional strategy that allows her "to remain in the tomboyish role of the angel-aggressive little girl" who haunts her own fictions and structures them around a "primitive fascination with death and bodily privation."

Using works that O'Connor wrote before *Wise Blood*, Virginia Wray in "The Importance of Home to the Fiction of Flannery O'Connor" (*Renascence* 47: 102–15) demonstrates that O'Connor was subconsciously writing about and coming to terms with her native South before her medical condition required her to return there. In fact, a period of chosen exile from the South was integral to O'Connor's successful use of her native ground in her post-1950 writing. Michelle Pagni Stewart in "A Good Trickster Is Hard to Find: A Refiguring of Flannery O'Connor" (*ShortS* 3, i: 77–83) draws parallels between O'Connor's "A Good Man Is Hard to Find" and "The Day the Crows Stopped Talking" by Harvest Moon Eyes. According to Stewart, reexamining O'Connor's story in light of that of Moon Eyes adds a new literary dimension to O'Connor's well-known tale; the Misfit in "A Good Man" may share the characteristics of the Native American trickster figure, who, feeling alienated from the community, "act[s] defensively, ultimately causing more harm to the community" as well as to himself. The Misfit is also the focus of Hal Blythe and Charlie Sweet's "The Misfit: O'Connor's 'Family' Man as Serial Killer" (*NConL* 25, i: 3–5), which sees the Misfit, the grandmother, and Bailey's family as products of dysfunctional families. To the Misfit, Bailey's family must be destroyed because its members remind him of his hatred for his own despicable family. In " 'That's a Greenleaf Bull': Totemism and Exogamy in Flannery O'Connor's 'Greenleaf' " (*ELN* 32, iii: 69–76) Jonathan Schiff argues that Mr. May experiences a moment of grace, renounces his totemism, and turns to Christianity. David J. Knauer in "Flannery O'Connor: 'A Late Encounter' with Poststructuralism" (*MissQ* 48: 277–89) presents "the poststructural modes of cultural materialism, Lacanian psychoanalysis, and deconstruction" as valid ways by which to read O'Connor's work. Using "A Late Encounter with the Enemy," Knauer refutes Frederick Crews's belief that poststructuralism cannot be applied to O'Connor's writing. D. G. Kehl in "Flannery O'Connor's 'Fourth Dimension': The Role of Sexuality in Her Fiction" (*MissQ* 48: 255–76) explores the many roles of sexuality in O'Connor's

writing: rape, prostitution, sexual initiation, sadism, voyeurism, transvestism, and homosexuality, for example. O'Connor uses sexuality frequently but judiciously in order to reveal the misuse of Freudian psychology, warped societal values, cultural fraud, sexual tension, the equation
of religion with sex, and sexual parody. O'Connor's Catholicism is the
subject of Michael Patrick Gillespie's "Baroque Catholicism in Southern
Fiction: Flannery O'Connor, Walker Percy, and John Kennedy Toole,"
pp. 25–47 in *Traditions, Voices, and Dreams*. Gillespie compares O'Connor's use of religion in her work with that of Toole and Percy, "emphasizing the way each writer draws on Catholicism to escape the influence of
Faulkner and the predictable label of regional writer."

Welty scholarship declines this year. In addition to the *EuWN*, which
offers its usual modest fare, Welty is represented by only three articles
and one interview. According to Sharon Deykin Baris in "Welty's Philosophy of Friendship: Meanings Treasured in *The Ponder Heart*" (*SLJ* 27,
ii: 43–61) Welty's novel is about more than laughter; it is about "human
understanding" and the fulfillment that can be gained by "making room
for others' lives and stories." Female sexuality is the subject of Danielle
Fuller's "'Making a Scene': Some Thoughts on Female Sexuality and
Marriage in Eudora Welty's *Delta Wedding* and *The Optimist's Daughter*"
(*MissQ* 48: 291–318). Fuller examines the way that Welty presents female
sexuality in the two novels, calling attention to the gendered power
games that Welty's female characters are forced to play. In "Meditations on Nonpresence: Re-visioning the Short Story in Eudora Welty's
The Wide Net," pp. 98–113 in *Modern American Short Story Sequences*,
Susan V. Donaldson explores Welty's use of the epiphany or a "still
moment." The stories in *The Wide Net* form a sequence, one in which
the characters seek that "still moment," only to find that the unity sought
is illusory. Patricia Grierson briefly notes Welty's appreciation of Tennessee Williams's work in "An Interview with Eudora Welty on Tennessee Williams" (*MissQ* 48: 583–85).

Katherine Anne Porter is the subject of one book and one article. In
Katherine Anne Porter: A Sense of the Times (Virginia), a well-documented
biography, Janis P. Stout studies Porter's life and works from a number of
angles. Subjects touched on include Porter's intellectualism, her relationship to the South, her many letters, her unstable family life, her efforts to
establish an identity, her numerous travels, the thematic concerns of her
writing, the influence of Mexico, and her relationship with the Agrarians
and other literary figures. In "'A little stolen holiday': Katherine Anne

Porter's Narrative of the Woman Artist" (*WS* 25: 73–93) Mary Titus focuses on the tension experienced by the women of Porter's generation who were not supposed to combine their maternal roles with their active ones. "Holiday," a neglected Porter story that depicts a patriarchal world, "represents Porter's most positive fictional resolution of the conflicts between being a woman and being an artist."

c. Harriette Simpson Arnow and Margaret Mitchell Arnow enthusiasts will welcome *Harriette Simpson Arnow: Critical Essays on Her Work*, ed. Haeja K. Chung (Mich. State), a blend of new scholarship, previously published essays, and lectures by Arnow. Of the 20 selections included, nine provide new readings of Arnow's works. In "Harriette Simpson Arnow's Life as a Writer" (pp. 15–31) Sandra L. Ballard provides an insightful overview of Arnow's life and writing, showing a relationship between some of Arnow's own experiences and those of her characters. Danny L. Miller in "Harriette Arnow's Social Histories" (pp. 83–96) studies *Seedtime on the Cumberland* and *Flowering of the Cumberland*, relevant nonfiction works that have been overshadowed by Arnow's novels, although, like her long fiction, they demonstrate her concern with "community and community relations." In "The Harbinger: Arnow's Short Fiction" (pp. 101–15) Chung examines a number of the short stories, some published, some unpublished, arguing that Arnow's short fiction is crucial to her canon; her stories reveal the diversity of her talent and pave the way for her to accomplish even more in characterization and theme in her later novels. Joan R. Griffin in " 'Fact and Fancy' in *Mountain Path*" (pp. 117–27) examines the first novel of Arnow's trilogy (*Hunter's Horn* and *The Dollmaker* are the others). Using both "fact and fancy," Arnow points out the dignity that exists in lives of the Kentucky Hill people, who value land, community, and family. Especially significant is Beth Harrison's " 'Between the Flowers': Writing Beyond Mountain Stereotypes" (pp. 129–39). Harrison reads Arnow's unpublished novel as "an anti-*bildungsroman* of the female protagonist." "Between the Flowers" is particularly important because it breaks new ground by joining a new genre in naturalistic writing, the " 'female pastoral' in which rural women characters finally become the heroes of their own stories." The use of the pastoral is also a focus of Kathleen R. Parker's "American Migration Tableau in Exaggerated Relief: *The Dollmaker*" (pp. 203–17). According to Parker, in *The Dollmaker* the "pastoral ideal" is contrasted with "urban reality" through the character of Gertie Nevels who must come to terms with a shift from a rural to an urban capitalistic environment, where her role as the main family breadwinner is displaced by a new maternal role, that of the family homemaker. Sandra L. Ballard in "The Central Importance of *Hunter's Horn*" (pp. 141–52) considers the novel as crucial to Arnow's other writing. In *Hunter's Horn*, Arnow achieves more complexity in the development of character and theme. Nunn Ballew, her protagonist, is capable of feeling guilt and his daughter Suse of possessing feminist beliefs. Charlotte Haines in *"The Weedkiller's Daughter* and *The Kentucky Trace:* Arnow's Egalitarian Vision" (pp. 219–37) is interested in the relationship between Arnow's final novels, which are similar to her social histories, *Flowering of the Cumberland* and *Seedtime on the Cumberland.* All four works underscore Arnow's nostalgia for the Cumberland region. In "Fictional Characters Come to Life: An Interview" (pp. 263–80) Chung recounts her conversation with Arnow in August 1983 in Ann Arbor. Arnow comments extensively on her own writing as well as her love of history and her reading interests. In "Harriette Simpson Arnow's Authorial Testimony: Toward a Reading of *The Dollmaker*" (*Crit* 36: 211–23) Chung argues that readers should pay more attention to Arnow's own view of her protagonist. Arnow portrays Gertie as having weaknesses as well as strengths; Gertie especially needs to be more articulate. Danny L. Miller in " 'For a living dog is better than a dead lion': Harriette Arnow as Religious Writer" (*SoAR* 60, i: 29–42) examines the religious aspects of *The Dollmaker,* especially the parallels to the biblical book of Job. Both Gertie and Job are innocent people who endure tremendous suffering, who pose religious questions about "divine justice, the nature of sin, and the causes of suffering," who want personal relationships with God and "a loving and living Christ," and who gain knowledge through suffering.

One Mitchell item deserves mention. Margaret D. Bauer in " 'Put Your Heart in the Land': An Intertextual Reading of *Barren Ground* and *Gone With the Wind*" in *Ellen Glasgow: New Perspectives* pairs Glasgow's and Mitchell's novels, which, when read as companion texts, enhance *Gone With the Wind* by demonstrating how it "defies the conventions of popular romance novels and plantation fiction."

d. Zora Neale Hurston   Using critical approaches from such fields as psychoanalysis, sociology, womanism, and biography, Deborah G. Plant in *Every Tub Must Sit on Its Own Bottom: The Philosophy and Politics of Zora Neale Hurston* (Illinois) studies Hurston's philosophical and political views and her many accomplishments. Rather than viewing her as a feminist, as many scholars have, Plant argues that Hurston is instead "a writer of resistance," who is intelligent, a self-reliant individualist, and "a model of empowerment."

Their Eyes Were Watching God continues to arouse much critical debate. Nancy Chinn in "Like Love, 'a movin thing': Janie's Search for Self and God in *Their Eyes Were Watching God*" (*SoAR* 60, i: 77–95) argues that while some scholars do not see God as prominent in the text, God is indeed an important presence there. It is Janie's love for Tea Cake that permits her to reject conventional ways of seeing God and instead "turn her eyes inward," looking within herself for the meaning of God and the peace that accompanies such a search. In "The Erotics of Talk: 'That Oldest Human Longing' in *Their Eyes Were Watching God*" (*AL* 67: 115–42) Carla Kaplan argues "that Janie's various refusals of public voice, self revelation, and fighting back do constitute an important form of political protest." By giving Janie a female audience, Pheoby, for the voice that Janie has always had, Hurston moves away from the conventional romance novel and thus makes the text even more contradictory. Hair is the unusual subject of Bertram D. Ashe's " 'Why don't he like my hair?': Constructing African-American Standards of Beauty in Toni Morrison's *Song of Solomon* and Zora Neale Hurston's *Their Eyes Were Watching God*" (*AAR* 29: 579–92). Ashe shows the ways in which Morrison and Hurston reveal how the female characters struggle to retain their own preferred styles of hair instead of succumbing to the styles desired by black males. For instance, Janie's spouses can be contrasted by their attitudes toward Janie's hair. In "Should Their Eyes Have Been Watching God?: Hurston's Use of Religious Experience and Gothic Horror" (*AAR* 29: 17–25) Erik D. Curren focuses on a neglected aspect of Hurston's novel: the sudden shift in genre "from optimistic quest to gothic horror." Hurston's purpose behind this shift is to show that the black folk community is as susceptible to prejudice, stereotypical behaviors, and snobbishness as is the white society whom they unconsciously emulate. Scholars will welcome Paul Cairney's "Writings about Zora Neale Hurston's *Their Eyes Were Watching God: 1987–1993*" (*BB* 52: 121–32), an annotated bibliography of more than 70 critical responses to Hurston's novel. Cairney prefaces his annotations with a five-page detailed summary of the text's previous scholarly interpretations. The Hurston neophyte will find useful Cheryl A. Wall's "Zora Neale Hurston's Traveling Blues," pp. 139–99 in *Women of the Harlem Renaissance*

(Indiana). An informative overview of Hurston's life and work, the chapter acknowledges the many contributions that Hurston made to African American folklore, especially those that came with the publication of *Mules and Men*.

e. Erskine Caldwell, Peter Taylor, and Thomas Wolfe   Erskine Caldwell is represented by Wayne Mixon's *The People's Writer: Erskine Caldwell and the South* (Virginia). Mixon provides an informative study of Caldwell's life and writing, both his accomplishments and his failures, relying on archival manuscripts and the stories of people who knew him and his family. Mixon explores Caldwell's views on racism, his deep ties to the South, his role as a Southern writer, and his interest in social reform. While Caldwell overlooked some of the better traits of the South, he still represented "the people's South" more accurately than did some of his contemporaries.

Taylor's work inspires an essay collection, *The Craft of Peter Taylor*, ed. C. Ralph Stephens and Lynda B. Salamon (Alabama). In "The Mystery of Art: Peter Taylor's Poetics" (pp. 9–19) Albert J. Griffith explores Taylor's views on the craft of writing: that theme is more important than plot, that it is vital to capture the essence of a place, that writing involves interpretation, that prose works could first be written in verse, and that compression is essential. Elizabeth Hardwick in "Locations Within Locations" (pp. 20–26) discusses the importance of Taylor's settings, which are multilayered, the individual kinds of houses and their occupants being as significant as the streets and the neighborhoods themselves. In "The Agrarians: The Halcyon Kinship" (pp. 27–36) Ward Scott focuses on Aunt Munsie, a character in "What You Hear from Em?," who represents the conflict between the old agrarian world and the new industrialized one. Creighton Lindsay in "Troubled Gardens: Peter Taylor's Pastoral Equations" (pp. 37–44) places Taylor in the American pastoral tradition, even though his settings are not pastoral per se; instead, Taylor uses "pastoral insets" and inversions that frequently take the form of "troubled gardens" or meditations on the natural world rather than the traditional Southern idyllic Arcadias that promote human growth and maturation. In "Peter Taylor and the Negotiation of Absence" (pp. 45–55) Christopher P. Metress argues that absences are a crucial part of Taylor's writing. As works such as "Two Pilgrims," *Presences*, "A Spinster's Tale," *The Widows of Thornton*, and *The Oracle of Stoneleigh Court* reveal, "absence is essential, and our lives are determined by how well we negotiate this discovery . . . and come to terms with the potency of this absence." Linda Richmond in "Peter Taylor and the Paternal Metaphor" (pp. 56–64) focuses on father figures in *A Summons to Memphis* and "Dean of Men," demonstrating through the psychoanalytic models of Lacan and Freud that such figures can possess enough power to shape their offspring's identities. Two Taylor short stories, "The Other Times" and "The Old Forest," are the subject of David M. Robinson's " 'Some Kind of Sign': The Psychological Dynamics of 'The Other Times' " (pp. 67–74). Robinson argues that although both stories revolve around the narrator's search for maturation, "The Old Forest" is a better work because of its inclusion of "the complex psychological portraits of two women, Caroline Braxley and Lee Ann Deehart," and its symbolic use of the forest. Ann Beattie also examines "The Old Forest" in "Peter Taylor's 'The Old Forest' " (pp. 105–10). According to Beattie, the story is "about the road not taken"; Nat should perhaps have had the courage to marry the spontaneous Lee Ann Deehart rather than the orderly Caroline. In "The Thrust for Freedom in Peter Taylor's Stoems" (pp. 75–84) Ronald J. Nelson reminds the reader of four of Taylor's generally neglected "stoems" or "poem-like stories": "Her Need," "Three Heroines," "The Hand of Emmagene," and "The Instruction of a Mistress." Because they are active rather than passive, Taylor's protagonists achieve tragic integrity, even if they fail at their efforts to free themselves from the forces of destiny. "The Hand of Emmagene" is the topic of Linda Kandel Kuehl's "Emmagene's Killing Cousins" (pp. 85–95) as well. Kuehl's interest is the ironic narrator, who, in relating the story of Emmagene's suicide, deceives himself by unknowingly alerting others to the role that he played in his cousin's death. In "Memory, Rewriting, and the Authoritarian Self in *A Summons to Memphis*" (pp. 111–21) Robert H. Brinkmeyer, Jr., argues that Phillip is really telling a story about his mother, not his father. In fact, Phillip, who learns nothing from telling his story, misses the options he could take in his life, an indication that, like his mother, he too is "sterile" and his life only "blank." The volume concludes with Christopher P. Metress's "An Oracle of Mystery: A Conversation with Peter Taylor" (pp. 143–56). Metress recounts his 11 August 1993 conversation with the author, which focused on Taylor's love of Sewannee, Tennessee, his short fiction, the themes of *The Oracle at Stoneleigh Court,* the Southern tradition of storytelling, and his rendering of *A Stand in the Mountains* from novel to play.

In "Sherwood Anderson and Thomas Wolfe" (*RALS* 21: 58–67)

Hilbert H. Campbell discusses the meeting of the two writers, their admiration for each other's work, and the eventual end of their friendship. Campbell draws on previously unpublished material from a variety of sources: the 1936–38 diaries of Anderson's wife, letters from Anderson to Wolfe and James Boyd, and Anderson's "Tom Wolfe's Town." *TWN* is responsible for most of the other published work on Wolfe this year. Two articles focus on *Look Homeward, Angel*. John R. Bumgarner, M.D., in *"Look Homeward, Angel:* An Epidemiologic Study" (19, i: 10–13) provides evidence that both Wolfe's protagonist, Eugene Gant, and Wolfe himself may have suffered from tuberculosis. In *"Look Homeward, Angel* as Autobiography and Artist Novel" (19, i: 44–53) Phillip A. Snyder applies contemporary theory to the novel and concludes that "Wolfe seems to be asserting that reality may be a construct of language." By using the characteristics of the Künstlerroman, Wolfe finds a potential method by which to enter an autobiographical text. James D. Boyer in "Thomas Wolfe's 'Farewell to the Fox' " (19, ii: 13–19) argues that the "A Farewell to the Fox Letter" is an effective ending for *You Can't Go Home Again*. The letter gives unity to a somewhat episodic novel and adds complexity to the novel's ending by showing that the author has changed his views about the writer's function. Stephen K. Simmerman and Martin Wank compare Wolfe's work to that of other writers. Simmerman in "H. L. Mencken and Thomas Wolfe: Divergent Styles and Shared Ideologies" (19, ii: 32–42) suggests the two writers had similar, yet different family backgrounds, and both were nonconformists who struggled against the status quo. In "Melville and Wolfe: The Wisdom of Ecclesiastes" (19, ii: 1–8) Wank notes the influence of the biblical book of Ecclesiastes on Wolfe and Melville. Wolfe moves beyond Melville to embrace the optimism of Emerson that is grounded in the faith of both God and mankind instead of adopting Melville's bleak view of universal destruction. Brooklyn's influence on Wolfe is considered in William Pencak's " 'Only the Dead Know Brooklyn—Or Do 'The Bums at Sunset'?" (19, ii: 44–51). According to Pencak, "Brooklyn gave to Thomas Wolfe the purpose and humanity his life had previously lacked," as can be seen in the literary works which he set in that locale. Two articles deal with the influence of Germany on Wolfe: Steven B. Rogers's "The Postwar German Vogue of Thomas Wolfe" (19, ii: 20–29) and John L. Idol, Jr.'s "Germany as Thomas Wolfe's Second Dark Helen: The *Angst* of *I Have a Thing to Tell You*" (19, i: 1–9). Rogers provides a detailed discussion of Wolfe's German translations and explains the resurgence of interest in

Wolfe's works after World War II, and Idol recounts Wolfe's love of Germany and the Angst that he suffered when he witnessed the actions of the Nazis. Wolfe included the Angst in *I Have a Thing to Tell You,* even though he knew that the novella's publication might bar him from ever returning to Germany. In "Thomas Wolfe's Bascom Hawke and Bascom Pentland: A Comparative Study" (19, i: 41–43) John S. Phillipson compares "A Portrait of Bascom Hawke" with the Bascom Pentland character in *Of Time and the River,* noting that the Bascom figure is less important in the novel than in the novella. In " 'Devils of Dissonance and Unrest': A Revelation in *K-19: Salvaged Pieces*" (19, i: 14–19) Douglas S. Johnson reminds Wolfe scholars of the significance of the two fragments of an unfinished novel that Scribner's decided not to publish: that Wolfe's and/ or the narrator's mental state(s) reflect a paranoid personality, which adds weight to David Rosenthal's 1979 speculation that Wolfe may have possessed a "schizotypal, paranoid personality." Each issue of *TWN* concludes with "The Wolfe Pack Bibliography" (19, i: 82–85; 19, ii: 111–14).

f. James Gould Cozzens, Carson McCullers, and Caroline Gordon
Anne Colclough Little in "The Manuscripts of James Gould Cozzens's *By Love Possessed*" (*RALS* 21: 189–205) argues that Cozzens was not a bigot. To the contrary, according to Little, Cozzens examines bigotry, not champions it in the novel, nor does he attack religion; instead, he condemns people who "live by emotion rather than by reason."

In *Wunderkind: The Reputation of Carson McCullers, 1940–1990* (Camden House) Judith Giblin James provides a thorough and insightful chronological overview of the critical responses of the last 50 years to McCullers's works, noting that New Criticism has dominated much of the scholarship devoted to them for several reasons: the New Critics' "desire to see [McCullers's] writing as apolitical, timeless, universal," their emphasis on poetry or the lyrical qualities of prose, and their interest in works that grew out of the South. McCullers's decadence and her naturalism have particularly been ignored. "Read her," James argues, in whatever way there is for her to be read, and realize that despite some of the narrow, limited readings that exist, "she was a seismograph completely sensitive to the direction of social change, a medium for registering slight reverberations of cultural shift. . . . There is much left to be done."

A significant contribution to Caroline Gordon scholarship is Nancylee Novell Jonza's *The Underground Stream: The Life and Art of Car-*

oline Gordon (Georgia), a provocative and detailed chronology of Gordon's life and literary career. Jonza places Gordon in a female literary tradition. As she argues, Gordon wrote on two levels: one that clearly reveals "patriarchal values" and the other an "underground stream" that sheltered her feminist viewpoints. Jonza ground her research in material only recently made accessible, such as Gordon's letters, previously unpublished works, journalistic writing, and manuscript drafts.

iii Expatriates and Émigrés

a. Vladimir Nabokov Nabokov inspires two book-length studies, three book chapters, and several articles. A significant contribution to scholarship is *The Garland Companion to Vladimir Nabokov*, ed. Vladimir E. Alexandrov (Garland). Encyclopedic in length, the volume contains a wealth of information about Nabokov's life and work (including a detailed chronology), an extensive bibliography of primary and secondary sources, and numerous well-documented entries on individual Nabokov texts, literary influences, and general subjects by 42 contributors. The volume is intended to serve a wide variety of audiences, from the student to the scholar, especially the non-Russian reader. Lance Olsen in *Lolita: A Janus Text* (Twayne) notes the dual role played by the novel. Like Janus, the Roman god with forward and backward faces, *Lolita* can embrace two literary movements at once: modernism and postmodernism, emphasizing both the epistemological and the ontological.

In "*Lolita* in *Peyton Place*," pp. 3–16 in *Lolita in Peyton Place: Highbrow, Middlebrow, and Lowbrow Novels of the 1950s* (Garland), Ruth Pirsig Wood notes similarities between Nabokov's novel and that of Grace Metalious. Both *Lolita* and *Peyton Place* deal with adolescent girls who move from innocence to experience, who lack fathers, and who are victimized. In addition, the novels share the same moral concern without being judgmental: "the effects of sexual self-indulgence and of sexual repression." In "Nabokov's *Lolita*/Lacan's Mirror," a chapter in *Hide and Seek: The Child Between Psychoanalysis and Fiction* (Illinois, pp. 201–45), Virginia L. Blum thoroughly grounds her study of the novel in Lacanian psychoanalysis, arguing that the Lacanian and Nabokovian models "are both premised on a narcissistic relationship with their audiences—and both enterprises depend ultimately on a child in the mirror." Satiric literalization is the subject of Rita A. Bergenholtz's "Nabokov's *Lolita*"

(*Expl* 53: 231–35). Humbert's confession, states Bergenholtz, is "a parody of spiritual autobiography," wherein Humbert wants others to believe that his death results from a broken heart, not an actual coronary illness. In "*Lolita* and Aristotle's Ethics" (*P&L* 19: 32–47) Peter Levine provides an alternative reading of *Lolita*: that of viewing the story from Lolita's point of view, not just Humbert's. Such a reading, when examined in terms of Aristotle's literary criteria, concludes that *Lolita* is a text that argues "against moral theory." Christy L. Burns in "The Art of Conspiracy: Punning and Paranoid Response in Nabokov's *Pnin*" (*Mosaic* 28, i: 99–117) explores in depth Nabokov's use of "postmodern paranoia" in *Pnin*, demonstrating how Nabokov "takes paranoid constructs and turns them into an admixture of metafictional humor and a more serious reflection on the nature of representation." Pninian parody is also the subject of Magdalena J. Zaborowska's "The Untold Story: Vladimir Nabokov's *Pnin* as an Immigrant Narrative," pp. 263–77 in *How We Found America*. Zaborowska provides insight into *Pnin* by reading the novel not only as an immigrant narrative, but as one that parodies male and female immigrant narratives and American immigrant romances. She draws parallels between *Pnin* and Abraham Cahan's *The Rise of David Levinsky* and even more importantly between *Pnin* and Susanna Rowson's sentimental *Charlotte Temple*.

b. Djuna Barnes, Anaïs Nin, and Paul Bowles   Barnes is the subject of one book and one article this year. Phillip Herring in *Djuna: The Life and Work of Djuna Barnes* (Viking) takes the reader into the world of an intensively private writer who socialized with such other well-known literary figures as Kay Boyle, Ezra Pound, and James Joyce, and whose work was endorsed by T. S. Eliot, but who spent the last 40 years of her life as a recluse. Herring explores Barnes's reputation beyond her most famous work, *Nightwood*, explaining as well the contributions to modernism made by her other writing and detailing the events of her life most responsible for the bitter anger that characterizes much of her work. Lianne Moyes in "Composing in the Scent of Wood and Roses: Nicole Brossard's Intertextual Encounters with Djuna Barnes and Gertrude Stein" (*ESC* 21: 206–25) discusses the way in which intertextuality in Brossard's *Picture Theory* "facilitates Brossard's exploration of the relationship between the writing of contemporary lesbians and that of Barnes and Stein."

In "The Three Faces of June: Anaïs Nin's Appropriation of Feminine

Writing" (*TSWL* 14: 309–24) Lynette Felber addresses the dilemma that Nin faced in taking on the role of a women's writer. By trying to use both male and female discourse in *House of Incest,* her first *Diary,* and *Henry and June,* Nin may have distanced herself from the traditional male literary canon as well as from the female "revisionist canon." In a second article, "Mentors, Protégés, and Lovers: Literary Liaisons and Mentorship Dialogues in Anaïs Nin's *Diary* and Dorothy Richardson's *Pilgrimage*" (*Frontiers* 15: 167–85) Felber examines the "literary liaisons" of Henry Miller, Nin, H. G. Wells, and Dorothy Richardson and the "mentoring conflicts" that take place, especially when the mentors are also lovers. According to Felber, Nin and Richardson "define themselves *against* their male mentors, re-viewing themselves positively as Others, a strategy that contributes to finding their voice as *women* writers and often leading them to innovations in form and genre."

Asad Al-Ghalith in "Overlooked Prominence: Two Short Stories of Paul Bowles" (*CLAJ* 39: 208–18) examines two neglected Bowles stories, "The Waters of Izli" and "Madame and Ahmed." Like Bowles's earlier works, these tales include the "height/water technique," characters who have difficulty making friends or communicating well with others, and characters whose actions are not judged; however, the stories are unusual in Bowles's canon because of their lack of harmful deceit and their absence of traits common in Bowles's stories, such as substance abuse, supernatural events, or extremely violent acts.

iv Easterners

a. Saul Bellow Thanks to Marianne M. Friedrich, Saul Bellow's short fiction now receives some overdue attention. In *Character and Narration in the Short Fiction of Saul Bellow* (Peter Lang) Friedrich provides a thorough, yet concise, overview of previous critical commentary on the short stories before turning to an analysis of "the correlation of character and form," a heretofore neglected aspect of Bellow's stories. Friedrich explores the interweaving of character and form in "Dora," "Looking for Mr. Green," "Leaving the Yellow House," "A Silver Dish," *What Kind of Day Did You Have?,* "Cousins," and *A Theft.*

Unfortunately, space limitations preclude the annotation of the many fine articles on Bellow this year. Ben Siegel in "Simply Not a Mandarin: Saul Bellow as Jew and Jewish Writer," pp. 62–88 in *Traditions, Voices, and Dreams,* informatively presents Bellow's beliefs about the role of the

Jewish writer. While Bellow categorizes himself as a "modern writer," not a Jewish one, he applies the term "Jewish writer" to others. Moreover, his own works contain some highly Jewish traits; e.g., the emphasis on Yiddish heritage and the use of Jewish neighborhood settings. *Mr. Sammler's Planet* is the focus of several essays. Derek Wright in "The Mind's Blind Eye: Saul Bellow's *Mr. Sammler's Planet*" (*IFR* 22: 20–24) examines the eye motif. Because Bellow reverses "the external, observing eye and the informing, intellectual eye," Mr. Sammler misses the very events that he should experience in life. In "Mr. Sammler's War of the Planets," pp. 33–49 in *The Critical Responses to H. G. Wells,* Allan Chavkin explores the influence of Wells on Bellow's protagonist, arguing that Wells, who is frequently alluded to in the novel, is a focal point of Sammler's "crisis meditation." In the course of the novel Sammler moves from a positive to a negative view of Wells. Dick Wethington in "Re/Establishing Boundaries in Bellow: Postmodernism and *Mr. Sammler's Planet*" (*SBN* 13, ii: 3–18) posits that Sammler struggles with the "postmodern condition" until the end of the novel when he shifts back to modernism, where he can embrace the belief "that we can truly know ourselves and our world, and that we must act in it." Postmodernism is also the focus of Margaret Mahoney's "Aspects of Postmodernism in *More Die of Heartbreak*" (*SBN* 13, ii: 81–98), which argues that the novel contains three postmodernist traits: black humor, the "ironic allusive mode," and the use of an "absurd" hero. In "Reconciliation and the Natural Knowledge of the Soul in *Mr. Sammler's Planet*" (*SBN* 13, i: 3–21) Douglas Hoggatt refutes the idea that Sammler is not a didacticist used by Bellow to point out society's flaws; rather, through Sammler, Bellow contends that people must be in harmony with their world in order to value the quality of human existence.

Both *Henderson the Rain King* and *Seize the Day* are the subjects of several essays. In "Transcendentalism and Bellow's *Henderson the Rain King*" (*SAJL* 14: 46–57) M. A. Quayum examines Bellow's novel in the light of American Transcendentalism, linking the moral philosophies and language of Henderson and Dahfu with those of Whitman and Emerson. In "Bellow's *Henderson the Rain King* as an Allegory for the Fifties" (*ASInt* 33, i: 65–74) Quayum also claims that "Bellow provides an allegory of the bipolar culture of the fifties" by endowing both his American and his African protagonists "with the fragmentary and dismembered consciousness of the age." Darryl Hattenhauer in "Tommy Wilhelm as Passive-Aggressive in *Seize the Day*" (*MQ* 36: 265–74) persuasively argues that Bellow's protagonist is passive-aggressive, not only narcissistic and masochistic as previous scholars have noted. Hattenhauer's reading challenges critics who contend that the novel's ending is optimistic. In "On Saul Bellow's *Seize the Day:* 'Sunk though he be beneath the wat'ry floor' " (*Salmagundi* 106–07: 75–80) Elizabeth Frank notes resemblances between Melville's *Billy Budd* and "Bartleby the Scrivener" and Bellow's novella. All three works deal with conflicts between paternal figures and sons. In "Narcissus and Hermes: The Intersection of Psychoanalysis and Myth in *Seize the Day*" (*SBN* 13, ii: 30–48) Heide Elam explores the relationship of the protagonist, who is afflicted with Kohutian self-disorder, to "Narcissus" and that of Tamkin to "Hermes." According to Elam, the trickster's abandonment of Tommy Wilheim provides catharsis at the end of the novella. Jerrald Ranta's "Time in Bellow's *Seize the Day*" (*ELWIU* 22: 300–315) addresses a heretofore ignored theme; three types of time merge in the novella— Gregorian, Jewish, and "a 'modern' scientific version of man's activity in time." In "An Epistolary Road Map for a Modern-Day Moses: The Kierkegaardian Strait Gates in Saul Bellow's *Herzog*" (*SBN* 13, i: 27–39) Ming-Qian Ma views *Herzog* as vastly different from other Bellow works in that it is paradoxically "constructed in a double discourse": "by starting to write letters, he [Herzog] takes a leap out from the aesthetic into the ethical into the religious." Kathleen McCoy in *"Dangling Man* and *Herzog:* First Novel as *Ur-Text"* (*SBN* 13, ii: 66–80) examines *Dangling Man* as a prototype from which the more fully developed *Herzog* emerges two decades later. Both Joseph and Herzog show symptoms of mental instability, share similar physical traits and mannerisms, suffer from alienation, desire a return to reality, and remain optimistic about the modern world. However, Herzog, who is endowed with more wisdom and love than his predecessor in *Dangling Man,* "emerges a new Jewish figure for the post-Holocaust age." Laurie Grobman in "African Americans in Roth's 'Goodbye Columbus,' Bellow's *Mr. Sammler's Planet* and Malamud's *The Natural"* (*SAJL* 14: 80–89) explores the stereotypical depiction of most of the African American characters in these works, arguing that Jewish writers must make more of an effort to promote progress in Jewish-African American relationships.

b. Bernard Malamud   Ethnic relations are the subject of several Malamud essays. Daniel Walden in "The Bitter and the Sweet: 'The Angel

Levine' and 'Black Is My Favorite Color' " (*SAJL* 14: 101–04) discusses Malamud's interest in black-Jewish relations. In "Jewish-Gentile Relations and Romance in *The Assistant*" (*SAJL* 14: 58–63) Claudia Gorg focuses on the novel's subplot, which deals with Frank Alpine and Helen Bober's romance. Through the subplot, which demonstrates the complex nature of the Jewish-gentile relationship, Malamud implies that such relationships may succeed, despite the intervening obstacles. Gary Sloan in "Malamud's Unmagic Barrel" (*SSF* 32: 51–57) argues that Salzman possesses no magic powers; instead, he clearly manipulates Finkle by showing him photographs of unsuitable clients and packaging Stella to meet Finkle's unconscious sexual gratification. Mary Rose Sullivan in "Malamud in the Joycean Mode: A Retrospective on 'The Magic Barrel' and 'The Dead' " (*SAJL* 14: 4–13) considers the influence of Joyce's story on Malamud's. "The Magic Barrel" and "The Dead" are thematically, structurally, and stylistically similar. Malamud particularly emulates Joyce in his inclusion of an epiphany that will drastically affect the emotional state of the protagonist. Malamud extends the device beyond Joyce, however, in that his protagonist learns from his epiphany and emerges a better man, whereas Joyce's character does not. In "Isaac's Arithmetic: A Note on Malamud's 'Idiots First' " (*ANQ* 8, iii: 26–29) Earle V. Bryant notes how Malamud hints at the time when Mendel's night journey begins. Siegfried Mandel in "Bernard Malamud's 'Alma Redeemed': A Bio-Fictional Meditation" (*SAJL* 14: 39–45) shows how Malamud experimented with the story of the lives of Gustav and Alma Mahler, blurring the fictional/biographical boundaries and drawing the reader into the text through the questions that such blurring poses. In "Surviving the End: Apocalypse, Evolution, and Entropy in Bernard Malamud, Kurt Vonnegut, and Thomas Pynchon" (*Crit* 36: 163–76) Peter Freese examines patterns of death and rebirth, destruction and renewal in Malamud's *God's Grace*, Vonnegut's *Galápagos*, and Pynchon's *The Crying of Lot 49*, concluding that each author believes that "hope can be wrested from despair and that by imagining the end and pondering the reasons for its coming we might help to prevent or at least to postpone it." Gabriella Morisco in "Bernard Malamud: An American Reading of Fedor Dostoevsky" (*SAJL* 14: 14–27) explores Malamud's use of *Crime and Punishment* as a paradigm for *The Assistant*. According to Morisco, while each novel is structured differently and "the function of savior" is assigned to different genders, both novels contain the same thematic concerns, treat the issue of time similarly, end with silence, and depict their protagonists reading the Bible. In "Cityscape as Moral Fable: The Place of Jewish History and American Social Realism in Bernard Malamud's Imagination" (*SAJL* 14: 28–38) Sanford Pinsker demonstrates that Malamud changed the notions of "cityscape" and "social realism," mainly because he devotes less attention than some of his contemporaries to "establishing the niceties of time and place." Instead, Malamud is more concerned with moral issues, with his characters' quests for more humanity. Yolanda Ohana in "An Interview with Bernard Malamud: A Remembrance" (*SAJL* 14: 64–71) provides the transcript of her 1984 interview with the author. Some of the topics covered include Malamud's relationships with other writers, his role as an American writer, the film versions of some of his works, the significance of audience in writing, the sources for some of his novels, and his future projects.

v Westerners

As in 1994, Westerners attract relatively little attention. Laura R. Villiger resurrects Mari Sandoz in *Mari Sandoz: A Study in Post-Colonial Discourse* (Peter Lang, 1994). Villiger's study seeks to fill the void left by the many scholars who have neglected this Nebraska writer's works, arguing that Sandoz's fiction is significant for the attention that it pays to the postcolonial process in American history, especially in its focus on ethnicity. Sandoz presents both the point of view of Native Americans and Anglos "from *within*" so that readers can see each culture's distinct qualities and understand more clearly why the two cultures felt threatened by each other.

Nancy Owen Nelson in "Land Lessons in an 'Unhistoried' West: Wallace Stegner's California," pp. 160–76 in *San Francisco in Fiction*, shows the relevance of the California novels to Stegner's environmental concerns. *Angle of Repose* is especially important in that it involves "the reconciliation of the self with both past and present" and posits that mankind must behave responsibly and "struggle to establish an acceptable relationship to the land," drawing on conservation, preservation, and development. In "'Turned on the Same Lathe': Wright Morris's Loren Eiseley" (*SDR* 33, i: 66–83) Joseph J. Wydeven contends that Eiseley deserves more credit than he has received for influencing Morris's work.

vi Iconoclasts and Detectives

a. Jack Kerouac and William Burroughs   Robert Holton in "Kerouac Among the Fellahin: *On the Road* to the Postmodern" (*MFS* 41: 265–83) explores Kerouac's interest in the "fellahin," his term for any group of people whose cultures fall outside the boundaries of the so-called modern world. However, Holton points out that Kerouac uses the fellahin as a means of simplifying the complexities of his own life more than as a way of empathizing with those poised outside cultural barriers. Michael Kowalewski in "Jack Kerouac and the Beats in San Francisco," pp. 126–43 in *San Francisco in Fiction,* provides a good overview of the role of the Beat generation and the ways in which Kerouac's writing demonstrates the importance of San Francisco to the writers in that movement. In "Narrative After Deconstruction: Structure and the Negative Poetics of William Burroughs's *Cities of the Red Night*" (*Style* 29: 36–57) Daniel Punday uses the novel to demonstrate how Burroughs in his more recent fiction "no longer assaults language directly, but now constructs a carefully structured narrative that turns back and points beyond itself to the language within which both reader and text operate" to the point where language itself functions almost as one of the novel's characters.

b. Henry Miller   Miller is represented by one book, Brassaï's *Henry Miller: The Paris Years* (Arcade), the first English-language translation of the French *Henry Miller, grandeur nature* (1975). Brassaï, a talented photographer, provides an interesting memoir of Miller's Paris years by means of a blend of photography, previously unpublished letters, memories of conversations, occasional discussions of Miller's works, and details of Miller's friendships with other writers, including Nin and Lawrence Durrell.

c. H. P. Lovecraft and Others   The Lovecraft neophyte will appreciate Curt Wohleber's "The Man Who Can Scare Stephen King" (*Amer-Heritage* 46, viii: 82–90), which offers an interesting and accessible overview of Lovecraft's life and work, including samples of his prose. S. T. Joshi in "A Literary Tutelage: Robert Bloch and H. P. Lovecraft" (*StWF* 16: 13–25) examines Lovecraft's influence on Bloch, with whom he regularly corresponded but never met.

In "Stranger Than Fiction" (*Out* June 1995: 70, 72, 150) Brooks Peters concisely surveys Patricia Highsmith's life and work, noting that Highsmith was not only a mystery and suspense writer, but a gay author whose lesbian novel *The Price of Salt* has been widely read and is still in print after four decades.

Ray Bradbury is represented by one substantial essay, Kevin Hoskinson's "*The Martian Chronicles* and *Fahrenheit 451:* Ray Bradbury's Cold War Novels" (*Extrapolation* 36: 345–59). Hoskinson, in arguing that Bradbury's intention in these two novels is "to expose the 'meanness' of the cold war years," identifies four main cold war themes that Bradbury uses: distrust, "the fear-of-nuclear-holocaust," the fragility of life, and "the dichotomous nature of the Cold War Man."

d. Dashiell Hammett, Raymond Chandler, and Others   The detectives inspire two book-length studies this year. William Marling's *The American Roman Noir* examines the effects of the wealth of the 1920s and the depression of the 1930s on the United States and three of its most popular writers. Marling grounds his material in a close study of prodigality, technology, and the economy; he then turns to discussions of Hammett, James M. Cain, and Chandler, copywriter, journalist, and oil executive, respectively, arguing that each of them attempted in his works to explain the "milieu of prodigality" that pervaded the society and era in which he wrote. Chandler's accomplishments are enumerated in *The Critical Response to Raymond Chandler,* ed. J. K. Van Dover (Greenwood), a compilation of 16 essays, most of them previously published, that serve as historical highlights of the critical reception of Chandler's fiction. In the introduction (pp. 1–17) Van Dover surveys the critical appraisals of Chandler's work, noting divergent views. Van Dover contributes two other original selections: "Chandler and the Reviewers: American and English Observations on a P.I.'s Progress, 1939–1964" (pp. 19–37) and "Narrative Symmetries in *Farewell, My Lovely*" (pp. 203–10).

In "The 'Heart's Field': Dashiell Hammett's Anonymous Territory," pp. 96–110 in *San Francisco in Fiction,* Paul Skenazy takes issue with critics who have categorized Hammett as a regionalist. Hammett's settings are merely locales and backdrops, not situations and events; thus, San Francisco plays no important environmental role in Hammett's fiction. Edward M. Wheat in "The Post-Modern Detective: The Aesthetic Politics of Dashiell Hammett's 'Continental Op'" (*MQ* 36: 237–49) argues that Hammett's detective, though created during the modernist movement, operates in a postmodernist world, where society is disorderly, chaotic, and corrupt, and where absolute truth cannot be determined or justice necessarily served. In "Dutch Jake Wahl and Pete the Finn: A Brief Look into the Representation of Ethnic Crime in Dashiell Hammett's *Red Harvest*" (*Clues* 16, i: 99–110) Jopi Nyman examines the connection between the criminal underworld, especially the American Mafia, and ethnicity. Nyman concludes that Hammett makes the ethnic characters criminals in order to show that corruption in the 1920s was widespread and not confined to any one social group. Paul P. Abrahams in "On Re-Reading *The Maltese Falcon*" (*JACult* 18, i: 97–107) notes Hammett's unique contributions to the American detective novel. For example, *The Maltese Falcon* differs from earlier hard-boiled detective novels in that its experiences are action-based and autonomous, not reason-based; it does not include violence for the sake of violence; "the hero is inseparable from the problem"; and his "story is a matter of becoming rather than being." Gregory Forter in "Criminal Pleasures, Pleasurable Crime" (*Style* 29: 423–40) argues that readers of hard-boiled detective novels engage in a "psychic self-destruction" in which they sadistically enjoy the threat of their own deaths as well as those of the characters. Using Hammett's *The Glass Key* as an example, Forter shows how Hammett represents a type of sexual encounter with the corpses, a perverse feminization that helps coerce readers "into identifying with a man who identifies with the mother in the image of a corpse."

Philip K. Dick is the topic of one article, Cassie Carter's "The Meta-colonization of Dick's *The Man in the High Castle:* Mimicry, Parasitism, and Americanism in the PSA" (*SFS* 22: 333–42). According to Carter, scholars have neglected to explore the fact that Dick does not set the novel in the area controlled by his fictional Nazis who occupy most of his United States. Instead, Dick focuses primarily on the Japanese PSA colony, a strong indication that he is questioning "the imperialist/fascist underpinnings of Americanism," not only the political views of other powers.

Arkansas State University

16 Fiction: The 1960s to the Present

Jerome Klinkowitz

"Modernism, as I see it," Ihab Hassan explains in *Rumors of Change* (Alabama), "was essentially authoritarian in form and aristocratic in its cultural spirit. . . . Postmodernism, on the other hand, is essentially subversive in form and anarchic or eclectic in its cultural spirit." His "essays of five decades," as this volume is subtitled, reach back to William S. Burroughs and forward to work by Ronald Sukenick and Raymond Federman to support this broad but insightful contrast. Keeping his distinction in mind is especially helpful in perceiving how the subsequent generation of critics, nearly all of whom entered graduate school with the postmodern age already acknowledged, are finding specific directions within the contemporary canon.

i General Studies

Hassan's overview of the postmodern condition informs both cultural and more specifically literary studies. That there was a movement from repression to liberation during this era is established by Alan Nadel, whose *Containment Culture: American Narratives, Postmodernism, and the Atomic Age* (Duke) includes Joseph Heller's *Catch-22*, John A. Williams's work, Alice Walker's *Meridian*, and Joan Didion's *Democracy* as examples of how various the breakout from postwar cultural confinement could be. Against an official culture that sought to contain everything from politics and sexuality to race and gender, Heller's novel is indicative of a new style of literary art that "manifested a national narrative whose singular authority depended upon uncontrollable doubling, a gendered narrative whose couplings depended on unstable distinctions, a historical narrative that functioned independently of events, [and] a form of writing that undermined the authority of its referents."

My thanks to Julie Huffman for help with the research toward this essay.

Williams and Walker, Nadel believes, are able by their "marginalized discourse" to remain outside this mainstream of statement and counterstatement, while Didion's *Democracy* "challenges the work of all narratives—by indicating that they purchase survival at a political price," a notion that is only subliminally present in the texts of the 1940s and 1950s that inaugurate Nadel's study (John Hersey's *Hiroshima,* J. D. Salinger's *The Catcher in the Rye,* and films by Disney and De Mille). Nadel is particularly adept with popular sources, reminding readers how "popular culture" is often an institutionalized tool for the suppression of imagination—his fundamental thesis is that both the film world and publishing adhered to an artistic version of Ambassador George F. Kennan's containment-of-communism policy that defined the cold war. Yet popular culture can be a focus for dissent and revolution, as Carol Polsgrove shows in *It Wasn't Pretty, Folks, But Didn't We Have Fun? Esquire in the Sixties* (Norton). Drawing on editor Harold Hayes's papers, Polsgrove details *Esquire's* role in promoting Norman Mailer's personal journalism and Mailer's own attempts (frustrated by fiction editor Rust Hills) to expand his fictive themes and styles. Because of Tom Wolfe's pioneering work in *Esquire,* the "New Journalism" would become a factor in debates over fiction, Wolfe himself arguing that the novel had abandoned its traditional role of social reflection. Of special interest is fiction editor Gordon Lish's role in acquiring short stories (by Raymond Carver and others) in the neorealistic mode that became known as "minimalism."

Literary politics figures into the transitional scene as well, again corresponding to Hassan's authoritarian-libertarian split. A major enthusiast of Gordon Lish's fiction-editing at *Esquire* was Joe David Bellamy, whose *Literary Luxuries: American Writing at the End of the Millennium* (Missouri) provides inadvertent evidence that a network of conservatively biased gatekeepers exists among slick commercial publishers, creative writing programs, and the National Endowment for the Arts (where Bellamy directed the literature program during its era of greatest controversy in the early 1990s). Bellamy's memoir presents the sincere belief that American literature will perish if it is denied abundant grants support. Richard Kostelanetz's investigative scholarship clarifies the point, which is that the style of writing Bellamy endorses would die off were it not for the mutually supportive alliances formed among academic establishments, grants organizations, and publishers reliant on an easily marketable product. In *An ABC of Contemporary Reading* (San

Diego) Kostelanetz explains how left-leaning thematics result in aesthetically conservative formal techniques; his chapters "Avant-Garde"
(pp. 7–25) and "Critics" (pp. 179–85) explain just how these forces work
and are best resisted. Especially valuable is Kostelanetz's *Crimes of Culture: Three Decades of Citizens' Arrests* (Autonomedia) for its outsider's
view of the inside deals cut among the interest groups that too often
determine the nature of contemporary literature. Keys to Kostelanetz's
investigative methods include finding patterns of exclusion in the exercise of power and exposing the practice of doing business on the basis
of quid pro quo, two styles of arts administration that others defend as
insuring quality and universal values.

With Hassan's and Nadel's basic contrasts in mind and with Bellamy's
and Kostelanetz's opposing visions indicating the two most radically
different ways of approaching the period, one can better appreciate the
agendas that inform this year's major studies of contemporary fiction. In
Traditions, Voices, and Dreams editors Melvin J. Friedman and Ben Siegel
commission 14 essays by leading scholars (Linda Wagner-Martin, James
Nagel, Elaine Safer, Thomas Schaub, and James L. W. West III among
them) in an attempt to produce a volume equal to Joseph J. Waldmeir's
1963 classic, *Recent American Fiction: Some Critical Views.* The result is a
conservatively mainstream view, encompassing such familiar topics as
baroque Catholicism in Southern fiction, William Styron's narrative
personae, Saul Bellow's Jewish presence, the influence of Henry James on
Cynthia Ozick and Philip Roth, and more general essays on John Barth,
Thomas Pynchon, Norman Mailer, John Updike, Kurt Vonnegut, E. L.
Doctorow, Joyce Carol Oates, and Marilynne Robinson. Canonical
expansion is accommodated by means of strong pieces by Suzette A.
Henke on "Women's Life-Writing and the Minority Voice: Maya An-
gelou, Maxine Hong Kingston, and Alice Walker" (pp. 210–33), James
Nagel on "Desperate Hopes, Desperate Lives: Depression and Self-
Realization in Jamaica Kincaid's *Annie John* and *Lucy*" (pp. 237–53), and
Gloria L. Cronin on "Fundamentalist Views and Feminist Dilemmas:
Elizabeth Dewberry Vaughn's *Many Things Have Happened Since He
Died* and Break the Heart of Me" (pp. 254–78). Especially reliable for its
grasp is Melvin J. Friedman's "Introduction: A Brief Overview of the
Recent American Novel" (pp. 9–19), where the case is made for both old
typologies (Southern rural, Jewish-American urban) and new (not just
women and minorities but a fresh style of diversity that encompasses
innovative fiction as well).

Two exceptionally strong studies focus on specific points in the transition to fully postmodern fiction. Barbara Tepa Lupack sees liberated individualism in a narrowly authoritarian world as both the thematic and technical essence of what novelists in the 1960s and 1970s were suggesting to be the era's most significant point of struggle. Her *Insanity as Redemption in Contemporary American Fiction: Inmates Running the Asylum* (Florida) selects five representative novels and studies the nature of their experiments: Joseph Heller's delight in the institutional illogic of *Catch-22*, Ken Kesey's complexity of role reversal in *One Flew Over the Cuckoo's Nest*, Kurt Vonnegut's transformation of time and space in *Slaughterhouse-Five*, Jerzy Kosinski's subversion of perceived order in *Being There*, and William Styron's restructuring of the pathologies of madness in *Sophie's Choice*. In each case Lupack is careful to note how what is assumed to be an individual's insanity functions as a critique of larger institutions that set such definitions, while throughout her study she relates artistic trends to social developments. Specific employment of postmodern theory is Steven Weisenburger's strength in *Fables of Subversion*. Mikhail Bakhtin's notions of carnival, his dialogical as opposed to the monological view of order(s), and principally the Russian theorist's reemployment of Menippean satire provide Weisenburger with tools for exploring novelists' suspicions of "all structures, including structures of perceiving, representing, and transforming. Narratives, especially, are among the most problematic of such structures, and satire becomes a mode for interrogating and counterterrorizing them." Weisenburger approaches Bakhtin by way of Julia Kristeva, who puts less emphasis on the novel's panoply of voices and more on its subversion of previously unquestioned hierarchy. Thus, it is no surprise that Weisenburger founds his thesis on the "late-modernist disruptions" of Nathanael West, Flannery O'Connor, and John Hawkes, proceeds through the thematics of black humor (where he places the work of Kurt Vonnegut), devotes much attention to Robert Coover and Ishmael Reed as sociopolitical satirists, and rests his argument on what he calls the "encyclopedic satires" of Thomas Pynchon and William Gaddis.

Whereas Bakhtin and Kristeva broaden one's agenda for organizing contemporary fiction, a reliance on the vision of Walter Benjamin narrows it, as Joseph Tabbi inadvertently demonstrates in *Postmodern Sublime*. "The postmodern writer is not trying to compete with the scientist or the journalist by claiming an objectivity and authorial impersonality that would rise above history," Tabbi explains. "Rather, like

Benjamin's angel of history, the contemporary naturalist writer disappears into the wreckage of everyday culture, wherein the culture might find its own direction against the continuing storm of a progressivist history." This formulation sets the stage for a technical reading of Norman Mailer's *Of a Fire on the Moon,* an engineering report on Pynchon's activities in *Gravity's Rainbow,* similar probings of work by Joseph McElroy and Don DeLillo, and an inevitable (given this direction) conclusion that celebrates cyberpunk as the goal in "late modernism's" passage "from a monolithic existence in text into multiple technologies of reference." In terms of Hassan's paradigm, Tabbi thus transcends the spirit of postmodernism entirely in order to embrace the authority of the machine, indicating cyberpunk's essentially totalitarian nature. Like Tabbi, Richard Walsh also concludes with Kathy Acker, but by selecting slightly different authors and avoiding the need to hitch onto the cyberpunk bandwagon (as does Tabbi with the work of William Gibson) his *Novel Arguments: Reading Innovative American Fiction* (Cambridge) makes an entirely different assessment of fiction's present state and future hopes. By using Bakhtin, Kristeva, and Saussure rather than Benjamin and Baudrillard, Walsh is able to construct a theoretical platform that supports his understanding of how play, self-consciousness, and immanence are not hazards of metafictional self-absorption but rather vehicles for engagement with readers and the world. As does Lupack, Walsh selects key novels for the way that they relate not to narrow issues such as technology and mind but to larger concerns of their age: Donald Barthelme's *The Dead Father,* Ishmael Reed's *Flight to Canada,* Robert Coover's *The Public Burning,* Walter Abish's *How German Is It,* and Kathy Acker's *Don Quixote.* These works interrogate power rather than wield it, satirize history rather than imperiously rewrite it, and revel in the exuberance of carnival rather than take masochistic pleasure in the arrogance of control. Written as a doctoral dissertation for Tony Tanner, *Novel Arguments* is one of those rare graduate school projects that makes "reviewing the criticism" a genuinely constructive act; far better than many other such treatments, Walsh's book demonstrates how certain early responses to innovation were grounded in misapprehension and directed scholarship into some regrettable blind alleys.

Yet critics have and always will swing widely and sometimes wildly in their own carnivalistic exuberance. Some of these qualities are evident in the pieces Lance Olsen has commissioned for *Surfing Tomorrow: Essays on the Future of American Fiction* (Potpourri), pieces in which critics become willfully infected with the innovative nature of their subjects. In a post-Heisenberg world, such candor is admirable, especially when it refuses to don the mantle of authority. Hence, the speculations offered have their value, such as Olsen's belief that the future lies in cyberpunk writing, Mark Amerika's broader advocacy of what he and Larry McCaffery call "Avant-Pop" (in which innovation and popular culture combine to recontextualize literary networks), and Curtis White's well-founded argument that economic trends in publishing have established what can honestly be called "state fiction." These hypotheses have been advanced before, and they profit here from being reformulated and refined. The two breakthrough essays, however, are Marjorie Perloff's "Great American Novel" (pp. 77–79), which indicts Toni Morrison for selling out to shallow commercial interests with *Beloved,* and Robert A. Morace's "Newor(l)der" (pp. 71–76), which relates the direction of fiction to the new cultural conservatism of the 1980s.

Agendas, therefore, can be useful in making sense of fiction's development—but only when particular prejudices are made evident within an intelligible set of larger boundaries. Some critics ably deconstruct themselves, making clear the basis for their assumptions; thus, Tabbi's intellectualization of technology makes it obvious that starting with Mailer and Pynchon and proceeding through McElroy and DeLillo will take one to the center of cyberpunk, whereas Lupack's choice of popularly accessible postmodernists leads her to a more socially pertinent conclusion. Even Bellamy's *Literary Luxuries* has its value, not just for showing how the mind of an arts administrator works but for suggesting how the grants consortia and creative writing industry have helped determine the nature of recent fiction. Two generalist essays indicate how this critical dialogue may continue. Both utopianism and postmodernism are as American as apple pie, Marianne DeKoven suggests in "Utopia Limited: Post-Sixties and Postmodern American Fiction" (*MFS* 41: 75–97); "historiographic fiction" (a style of text favored by Weisenburger and Walsh) such as Toni Morrison's *Beloved* and E. L. Doctorow's *The Waterworks* uses post-utopian settings from the early 1870s to ground the writers' own post-utopian styles, supporting DeKoven's thesis that "like the post-Reconstruction period, the period following the demise and defeat of the 60s—a period I would argue continues into the present—is also a post-utopian moment." A somewhat different view is taken by Miriam Marty Clark, whose "Contemporary Short Fiction and the Postmodern Condition" (*SSF* 32: 147–59) says that instead of abandoning the previous decade's experiments, neorealistic stories of the 1980s "mark out the radical troubling of realist claims; beyond their modernist inheritance they surrender in small ways and little narratives the expectation of epiphany, the hope for metaphysical consolation in a fragmenting world, a lingering commitment to a transcendent subject."

ii Women

"The clash between liberal and feminist, subdued when it comes to language reform and the recovery of women's history, explodes on the issue of pornography." Thus Wendy Steiner acknowledges the debate that affects the issue of sexuality in art. In *The Scandal of Pleasure* (Chicago) she covers a great many topics. Of special interest to scholars of contemporary fiction is her second chapter, "The Literalism of the Left: Fear of Fantasy" (pp. 60–93), for here Steiner offers specific analysis of the problem that Richard Kostelanetz, Ronald Sukenick, and Ishmael Reed have raised before: why social emancipation so often involves aesthetic restriction. There have been ways that changes in representation alter reality, Steiner admits, citing "this process of change" in Alice Walker's *The Color Purple* and Gloria Naylor's *Linden Hills* and acknowledging Catharine MacKinnon's belief that changing "social reality" as perceived will "change the material facts of women's existence." But the company parts when it comes to pornography, which liberals see as fictive in its use of language rather than instrumental, insisting that "aesthetic representation is not the same as action." The problem with this formulation comes not when pornography is excused as fiction but when fiction with sexual content is condemned as pornography. At issue is the question of pornography's causality, which Steiner considers not by any casuistry of her own but by undertaking a sound literary analysis of Andrea Dworkin's novel, *Mercy*, where the critic finds indulgence in "a shocking and ultimately self-subversive literalism." Steiner's investigation comes up with telling revelations, such as how a censorship law modeled on MacKinnon's and Dworkin's beliefs prohibits the representation of certain acts but not the acts themselves. "To see art as the enactment of a one-way power relation is adequate neither to women or to art," Steiner concludes. "No one is innately, inevitably, or uninterruptedly a victim, and there is no way to experience art—however minimalist it may be—that does not involve both mastery and submission on both sides. The wonder that overtakes us in great art need not diminish women or preclude political relevance."

The Scandal of Pleasure reflects a growing trend in which certain attitudes among feminist criticism are interrogated and reevaluated. Central to Charlotte Templin's thesis in *Feminism and the Politics of Literary Reputation: The Example of Erica Jong* (Kansas) is the belief that subsequent interest in relationships of women to other women and to their families discounted critical enthusiasm for Jong's heterosexuality. Templin seeks to understand this writer's career in the context of publishing conditions as well, and she is brilliant in her investigation of various critics' backgrounds. Wishing to see *Fear of Flying* and Jong's other work not as "a site of meaning production or the formulation of ideology," Templin must nevertheless conclude that "Jong's case is indeed one of mediazation of literary reputation."

Two worthwhile studies measure Alice Walker and Shirley Ann Grau against possible confinements of their art. In *Womanist and Feminist Aesthetics: A Comparative Review* (Ohio) Tuzyline Jita Allan studies Alice Walker's "womanism" for its wholistic worldview and positive alternative to the patriarchal, but Allan sees a problem in "the essentialist implication of womanism" as a self-definition that excludes similar white feminists, especially when it is assumed "that by virtue of being white or nonwhite, a feminist is necessarily a womanist." Sally Bishop Shigley's "Refuge or Prison: Images of Enclosure and Freedom in Shirley Ann Grau's *Nine Women*" (*ShortS* 3, ii: 54–68) argues that "If not a strictly 'feminist' book," Grau's story cycle "presents a focus that is definitely humanist, as it expresses both the need for shelter and enclosure from the sometimes too real aspects of the world and the danger inherent in finding such security." On the other hand, Kathy Acker's *Great Expectations* releases the "subversive potential of male masochism" by making "aggressive appropriations" of prior male texts, texts that mark women as "other"; as a result, according to Carol Siegel in *Male Masochism: Modern Revisions of the Story of Love* (Indiana), gender is "not so much shifted as redefined." Other prior texts, such as romance, survive the disapproval of earlier feminists because "We may . . . no longer *believe* in love, but we still all fall for it," say editors Lynn Pearce and Jackie Stacey in their introduction to *Romance Revisited* (NYU); at the same time, romance novels have themselves changed in order to remain attractive, doing so by emphasizing their narrativity—as something already written, the subgenre inspires continual reinscriptions and provides textual space for exploration. There also exist "feminist revisions of fairy tales," as demonstrated by Nancy A. Walker in *The Disobedient Writer;* one way to revise is identifying "patterns of thought and behavior with their fairy-tale equivalents," while another is "to change the story by rewriting it on its own terms." As for the master narrative of family romance, Dana Heller probes the fault lines in *Family Plots: The De-Oedipalization of Popular Culture* (Penn.), in the process changing the semiotics of its description. As opposed to the modern separations of space, postmodernism erases these in favor of gender-culture realignments as undertaken by Evan S. Connell, Anne Tyler, Jane Smiley, Amy Tan, and Toni Morrison. Of special interest is her understanding that cyberpunk is reactionary, serving the American public's "hunger for illusion" by restoring woman's image as "the angel in the house" from Victorian days. More forward-looking than cyberpunk are the texts studied by Jeanne Perreault in *Writing Selves: Contemporary Feminist Autography* (Minnesota). Here "autography" is not autobiography or nonfiction prose but rather a new style of writing that brings into being a self that the writer names "I." Such work is emancipatory but also, in its reinterpretation of other texts, does change the world as Wendy Steiner acknowledges can happen. Authors studied here are Audre Lorde, Kate Millet, Adrienne Rich, and Patricia Williams.

A hallmark in scholarship is the publication of *Oxford Companion to Women's Writing in the United States.* Of great value is its combination of author studies and treatments of topics, and as a resource it will be the first place that future scholars look before commencing their work. Yet more work needs to be done. For example, even its thousand double-columned pages have room, under the letter Q, for a detailed treatment of Queer Theory and a cross-reference to Quilting but no space for mention of experimental novelist and poet Susan Quist. Throughout, priority is given to the thematic, which is especially unfortunate for the postmodern period. Grace Paley, for example, is presented as a Jewish-American writer notable for her interest in family and political activism—nothing is said about her innovations with structure and technique. In a similar manner Needlework is discussed for its quality of women's experience in both history and metaphor but not for the nature of its expressive form. Postmodern writing itself is handled in terms of self-reflexivity. As too often happens in other criticism, this volume tends to narrow its definition to metafiction only, a specific rather than general style and one in which Grace Paley, an avowed postmodernist, does not write. Hence, the major innovations in her storytelling are uncomprehended in favor of saying that her stories "reverberate with wit and grace."

iii Paule Marshall, Ishmael Reed, and Other African Americans

As African American literature itself once negotiated for its place in the canon, multiculturalism and diversity within the broad sweep of African American writing is just lately achieving full and proper recognition. Measures of control have been similar: just as white scholars in the past might choose to treat one African American author at a time and then only as an anthropological curiosity ("Oh, how he must have struggled!" reads the subtext), so have less common backgrounds been given less attention within the field. Two examples have been the Caribbean-American and the ancestrally free, both of which are now receiving overdue attention. Two books on Paule Marshall contribute to the former: Dorothy Hamer Denniston's *The Fiction of Paule Marshall: Reconstructions of History, Culture and Gender* (Tennessee) and Joyce Pettis's *Toward Wholeness in Paule Marshall's Fiction* (Virginia). Denniston tracks a movement in vision from stateside mainstream concerns in Marshall's work to Pan-Africanism, with stops along the way at African American and African-Caribbean interests. The writing itself incorporates African oral traditions, roots in the West Indian/American stories of "home" and the complexity of what "home" means. Pettis digs even deeper into the problematics of dual cultural heritage, seeing evidence of fractured psyches in the African-Caribbean contrast with mainland culture on the one hand and with African heritage on the other. Such ruptures prompt a desire to regain losses and give Marshall a strong structural nexus for her work. As for Ishmael Reed, his 30-year career has often been at odds with passing fashions, from his emphasis during the militant 1960s on his freeman heritage to his espousal of multiculturalism during subsequent debates over the "Black Aesthetic." Editors Bruce Dick and Amritjit Singh make an important contribution to clarifying Reed's continuing importance with their *Conversations with Ishmael Reed* (Miss.). In nearly 400 pages of insightful dialogue Reed reveals his own activities as central to contemporary concerns—a situation all the more remarkable because his pertinence to issues of 1995 is documented from cutting-edge comments made as early as the 1960s and 1970s.

Generalist studies grow stronger each year, given scholars' more sophisticated methods and broader concerns. Gunilla Theander Kester
works her way through Toni Morrison's *The Bluest Eye,* Gayl Jones's *Eva's
Man,* Charles Johnson's *Oxherding Tale,* and Sherley Anne Williams's
Dessa Rose in *Writing the Subject: Bildung and the African American Text*
(Peter Lang), crediting American suspicions of organized society and
considering the way African American writing has questioned the nature
of closure. A twofold doubleness characterizes such narratives, she points
out: fact versus fiction and European versus American. In these ways
such work anticipates a more generalized postmodernism. *The City in
African-American Literature* provides a forum for editors Yoshinobu
Hakutani and Robert Butler to present several important essays on
contemporary fiction. The collection's strength is that it maintains the
same standard of scholarship for today's urban scene as evidenced in
Michel Fabre's treatment of Richard Wright in Paris and John Conder's
understanding of how Chicago figures in Willard Motley's work; authors
studied here include Charles Johnson, James Baldwin, Toni Morrison
(for her novel *Jazz*), Gloria Naylor, John A. Williams, and Samuel R.
Delany. Overall, as the editors point out, the city has a "surprisingly
positive image" in African American literature, thanks to the sorry fact
that slavery effectively stamped out any idealistic memory of "a pre-
urban homeland in Africa."

Slavery itself focuses Gloria Naylor's introduction (pp. xiii–xx) to her
*Children of the Night: The Best Short Stories by Black Writers, 1967 to the
Present* (Little, Brown). "Its existence helped to shape a cohesive national
identity for the majority of Americans" who were *not* slaves, she observes;
given that this majority culture offers no voice for affirmation, African
American writing thus must create its own light. Ann E. Trapasso notes
"the number of contemporary slave novels" in her "Returning to the Site
of Violence: The Restructuring of Slavery's Legacy in Sherley Anne
Williams's *Dessa Rose*" (pp. 219–30) as contributed to editor Deirdre
Lashgari's *Violence, Silence, and Anger.* Williams's "revisionist historical
perspective" is necessary for the writer's own sense of healing, yet her own
characters' returns are made after their own reeducations, thus sustaining
"a delicate balance between representing the horrors and demystifying
them." Deborah E. McDowell amplifies this same point in *"The Changing Same." Dessa Rose* poses women's bodies as written objects, so that
there is a personal need for "re-presenting" slavery beyond the status of
silenced victim. In similar manner Toni Morrison's *Sula* encourages a

positive image by casting the problem of self versus other as a matter of hierarchies, while Alice Walker's *The Color Purple* engages a "private narrative fiction" that implies a certain readership within a cultural matrix (a reminder that Walker's work is a self-reflexive novel with a strong emphasis on the physical quality of writing, all as a way of rejecting the imperative that African American authors must be "uplifting" in their work).

Editor Joe Weixlmann's *African American Review* continues to be the single strongest repository for scholarship in the field, thanks to its policy of responsible inclusion. Here one finds sophisticated yet utterly intelligible treatments of postmodern theory, as in Philip Page's "Traces of Derrida in Toni Morrison's *Jazz*" (29: 55–66), together with traditional yet insightful thematic studies, such as " 'Love 'em and Lynch 'em': The Castration Motif in Gayl Jones's *Eva's Man*" (29: 393–410) by Carol Margaret Davison. Especially welcome this year are two studies that draw on a fiction writer's own critical commentaries: "Charles Johnson's Quest for Black Freedom in *Oxherding Tale*" (29: 631–44) by James W. Coleman, and Celestin Walby's "The African Sacrificial Kingship Ritual and Johnson's *Middle Passage*" (29: 657–69). While the journal continues to attract essays on such heavily studied figures as Alice Walker and Toni Morrison, its value remains in encouraging work on newer subjects. This year, for example, is not too early to consider a novel published in 1992, as shown by Maxine Lavon Montgomery in "Authority, Multivocality, and the New World Order in Gloria Naylor's *Bailey's Cafe*" (29: 27–33). Here, Naylor is seen as more confidently ambitious in her search for an authorial voice, with interesting results: "The systems privileged at the novel's end—oral, female, and collective—not only bear a recursive relation to those present in the unwritten modes serving as the text's beginnings, they also suggest an end to the old dispensation of a male dialectic," which is a culmination of concerns explored in Naylor's first three novels.

Anticipating Alice Walker's own reflections on film versus novel as scheduled for 1996 publication in *The Same River Twice* (Scribner's), Jacqueline Bobo undertakes a helpful analysis of *The Color Purple*'s two formats in *Black Women as Cultural Readers* (Columbia). Whereas the novel takes negatively constructed images and imbues them with power, the film bypasses historical and literary conditions that have helped produce Walker's text, thus leading to a different style of reception. With Oprah Winfrey purchasing film rights to *Beloved*, Toni Morrison may soon be facing a similar challenge in dealing with representations of her work. The challenge any film producer may face is suggested by Carl F. Malmgren; his "Mixed Genres and the Logic of Slavery in Toni Morrison's *Beloved*" (*Crit* 36: 96–106) notes the complexity of this work being "an unusually hybridized text—part ghost story, part historical novel, part slave narrative, part love story." That a film version may well emphasize the third of these genres is a suspicion aroused by Mark Ledbetter's "An Apocalypse of Race and Gender: Body Violence and Forming Identity in Toni Morrison's *Beloved*" in editor William G. Doty's *Picturing Cultural Values in Postmodern America* (Alabama, pp. 158–72). The submission of human bodies in the slave experience, Ledbetter indicates, so disfigures them that—beyond all reasons—only Judaeo-Christian concepts are left to explain the situation. Yet this traditionally apocalyptic vision is too narrowly male, and so Morrison reconfigures her view in terms of birth and rebirth (as opposed to terror and the chaos of closure). Barbara Claire Freeman sees an even greater challenge in dealing with this novel. In *The Feminine Sublime: Gender and Excess in Women's Fiction* (Calif.) she finds *Beloved* handling race as something ultimately no more representable than the Kantian Sublime. Race has, instead, a ghostly presence, much like the presence of African American literature itself in the national canon. At issue is comprehending the presence of that which has not left a mark, a trace that in Morrison's case involves the loss of a beloved body.

Relationships seem the essence of another Morrison novel. To editor Valerie Smith's *New Essays on* Song of Solomon (Cambridge) Wahneema Lubiano contributes "The Postmodernist Rag: Political Identity and the Vernacular in *Song of Solomon*" (pp. 93–116). It is Pilate who mediates the polarities of Guitar and Milkman, interweaving history and personhood in a postmodern way, specifically as "a funky pastiche of the modern and the folk." Mother-to-son relationships interest Joyce Elaine King and Carolyn Ann Mitchell; their *Black Mothers to Sons: Juxtaposing African American Literature with Social Practice* (Peter Lang) surveys the power of real mothers for the healing power of their family lore. Their key reminder is that black sons are not as free "to do" as are white sons; their study concludes that neither class nor education insulates from racism. "Genealogical archaeology" is what makes *Song of Solomon* Morrison's most challenging novel, Michael Awkward suggests in *Negotiating Difference: Race, Gender, and the Politics of Positionality* (Chicago). Rather than simply draw on myths, the writer transforms them to characterize

"the immense, and in many respects injurious, changes that have occurred over the course of the history of blacks in America." Afrocentric
and feminist politics are thus complexly inscribed on Morrison's otherwise appropriated texts.

Authors' backgrounds and especially the artistic use they make of
them inspire good work on John Edgar Wideman, Ernest Gaines, James
Alan McPherson, and Chester Himes. There is a movement from repressed Africanism to an acceptance of it as traced by Doreatha Drum-
mond Mbalia in *John Edgar Wideman: Reclaiming the African Personality*
(Susquehanna); Wideman's "early Eurocentric perspective," notable in
his views of female beauty (as in *Hurry Home*), eventually yield to the
self-redemption of *Philadelphia Fire*. John Lowe's editing of *Conversations with Ernest Gaines* (Miss.) includes his own previously unpublished
"An Interview with Ernest Gaines" (pp. 297–328), which establishes the
importance of Louisiana and 1948 for understanding *A Lesson Before
Dying*—Gaines remarks that the same situation exists today, but it is less
of a challenge to portray. Race relations are central to Herman Beavers's
work in *Wrestling Angels into Song: The Fictions of Ernest J. Gaines and
James Alan McPherson* (Penn.). African Americans can be a resource by
which whites define their own identities, Beavers finds, with Gaines
having blacks and whites interact according to strict codes, and McPherson establishing his characters in contractual relations regarding gender
and race. Michel Fabre and Robert E. Skinner edit a broad range of
interviews that sort out bogus publications from the real, an important
step in establishing a responsible biography and canon for an author too
often studied in terms of clichés; their *Conversations with Chester Himes*
(Miss.) thus makes another argument in favor of the interview as criticism and even as scholarship.

iv Indian and Asian American Writers: Bharati Mukherjee, Maxine Hong Kingston, and Others

Abandoned narratives can be as important as appropriated ones. This
principle is established by Kristin Carter-Sanborn in " 'We Murder Who
We Were': *Jasmine* and the Violence of Identity" (pp. 433–53) from
editors Michael Moon and Cathy N. Davidson's *Subjects and Citizens*. It
is the British story of "Victorian education and identity" that Bharati
Mukherjee must discard; her bildungsroman is bracketed by *Great Ex-*

pectations and *Jane Eyre* and is structured by the presence of these rejected narratives.

Maxine Hong Kingston's *The Woman Warrior* profits from Amy Ling's Bakhtinian reading. Her "Maxine Hong Kingston and the Dialogic Dilemma of Asian American Writers" (pp. 150–66) in editor Harriet Pollack's *Having Our Way: Women Rewriting Tradition in Twentieth-Century America* (Bucknell) is based on the ability to "read the entire text as an extended exploration of the internal dialogism of three words: *Chinese, American,* and *female,*" depending on what these terms mean in various contexts and from different perspectives. This ability, Ling indicates, allows Kingston to be something other than an "ethnic explainer" when writing as an Asian American fictionist. An important step toward recognizing the breadth of Kingston's canon is made by Jennie Wang in *"Tripmaster Monkey*: Kingston's Postmodern Representation of a New 'China Man'" (*MELUS* 20, i: 101–14). This character, Wittman Ah Sing, is nothing less than "the maker/magician created in the wake of Joyce's 'bygmaster,' conceived in the mind's fancy of a metafictionist." Something larger than recapturing Chinese-American history is at hand, for "Ah Sing is not Chinese but American: he is today's maker of American literature, creator of his race, his people, his community." Further reasons why Kingston is a postmodern writer and *The Woman Warrior* a highly experimental novel are provided by Marlene Goldman in "Naming the Unspeakable: The Mapping of Female Identity in Maxine Hong Kingston's *The Woman Warrior*" (pp. 223–32) as published in *International Women's Writing*. From this same collection comes "Born of a Stranger: Mother-Daughter Relationships and Storytelling in Amy Tan's *The Joy Luck Club*" (pp. 233–43) by Gloria Shen, in which 16 "her stories" challenge the novel's traditional form as a single "his story." Yet even individual male points of view are capable of challenge, as Jinqi Ling demonstrates in "Race, Power, and Cultural Politics in John Okada's *No-No Boy*" (*AL* 67: 359–81). Writing in a cold war era that "promoted tendencies to embrace a common national character and a 'seamless' American culture," Okada had to subvert expectations that only an "alien but 'safe'" minority culture could be accepted.

Similar pressures inform K. Scott Wong's "Chinatown: Conflicting Images, Contested Terrain" (*MELUS* 20, i: 3–15). As Jinqi Ling noted for Japanese-American writing, cold war culture favored autobiographies by Asian Americans rather than works of fiction. "Chinatown" itself as an image undergoes a similar process in which "Portrayals of Chinatown constructed by observers and writers who focused on what they found repugnant about Chinese life in America actually reveal more about the observers than the observed and disclose broader racial and class biases"—the very biases that the "containment culture" described by Alan Nadel claimed did not exist. In *The Immigrant Experience in American Fiction: An Annotated Bibliography* (Scarecrow) Roberta Simone covers all groups, but she is especially alert in reminding readers of how extensive has been the attention given to Asian American writing, from Frank Chin and Emma Gee's anthologies of the 1970s to Jessica Hagedorn's and Sylvia Wantanabe's of the 1990s.

v Oscar Zeta Acosta and Other Writers of the West and Southwest

Though his initial claim to fame was as the sidekick of Hunter S. Thompson, Oscar Zeta Acosta achieves prime prominence thanks to a veritable tide of scholarship this year. Leading the crest is Ilan Stavans's *Bandido: Oscar "Zeta" Acosta and the Chicano Experience* (HarperCollins). Stavans writes an ideal literary biography, which is possible because so much of Acosta's life was devoted to transcribing the energy of experience. Of special value is work done on the threatened litigation over Acosta's proprietorship of *Fear and Loathing in Las Vegas,* a text that may now be seen as more of an appropriation by Thompson than the spirited creation some critics have assumed it to be. This litigation empowered Acosta as a writer, for as a result of his protestations, contracts were obtained for the two volumes published under his own name. It is the second of these that attracts most attention, deservedly so because it is the author's fuller imaginative effort. "Los Angeles from the Barrio: Oscar Zeta Acosta's *The Revolt of the Cockroach People*" (pp. 239–52) is Raymund A. Paredes's contribution to editor David Fine's *Los Angeles in Fiction.* Here, the city of Nathanael West and Joan Didion is made unique, thanks to its unsavory reputation being linked with the abuse of Mexican-Americans. Central to this study are indications of Hunter S. Thompson's stylistic influences, though from Stavans's study it might seem that the influence worked the other way round. Central to an understanding of what this writer is about is "The Figure of the *Vato Loco* and the Representation of Ethnicity in the Narratives of Oscar Z.

Acosta" (*MELUS* 20, ii: 119–32) by James Smethurst. As the "crazy guy/lowrider" of Chicano literature, Acosta projects himself as the alternative to mainstream culture—whether mainstream American or Mexican, so that "a strident sense of difference constructed with cultural materials" defines identity apart from either national group. This sense of fluidity resists both assimilation and nationalism and privileges the sense of rugged individualism that since the 1940s has characterized Chicano writing. Both of Acosta's books "deconstruct various essentialist or static models of Chicano identity," but the figure of the *vato* allows him to propose not so much a figure for ethnicity as a model for ethnic writing, in which fluidity is the key. Carl Gutiérrez-Jones extends this notion in *Rethinking the Borderlands: Between Chicano Culture and Legal Discourse* (Calif.), proposing that in *Revolt of the Cockroach People* Acosta searches for a balance between political militancy and a Kerouacian delight in self-exploration. There is a sense of distinctiveness to the Chicano experience, Acosta's work suggests, thereby providing an excuse for exclusion. But that distinctiveness takes multiple roles in which issues of gender and sexuality compromise the struggle being undertaken for an empowering language.

There is an impulse for art, a love of the past, and a deeply human link of "accomplishment and renewal" that evidences itself in the work of an important Southwest writer, as proposed by Gene Steven Forrest in "Myth and Recurring Time in *El Cóndor and Other Stories*" (pp. 132–47) from editors María I. Duke dos Santos and Patricia de la Fuente's *Sabine R. Ulibarrí: Critical Essays* (New Mexico). On the other hand, a vivid exposition of contemporary conditions regarding the relation of the land to community inspires the treatment of John Joseph Mathews's *Sundown* by Robert Allen Warrior in *Tribal Secrets: Recovering American Indian Intellectual Traditions* (Minnesota). There is a descent into self-destruction portrayed in this novel traceable to assimilative schooling that effaces Osage traditions. Two general studies of Native American writing examine more complicated narrative strategies. James Ruppert's *Mediation in Contemporary Native American Fiction* (Okla.) considers the "implied readerships," "mediation," and "multiple narratives of identity" created in these texts; Ruppert finds that such approaches do not privilege the native culture but rather establish the space necessary to examine cultural interplay, something that works especially well in Gerald Vizenor's *Bearheart*. Alan R. Velie edits *Native American Perspec-*

tives on Literature and History (Okla.), a volume that includes his own "The Indian Historical Novel" (pp. 77–92) in which he discusses how objectivity is complicated by the methods of Vizenor and James Welch.

A gratifying sense of inclusiveness distinguishes editors Richard W. Etulain and N. Jill Howard's *Biographical Guide to the Study of Western American Literature,* a compilation that makes such intelligent considerations as Norman Mailer's Southwestern interests, Bernard Malamud's experience in the Pacific Northwest with *A New Life,* and even Ronald Sukenick's Western influences in his innovative fiction. Continued interest in Cormac McCarthy as a Western and not just a Southern writer is expressed by Bernard A. Schopen in " 'They Rode On': *Blood Meridian* and the Art of Narrative" (*WAL* 30: 179–94), with a reminder that it is McCarthy's artistic talent and not his subject matter that motivates the novel—it is the effect of language controlling the reader's response and calling attention to itself by virtue of its literariness. Larry McMurtry's fiction can be read in at least two ways, if we are to believe somewhat contrary studies by Roger Walton Jones and Deborah L. Madsen. Jones's *Larry McMurtry and the Victorian Novel* (Texas A & M, 1994) finds the author's inspiration to be George Eliot and Thomas Hardy, especially their Victorian sense of how a world is conveyed; McMurtry's contribution is a sense of reconciliation among the individual and society and nature with civilization, a reconciliation accomplished by means of his characters' "moral values." For editors Jane Dowson and Steven Earnshaw's *Postmodern Subjects / Postmodern Texts* (Rodopi) Madsen writes "Postmodern Westerns: Larry McMurtry and the Poetics of Nostalgia" (pp. 129–42), in which McMurtry's influences are anything but Victorian. Instead, Madsen contrasts the traditional mystical communion of cowboy and hostile home with a more postmodern version of nature betraying trust (*Horseman, Pass By*) to the extent that the familiar Western worldview can no longer be located. Only later in *Lonesome Dove* and *Buffalo Girls* does the writer become self-consciously nostalgic, basing his mood on the contradiction that the mystique of an untamed West was based on the activities of men attracted there to tame it.

vi William Styron, Gail Godwin, and Other Southerners

The Family Saga in the South (LSU) continues the welcome trend of treating white and black authors comparatively rather than in isolation, as once was the case. In this study Robert O. Stephens makes good use of Shirley Ann Grau's theme (in *The Keepers of the House*) of how knowledge is transmitted by means of family stories; for an African American writer such as Toni Morrison the situation shifts to redefining family so that it can be located in public history (the key here is noting how in *Song of Solomon* family lore is reinvented for each generation). Stephens takes special interest in new fiction that modifies tradition, such as work by Reynolds Price that looks beyond the Civil War for defining elements in memory. Oral performances within contexts larger than the family problematize the act of listening, says Jocelyn Hazelwood Donlon in "Hearing Is Believing: Southern Racial Communities and the Strategies of Story-Listening in Gloria Naylor and Lee Smith" (*TCL* 41: 16–35). Cocoa Day, Naylor's "listener" in *Mama Day,* and Jennifer Bingham in Smith's *Oral History* each listen to tales from beyond the grave; though different African American and white Appalachian traditions are involved, both writers "ultimately reveal their distrust of 'the American reader,' whose historical reluctance to hear stories of difference compels the authors' use of narrative ploys."

Two important volumes help William Styron regain attention. Gavin Cologne-Brookes sees the author progressing from lofty modernism to a more socially engaged position. *The Novels of William Styron: From Harmony to History* (LSU) finds that Styron's structures for order are increasingly undermined, much as happens in successive works by James Baldwin, Toni Morrison, E. L. Doctorow, and Kurt Vonnegut. Yet this is not a retrograde deviation from modernism but a move toward active responsibility, building on principles from both modernism and the postmodern. *Darkness Visible* inspires two original essays commissioned by Daniel W. Ross for his *The Critical Response to William Styron* (Greenwood): Jeffrey Berman's "Darkness Visible and Invisible: The Landscape of Depression in *Lie Down in Darkness*" (pp. 61–80), in which complex relationships of characters are now more readily traceable to psychological conflicts, and Thorton F. Jordan's "Surmounting the Intolerable: Reconstructing Loss in *Sophie's Choice,* 'A Tidewater Morning,' and *Darkness Visible*" (pp. 257–68), where isolation is seen to be a factor in both Styron's life and fiction, an unconscious force contributing to his need for "reconstruction." A reprinted essay by James M. Mellard, "This *Un*quiet Dust: The Problem of History in Styron's *The Confessions of Nat Turner*" (pp. 157–72), reminds scholars of how newly generated knowledge of history and self allow the author to deal with repressed materials, a topic of even greater importance now in the wake of *Darkness Visible*.

The relationship between philosophy and literature is a perennial theme in Percy studies, to which Patrick H. Samway, S.J., contributes *A Thief of Peirce: The Letters of Kenneth Laine Ketner and Walker Percy* (Miss.). From his post at Texas Tech, Ketner engaged Percy on the matter of C. S. Peirce's presence in the fiction and helped draw out the understanding that "signs are capable of helping us form new ideas and new habits as we move into the future." Another writer breaking out from isolation is studied by Robert W. Croft in *Anne Tyler: A Bio-Bibliography* (Greenwood); Tyler's roundabout ways back to expressing her Baltimore background can be related to her parents' Quaker activism and her own subsequent marriage and motherhood, along the way learning the artful use of mountain dialects in North Carolina. There is an evolving sense that mediates the extremes of "modernist abandonment and postmodern deconstruction of the self," according to Lihong Xie, whose *The Evolving Self in the Novels of Gail Godwin* (LSU) uncovers a decentering dialogic that moves toward an eventually more centered self in which essence is replaced by process. Godwin's social heteroglossia and multicentered world thus transcend the ideology of patriarchal oppression. James Dickey's first novel remains a worthwhile resource for Martin Bidney; his "Spirit-Bird, Bowshot, Water-Snake, Corpses, Cosmic Love: Reshaping the Coleridge Legacy in Dickey's *Deliverance*" (*PLL* 31: 389–405) explores the tension "between metaphysical meaning and the sense of ungovernable chaos" that informs this writer's work.

vii   Jewish American Writers: Philip Roth and Woody Allen

Paucity of work in this subfield is balanced by depth and range. A major statement is made by Elaine M. Kauvar in "This Doubly Reflected Communication: Philip Roth's 'Autobiographies'" (*ConL* 36: 412–46). Long concerned with his own subjectivity, Roth has since 1988 expanded that interest from autobiographical fiction to fictive autobiography, though the complex nature of his undertaking has discredited both of these terms as overly simplistic. It is Kauvar's thesis that *The Facts, Patrimony,* and *Operation Shylock* constitute a trilogy, with the testing procedures of the first determining content and form of the latter two volumes. Along the way issues crucial not just to Roth's fiction but to the writing of our age are considered: how reality is represented and the extent to which "memories are not factual events" but instead the result of conscious editing and unconscious fantasy.

Woody Allen's literary contributions have been studied from time to time, but not as consistently as they should be. His special merit is clarified by Michiko Kakutani, whose interview "Woody Allen: The Art of Humor I" (*ParisR* 136: 200–222) includes a description of how Allen began publishing fiction in the *New Yorker* (and how the editors of that magazine cautioned him not to be derivative of S. J. Perelman).

viii The Mannerists: John Updike and John Cheever

"Updike Ignored: The Contemporary Independent Critic" (*AL* 67: 531–52) makes a statement in its title that James A. Schiff supports by means of thorough examination and brightly reasoned argument: that this fiction writer's extensive and valuable literary criticism has been given ill attention because after the 1930s and 1940s the critic has been transformed from a public to an academic figure. The final novel of the *Rabbit* tetralogy inspires what is surely the most complex (yet conclusive) essay ever written on this author of supposedly superficial fiction, "Sounding the Black Box: Linear Reproduction and Chance Bifurcations in *Rabbit at Rest*" (*ArQ* 51, iv: 69–108) by Salah El Moncef, in which one sees "one of Updike's most ambitious narrative projects: the reconstruction of a complex structure of general equivalence between the effects of *biological* destabilization at the level of the 'psychosomatic economy' of the subject and the effects of *logical* destabilization at the level of the political economy of the social body." More in line with traditional Updike scholarship but adding its own special insight is "John Updike's *Olinger Stories*" (pp. 151–69), a contribution by Robert M. Luscher to editor J. Gerald Kennedy's *Modern American Short Story Sequences*. There are impulses in Updike's sequence, Luscher shows, that work toward dismantling the very things that a tight community makes possible, giving his story cycle a unity based on the notions of independence, fragmentation, and departure.

Kennedy's collection also includes an especially strong piece by Scott Donaldson on John Cheever, "Cheever's *Shady Hill*: A Suburban Sequence" (pp. 133–50). Derided for its materialism and conventionality, Cheever's fictive community in fact suffers from a closeted nature in which ambiguities and pessimism and optimism are confined (to excel-

lent narrative effect). Agreeing with recent trends in Cheever scholarship, Donaldson squares this fictive practice with Cheever's own ambiguous personality, a style of writing and living that often allowed for great
eruptions of magic within an otherwise mundane world. Cheever also
figures in an important segment (pp. 48–52) of *Writing Was Everything*
(Harvard), Alfred Kazin's memoir dating back to days of reviewing for
the *New Republic* when he first met this author. The occasion here is
Kazin's reflection on the publication of Cheever's journals. "In his polite
hopelessness," Kazin writes, "Cheever . . . knew exactly the emotional
tone he was writing from and aiming for. As he put in the middle of one
story, 'Why, in this half-finished civilization, this most prosperous,
equitable and accomplished world, should everyone seem so disappointed?' That, it not surprisingly turned out, was what his private
journals were all about, and done with his usual cleverness and show of
style."

ix Richard Yates, Paul Auster, and Other Realists Old and New

Richard Yates, who died late in 1992, is only now attracting the style of
criticism his work deserves. Ronald J. Nelson strives to perceive the
essence of Yates's art by delving beneath generalities of plot in order "to
probe the characters and situations" that let the author find depth where
others might see only surface; "Richard Yates's Portrait of the Artist as a
Young Thug: 'Doctor Jack-o'-Lantern' " (*SSF* 32: 1–10) thus shows how a
character's own limited vision need not restrict the writer's use of him or
her. Other realists work with a heavier hand, and in "John Gardner's
Dialogue with the Book of Job" (*MQ* 37: 80–91) Sally Ventura finds
it easy to list the biblical citations in *The Sunlight Dialogues,* given
Gardner's somewhat pompous claim of "hoping to write something as
great as *Moby-Dick.*" That Gardner was also motivated by his Tolstoyean
standards as expressed in *On Moral Fiction* makes his methods somewhat
less than subtle. A similar danger underlies studies of Raymond Carver,
especially when the critic confuses praise for this writer's mastery of
lowlife realism with admiration for his recovery from various misfor-
tunes and vices that figure as themes in his stories (such as bad marriages
and alcoholism). Sam Halpert's *Raymond Carver: An Oral Biography*
(Iowa) walks a narrow line in skirting such temptations, and it suffers
from having Tess Gallagher's comments withdrawn. But there are valuable observations here from Carver's first wife and from many of his

writer friends, including his early teacher Dick Day's insight that "Ray
didn't have a philosophical bone in his body. He wasn't interested in
larger structures or intangible ideas" but rather just "drove home image
after image" from his own experience. Kirk Nesset extends this view in
The Stories of Raymond Carver: A Critical Study (Ohio), crediting not just
Carver's difficult life and his admiration for traditionalism in the manner
of Hemingway, Anderson, O'Hara, and Cheever (as tempered by Turge-
nev and Chekhov) but appreciating how he cut short postmodernism's
"inward spiral" by "reinscribing" postmodern conditions as "realer than
real," exploiting along the way our era's "obsession with the limits of
language."

Just as the poorest work about Southern fiction limps to truistic
conclusions with the aid of crutch-words such as "guilt" and "apotheo-
sis," scholarship on realism in general and the American Midwest in
particular sometimes reduces vision to a superficial rendering of Grant
Wood's *American Gothic* and simplifies landscape as a Lionel train set. In
Writing from the Center (Indiana) Scott Russell Sanders risks falling into
this trap when he claims Midwestern values translate into a literary tone.
The danger is a real one; it is hilarious but also painful to watch one critic
be tripped up by a master of such banalities in Scott Cawelti's "An
Interview with Barry Hannah" (*ShortS* 3, i: 105–16), during which this
Iowa-based newspaper columnist begins by challenging Hannah on the
Confederate flags flown so conspicuously to this day in Oxford, Mississippi, only to be foolishly charmed by Hannah's tongue-in-cheek
response, claiming that what Ishmael Reed has called "America's swas-
tika" is "honorable, it means valor, old values, valor [*sic*], courtesy, things
that Iowa's for, actually—a front porch, neighbors, we're on the same
side" (against what, Cawelti fails to ask). Sanders is more specific about
the seat of his values, which is a sense of writers from the Midwest being
"firmly in place"—not just in regard to their own communities and
locales, but to the extent of appreciating the tragedy of abused lands and
broken communities in the work of Toni Morrison. Less successful is
Michael Martone's "The Flyover" (pp. 3–12) from editors Mark Vinz
and Thom Tammaro's *Imagining Home: Writing from the Midwest* (Minnesota), where the notion of "flyover country" (as East and West Coast
travelers sometimes call the region) is praised as a style of camouflage, an
acutely intellectualized judgment having little to do with the style of lives
being lived by those not off on lucrative writer-in-residence junkets.

A warmer sense of realism's inclusions is displayed by James R. Giles in his scholarly masterpiece, *The Naturalistic Inner-City Novel in America*. This study's brilliance lies in its coverage of writers and novels not usually enshrined in realism's pantheon (perhaps because they do not lend themselves to mass-market merchandizing and pontificational teaching). In his broader view Giles finds that Hubert Selby's *Last Exit to Brooklyn* codifies violence as a reaction to alienation and boredom; its narrative strategy allows no "reassuring distance" for the reader, but instead mandates a deep identification with these characters lost almost beyond hope. On the other hand, John Rechy's *City of Night* exploits a "spectator mentality" in its narrative voice as a way of revealing our culture's "suppressed awareness of its own androgny." Most interesting is Giles's treatment of Joyce Carol Oates's *them*, the novel so atypical of Oates's other work that employs the metafictional dimension of letters to contrast art with reality, demonstrating how art can reveal where human spirituality has been destroyed. Oates's achievement, Giles shows, is in creating an inner-city narrative persona that cannot remain detached from the urban scene. One of Giles's strongest authors also figures in an important contribution to *Cruising the Performative: Interventions into the Representation of Ethnicity, Nationality, and Sexuality*, ed. Sue-Ellen Case, Philip Brett, and Susan Leigh Foster (Indiana). It is Rechy's lessknown novel *Numbers* that allows Ricardo L. Ortiz to probe the author's textual strategies for the containment of "indiscretions"; there is a "raging exhibitionism" that "John Rechy and the Grammar of Ostentation" (pp. 59–70) helps readers understand as the author's fine ability to "show himself showing us" his protagonist.

Paul Auster shows signs of being the critics' choice as the realist who takes best advantage of the postmodern condition. A good introduction to this proposition is given by Steven E. Alford in "Mirrors of Madness: Paul Auster's *The New York Trilogy*" (*Crit* 37: 17–33). Like many of the more apparent metafictionists, Auster looks back to Cervantes, seeing not a picaresque adventure but rather a strategy for allowing the text to generate not only characters and action but author and reader. Similar complexities distinguish the materials of editor Dennis Barone's *Beyond the Red Notebook: Essays on Paul Auster* (Penn.), most of which emphasize how the author foregrounds elements of storytelling and narrativity rather than subject. Most valuable are Madeleine Sorapure's "The Detective and the Author: *City of Glass*" (pp. 71–87), which considers how this novel "calls into question the presuppositions of the traditional detective novel" by undermining notions of master plot and master plotter, and

"Paul Auster's Pseudonymous World" (pp. 34–43) by Marc Chénetier, where language is seen as being stripped of all transcendence and left to find its motivations in overt power plays.

x Innovative Fiction from Barth to Vonnegut

The great wave of experiment in recent American fiction is usually seen to have begun with the comedy of Ken Kesey, Joseph Heller, and Kurt Vonnegut as combined with the more intellectually involved doings of John Barth, Thomas Pynchon, and the recently less-studied John Hawkes. There has always been a suspicion, however, that earlier and much quieter developments among writers better known as poets may have anticipated this boom. A special issue of *RCF* (15, iii) guest-edited by Douglas Gunn makes the case that Robert Creeley, much like William Carlos Williams before him, undertook important innovations in *The Island* (a novel) and *The Gold Diggers* (stories) that set standards by by which subsequent work of more popular authors will be judged. What Creeley brings to fiction is a special privileging of voice, says Michael Stephens in "The Poet in Robert Creeley's Prose" (pp. 110–15), crediting an emphasis on "breath and syllable" adopted from Williams's fiction and Charles Olson's poetry and journals. Echoing his own classic essay "The Various Isolated: W. C. Williams' Prose" (first published in issue number 15 of *New American Review* for 1972, pp. 192–207, and collected in *Something Said* [see *ALS 1984*, pp. 294–95]) Gilbert Sorrentino reminds scholars that "the writer's placement and adjustment of the materials given him create the form and meaning of his work," making "external impositions of what might be called 'correct procedure' seem frivolous, so say the least, in the face of form's necessity." Thus, Sorrentino's "The Monster Come to Dinner" (pp. 107–09) reasserts the position that apparently "random and broken" fiction such as Creeley's in fact "abandons sequential narrative for the discoveries that occur when signifiers combine to produce what Lacan calls 'The creative spark of the metaphor'" that flashes between the signifiers of reality.

John Barth's position becomes anterior to Creeley's in terms of innovation, for as Alan Lindsay shows in *Death in the Funhouse: John Barth and Poststructuralist Aesthetics* (Peter Lang) this author fits in more comfortably with Charles Jencks's architecturally based definition of postmodernism as historical reappropriation than he does among Ihab Hassan's paradigms of change. For Lindsay, Barth is essentially a poststructuralist writer, showing evidence in his early work of appreciating the death of the author and the pleasures of the text but later on retreating to a more conservative, socially relevant position. Barth's own *Further Fridays: Essays, Lectures, and Other Nonfiction, 1984–1994* (Little, Brown) continues where his *The Friday Book* (see *ALS 1984*, p. 295) leaves off; illustrative of his position is "Postmodernism Visited: A Professional Novelist's Amateur Review" (pp. 291–310). On the occasion of these 1991 Stuttgart Seminars, Barth tells his colleagues that his own postmodernism is "an essentially Modernist criticism of Modernism; one that . . . not only declines to throw out the baby with the bathwater, but maintains a high regard for that bathwater as well." In describing the postmodernism of others, Barth admires Fredric Jameson's architectural model of historicist play and allusion, another confirmation that the author's fiction is not the revolutionary material some critics have thought it to be.

Thomas Pynchon's reputation, weakened by critical disappointment with his *Vineland,* is sustained by capable studies of his earlier work. *PNotes* 32–33 [1993] features "Pynchon's *V.* and the Rhetoric of the Cold War" (pp. 5–32) by Paul W. Celmer, Jr., whose reading of *The Truth About the Foreign Policy Association* published in 1960 by an American Legion post reveals subtle influences that help shape Pynchon's art. This same issue includes an exceptionally well-researched note by Jonathan R. Eller and William E. McCarron, "Pynchon and Glenn Miller" (pp. 193–96), in which *Gravity's Rainbow* is praised for another aspect of its thoroughness with 1940s popular culture. In *Literary Realism and the Ekphrastic Tradition* (Penn. State) Mack Smith goes so far as to claim a "paracinematic reality" for this novel, based on Pynchon's ability to have one signifier dominate others in his structures; his "use of cinematic descriptions, forcing the reader to view the novelistic actual world through a film frame, shows how all responses are mediated by sign systems and discourses."

Among her many strengths Susan Sontag's importance as a novelist is enhanced by Liam Kennedy's study, *Susan Sontag: Mind as Passion* (Manchester). Whereas *The Benefactor* is best considered as "an extended treatise on subjectivity" with its characters serving as vehicles for ideas and its violations of conventions working less as innovations than as self-conscious gestures of absurdity, *Death Kit* succeeds as a more effective narrative. Its "reflexive aims" are achieved, Kennedy proves, by giving desire a narrative impulse; this impulse becomes "a compulsion toward death, but it undergoes repetitions and detours in this movement, constantly approaching yet deferring its ultimate object." A more sympathetic view of this author's characterizations emerges from Marithelma Costa and Adelaide López's "Susan Sontag: The Passion for Words" (pp. 222–36) as included in *Conversations with Susan Sontag,* ed. Leland Poague (Miss.). Her characters, it evolves from the interview here, embody a voice that articulates their own unique language. Edward Hirsch draws her out on similar issues in his "Susan Sontag: The Art of Fiction CXLIII" (*ParisR* 137: 176–208), a dialogue that integrates Sontag's intellectual concerns with her fictive talents.

Ken Kesey, Joseph Heller, and Kurt Vonnegut are served well in various commentaries. Peter Najarian's "The Big Game" (pp. 105–17) supplies editor Peter Stine's *The Sixties* (Wayne State) with a familiar narrative about visiting Kesey's farm, yet its value resides in a contrastive portrait of Richard Brautigan as so different from his predecessor—shy, private, and devoured by fame, existing so much better in the earlier Beat era when he was ignored. Restoring the humor that is otherwise overlooked in the category "black humor" is Daniel Green's goal in "A World Worth Laughing At: *Catch-22* and the Humor of Black Humor" (*SNNTS* 27: 186–96); jokes are "both the foundation of individual scenes and episodes" and serve as "a central organizing principle of the novel as a whole," a proposition that makes Heller's novel much simpler than some language-based critics have proposed. Vonnegut has also suffered for the original nature of his comedy, not because critics have sought to make him overly complex, but because they cannot accept his unassuming originality, according to John Irving's response in "The Man in the Back Row Has a Question" (*ParisR* 136: 100–101). Editor Haskell Springer's *America and the Sea* accommodates Vonnegut criticism in "Prose Since 1960" (pp. 307–26), an essay by Dennis Berthold that sees the old fear of oceans as alien and hostile being replaced by new feelings of positive and sustaining forces boding all the better for human life, a thesis propounded by examinations of *Cat's Cradle* and *Galápagos*. *Galápagos* figures centrally in "Surviving the End: Apocalypse, Evolution, and Entropy in Bernard Malamud, Kurt Vonnegut, and Thomas Pynchon" (*Crit* 36: 163–76), in which Peter Freese finds "new beginnings to be wrested from an all-embracing apocalypse" that earlier writers would have surrendered to as an end. *Cat's Cradle* and *Slaughterhouse-Five* challenge any categorical assimilations, especially those of time and space, according to Ronald Granofsky in *The Trauma Novel: Contempo-*

rary Symbolic Depictions of Collective Disaster (Peter Lang), a study that also demonstrates how time is made meaningless in Jerzy Kosinski's novels that posit a dominant self against collective trauma. Vonnegut's own "ironic distance as a novelist" has much to do with his anthropology studies at the University of Chicago, both for the discipline itself and the way the department systematically marginalized him as a student, as Vonnegut reports in "A Very Fringe Character" (pp. 235–42) for editor Molly McQuade's *An Unsentimental Education: Writers and Chicago* (Chicago).

Donald Barthelme's centrality to popular culture not just of his own but of all eras is clarified by Jack Zipes in "Recent Trends in the Contemporary American Fairy Tale" (pp. 1–17) from *Functions of the Fantastic: Selected Essays from the Thirteenth International Conference on the Fantastic in the Arts,* ed. Joe Sanders (Greenwood). In the traditional struggle of the imagination against "the hard reality of exploitation and reification (representing the rise of inhumane technology)" Barthelme and Robert Coover break their postmodernized fairy tales into fragments—not so that they can reassemble the narrative as a whole, but to show different ways of viewing stories. Barthelme himself shows well in Herbert Mitgang's *Words Still Count with Me: A Chronicle of Literary Conversations* (Norton), both in Mitgang's central essay, "Donald Barthelme" (pp. 174–76), and in comments from Susan Sontag and Italo Calvino; collections such as this one are especially worthwhile when indexed, as has been done here. Mitgang describes how Barthelme considers his work socially relevant yet artistically tough; Carl D. Malmgren proves this point in "Exhumation: *The Dead Father*" (pp. 25–40) for editors Theo D'haen and Hans Bertens's *Narrative Turns and Minor Genres in Postmodernism* (Rodopi), concluding that burying the dead father is not a point of closure but rather a rehearsal of something that must be done and redone until it has been got right.

"Avant-Pop" and "Cyberpunk" are partially overlapping terms for what critics (most of them practitioners as well) call the next stage in the evolution of American fiction. As veterans of the innovative fiction wars dating back to the 1960s, Ronald Sukenick and Raymond Federman are transitional figures, both in their newer work and in Larry McCaffery's reinterpretation of their classic novels published before some of the style's younger writers were born. The development of *Black Ice* magazine as an alternative to the Fiction Collective's own alternative program is detailed in "The Fiction of Fiction: An Interview with Ronald Sukenick" con-

ducted by Ted Rooney (*Poetry Flash* 261: 1, 4–6, 8–11). Federman expands Sukenick's arguments for serious fiction in an age virtually buried
under cheap commercialism by launching "Avant-Pop: You're Kidding!
Or, The Real Begins Where the Spectacle Ends—A Manifesto of Sorts"
(pp. 94–97) on the occasion of editors Hanjo Berressem and Bernd
Herzogenrath's *Near Encounters: Festschrift for Richard Martin* (Peter
Lang), while a much younger avant-popper (Tom Patten) responds to
the old master's methods in "Federman: The Workshop" (*IowaR* 25, i:
84–89). What the term means is explicated by Larry McCaffery in his
editor's introduction ("Avant-Pop: Still Life After Yesterday's Crash,"
pp. xi–xxix) to *After Yesterday's Crash: The Avant-Pop Anthology* (Penguin). As opposed to what he celebrated as a marriage of science fiction
and innovative writing using artificial intelligence and new textures of
communication in *Storming the Reality Studio: A Casebook of Cyberpunk
and Postmodern Fiction* (see *ALS 1991,* pp. 274–75), McCaffery now
broadens his view to include nonelectronic work that nevertheless generates itself by interfacing with and drawing from media such as films,
television, advertising, and popular music. Other scholars are less win-
some about such developments and regret that "the autonomous agency
suggested by the hacker cowboy of cyberpunk" is in fact a vehicle for
creating "an ideal geography for the dynamics of postnational capitalism"; thus, it is wise to heed Sharon Stockton's warning in " 'The Self
Regained': Cyberpunk's Retreat to the Imperium" (*ConL* 36: 588–612)
that "cyberpunk should call to mind for us more than the vision of the
unified self regained—reflected, remembered, and reappearing—in the
free space of the electronic network. By the same token, early capitalism
cannot so easily be reified yet again as the foundation of the self."

xi Sport, War, Science Fiction, and Detective Novels

Batboys and the World of Baseball (Miss.) by Neil D. Isaacs does much
with unique perspectives of narratology drawn from accounts by real-life
batboys, but this study has literary dimensions as well, including novelist
Gerald Rosen's use and later expansion of his experience as a batboy in
Growing Up Bronx and *Writing Baseball.* The parallel but more serious
contest of war is reemphasized in Steven Kaplan's *Understanding Tim
O'Brien* (So. Car.). This writer's chief theme is that of courage effected by
choice, while his technical innovations open new roads for the consciousness into reality. By virtue of his artful repetitions O'Brien thus

captures the fluidity of all experience, especially as reorganized by the disruptions of conventional warfare in Vietnam. A very specific study of O'Brien's experiments is undertaken by Catherine Calloway in " 'How to Tell a War Story': Metafiction in *The Things They Carried*" (*Crit* 36: 249–57). A more psychological approach in narrative structures is described by Ruth D. Weston in "Debunking the Unitary Self and Story in the War Stories of Barry Hannah" (*SLJ* 27, ii: 96–106). Of great help in appreciating the difficulty of any such descriptions is Renny Christopher's *The Vietnam War / The American War: Images and Representations in Euro-American and Vietnamese Exile Narratives* (Mass.), a wonderfully detailed and insightful study of how Americans have excluded Vietnamese characters from narratives set in their own country (and of what happens to the canon of war stories when it is expanded to include the Vietnamese point of view).

The subgenres of science fiction and detective novels remain fields where women-oriented studies thrive. A major contribution is Joanna Russ's *To Write Like a Woman: Essays in Feminism and Science Fiction* (Indiana). There is a broad consensus on "what to do with the rest of society" in various feminist utopias, Russ believes, such as social units becoming communal and even tribal as they pursue balanced ecologies and sexual permissiveness while avoiding class distinctions and violence. Feminism's interest in both writers and readers of crime fiction prompts Kathleen Gregory Klein to edit *Women Times Three: Writers, Detectives, Readers* (Bowling Green) and propose that the interactive influence of reader, writer, and text is studied most productively when women's involvement is common to all three areas; the essays that Klein commissions examine writers from Sara Paretsky to Barbara Wilson and explore gender issues in the detection process that shapes such narratives. Linda C. Pelzer's *Mary Higgins Clark: A Critical Companion* (Greenwood) praises this writer for producing thorough characterizations rather than facile puzzles; in Clark's novels, both heroine and villain are complete, and the author's own career is marked by deepening psychological insight. A good look into a writer's lifestyle (as influenced by Hemingway) and working routine (including the germination of "concept novels") is provided by Ernie Bulow and Lawrence Block in their *After Hours: Conversations with Lawrence Block* (New Mexico), while an excellent reference work is produced by Myron J. Smith, Jr., and Terry White in the third edition of their *Cloak and Dagger Fiction*.

University of Northern Iowa

17 Poetry: 1900 to the 1940s

Timothy Materer

A greater variety of scholarship is welcome this year after the recent dominance of books on Wallace Stevens and William Carlos Williams. Although there are two books on Williams and three on Stevens, there are also three on Marianne Moore and, surprisingly, three on Robinson Jeffers. Books also were published on W. H. Auden, Witter Bynner, Langston Hughes, Edna St. Vincent Millay, Robert Penn Warren, and Richard Wilbur as well as three general studies of American poetry. I begin with the books and articles on Marianne Moore because of their high quality and their demonstration that Moore is as central to modern American poetry as Stevens or Williams.

i Marianne Moore

Both Cristanne Miller's *Marianne Moore: Questions of Authority* (Harvard) and Linda Leavell's *Marianne Moore and the Visual Arts* (LSU) explore Moore's response to a culture that was both modernist and sexist. Yet these books display remarkably little overlap, which suggests the richness of Moore's work as well as the quality of these studies. Miller's book is more deeply engaged with theoretical issues, while Leavell's has a greater range (including the arts of photography, painting, and collage) and livelier readings of Moore's works. Both are based on original research into Moore's papers and manuscripts.

The basic "question" of authority is how to establish one's power to speak through the art of poetry without pretensions to "genius." Moore attempted to avoid what Miller calls "the romantic sublime . . . and the modernist impersonal modes" as well as the 19th-century sentimental tradition against which Edna St. Vincent Millay struggled. Miller discusses Lacanian/Kristevan approaches to *"écriture feminine"* but concludes that poets like Moore reject the notion of "disruptive, nonverbal, extralinguistic strategies as either expressing or constructing an order beyond phallocentrism."

According to Miller, Moore wanted to establish a "communally focused authority that avoided egocentric and essentialist assertions of a subjective self." In poems like "The Plumet Basilisk," Moore's "authority" lies in the accuracy of her information and "the suggestiveness of the commentary she embeds in the apparently objective detail." As she attempts to write in a nongendered voice, Moore is also highly sensitive to racial politics. Although Miller is perhaps too sensitive in claiming that Moore is not untainted by the language of racism, this scrupulousness makes her description of Moore's liberal and compassionate social views all the more convincing. Later chapters trace the "shift in Moore's work toward the more personal, popular, occasional, and openly appreciative" as World War II inspired in her a more public and didactic scope. However, Miller again seems too sensitive in feeling that Moore in this late stage of her career (the eccentric in a cape and tricornered hat) "inadvertently supported a regressive image of womanhood." (Later, we will see a different view of Moore's persona.) Beyond its searching exploration of poetic authority, this book's accomplishment is to demonstrate Moore's "largely unacknowledged concern for national and international (moral) political issues."

In *Marianne Moore and the Visual Arts* Leavell also analyzes how Moore established her authority as a modernist poet, but Levell's argument is less abstract and livelier than Miller's because this well-illustrated work places Moore's art in the exciting context of the modernist visual arts. The account of how the works and theories of Edward Steichen and Alfred Stieglitz (her visit to his gallery in 1915 was a formative moment) shaped her way of seeing is fascinating and original. The influence of paintings on Moore is important, but Leavell's most interesting findings concern the impact of certain photographs on her work. Photography in Stieglitz's style "defined a new way of seeing that had ethical as well as aesthetic implications" because for Stieglitz "straight photography" meant sharp focus and "minimum manipulation of the negative."

The visual context allows Leavell to picture Moore's modernist credentials as equally as impressive as those of Eliot, Pound, or Stevens. In Leavell's consideration of the valid points of comparison between visual and verbal art, she concludes that modernism should be considered a set of problems posed by "analytic cubism, by collage, by primitivism, and by American technology" and not as solutions, such as compressed perspective and free verse. For example, Moore's poetry deals with analytic cubism's questioning of the relation of form to subject and with the challenges of collage, which "redefines art as selecting rather than making." Leavell shows a particular sensitivity to the way that Moore sensed ethical issues within the artistic revolution such as the "resistance to aesthetic, social and even spiritual hierarchies." Thus, like Miller, she examines questions of authority. This book ranks with Glen MacLeod's *Wallace Stevens and Modern Art* (*ALS 1993*, pp. 283–84) as an essential scholarly and critical account of modernist art and poetry.

In *The Web of Friendship: Marianne Moore and Wallace Stevens* (Michigan) Robin G. Schulze does not characterize the two poets, in Harold Bloom's manner, as anxious rivals; nor does she follow Sandra Gilbert and Susan Gubar's model of "communal nurturance and shared generosity" among women writers, which she considers as "gender-essentialist" as Bloom's. Instead, she poses a model of "poetic influence as extended conversation" as the two poets gauge their progress against each other through the period of *Others,* to the publication of Stevens's *Harmonium* and Moore's *Selected Poems,* to their later correspondence about their shared aesthetic and social views. Moore's early suspicion about Stevens's aestheticism became by the time of her review of *Harmonium* a concern with Stevens's philosophical skepticism, which she felt challenged "the construction of all stable, comforting, or coherent ideals." Her chapter on "Finding the Proper Way to Fly" is an analysis of "The Plumet Basilisk," "The Jerboa," and "The Frigate Pelican" as poems about art, isolation, and social responsibility. In "The Frigate Pelican" Moore abandons her fear that romantic impulses are necessarily escapist.

Stevens was nearly as fascinated with Moore's work as a model of poetry as Moore was with Stevens's. She represented for him a new kind of romanticism that would delight in the pleasure of the imagination without seeming to disdain common social realities. After her many detailed and rather exhausting readings of poems in which the two poets reflect on each other, Schulze's final chapter is a welcome narrative of the years when they became closer, especially through their mutual friendship with Mrs. Henry Church. The most curious event in these years was Stevens's insistence that Moore accompany Mrs. Church on a trip to Europe. When Moore forgave Stevens for his rudeness ("a few verbal

pineapples"), Stevens replied gratefully that "the web of friendship between poets [is] the most delicate thing in the world."

Cynthia Hogue's *Scheming Women*, a study of Emily Dickinson,
H.D., and Adrienne Rich, also treats Moore in the chapter "Less is
Moore: Marianne Moore's Poetic Subject" (pp. 73–115). Like Miller,
Hogue explores the way in which poets find a method to disrupt and
redefine "relations of subjectivity to positions of power." Unlike Miller,
Hogue emphasizes the poet's subjectivity and attempts to show, what
Miller denies, that Moore did create an *"écriture feminine."* In a technique of "equivocations," Moore erases her "self" and makes idealized
images of femininity and maternity ambivalent. Thus, Hogue would
disagree with Miller about the persona that Moore took on in later life.
To Hogue the tricorn hat and cape is a form of "transvestism" and a
calculated response to "festishized femininity." Although Hogue's analysis is always interesting, she makes Moore appear an implausibly self-
conscious and assured feminist.

Clive Bloom and Brian Docherty, the editors of *American Poetry: The
Modernist Ideal,* which I review more fully later, claim that Moore fits
neither the Whitman-Pound nor the Poe-Eliot tradition but instead
writes a Wordsworthian poetry of detailed description of the natural
world. However, Lorrayne Carroll's essay on Moore (pp. 105–19) places
her firmly in the Eliot tradition by focusing on her poem "Marriage." In
"Presenting Miss Moore, Modernist: T. S. Eliot's Edition of Marianne
Moore's 'Selected Poems' " (*JML* 19: 129–51) Andrew J. Kappel shows
how Eliot established Moore as a modernist poet by publishing her
Selected Poems (1934). Finally, after so much discussion of Moore's undermining of authority, it is fascinating to read Chris Beyers's "Marianne
Moore's and John James Audubon's Frigate Pelican" (*Sagetrieb* 13, iii
[1994]: 51–70). An important exception to Moore's customary treatment
of sources occurs when she draws respectfully on Audubon's writings in
"The Frigate Pelican."

ii Wallace Stevens

Janet McCann's *Wallace Stevens Revisited: The Celestial Possible* (Twayne)
is a well-organized introduction to the poet, with extensive though
sometimes labored explications of the major poems, that also contains
some interesting biographical speculation about Stevens's spiritual de-

velopment. McCann frankly states of his deathbed conversion to Catholicism that he was "not forced to sign on the line by zealous nuns," and she rejects the claim of Stevens's biographer Joan Richardson that it was a "prank." She believes that Stevens's correspondence with the Irish poet Tom McGreevy and Sister Bernetta Quinn, O.S.F., reveals that the poet's attraction to Catholicism preceded his deathbed conversion. She argues that at every stage of his metaphysical quest he was testing his fiction against the idea of God to find "what may suffice" in place of this idea and finding that nothing else can.

In Anca Rosu's *The Metaphysics of Sound in Wallace Stevens* (Alabama) the word "sound" has both a literal and metaphoric meaning. She focuses on literal sound devices such as simple repetition, incremental repetition, chant, song, refrain, and nonsense syllables. In sometimes labored but usually sensitive readings Rosu gives what she calls "microscopic" attention to sound devices as they affect the meaning of a poem. She has a good ear for "changes from one discourse to another" and what she calls "discursive fluctuations" in Stevens's verse, which both implies the presence of an audience and disrupts that audience's presumed expectations. One of the best analyses is of "Anecdote of the Jar" as a charm or spell. However, Rosu's concept of "sound" is unclear when it becomes a metaphor for Stevens's philosophical orientation. When Rosu writes that Stevens's sound effects "give essentially another value to language," she cannot possibly mean that Stevens is alone in doing so, yet she seems to imply just that. It is telling that Rosu ignores the criticism of Stevens and the heritage of French symbolism ("De la musique avant tout chose") since that would remove any appearance that Stevens is somehow unique or that Rosu has noticed something which other critics have not.

Stevens's "nonsense" sounds are indeed meaningful in Rachel Blau DuPlessis's " 'HOO, HOO, HOO': Some Episodes in the Construction of Modern Whiteness" (*AL* 67: 667–700). DuPlessis argues that in Stevens's and Eliot's poetry the word "hoo," used by Vachel Lindsay in "The Congo" (1914), signifies the language of Africans and implies the superiority of white discourse: "The syllable affirms white 'rights' in black materials." Stevens's "Owl's Clover" ("a public poem against public poetry") is analyzed in Joseph Harrington's "Wallace Stevens and the Poetics of National Insurance" (*AL* 67: 95–114). The poem reveals the interest of both a poet and business professional in "rights to privacy and property and with the separation of spheres that undergirds those rights." Stevens's insurance background also figures in Elizabeth Rosen's "The Lawyer in the Poet: Stevens' Use of Legal Terminology" (*WSJour* 19: 3–18).

The Fall issue of *WSJour* is devoted to Stevens and Elizabeth Bishop. Although they both were associated with the Key West artistic community, the two poets never met, and Stevens's references to Bishop were few and noncommittal. In "Wallace Stevens and Elizabeth Bishop at Key West: Ideas of Order" (19: 155–65) Albert Gelpi compares Stevens's "Idea of Order" to Bishop's "At the Fishhouses" to explore their relationships to a Coleridgean concept of the creative imagination. He regrets both in Bishop and generally in contemporary poetry a loss of "the sublime notion of a capable and empowering imagination." Charles Altieri counters the trend of Bishop's critics to praise her at Stevens's expense in his "Ann Lauterbach's 'Still' and Why Stevens Still Matters" (19: 219–33). He disagrees that Stevens's sense of the sublime, unlike Bishop's, is solipsistic. Like Gelpi, Altieri thinks contemporary poets have lost something in moving away from "the more dialectical model of reflection and self-reflective identities that Stevens elaborated."

iii William Carlos Williams

The feisty preface to Robert J. Cirasa's *The Lost Works of William Carlos Williams: The Volumes of Collected Poetry as Lyrical Sequences* (Fairleigh Dickinson) attacks theoretical criticism to defend his own brand of "performance" criticism. However, I cannot agree that a theoretical criticism which "brood[s] nihilistically over all the paradoxical mechanisms of meaning" is as disastrously prevalent as Cirasa implies. Cirasa's objection to theory seems motivated by the need to defend his own problematic critical approach of poem-by-poem readings of all of Williams's major collections. Employing what he calls M. L. Rosenthal's "entirely new critical approach," he says we must *"perform* or creatively *re*construct (rather than deconstruct) particular works of literature." Cirasa is drawing on Rosenthal's and Sally M. Gall's thesis in *The Modern Poetic Sequence* (see *ALS 1993*, pp. 349–51) that the sequence is basically a new genre of poetry that constitutes its "genius." They define it as "a grouping of mainly lyric poems and passages, rarely uniform in pattern, which tend to interact as an organic whole." Since a "sequence" amounts to a separate poetic work, Cirasa can argue that the collections of lyrics

Williams himself assembled are in a sense "lost works": specifically, his *Collected Poems 1921–1931* and *The Complete Collected Poems 1906–1938.* Cirasa aims to demonstrate the organic nature of the thematic and technical interrelations of the poems within these volumes. To me, his critical approach seems premised on a number of exaggerated claims: the domination of theory, the notion that a "sequence" is a special modern genre, and that "performative" criticism is a new kind of criticism (whether or not Rosenthal invented it). There is nothing new about showing how poems in a poet's oeuvre play off against and enrich each other.

Despite my reservations, I think that Cirasa's efforts more often reward rather than weary the reader. For example, his analysis of the *Collected Poems 1921–1931* shows how the opening poem of the volume's first sequence, "All the Fancy Things," provides a theme and creates a character (a woman like Williams's mother) that ties in with the remaining poems in the sequence and indeed throughout the volume. The collection's next poem, "Young Sycamore," gains a new dimension if we think of it as a son's urgent remonstrance to his aged mother's self-absorption. Poems about a failure to appreciate the common things of life (such as "Brilliant Sad Sun," again from the perspective of an old woman) are intertwined with vivid appreciations of them, so that in context the poems about the cat stepping into the flowerpot and the stolen plums seem even richer. The cogent analysis of the organizing of his final volumes (*The Collected Earlier Poems* and *The Collected Later Poems*) reveal the complicated personal reasons for their chaotic shapes.

The introduction to Daniel Morris's *The Writing of William Carlos Williams: Publicity for the Self* (Missouri) is as self-conscious as Cirasa's preface. Much as Cirasa apologizes for actually discussing the meaning of Williams's poems, so Morris warns us that his book will consider a relationship "between anterior reality and texts" as well as "perform close textual analysis"—as if this approach needed defense or explanation. He also ponderously characterizes his "literary-cultural approach" as a "third moment of modernist criticism" which holds that modernist works "contained within them the seeds of their own de(con)struction." The "de(con)structive" analysis reveals the contraction that Williams wanted both to defy and to win an audience. He focuses on Williams's relatively conventional fiction, beginning with *A Voyage to Pagany* (1928), because it reveals this interest in acquiring a general public.

Williams was fascinated by Ernest Hemingway's image as a sportsman and friend of movie stars. As Williams achieved some measure of popularity, he was seen (as in a series of reviews in *Time*) "as a figure of public trust, as this figure was constructed by Williams in the narrative fiction," with of course an emphasis on Williams as a doctor who delivered thousands of American babies. In this chapter and throughout, excellent use is made of Williams's correspondence with James Laughlin, publisher of the avant-garde, who could not satisfy Williams's need for greater publicity and wider distribution.

Morris's analysis of Williams's "doctor" stories, which recalls Miller's analysis of Moore in *Questions of Authority,* shows how Williams could "be accused of reifying his own personal identity in order to make his work a popular commercial production." But unlike some books with a cultural thesis, Morris does not criticize Williams merely for being a man of his time, for craving success, or even for clinging to a contradictory self-image. His desire for success is one with his desire to make "contact" with the "community of ordinary American readers." Moreover, in *Paterson V* his hard-won authority is abandoned when he conceives of himself in "the restricted role of a teacher" of a new generation of poets. Morris's (de)construction is perceptive and sympathetic.

In Bruce Comens's *Apocalypse and After: Modern Strategy and Postmodern Tactics in Pound, Williams, and Zukofsky* (Alabama) the word "strategy" (as in "global strategy") refers to an attempt to control the development of history and culture, which becomes less and less possible in the nuclear age. While Ezra Pound attempted such a strategy, Williams understood from the beginning that one could deal with life only in terms of fragmentary tactics. (An exception was Williams's endorsement of social credit as a "cure" in *Paterson.*) In *Spring and All* Williams "imagines the apocalypse . . . to disrupt and so free us from apocalyptic, or strategic, patterns of thought and culture." Williams's ambivalent reaction to Hiroshima appears in a statement to Laughlin that the explosion "is mind quelling, touches more than the imagination—a blast of the history of the Milky Way. It's got to end something but quick." Comens explores this ambivalence in an interesting reading of "Asphodel." Although a nuclear apocalypse reveals the uselessness of "strategy," it is also "the ultimate expression or embodiment of strategic domination." As Williams writes, "the bomb speaks" its message of apocalypse, and "we come to our deaths/in silence." But in "Asphodel" accepting death as the "condition of life enables the activity of love" and so of "the end of the bomb's domain." This dark conclusion suits Williams's conception of "tactics" that are tentative and never really solutions.

In *Orientalism and Modernism* Zhaoming Qian speculates about where Williams would have read Oriental poetry (in works by H. A. Giles, Arthur Waley, and Amy Lowell as well as Pound) and claims that he was most influenced by the Tang poet Bo Juyi. Many of his speculations, however, seem unlikely. There's no reason to think, for example, that Williams owes to Bo Juyi alone, or even primarily, the "ability to envisage sorrow in joy" or that he acquired from the Chinese the Taoist "notion of nonbeing/being" in "The Red Wheelbarrow." Virginia M. Kouidis's "William Carlos Williams Among the Nightingales: The Erotics and Poetics of the Modernist Love Song" (*Sagetrieb* 13, iii [1994]: 5–30) discusses Williams's "Chinese Nightingale" (1917) as a response to Vachel Lindsay's sentimental ballad "The Chinese Nightingale" (1917) and an implied criticism of Eliot's and Pound's modernist love poems.

iv Robinson Jeffers

In *Robinson Jeffers: Dimensions of a Poet,* ed. Robert Brophy (Fordham), the editor's "Robinson Jeffers: Poet of Carmel-Sur" (pp. 1–18) is an impressively concentrated account of Jeffers's life and career, the elemental themes of his poetry, and his philosophical "inhumanism." The biographical elements include a demanding father and youthful, vivacious mother, foreign travel and study, an affair with the married woman who became his wife, Una, the building of Tor House and Hawk Tower stone by stone on the rugged Carmel coast, and the precipitous rise and decline of his popularity. Alex Vardamis "In the Poet's Lifetime" (pp. 19–29) focuses on the fascinating story of Jeffers's transformation from an obscure regionalist to the poet on a *Time* magazine cover in 1932, followed by a decline in the late '30s as a result of the New Critics, the demands for social relevance (although Jeffers considered mankind irrelevant), his opposition to World War II, and a return to relative obscurity before his death in 1962. Following the autobiographical essays is Robert Zaller's "Robinson Jeffers and the Use of History" (pp. 30–47), on the poet's Hegelian and Nietzschean inspirations, and two essays that discuss his narrative poems "Thurso's Landing" and "Roan Stallion." Kirk Glaser's "Desire, Death, and Domesticity in Jeffers's Pastorals of Apocalypse" (pp. 137–76) reviews the poetry with the generous quotations needed to get a sense of Jeffers's sweep. William Everson's "All Flesh Is

Grass" (pp. 204–38) argues that Jeffers is not a philosopher but a mystic and prophet like William Blake. A symposium on "Robinson Jeffers and the Female Archetype" (pp. 110–36) generates some unproductive disagreements. Diane Wakoski's reply to the symposium sensibly questions the relevance of the issue to Jeffers, because for him "sexual identity, either male or female, is fraught with misery."

A problem with this kind of collection, as with the Millay collection reviewed later, is that the essays are more expository than critical and are focused on a neglected poet to the extent that the authors make few comparisons with other literary figures. However, Alan Soldofsky's "Nature and the Symbolic Order: The Dialogue Between Czeslaw Milosz and Robinson Jeffers" (pp. 177–203) is a truly critical comparison of Milosz, the Lithuanian-born Polish poet and avowed humanist, with the poet he came to admire while he was living in exile in Berkeley. Milosz challenged Jeffers's vision as philosophically naive: "Jeffers, who professed, as he called it, 'inhumanism,' took refuge in an artificial world which he invented using ideas taken from biology textbooks and from the philosophy of Nietzsche." Soldofsky answers Milosz's criticism by asserting that Jeffers's Tor House itself shows that his experience of nature is not unmediated but symbolic and indeed humanized.

Like Brophy's collection, Terry Beers's ". . . a thousand graceful subtleties": Rhetoric in the Poetry of Robinson Jeffers (Peter Lang) is naturally concerned with defending Jeffers's reputation. He believes that, although the New Critics' emphasis on the texture of self-contained poems did not suit Jeffers's poetry, their focus on the rhetoric of poetry should have. None other than John Crowe Ransom defended Jeffers against Ivor Winters's attack on the "logical" structure of Jeffers's poetry on the grounds that Winters's sense of rhetorical structure was too limited. Beers treats the rhetoric of Jeffers's poetry in each of the Aristotelian categories of *pathos, ethos,* and *logos.* (In its tidy but too schematic organization, the three middle chapters demonstrate Jeffers's use of each category.) An appeal to the feelings of an audience (*pathos*) from a speaker who bears authority and integrity (*ethos*) and presents a logically compelling argument (*logos*) are all relevant to Jeffers's work because, as Beers frankly admits, Jeffers was a didactic poet. In the *pathos* chapter Beers relates Jeffers to William Wordsworth as a poet who gives us elemental characters who take on the qualities of their environment. Granted that the characters of the Big Sur landscape are violent and incestuous, he reminds us not to assume that their emotions, which must be purged, are approved by Jeffers. Similarly, the *ethos* of his characters is both self-destructive and heroic. Instead of opposing or attempting to escape elemental forces, Jeffers's characters must learn to submit to them. Beers's conclusion tries to mitigate the harshness of Jeffers's vision by describing his emphasis on the family as the privileged unit in which nature's drama is played out (though, as he well knows, family interactions in the narratives are invariably violent and tragic) and through a largely unsupported claim that Jeffers is an Emersonian. Although Jeffers's readers should find this book a clarification of the poet's techniques, its narrow scope will win no new readers.

After reading these two books I feel that Tim Hunt focused on the right issue in the Introduction (pp. 1–10) to *Robinson Jeffers and a Galaxy of Writers*. He argues that the isolated, prophetic Jeffers that early critics either loved or hated must now be seen in context with his contemporaries and with the poets he influenced. Jeffers comes into focus here in a volume that makes invaluable yet previously neglected comparisons with Lawrence, Yeats, and Frost. Two essays also contrast Jeffers with T. S. Eliot, and there are illuminating studies of Jeffers's influence on poets like William Merwin, Gary Snyder, and James Dickey. The influences on Jeffers are considered in two essays on his complex debt to Emerson and Thoreau: Colin Falck's "Robinson Jeffers: American Romantic?" (pp. 83–92) and Alan Brasher's " 'Their Beauty Has More Meaning': Transcendental Echoes in Jeffers's Inhumanist Philosophy of Nature" (pp. 146–59).

Jeffers's deepest affinity is with W. S. Merwin and Gary Snyder because they are closest to sharing his "inhumanist" vision that the earth would be better without the polluting, self-conscious presence of mankind. Neal Bowers's "Jeffers and Merwin: The World Beyond Words" (pp. 11–26) begins with a denunciation of the view of the world as a text, "merely a human extension, subject to the vagaries of human thought and language," which he attributes not only to critics but poets like Frost: "nature is an allegorical mirror, as in Frost's work, or an echo of one's own pathetic condition." This comment is unfair to Frost, as is the equally harsh comment that the Sierra Club has made Jeffers its "coffee-table poet, aligning the Carmel recluse with a stewardship" he would have despised. But Bowers makes a strong case for Jeffers's influence on Merwin's poetry through analyzing Merwin's allusions to "trees wearing names that are not their own" and the poet's regret that our speech lacks a "noun for standing in mist by a haunted tree/the verb for I." Both poets see the danger of art affirming the dominance of human perception.

Patrick D. Murphy's "Robinson Jeffers, Gary Snyder, and the Problem of Civilization" (pp. 93–107) discusses a similar contrast between poets, but makes a more searching criticism of Jeffers. He sees a direct response to Jeffers in Snyder's "T-2 Tanker Blues": "I will not cry Inhuman & think that makes us small and nature/great, we are enough, and as we are." He attributes the bleakness of Jeffers's philosophy to his remaining "trapped" in Western metaphysics (as opposed to Snyder's absorption of Zen) and his lack of "sufficient community practice outside of the arts by which to test his own appraisals of human immaturity and evolutionary potential."

Among the moderns, Jeffers has the least affinity with Eliot and the most with Lawrence. In Mary McCormack's "The Women of Robinson Jeffers and T. S. Eliot: Mythical Parallels in 'Give Your Heart to the Hawks' and *The Family Reunion*" (pp. 135–45) the parallels are of little interest because so little is made of the antipathy (had they cared to read each other) between their worldviews. (Jeffers's hostility to Christianity is considered in Wayne Cox's "Robinson Jeffers and the Conflict of Christianity" [pp. 122–34].) Gilbert Allen's "Passionate Detachment in the Lyrics of Jeffers and Yeats" (pp. 60–68) shows that the poets of Tor House and Thoor Ballylee are considerably different despite the elemental joy and fierce hatred expressed in their works: "For Yeats . . . the past is cultural; for Jeffers, the past is geological." Jeffers is not, like Yeats, a romantic absorbed in his own creative perception of nature and personal involvement in history. In " 'Enter and Possess': Jeffers, Frost, and the Borders of the Self" (pp. 69–82) Kyle Norwood notes that both poets portray isolated figures "confronting the incommensurable." But Frost does not have Jeffers's thirst for the absolute and disdain for the self in contrast to a divine Other. The best of these comparative essays is Calvin Bedient's "Robinson Jeffers, D. H. Lawrence, and the Erotic Sublime" (pp. 160–81). As in the comparison with Frost, Jeffers appears unsympathetically fierce in comparison with Lawrence, whose "feeling for beauty, like his feeling for life, is sweeter" and who is "less a devotee of divine 'desolation.' " Bedient's comparison of Jeffers's "Roan Stallion" with Lawrence's novella *St. Mawr* is the kind of specific, comparative criticism Jeffers's work needs. The volume also contains a panel discussion among Charles Altieri, Terence Diggory, Albert Gelpi, and James E. Miller, Jr. (pp. 182–202) that shows how Jeffers's sense of community (or lack of it) distinguishes him from other modernists. Readers of modern poetry who have neglected Jeffers's work need to fill this gap, and this volume should be the companion to their reading.

v Robert Penn Warren

In a 1976 interview Warren described himself as a "yearner" rather than a religious person. Although Warren's self-description is calculated modesty, he indeed appears no more than a "yearner" in Robert S. Koppelman's *Robert Penn Warren's Modernist Spirituality* (Missouri). Koppelman's conception of "Modernist spirituality" is entirely too vague. David Jarraway's *Wallace Stevens and the Question of Belief* (see *ALS 1993*, pp. 281–82) may have overwhelmed the reader with references to Heidegger, Levinas, and Kierkegaard, but he put Stevens's modernist spirituality in perspective with other religious thinkers. Koppelman simply accepts Warren's account of his spiritual development at face value. His analysis of how Warren's life as a teacher and his theories of metaphor contributed to his spiritual quest is interesting, and he perceptively relates Warren's poetry to his novels. However, this is an exposition of Warren's ideas rather than a critical study. Since Warren had a religious temperament but a scientific background, he tried to believe "in redemption through engagement with literature and participation in the world." Warren thus appears, in Koppelman's account, to develop an aesthetic and not a modernist sensibility like Stevens's, who is never mentioned in the book despite dealing with the same spiritual and poetic issues. Koppelman's description of Warren's sensibility as "based on the organic unity of nature and the significance of events" gives us a romantic poet who feels that time and history are connected. Romanticism and aestheticism then combine in Warren's belief that Christianity is "a great Spiritual metaphor." When Koppelman refers to this as a "spiritual aesthetic," he does not consider the implications of his paradoxical term. One does not need Kierkegaard to realize that the two words involve different orders of thought that are not as reconcilable as Koppelman implies. The book briefly alludes to the influence of William James but does not use James to clarify the terms Warren might have used to justify his religious ambivalence. Koppelman's discussion of Joseph Conrad's "necessary lie" is similarly undeveloped. If Warren is indeed a poet to rank with Moore, Williams, or Stevens, his critics need to write books that are more comparative and critical.

In a special issue of *MissQ* devoted to Warren, Victor Strandberg's "Robert Penn Warren and the Classical Tradition" (48: 17–28) addresses similar issues to those in Koppelman's book. He notes that the Christian spiritual patterns (such as the Fall and redemption) and allusions in his work may suggest that Warren is "an essentially Christian writer." However, most of the Christian allusions are to the Old Testament, and his classical allusions seem more respectful and influential. Strandberg traces this influence to Warren's father, who was a trained classicist, indifferent to religion but committed to classical qualities of restraint and self-discipline. Strandberg concludes that Warren's "ethics were stoic, his metaphysics pantheistic." Nothing "modernist" here!

Four of the essays in *MissQ* focus on Warren's poetry. Randolph Paul Runyon's "Repeating the 'Implacable Monotone' in Thirty-Six Poems" (48: 39–56) analyzes the intricate sound patterns in Warren's first volume, *Thirty-Six Poems* (1935), and shows how the patterns are developed in subsequent volumes. Mark D. Miller's "Faith in Good Works: The Salvation of Robert Penn Warren" (48: 57–72) is concerned with the spiritual "drought" Warren suffered from 1942 until 1952, during which he could not finish a lyric poem. Miller argues that the "drought" years were filled for Warren with a search for a myth that would anchor his poems and give them significance in his own eyes. As the article's title indicates, an essentially Christian pattern of guilt and redemption gave Warren the necessary framework. Both Runyon and Miller analyze this drought and accept Warren's own explanation that, in personal terms, it was broken during the time he spent in Italy after his remarriage and birth of his two children. However, in "Racism and the Personal Past in Robert Penn Warren" (48: 73–82) James A. Perkins contends that Warren's travels through the South to research his books *Segregation* and *Who Speaks for the Negro?* were equally important in restoring his inspiration. His list of the 31 poems Warren began after conducting the interviews for these books all deal with childhood memories of the South. Perkins concludes that Warren's work on the race question "led him to an emotional reconciliation with the South and allowed him to recover his childhood memories as a subject for poetry." Finally, Lesa Carnes Corrigan's "Snapshots of Audubon: Photographic Perspectives from Eudora

Welty and Robert Penn Warren" (48: 83–92) shows that the imagistic techniques in Warren's *Audubon: A Vision* were inspired not only by Welty's story "A Still Moment," but also by her reflections on the way photography captures an image.

vi H.D. (Hilda Doolittle)

Helen Sword's *Engendering Inspiration: Visionary Strategies in Rilke, Lawrence, and H.D.* (Michigan) also raises questions of authority. Although the "adoption of a prophetic, visionary stance has offered a standard means to poetic authority," it paradoxically implies "supreme self-effacement." Sword cites the cases of Moore and Philip Larkin to explore the paradox that in avoiding any appeal to the visionary the "omission in itself testifies to the influence and importance of the prophetic paradigm." This book also raises gender questions because male poets such as Eliot, Crane, and Yeats have been called "religious" or "prophetic" whereas H.D.'s visionary quality has too often been dismissed as "escapist."

Sword's fascinating analysis of H.D.'s 20-year process of absorbing her visionary experiences in Greece, as well as her response to events as "real" as the London blitz in *Trilogy,* corrects the misinterpretations of her visionary qualities. H.D.'s early adoption of Apollo as a patron signifies her commitment to rationality as well as inspiration, and Sword's analysis of her psychoanalysis with Freud emphasizes the same commitment. In H.D.'s later poetry, Sword describes the way her visionary experiences, including her seances during World War II, exhausted her and led her to adopt a more contemplative mystical mode in *Helen in Egypt.* Sword's treatment of H.D.'s style is far subtler than Hogue's (see below), but she makes the similar point that H.D. viewed language "as an unending play of significations." Sword's distinctions among prophetic, ritual, poetic, and erotic modes in H.D. is an important contribution to understanding her poetry, which is often described as having little variety; and she does a service to H.D.'s reputation by putting her in context with Rilke and Lawrence as visionary poets "caught between power and impotence, between desire and danger."

In *Ritual and Experiment in Modern Poetry* (St. Martin's) Jacob Korg argues that both ritual and experiment explore the unknown, but ritual "sets aside the problem of cognition and adopts an attitude of unquestioning belief, while experiment proposes to penetrate and illuminate the unknown." He shows that poets may tend toward one quality or another or express both poles. His conclusion about H.D., which is predictable in terms of his argument but nevertheless overstated, is that "the conjunction of religious emotion and new poetic techniques produced a more unified, more plausible merging of the ritual and experimental spirits in poetry than that achieved by any of H.D.'s contemporaries." In her chapter "Equi/Vocations: H.D.'s Demasculinization of the Subject in *Helen in Egypt*" in *Scheming Women* (pp. 117–57) Cynthia Hogue claims that "for H.D., metaphor represents a masculinist drive to mastery" and attempts to show that H.D. subverts "metaphoric structure" through "metonymic play." Yet it seems obvious that she uses metaphor as frequently as any poet and that Hogue's claim that H.D. has created a "whole new poetry" is inflated. However, her analysis of H.D.'s rewriting of the Helen myth and the epic form in her late poem *Helen in Egypt* is valuable. Finally, a special issue of *Sagetrieb* (14, i–ii) contains three interesting articles on H.D.'s poetic style: William Wenthe's " 'The Hieratic Dance' ": Prosody and the Unconscious in H.D.'s Poetry" (pp. 113–40), Lawrence H. McCauley's "The Wail Cannot Di-Jest Me: Puns, Poetry, and Language in H.D.'s *Trilogy*" (pp. 141–60), and Scott Boehnen's " 'H.D., War Poet' and the 'Language Fantasy' of *Trilogy*". (pp. 179–200), as well as two articles on *Helen in Egypt*. Finally, Burton Hatlen's "The Imagist Poetic of H.D.'s Sea Garden" (*Paideuma* 24, ii–iii: 107–30) gives an important reconsideration of H.D.'s early work by contending that Imagism implied not an impressionistic, passive apprehension of the world but a dynamic, phenomenological one. Finally, my own chapter in *Modernist Alchemy* places her occult or visionary poetry in context with poetic occultism from Yeats and Pound to Sylvia Plath and James Merrill.

vii Edna St. Vincent Millay

Parts 1 and 2 of Diane P. Freedman's *Millay at 100: A Critical Reappraisal* (So. Ill.) consider why Millay is widely read yet critically obscure and give a "revisionary perspective" on the poetry, especially its treatment of "women in love and children beloved." Parts 3 and 4 consider the theme of time and Millay's "multiple constructions of identity" in her fiction. Jo Ellen Green Kaiser's "Displaced Modernism: Millay and the Triumph of

Sentimentality" (pp. 27–40) suggests that Millay is not a modernist like Woolf, H.D., or Stein but that her "very feminine sentimental ideology made it a superior position in the early twentieth century for effecting political change." In "Uncanny Millay" (pp. 3–26) Suzanne Clark says that Millay challenges the "gendered identity assumed by the modernist aesthetic." Millay's impersonality, unlike Eliot's (and like Moore's), involves an "ordinary embodied self." Part 3 contains still more essays on Millay's figuration of the body and three essays on the sonnets. The comparative technique of Marilyn May Lombardi's "Vampirism and Translation" (pp. 130–41) on the influence of French and English decadence produces one of the livelier pieces. In " 'Directions for Using the Empress': Millay's Supreme Fiction(s)" (pp. 163–81) Sandra M. Gilbert cites Woolf, Dorothy Parker, Louise Bogan, and Marilyn Monroe (as the inventor of her "MM" persona) in her analysis of Millay's not wholly successful attempt to "use the artifice of 'femininity' without being used by it." Millay's sonnets receive yet more attention in Irene R. Fairley's "Edna St. Vincent Millay's Gendered Language and Form: 'Sonnets from an Ungrafted Tree' " (*Style* 29: 58–75), which argues that Millay's poetic language is at its imaginative best in these poems as she achieves a reflective style through the use of time jumps, dreamlike associations, and ellipses that "capture the rhythm of thought."

viii Langston Hughes

Langston Hughes: The Man, His Art, and His Continuing Influence, ed. C. James Trotman and Emery Wimbish, Jr. (Garland), focuses on Hughes's fiction, but three essays explore the influence of the blues on his poetry. Steven C. Tracy's "Langston Hughes: Poetry, Blues, and Gospel" (pp. 51–61) explains that Hughes's love of the blues was not characteristic of writers like Alain Locke, James Weldon Johnson, and W. E. B. Du Bois, who preferred the more respectable spirituals. It was thus Hughes, as Cheryl A. Wall recounts in "Whose Sweet Angel Child? Blues Women, Langston Hughes, and Writing During the Harlem Renaissance" (pp. 37–50), who produced the first characterization of a blues singer in American fiction. Inspired by Ma Rainey and Bessie Smith, Hughes's blues woman has a moral and spiritual power that is entirely secular and based on a devotion to freedom rather than Christianity. In "Langston Hughes's *Nigger Heaven Blues*" (pp. 87–96) Bruce Kellner tells the remarkable story of how Hughes helped Carl Van Vechten avoid having his novel *Nigger Heaven* suppressed for its unauthorized use of popular blues songs by writing 16 lyrics that matched both Van Vechten's narrative and the censored space on the printer's plates.

ix E. E. Cummings

Martin Heusser's "The Visual Rhetoric of e. e. cummings' 'poempictures' " (*W&I* 11: 16–30) and Michael Webster's "E. E. Cummings: Romantic Ideology and Technique" in *Reading Visual Poetry after Futurism* (Peter Lang, pp. 111–40) usefully focus on Cummings as both a visual and verbal artist. Heusser distinguishes three types of "poempicture": iconic or mimetic poems in the manner of "shaped poetry"; poems in which the typography makes an aesthetic, purely formal pattern; and "catabolic" poems where the "disintegrative impulse" reveals a strain of Dadaism. The essay contains a perceptive analysis of Cummings's poempicture "t,h;r:u;s,h;e:s." (Incidentally, by writing "e. e. cummings" Heusser continues the mistaken folklore that Cummings preferred the lowercase spelling.) Webster illuminates Cummings's poetry by placing him in context with other "visual" poets such as F. T. Marinetti, Apollinaire, and Kurt Schwitters. He defends Cummings from the critics who dismiss poetry written for the "eye" alone by showing that he shared a rich avant-garde tradition which existed coherently with his romantic individualism. Although Cummings was influenced by the Futurist disparagement of syntax and punctuation, Webster shows that he manipulated spelling, syntax, and punctuation to achieve an iconic design; and unlike Kurt Schwitters, he never wrote nonrepresentational poetry. *Spring* is full of excellent material generated by last year's centennial conferences, including Milton A. Cohen's "Disparate Twins: Spontaneity in Cummings' Poetry and Painting" (4: 83–94).

x W. H. Auden

The Auden chapter (pp. 29–89) in Katy Aisenberg's *Ravishing Images: Ekphrasis in the Poetry and Prose of William Wordsworth, W. H. Auden and Philip Larkin* (Peter Lang) draws on the work of W. J. T. Mitchell to question the notion that the visual allows a privileged or even unmediated view of the truth. It is his iconophilic critics, not Auden, who claim that his visual approach to experience has a special authority. Although

"Musée Des Beaux Arts" is praised as a precise and masterly poem, Aisenberg maintains that it is really "a careful illustration of the danger of pretending to have complete mastery or sympathetic understanding."

"In Solitude, for Company": W. H. Auden After 1940: Unpublished Prose and Recent Criticism, ed. Katherine Bucknell and Nicholas Jenkins (Clarendon), contains a mix of criticism, bibliography, reminiscence, and primary materials. Of the three unpublished essays by Auden, the most interesting is the 1971 "Phantasy and Reality in Poetry" (pp. 177–96). The biographical section consists of the amusing and frank letters Auden wrote from 1941 until 1973 to James and Tania Stern (pp. 31–109) and a memoir by the Austrian writer Stella Musulin (pp. 207–23) about Auden's life in Kirchstetten and the awkward circumstances surrounding his funeral. The criticism includes articles on "For the Time Being," a symposium on "In Praise of Limestone," and Ian Sansom's " 'Flouting Papa' " (pp. 273–87), on Randall Jarrell's decidedly Oedipal literary relationship with Auden. *Auden* by Richard Davenport-Hines (Pantheon) is well-researched and highly readable. His accounts of Auden's relationships with his father, his brother John, Christopher Isherwood, and Chester Kallman are especially interesting. According to Davenport-Hines, Auden's homosexuality was the key to his life, and he gives an interesting account of Auden's ambivalence about gay life. In Richard R. Bozorth's " 'But Who Would Get It?': Auden and the Codes of Poetry and Desire" (*ELH* 62: 709–27) Auden's description of poetry as a "game of knowledge" is reinterpreted as "an activity of coding." As a gay poet, Auden subtly addresses the conflicts of repression and liberation, public and private, speakable and unspeakable, and knowledge and ignorance.

xi Robert Frost

Relatively little criticism of Frost appeared this year, but his readers will welcome Jeffrey S. Cramer's *Robert Frost Among His Poems: A Literary Companion to the Poet's Own Biographical Contexts and Associations* (McFarland) and the Library of America's *Robert Frost: Collected Poems, Prose, and Plays,* selected and annotated by Richard Poirier and Mark Richardson. Cramer's commentary places each poem (and dates it) in the "biographical, historical and geographical context of his life and time" as well as annotating words and phrases. He also provides a bibliography, and sometimes entire texts, of Frost's uncollected and unpublished poetry. The Library of America's Frost volume contains *Complete Poems* and *In the Clearing* as well as a selection of 94 unpublished poems, including 17 that are printed for the first time. Also included are three plays and a selection of 88 lectures, essays, stories, and letters that give a thorough picture of Frost's accomplishments as a prose writer. William Logan's essay on "The Other Other Frost" (*New C* 13, x:21–34) is simply a view of the saturnine Frost identified by Randall Jarrell and Lionel Trilling through poems that are not often chosen by anthologists. Although it has nothing new to say, it is a fine appreciation and demonstrates that poets like Frost would seem as great even if the public knew them through a wholly different set of poems. The question of how a poet can claim authority arises in Mark Richardson's "Believing in Robert Frost: A Study of Authority in His Poetics" (*TSLL* 37: 445–74), and Frost's view of literary immortality is considered in Lewis Klausner's "Frost's Claims to Immortality: The Bones of Bequest" (*SWR* 80: 137–48). John Zubizarreta uses Octavio Paz's 1945 interview with Frost as a place to start comparing the works of the two poets in "Octavio Paz and Robert Frost" (*CL* 47: 235–50). The year's best essay on any poet is Derek Walcott's review, "The Road Taken," of the Library of America volume (*NRep,* 27 Nov., pp. 29–36). Written for a general reader, it is a condensed survey of Frost's career that is brilliant with vivid phrases, insights into Frost's personae, perceptive criticisms of his poetic forms and rhythms, and striking comparisons of Frost with other poets (such as Jeffers). His comments on Frost as an "autocratic" and not a democratic poet and as an "icon of Yankee values" are sharp but also, as in his analysis of a racist passage in a letter, both realistic and sympathetic.

xii Witter Bynner and Richard Wilbur

Two books by James Kraft on Witter Bynner give us a comprehensive look at this minor but appealing American poet: *Who Is Witter Bynner? A Biography* and *The Selected Witter Bynner; Poems, Plays, Translations, Prose, and Letters* (New Mexico). His reputation rests on the poems alone, but the best of them are unoriginal translations from the Chinese or lyrics he wrote as a member of the Spectra School, which was a spoof on Imagism.

Rodney Stenning Edgecombe's *A Reader's Guide to the Poetry of Richard Wilbur* (Alabama) emphasizes Wilbur's "quarrel with Poe" about the balance of the physical and spiritual in human nature and the poet's respect for the local and native materials that Wilbur shares with William Carlos Williams. Both themes are intelligently developed, but it is impossible to read through this work. As Edgecomb says, one needs Wilbur's *New and Collected Poems* at hand as one reads the analyses; indeed, this book should be next to Wilbur's poems on the bookshelf. Philip White's "'Walking to Sleep' and Richard Wilbur's Quest for a Rational Imagination" (*TCL* 41: 249–65) also takes up the "quarrel with Poe" in a sensitive reading of "Walking to Sleep" as a modern version of a Romantic "crisis poem."

xiii General Studies

The thesis of William Doreski's *The Modern Voice in American Poetry* is that our poetry has been shaped not so much by the development of the lyric from its Romantic roots as by "historical and dialogic modes of discourse." He finds in American poets a return to "more interdiscursive lyric, monologic, and dialogic forms . . . to expand the rhetorical range of their poetics." Although the thesis is unoriginal, the rhetorical readings of individual authors are valuable. He argues that whereas Frost expands the range of dramatic monologue and dialogue, Stevens develops a rhetoric untainted by European tradition, Williams grounds the poem in a compressed, idiomatic speech, and Moore expresses a "passion for found speech, the unmediated rhetorical effect." This book is distinguished for its readings of poems like Frost's "Directive," Williams's "Brilliant Sad Sun," and Moore's "Black Earth" than for its thesis about American poetry.

In comparison to the essay on Moore reviewed earlier, the other essays in *American Poetry: The Modernist Ideal* are valuable only to new readers or students of poetry. The authors, all but one of them English, emphasize the specifically American poetic qualities, but otherwise the essays vary widely in approach and quality. Pat Righelato on Stevens (pp. 81–92) is clearly focused on the Transcendental roots of his poetry, and Brian Docherty's useful chapter on Cummings (pp. 120–30) emphasizes his New England heritage. David Seed's emphasis on H.D.'s transcendentalism (pp. 10–27) registers an important reservation to the conception of H.D. as an Imagist.

Alan Golding's *From Outlaw to Classic* not only clarifies the way canons are made, but also how the taste of America's poetry-reading public has been formed. He admits the attractiveness of the poet-centered model of canon formation in which great poets welcome new

ones to their fold; but the importance of the institutional model is clear
from the role of anthologies, textbooks, and universities that, after all,
form the taste of the established poets. Chapter 2 on "Poets Canonizing
Poets: John Berryman's 'Homage to Mistress Bradstreet' " and chapter 3
on "The New Criticism and American Poetry in the Academy" are
especially relevant to the poets covered in this chapter. Golding's analysis
of *The Harvard Book of Contemporary Poetry* and *The Norton Anthology of
Modern Poetry* is a fascinating revelation of cultural predispositions. He
also demonstrates that Brooks and Warren's emphasis on metrical forms
in *Understanding Poetry* led to the work's preponderance of Frost and
neglect of Williams. Golding's book helps us understand the current
struggles in English departments where scholars, critics, creative writers,
and theorists justify their existence by defending their canons.

University of Missouri, Columbia

18 Poetry: The 1940s to the Present

Lorenzo Thomas

There is a verse in an old Bob Dylan song that describes Ezra Pound and T. S. Eliot arguing over some important matter of poetics while Calypso singers—masters of a genuinely extemporaneous poetry—laugh at the two High Modernists. Dylan delivered these lines with a delightful sneer of superiority, but his fictive situation is not unlike the critical concerns that surfaced this year. In addition to studies of individual poets (with Elizabeth Bishop, Gwendolyn Brooks, and John Ashbery garnering a great deal of attention) two complementary and serious issues—usually referred to as "canon formation" and "identity politics"—were the focus of much critical debate.

i The State of the Art

The issue of the literary canon, much discussed in the mid-1980s, has been revisited primarily because of the appearance of a number of new poetry anthologies—some of them intended for classroom use and others aimed at the general public. Critics have raised serious questions about how and why particular works become known as "great poems" or are authorized for classroom study. Alan Golding's *From Outlaw to Classic* is an important contribution to this discussion. Golding carefully identifies two current ideas about canon formation: one view suggests that critics, teachers, and the editors of anthologies create a canon primarily for political reasons, which are then disguised by claiming "intrinsic value" for the works selected; another view is that poets create canons through the practice of allusion and imitation. Golding shows that even if "poets canonizing poets" is accepted as a counterforce to the academy, it also is another way to hide the hand of the anthologist. Golding's chapter on anthologies—from Samuel Kettell's *Specimens of American Poetry* (1829) to the most recent Norton volumes—offers specific historical evaluations that are too often lacking from discussions that seem increasingly to rely on the demographics of which poets are "in" or "excluded." Other chapters trace the influence of the New Critics and discuss how "in the current treatment of Language writing we are seeing the canonization of an avant-garde in progress." Golding's view that "the goal for any avant-garde [is] not to avoid commodification or institutionalization so much as to use it" will certainly inspire vigorous debate.

Outspokenly acerbic, Jed Rasula weighs in with *The American Poetry Wax Museum: Reality Effects, 1940–1990* (NCTE) and "The Empire's New Clothes: Anthologizing American Poetry in the 1990s" (*AmLH* 7: 261–83). In his critical history Rasula describes how the New Critics and modernism devolved into a stultifying postwar conformity, and he declares that more recent developments reveal "a spectacle of confusion and dismay." While he feels that the most exciting poetry of the 1980s and '90s has been produced by the Language poets, he charges that this work has been ignored by anthologists. What Rasula terms our "official verse culture" is, he asserts, based on a "perpetuation of the familiar . . . every bit as pervasive in the purportedly highbrow world of the poetry anthology as it is in the lowbrow one of sitcom." Hank Lazer's essay "Anthologies, Poetry, and Postmodernism" (*ConL* 36: 362–83) argues that recent anthologies—some of which are widely adopted as textbooks—do not accurately represent the rich variety of contemporary poetic production. "An irony worth pondering," he writes, "is that under the rubric of diversity and difference, we are presented with poetry that extends the hegemony of a predominantly white, mainstream, highly professionalized and intensely regulated writing practice."

The structural constraints on writers and readers imposed by the mechanics of literary publishing and distribution is the topic of Charles Bernstein's "Provisional Institutions: Alternative Presses and Poetic Innovation" (*ArQ* 51, i: 133–46). He notes that the *New Yorker's* 750,000 readers and small press editions of 2,000 copies are as important as poetic theories in determining the state of the art. Joe David Bellamy also discusses the protocols of literary publishing and the role of the universities in *Literary Luxuries: American Writing at the End of the Millenium* (Missouri). Concerned particularly with the impact of creative writing courses, Bellamy does not require that system to be a "farm team" for great poets. Such courses, he argues, provide opportunities for "self-discovery and self-creation" that are otherwise lacking in our higher education curriculum. Poets who teach such courses, and workshops at the many writers' conferences held each summer, are represented in *Writing It Down for James: Writers on Life and Craft,* ed. Kurt Brown (Beacon). Among those who share their experiences and ideas are John Malcolm Brinnin, Ruth Whitman, M. Nourbese Philip, Pattiann Rogers, and Edward Hirsch.

Ross Talarico's unusual *Spreading the Word: Poetry and the Survival of Community in America* (Duke) goes further than the lectures collected in *Writing It Down for James.* Each of Talarico's chapters include writing strategies developed in poetry workshops open to the general public that he conducted in Rochester, New York. Talarico's purpose in this book is much more ambitious than approaches to writing, however. Walt Whitman believed that "to have great poets, there must be great audiences, too"; but the citizens that Talarico meets in his travels across the United States "didn't really know what poetry is, let alone what a poet might be." This problem, he suggests, is a reflection of a deeper cultural syndrome that he calls "deliteracy." American society, he writes, "rewards those who use language to deceive others, and abandons those who use it in attempts to enlighten." Talarico argues in the end that only active popular participation in poetry—on every level of production and appreciation—can remedy this situation.

ii General Studies

The ancients thought of poetry as one of the magic arts, and Timothy Materer examines some survivals of this attitude in the fascinating *Modernist Alchemy.* Chapters are devoted to Robert Duncan, Sylvia Plath, and James Merrill, among others. Materer makes it clear that interest in "the supernatural" is not synonymous with occult studies and that the use of occult lore by poets does not always indicate the absence of skepticism. *Modernist Alchemy* is both learned and lucid, and its usefulness to serious readers of 20th-century American poetry is not as limited as the title might suggest. Materer points out, for example, that Duncan employs alchemy as metaphor much as C. G. Jung did, that Plath's experiments with spiritualism indicate a serious religious yearning, and that Merrill's *The Changing Light at Sandover* is an impressive exploration of the unconscious mind. *Modernist Alchemy* should enhance the study of any of these poets.

That poetry may sometimes be necessary—despite William Carlos

Williams's famous statement—is the theme of several articles. In "Metaphors in Poems About AIDS" (*CimR* 112: 127–37) Beret E. Strong argues that when love and death have become "a literal equation," poets are pressed to find new formulations to offer perception, solace, and constructive alarm. Strong discusses poems by Thom Gunn, Miller Williams, Robert Creeley, Felice Picano, Mark Doty, and several others. Mindful of the topic's importance, she is not shy about identifying some metaphors as redemptive and others as inadequate. In "The State You Are Entering: Depression and Contemporary Poetry" (*NER* 17: 110–23) David Wojahn considers how the melancholia of the ancients became a clinical malady for the "middle generation" of poets—Robert Lowell, Plath, John Berryman, Randall Jarrell, and Anne Sexton. "Throughout the 1960s," he writes, "poems about psychiatric hospitalizations are about as ubiquitous as bellbottoms and lava lamps—and the genre today seems almost as dated." Wojahn's comments on poems by Theodore Roethke and Frederick Seidel are particularly informative.

"The Smile of Accomplishment: Sylvia Plath's Ambition" (*IowaR* 25, i: 1–28) is Patricia Hampl's examination of the development of a young poet. That Plath was ambitious is well-known, but she was also, as Hampl shows, a young woman who was uncertain "how high I could set my goals." Commenting on passages from Plath's journals and poems, Hampl also explains how Plath served as an inspiration for her own youthful desire to "trust poetry."

One of the year's best offerings, the excellent and useful *American Poetry: The Modernist Ideal* includes brief introductions to 15 poets, including Kenneth Rexroth, Frank O'Hara, Allen Ginsberg, Charles Olson, Edward Dorn, Creeley, and Denise Levertov. Editors Clive Bloom and Brian Docherty have assembled a distinguished group of scholars to write the chapters.

iii Major Voices: Robert Lowell and Elizabeth Bishop

Richard Tillinghast's "Robert Lowell on Native Ground" (*VQR* 71: 86–100), a memoir of his first meeting with the poet as a Harvard student in 1962, offers a pleasant evocation of Lowell's humor and the creative generosity he bestowed on his students. As a writing teacher, Lowell "transmitted a total dedication to the effort of laying words down on the page like a fresh coat of paint." Elsewhere, Tillinghast considers the controversy surrounding Lowell's lack of decorum (or discretion) regarding personal correspondence in "Robert Lowell's *The Dolphin*—'Ransacking My Bags of Dust for Silver Spoons' " (*SCR* 27, i–ii: 287–94). Those who have enjoyed Tillinghast's frequent appearances in journals will welcome the publication of his *Robert Lowell: Damaged Grandeur* (Michigan). Also recommended is Henry Hart's *Robert Lowell and the Sublime* (Syracuse). David Laskin's *A Common Life* includes a study of the "passionate admiration for each other's works" that defined the relationship of Lowell and Elizabeth Bishop. In decorously readable prose, Laskin describes how each poet challenged, inspired, and sometimes annoyed the other. It is praise to point out that some of Laskin's conclusions might be sensational in the hands of a less gifted writer.

Joseph Epstein in "Elizabeth Bishop: Never a Bridesmaid" (*HudR* 48: 34–52) reexamines the poet's success and concludes that Bishop was an excellent "caretaker of her career," ever alert to the rhyming ratio of supply and demand. Bishop was not a prolific writer, and Epstein suggests another possible reason for her reticence: "An insane mother, an incipient drinking problem, worry about her own sexual proclivities—this was rather heavy baggage for a young woman to carry around." This statement is offered as a summary of Epstein's reading of available biographies rather than a lapse of gallantry. He now believes that serious critics of her poetry, her "often cool and well-made verbal contraptions," will have to confront these facts. Unimpressed by most recent Bishop criticism, Epstein depicts her as a brave person and a minor poet.

Facing the unpleasant facts of Bishop's life, and showing how she transmuted them into art, is precisely the approach taken by Marilyn May Lombardi in *The Body and the Song: Elizabeth Bishop's Poetics* (So. Ill.). The metrical precision of Bishop's poetic forms, says Lombardi, "are her costumes, sensible fashions to clothe her unorthodoxy." Based on extensive research in unpublished archival materials, Lombardi's impressive study includes chapters that focus on Bishop's sense of self and use of literary models, but Lombardi depends on the tools of intelligent and empathetic literary criticism and eschews reliance on formal psychoanalytic theory. An interesting contribution is Lombardi's exploration (pp. 165–91) of the relationship of Bishop's work to that of visual artists such as Leonor Fini, Max Ernst, and other surrealists. Pointing out analogies between Bishop's fascination with the Sears Roebuck catalog and her delight in Joseph Cornell's three-dimensional collage, Lombardi provides yet another avenue for readers to enjoy the breathtaking "met-

onymic substitutions" characteristic of Bishop's poems. James Longenbach's fine essay "Elizabeth Bishop's Social Conscience" (*ELH* 62:
467–86) depicts the multiple anxieties that Bishop inspired in younger
writers such as Adrienne Rich, but he also explains that Bishop was never
quite what others thought she was. Longenbach argues that Bishop was
aware of the possibility of being intimidated by her own reputation,
which she struggled against by maintaining an interest in politics and
"social problems" that she never expressed overtly in her poems. Longenbach presents a balanced and informative reading of Bishop's poems and
letters, giving a clear sense of what it cost her to maintain her "painful
reticence." Shira Wolosky in "Representing Other Voices: Rhetorical
Perspective in Elizabeth Bishop" (*Style* 29: 1–15) employs a Bakhtinian approach that provides insight into poems such as "Songs for a Colored Singer," "Manuelzhino," and others that express Bishop's social
awareness.

   Becoming Canonical in American Poetry, Timothy Morris's finely
nuanced and provocative critique of feminist theory, includes a chapter
describing how Bishop graduated from being "a subset" of Marianne
Moore to the status of a major poet. "Constraint and Recuperation in the
Early Reception of Elizabeth Bishop" (pp. 104–30) suggests that this
"potentially subversive" poet—the phrase is a term of approval in this
text—has been read differently since her death in 1979 as much because
of changes in the nation's sociopolitical climate as because of the opinion
of literary critics. Nonetheless, Morris warns that Bishop's work presents
persistent difficulties for those who desire to "process her image into the
mold of Whitmanic hero." Jeffrey Powers-Beck in "'Time to Plant
Tears': Elizabeth Bishop's Seminary of Tears" (*SoAR* 60, iv: 69–87)
considers the influence of poems by George Herbert and Gerard Manley
Hopkins on Bishop's attempts to achieve "poetic consolation," and a
number of articles on Bishop's affinities to Wallace Stevens appear in
WSJour (19, ii). Contributors there include Celeste Goodridge, George
S. Lensing, and Barbara Page.

   In the tradition of Walter Savage Landor, Laurence Stapleton's *Some
Poets and Their Resources: The Future Agenda* (Univ. Press) presents
imaginary conversations between two "common readers" on eight 19th-
and 20th-century writers. His final chapter (pp. 113–42) finds Stapleton's
two friends discussing Seamus Heaney, Elizabeth Bishop, Richard Wilbur, and "the poet's awareness of man's place in nature [and] the integrity

of the creative process." Those who are feeling overtaxed by the rigorous theoretical approach (and acrimony) of much recent criticism might find refreshment here.

iv Richard Wilbur, James Merrill, Gwendolyn Brooks

An issue of *C&L* (42, iv) is devoted to Richard Wilbur and includes an interview with the poet by Jewel Spears Brooker. Contributors of critical essays include Cleanth Brooks, Clara Claiborne Park, Bruce Michelson, and Marjorie Scheidt Payne, who notes Wilbur's affinities to Milton, Dante, and C. S. Lewis. In the world of Wilbur's poems, says Michelson, religious faith is not a facile pose. "Wilbur's poems," he writes, "enact a reality where experience is what it is—sensory, psychological, spiritual— and where nothing is shunned by the mind, Christianized or not." A useful addition to Wilbur studies is Rodney Stenning Edgecombe's *A Reader's Guide to the Poetry of Richard Wilbur* (Alabama).

James Merrill's death this year occasioned the expected outpouring of tributes, but the appreciations offered by Rachel Hadas, Richard Kenney, Helen Vendler, Stephen Yenser, and Steven Meyer at a Washington University symposium were a bouquet presented before Merrill's transition. The transcript of the panel is found in "James Merrill: A Life in Writing" (*SWR* 80: 159–85). Stephen Yenser's "James Merrill: His Poetry and the Age" (*SWR* 80: 186–204) views the poet's career and locates him among his contemporaries. Yenser describes a protean Merrill: "he disseminates multitudes; his work demolishes classifications and is therefore fundamentally American." Along the way, Yenser offers useful comments on a number of other poets. While W. H. Auden appears in *The Changing Light at Sandover,* summoned by Merrill's ouija board, Jeffrey Donaldson is content to use more ordinary methods of inquiry to trace Merrill's allusions to Auden's "Letter to Lord Byron" (1936) and the libretto—written with Chester Kallman—for Igor Stravinsky's *The Rake's Progress* (1951). Donaldson accomplishes this splendidly in "The Company Poets Keep: Allusion, Echo and the Question of Who Is Listening in W. H. Auden and James Merrill" (*ConL* 36: 35–57), suggesting that both poets talk to their colleagues in another dimension, partly because of an uncertainty regarding the attention of an audience here and now.

Stephen Caldwell Wright's edited *On Gwendolyn Brooks: Reliant Contemplation* (Michigan) collects reviews and critical essays covering every aspect of the poet's career from 1945 to the present. It is interesting to compare Rolfe Humphries's early hesitancy with recent criticism such as Joyce Ann Joyce's "The Poetry of Gwendolyn Brooks: An Afrocentric Exploration" (pp. 246–53) or Henry Taylor's "Gwendolyn Brooks: An Essential Sanity" (pp. 245–75). Other critics represented here include M. L. Rosenthal, George E. Kent, Haki R. Madhubuti, Robert Farnsworth, Houston A. Baker, Jr., and R. Baxter Miller. Brooks's *Annie Allen* (1949), which received the Pulitzer Prize, is given an impressively rigorous postmodernist reading by Ann Folwell Stanford in "An Epic with a Difference: Sexual Politics in Gwendolyn Brooks's 'The Anniad' " (*AL* 67: 283–302). Stanford argues that the poem sequence "furthers a resistance to white racist hegemony [and] extends its analysis to the confining ideology that (mis)shapes gender and distorts sexual relationships." Nevertheless, Stanford finds that Brooks "fails to empower her female characters, especially Annie Allen, who is locked within the systems the poetry scrutinizes."

Cheryl Clarke offers a careful study of narrative strategies in "The Loss of Lyric Space and the Critique of Traditions in Gwendolyn Brooks' *In the Mecca*" (*KR* 17, i: 136–47). "Brooks's entire oeuvre," writes Clarke, "has been studies of black subjectivity, of African American oral and written traditions, sources of knowledge and faith systems; of the psychic and physical effects of racism on the lives of black and white people; and of the richness of the lyric." Noting that Brooks originally conceived *In the Mecca* (1968) as a novel, Clark treats it as such, applying Henry Louis Gates, Jr.'s theory of "signifyin(g)." This approach is useful, but it does not allow Clarke to consider Brooks's work in the context of other modernist long poems. Craig Hansen Werner's *Playing the Changes: From Afro-Modernism to the Jazz Impulse* (Illinois, 1994) includes important chapters on Brooks (pp. 142–61) and Melvin B. Tolson (pp. 162–82) as well as significant discussions of Etheridge Knight, Henry Dumas, and Audre Lorde (pp. 103–41). Werner does an excellent job of describing Brooks's use of traditional stanzaic forms and her development of a more idiosyncratic free-verse style that he compares to the blues.

v John Ashbery, Frank O'Hara, Rita Dove, and Jorie Graham

That Ashbery has achieved the rank of a major poet is indicated by the growing body of critical attention to his work. *The Tribe of John: Ashbery and Contemporary Poetry*, ed. Susan M. Schultz (Alabama), joins David

Lehman's *Beyond Amazement: New Essays on John Ashbery* (see *ALS 1980*, pp. 407–08) as an indispensable reference. Two contributors to Lehman's volume—John Koethe and Fred Moramarco—are joined by a dozen other critics in Schultz's collection. Schultz's volume is timely because, of those who began publishing in the 1950s, Ashbery and Amiri Baraka may have become the most widely influential among younger poets. The core of Schultz's book focuses on this development. John Gery (pp. 126–45) identifies Ashbery's influence in the works of writers as different as Marjorie Welish, Clark Coolidge, and Jorie Graham. Essays by John Ernest and James McCorkle discuss Ashbery's affinities to William Bronk and Ann Lauterbach. In "The Music of Construction: Measure and Polyphony in Ashbery and Bernstein" (pp. 211–57) John Shoptaw disputes "the idea that Language poetry is nonreferential and meaningless." Thankfully, Shoptaw uses clear language and generous textual quotations to make a difficult argument more accessible. Looking directly at Ashbery's oeuvre, Charles Altieri considers him as a love poet, and Stephen Paul Miller attempts to elucidate the political commentary (on the Vietnam War and on the Reagan era) he finds in various poems. Fred Moramarco usefully compares Ashbery to Wallace Stevens (pp. 38–59). Other contributors include Charles Bernstein, George Bradley, Connie Costello, Jonathan Morse, Donald Revell, and Andrew Ross.

Bin Ramke's thought-provoking "How French Is It? Recent Translations and Poems by John Ashbery" (*DQ* 29, iii: 118–24) reviews Ashbery's translations of the poems of Pierre Martory, a longtime friend. Ramke suggests that Ashbery's own work is influenced by French language and culture and that "Ashbery at his best is a religious poet, as long as we leave God out of it."

"What I am trying to get at," Ashbery has said, "is a general, all-purpose experience." Catherine Imbriglio quotes the statement but does not seem convinced. In "'Our Days Put On Such Reticence': The Rhetoric of the Closet in John Ashbery's *Some Trees*" (*ConL* 36: 249–88) Imbriglio explicates "The Thinnest Shadow," "The Instruction Manual," and other poems, contending that they are concerned with "the difficulties of articulating sexual difference in the face of repressive social and cultural prohibitions." Though Steven Meyer—as do all of Ashbery's critics—admits confusion when reading new poems, he helpfully identifies the source of Ashbery's enormous popularity in "the unexpected turns of demotic speech," which makes readers enjoy the possible poetry in everyday expressions. In "Ashbery: Poet for All Seasons" (*Raritan* 15, ii:

144–61) Meyer also points out that Ashbery "never lets one forget that one is reading poetry, not overhearing conversation." The article suggests that Ashbery learned these techniques from Gertrude Stein, Auden, and French poets such as Martory, while also continuing to study Wordsworth and early forms such as the ballad. For readers just beginning to explore Ashbery's work, Meyer's essay is a brilliantly accessible introduction.

Mutlu Konuk Blasing contends that "historical coherence and cultural consensus are very much in doubt" in our era and that our poetry reflects this actuality. In *Politics and Form in Postmodern Poetry: O'Hara, Bishop, Ashbery, and Merrill* (Cambridge) Blasing offers informed close readings of these poets. His chapter on Frank O'Hara (pp. 30–66) demonstrates his skill in explicating a poet who "replays certain modernist conventions but shows how they play differently in the current cultural economy." Offering useful insights on the New Formalists and Language poets, Blasing argues that the four poets discussed in detail exemplify the age's skeptical response to "humanist belief in the values of progress, modernity, science, and natural truth." Hartmut Heep vehemently challenges current modes of criticism in "May I Offer You a Drink? Sex and Sexual Subtexts in Frank O'Hara's Poetry" (*Journal of Homosexuality* 30, i: 75–87). Heep does not find anything new in O'Hara's "A Step Away from Them," but he insists that the poet's "homo-semiosis functions by homo-consexualizing non-sexual signifiers."

Helen Vendler's *The Given and the Made: Strategies of Poetic Redefinition* (Harvard) is based on lectures she delivered in England in 1993. Vendler offers considerations of Robert Lowell, John Berryman, Rita Dove, and Jorie Graham, seeking to identify "some personal *donnée* which the poet could not avoid treating, and to see how he or she found symbolic equivalents for it, and developed that material imaginatively over time." She sees Graham as a poet of "philosophical wonder" whose work is enhanced by a trilingual education. Berryman's work is interestingly termed "the Freudian lyric," while Lowell is presented as a poet whose illustrious American geneaology "gave him history" as both a public and private discourse. While this approach is interesting, it has limitations. Vendler herself is aware of the inadequacy of the "given" she assigns to Dove, and she admits to "neglecting, for the most part, the handsome poems Dove has written that do not take blackness as one of their themes—notably, her poems on travel and motherhood, and on aesthetic experience." Vendler's *Soul Says: Recent Poetry* (Harvard) also contains short essays on Dove, Graham, and other poets. Emily Walker Cook argues convincingly in " 'But She Won't Set Foot/In His Turtle-dove Nash': Gender Roles and Gender Symbolism in Rita Dove's *Thomas and Beulah*" (*CLAJ* 38: 322–30) that the characters in Dove's Pulitzer Prizewinning poem sequence show the reader how people can survive and counter "preestablished [social] constraints."

vi A Variety of Voices: Robinson Jeffers, James Dickey, Adrienne Rich, and Others

In his useful annotated bibliography, *Robinson Jeffers: Dimensions of a Poet* (Fordham), Robert Brophy glosses Jeffers's 1949 manifesto *Poetry, Gongorism and a Thousand Years* as a statement that a great poet is "one who avoids trends and writes to be understood in the far future." Jeffers's death in 1962 does not quite qualify him for antiquity, but Brophy's fine collection of essays by eight colleagues—along with *Robinson Jeffers and a Galaxy of Writers*—will certainly, to paraphrase John Ashbery, help the academy of the future to open its doors. The *Galaxy of Writers* collection includes considerations of Jeffers's influence on a wide range of poets, including Stevens, Gary Snyder, W. S. Merwin, and Robert Hass.

The chronically underrated Weldon Kees (1914–1955) is reintroduced to a new generation of readers by James Ballowe in "Weldon Kees: Loathed All Roses" (*NDQ* 62, iii: 181–97). Kenneth Fearing, another undeservedly overlooked poet, was recently returned to print with *Complete Poems* (National Poetry Foundation) ed. with an informative critical introduction by Robert M. Ryley. Robert Penn Warren is the subject of an issue of *MissQ* (48, i). In addition to a bibliographical survey compiled by Jonathan R. Eller and C. Jason Smith, James A. Grimshaw contributes "Cleanth Brooks and Robert Penn Warren: Notes on Their Literary Correspondence" (pp. 93–104), and Randolph Paul Runyon considers Warren's poetry in "Repeating the 'Implacable Monotone' in *Thirty-six Poems*" (pp. 39–56). Cleanth Brooks's previously uncollected essays, published as *Community, Religion, and Literature* (Missouri), include "Episode and Anecdote in the Poetry of Robert Penn Warren" (pp. 126–42) and "John Crowe Ransom: As I Remember Him" (pp. 143–69).

The Craft of Peter Taylor, ed. C. Ralph Stephens and Lynda B. Salamon (Alabama), brings together essays on the poet, playwright, and fiction writer who—according to Walter Sullivan in "Peter Taylor (1917–1994)" (*SR* 103: 299–300)—was "one of the last authors who could properly claim a place in the southern literary renaissance." The volume includes contributions by Cleanth Brooks, David H. Lynn, Albert J. Griffith, and Elizabeth Hardwick, among many others. Linda Kandel Kuehl also deals with Taylor's experimental drama in "Public Occasions and Private Evasions in the Plays of Peter Taylor" (*SoQ* 34, i: 49–62).

Robert Kirschten's "The Momentum of Word-Magic in James Dickey's *The Eye-Beaters, Blood, Victory, Madness, Buckhead and Mercy*" (*ConL* 36: 130–61) vigorously argues that this often disparaged 1968 collection contains "at least seven of Dickey's major poems and con-stitutes one of the central transitional texts in Dickey's poetic canon." What many critics missed, says Kirschten, is that Dickey had abandoned "poems characterized by statements that have an empirical or external referential direction" in favor of a more ancient, ritualistic type of wordplay. Dickey's poems, he seems to suggest, were not intended to appeal to the intellect but to affect other levels of consciousness. Michael B. Jasper presents a considerably less occult view in " 'Dead from the Waist Down': A Comparative Reading of Dickey's 'Mangham' and Robert Browning's 'A Grammarian's Funeral' " (*JDN* 12: 12–20). Jasper argues that Dickey devises an ironic dramatic monologue to underscore the importance of establishing a creative engagement with the world. The poem, according to Jasper, does express the poet's endorsement of Pythagorean asceticism as an effective path to enhanced awareness.

Like Dickey, Adrienne Rich attracts vigilant partisans. " 'Unnameable by Choice': Multivalent Silences in Adrienne Rich's *Time's Power*" by Jane Hoogestraat (pp. 25–37) appears in Deirdre Lashgari's *Violence, Silence, and Anger*. Hoogestraat begins with the assumption that "much of the experience of women has been lost to history, in part because it could not be safely spoken about or even safely seen at the time." As a result, she claims, Rich is wary of even feminist theories and relies on poetry to "envision alternatives" to an oppressive status quo. Rich is one of many, however, who ignite Bruce Bawer's ire. "Violated by Ideas: Reflections on Literature in an Age of Identity Politics" (*HudR* 48: 19–33), a polemical review of several books and journal articles, allows Bawer to deplore the fact that poetry may have become politicized to the extent that, for some critics, "artistry can in fact be an impediment."

In a wide-ranging essay, "Singing America: From Walt Whitman to Adrienne Rich" (*KR* 17: 103–19), Peter Erickson attempts to focus on Rich's developing views of multiculturalism. Whitman's legacy, says Erickson, is "the idea that a new American literary tradition involves a sharp break, not an evolutionary change." His discussion shows how several poets—including Langston Hughes and June Jordan—have approached Whitman and, in Erickson's view, "Whitman's limitations." While most of the article concerns Rich's views as expressed in the essays collected in *What Is Found There* (1993), Erickson also looks to her poetry, noting that her "mid-career shift in emphasis from rewriting the masters to rewriting herself" indicates that Rich herself "has paradoxically become a canonical figure." Also of interest is Jeffrey A. Walker's "Remapping Freudian America: Adrienne Rich and the Adult Son" (*NDQ* 62, iii: 76–93). In *Scheming Women* Cynthia Hogue considers Rich's "ambivalence about maternal conventions" as a factor in her movement toward political activism.

"Galway Kinnell: A Voice to Lead Us" by Karen Maceira (*HC* 32, iv: 1–14) is a thorough but concise review of Kinnell's work from the 1960s to the present. Maceira discusses Kinnell's development of a unique voice through his eclectic use of free verse and elements of traditional meter, and she concludes that his "contemporary existential view of life" nevertheless contains an affirmation of human possibilities. Andrew J. Angyal's *Wendell Berry* is another volume in the excellent TUSAS. Angyal covers Berry's entire career as poet, novelist and essayist, philosopher and farmer, situating him in the tradition of the Jeffersonian agrarian and the individualistic engagement of Thoreau. Also included is an outstanding assessment of Berry's poetry (pp. 116–40) and Angyal's interview with him. As with each of the titles in this series, this one contains a useful bibliography.

Essays on Berry by Jack Hicks, Patrick D. Murphy, and Steven Wieland appear in *Earthly Words: Essays on Contemporary American Nature and Environmental Writers,* ed. John Cooley (Michigan, 1994). The book also includes Ed Folsom's "Gary Snyder's Descent to Turtle Island: Searching for Fossil Love" (pp. 217–36). Usually regarded as a mentor to Snyder and the Beat Generation poets, Kenneth Rexroth is viewed as something of a regionalist in Donald Gutierrez's "The West and Western Mountains in the Poetry of Kenneth Rexroth" (*NDQ* 62, iii: 121–39). Anne Waldman—a resident of Colorado but hardly a regional poet—is sometimes associated with the Beats and with the "second generation" of the New York School. Her work is the focus of an issue of *Talisman* (13) that includes an interview with her and essays by W. C. Bamberger, Edward Foster, Chris Funkhouser, Douglas Oliver, Kristin Prevallet, and Katie Yates.

Robert Kelly has found an erudite and perceptive reader in Edward Schelb. Tracing the many threads of world culture that Kelly weaves is the task that Schelb assumes in "The Charred Heart of Polyphemus: Tantric Ecstacy and Shamanic Violence in Robert Kelly's *The Loom*" (*ConL* 36: 317–49). Schelb establishes Kelly as a poet who has extended (and expanded) the concerns of such predecessors as Robert Duncan and Charles Olson and who shares an encyclopedic interest in "magical" practices with colleagues such as Richard Grossinger. As a result, *The Loom* (1975) can be fully understood only if one is aware of ideas ranging from Mahayana Buddhism to traditional Dogon cosmology of West Africa described in Marcel Griaule's *Conversations with Ogotommeli* (1965). Schelb skillfully provides clues and cues to guide the reader through the "rite of self-transformation" that Kelly's poem performs.

vii   A Variety of Women's Voices: Tess Gallagher and Others

Ron McFarland's *Tess Gallagher* (BSWWS) is a concise introduction to Gallagher's poetry and fiction. McFarland offers a biographical sketch and a chronological discussion of her published collections from *Stepping Outside* (1974) to *Moon Crossing Bridge* (1992). This series is intended to be accessible to students, and, while a selected bibliography of secondary sources is included, McFarland makes no attempt to summarize critical commentary on Gallagher's work. His essay does, however, provide readers with much informative detail to contextualize and explicate her poems. McFarland also outlines the trajectory of a poet's career, and, in what may be considered lagniappe, he shares his knowledge of small press publishing, a major source of contemporary poetry books.

Deirdre Lashgari's anthology *Violence, Silence, and Anger* includes her essay "Disrupting the Deadly Stillness: Janice Mirikitani's Poetics of Violence" (pp. 291–304). Lashgari reads Mirikitani's *Shedding Silence* (1987) as a gesture of healing that is also, necessarily, disturbing to the reader. Mirikitani, she writes, "insists that we see what Western, and especially European American, feminists often miss, or miss-see—the complexity of the silences as well as the angers of people of color as they respond to multifaceted violence." Miriam DeCosta-Willis redirects attention to an unusual writer in "Southern Folk Roots in the Slave Poetry of Elma Stuckey" (*CLAJ* 38: 390–403). A resident of Memphis, Stuckey (1907–88) published her work in African American newspapers and magazines before issuing collections in 1976 and 1987. DeCosta-Willis sees her as an authentic conduit to Southern folk expression; her poems are sometimes inspired by slave songs learned from her grandfather, but always they are presented in "the black tradition of beautiful talk."

Among women poets now beginning to attract serious critical attention are Betty Adcock and Alice Fulton. In " 'Rich with Disappearance': Betty Adcock's Time Paradoxes" (*Shenandoah* 45: 58–67) Fred Chappell confronts poems that are sometimes ironic, sometimes self-doubting, informed by the realization that "the most durable thing in the world is loss of loved ones." Emily Grosholz in "Distortion, Explosion, Embrace: The Poetry of Alice Fulton" (*MQR* 34: 213–29) presents a poet who is as familiar with loss as is Adcock and who is aware that "the price of the artful constructions that hold things fast, is that they distort as well as secure."

viii The Objectivists, Black Mountain, and Language Poets

Objectivist poet Charles Reznikoff is the focus of an issue of *Sagetrieb* (13, i–ii). In addition to letters and an early essay written by Reznikoff, there are articles by Milton Hindus, Stephen Fredman, Genevieve Cohen-Cheminet, Bruce Holsapple, Tom Lavazzi, and Matthew Sweney. Editor Burton Hatlen contributes "Objectivism in Context: Charles Reznikoff and Jewish-American Modernism" (pp. 147–68). Hatlen speculates that the Objectivist poets—Reznikoff, George Oppen, and Louis Zukofsky—created poetic texts intended to "mediate the demands of tradition (specifically Jewish tradition) and modernity" and that this work grows directly from their experiences in immigrant families. In his interesting *Apocalypse and After: Modern Strategy and Postmodern Tactics in Pound, Williams, and Zukofsky* (Alabama) Bruce Comens argues that 20th-century wars—and particularly the threat of global nuclear destruction—have not only changed our perception of history but the form of the epic poem. Comens's close readings of *The Cantos, Paterson,* and Zukofsky's *A* are intended to demonstrate "formal literary developments in relation to their social contexts."

Olson, Robert Creeley, and Robert Duncan are given close attention in *Understanding the Black Mountain Poets* (So. Car.) by Edward Halsey Foster. Written to serve as a reader's introduction to these poets, the book also situates them in a literary continuum ranging from Emerson to the Language poets. Foster has also provided an excellent and extensive "Select Bibliography" for each poet.

The articulation of a literary continuum, such as the one described by Foster, has been a primary concern of the poets once associated with Charles Bernstein and Bruce Andrews's journal $L=A=N=G=U=A=G=E$. Luke Carson explains the Language poets' interest in a difficult poet who renounced her art in "'This Is Something Unlosable': Laura Riding's 'Compacting Sense'" (*TSLL* 37: 414–44). Applying the theory of Jacques Lacan to Riding's work, says Carson, exposes "the truth of language as equivocation, as deception." Such a goal seems consistent with the practice of the Language poets themselves. In "An End of Abstraction: An Essay on Susan Howe's Historicism" (*DQ* 29: 74–97) John Palattella returns to a 1974 essay by Howe on the antireferential art of painter Ad Reinhardt and poet Ian Hamilton Finlay in an attempt to find a useful analogy for Howe's poetry. Palattella also offers a feminist analysis and concludes that Howe, by creating "a poetics [that is] constantly redefining its partial truths," avoids the snares of authoritarianism.

A different angle of approach is taken by Ming-Qian Ma in "Articulating the Inarticulate: Singularities and the Counter-method in Susan Howe" (*ConL* 36: 466–89). His reading differs from Palattella's by situating Howe squarely within the ranks of Language poets. Howe's palimpsestic texts, Ma claims, reassert writing as a present-tense activity, thereby inviting readers to join her in an interrogation of the early American literature sources she frequently employs. Lynn Keller's "An Interview with Susan Howe" (*ConL* 36: 1–34) provides helpful clues to deciphering the poet's innovative texts. Particularly interesting is Howe's discussion (along with facsimiles of her annotated typescripts) of the manner in which she determines how her nonlinear pages—which sometimes resemble the musical scores of John Cage or early Dada typography—are to be read aloud.

According to Garrett Kalleberg, Ann Lauterbach's poetry evades both biographical interpretation and legible allusion while affirming "the inadequacy of thought." Kalleberg's "A Form of Duration: On Ann Lauterbach's *And for Example*" (*DQ* 29: 98–109) suggests that the result of Lauterbach's aesthetic stance is a poetry at once mysterious, oracular, and demanding of the reader's complete attention. In "Penelope Reworking the Twill: Patchwork, Writing, and Lyn Hejinian's *My Life*" (*ConL* 36: 58–81) Craig Douglas Dworkin employs conventional academic citations as well as italicized "appropriations" from Hejinian's text to suggest, perhaps, that *My Life* (1988) requires a very active reader, indeed. Noting the "deliberately fractured and fractal nature of Hejinian's work," Dworkin compares this autobiographical poetic text to a quilt that, in the act of its making, draws together the quilter's personal and social identities. This useful metaphor does not, however, afford Dworkin much in terms of clarifying what he calls an "indeterminate text [that] disappears into a labyrinth of potential reference." In other words, Dworkin replicates rather than *explicates* (i.e., "unravel[s]") Hejinian's style.

ix Native American and Chicano/a Voices

The word "multicultural" is often misused and misunderstood, but it is a fact that diverse ethnic perspectives are gaining greater recognition in American literature. Contemporary Native American poetry is the focus of an issue of *Studies in American Indian Literature* (7, ii). Susan B. Brill's "Discovering the Order and Structure of Things: A Conversive Approach to Contemporary Navajo Poetry" (pp. 51–69) uses Mikhail Bakhtin's theory of discourses, modified by Arnold Krupat's *Ethnocriticism* (1991), to achieve an understanding of the aesthetic employed by Navajo poet Luci Tapahonso. Anthropology is not an adequate response to such work, but—as Brill notes—an "indigenous" Navajo or Native American critical theory (derived from the ideas of the poets themselves or the values of their cultural community) has not yet been fully articulated. An essay by Janet McAdams, "We, I, 'Voice,' and Voices: Reading Contemporary Native American Poetry" (pp. 7–16), warns critics against "collapsing of 'voice' as a literary strategy into 'subjectivity' as an identity category." McAdams insightfully examines works by Ray A. Young Bear and Linda Hogan, poets who clearly deserve something better than marginalization or political categorization from "well-meaning" readers. Hogan, Maurice Kenny, Wendy Rose, Carter Revard, and Simon J. Ortiz are read in the light of Gloria Anzaldúa's theories in Robin Riley Fast's "Borderland Voices in Contemporary Native American Poetry" (*ConL* 36: 508–36). Fast argues that Anzaldúa's paradigm is applicable because "borders are often imposed by the powerful to contain and control the disempowered (as in our history of Indian removal, reservations, and relocation)." The essay also invokes Bakhtin as a useful way of discussing poems that are often ironically and simultaneously addressed to an audience composed of both insiders and potentially hostile non-natives. Joy Harjo, one of the foremost Native American poets, gets to speak for herself in *The Spiral of Memory: Interviews,* ed. Laura Coltelli

(Michigan). The interviews, dating from the 1970s to the present, include Harjo's thoughts on aesthetics as well as culture and politics.

Two important works affirm that the development of an indigenous criticism for Mexican American literature is proceeding. *Women Singing in the Snow: A Cultural Analysis of Chicana Literature* (Arizona) is Tey Diana Rebolledo's compact history of writing by Mexican American women since the 1930s. Rebolledo skillfully addresses issues ranging from mythology, popular culture, and oral traditions to the task of constructing an identity as a writer by women who have traditionally been inhibited by gender and social class while facing questions about linguistic choices and desired audiences. As a critic, Rebolledo is concerned to depict "the historical, social and cultural processes that formed the writers" and to explain how they "have managed to make themselves the subjects of their own discourses." Rebolledo partly embraces a feminist project, but she also emphasizes that Chicana writers celebrate "multiple identities." In addition to analyzing poetry by Lorna Dee Cervantes, Sandra Cisneros, Evangelina Vigil, and others, Rebolledo draws on theoretical paradigms offered by Pat Mora, Juan Bruce-Novoa, María Herrera-Sobek, Ana Castillo, and Anzaldúa. Her critical authority is enhanced by the fact that she works not solely from texts but participates in collegial conversation with the creative writers as well as with critics.

Rafael Pérez-Torres's *Movements in Chicano Poetry: Against Myths, Against Margins* (Cambridge) begins with the assertion that Mexican American literature is a simultaneously postmodern and postcolonial discourse. Pérez-Torres offers an excellent historical assessment of Chicana/o literary criticism and polemical texts as well as meticulous discussions (with intelligent and accessible explications) of a wide range of poems. In addition to poets such as Rodolfo "Corky" Gonzalez, Alurista, Ricardo Sanchez, and Abelardo Delgado, who were the voices of the 1960s cultural consciousness-raising El Movimiento, Pérez-Torres examines a second generation that includes Jimmy Santiago Baca, Carmen Tafolla, Ana Castillo, Anzaldúa, Cervantes, Cisneros, and Vigil, along with several others. Erudite and informative, this book is a major achievement for Pérez-Torres and an indispensable guide for readers. Notable for clarity and objectivity, *Movements in Chicano Poetry* assures the permanent presence of these artists in American literary history.

University of Houston–Downtown

19 Drama

James J. Martine

Drama critic Walter Prichard Eaton once observed, "To take the theatre seriously always surprises many serious people." This is a year of surprises. Writing about American drama had not wandered far down the alley of political correctness and critical abstruse arcanums—at least not as far down as the commentaries on related genres; thus, it was easy to escape back to the thoroughfares of common sense. In the past few years, for example, Tennessee Williams's reputation had been tarnished by perceived self-loathing, and Arthur Miller had been denigrated as a closet capitalist, male chauvinist homophobe. This year, studies on Williams are amplified by a major biography and a comprehensive bibliography, and Miller's reputation has been righted by two excellent collections of essays. Fashion and critical styles change, of course, but American drama, often seen as the backstreet illegitimate sister of the arts, has been restored to proper garb. Scholarship once more looks, and reads, like scholarship, and evidence of the just plain hard work of research worthy of note remains, as the birds of theoretical fancy have flown. Pretentious, inflated, and overblown abstract rhetoric is replaced by readable English. Critics may continue a discussion of the causes and effects of a continued academic neglect of American drama and theater, but the publication record indicates otherwise. As quality has risen, so has quantity. So many worthy books were published this year that there is no room for even a mention of some journal articles. Styles of criticism over the past dozen years, fashions and foppery, diminish in number and frequency of appearance, and more traditional scholarship and scholarly method, informed by fresh concerns, come back—as do playwrights who seemed about to slip into eclipse to tangential studies and political investigations. Everything old is new again.

i Reference Works and Anthologies

Greenwood, along with Oxford and Cambridge, continues to press its preeminent position as publisher of serious reference works in American drama. *American Playwrights, 1880–1945: A Research and Production Sourcebook,* ed. William W. Demastes (Greenwood), is an excellent complement to *American Playwrights Since 1945: A Guide to Scholarship, Criticism, and Performance* (see *ALS* 1989, p. 466). Demastes's volume covers 40 playwrights, and each entry consists of a biographical overview; a selective list of major plays, premieres, and significant revivals with dates and summaries of critical receptions; less significant plays; a general assessment of the dramatist's career incorporating summary references to published evaluations from critics and scholars; a listing of archival sources; and both primary and secondary bibliographies. The playwrights included range from the "canonized," such as Maxwell Anderson, S. N. Behrman, Glaspell, Hellman, George S. Kaufman, Elmer Rice, Thornton Wilder, Odets, and O'Neill; through writers such as Henry James, William Dean Howells, and Irwin Shaw who are better-known in other genres; to less-celebrated craftsmen like Clyde Fitch, Augustus Thomas, and Abram Hill. Nor have matters of gender and race been neglected as entries on women and people of color have been included. The entries throughout are thorough. Demastes and his scholarly battalion of often younger contributors have made a dependable contribution to serious study, usable by specialist and novice.

Copious footnotes are helpful without being cumbersome or intrusive in *Plays by Early American Women.* The extensive appended bibliography (pp. 369–444) lists 165 women who published plays between 1850 and 1900. The list of plays and publication data are a treasure trove opening broad new areas in American literary scholarship, and Amelia Howe Kritzer's introduction (pp. 1–28) is the product of impressive and thoughtfully presented research. Not only is the scholarly apparatus excellent, but the plays represent the lives of women, often in interaction with a historical event. Among these plays are several that have fallen into obscurity or have been excluded from the American canon. Not all of the included playwrights were born in the United States, but all of them spent the productive parts of their lives here. The plays will be of interest to Americanists irrespective of genre or gender. Included are Mercy Otis Warren's successful 1775 dramatic satire *The Group* (pp. 29–53); Susanna Haswell Rowson's first known dramatic work, the 1794 comic opera *Slaves in Algiers* (pp. 56–95); Judith Sargent Murray's 1796 comedy *The Traveller Returned* (pp. 97–136), which offers a unique feature in the type of a "rake reformed" who is female; Sarah Pogson's 1807 romantic verse drama *The Female Enthusiast* (pp. 137–81); Mary Carr's 1815 patriotic celebration *The Fair Americans* (pp. 183–215); Frances Wright's 1819 tragedy *Altorf* (pp. 217–78); Louisa Medina's 1838 melodrama *Ernest Maltravers,* adapted from a Bulwer-Lytton novel (pp. 279–319); and Charlotte Mary Sanford Barnes's 1848 docudrama *The Forest Princess* (pp. 321–68). This last play focuses on Pocahontas and is remarkable for its time in its respectful treatment of Native Americans. Kritzer has done worthy work.

Classic Plays from the Negro Ensemble Company, ed. Paul Carter Harrison and Gus Edwards (Pittsburgh), gathers 10 plays between a reflective and fully developed foreword (pp. xi–xxiv) by Douglas Turner Ward, the Negro Ensemble Company's artistic director, and an afterword (pp. 589–94) by the editors on the enduring presence of African Americans in American theater. These plays are part of that theater's mainstream, though some are more famous than others: the Pulitzer Prize-winning *A Soldier's Play* (1982) by Charles Fuller (pp. 1–53) and the thunderously acclaimed *Ceremonies in Dark Old Men* (1969) by Lonne Elder III (pp. 55–118) are justly celebrated; the towering poetic masterpiece *Dream on Monkey Mountain* is a 1971 drama (pp. 375–431) that came to deserved recognition with the 1992 Nobel Prize awarded to Derek Walcott. The volume also contains the earthy lyricism and sly humor of the three-character *Home* (1979) by Samm-Art Williams (pp. 119–73); Phillip Hayes Dean's elegiac 1971 threnody to a regional Southern past, *The Sty of the Blind Pig* (pp. 175–228); Judi Ann Mason's mature, starkly severe female perspective *Daughters of the Mock* (1978), which has achieved almost cult status (pp. 229–62); Leslie Lee's 1975 triumphant homage to the indomitable spirit and tenacious survival of an archetypal black woman *The First Breeze of Summer* (pp. 301–73); the raucous, passionate, roaring 1972 play *The River Niger* by Joseph Walker (pp. 433–508); Edwards's own provocative and gripping *The Offering* (1977) (pp. 263–300); and Harrison's *The Great MacDaddy* (1974) (pp. 509–88). *American Drama: From the Colonial to the Contemporary,* ed. Stephen Watt and Gary A. Richardson (Harcourt, 1994), is a cumbersome 1,157-page collection of 32 plays and performance pieces intended for classroom use. The dramas range from Royall Tyler's *The Contrast* (1787) to Dion Boucicault's *The Octoroon* (1859), representing the Colonial period to the Civil

War; Augustin Daly's *Under the Gaslight* (1867) to Rachel Crothers's *He and She* (1911), covering the Civil War to World War I; Susan Glaspell's *Trifles* (1916) to Williams's *Cat on a Hot Tin Roof* (1955), representing modern plays; and Edward Albee's *The Zoo Story* (1959), Amiri Baraka's *Dutchman* (1964), Mamet's *Oleanna* (1992), and Cherríe Moraga's *Giving Up the Ghost* (1994) among contemporary dramas. There also are plays by Shepard, Rabe, Adrienne Kennedy, Marsha Norman, Ntozake Shange, August Wilson, and David Henry Hwang. Ten selections by women playwrights are included, and the significant contributions by dramatists of color demonstrate once again how rich mainstream American drama is. Watt and Richardson provide four essays on social, historical, and cultural contexts, along with brief headnotes on each drama. If the volume seems awkward in the hand, the drama it includes makes for a bargain.

Last year, Penguin Mentor produced separate inexpensive anthologies of Puerto Rican plays and the best of off-Broadway Obie-winning plays. This year they publish *Awake and Singing: 7 Classic Plays from the American Jewish Repertoire,* ed. Ellen Schiff (Mentor), which gathers significant works that appeared from 1920 through 1960. A promised companion volume will provide a selection of plays of the last four decades. The present volume includes such celebrated works as Clifford Odets's watershed, quintessentially American Jewish play *Awake and Sing* (1935); Arthur Laurents's memorable *Home of the Brave* (1945), which stands in the vanguard of America's concern with psychological problems fostered by the breakdown of prevailing mores and by wartime experiences; and Paddy Chayefsky's coup de théâtre, the highly successful *The Tenth Man* (1959). Less well-known but equally worthy are Aaron Hoffman's charming but mischievously titled *Welcome Stranger* (1920); Elmer Rice's cosmopolitan and passionate *Counsellor-at-Law* (1931); Sylvia Regan's ambitious *Morning Star* (1940), with the tragic Triangle Waist Co. fire that took 146 lives in 1911 as its historical background; and S. N. Behrman's gentle mood play *The Cold Wind and the Warm* (1958). Schiff supplies an interesting introduction and brief headnotes that provide the context for each drama, and she has selected plays that retain dramatic vitality and the capacity to entertain. Another collection containing a cross section of plays is *Selected Plays of Jerome Lawrence and Robert E. Lee,* ed. Alan Woods (Ohio State), which includes the product of their collaboration from *Inherit the Wind* (1955) and *Auntie Mame* (1956) to *First Monday in October* (1977). Also included are *The Gang's All Here,*

Only in America, A Call on Kuprin, Diamond Orchid, and *The Night Thoreau Spent in Jail.* While the plays are the volume's raison d'être, Woods provides a carefully documented general introduction (pp. ix–xxv), reliable introductions to each play, including forewords by Lawrence and Lee, cast lists, data on initial and important productions, and a concluding chronology. There is a brief foreword by Norman Cousins, and the Theatre Research Institute at Ohio State provides 18 rare photographs.

A salute is owed to Jackson R. Bryer, who over the past 30 years has published books in American literature and modern drama. This year *The Playwright's Art: Conversations with Contemporary American Dramatists,* ed. Bryer (Rutgers), is a collection of interviews (an increasingly more common scholarly interest) with Edward Albee, Robert Anderson, Alice Childress, John Guare, A. R. Gurney, Beth Henley, David Henry Hwang, Larry L. King, Jerome Lawrence, Terrence McNally, Ntozake Shange, Neil Simon, Jean-Claude van Itallie, Wendy Wasserstein, and Lanford Wilson. The interviews, done by Bryer and a coterie of collaborators, average 20 pages each, are consistent in quality, and the playwrights' reflections range from broad philosophical observations to production problems and influences. Bryer's authoritative introduction (pp. vii–xvii) describes and accounts for the major changes in American theater since World War II, going beyond the scope of the writers included. It is among the best brief overviews of the last 50 years of theater in the United States. *American Drama,* ed. Clive Bloom (St. Martin's), presents American drama as viewed from abroad—specifically from England. Bloom's supercilious, superficial, and superfluous introduction (pp. 1–5) characterizes American serious theater as the illegitimate child of commercial Broadway and the West Coast film industry. Barbara Ozieblo provides the patronizingly requisite p.c. chapter on Susan Glaspell (pp. 6–20). Eric Mottram devotes a satisfactory essay to O'Neill (pp. 21–45), although he finds the "peculiarly American identification of the self with universals" in O'Neill and others "a risk at any time, but critical when transferred to national conduct." Michael Woolf is allowed two dozen pages to restore Clifford Odets to eminence (pp. 46–69), and he returns in an essay on Neil Simon (pp. 117–30) to explore a characteristic and continued necessity of American Jewish culture to revisit past experience. Mark Lilly's chapter on Tennessee Williams (pp. 70–81) starts with the premise that Williams's work attempts to express "the author's experience of sexuality and desire as a gay man who is not permitted, or does not dare, to write of the gay experience directly." A. Robert Lee's interesting chapter on Imamu Amiri Baraka (pp. 97–116) explores a double set of meanings in black American drama. Michael J. Hayes makes quick work of rock music and the use of language in his chapter on Sam Shepard (pp. 131–41). Darryll Grantley in an essay on Marsha Norman (pp. 142–64) looks at *Getting Out* and *Third and Oak* before focusing on the harrowing Pulitzer Prizewinning *'night Mother;* Grantley's balance is just right with room for commentary on *The Holdup* and *Traveller in the Dark.* The chapter on David Mamet (pp. 165–77) by Edward J. Esche describes the playwright's dramatic theory, discusses Shakespeare's problem plays as possible influences, and closely examines two moments in *American Buffalo* and *Reunion.* Charlotte Canning brings the volume to a close with a chapter on contemporary feminist theater (pp. 178–92). On the whole, Bloom's book is intended to offer "a comprehensive introduction to the subject for students who require detailed but clear information" (p. vii). But there are anomalies: Chris Banfield's article on Arthur Miller (pp. 82–96) is superficial beyond explanation. It dismisses Miller's masterpieces in two pages and (oddly for an article published in 1995) ignores entirely *The Ride Down Mount Morgan* and *Broken Glass,* which I could under-stand had the essay appeared ten years earlier. Banfield pontificates that "there is no single reason why Arthur Miller's popularity as playwright declined . . . ," and "Arthur Miller has not maintained popularity and critical interest in his native America." Even if these claims were valid, the "single reason" might be glib scholarship such as this essay. It invites aggressive editing.

ii Theater History

Gerald Bordman's *American Theatre: A Chronicle of Comedy and Drama, 1914–1930* (Oxford) is the second volume in what was originally con-ceived as a three-volume (now expanded to include a planned fourth examining Colonial and pre-Civil War stages) history of America's non-musical theater. No matter what the final number in the set, Bordman's contribution to scholarship is marked. The present volume deals almost entirely with first-class houses in New York, since by 1914 films had put an end to cheap touring shows, and the words of approbation for the initial volume (see *ALS 1994,* p. 366) echo here along with the minor advisory: the year-by-year organization makes fine reading and good history, but it presents difficulty for use in research. Thus, 37 separate references to Eugene O'Neill and 46 to David Belasco appear in the indexes. All in all, an excellent history. *The Oxford Illustrated History of Theatre,* ed. John Russell Brown (Oxford), on the other hand, is not a place where an Americanist is going to feel at home. The volume treats mostly British theater and world drama. Of the volume's 582 pages, perhaps a dozen paragraphs are devoted to things American: two paragraphs on the Astor Place riots; *Uncle Tom's Cabin* gets two pages; and paragraphs on American vaudeville, the minstrel show, and the Ziegfeld Follies. O'Neill, Odets, Williams, and Miller receive mere mention. Two paragraphs sum up 18th-century America; there is nothing on the United States in Martin Esslin's chapter on modern theater, 1890–1920. To be fair, a great deal of theater exists in the world, and Oxford has published Bordman's volumes on American theater.

The Dawning of American Drama: American Dramatic Criticism, 1746–1915, ed. Jürgen C. Wolter (Greenwood, 1993), aims to systematically investigate periodicals of the 18th and 19th centuries in search of cultural memorabilia. Its purpose is to provide researchers with bibliographical lists and an anthology of representative texts from 170 years of dramatic criticism in the United States. While the bulk of the book reprints texts in "An Anthology of American Dramatic Criticism, 1746–1915: Jeremiads and Eulogies," the nuclei are 496 items in the "Chronological List of Dramatic Criticism in American Periodicals, 1746–1915" and an "Alphabetical List of the Periodicals Consulted." This survey of the development of U.S. theatrical criticism deserves a place on the shelf alongside this year's contributions by Watt and Richardson, Kritzer, and Jared Brown's *The Theatre in America During the Revolution* (Cambridge). Even though Revolutionary theater was predominantly British, Brown's book is a nice addition to the study of our national literature. Acknowledging the strong British influence in American cultural affairs for many decades, Brown illustrates how the approaching Revolution could be heard in both Whig and Tory plays, most of which were written to be read rather than performed in the years before the first shots were fired. Keeping its principal focus on 1775 to 1783 and the nascent American theater (the Continental Congress effectively stamped out professional theater until 1781), the volume concludes that the theater was used assiduously by both sides to help achieve political and military objectives. An appendix (pp. 173–87) provides a list of known theatrical productions given during the Revolution.

Despite its cautionary aspects relating the terrors of alcoholism, Maureen Stapleton and Jane Scovell's *A Hell of a Life: An Autobiography* (Simon & Schuster) is an interesting collection of anecdotes, set pieces, and bagatelles of theater history. Stapleton won a Tony for the role that she originated of Serafina in Williams's *The Rose Tattoo,* reprised the part in 1966 and 1973 revivals, and appeared in *Orpheus Descending,* the 1965 revival of *The Glass Menagerie,* and as Big Mama to Laurence Olivier's Big Daddy in a 1976 TV version of *Cat on a Hot Tin Roof.* She has enough tales about Tennessee Williams to keep a contemporary Scheherazade busy. Her prose is salty and direct, and some episodes scatological—a prized note from Williams is displayed among four dozen photographs tucked into the book's center. Unique cameos are presented of Lillian Hellman, Arthur Miller, Neil Simon, and Marilyn Monroe. Inspired by the debate over ethnocultural representation in the musical, Robin Breon's *"Show Boat:* The Revival, the Racism" (*TDR* 39, ii: 86–105) provides a detailed look at both the show and 66 years of social and theater history. Using the dramas of John Guare, David Rabe, Sam Shepard, and David Mamet for illustration, John Orr's "Paranoia and Celebrity in American Dramatic Writing: 1970–90," pp. 141–58 in *The Theatrical Gamut: Notes for a Post-Beckettian Stage,* ed. Enoch Brater (Michigan), examines a thin dividing line between paranoid delusion and the quest for celebrity as a dominant feature in American dramatic writing since the Vietnam War. Anyone interested in practical theater history must read Steve Nelson's "Broadway and the Beast: Disney Comes to Times Square" (*TDR* 39, ii: 71–85), which carefully describes what has happened and will continue to happen to the foremost center of American theater in its recent lunge toward spectacle; the implications for the future of American drama generally are less significant for scholars, critics, and historians concerned with theatrically innovative forms than might be supposed. As always, I made a point to seek out Gerald Weales's "American Theater Watch, 1994–1995" (*GaR* 49: 697–707), which allows a distinguished scholar to make observations on Terrance McNally's *Love! Valor! Compassion!* and *Master Class,* Sam Shepard's *Simpatico,* Tony Kushner's *Slavs!,* David Mamet's *The Cryptogram,* and Mac Wellman's *Swoop.* Weales also introduces *Dog Opera* by Constance Congdon to a wider scholarly audience and comments on playwrights Richard Nelson, Arthur Laurents, and others. Glenn Loney's "Survival Strategies in New York Theatres" (*NTQ* 41: 79–90) reflects in broad terms on the state of the New York theater. He discusses Eric Bogosian, Claudia Shear, and new musicals and musicals in revival, reserving special approbation for Anna Deavere Smith.

iii Criticism and Theory

A much better blend of England's John Bull and America's Brother Jonathan than Clive Bloom's collection is Ruby Cohn's *Anglo-American Interplay in Recent Drama* (Cambridge), which pairs a half-dozen contemporary Anglo dramatists with six American counterparts. In each pairing, the experienced eye of Cohn perceives similarities that usually expose culturally based differences. Her initial chapter, "Funny Money in New York and Pendon: Neil Simon and Alan Ayckbourn" (pp. 9–35) is devoted to comic exposition of middle-class mores, although I wished for fuller attention to *The Norman Conquests;* "Artists' Arias: Edward Bond and Sam Shepard" (pp. 36–57) examines the plight of the artist in society; "Phrasal Energies: Harold Pinter and David Mamet" (pp. 58–93) notes the shared sense of linguistic play. Cohn insists that her next two chapters, "Reading and Teaching: Maria Irene Fornes and Caryl Churchill" (pp. 94–116) and "Males Articulating Women: David Hare and David Rabe" (pp. 117–40), should be read in tandem since they react to patriarchies on both sides of the Atlantic. The final chapter, "Englobing Intimacies: Christopher Hampton and Richard Nelson" (pp. 141–66), calls attention to two unspectacular, workmanlike, and skilled playwrights, neither of whom has received the critical consideration that Cohn believes he deserves. A significant study is Tejumola Olaniyan's *Scars of Conquest/Masks of Resistance: The Invention of Cultural Identities in African, African-American, and Caribbean Drama* (Oxford), which investigates the preoccupation with refashioning the cultural self in the drama of English-speaking peoples of African origin. Aware of the euphoria over political decolonization, Olaniyan stresses an unabated *cultural* imperialism. In this work, dramatic texts, theoretical reflections, poetry and fiction when appropriate, biography, reviews, critical reception, and the writer's general discursive context are all considered. Rather than attempting too much or weakening its argument with too broad a sample, the volume centers on four dramatists. Two Nobel laureates are considered: "Wole Soyinka: 'Race Retrieval' and Cultural Self-Apprehension" (pp. 43–66) and "Derek Walcott: Islands of History at a Rendezvous with a Muse" (pp. 93–115). "LeRoi Jones/Amiri Baraka: The Motion of History" (pp. 67–92) traces Baraka's development from romantic rebellion against bourgeois norms through an equally restrictive, doctrinaire Marxism, to an open Marxism-feminism. Recognizing that gender has been a profound nemesis of black cultural identity, Olaniyan in "Ntozake Shange: The Vengeance of Difference, or The Gender of Black Cultural Identity" (pp. 116–38) gives a detailed consideration to the feminist artist. The book's conclusion wrestles with the questions of whether an empowering post-Afrocentric drama can flourish within Eurocentric institutions without its own supporting structures and whether an authentic black cultural identity can be symbolized in European languages. Olaniyan asks if an epistemological shift from the West is needed. The answer would seem to be apparent in the four playwrights themselves, trained and skilled in Western literary and dramatic tradition, who rediscover their art and their different cultures through engagements with this tradition.

Una Chaudhuri's *Staging Place: The Geography of Modern Drama* (Michigan) is not always easy reading, yet it is an interesting book about the imagination of place in modern drama, attempting to form a new methodology for drama and theater studies, a "geography" capable of supplementing the more familiar history. The book tracks not only figures of home, homelessness, exile, and immigration, but recurring tropes such as addiction and burial that accompany the dramatic discourse of place, along the way commenting on apparently innocuous examples of "blatant American economic imperialism" like Disneyland and an advertising campaign for Pepsi-Cola. While European and British plays are included, Americanists will want to see Chaudhuri's comments on Shepard's *Buried Child,* Spalding Gray's *Terrors of Pleasure,* Eric Overmyer's *On the Verge,* Maria Irene Fornes's *The Danube,* Tony Kushner's much-heralded *Angels in America,* and Suzan-Lori Parks's less well-known *The American Play.* Chaudhuri acknowledges that the deepest debt in writing this book is to Robert Vorlicky, "the most generous intellectual companion a writer could have." Vorlicky's *Act Like a Man: Challenging Masculinities in American Drama* (Michigan) provides statistics and data on ethnicity, sexual preference, and favored site of setting, but the author is most interested in, and interesting on, the unique perspective on mutual determinations of drama and culture, especially the relationship of realism to changing gender codes afforded by the American male-cast canon that includes more than a thousand produced plays, of which 500 have been published. The dramatic system of the male-cast play, Vorlicky demonstrates, is rooted in American culture and language. He discusses how the dialogue of Mamet's *Glengarry Glen Ross* depends on masculine mythologies, then refines his discussion to a specific topic within the male ethos, the absent woman, illustrating his argument by reference to Alice Gerstenberg's one-act *At the Club* (1930) and Sidney Morris's three-act *If This Isn't Love!* (1982). He then turns to three plays that demonstrate uncooperative communication: O'Neill's *Hughie* (1959), Amiri Baraka's *The Toilet* (1963), and Albee's *The Zoo Story* (1960). The center of Vorlicky's book deals with seven plays characterized by sustained personal dialogue. He focuses on David Rabe's *Streamers* (1977), Miguel Piñero's *Short Eyes* (1975), and Robin Swados's AIDS hospice play *A Quiet End* (1991). The author then identifies dramas in which the majority of characters choose self-identifications based on racial, ethnic, and sexual differences: Philip Kan Gotanda's Japanese-American *Yankee Dawg You Die* (1991); Dick Goldberg's Jewish domestic *Family Business* (1979); Mamet's working-class *American Buffalo* (1977); and Alonzo D. Lamont, Jr.'s African American *That Serious He-Man Ball* (1989). In this groundbreaking study, Vorlicky analyzes these 13 plays set in the United States to illustrate his point, but by no means is the book restricted to those plays. "Not all men experience phallic power in the same way," he explains, and he sees this difference as crucial to his project. His study suggests that if "gender is viewed as a fluid construct, then all men are necessarily differently masculine from each other," just as women are differently feminine from each other. Thus, individualization is determined by the unique variation of "coexisting gender codes." Appended is a "Selected Bibliography of Additional Male-Cast Plays and Monodramas" (pp. 329–49).

Caleen Sinnette Jennings's "America on Stage: The World in the Classroom" (*NTQ* 41: 66–71) suggests introducing American theater studies to students from a wide variety of national and social backgrounds and provides a syllabus and commentary on methodology. As to method here, like the editors of *TJ*, I have no desire to participate in the ghettoization of lesbian and gay scholarship, preferring instead to cite relevant essays by David Savran, Robert F. Gross, and Anne Fleche at appropriate places in this chapter, but I would be remiss not to point out a special issue (*TJ* 47, ii) devoted to "Gay and Lesbian Queeries"—their term—featuring essays by Tim Miller and David Roman, Kate Davy, and Lynda Hart and Peggy Phelan on the strength of queer theory.

iv Eugene O'Neill

Grown in the rare intellectual climate at the "hothouse for cultural studies" at Wesleyan and guided by Alan Trachtenberg and Richard Ohmann, the intellectual concepts of Joel Pfister's *Staging Depth: Eugene O'Neill and the Politics of Psychological Discourse* (N.C.) are challenging. Pfister follows O'Neill's career as the dramatist reassessed realism and embraced notions "resonant with psychological, pathological, therapeutic, and aesthetic associations." *Strange Interlude* and its interior monologues made overt use of modern depth psychology despite O'Neill's repeated denials of having been influenced by any contemporary psychologist, including Freud. As psychoanalysis acquired a cultural capital, however, O'Neill learned how to benefit from its popular image. *Staging Depth* examines the material, cultural, and ideological forces that gave power to the concept of depth as a psychological and aesthetic category from 1910 to the 1940s. Pfister argues that O'Neill's "psychological self" was in fact a political "self" used to mystify various class, racial, ethnic, and gender identities. Pfister takes issue with scholars who approach O'Neill's plays as a form of biography, and he rereads the dramas in terms of pop psychology for a professional-managerial class. Pfister's revisions culminate in his final and best chapter, "The Trappings of Theatre, Gender, and Desire," which deals with the connections between O'Neill's work and that of Susan Glaspell, his Provincetown friend and colleague. Pfister's revisionist reading of *Long Day's Journey Into Night* (pp. 203–15), which he contends illustrates O'Neill's consciousness of gender stereotypes, is as au courant as is possible. Still, this challenging and rewarding book seeks to appraise O'Neill's legacy and includes 28 illustrations and photographs—some quite beautiful. On the other hand, *The Proverbial Eugene O'Neill: An Index to Proverbs in the Works of Eugene Gladstone O'Neill*, ed. George B. Bryan and Wolfgang Mieder (Greenwood), is a directory to proverbs in O'Neill's 50 dramas and numerous letters, articles, and notebooks, which has been compiled for no obvious purpose. The heart of the book is a key-word index that identifies the locations of the proverbs in the dramatist's oeuvre. The book proves O'Neill appreciated colloquial speech patterns, but it is not a concordance. So what that O'Neill used "to hell with someone or something" 59 times, "that old devil sea" 22 times, "to beat it" nine times, or "to be dyed-in-the-wool" three times?

For some journals the "double issue" is now the rule rather than the exception; *EONR* (18, i and ii) prints 21 items, including revisions of six of the 53 scholarly papers delivered at the May 1995 O'Neill conference at Suffolk University. The featured articles are Normand Berlin's "Olivier's Tyrone" (pp. 135–42), which presents the celebrated actor's initial resistance to and triumph in, the "autobiographical job" of playing the parsimonious father in *Long Day's Journey;* Travis Bogard's nostalgic recollection of losing his theatrical naïveté upon attending separate performances by Alice Brady and Alla Nazimova in "Alice and Alla" (pp. 65–77); Laurin R. Porter's careful understanding of O'Neill's representation of America's spiritual malady in "Self and Other: The Problem of Possession in O'Neill's Historical Cycle" (pp. 109–15); Haiping Liu's "The Invisible: A Study of O'Neill's Offstage Characters" (pp. 149–61), a unique concentration on characters who make no stage appearance but are brought to life through utterances of characters on stage; Madeline Smith and Richard Eaton's suggestions in "The Truth About Hogan" (pp. 163–70) about how O'Neill manipulated and altered biographical matter in *A Moon for the Misbegotten;* and Richard Brucher's "O'Neill, Othello, and Robeson" (pp. 45–58), one of a trio of essays on the playwright's sympathetic creation of roles for black actors. Gabriele Poole's "'Blarsted Niggers!': *The Emperor Jones* and Modernism's Encounter with Africa" (pp. 21–37) examines the play's ambivalence, and Rebecca B. Gauss reflects on its operatic adaptation in "O'Neill, Gruenberg, and *The Emperor Jones*" (pp. 38–44). Also included are Thomas S. Elliott's "Altar Ego: O'Neill's Sacrifice of Self and Character in *The Great God Brown*" (pp. 59–64); Robert Meade's "Incest Fantasy and the Hero in *A Touch of the Poet*" (pp. 79–94); and Maria T. Miliora's "Narcissistic Fantasies in *A Touch of the Poet:* A Self-Psychological Study" (pp. 95–107). Three other pieces peep at minor aspects of O'Neill's masterpiece: Joseph Cordaro makes a new pass at the often cited apparent Mary Shelley blunder in "Long Day's Journey into *Frankenstein*" (pp. 116–28); Robert Fulford in "A Theatrical Journey into Long-Lost Lingo" (pp. 129–31) reflects on the increasing value of the 1912 American vernacular for a contemporary audience; and Bert Cardullo in "Dreams of Journey" (pp. 132–34) places the drama in the genre of the dream play. Mariko

Hori searches for affinities to non-Western theater traditions in "Aspects of Noh Theatre in Three Late O'Neill Plays" (pp. 143–48); and Stephen A. Black in "O'Neill in Mourning" (pp. 171–88) essentially reprints a 1988 *Biography* essay. Two comparative pieces conclude the volume: Peter L. Hays's "O'Neill and Hellman" (pp. 189–92) and Michael Abbott's "The Curse of the Misbegotten: The Wanton Son in O'Neill and Shepard" (pp. 193–98). The volume's front-matter includes a brief foreword by Fred Wilkins, the journal's editor, and Athenaide Dallett's "Old Beauty and Gutter Tramps: O'Neill on Stage" (pp. 13–20), in which Jason Robards, José Quintero, and Arthur and Barbara Gelb reminisce about the dramatist and his drama.

v Sam Shepard

Even as British theater critics raved over the stunning new production of the London revival of Shepard's *True West,* finding the play even better than its first appearance there a decade before, scholarly interest in the playwright paused for breath. Ruby Cohn devotes a chapter to Shepard in *Anglo-American Interplay,* and *The Theatrical Gamut* contains two essays about the playwright: Bill Coco in "The Dramaturgy of the Dream Play: Monologues by Breuer, Chaikin, Shepard" (pp. 159–70) sees Strindberg's *Dream Play* as the "precursor" of Joseph Chaikin's and Sam Shepard's 1985 radio collaboration *The War in Heaven;* and Gerry McCarthy in " 'Codes from a Mixed-up Machine': The Disintegrating Actor in Beckett, Shepard, and, Surprisingly, Shakespeare" (pp. 171–87) provides a comparativist perspective on Shepard. Responding to claims of misogyny in Shepard's treatment of female characters, Carla J. McDonough's "The Politics of Stage Space: Women and Male Identity in Sam Shepard's Family Plays" (*JDTC* 9, ii: 65–83) proposes that Shepard's women, even those off-stage or in the margins, offer hope for survival.

vi Tennessee Williams and Arthur Miller

As interest in Shepard burrowed, scholarly publication burgeoned on two long-familiar figures who in recent years might have seemed in danger of becoming anachronisms. The 50th anniversary of Williams's first success, *The Glass Menagerie,* was marked by a hugely acclaimed production of that play in London. Two years ago in this space, in estimating the merits of a Williams biography, I concurred with critics that we still had to wait for a better life study. Unlike Beckett's Estragon and Vladimir, however, our wait has not been long—at least for the first volume of the work. Lyle Leverich's *Tom: The Unknown Tennessee Williams* (Crown) is the work of a theatrical producer and manager, and though the author stresses that this is not an authorized biography, he was chosen by Williams to be his biographer and he enjoyed full access to his papers, journals, and correspondence. The death last year of Maria St. Just, Williams's zealous literary executor, left the author free to quote from those sources. While Leverich does not attempt to psychoanalyze his subject's paradoxical character, he does identify two major formative influences in Williams's development as a poet and playwright, deals honestly with his personal life and the dramatist's unrequited love for his father, treats his two overriding devotions (his career as a writer and his sister Rose), and explains the less romantic reason than the dramatist liked to pretend that Tom became Tennessee. Beginning his book with the desperate final month of Williams's life, the antic circumstances following his demise, and a bizarre death that the dramatist might have written for one of his characters, Leverich moves through the playwright's family, youth, education, and early works. This is not a critical biography in the academic sense, though Leverich documents carefully; his notes and sources are extensive. Appropriate to its subject, Leverich's prose style and structure are dramatic. This is a popular—that is to say readable—biography, a big book in every good sense of the words, the first of a planned two volumes. This first volume takes Williams to 1945, leaving him absorbed in writing *A Streetcar Named Desire*. What awaits Williams in the second volume is what he called "the catastrophe of success." Inspired by Leverich's book, John Harris's "The Young Tennessee" (*Theater Week*, 6 Nov., pp. 14–19), includes conversations with Leverich and Williams's close friend Donald Windham. John Quilty's "The Suddenly Last Summer House" (*Theater Week*, 6 Nov., pp. 20–23) is a photo-essay on the two-story garden room in New Orleans reported by some to have served as the model for the stage setting of the Williams play. The dramatist was also the subject of a worthy bibliography. George W. Crandell's *Tennessee Williams: A Descriptive Bibliography* (Pittsburgh) is a careful and comprehensive work that such a major figure deserves. Crandell completes the authorized Williams bibliography begun in the early 1960s by Andreas Brown but later abandoned. With access to a typescript copy, notes, and correspondence, he has gone beyond Brown's efforts to produce a model scholarly bibliography. This descriptive bibliography is limited to works *by* Williams, listing them chronologically, including all printings of all editions through 1991. The volume's terms and methodology are meticulous. Each entry begins with facsimiles of the title page and copyright page; all relevant details on contents, typography and paper, publication, printings, and performances are included. The volume also includes sections on recordings of Williams reading from his works and recorded interviews and translations of Williams's plays, poetry, and prose arranged alphabetically by language and title.

Philip C. Kolin, who published seven articles this year on Williams, including a pair in *NConL* and an entry in *SoAR*, made a significant contribution as guest editor of a special issue of *MissQ* devoted entirely to the dramatist and containing three introductory comments, three celebratory poems, a dozen scholarly articles, and five interviews, among them Robert Bray's "An Interview with Dakin Williams," the writer's brother (48: 776–88). The principal features of the issue are Kimball King's "Tennessee Williams: A Southern Writer" (48: 627–47) on Southern literary conventions, regional bias, and Williams's love/hate relations with the culture into which he was born; Thomas P. Adler's "Culture, Power, and the (En)gendering of Community: Tennessee Williams and Politics" (48: 649–65), which comments on the apocalyptic endings of several Williams works; Colby H. Kullman's "Rule by Power: 'Big Daddyism' in the World of Tennessee Williams's Plays" (48: 667–76), which points out complex and contradictory concepts that have become a part of the English idiom; John Wylie Hall's "The Stork and the Reaper, The Madonna and the Stud: Procreation and Mothering in Tennessee Williams's Plays" (48: 677–700), which traces the progression in Williams's plays from the depiction of the Madonna to the Earth Mother; Mark Royden Winchell's "Come Back to the Locker Room Ag'in, Brick Honey!" (48: 701–12), which sees an advance in Williams's treatment of homosexuality in *Cat on a Hot Tin Roof* over the innocent ideal of male companionship; and John Gronbeck-Tedesco's "Ambiguity and Performance in the Plays of Tennessee Williams" (48: 735–48), which discusses actual performances of particular actors in Williams's plays. The issue also includes Kolin's "The Japanese Premiere of *A Streetcar Named Desire*" (48: 713–33); Francesca M. Hitchcock's "Tennessee Williams's 'Vengeance of Nitocris': The Keynote to Future Works" (48: 595–608), on a piece of fictional juvenilia; Allean Hale's "Tennessee Williams's

St. Louis Blues" (48: 609–25), on the role of that city in Williams's art; John Timpane's "Gaze and Resistance in the Plays of Tennessee Williams" (48: 751–61); and two related items: Harry W. McCraw's "Tennessee Williams, Film Music, Alex North: An Interview with Luigi Zaninelli" (48: 763–75) and William Plumley's "Tennessee Williams's Graphic Art: 'Two on a Party'" (48: 789–805).

Kolin is also the author of "On a Trolley to the Cinema: Ingmar Bergman and the First Swedish Production of *A Streetcar Named Desire*" (*SCR* 27: 277–86), continuing his ongoing essays on foreign productions of the dramatist's plays. His "Black and Multi-Racial Productions of Tennessee Williams's *The Glass Menagerie*" (*JDTC* 9, ii: 96–128), augmented by 16 photos, explores both sociological and theoretical implications of these productions; and his "'No masterpiece has been overlooked': The Early Reception and Significance of Tennessee Williams's 'Big Black: A Mississippi Idyll'" (*ANQ* 8, iv: 27–34) describes archival materials at the University of Missouri.

Anne Fleche has contributed two noteworthy articles on the dramatist this year, "When a Door Is a Jar, or Out in the Theatre: Tennessee Williams and Queer Space" (*TJ* 47: 253–67) and "The Space of Madness and Desire: Tennessee Williams and *Streetcar*" (*MD* 38: 496–509). *MD* adds two more essays, Marian Price's "*Cat on a Hot Tin Roof:* The Uneasy Marriage of Success and Idealism" (38: 324–35), and Andrew Sofer's "Self-Consuming Artifacts: Power, Performance and the Body in Tennessee Williams's *Suddenly Last Summer*" (38: 336–47). The same play is the subject of Robert F. Gross's "Consuming Hart: Sublimity and Gay Poetics in *Suddenly Last Summer*" (*TJ* 47: 229–51), which identifies several levels of plot and authorial triangles in a fresh and complex reading.

There have been studies of how poems end; there is Frank Kermode's seminal study of endings of fiction; and there have been studies of closure in drama. This year June Schlueter's *Dramatic Closure: Reading the End* (Fairleigh Dickinson) "explores closure within both a traditional Aristotelian paradigm and contemporary reader-response theory, necessarily revising narrative insights to accommodate the special features of drama as a literary and performance form." Schlueter presents examples from *Oedipus* to *King Lear*. Of special interest to Americanists are the brief chapters devoted to Tennessee Williams and Arthur Miller: "Reading Toward Closure: *A Streetcar Named Desire*" and "*The Ride Down Mount Morgan:* Scripting the Closing Scene."

One of the initial volumes in a promising Plays in Production series, Brenda Murphy's *Miller: Death of a Salesman* (Cambridge) is a welcome addition to the scholarship on this classic American play. The volume again demonstrates how clearly Murphy writes and how tenaciously she researches. Using notebooks and various drafts of Miller's script, the director's notes of Elia Kazan, and the work of Jo Mielziner (a method she used so well in her Williams book), Murphy provides an account of the play's original New York production, which takes up a third of the volume. She then moves on to *Salesman's* stage history, listing nearly 50 productions that have been significant in the play's stage life, treating along the way such important matters as interracial casting in production. The volume lists productions in English, other languages, and other media, and includes a chronology, bibliography, discography, videography, and photographs and sketches from key productions. Murphy has been too modest in saying that her hope is that this volume will serve as a starting point for future research. This is a remarkable research project well done, a sine qua non for anyone planning to analyze or stage a production of the play. Anyone who *teaches* the play should consult *Approaches to Teaching Miller's* Death of a Salesman, ed. Matthew C. Roudané (MLA), a recent addition to the MLA's series Approaches to Teaching World Literature, in which 14 contributors describe how they introduce the play to students. Roudané's thorough introduction (pp. 3–26) contains information on editions, bibliographies, biography, critical studies, and performances. Susan Harris Smith's "Contextualizing *Death of a Salesman* as an American Play" (pp. 27–32) considers the traditional view that it is the quintessential American drama, and four essays address Miller's techniques and themes: Alexander G. Gonzalez's "Utilizing the Initial Stage Directions in *Death of a Salesman*" (pp. 33–36) attends to the didascalia; Susan C. Haedicke's "Celebrating Stylistic Conventions: *Death of a Salesman* from a Theatrical Perspective" (pp. 37–44) uses a method that resembles attendance at a production; Thomas P. Adler's "Miller's Mindscape: A Scenic Approach to *Death of a Salesman*" (pp. 45–51) discusses scenic design, the memory structure of the play, and questions of closure; and Barbara Lounsberry explores the use of expressionism in the play's structural design in " 'The Woods Are Burning': Expressionism in *Death of a Salesman*" (pp. 52–61). Martin J. Jacobi in "The Dramatist as Salesman: A Rhetorical Analysis of Miller's Intentions and Effects" (pp. 62–73) does what its title indicates; and William W. Demastes's "Miller's Use and Modification of the Realist Tradition" (pp. 74–81) discusses Miller's reinvention of traditional notions of the realistic image. Both "The Crisis of Authenticity: *Death of a Salesman and the Tragic Muse*" (pp. 82–101) by Stephen Barker and "The Sociosymbolic Work of Family in *Death of a Salesman*" (pp. 102–14) by Linda Kintz employ current critical theory in their arguments, while Janet Balakian's "Beyond the Male Locker Room: *Death of a Salesman* from a Feminist Perspective" (pp. 115–24) discloses the complex role of Linda Loman, who is seen as both marginalized and indomitable. Paula Marantz Cohen's "Why Willy Is Confused: The Effects of a Paradigm Shift in *Death of a Salesman*" (pp. 125–33), James Hurt's "Family and History in *Death of a Salesman*" (pp. 134–41), and June Schlueter's "Remembering Willy's Past: Introducing Postmodern Concerns Through *Death of a Salesman*" (pp. 142–54) address inevitable issues for class discussion. All of the essays are necessarily brief to suit their pedagogical purpose, and Ruby Cohn's "Oh, God I Hate This Job" (pp. 155–62) is an appropriate coda to the volume in its comparative survey of the role of the salesman from O'Neill's Hickey in *The Iceman Cometh* to Mamet's *Glengarry Glen Ross.*

The Achievement of Arthur Miller: New Essays, ed. Steven R. Centola (Contemporary Research), is the best collection of essays on Miller in two decades. Centola provides an introduction (pp. 11–16) that is knowledgeable and honest on Miller's status and reputation, and his "Temporality, Consciousness, and Transcendence in *Danger: Memory!*" (pp. 135–42) associates the two one-act plays with Miller's earlier drama and Jean-Paul Sartre's theater of situations. Matthew Roudané's "From Page to Stage: Subtextual Dimensions in the Theater of Arthur Miller" (pp. 31–41) considers the complex signals in Miller's stage directions. Christopher E. W. Bigsby's "A British View of an American Playwright" (pp. 17–29) offers explanations for Miller's receding popularity in the United States and his success abroad. Relying on unpublished manuscripts, Brenda Murphy's "The Reformation of Biff Loman: A View from the Pre-Production Scripts" (pp. 51–57) discusses the transformation of Biff's character essential to Miller's thematic purpose. Robert A. Martin's "Arthur Miller's *After the Fall:* The Critical Context" (pp. 119–26) reacts to detractors of that play. Gerald Weales's "Watching the *Clock*" (pp. 127–34) reevaluates the underrated *The American Clock,* and June Schlueter's "Scripting the Closing Scene: Arthur Miller's *The Ride Down Mount Morgan*" (pp. 143–50), reprinted from *Dramatic Closure,* explains that play's central conflict. Among the fresh voices in the volume,

James A. Robinson reconsiders the familiar subject of the father-son relationship from an apprentice play to the later dramas in "Fathers and Sons in *They Too Arise*" (pp. 43–49). *Death of a Salesman* is the subject of three other essays: Janet Balakian's "*Salesman:* Private Tensions Raised to a Poetic Social Level" (pp. 59–67) points out the overpowering impact of social laws on the individual psyche; Charlotte Canning's "Is This a Play About Women?: A Feminist Reading of *Death of a Salesman*" (pp. 69–76) sees the play's women not as marginalized but central; while the volume's most controversial essay, Paula Langsteau's "Miller's *Salesman:* An Early Version of Absurdist Theatre" (pp. 77–85), views the play as absurdist drama. Timothy Miller, a Milton scholar, validates the playwright's portrayal of 17th-century attitudes in "John Proctor: Christian Revolutionary" (pp. 87–93); and Terry Otten's "Arthur Miller and the Temptation of Innocence" (pp. 109–17) proposes that Miller uses the Fall myth to portray the corruption of American values. Both Qun Wang's "The Tragedy of Ethical Bewilderment" (pp. 95–100) and Jeanne Johnsey's "Meeting Dr. Mengele: Naming, Self (Re)Presentation and the Tragic Moment in Miller" (pp. 101–07) approach Miller's plays from a philosophical perspective. In "The Last Yankee: An Interview with Arthur Miller" (*AmDram* 5, i: 78–98) Centola leads the playwright to comment on *The Ride Down Mount Morgan, The Last Yankee,* and especially *Broken Glass.* Gerald Weales also authored "Arthur Miller Takes the Air" (*AmDram* 5, i: 1–15), which examines typescripts passed over by bibliographers and provides a close look at Miller's radio plays.

In *Psychological Politics of the American Dream* Lois Tyson devotes the central chapter, "The Commodity Comes Home to Roost: Repression, Regression, and Death in Arthur Miller's *Death of a Salesman*" (pp. 63–86), to the Loman family's sexuality: Willy's extramarital affair and an unhealthy Oedipal situation for Linda, Happy, and Biff. Reading the play as structured by a series of detailed descriptions of the stages in Willy's psychological breakdown, Tyson reads the five so-called memory scenes as regressive episodes and proposes that it is in the American dream itself that the play's psychological and political strands are inextricably entwined. Tyson concludes that "the play tells the truth about commodity psychology and the American dream despite the desire of Miller and his critics to hide it." Though some reviewers have found Tyson's readings forced and her prose jargon-ridden, this is a different approach to the ongoing literary debate about the American Dream. Also noteworthy are Stephen Marino's "Arthur Miller's 'Weight of Truth' in *The Crucible*" (*MD* 38: 488–95), which provides a linguistic analysis tracing the repetition of the word "weight" as it relates to one of the play's crucial themes; H. C. Phelps's "Miller's *Death of a Salesman*" (*Expl* 53: 239–40), which takes a new look at the role of Linda and Happy in Willy's ultimate act; Hersh Zeifman's "All My Sons After the Fall: Arthur Miller and the Rage for Order" (*The Theatrical Gamut*, pp. 107–20), which connects the rage for order as the driving force behind the conflict between Chris Keller and his father to a prosecutorial direct reversal in *After the Fall;* and Kimberly K. Cook's "Valentin and Biff: Each Unhappy in His Own Way?" (*JEP* 16, i–ii: 47–52), which compares the sons of the Bellegarde family in James's *The American* and the Loman family in *Death of a Salesman.*

vii Edward Albee and David Mamet

Maggie Smith returned to the London stage in what theater critic Sheridan Morley called Albee's "chillingly brilliant" *Three Tall Women,* and a pair of excellent scholarly articles on other Albee plays appeared this year. Bonnie Blumenthal Finkelstein's "Albee's Martha: Someone's Daughter, Someone's Wife, No One's Mother" (*AmDram* 5, i: 51–70) is a suggestive reading of *Who's Afraid of Virginia Woolf?* proposing that Albee's play is critical of stereotyped gender roles, the more striking in that it predates *The Feminine Mystique* (1963) and the modern women's movement. In "An Elegy for Thwarted Vision: Edward Albee's *The Lorca Story: Scenes from a Life*" (*JDTC* 9, ii: 142–47) Jeane Luere comments on the dramatist's present venture, a commissioned work that, like *Three Tall Women,* will proceed to commercial venues when Albee thinks it ready.

In addition to the chapter on Mamet in Cohn's *Anglo-American Interplay,* several good essays on the playwright appeared. Verna Foster's "Sex, Power, and Pedagogy in Mamet's *Oleanna* and Ionesco's *The Lesson*" (*AmDram* 5, i: 36–50) is a comparative study which suggests that Mamet's play is less an antifeminist statement than an indictment of the moral bankruptcy of American higher education. Christine MacLeod's "The Politics of Gender, Language and Hierarchy in Mamet's 'Oleanna'" (*JAmS* 29: 199–213) goes beyond perceived antifeminist bias in the play, acknowledges that hierarchical power and linguistic practices are not simply dependent on gender differences, and finds, like Foster, that the play is part of Mamet's overall critique of a capitalist system based on competitive individualism. While not denying the significance of gender issues, MacLeod concludes that the play's struggle for supremacy owes more to the competitive compulsion of social Darwinism than sexual hostility. Jerry Tallmer's "Laughing at Death" (*Playbill:* 30 April, pp. 65–68) is an article on *Death Defying Acts,* a bill of three new one-act comedies that includes Mamet's cynical view of the legal profession, "An Interview." This year also saw Stephen McKinley Henderson direct *Oleanna* in Buffalo with an all-black cast; Mamet occupied himself publishing fiction—*Passover*—and directing his own adaptation of a 1932 J. B. Priestley comedy-drama of manners, *Dangerous Corner,* as well as directing the American Repertory Theater's premiere of his *The Cryptogram* at New York's Westside Theater.

viii Closed Canons

In the past 12 months numerous articles and a quartet of books have appeared on playwrights past. *AmDram* provides a tandem of essays on Maxwell Anderson. Jennifer Jones's "A Fictitious Injustice: The Politics of Conversation in Maxwell Anderson's *Gods of the Lightning*" (4, ii: 81–96) is an excellent evaluation of Anderson's social protest drama to commemorate the lives of the two Italian immigrants seven years before his Pulitzer Prizewinning *Winterset* became the definitive dramatic response to the Sacco and Vanzetti case; and Tony Speranza's "Renegotiating the Frontier of American Manhood: Maxwell Anderson's *High Tor*" (5, i: 16–35) sees that play, coming during the waning years of the Great Depression and new social and economic realities, as revising the romantic, individualistic notion of American manhood and the New Woman into a comradely ideal between the sexes. Though Anderson is nearly forgotten, Susan Glaspell's resurrection continues. Elin Diamond devotes four paragraphs of "'The Garden Is a Mess': Maternal Space in Bowles, Glaspell, Robins" (*The Theatrical Gamut,* pp. 126–39) to commentary on Glaspell's *The Verge.* For some time Glaspell's works have deserved a good collection of critical essays, and one has finally been published. *Susan Glaspell: Essays* contains 16 articles divided into five parts. The first is devoted to the one-act *Trifles* and its short story offshoot "A Jury of Her Peers," both feminist classics. Linda Ben-Zvi's "'Murder, She Wrote': The Genesis of Susan Glaspell's *Trifles*" (pp. 19–48) details the actual murder case on which the play is based, and Elaine Hedges in "Small Things Reconsidered: 'A Jury of Her Peers'" (pp. 49–

69) expands on the historical background to Glaspell's writings. Karen Alkalay-Gut in "Murder and Marriage: Another Look at *Trifles*" (pp. 71–81) and Liza Maeve Nelligan in " 'The Haunting Beauty from the Life We've Left': A Contextual Reading of *Trifles* and *The Verge*" (pp. 85–104) question initial readings of the play and story on the grounds of privileged gender difference and female victimization. Nelligan's article serves as a bridge between *Trifles* and *The Verge,* a work that more directly addresses feminist issues. Barbara Ozieblo ("Suppression and Society in Susan Glaspell's Theater," pp. 105–22) and Marcia Noe (*"The Verge: L'Écriture Féminine* at the Provincetown," pp. 129–42) treat *The Verge* as a model for later playwrights. Additional essays consider other Glaspell plays. In "Beyond *The Verge:* Absent Heroines in the Plays of Susan Glaspell" (pp. 145–54) Jackie Czerepinski explores the device of the absent female figure up to and including the Pulitzer Prizewinning *Alison's House;* in "Glaspell and Dickinson: Surveying the Premises of *Alison's House*" (pp. 195–218) Katharine Rodier traces the relationship of that play to the poet's biography; and in "Conflict of Interest: The Ideology of Authorship in *Alison's House*" (pp. 219–35) Karen Laughlin makes the case that the play deserved the Pulitzer. J. Ellen Gainor's "*Chains of Dew* and the Drama of Birth Control" (pp. 165–93) relates Glaspell's 1922 play to topical controversy. Sharon Friedman contributes "Bernice's Strange Deceit: The Avenging Angel in the House" (pp. 155–63), on Glaspell's first full-length play; and Gerhard Bach, one of the first critics to reclaim Glaspell, pleads the case for her revival in "Susan Glaspell: Mapping the Domains of Critical Revision" (pp. 239–58). Perhaps the most noteworthy essays on Glaspell's dramatic writing, however, are Karen Malpede's "Reflections on *The Verge*" (pp. 123–27), in which she compares Claire Archer and Hedda Gabler; and Judith E. Barlow's "Susan's Sisters: The 'Other' Women Writers of the Provincetown Players" (pp. 259–300), an exciting article that opens a new world of unpublished plays for scholarly inspection, including works by Djuna Barnes, Neith Boyce, Rita Wellman, and Alice Rostetter. Barlow's is the outstanding essay in an outstanding collection. Glaspell's most original contribution to American drama, the strategy of constructing a play around a central character who never appears onstage, is the subject of Noe's "Reconfiguring the Subject/Recuperating Realism: Susan Glaspell's Unseen Women" (*AmDram* 4, ii: 36–54). Noe concludes that both the woman who wrote the radically feminist *Trifles* and *The Verge* and her unseen females ultimately prevail.

AmDram 4, ii delivers three essays on writers whose stars at present seem in eclipse. Because his work was collaborative, George S. Kaufman's contribution to American theater until recently has been ignored. Using an approach focusing on women's roles, David K. Sauer's "George S. Kaufman's Exploitation of Women (Characters): Dramaturgy and Feminism" (pp. 55–80) examines how his dramaturgy changed in his first five plays. Gabriel Miller's "Clifford Odets's and Elia Kazan's 'Mother's Day': A Lost Fragment of the Thirties" (pp. 17–35) provides a first look at three incomplete drafts, a brief fragmentary piece of collaboration. Carefully providing historical context, Barry Witham's *"Between Two Worlds: Elmer Rice Chairs the Thirties Debate"* (pp. 1–16) is an interesting look at the ill-fated 1934 production of Rice's misunderstood attempt to dramatize rapprochement between the Soviet and American systems. Rice is due for a critical renaissance in the coming year, and Witham's essay is a balanced way to approach him.

Mark Fearnow's *Clare Boothe Luce: A Research and Production Sourcebook* (Greenwood) appears in the Modern Dramatists Sourcebooks series, and like all the volumes in that series, it contains a brief chronology, a synopsis of her life and career, and plot summaries and critical overviews of 19 plays from *Abide with Me* to *The Women*. There is also an annotated primary bibliography, a listing of archival sources, an exhaustive annotated secondary bibliography, a list of important productions and credits, and two indices. This volume is, as is the case with other of the Greenwood Sourcebooks, a satisfactory place to begin work on any dramatist. Beginning in the 1970s, scholarly work on William Saroyan diminished, and his death in 1981 did little to stimulate academic attention. He is probably better remembered for rejecting the Pulitzer Prize awarded to *The Time of Your Life* than for the play itself. This year, *Critical Essays on William Saroyan,* ed. Harry Keyishian (Hall), which includes seven reviews and 13 articles, nine of them reprints, is issued in the Critical Essays on American Literature series under the general editorship of James Nagel. The four original essays deal with Saroyan's fiction, memoirs, and use of language in general. Of the reprints, Stark Young's 1939 review of *The Time of Your Life* (pp. 38–39), James H. Justus's "William Saroyan and the Theatre of Transformation" (pp. 65–71), Thelma J. Shinn's "William Saroyan: Romantic Existentialist" (pp. 96–104), Kenneth W. Rhoads's "Joe as Christ-Type in Saroyan's *The Time of Your Life*" (pp. 105–23), Robert G. Everding's *"The Time of Your Life:* 'A Figment in a Nightmare of an Idiot' " (pp. 124–33), and John A.

Mills's "'What. What-not.' Absurdity in Saroyan's *The Time of Your Life*" (pp. 134–47) can be read again. Paul Lifton's *"Vast Encyclopedia": The Theatre of Thornton Wilder* (Greenwood) is another volume in that publisher's Contributions in Drama and Theatre Studies series. The volume integrates literary analysis with interpretations of theatrical techniques. Lifton explores both symbolist and naturalistic aspects of Wilder's drama and his relationships to Brecht and Pirandello, concluding with parallels in his writings to classical Greek and Roman, medieval European, Elizabethan, Renaissance Spanish, Japanese, and Chinese cultures. Even an unanticipated but relevant chapter is devoted to the direct influence of existentialist thought—principally that of Kierkegaard and Sartre—on Wilder's thinking. Despite the myriad echoes and resonances in the vast encyclopedic scope of Wilder's plays, Lifton's best chapter is "The Unique Character of Wilder's Theatre" (pp. 203–10), which acknowledges the dramatist's singular vision and unmistakable trademarks.

ix The Quick

Last year's collection of 16 short plays by Israel Horovitz was joined by *Israel Horovitz: A Collection of Critical Essays,* ed. Leslie Kane (Greenwood, 1994), a gathering of 13 essays, 12 of them original, and an interview. Kane contributes a chronology, an introduction, and an essay, *"The Widow's Blind Date:* 'A Shitload of Getting Together' " (pp. 79–90), an expanded version of a 1993 article that traces *Widow* from its first reading to its final stage version. Kane's delightful interview (pp. 179–209), twice the length of any other piece, is the best part of the book and allows the dramatist to reflect on his relationships with Beckett, Ionesco, Wendy Wasserstein, drama critic Frank Rich, and his dismissal from CCNY, among other topics. Horovitz is very funny and he drops names as though he were at a show business cocktail party. The volume's academic commentaries vary in merit and method. " 'We Gotta' Hang Together': Horovitz and the National Cycles of Violence" (pp. 15–25) by William Demastes suggests that the physical, verbal, and psychic violence typical of Horovitz's drama are the result of a breakdown of social structures; Robert Combs's comparative essay "O'Neill and Horovitz: Toward Home" (pp. 39–49) places Horovitz, traditionally thought to have been influenced by Ionesco and Beckett, in the long shadow of O'Neill; while Dennis A. Klein's "The Influence of Aeschylus's *Oresteia*

on Israel Horovitz's *Alfred Trilogy*" (pp. 51–68) points to parallels between the texts. Robert Skloot's "Ins and Outs: The Ethnic World of
Israel Horovitz" (pp. 27–38) focuses on the "newcomer/outsider" theme
and maintains that Horovitz's comic world is disrupted by violence born
of ethnic tension, and Susan C. Haedicke's "Portraits of Wo(Men) in
Israel Horovitz's *North Shore Fish* and *Park Your Car in Harvard Yard*"
(pp. 125–39) offers a feminist perspective on these plays that finds they
marginalize women. Anne C. Hall, on the other hand, in "Machismo in
Massachusetts: Israel Horovitz's Unpublished Screenplays *The Deuce* and
Strong-Men" (pp. 141–49) finds masculine flexibility rather than macho
rigidity depicted in the texts. Also included are Thomas F. Connolly's
theatrical local color piece, "The Place, the Thing: Israel Horovitz's
Gloucester Milieu" (pp. 113–24); John Watkins and Andrew Elfenbein's
contribution to the contemporary minefield of social politics, "The
Unkindness of Strangers: Violence and Homosexual Subtexts in Israel
Horovitz" (pp. 91–101); Steven H. Gale's "Israel Horovitz's *Strong-Man's
Weak Child/Strong-Men:* From Stage Play to Screenplay" (pp. 151–65)
deals with the creative process in each medium; Martin J. Jacobi's "Ed
Lemon: Prophet of Profit" (pp. 167–78) discusses the absurdity of *Mack-
erel;* Liliane Kerjan's "Double Mixed Memories" (pp. 69–78) considers
the minimalist pieces of the *Quannapowitt Quartet;* and Robert Scanlan's
"The Influence of Samuel Beckett on Israel Horovitz" (pp. 103–12) takes
up the question of an enduring friendship and influence pro tem. Rudolf
Erben's *Mark Medoff* (BSWWS) is a 55-page pamphlet providing a
concise introduction useful to general readers and students. The format
allows for only a short biography; Erben divides his commentary into
good and bad guys, hero and heroine plays, but appropriate attention is
given to *When You Comin Back, Red Ryder?* and *Children of a Lesser God.*

The brief revival of *for colored girls who have considered suicide/when
the rainbow is enuf* in July 1995 virtually coincided with the publication
of Neal A. Lester's *Ntozake Shange: A Critical Study of the Plays* (Garland). This study of five published plays does not propose to be a
definitive analysis of Shange's theater pieces. Experimental in form,
rejecting standard English in favor of black vernacular and profanity,
aggressively portraying a sexist, racist, and oppressive capitalist society,
and forthrightly political, Shange's works will not appeal to an over-
refined audience. Creating her own rules of spelling, punctuation, cap-
italization, word usage, and syntax, Shange uses an unconventional form
that combines poetry, prose, song, dance, and music to arouse an au-

dience's emotional response. Lester's book, a revision of his doctoral thesis, analyzes the techniques of Shange's "choreopoem" and argues that her name is "relatively new in literary scholarship" because the format of her dramatic presentations and her "radical attacks on racism and sexism" are misunderstood. Lester, for example, denounces John Simon for "his own personal racial and gender biases." Reading the choreopoem *From Okra to Greens* (1985) as a commentary on the complicated lives of females in a male-dominated society, Lester supports Shange's portrayal of "the inseparability of race and gender issues and national and international political concerns."

Kim Pereira's *August Wilson and the African-American Odyssey* (Illinois) is a concise critical study of four plays—*Ma Rainey's Black Bottom, Fences, Joe Turner's Come and Gone,* and *The Piano Lesson*—bounded by an introduction and a brief conclusion, all of which seek to demonstrate how Wilson uses the themes of separation, migration, and reunion to portray the physical and psychological hegiras of African Americans, although Pereira is careful to allow that tales of communities of people reinventing their cultural identity are as universal as Native American tales or the legends of India, Israel, or Ireland. By considering the plays in the order of their composition Pereira chronicles Wilson's artistic maturation. Interested readers may also want to check Ben Brantley's "The World That Created August Wilson" (*New York Times:* 5 Feb., sec. 2, pp. 1, 5).

Audiences of Adrienne Kennedy's *Funnyhouse of a Negro* and *A Movie Star Has to Star in Black and White* should note Margo Jefferson's "A Family's Story Merges With The Nation's" (*New York Times:* 8 Oct., sec. 2, pp. 4, 43). In another venue David Savran's "Ambivalence, Utopia, and a Queer Sort of Materialism: How *Angels in America* Reconstructs the Nation" (*TJ* 47: 207–27) places Tony Kushner's play in the unenviable position of having to rescue American theater from its "sorry state." Savran asserts that *"Angels in America* has almost singlehandedly resuscitated . . . serious drama." Why has so much written about gay drama been apocalyptic *and* messianic? Last year Bradley Boney saw the theater as going, going, gone (see *ALS 1994,* p. 375) unless saved by gays, women, and persons of color. American drama does not need to be saved; it adapts and assimilates. Ironically, once through the preliminary excesses, Savran's formal exegesis of Kushner's complicated play is a model of critical excellence. Richard Hornby takes time in "Aging Actresses" (*HudR* 48: 108–14) to comment on *What's Wrong with This Picture?,* the first play by Donald Margulies to reach Broadway. Hornby concludes his "LA's 99-Seat Theatre" (*HudR* 48: 451–58) with the prediction that Terrence McNally's *Master Class,* which Hornby considers underdeveloped and lacking structure, would fail on Broadway. So much for Hornby as Cassandra. In "Mathematical Drama" (*HudR* 48: 279–86) Hornby concludes that Steve Martin partially succeeds in his attempt to write like Tom Stoppard in *Picasso at the Lapin Agile* but that Joyce Carol Oates's *The Truth Teller* is overloaded with plot, and its humor is "as subtle as a lead brick."

Although Suzan-Lori Parks's plays are highly political and focus on race, Linda Ben-Zvi's " 'Aroun the Worl': The Signifyin(g) Theater of Suzan-Lori Parks" (*The Theatrical Gamut,* pp. 189–208) detects and describes a distinctive language that fashions their dramatic world. Steven Drukman in "Suzan-Lori Parks and Liz Diamond" (*TDR* 39, iii: 56–75) finds jazz a useful way of thinking about the theatrical collaborations of the playwright and director in a lengthy and informative interview. Susan and George Gore's "Theater Chronicle: Americans in London" (*SR* 102: 694–99) reviews the differing response of English critics to Mamet's *Glengarry Glen Ross* and *The Cryptogram;* Miller's *Broken Glass;* and Wendy Wasserstein's *The Sisters Rosensweig.* And with the reference to the British critics, this chapter closes, having come almost full circle.

St. Bonaventure University

20 Themes, Topics, Criticism

Gary Lee Stonum

Monographs conspicuously outnumber articles this year, reflecting a continuing trend. Not only has the comparative prestige of books and essays in literary studies undergone a long-term shift, but a more recent change has taken place in our sense of what makes for a fitting scholarly enterprise. Once upon a time, literary critics could be charged with focusing too much on local interpretive squabbles or esoteric theoretical debates, hence with neglecting the great questions that might have commanded wider public attention. Now, however, the discipline bestows its highest accolades on work that looks out on a broad terrain and that advances large claims about the history and meaning of national culture.

This enlargement of our scope and ambition brings with it practical, institutional challenges and also methodological ones. In expecting historical breadth and innovative social or political visions from our work, we can easily pressure ourselves into settling for hasty, flimsy, or undernourished arguments. The brightest and boldest younger scholars must particularly experience this pressure, for institutional constraints oblige them to publish monographs early in their careers and disciplinary constraints now direct this effort toward projects that ideally demand rich historical perspective and unusual intellectual maturity, not to mention years of work in the archives.

The challenge may only be one reflection of a speedup in production lines visible throughout American society, but it has a methodological corollary that is specific to literary studies. The methodological challenge arises from attempting to correlate the interpretation of fine textual details with a demonstration of social or historical significance. When the most common kind of scholarly monograph was the intensive reading of (some aspect of) Author X's works, such a problem rarely arose.

Better, deeper, richer readings are to some extent their own reward, and they are certainly their own proof. However, to the extent that close reading remains the central form of argumentation and exposition in our field, a new interpretation usually precludes in its very novelty or subtlety the possibility that the text functioned for earlier audiences with the meaning and value now discerned. Determining a crux in, say, Harriet Beecher Stowe, does not necessarily revise our understanding of the abolitionist movement or the moral authority of Victorian women. Yet even some of our most promising critics write as if boldly interpreting a handful of texts might constitute a form of historical argumentation. The problem grows worse, moreover, if the texts seem selected capriciously or tendentiously.

i Identities

The challenge of linking textuality and social forces is directly and impressively met in Priscilla Wald's *Constituting Americans,* one of three major books that addresses some facet of the relation between race and other forms of national or cultural identity. Wald proposes a method in which materials of obvious historical significance usefully get read for literary form, and literary materials get read symptomatically as engagements with social issues. Peremptorily but credibly linking personal and national identity to storytelling, she examines a series of narratives ranging from Douglass's autobiographies to Stein's *The Making of Americans,* often juxtaposing them with documents such as political speeches and legal opinions, which are less obviously narrative in form. Like J. Hillis Miller reborn as a New Historian, Wald looks for uncanny moments in the text, that is, awkward, ungrammatical, or otherwise formally incongruent details, out of which she reads social and political anxiety about the story being told or about the form of authorial subjectivity being articulated.

Wald's procedures are a little less methodical than she represents them, for both of her key concepts—narrative and the uncanny—prove to be roomy categories. Nevertheless, her method has the advantage of avoiding the ad hoc ingenuity and hence questionable scope and authority of some New Historicism. In addition, she provides good readings of several important moments in the history of American authorship, which she views in the context of the collective and self-constituting authorship represented in the opening worlds of the Constitution, "We the People," and thus as part of the task of nation-building at various points in American history. Wald is especially interested in how racial and familial identities complicate national ones.

Walter Benn Michaels also looks at identity—racial, cultural, and especially national—in *Our America,* although his interest is more in the (il)logic of "identitarianism" than its history or its literary consequences. With characteristic brilliance and iconoclastic glee, Michaels argues that pluralism requires racism. Personal and group identity, if they are to be anything more than matters of custom and historical contingency, need some notion of essence, he insists, and for anthropologists, polemicists, and nativist writers (Hemingway, Faulkner, Cather, and Williams but oddly not such cosmopolitan racists as Pound), such essence always proves to be an elusive je ne sais quoi of race and blood.

By comparison to earlier racialisms, moreover, which usually insisted on the superiority of one group but thus had to presuppose some reasonable basis of comparison, during the 1920s literary and intellectual modernists invented a cultural relativism that tended to regard one group's essence as incommensurable with any other's. The most esoteric quality seems to have been Americanism, but a similar and more obviously racial mystification is that which forever distinguishes Hemingway's Jake Barnes from Robert Cohn.

Michaels's argument is obviously provocative and timely, particularly in implying that such modernism is a forgotten parent of multiculturalism and that both ideologies nervously depend on racial obscurantism. He also makes a number of dazzling connections between canonical modernist literature and such events as the Immigration Act of 1924. On the other hand, his book seems oddly unfinished, even slipshod. More than developing an argument or setting forth an account, Michaels reiterates a series of assertions without much bothering to set them in order and apparently without worrying that he often repeats himself.

Robyn Wiegman's *American Anatomies* offers an unsettling but direct answer to the question at the heart of Michaels's inquiry—not the nature of Americanism but the nature of race. Race is precisely skin-deep, she shows, because skin is what shows, this having been the case through several centuries of what she argues is an obsession with the visible. The catch is that our attention to the body's visible surfaces has sponsored a number of beliefs about the deep or internal meaning of what can be seen. These are the reductive or essentialist beliefs that Michaels mocks as irrational. Wiegman, however, doubts that they can be dismissed so facilely.

Wiegman is especially interested in how contemporary celebrations of diversity (an ethical position with which she otherwise sympathizes) often perpetuate a troubling regime of separate-but-equal. She also offers a number of intricate meditations on race and gender, exploring with meticulously self-critical sophistication what she sees as the cultural feminization of black men in the 19th century and as the historically widespread uses of a racial Other to signify or substitute for the feminine. Wiegman directs herself mainly to feminist theory and to cultural studies, but this last theme has special literary interest. Drawing on Leslie Fiedler's famous pronouncements about Huck and Jim and on subsequent examination of cross-racial male bonding from the perspective of queer theory, she points out that the terminology of such criticism regularly and unwarily slips from the racial to the gendered. One problem with this slippage, she argues, and with several other cultural formations she studies, is that they unwittingly project a simplistic myth of integration, one that disregards multiform differences and complexities in favor of a smooth, untroubled unity. The result usually bolsters the rule of the dominant, she argues, noting that a conspicuous increase in visible black bodies in movies and on television has been keeping pace with a decline in race relations.

Whereas both Wiegman and Michaels seek to make trouble, she by questioning the premises of identity politics and he by finding modernism's appeals to race both pervasive and incoherent, two other veteran critics put a happier face on the topic. In "Interrogating 'Whiteness,' Complicating 'Blackness': Remapping American Culture" (AQ 47: 428–66) Shelley Fisher Fishkin surveys studies in recent years of how nominally white and nominally black cultures have mutually influenced one another. Fishkin effusively celebrates such hybridization, but she also does not shrink from noticing controversy, particularly the uneasiness some African Americans have expressed about acknowledging white or bourgeois influences.

Betsy Erkkila in "Ethnicity, Literary Theory, and the Grounds of Resistance" (AQ 47: 563–94) examines one episode of this controversy, the protest raised a decade ago by black critics, especially women, against the prestige of French theory, especially a poststructuralism that seemed to devalue authorship just when numbers of black men and women were achieving that status. Erkkila endorses their presumption that challenging an ideology of authorship or dismantling specific theories of subjectivity helps discredit authors and selfhood entirely. She also claims that challenges to the canon by women and blacks prepared the way for the reception of deconstruction, contrary to a common telling of the story in which deconstruction's vogue came earlier.

In *Parables of Possibility* Terence Martin revisits several truisms about the national character and a number of classic texts long regarded as central to it. Troubled by the increasing implausibility of imagining the prototypical American self as a white kid lighting out for the territory but still as devoted to such clichés as any proponent of the myth-symbol-image school in the 1950s, Martin observes solemnly that we are no longer a youthful nation and that we can no longer legitimately take inspiration from Adamic enterprises, endless frontiers, and an inexhaustibly promising future.

Martin's more original contribution is to study a rhetoric of negation that is prominent in the old myths of starting anew. Again and again new worlds and the New World are described in terms of what they are not and of what they exclude, defy, or depart from. Martin sees this common rhetorical pattern as linked to what he calls the negative character in fiction, a figure that functions to measure the world in which readers live by the worlds in which the figure is unable to live. Misfits such as Natty Bumppo and Huck Finn are classic examples of the type, which, however, is defined so loosely that it would have to include such neo-Americans as Anna Karenina, Joseph K, and Shakespeare's Richard II.

Equally old-fashioned in her allegiance to standard ideas about American selfhood, Pamela A. Boker in *The Grief Taboo* marshals an eclectic batch of psychoanalytic ideas to redescribe the melodrama of beset manhood as the male's repressed grief for his feminine side or his pre-Oedipal mother. Fecklessness can thus derive from a failure to grieve.

ii Genres

Two very different books examine travel writing as a key indicator of American character, and both draw heavily on recent theoretical considerations of tourism, ethnography, and imperial or postcolonial border crossings. William W. Stowe's *Going Abroad: European Travel in Nineteenth-Century American Culture* (Princeton, 1994) bids fair to become the standard account of premodernist writings about travel. Amiably synthesizing diverse accounts of the relations among power, representation, and subjectivity, Stowe offers a historically alert anatomy of the genre and a fine set of readings of the major authors who contributed to it. His chief claim is that travel and travel writing are inextricably conventional, even ritualistic social performances and that their function is to establish distinction. Americans traveled and wrote about their travel in order to claim an elevated social position and to legitimize that privilege by demonstrating their superior taste and sensitivity.

By contrast to Stowe's confidently Bourdieuvian sociologizing, Terry Caesar in *Forgiving the Boundaries* doubts that American travel writing reveals any consistent practices or formal principles. Caesar does repeatedly insist that the representation of travel keeps turning into the travel of representation, a formula I confess to finding impenetrable, but in several respects his study resembles the literature he writes about. It is, in other words, a rambling tour of often fascinating textual details and representational conundrums as well as a conspicuous pastiche of earlier writings on the subject. Whereas Stowe keeps to the previous century, Caesar ranges from 1810 to the present, and he pays somewhat less attention to ostensibly nonfictional travel writing than to novels in which some relation figures between home and abroad.

Alan Golding's *From Outlaw to Classic* sets a high standard for the analysis of canon formation, an activity in which Americanists have an interest that long predates current battles. By presenting a series of case studies that address different historical and institutional issues, Golding manages to avoid overly sweeping claims while still keeping the whole territory in view. For example, he offers a brief history of poetry anthologies that stresses their often different purposes and standards rather than some singular thesis that they can be made to demonstrate. Whereas other scholars have unduly emphasized the omnibus anthologies now dominating the academic market, Golding gives equal time to partisan collections meant to boost a particular school and to other volumes that conscientiously struck different balances between historical representativeness and universal merit.

Elsewhere, Golding argues for a synthesis of the two extant models of canon formation, one proposing that poets themselves establish traditions, and the other that institutions, especially academic ones, do so. Different examples support different aspects of the two models. In the 1950s, for example, Olson, Duncan, and Creeley largely promoted their own verse and the Pound/Williams line from outside the university, via the little magazine *Origin,* but their effort was then assimilated into and ratified by academic institutions increasingly less sympathetic to New Critical mandarinism. However, a different balance between aesthetic claims and institutional ones can be seen in John Berryman's interested use of Anne Bradstreet, the distinctive professional situation of the many New Critics who were both poet and professor, and the ambivalent or conflicted stance Language Poets take toward the contemporary university.

Two otherwise estimable books about genre and mode succumb to the temptation of delivering historical declarations that lack firm support. In *Becoming Canonical in American Poetry* Timothy Morris touches on some of the same questions as Golding but from a more polemical perspective. He provocatively claims that there has always been a single standard for canonicity in American poetry, which he calls a poetics of presence. Moreover, although the values of presence date to the 1810s, they can be identified specifically with Whitman's poetry and indeed are said to have established the ground for Whitman's early and widespread recognition as the American Homer. The same standard of canonicity applies to Dickinson, whom Morris characterizes as having been regarded by male critics as a sort of female Whitman.

None of these rather astounding claims gets vigorous argument, and the concept of presence—a compound of originality, organicism, and monologism—becomes increasingly nebulous as Morris carries his study into the 20th century. On the other hand, because Morris regards canonical status as practically identical to the place that a poet occupies in bibliographies and on reading lists, a premise that best fits writers who gained their reputations in recent times, his most informed observations have to do with Marianne Moore and Elizabeth Bishop, particularly with newer and in his view much improved views about these two poets. Morris pays little attention to the apparatus of literary reputation in earlier times, however, and his account of earlier poetry is correspondingly weaker.

Cindy Weinstein announces a fascinating thesis about the historical contexts of modern allegory in *The Literature of Labor and the Labors of Literature.* She proposes that allegorical characters signify cultural anxiety about the threat that mechanization and industrialization pose to cherished ideas about the work ethic and the dignity of the individual. They also testify to a related uneasiness about literary labor in Victorian America, one most visible in the genteel idea that literature should seem casual and effortless. Unfortunately, Weinstein never develops or fully explains these claims, instead taking them as pretext for a series of ad hoc readings that sometimes can only be described as labored. Oddly, in a book that promises to historicize such a quintessentially formalist notion as allegory, she offers little discussion of the social and historical contexts that she invokes. The most startling example of this absence appears in her declaration that "changing expectations for work and workers in mid-nineteenth-century America produced melancholy on a vast scale." The claim might seem to deserve an entire monograph's worth of substantiation, perhaps even a life's work, but Weinstein offers nothing further than a footnote to Walter Benjamin's book on 17th-century German *Trauerspiel.*

iii Literary History

In *American Women Writers and the Work of History* Nina Baym ranges through much of the historical literature produced by American women during the antebellum years. She magisterially anatomizes both the histories that American women wrote and the history of their writing such treatises, schoolbooks, poems, travel narratives, novels, plays, and memoirs. The result is an impressive work of scholarly retrieval, one that articulates, substantiates, or extends a number of significant arguments.

As might be expected of a critic long devoted to a centrist feminism, Baym stresses a revised and moderate view of True Womanhood, arguing that the separation of spheres had advantages as well as disadvantages for women writers. Not only did the Victorian pedestal on which women's greater spiritual authority was installed give them a certain license for writing history (and for domestic fiction and moral tracts as well), the cultural division between domestic and public worlds could actually work to make the historical education of the young a species of women's work: "Home was where the most important national product—the citizen—was manufactured." As well as contributing importantly to debates about the cultural status of women at the time, Baym provides a broad view of the cultural opinions they promulgated. In effect, we get a compendium of the doxa of New England (source of nearly all of the writings she examines) at the time of its greatest influence on the nation, and this in turn provides us with a sourcebook of contexts for nearly every contested issue in antebellum literary history.

Three themes stand out. First, confirming Emerson's lament in *Na-*

ture, history was highly venerated as an educational tool, and it was sometimes specifically viewed as fostering the social, by contrast to a study of nature that Emerson and others regarded as nurturing the unfettered ego. In Baym's telling, the often female party of Memory is at least an even match for the party of Hope. Second, as an Enlightenment and Revolutionary-era faith in reason's universality gave way to a Victorian belief in gender differences, woman writers of history actively promoted domestic ideology as a source of authority. A key figure for recounting historical truths is the "didactic mother," who gathers her children around the fireside to instruct them about Washington, Savonarola, and Queen Elizabeth. A descendant of the better-known "republican mother," she is a figure whom literary scholars are said to have neglected, presumably because she tends to be absent from the fiction of the time. Such fiction favors independent or rebellious daughters, Baym observes, so it has to underplay scenes of effective maternal tutelage.

Finally, Baym insists that throughout the several hundred works she examines an overriding constant amid differences of ideology, genre, and personal opinion is the Protestant view of history's meaning and direction. According to this two-ply myth, idol worship and brute force (both associated with pagan and especially Catholic regimes) are progressively displaced by an internalized spiritual power, and at the same time the people acquire more and more direct access to political power, the two strands intertwining in the emergence of Protestant republics and specifically of a United States dominated by New England and its emissaries.

Information about doxa, especially the opinions transmitted by textbooks and popular culture, is also a contribution of Raoul Granqvist's *Imitation as Resistance: Appropriations of English Literature in Nineteenth-Century America* (Fairleigh Dickinson). The book is otherwise a strikingly anachronistic example of the old historicism in literary scholarship, one that displays fewer of the genre's virtues (modesty, thoroughness, respect for evidence) than its vices (historiographical and epistemological naïveté combined with a propensity for armchair remarks such as "all [immigrants] came from backgrounds equally poverty-stricken and barren of opportunity").

Christopher J. Knight's *The Patient Particulars: American Modernism and the Technique of Originality* (Bucknell) takes seriously the frequent claim of modernist writers to be presenting the world as it is rather than merely representing it through some idea, medium, or style. It also takes seriously, even solemnly, the cognitive skepticism of recent theory, proposing to reconcile the two views by understanding literary history as a history of epistemological beliefs. Knight's modernists employ what Zola confusingly called the "technique of originality." By this term Knight primarily refers to the protominimalism for which Hemingway was especially famous. More specifically, it designates the shrinking of a text's frame or border so as to better seem to be presenting objects directly and immediately.

Craig Hansen Werner's *Playing the Changes: From Afro-Modernism to the Jazz Impulse* (Illinois) is the latest contribution to mapping connections between Anglo modernism and black literature. It is also the most thorough, for by contrast to previous scholars, who have mainly examined narrative, Werner considers a wide range of genres—fiction, verse, drama, autobiography, and many forms of music—and he at least glances at a number of examples of each kind. The result is an extraordinarily generous literary history, which welcomes the achievements of everyone and is at pains to defend works against their attackers. Werner appreciates both the Black Arts Movement and the less polemical art it attacked, for example, and he strives to make peace between James Baldwin and all those he either provoked or received provocation from. Werner's eclecticism precludes advancing a sharp thesis, but he provides support for several broad claims. He extends Henry Louis Gates's argument about the affinity between deconstruction and the Africanist tradition of signifying, for instance. And he thoroughly tests and enriches various claims about the link between literature and black music, including gospel forms as well as the more frequently studied jazz and blues traditions.

Over the last dozen years or so the flourishing literature on postmodernism has established some well-worn grooves: proposals about how postmodernism is to be linked to modernism and/or modernity, debates about whether postmodern culture is most ably theorized by Jameson, Lyotard, Baudrillard, or some combination thereof, and arguments positioning the literature at various points on a scale running from an effective political and cultural instrument to a helpless, even shameless creature of late capitalism. In *Postmodern Sublime* Joseph Tabbi outlines moderate and thoughtful positions on each of these questions by examining how several novelists struggle with a somewhat less familiar one: the relation between linguistic and technological systems, that is between the machinery of representation and machinery in the strict sense. Tabbi represents this relation as a version of the sublime encounter between the authorial self's powers and some unrepresentable excess or alterity. He links it also to Donna Haraway's figure of the cyborg. The result is a refreshingly ethical view of contemporary novels that more often simply get lamented for their antihumanist gigantism or celebrated for their encyclopedic ambition. Tabbi argues that at its best the technological sublime of postmodernism gets beyond a modernist insistence on subduing machinery and mechanical forces, and that it also avoids the facile nihilism of the merely solipsistic, ironic, or simulacral text. The happier but somewhat obscurely described alternative he sees in Pynchon and especially Joseph McElroy is a textual field in which self and other relate nondialectically. One model for such nondialectical linkage is Ludwig von Bertalanffy's notion of multifinality.

Steven Weisenburger's *Fables of Subversion* uses genre theory to categorize postmodern fiction, arguing that much of the most adventurous fiction in the second half of this century needs to be understood as a distinctive form of satire. This contemporary form is what he calls degenerative satire, by contrast to the generative form that was practiced by the Augustans and others and that underlies the prevailing, formalist accounts of satire. Generative satire presupposes norms and seeks to correct vices in the objects it attacks. Degenerative satire, on the other hand, might as well be called deconstructive (or carnivalesque) for, rather than affirming some norm, it ultimately calls into question all norms and models, including often its own narrative form. The distinction serves to defend the social and political effectiveness of postmodern fiction, particularly against claims that such writing falls into the dustbin of pastiche, and it also interestingly looks back on the failure of traditional theories of satire to account sufficiently for grotesque images and styles, carnivalesque discursive arenas, or regressive plots. Weisenburger's strongest suits are interpreting a text and spying fresh literary genealogies. He convincingly shows, for example, how both Flannery O'Connor and John Hawkes draw structurally from Nathanael West and at the same time provide models for Vietnam-era fabulation. In other words, he identifies a line of descent where other critics have seen mainly dissent. On the other hand, the price of this historiographical insight is that it blurs the theoretical distinction between generative and degenerative satire.

iv Critics and Methods

After several years in which its influence has waned, deconstruction may again be the specter haunting American criticism. Fittingly, in "The Time Is Out of Joint," Jacques Derrida's keynote to *Deconstruction Is/In America: A New Sense of the Political*, ed. Anselm Haverkamp (NYU), he calls on the tergiversations of *Hamlet* to affirm what deconstruction's friends and enemies both have regarded as ghostly—namely, its political import. No essay in the volume bears specifically on American literature, but all of them reflect a tension between political urgency and cognitive or textual skepticism that defines much current criticism and theory in the United States.

A prime example of this spectral tension appears, uncannily enough, in a posthumous work. Joseph N. Riddel's *Purloined Letters* extends the deconstructionist case for American exceptionalism. Although the essays collected in Riddel's volume all predate New Historicism, they offer a particularly fervent version of American deconstruction's quarrel with politically tendentious criticism. Riddel reads Emerson, Poe, and other canonical writers as demanding of American literature an originality that they keep discovering as necessarily hybrid and derivative. He sees American literature, in other words, as writings without proper ground, whereas at least some multiculturalists see it as a ground without proper writings. Put another way, multiculturalists are more likely to stress the degree to which a national literature should reflect cultural divisions and thus work to displace the elite canon that fails sufficiently to do so.

An even ghostlier intervention is offered by William V. Spanos, who has for decades been arguing without much impact for what he calls ontological criticism, a method derived from Heidegger that is meant to encompass both deconstruction and ideological critique. He is not likely to win more converts with the turgid prose of *The Errant Art of* Moby-Dick, which champions an antiorganicist and antispatial understanding of literary form as the apt complement to Donald Pease's work on cultural rhetorics.

The backlash against poststructuralist theory is ably represented in *The Emperor Redressed: Critiquing Critical Theory*, ed. Dwight Eddins (Alabama). Whereas Richard Levin in "The Current Polarization in Literary Studies" (pp. 62–80) conventionally but reluctantly links such theory to what he laments as the politicization of scholarship, Frederick Crews in "The End of the Poststructuralist Era" (pp. 45–61) more plausibly sees theory as a mandarin willfulness from which politically engaged New Americanists are now happily beginning to wean themselves. A more trenchant argument against one allegedly willful kind of deconstruction appears in "Paul de Man and the Postmodern Myth of Nietzsche's Deconstruction of Causality" (pp. 313–36), Manfred Pütz's contribution to a volume he also edited, *Nietzsche in American Literature and Thought*. Pütz contests nearly every detail in de Man's vastly influential reading of Nietzsche, particularly de Man's emphasis on language's figurality as a source of metaphysical error.

The most ambitious reflection on the age of theory, Mark Edmundson's *Literature Against Philosophy*, rests ultimately on the ancient contrast between art (energy, presence, pleasure) and thought, especially of the academic, philosophical, or disciplinary sort. Along the way, however, Edmundson offers a number of fine, often sympathetic observations about the impact of Derrida, de Man, Foucault, and Bloom. He is especially good at characterizing some of the less obvious facets of their appeal, as when he notes that in de Man "every deconstructive reading that works is a teacher's reading of a student." In other words, it functions to reinforce a teacher/reader's authority and hence to legitimize the hierarchical structure of university instruction.

Although Lawrence Buell's *The Environmental Imagination* is for the most part a history of Thoreauvian nature writing, it also has been hailed as the first major work of ecocriticism; the book's value derives as much from its sensitivity about method as its comprehensive view of Thoreau's stature and influence. Buell takes pains to defend green writing and thinking from several camps that would regard it skeptically or condescendingly. In the face of charges that such literature is woefully masculinist, for example, he notes the number and significance of women writers within its ranks, and to counter suspicions of imperial or neocolonial bias he leavens his primarily American materials with English, Australian, Canadian, and African parallels. More important, against literary theory's suspicion of representation and empiricism, he mounts a plea in favor of the coexistence of referentiality and intertextuality.

The more positive thrust of Buell's work is to argue that we need to take environmental writing more seriously. As is often the case with such pleas, he makes it on the grounds of the truth of the content rather than the qualities of the writing. Buell wryly observes, for example, that an obverse counterpart to Marxist reification seems to hold with respect to nature. Rather than we bourgeois scholars foolishly supposing our culturally and materially constructed world to be natural and hence something to which we are inevitably subject, we foolishly believe—thanks to the apparent success with which we regulate the environment—that we are not fundamentally subject to nature.

A bolder and more important challenge to critical orthodoxy is offered by Elisa New's "Beyond the Romance Theory of American Vision: Beauty and the Qualified Will in Edwards, Jefferson, and Audubon" (*AmLH* 7: 381–414). New argues against a now common identification of the act of seeing with the subject's appropriation of the object, a link that often extends to equating the gaze with a violent, imperial, and usually Oedipal will. Such an equation, the authority of which she attributes to Michel Foucault (but which probably derives as much from poststructuralist film theory), excludes or occludes other, more laudable kinds of vision, in which the eye neither precisely imprints itself nor takes imprint. The equation particularly simplifies Jonathan Edwards's proto-pragmatist account, in which relational Being precedes any division of subject from object, and ocular activity is ideally the consent to experiencing such undividedness, a quality that Edwards identifies as beauty.

Audubon is the least benign example that New considers, but she does not flinch from the seemingly damning fact that he sights his birds along a gun barrel. Tendentiously, she makes this part of Audubon's point, the moment of his art expressing the "somatic poetry" of the relation between the life of the object and that of the visionary viewer. Moreover, in contrasting this interpretation to Annette Kolodny's, whom she aptly views as a forerunner of New Americanist ideological criticism and of a conception of American culture giving new primacy to the romance as an imperialist genre, New seems to clear the way for a sweeping revaluation of national traditions of representation.

Case Western Reserve University

21 Scholarship in Languages Other Than English

i French Contributions: Daniel Royot

a. General Several major causes accounted for significant reorientations in American literary studies. The rampant anti-Americanism of the French media did not deter the public from hailing such novelists as Richard Ford and James Welch at the Paris book show. In this respect, Marc Chenetier assessed the value of French versions of American fiction by resorting to his own experience as translator in "Traduire l'Américain" (*Prétexte* 3: 59–64). The sudden popularity of Paul Auster's fiction was reflected not only in a substantial number of articles, but in his being promoted as a classical author in the yearly postgraduate program of the *Agrégation* and *CAPES* nationwide examinations, which spurred the development of many study aids within a few months. As small publishing houses are now cropping up, however, the opportunities offered to young scholars sometimes hardly compensate for the uneven quality and poor editing of some of those aids.

The new trends of criticism in the United States have enlisted so many French philosophers and linguists that the *RFEA* devoted its July issue to "la critique littéraire aux Etats-Unis." As editor of the volume, André Bleikasten evaluates the current importance of literary theory in the American academy. Many French thinkers from Derrida to Kristeva have played a significant part in the debates raging over the function and meaning of literature. Bleikasten considers the use made of imported theories and methodologies. He points to the "lexical kits," "Althusserian spices," foregone conclusions about alleged misreadings, subversive strategies, and the habits of quoting ad nauseum an approved intertextual discourse ("Y-a-t-il une critique américaine?" (65: 405–18). In "Simulacre/De la vérité littéraire (Critique et perversion)" (65: 419–34) Christian Susini vindicates Kenneth Burke's seminal contribution to the study of literature and language with reference to the concepts of "simulacrum," "re-enactment," and "chart" to define the elements of "vibrantly active" textual interpretations. Jean-Claude Barat attempts to trace the development of theoretical issues at stake behind the still ongoing debate over Wordsworth's poem "A Slumber Did My Spirit Seal." He supports John Searle versus Derrida and deplores the emphasis of context over text. Quoting Rorty, however, Barat welcomes "the clash of rhetorical words" as a proof of vitality and pluralism, although aware that Camille Paglia once threatened to dump the French in Boston Harbor and let them swim home. Barat aptly questions the epistemic buoyancy of high-pressure deconstructionism, while noting that the critic becomes a grotesque in the wake of *Winesburg, Ohio,* when the truth he embraces proves to be a falsehood ("Le conflit des interprétations dans la critique américaine," 65: 435–47). In "L'éternel féministe: un discours critique et ses mythes" (65: 448–59) Claire Joubert recognizes the incisiveness of feminist criticism, yet she regrets the loss of critical power resulting from a textual practice based on what has to appear as reactionary, reflectionist, and subjectivist aesthetic views. For Joubert, feminist fables, mother theories, and mother texts invert and, therefore, fail to subvert the fundamental tropes of patriarchal discourse. Especially referring to Shoshana Felman, Marie-Christine Lemardeley-Cunci acknowledges the invention of a new reading style that combines theory and autobiography. After gynocriticism has mapped out a new literary landscape for women, psychoanalytical criticism is probing textual traces ("Qu'est-ce qu'elles veulent encore? Un regard freudien sur la critique littéraire féministe," 65: 460–70). Evelyne Labbé's article outlines the uses and abuses of contextualist practices derived from New Historicist procedures. Referring to the treatment of Henry James as a touchstone for the critical models propounded by David Minter's *A Cultural History of the American Novel* in 1984, Labbé recalls recent ways of historicizing the myth of James and contextualizing him as a disturbing figure of heterogeneity ("Henry James, Sitting Bull et les autres," 65: 471–80). William Dow concludes the survey with "Report from the Other Academy: Non-American Voices and American Literature" (65: 484–95), stating that the reigning "American critical myopia" results from the coerciveness of a multicultural ideology, seemingly averse to ethnocentrism, yet impervious to the insights of foreign Americanists.

b. Colonial, 18th-Century, and 19th-Century Literature The gathering of three centuries within this section alarmingly reveals that works before World War I tend to fall into neglect, save by young scholars still devoted to literary history. Catherine Bécasse demonstrates that William Bradford's narrative was intended to obscure the open space of New England, while chiefly relying on spiritual experience, as opposed to Cotton Mather's writings, which encouraged contemporaries to confidently contemplate the space to be conquered ("Espace du Nouveau Monde et écriture de l'histoire, William Bradford, *The History of Plymouth Plantation*, 1620–1647," *L'espace littéraire dans la littérature et la culture anglo-saxonnes*, ed. Bernard Brugière [PSN], pp. 41–50).

The complex vision of the Revolutionary crisis is seen taking different forms on the frontier and in more settled areas by Robert Sayre, who interprets J. Hector St. John de Crèvecoeur's *Letters from an American Farmer* as a partial view of a society in which greed appears to be the essential motivator in the struggle of classes ("L'expérience et l'interprétation de la crise chez Crèvecoeur," *RFEA* 64: 279–87). *Trois récits fantastiques américains: "Rip Van Winkle" et "La légende du Val Dormant" de Washington Irving, "Peter Rugg, Le disparu" de William Austin* (Corti) is an original translation by Alain Geoffroy of three tales introduced by Bernard Terramorsi, whose controversial interpretation of early American fiction associates the fantastic with "political mythology." For failing to "trace the protagonists," the narratives are said to liken the country's historical foundation to an "eclipse" or, worse, to a devilish stratagem. As Terramorsi contends, neither Rip nor Peter Rugg return with a political message. The "nightmarish loss of point of view" results in a kind of aporia, the birth of the nation becoming a blind spot through its fantastic representation of "the endless mourning of the lost object, of a past . . . that cannot vanish." In "Réserves de la crise dans *The Scarlet Letter*" (*RFEA* 64: 193–204) Françoise Sammarcelli concentrates on an excerpt from chapter 7 of Hawthorne's novel to account for its "power of specularity." The text is seen as dramatically transmuted into "a moment of critique." On her part, Leona Toker defines the critical moments in Hawthorne's fiction through a process of individual resistance to the dangers of utopia, defined as "a threat to the sacred space of the human heart" ("Représentation de la crise dans l'oeuvre de Nathaniel Hawthorne: le mode carnavalesque," pp. 97–109 in *Eclats de voix*, ed. Christine Raguet-Bouvart [Rumeur]). In a stimulating note ("William

Saroyan, Walt Whitman et la ponctuation," *EA* 48: 198–200) Roger Asselineau refers to cross-cultural uses of punctuation with special reference to Paul Claudel, André Gide, William Saroyan, and Walt Whitman. His study is based on Saroyan's story, "Histoire d'un petit garçon, d'une petite fille et d'un 'hot dog'" (1975).

Literary realism and naturalism have enlisted the critical energies of prominent scholars. Patricia Bleu concentrates on James's evocation of London in "Londres, figure du désir dans *The Princess Casamassima*" (*Albion*, pp. 115–30). Bleu suggests Hyacinth Robinson makes a virtue of powerlessness, using words as "a device of seduction," while London serves as a source of mystery; in "the dense categories of dark arcana, the object becomes the reflection of desire, a mirror for desire's own image." In "American Land-, Ocean- and Urban Scapes in Henry James" (*Cahiers Victoriens et Edwardiens* 41: 121–32) Christine Raguet-Bouvart points to James's evolution from a simplistic vision of transatlantic themes toward a more cosmopolitan approach in the late 1890s. *Americana* devotes a pair of articles to *The Red Badge of Courage*. Roger Asselineau interprets the novel in relation to expressionism, as illustrated in Norwegian painter Edvard Munch's artistry. Crane's "sultry nightmare" thus goes beyond impressionism ("Du réalisme à l'expressionisme dans *The Red Badge of Courage*," 12: 11–16). Marc Saporta compares Paul Watkins's *Night Over Day Over Night* with Crane's work to appraise the emotional impact and fundamental paradox of retrospective writings by authors who were never on the battlefields ("Le paradoxe de l'écrivain," 12: 17–27). Claude Dorey's interpretation of Crane's "An Episode of War" deals with the irony undermining all areas of the narrative process, thus calling forth a world tricked out in deceitful apparel where the drama is depleted and the inane is set in relief. Dorey assumes that the raw materials of Crane's epistemology are spiritualized into emblems, and lethal representation conjures up a world as flat as a sheet and inscribed with erasures ("'An Episode of War,' de Stephen Crane: l'épisode, spectacle et oubli," *RFEA* 64: 205–14).

c. 20th-Century Fiction to World War II In *Ernest Hemingway in France 1926–1994, a Comprehensive Bibliography* (PUR) Geneviève Hily-Mane offers a belated tribute to Hemingway's reputation on the banks of the Seine. His success has never flagged, as proven by the popularity of editions by publishers like Gallimard and Hachette. Although Hemingway was always overshadowed by Faulkner in French academia, Roger

Asselineau recently suggested that the interest among scholars has not dried up, even though few articles have appeared in the past few years. As a token of a looming Hemingway revival, a study by George-Michel Sarotte reappraises *The Sun Also Rises* by considering Jake as an ideal narrator, able to identify with any of the characters. In a world dominated by "verbal virility," Hemingway's style reflects a kind of "genderlessness" bordering on "androgynous silence" ("L'homme blessé, Pedro Romero et la crise d'identité de Jacob Barnes dans *The Sun Also Rises* d'Ernest Hemingway," *Eclats de Voix,* pp. 11–28). Turning to Fitzgerald, Marie-Christine Lemardeley-Cunci elaborates on the theme of the garden to substantiate the function of the vanished object in relation to Nicole's own equivocal sense of space in *Tender is the Night* ("L'espace louche: à propos de *Tender is the Night," L'espace littéraire dans la littérature et la culture anglo-saxonnes,* pp. 13–18).

Among a flood of articles on *Sanctuary,* André Bleikasten offers a revaluation of Temple, now considered with sympathy and understanding by feminist critics particularly eager to defend her, in "La réhabilitation de Temple Drake: *Sanctuary* et la critique féministe" in *Douze lectures de* Sanctuaire, ed. Bleikasten and Nicole Moulinoux (PURennes). For Bleikasten, most recent attempts to transform Temple into an innocent victim fail to acknowledge her fictional status and the effects on the reader of Faulkner's shrill rhetoric (*EA* 48: 442–52). Bleikasten expands his earlier studies on *Sanctuary* in a book (Didier-Erudition) in which he concludes that while tempted to yield to the fascination of evil and the lure of nothingness, Faulkner was able to break the insidious enchantment by the countermagic of his writing. Evoking André Malraux's famous preface to the French version of Faulkner's novel, Bleikasten sees in *Sanctuary* a "fascination held and withheld in words," and he adds that "of all Faulkner's novels it is beyond contest the darkest, written like none of the others in the ink of melancholy." In "Inner Divisions: The Character in Faulkner's *As I Lay Dying*" (*RANAM* 28: 37–50) Aurélie Guillain views characterization as twofold: characters are heard as voices telling their own part of the tale, but they also are mentioned and described in the other characters' monologues. In some cases the fictional creature's appearance in his own "gaze" and its appearance in the other's gaze do coincide. But in others, these aspects of characterization seem to be irreconcilable and result in inner division. Another distinguished Faulkner specialist, Alain Geoffroy, suggests that although the real is basically resistant to the style of writing in *Sanctuary,* it is nevertheless the primary source of it, the umbilicus of literary fiction, like the hollow in a vortex. Imprisoned in Temple's gaze, Popeye is turned into a mere couple of "peas." The metaphor of "inkwells" for Temple's eyes reduces the protagonist to a symbolic dimension. Faulkner thus relates the very process of writing to the unfathomable well opened to imagination. For Geoffroy, *Sanctuary*'s last lines bear witness to apparently restored tranquility after the turmoil. In the Luxembourg Gardens the whirlpool has given way to a harmless pond, as if innocence reigned again, shadowed only by the looming presence of death, which is the real par excellence, significantly the final words of the novel ("Like Peas in Two Inkwells: Text and Vortex in *Sanctuary,*" *Alizés-Trade Winds* 10: 23–33).

Hard-boiled fiction has now gained access to the status of classical works in American studies. Raymond Chandler's *The Big Sleep* attracted many studies, among them Patrick Badonnel and Claude Maisonnat's *Raymond Chandler:* The Big Sleep (Didier-Erudition). The book's eight chapters bear on the evolution of the thriller; the character as signifier; the hard-boiled "demoralised moralist"; conflict as narrative syntax; sexuality, society, and the individual; and the ambivalent chivalric stance. The authors regard Chandler's versatility and brilliance as the mainspring of Philip Marlowe's wisecracking and romanticism. Straddling a metaphysical abyss, Marlowe finds himself in the uncomfortable position of a man who has a foot in two ideological camps. As the authors explain, "Chandler was facing a conundrum at once ethical and metaphysical, which he could solve only by committing literary suicide, that is marrying Marlowe into money." Their general methodology is developed in "L'approche psychoanalytique de la nouvelle," pp. 143–64 in *Aspects de la Nouvelle,* ed. Paul Carmignani (PUPerpigan). Although centered on the short story, the article offers stimulating insights into a reasonable use of psychoanalysis in literary criticism. Isabelle Boof-Vermesse questions the existence of a single governing narrative structure in *The Big Sleep.* The narrative's unfolding is shown to be disturbed and undermined by the various patterns of imagery, which also involve the gothic coloring of the text. Chandler's novel is thus read less as an antiromance than as what could be termed a "baffled" romance. Springing from the mystery of some primitive scene, as represented by General Sternwood's greenhouse, alien anaphorae motifs, hitherto unaccounted for, assemble to constitute an alternative narrative, undercutting the genre's demand for closure ("Fils du récit, réseaux d'images: pour une lecture gothique de *The Big Sleep,*" *EA* 48: 453–64).

Both on a Paris stage and in the syllabus of the *Agrégation* Eugene O'Neill has now regained a faithful audience. Claude Coulon stresses determinism in O'Neill's portrayal of women through the divided image of the ideal mother and "Cybel dominated by the father image in herself" ("La femme chez O'Neill, première approche de *Strange Interlude,*" *Americana* 12: 41–46). In the same volume Colette Gerbaud discusses the values related to the pursuit of happiness by confronting the theme of self-denial ("*Strange Interlude* et la quête du bonheur," 12: 59– 68); and Nina's quest for truth is analyzed by Thierry Dubost, who emphasizes self-emancipation in the repression of desire in "Renaissance dans *Strange Interlude*" (12: 69–81).

d. Contemporary Literature The tone of current French criticism was set by Marc Chenetier with "L'écriture aux abords, entretien avec Jerome Charyn," mostly bearing on the technique of the detective novel, but also providing new perspectives on the new cultural environment in the United States (*Dramaxes,* ed. Denis Mellier and Luc Ruiz [ENS], pp. 113–28).

It was an annus mirabilis in Nabokovian studies. Suzanne Fraysse analyzes the relationships between the author, space, and the reader with reference to Nabokov's notion that "the creative artist makes his own world or worlds" ("Nabokov et l'espace de fiction," in *L'espace littéraire dans la littérature et la culture anglo-saxonnes,* pp. 128–35). Aside from individual contributions in various reviews, the two foremost Nabokov specialists, Christine Raguet-Bouvart and Maurice Couturier, were responsible for several publications, some of them collections of papers delivered at conferences. An issue of *Cycnos* (12, ii) entitled "Nabokov at the Crossroads of Modernism and Postmodernism," ed. Couturier, features contributors with international reputations, including Galya Diment, Alexander Dolinin, Don Johnson, John Burt Foster, Jane Grayson, and Ellen Pifer. Couturier also authored *Lolita* (Didier-Erudition) as a study aid for postgraduates. In that volume he stresses the function of Humbert as modern picaro and virtuoso in the manipulation of a double language. As protagonist and narrator, the central character is shown to win the admiration and complicity of the reader. Couturier deftly reveals the paradoxical mechanisms of the interaction between author, narrator, and reader through the interplay of their respective desires. Raguet-Bouvart's *Lolita, un royaume au delà des mers* has chapters on "roman du déplacement, doubles et reflets, exil, l'Amérique mythique, obstacles, la conquête du tyran." The book also collects articles published on *Lolita* as well as a full-scale chronology. *Europe* 791 invited Christine Raguet-Bouvart to edit a 150-page section on Nabokov with contributions by Dmitri Nabokov on his father, pp. 8–19; Suzanne Fraysse, "La création du lecteur," pp. 20–27; Marie Françoise Kempf, "Les yeux errants du voyageur," pp. 38–47; Ann-Déborah Lévy-Bertherat, "Le dilemme du bilinguisme," pp. 48–56; Drury Pifer, "Le théatre et le monde," pp. 57–63; Ellen Pifer, "De la Russie à Lolita," pp. 64–70; Leona Toker, "L'éthique du camouflage narratif," pp. 71–80; William Gass, "Debout parmi les poissons ébahis," pp. 81–84; Pietro Citati, "Le roman des gloses," pp. 85–88; Jonathan Raban, "Sentiments arides," pp. 89–93; Paul Bradford, "Nabokov oulipien," pp. 94–105; Brian Boyd, "L'art et l'ardeur d'Ada," pp. 106–15; and Bernard Kreise, "Nabokov critique," pp. 132–39. In "Etat de création ou état de crise: Vladimir Nabokov en quête d'une voix américaine" (*Eclats de Voix,* pp. 49–59) Raguet-Bouvart defines Nabokov's own brand of multilingualism in relation to the loss of his natural idiom and the painstaking acquisition of a new language. She adds a subtle appraisal of the self-assigned task of translation, which enables Nabokov to alter his identity at every new stage reached by his creative spirit ("Nabokov: de *Camera Obscura* à *Laughter in the Dark* ou la confusion des textes," *Palimpsestes* 9: 119–33).

Postmodern authors are still in favor, to judge from Anne Cristofovici's comments on John Hawkes, especially those on his capacity to picture violence as an expression of latent conflicts ("Le théatre des émotions et l'écran des rêves dans *Second Skin* de John Hawkes," *Americana* 12: 85–94.) Using the example of Raymond Carver's short story "Why, Honey?" Claire Maniez examines the notion of crisis in light of Umberto Eco's contention that the legitimacy of one interpretation should be measured against the *intentio operis* at work in a particular text. She thus proposes an analysis of the narrative strategy used by Carver, which conditions the reader's response and questions the legitimacy of some other available interpretations ("'Why, Honey?' de Raymond Carver: les limites de l'interprétation," *RFEA* 64: 183–92). Brigitte Félix reexamines the complexity of William Gaddis's works by questioning the notion of a critical moment on the opening page of each novel, seen as a challenge to the reader's desire to enter the "house of fiction" ("Interrogation sur le seuil [critique] des quatre romans de William Gaddis," *RFEA* 64: 214–25). In "The Conception of a Freak: Stanley Elkin's Cruel Poetics" (*RFEA* 64: 227–37) Thomas Pughe argues that cruelty and kindliness are the critical qualities of Elkin's work. "Cynthia Ozick ou l'au-delà du figurable" by Martine Chard-Hutchinson (*Eclats de Voix*, pp. 61–71) deals with the issue of representation through writing in Ozick's fiction.

Paul Auster's popularity in France prompted Annick Duperray to organize an international conference at the Université de Provence in Aix. She also edited the proceedings now published by Actes Sud under the title *L'oeuvre de Paul Auster: Approches et lectures plurielles*. *The Invention of Solitude* is discussed in Chard-Hutchinson's "Les espaces de la mémoire" (pp. 15–23), Françoise Sammarcelli's "L'invention d'une écriture: filiation et altérité" (pp. 24–37), William Dow's "Lueurs dans l'appréhension de l'authenticité" (pp. 38–50), Sophie Chambon's "L'invention de l'écriture et la fabrication du roman" (pp. 51–57), and Lucette Bozzetto-Ditto's "L'arbre et la ville invisible" (pp. 58–74). Several articles bear on *City of Glass:* Bertrand Gervais's "Au pays des tout derniers mots: une cité de verre aux limites du langage" (pp. 86–101), Denis Mellier's "Tuyauteries et théories à la noix: métafiction et signification" (pp. 102–13), Mireille Hardy's "Le blanchiment des repères" (pp. 114–27), William Marling's "Le *Fanshawe* d'Hawthorne: la filiation avouée d'Auster" (pp. 128–39), and Tomoyuki Iino's "Affaire classée: la naissance d'un romancier dans la trilogie new-yorkaise" (pp. 140–50). Also notable are Kathie Birat's "Le langage de l'argent: la métaphore comme monnaie d'échange dans *The Music of Chance*" (pp. 199–212), Jean-François Chassay's "*Moon Palace:* le palimpseste historique" (pp. 215–27), and Nathalie Cochoy's "Prête-moi ta plume: la face cachée de New York dans la Trilogie et dans *Moon Palace*" (pp. 228–42). The poetic dimension is approached by Christopher Metress in "Iles et archipels, sauver ce qui est récupérable: la fiction de Paul Auster" (pp. 245–57) and Marc Chenetier in his brilliant conclusion, "Un lieu flagrant et nul: la poésie de Paul Auster" (pp. 258–70). For Daniel Canty, Auster's *City of Glass* can be read as a fable of redemption. Only a calculating god could give moral meaning to Quinn's masquerade. The twin images of Pascal's paradoxical sphere and Emerson's transparent eyeball, as used by the narrator to describe the novel's universe and the ambitions of its protagonist, are the first indications of the deity's presence, while the role of air and light as metaphors of change and time support this hypothesis ("L'oeil d'Emerson et la sphère de Pascal: *City of Glass* de Paul Auster," *RFEA* 64: 376–83).

e. Ethnic Literature   One of the most valuable volumes in the field of ethnic studies was *Ecritures nord-américaines: un singulier pluriel: fractures/ruptures,* ed. Christian Lerat and Yves-Charles Granjeat (Maison). This collection of miscellaneous ethnic voices includes Jean Béranger's "Fractures et héritages dans *Ghost Dance* de Carole Maso" (pp. 13–28), Françoise Clary's "Fractures identitaires dans *The Bluest Eye* de Toni Morrison" (pp. 55–66), Bernadette Rigard-Cellard's "*Wolfsong* de Louis Owens: l'abattage des grands bois ou l'éternelle fêlure américaine" (pp. 29–42), Serge Ricard's " 'La fiancée de Frankenstein' au pays des Aztèques: la nouvelle métisse selon Gloria Anzaldúa" (pp. 143–56), Ada Savin's "La mémoire de la rupture: Richard Rodriguez de *Hunger of Memory* à *Days of Obligation*" (pp. 131–42), Elyette Benjamin-Labarthe's "*Sapogonia* d'Ana Castillo, ou le feuilleté des identifications" (pp. 157–70), Nicole Ollier's "Déchirures du Moi-Peau: *Cora* de Daphne Athas" (pp. 171–88), and Martine Chard-Hutchinson's "Yozip, cowboy juif ou Juif indien, *The People* de Bernard Malamud ou les ruptures de l'identité américaine" (pp. 189–98). Mention should be made of Jean Cazemajou's treatment of vision and language in the autobiographical writings of Annie Dillard (pp. 221–31); he shows the influence of ethnic statements on a genre of mainstream culture now more than ever pervaded by a sense of duality. In "Dionysos Among the Dinosaurs: The Migration of the Mythic Semes in Robert Kroetch's *Badlands*" (*RANAM* 28: 101–21) Héliane Ventura concentrates on the chapter "Squaw Wrestling," in which various rituals pertaining to Native American, Greek, and Christian traditions are enacted. Yves-Charles Granjeat opposes deadly order to "the subject in crisis," who derives a new energy from instability and disorder in "Le sens de la crise dans *White Noise* de Don DeLillo" (*Eclats de Voix,* pp. 73–83). Claudine Raynaud turns to the autobiographical elements in Adrienne Kennedy's *People Who Led to My Plays* (*Eclats de Voix,* pp. 85–96), a text "written against death" in which "Dreams, memories are appropriated to express the alienation of the 'half-caste.' " In *La double intervention culturelle,* ed. Max Vega-Ritter (Clermont-Ferrand: Centre de Recherches sur les Littératures Modernes et Contemporaines, pp. 21–34) Françoise Clary revisits Clarence Major's fiction ("Lexicographe et romancier, deux interventions sur le langage," pp. 21–

34). Referring to Henry Louis Gates's notion of "the black Other in Western culture," Clary sees scatological and sexual imagery as an aesthetic challenge in light of Ishmael Reed's words: "You can read my writing, but you sure can't read my mind."

Jean Cazemajou and Marcienne Rocard edited an issue of *RFEA* devoted to Mexican American culture, with special emphasis on the artist as a mediator between two antinomic words, able to transcend the initial paradoxes inherent in dual origins. Rocard's "An Amphibian: An Interview with Sandra Cisneros" (66: 585–89) and "Writing *Hors Catégorie:* An Interview With Cecile Pineda" (66: 591–94) highlight the problem of identity in relation to the process of Americanization. Among other contributors, Yves-Charles Granjeat discusses the complexity of Chicano literary achievements, between what remains of an ideology of cultural nationalism and other, subversive decentering forces that push it toward less-defined territories where boundaries exist only to be transgressed. He sees Alejandro Morales's *Reto en el Paraiso* as illustrating a multivoiced production whose countless elements reverberate against each other ("Chicano Literature: Back to Mexico and Beyond," 66: 512–19). In "L'intellectuel et le théâtre pauvre, El Teatro Campesino de Luis Valdèz" Elyette Benjamin-Labarthe assesses the value of El Teatro Campesino as mediation and integration by stating that the very spectacle of sedition enables Luis Valdèz to provide increased visibility to Chicano culture (*Elites et médiations dans le monde interculturel* [PUP], pp. 105–20). Most significant is Jean Cazemajou's "Poétique du récit dans *The Rain God* (1984) et *Migrant Souls* (1990) d'Arturo Islas," pp. 165–76 in *Confrontations et Métissages,* ed. Elyette Benjamin-Labarthe, Yves-Charles Granjeat, and Christian Lerat (Maison des Pays Ibériques). Cazemajou investigates the polyphonic value of narrative and dialogue. Past and present respond to each other through a technique evocative of motion pictures. Memory imposes a dilemma between the will to free oneself from the fetters of time and the commitment to "an exercise of commemoration."

f. Poetry As in past years, critiques were diverse and innovative, with no dominant methodology emerging. Arthur Golden's appraisal of "Respondez," a poem included in the second edition of *Leaves of Grass,* reveals Whitman's reluctant indebtedness to Emerson. Whitman reversed the spiritual assumptions that inform *Nature* by testing the uplifting words of Emerson in the "rough and tumble prose world of 1856, the harsh realities of failed social and political formulations in a democratic society" ("Whitman's 'Respondez,' 'A Rounded Catalogue Divine Complete,' and Emerson," *EA* 48: 319–27). Turning to Emily Dickinson, Antoine Cazé's study of "Crisis is Sweet" demonstrates that the reader shares in a multiple experience of crisis combining sexual climax, mystical revelation, and destruction of the poetic image. The poem thus reveals that the very process of definition entails a fundamental crisis of representation ("Aux limites de la crise: moment critique d'Emily Dickinson," *RFEA* 64: 173–81). Christine Savinel capitalizes on Dickinson's assertion that "while Shakespeare remains, literature is firm" to vindicate the role of irony in the achievements of both writers ("Emily Dickinson et Shakespeare: l'espace de l'inqualifiable," *L'espace littéraire dans la littérature et la culture anglo-saxonnes*, pp. 201–14). In "Wallace Stevens: la crise à la lettre C" (*Eclats de Voix*, pp. 147–59) Savinel examines the sublime in relation to Stevens's mirthful, solitary utterance as exemplified in the line "a chorister whose C precedes the choir." And she concludes that "the ultimate surprise is musical." Pascal Aquien links the loss of identity to fragmentation in W. H. Auden's universe, considering that, alienated by language, the exiled poet associates hell with the absence of a name. Hence, the anguished search for a paradise regained ("La dissémination du nom dans l'espace poétique chez Auden," *L'espace littéraire dans la littérature et la culture anglo-saxonnes*, pp. 231–46). Three contributions in *Eclats de Voix* deal with contemporary poets. In " 'Daddy' revu et corrigé: Sylvia Plath et le legs de l'art extrémiste" (pp. 111–24) Gayle Wurst links Plath's biography to her life commitments, the suicidal intent being at the heart of a mythology informing contemporary poetry. Evelyne Labbé studies Lowell's "The Flaw" and "Ice" as enacting the impossible representation of the subject's death (pp. 125–35). Marie-Christine Lemardeley-Cunci explores the paradox of Ann Sexton's blind belief in the unconscious as the source of obscurantism. Exquisite pain is emphasized to alleviate existential suffering, while the choice of mystic thinking breeds the same threats as Salvador Dali's soft watches ("Crises exquises: persistance de la douleur dans la poésie d'Anne Sexton," pp. 137–46.)

Elyette Benjamin-Labarthe returns to Chicano poetry with a revised edition of her anthology, *Vous avez dit Chicano, anthologie thématique de la poésie chicano* (PUB). Her major perspective is reiterated in "Poésie chicano: guerre des cultures, guerre des mots" (*RFEA* 66: 568–75). She contends that interlingual Mexican American verse destabilizes both English and Spanish in its refusal to respect the integrity of national codes. Beyond the stigma of linguistic anarchy, and far removed from the predictable postulates of sociolinguistics, it has refined code-switching into an aesthetics. Endowed with euphonic and yet jarring beauty, it stands out as a symbol of embattled cultures. Benjamin-Labarthe also develops the theme of bilingual poetry as a "transitory form of fighting" by showing how Chicano poets destabilize English and create an effect of mystery through wordplay and various strategies of linguistic subversion ("Bilinguisme poétique chicano: rejets, osmoses, mutations," pp. 199–218) in *La Frontière Mexique-Etats-Unis,* ed. Serge Ricard (Provence). Finally, Ada Savin analyzes the permanent questioning of feminine identity in an increasingly heterogeneous world, through which Cisneros reaches a comprehensive vision of society on both sides of the Mexican American border ("Le dialogisme poétique de Sandra Cisneros," *RFEA* 64: 576–83). *Sorbonne Nouvelle, Paris*

ii German Contributions: Christoph Irmscher

German contributions to American literary scholarship this year were so manifold, so diverse in terms of subject matter and method, that this novice reviewer's "rage for order" was put to a severe test. *Faute de mieux,* the following notes repeat—to continue the imagery borrowed from Wallace Stevens—just the "keener sounds" from what appeared both new and noteworthy, leaving aside some other works that I found a little less resonant.

a. Critical Theory This year's issue of *REALB* is a voluminous volume, indeed, but it is full of fresh and challenging ideas about what the editor calls the "historical and political turn in literary studies." Winfried Fluck's collection of essays from the pens of German and American critics is dedicated to the distinguished German Americanist Ursula Brumm, who has contributed a splendid essay on "the interest, fascination, even obsession" with conspiracy in the American imagination ("Consensus and Conspiracy in American Literature," 11: 29–41). If Sacvan Bercovitch has uncovered the cohesive force of "rites of assent" in American literature and history, Brumm shows more interest in "rites of dissent"—as reflected in, for example, the conspiracy themes that haunt Cotton Mather's *Wonders of the Invisible World,* Edward Everett Hale's

My thanks to Lauren Trussell-Cullen for her help in the preparation of the German section of this chapter.

"The Man Without a Country," and Don DeLillo's novel *Libra*. Udo Hebel's contribution on "Sanctioned Images: Court Orders, Synodal Resolutions, and the Cultural Contestation of Seventeenth-Century Puritan England" (II: 43–74) similarly wants us to recognize the important function of oppositional tendencies in Puritan New England. The representation of dissenters in the legal and synodal documents of the Puritans, Hebel writes, was intended "to make the implied collective self-image of 'us that are one in the Orthodox truth' . . . shine more brightly." Hebel's meticulously researched essay is a good example of how American studies can benefit from the gentle infusion of theories from other disciplines, such as legal studies or religious history.

From the volume editor's own contribution emerges the provocative and somewhat startling claim that the "historical and political turn" in literary studies has not really taken place—at least not to the extent that its loudest proponents would like to think. In fact, Fluck argues in his thoughtful "Cultures of Criticism: *Moby-Dick,* Expressive Individualism, and the New Historicism" (II: 207–28), New Historicism itself sorely stands in need of historicization. Fluck feels that it should finally acknowledge its "family resemblance to cultural practices of self-fashioning articulated first by books like *Moby-Dick.*" Melville's novel, as Fluck reads it, is a composite book with composite characters offering composite perspectives "on a whole range of cultural options of self-definition and self-empowerment." This, for Fluck, makes it a form of "expressive individualism," which he alternatively defines as the ability "to process a rapid sequence of cultural options." New Historicism, with its insistence on oppositionalism, its free linkage of different cultural contexts, does not undermine this individualist ideology; it merely carries it one step further. Fluck's argument effectively takes the bite out of New Historicism's "political" claims, which on closer inspection are, Fluck says, less radical positionings than part and parcel "of a broad anti-bourgeois critique of cultural oppression."

From a different angle, Herbert Grabes in "Errant Specialisms: The Recent Historicist Turn Away from Aesthetics" (II: 159–72) continues Fluck's critique. He is disappointed that New Historicism, although it promises to put literature back on the turntable of history, remains blind to the fact that aesthetic achievements (by following, for example, the laws of genre) are historically determined, too. A more direct attack on practitioners of revisionist literary history is Thomas Claviez's "Dimensioning Society: Ideology, Rhetoric, and Criticism in the Work of Sacvan

Bercovitch" (II: 173–205), which faults Bercovitch for repeating the same mechanisms of exclusion that he purports to criticize. And Ulla Haselstein in a complexly written essay on "Stephen Greenblatt's Concept of a Symbolic Economy" (II: 347–71) finds Greenblatt's theory wanting, too, since it does not consider "the interests and strategies of the Other" in the cultural exchange between Europeans and indigenous populations.

Predictably, several contributions are concerned with the well-known triad of race, class, and gender in American fiction and culture, and they do so on the firm basis of careful textual interpretations. In one of the most accessibly and engagingly written contributions ("Seduced and Enslaved: Sexual Violence in Antebellum American Literature and Contemporary Feminist Discourse," II: 299–324) Sabine Sielke deals with the "rhetoric of rape" and finds that the contemporary feminist "rape-crisis-discourse" strangely repeats and therefore reinstates 19th-century notions of female sexuality as presented in, for example, Harriet Jacobs's *Incidents in the Life of a Slave Girl* and Elizabeth Keckley's *Behind the Scenes. Or, Thirty Years a Slave, and Four Years in the White House.* As a rhetorical device, maintains Sielke, "rape" has lost its political precision; she suggests that rather than censoring or celebrating representations of sexual acts, we should begin to challenge our ways of reading them. Ulfried Reichardt looks at historical reconstruction of an African American past in David Bradley's *The Chaneysville Incident* (1981) and Charles Johnson's *Oxherding Tale* (1982) and concludes that *Oxherding Tale* is more conscious of the textually constructed nature of history itself ("Writing the Past: History, Fiction, and Subjectivity in Two Recent Novels about Slavery," II: 283–98). Read alongside these two clearly argued pieces, the central point of Ruth Mayer's essay (" 'Ther's Somethin' in Blood, After All': Late Nineteenth-Century Fiction and the Rhetoric of Race," II: 119–38), which would have benefited from editing, is more difficult to make out. Mayer promises to look at the "shifting, heterogeneous, a-logical" constructions of race in the Gilded Age and then briefly discusses three novels: Rebecca Harding Davis's *Waiting for the Verdict* (1867), George Washington Cable's *The Grandissimes* (1880), and Charles Chesnutt's *The Marrow of Tradition* (1901). In spite of some strange jargon (my own personal favorite is the "normative cathexis of reciprocity," which rears its ugly but mercifully blurry head in one contribution) Fluck's collection as a whole makes for interesting and rewarding reading, representing as it does the best in contemporary critical thinking on American literary theory and culture.

The proceedings of the meeting of the *Anglistentag* in Graz, Austria, in 1994 have now been made available in a typically massive volume by Niemeyer Verlag, and a special section of the volume is devoted to "New Developments in Literary Aesthetics." Wolfgang Iser links the "process of interpretation" with "translatability," by which he means the continual acts of transposition taking place within a given culture and between different cultures ("On Translatability: Variables of Interpretation," pp. 299–310). For Iser, translatability counters the idea of cultural hierarchy; when applied to interpretation, the act of reading becomes "productive" rather than "predicative." Herbert Grabes in "The Aesthetic in Recent Theory and Literary Art" (pp. 311–27) recognizes a "new artistic plenitude" in contemporary writing, in which intertextuality is not an unavoidable problem but a form of intelligent play. Therefore, Grabes feels that talk about the "end of art, the waning of true creativity in an age of commodification" is premature. Gerhard Hoffmann in "The Aesthetic, the Anti-Aesthetic and the Non-Aesthetic" (pp. 329–50) likewise thinks there is not a whole lot to worry about, in spite of what some might see as a dangerous "levelling" of aesthetic experience: "the aesthetic has come to include non-aesthetic, anti-aesthetic and even post-aesthetic elements"; it has "expanded towards non-aesthetic discourses" and has thus turned pleasantly "multi-aesthetic." In "Literature and Value: Back to a New Humanism?" (pp. 403–14) Walter Göbel tentatively argues for a "new humanism" with a clear emphasis on "intercultural negotiations," on poiesis rather than mimesis.

b. General Collections   *Images of Central Europe,* the sixth volume in Lothar Hönnighausen's interdisciplinary series "Transatlantic Perspectives," deserves special mention. Edited by the Austrian scholar Waldemar Zacharasiewicz, it is based on a summit of historians and literary critics at the University of Vienna in 1994. According to Zacharasiewicz, these 37 essays reflect the increasing interest in imagology, the study of auto- and heterostereotypes and their importance in forming cultural images. While the manifold reactions of Europeans to the New World have been investigated in now often-tiresome detail, *Images of Central Europe* looks at the relatively neglected reverse side of the encounter, "the factual and fictional confrontation of North Americans with cisatlantic manners and morals."

"Keep that earlier, wilder image bright," William Cullen Bryant recommended when painter Thomas Cole packed his suitcases for Europe, and, sure enough, many 19th-century American travelers found the Rhine beautiful but also wanting compared to the "noble grandeur" of the Hudson (Karl Ortseifen, "From the Hudson to the Rhine: American Views of the Rhine in the Nineteenth Century," pp. 68–76). Some essays appear to be more anecdotal than rigorously theoretical, but all are well-written, carefully researched, and invariably informative. Gerd Raeithel, for example, in "Mark Twain in Munich" (pp. 87–93) reports that Twain hated Munich ("the horriblest place") and that, not surprisingly, Munich left few, if any, traces in his writing. Kurt Albert Mayer in "Henry Adams: 'And I've Retouched My Austria'" (pp. 104–18) finds Adams growing more and more disenchanted with Austria and the Viennese capital ("Vienna is a bore"), while his own sense of historical doom was increasing, too. And from Arno Heller's "Hemingway in Austria" (pp. 159–66) we learn why the references to the Vorarlberg mountains in Hemingway's writing should not be used by the Austrian tourist board: it was here that Hemingway cheated on his wife, and the favorable memories of Schruns in "The Snows of Kilimanjaro" occur while the protagonist is dying of gangrene.

Elsewhere, strangeness makes sense, the gloomy speaker hopes in one of Philip Larkin's poems, but as the essays assembled in *Images of Central Europe* seem to indicate, American writers often have had a tendency to feel even stranger abroad than at home. At least for James Baldwin the experience was productive. Surrounded by the "white wilderness" of the Swiss Alps, in a village whose residents thought he had been sent "by the Devil," he finished his first novel, predicting that this world would be "white no longer" (Isabel Urban, "James Baldwin in Switzerland: 'Stranger in the Village,'" pp. 242–48). One of the most sophisticated essays in Zacharasiewicz's volume is Swiss scholar Hartwig Isernhagen's reflection on "Clichés at the Edge of the Zone? Southern Germany, Austria, and Switzerland in the Fictional Geography of *Gravity's Rainbow*" (pp. 249–60). Isernhagen discovers geographical "specificity" in Thomas Pynchon's novel and recognizes the importance of Zurich to a narrative in which the playful "textualization of the real" is, as Isernhagen puts it, offset by an impulse to "realize" the textual, to anchor it in representational space.

c. Colonial Literature   It is difficult to do justice to the richness of what I think is the most important book to come out this year—the second, posthumously published volume of Hans Galinsky's *Geschichte der amer-*

ikanischen Kolonialliteratur: Multinationale Wurzeln einer Weltliteratur in Entwicklungslinien und Werkinterpretationen (1542–1722), ed. Winfried Herget in collaboration with Brigitte Finkenbeiner (Wissenschaftliche). The mixture of carefully detailed textual analysis and wide-ranging historical summary is exemplary. His erudition enables him to move gracefully from biblical tradition to contemporary contexts, from Spanish or Portuguese texts to Edward Holyoke, Edgar Allan Poe, E. E. Cummings, or Ernest Hemingway. Galinsky's volume focuses on the work of authors born from 1610 through 1620 who came to the New World at a relatively young age. The domineering figure in this generation no doubt was Anne Bradstreet, whose contributions to American literature Galinsky subjects to meticulous scrutiny. While John Berryman devoted some of his best poetry to her, he disliked Bradstreet's "spiritless poems" and called her "boring"—rash pronouncements he might have regretted had he had the benefit of Galinsky's insights on Bradstreet's "Contemplations." Galinsky not only addresses the transformations of European literary traditions and the surprising influence of the erotic poetry of Catullus on Bradstreet's meditative reflections, but he succeeds in demonstrating that the progression from the senses to sense in "Contemplations" is reflected in Bradstreet's careful modeling of her language, the expert fusion of sensuous sound and rational syntactic patterning.

Equally impressive are Galinsky's later comments on Bradstreet's short autobiography, her verbal testament to her children, in which he discovers a "drama of consciousness" hitherto found only in the diaries of Thomas Shepard. Of particular importance in this part of the study is Galinsky's groundbreaking analysis of the first short story in the literature of New England, the "Prosopopeia of Solomons fall" from chapter 31 of Edward Holyoke's *The Doctrine of Life* (1658), the first example in the English language of a reworking of Old Testament material in narrative form. Galinsky pays attention to more general questions of genre as well as to seemingly minor textual details—rhythm, sound effects, syntax, repetition—all of which, in Galinsky's reading, become an impressive testimony to the virtually forgotten Holyoke's supreme verbal artistry.

d. 18th-Century Literature   One of this year's best contributions (and my personal favorite) is also one of the shortest—Peter Nicolaisen's slim, lavishly illustrated biography, *Thomas Jefferson* (Rowohlt). Nicolaisen's splendidly written book bears its considerable learning lightly; throughout, it is nourished by the author's pervasive sympathy for his subject, an underlying premise that even those readers who, like myself, continue to find offensive the racial exceptionalism propagated in *Notes on the State of Virginia,* will quickly come to respect. Nicolaisen's method of detaching himself from the less acceptable views of his subject and endorsing his more appealing, enduringly valid convictions ultimately proves to be highly effective; his chief tool is cool summary rather than excited evaluation. Equally competent on Jefferson's interests in architecture, gardening, natural history, philology, or diplomacy, Nicolaisen notes that this American president, in spite of his many talents and his undisputed historical stature, has always remained an ambivalent and strangely elusive figure. In spite of the roughly 18,000 letters he left (from which Nicolaisen's biography offers superbly translated excerpts), we know surprisingly little about Jefferson as a human being. Jefferson invariably faced the world, as Nicolaisen writes with an attitude of rational equanimity, politely intent on resolving the problems at hand and eager to avoid future conflicts, but never relenting in his desire to experiment with new ideas, projects, or technical gadgets. Not coincidentally, Nicolaisen quotes from a letter Jefferson sent to John Wayles Eppes in 1813: "The earth belongs to the living not the dead."

e. 19th-Century Literature   Three books based on doctoral dissertations dominate this year's studies. Among these, S. Karin Amos's *Alexis de Tocqueville and the American National Identity* (Peter Lang) is perhaps the most ambitious. Amos deals with the reception of *Democracy in America* among Victorian Americans, a challenging and interesting subject. Her heavily documented and, unfortunately, densely written study assesses the impact of Tocqueville's book on the American educational, academic, and national discourse. Amos comes to the conclusion that *Democracy,* which seemed all the more authoritative since it was written by a foreigner with no personal stake in the American experiment, equipped Americans at an opportune moment "with a most effective shield against European attacks."

Birgit Wetzel-Sahm's *"The Novel Ends Well That Ends Faithfully": Strategien der Konfliktlösung in Romanwerk von William Dean Howells* (Peter Lang) is a whopping (and closely printed) 465 pages, but it is definitely worth the effort. Based on readings of 34 (!) novels that Howells wrote between 1861 and 1920 (some of them virtually forgotten),

Wetzel-Sahm establishes a taxonomy of Howells's methods of resolving conflicts at the conclusions of his narratives. She shows that they typically undermine the premises of his more traditionally constructed plots.

Karin Schmidli's *Models and Modifications: Early African-American Women Writers from the Slave Narrative to the Novel* (Francke) grew out of a doctoral dissertation submitted at the University of Zurich in 1994. Drawing on texts that range from the first autobiographical narrative by a black woman, *The History of Mary Prince* (1831), to Emma Dunham Kelley's "Christian *bildungsroman*" *Megda* (1891), Schmidli clearly sees herself embarked on a mission: she wants her readers to recognize a distinct female experience *within* the African American 19th-century literary tradition. The narratives that she analyzes lead from a specific concern with the abolition of slavery toward the belief—in Kelley's case, for example—that racial injustice could be mitigated by the elevation of the black woman's soul. Schmidli is appalled by the neglect of Kelley, whose name has been absent from all major reference works, and she argues that "more black women authors have to be retrieved and re-evaluated in order to complete the picture of the African-American literary tradition."

Some essay-length contributions deserve mention. *Geburt und Tod im Kunstvergleich* (Wissenschaftlicher), ed. Gudrun Grabher, an interdisciplinary collection devoted to the truly liminal experiences of birth and death, offers an essay by the editor comparing the silences in Kate Chopin's *The Awakening* with Jane Campion's 1993 movie *The Piano* ("Ontologie des Schweigens: Todes- und Wiedergeburtsmetaphern in Jane Campions *The Piano* und Kate Chopins *The Awakening*," pp. 93–111). I was particularly impressed by Bärbel Czennia's "Der Tod auf dem Schlachtfeld: Verstösse gegen traditionelle Sehgewohnheiten in Stephen Cranes *The Red Badge of Courage*" (pp. 113–48), an idiosyncratic but convincing attempt to establish similarities among Crane's representation of death, Mathew Brady's Civil War photographs, and German artist Otto Dix's graphic works created in the years following World War I. Czennia shows that a literary text can adopt and transform the modes of seeing characteristic of other media, and thus, perhaps even more effectively and lastingly than a photograph or a painting, it shapes the reader's response to the drastic scenes it describes.

Among this year's contributions to *Amst* I would mention Klaus Lubbers's "Popular Models of National Identity in Currier & Ives's

Chromolithographs" (40: 163–81), though it bears only obliquely on literary scholarship. Lubbers usefully suggests that the model of national identity propagated in Currier & Ives prints, "the largest visual record of America," needs to be taken more seriously by literary historians; it was here that American pop culture began. The same issue of *Amst* contains Jochen Achilles's important study of the "magical spiritualization" of Poe's landscapes ("Edgar Allan Poe's Dreamscapes and the Transcendentalist View of Nature," 40: 553–73). Poe's fiction (notably "The Domain of Arnheim" and "Landor's Cottage") is a powerful anticipation of 20th-century forms of surrealism and thus of a time "when the synthesis of nature and culture seems to hatch huge and stony birds of prey, when castles in the air threaten to hit the earth like meteors . . . and when desire turns into the name of a streetcar." Poe's Eden is a "montaged" paradise, and Achilles brings home this point by concluding with brief references to Magritte's *Le Domain d'Arnheim* and *Le Château des Pyrenées*. These are pictorial expressions of the "otherness within ourselves," the recognition of which Achilles's essay thinks was still suppressed in Emerson's concept of nature and is now brought to the fore in Poe's ironic dreamscapes.

f. 20th-Century Literature   Twentieth-century American literature again yielded the richest harvest—too rich, in fact, to be served up here in other than small portions. I particularly enjoyed Astrid Böger's slim but tightly argued *Documenting Lives,* the first volume in the new series "Düsseldorfer Beiträge aus Anglistik und Amerikanistik," ed. Uwe Baumann and Herwig Friedl (Peter Lang). Böger reads James Agee's and Walker Evans's *Let Us Now Praise Famous Men* as a "dialogue" about representation; both Evans's photographs and Agee's convoluted, tormented text expose and reject conventional tropes of poverty and instead stress the dignity and beauty of their subjects. As Böger shows, *Famous Men* actively challenges the hierarchical distinction between the knower and the known; it seeks to understand or "praise" rather than change the lives of the Alabama tenants.

Vera Boie's *Writing Sexual Revolutions: Novel of Manners and Sexualität im Romanwerk von Sinclair Lewis und John Updike* (Königshausen) is an interesting comparison—a little off the beaten track—between the treatment of sexuality in three novels written by Sinclair Lewis in the 1920s (*Main Street, Babbitt, Dodsworth*) and John Updike's fictional response to the sexual revolution of the 1960s in his *Rabbit* tetralogy. Another contribution on Updike, Nicola Koch's clumsily titled *An Organized Mass of Images Moving Forward: Motive und Motivstrukturen im Romanwerk von John Updike* (Blaue Eule), aims to illustrate "the wealth of motifs which, with extraordinary compositional skill, Updike fuses into his complex narratives." In an appendix Koch reprints the interview she conducted in 1994 with the slightly bemused but on the whole supportive and encouraging Updike: "I am like the frog on the table you are dissecting," he cautioned. "So you cannot expect the frog to keep telling you what to do." Undaunted and with great thoroughness, Koch first analyzes the pervasive motif of the quest in Updike's novels and finds that it has connections with other motifs coming from sports, the arts, and the media. Updike's questers are, as a rule, unsuccessful, hence the motif addressed in Koch's final chapter—the hostile environment. The merit of Koch's book lies less in its overall thesis than in its plenitude of interpretive detail, its patient listing of motifs and metaphors.

Heide Ziegler's *Ironie ist Pflicht: John Barth und John Hawkes. Bewusstseinsformen des amerikanischen Gegenwartsromans* (Winter) is an ambitious, highly constructed attempt to ground an interpretation of the postmodern American novel in the concepts of irony proposed by two German Romantic thinkers, Friedrich Schlegel and Karl F. W. Solger. Ziegler sees irony as an attitude, not as a rhetorical gesture; by suspending the boundaries separating reality from fiction, irony crucially determines the relationship between author and reader. Postmodern literature, which according to Ziegler understands itself as a kind of "secular religion," manipulates as well as privileges readers who agree to participate in a play that allows them to join the author in projecting possible images of the world. For Barth, the communication between the narrator/author and the listener/reader is determined by the experience of love; Hawkes, however, demands the reader's self-immolation. While Barth, who uses a "temporal" form of irony (in, for example, *Lost in the Funhouse*), is obsessed with birth, Hawkes's "spatial" novels (Ziegler's main example is *Travesty*) reenact the experience of death; author and reader meet each other in nothingness or, rather, the free-floating space of the imagination.

No one would consider Bret Easton Ellis on a par with Barth or Hawkes, but after finishing Horst Steur's *Der Schein und das Nichts: Bret Easton Ellis' Roman* Less Than Zero (Blaue Eule), with its many observations on the function of verbal and scenic repetition in Ellis's text, I am almost convinced that there is more to this "MTV novel" and its challenge to the division between highbrow and lowbrow culture than meets the condescending critic's eye. I found particularly instructive the long chapter in which Steur criticizes the hurriedly produced German translation of Ellis's text.

In this year's only book-length contribution on modern African American literature, *The African Continuum and Contemporary African American Women Writers* (Peter Lang), Marion Kraft believes that she has discovered matrilineal African cultural traditions and narrative strategies in the works of contemporary African American women writers. Central to these African Americanisms, she alleges, is the figure of the double-voiced trickster-storyteller, whose presence Kraft discovers in the novels and autobiographies of Zora Neale Hurston, Maya Angelou, Audre Lorde, Alice Walker, Paule Marshall, and Toni Morrison.

Essay-length articles on 20th-century American prose include my own "Crossblood Columbus: Gerald Vizenor's Narrative 'Discoveries' " (*Amst* 40: 83–94), a reading of Vizenor's novel *The Heirs of Columbus* (1991). A comparison of *The Heirs* and Michael Dorris and Louise Erdrich's *The Crown of Columbus* (1991), it reveals Vizenor's narrative radicalism: the "discovery" of America turns into a text whose elements can be freely changed, rearranged, and reversed. Through the language games practiced by Vizenor's "crossblood" characters, narrative meaning becomes something to be endlessly reinvented rather than finally discovered. Maria Moss's "Demons at Play in Paul Auster's *The Music of Chance*" (*Amst* 40: 695–708) sees Auster using a "deadly serious" gamelike pattern as the structure for his novel in which he celebrates the "death of the postmodern author."

Studies of poetry this year include, first of all, Diana von Finck's *Ideen der Ordnung in der amerikanischen poetologischen Lyrik des 20. Jahrhunderts* (Peter Lang), which is about a type of verse that has attracted increasing interest: the poem whose main subject is the poem. Taking her cue from Alfred Weber's definition of the "poetological poem" as situated between the denotative discourse of the essay and the connotative evocativeness of the poem, von Finck scrutinizes the work of five American poets from two generations (William Carlos Williams, Wallace Stevens, T. S. Eliot, A. R. Ammons, and Robert Duncan) and finds that terms and metaphors for order indeed pervade these texts, supporting Armin Paul Frank's hypothesis that poetological reflection is the hallmark of modern poetry. Von Finck's overarching thesis that American modernists conceived of their activity mainly as the creation of order out of chaos sometimes forces her to sacrifice the sensuous richness and multiplicity of meaning in her texts to the monolithic structures of the schematic overview. For example, she is less interested in Stevens's word-play than in the conceptual principles that, to her, seem to forge his poetry into a coherent illustration of the power of the imagination "over the possibilities of things" or "the pressure of reality," in Stevens's own words. But Stevens's ambivalent metaphor for order, the jar in Tennessee, remains, significantly, "gray and bare"—an ironic reminder, I think, that as a poet Stevens always went in fear of abstractions and that in his best texts poetic theory and thus the "idea of order" become a form of sophisticated play that, unlike the gray jar, indeed "gives of bird and bush." Such reservations notwithstanding, von Finck's book is the best and most cohesive treatment available in German of Williams's and Stevens's poetry; her chapter on Williams's *Paterson* is the most accessible and clear-headed reading of this elusive text that I know. I wholeheart-edly agree with von Finck's final assessment that the "ideas of order" in Duncan's and Ammons's poetry, often classified as postmodern, do not venture far beyond the intellectual territory charted in the work of their modernist predecessors. "Poetry is necessarily theoretical," announces Language Poet Charles Bernstein, too, in an interview with Hannah Möckel-Rieke, appropriately conducted through e-mail and now re-printed (*Amst* 40: 59–67). In "Die 'unvollendete Moderne': Language Poetries und die amerikanische Lyrik der 80er Jahre" (*Amst* 40: 7–44) Hannah Möckel-Rieke chimes in when, in informed and sensitive read-ings of poems by Bernstein, Susan Howe, Kathleen Fraser, and Rosmarie Waldrop, she shows how some of the concerns of poetic modernism (among them the leveling of differences between the "high art" of the poem and other, more discursive statements) effectively survive even in the poetry of the 1980s and 1990s.

Sylvia Plath's poetry is the subject of an interesting dissertation sub-mitted in Freiburg by Monika Steinert: *Mythos in den Gedichten Sylvia Plaths* (Peter Lang). It is a refreshingly careful approach to Plath's work that takes the poetry on its own terms and remains unencumbered by the ongoing biographical brouhaha that has made Plath one of the most frequently discussed but most widely unread modern American poets. Steinert sees a development from an uncritical adoption of established cultural clichés toward a more playful, revisionist use of mythical per-sonae in Plath's poetry, as evidenced, for example, in "Ariel," where, in their quest for infinity, horse and rider become equals, not, as in the

Platonic version of the story, warring expressions for the soul and the body. Or as Wallace Stevens noted in his own version of Plato's little story ("The Noble Rider and the Sound of Words"), "it is not a choice of one over the other and not a decision that divides them"; instead, the poet's "choice and decision must be that they are equal and inseparable." Perhaps this is also the right way to view this year's German contributions to American literary scholarship.

Harvard University

iii Italian Contributions: Algerina Neri

Both 19th-century and 20th-century poetry, a field usually studied by a "happy few" Italian Americanists, is attracting young scholars. New translations, revised editions, and fine contributions on Emily Dickinson, Ezra Pound, T. S. Eliot, H. D., William Carlos Williams, and Robert Creeley mark this year's work, which has seen a return to favor of the Beat poets, too. The reprint of some pivotal works like Fernanda Pivano's 1964 anthology, *Poesia degli ultimi americani,* Emilio Cecchi's *America Amara,* or the great popularity of ethnic studies in Italy seem to be responsible for stimulating a long-desired need: a backward glance to 50 years of American studies in Italy, an analysis of the present situation, and a forecast of possible developments. Certainly, ethnic studies are not likely to lose their large following anytime soon.

a. General Work, Criticism Nobody could discuss American studies in Italy better than Agostino Lombardo. Bruno Cartosio and Alessandro Portelli interviewed him on this topic in "La via italiana agli studi americani: intervista con Agostino Lombardo" (*Acoma* 3: 70–74). Italian scholars have always felt the need to connect American literature, even more closely than other literatures, to its social and historical background. Noncanonical and minority strands have been, and are, part of the Italian approach, though Lombardo underlines the need to keep literature in its central place rather than losing its specificity in less-focused disciplinary approaches. Original Italian contributions to American studies can come only from our different and external cultural perspectives that allow us to see things that Americans themselves may not notice from within.

The forerunners of American studies have been reconsidered. Emilio Cecchi's travelogue, *America Amara* (1939), reprinted this year by Franco

Muzzio Editore, presents just one side of American reality. In "Le scoperte dell'America" (*Nuovi Argomenti* 5: 100–105) Tommaso Giartosio tries to read Cecchi's book out of its historical context; the severe judgments on the United States, which have been attributed to a sullen operation of political consensus, reflect instead what Cecchi felt. For Cesare Pavese, the United States was "the huge theater where everyone's drama was performed with much more frankness than anywhere else"; for Fernanda Pivano it was the encounter with American writers. Besides the reprint of her "cult anthology" of the Beat Generation, *Poesia degli ultimi americani* (Feltrinelli), she has published *Amici miei* (Mondadori), a collection of about 70 short chapters, each one a flashback through 40 years of meetings with American writers. A page-turner, though, devoid of any critical approach. Pivano's love affair with the Beats also materializes in her "Prevert d'America," an introduction to the poems that Lawrence Ferlinghetti has written on Italy, *Scene italiane* (Minimum Fax). Although neglected by critics, Italo Calvino's writings on the United States form an impressive body of work. In "L'America critica e fantapolitica di Italo Calvino" (*Acoma* 5: 111–20) Martino Marazzi critically examines Calvino's articles and diaries following his 1959–60 stay in the United States. Their ideological and political message today seems too imaginative and contrived. Even later in his life Calvino went back to the image of New York, the ideal city, "a geometric, cristal clear place, without past, without depth," a city of the mind, both concrete and "invisible." New York was the growing place of the writer Aldo Rosselli, who arrived there at five with his mother and grandmother to escape from Nazi and Fascist persecutions. *La mia America e la tua* (Theoria) is not Rosselli's autobiography, but a topographical succession of places, facts, and people through which his existence makes sense. Mario Maffi also dedicates his latest book to New York, *New York: L'isola delle Colline* (Saggiatore). Maffi's agile presentation of the city as a whole comes three years after his contribution about the Lower East Side, *Nel mosaico della città* (see *ALS 1992*, p. 338), which was written after 10 years of study, research, and trips. Now Maffi in *New York,* free from pressures, feels the need to go back to remember, to view again and compare what had been compressed in his earlier book. The result is an unceasing alternation of mixed feelings, like going up and down the switchbacks of Manhattan, the island built on a rock, "the island of the hills."

If Maffi's book dazzles with its kaleidoscope of images, Marco D'Eramo's *Il maiale e il grattacielo* (Feltrinelli) charts Chicago with a magnifying glass. His detective work leads to the study of a city and its history, which, D'Eramo thinks, is the history of modernity. Maffi goes on with his urban "archaeological diggins" in his "The Subway and the Cellar: breve viaggio nei sotteranei d'America" (*Acoma* 2: 16–21). Drawing on texts by such authors as Mark Twain, Jack London, Ralph Ellison, George Lippard, Edgar Allan Poe, and LeRoi Jones, his essay explores the subway as the Other of the city and the cellar as the Other of the self. These sites where the repressed must be confronted can also be the places where reconstruction of a new identity may begin. A more general study is Sergio Benvenuto's *Capire l'America: Un europeo negli States di oggi* (Costa and Nolan). Benvenuto, too, a philosopher and a psychologist, knows the art of going under the surface, and he gives some perceptive views on American ways.

Franco Moretti, professor of comparative literature at Columbia University, discusses his experience in "L'università del narcisismo: Mercato, ricerca, specialismi nell'università e nella critica americana" (*Acoma* 4:61–65). Moretti finds both strengths and weaknesses in the predominantly market-driven U.S. university system. He discusses multiculturalism, the rise of cultural studies and the New Historicism, the teaching of literature, the decline of the relationship between the university and the public sphere. Sacvan Bercovitch talks about university work, but also of growing up in a poor French district of Montreal, in his interview with Giuseppe Nori, "Cross-Cultural Adventures" (*RSAJ* 5: 111–20). Nori, who translated Bercovitch's *America Puritana* (see *ALS 1992*, p. 327), asks about Bercovitch's life and experience in order to understand his current critical position. American criticism in the '80s is presented in Peter Caravetta's tough and sound contribution, "Erranza della teoria tra filosofia, storia e letteratura: Problemi e prospettive del panorama americano degli anni 80" (*Allegoria* 19: 26–53). In the same issue Pietropaolo Domenico speaks about New Historicism in "La novità del nuovo storicismo americano" (pp. 139–42). Roberto Cagliero and Chiara Spallino publish *Dizionario di slang americano* (Mondadori 1994), a useful paperback that reflects the extreme vitality and elasticity of the American language, one able to absorb and transform words that come from the most unusual fields.

b. 19th-Century Literature In 1994 the Italian Association for North American Studies gathered at Trieste, a very suitable place, to discuss "Departure, Arrival, Transit: The Expatriate Eye Revisited." Some contributions by foreign and Italian scholars have been collected in *Prospero,* ed. Renzo Crivelli. In "The Fall of a Dream of a National/Monological Discourse in the Polylinguistic/Logical Texts of Exile Literature" (2: 113–29) Paola Zaccaria shows how exiles' works are the results of a subjectivity "on the move" that is "consequently able to translate the vision arising from the rupture of linguistic, national, cultural bonds only through a breaking of codified linguistic and aesthetic norms." In " 'A Levante per Ponente': Home Seeking Through Irony and Paradox in Royall Tyler's *The Algerine Captive*" (2: 64–71) Michele Bottalico discusses expatriation as a way of home-seeking, which is the real focus of Tyler's book. Bottalico uses Luigi Pirandello's terminology in his essay "On Humour" to analyze Tyler's rhetorical devices. In "A Frenchman Abroad: The Construction of National Identity in Cooper's *The Wing-and-Wing*" (2: 72–78) Leonardo Buonomo closely examines the use that Cooper made in the novel of French, English, and American characters abroad in order to show his disillusionment with his country's moral fiber. Set mostly in the bay of Naples, the novel was written many years after Cooper's sojourn in Italy. In "Il Sud di James Fenimore Cooper: l'esperienza periegetica e i testi" in *Viaggio nel Sud III,* ed. E. Kanceff and R. Rampone (C.I.R.V.I.), Gaetano Prampolini compares the different ways in which Cooper describes his Italian experience in his diary and letters, in *The Water-Witch,* in his travel book, and in *The Wing-and-Wing.* In another perceptive contribution Prampolini expands on Cooper's travel book on Italy, "Il Viaggio in Italia di James Fenimore Cooper" (*Bollettino del C.I.R.V.I.* 22: 362–70). Cooper, the first American writer to publish a travel book on Italy, seems to balance two ways of looking at Italy that became irreconcilable for future travelers: Italy as "the dream of Arcadia" (Hawthorne, Melville, James, Wharton) and Italy as a real place (Howells and Twain). To go on living in Arcadia, the writer must avoid history. This is what Washington Irving did when he arrived in Liverpool. In "Liverpool & Liverpool: l'immagine della città da Washington Irving a Herman Melville" (pp. 33–60) in *La città senza confini,* ed. Carlo Pagetti (Bulzoni), Barbara Nugnes points out how Irving removed the disquieting reality of the industrial city by not speaking about it in *The Sketch Book.* Some 30 years later, Melville's Redburn arrived at Liverpool, too, and there he experienced restlessness, bewilderment, that "charterless voyage" which is typical of modernity.

Paolo Collo collected *The Raven, Ulalume and Annabel Lee di Edgar Allan Poe* (Einaudi) in a fine, small edition that gathers works by writers translated by other writers in two foreign languages, in this case by Fernando Pessoa, Antonio Bruno, Gabriele Baldini, and Elio Chinol. In his afterword Collo highlights Pessoa's translations, showing how the Portuguese writer made the original message come back to life through the genius of his own language and culture. Thoreau's chapter on "Reading" in *Walden* catches the attention of Pier Cesare Bori. In " 'Le Sacre Scritture, o Bibbie dell'umanità' in *Walden* di H. D. Thoreau" (*Il piccolo Hans* 83–84: 257–72) Bori underlines the extraordinary political intensity of Thoreau's cultural proposal when he recognizes the plurality and validity of the sacred scriptures of different religions and traditions.

Last year Vito Amoruso edited a fine collection of Hawthorne's works (see *ALS 1994*, p. 439), and this year Carlo Pagetti publishes a paperback edition of *Twice-Told Tales, Racconti raccontati due volte* (Garzanti). It is the first complete edition of Hawthorne's book, which has been translated by Marco Papi. Pagetti's stimulating introduction with a very useful bibliography takes us into the writer's world where his tales "lead the reader into a neutral zone between reality and an imaginary world where human beings and ghosts may meet and even change their roles." In his subtle introduction to a fine edition of *The Marble Faun, Il Fauno di Marmo* (Giunti) Agostino Lombardo compares the novel and Hawthorne's diary, which was edited by Lombardo in 1959 and is still available. Angela Giannitrapani collects some essays she had written for a Messina magazine in *Memoria Critica* (Empiria). In "La terribile soglia" (pp. 9–14) she analyzes the emblematic value of the threshold in *The Scarlet Letter;* in "Maschere" (pp. 89–96) Giannitrapani compares Edward Taylor's and Emerson's poetry.

Melville fares well this year, too. An able contribution comes from Giuseppe Nori, *Il Seme delle Piramidi: L'evoluzione artistica e intellettuale di Herman Melville* (Andrea Livi). Last year Nori edited Melville's letters to Hawthorne (see *ALS 94*, p. 439), and this year he explores Melville's evolution from 1850 through 1857, starting from the correspondence with Hawthorne and Melville's essay "Hawthorne and His Mosses." These writings offer a unique perspective to light Melville's winding path, which led not only to his monumental novels, but to a reassessment of his thought and his literary work in the years after his "major phase." Virtually the same period comes under scrutiny in Giuseppe Lombardo's "To Strike the Uneven Balance: Dissimetria e Distanza nelle Prose Brevi (1853–1856) di Herman Melville" (*Nuovi Annali della Facoltà di Magistero di Messina 1994*, pp. 453–535). The short stories of this period are an interesting step in Melville's evolution. Both themes and language register his evolution toward the realization that asymmetry is a permanent state. In his controversial book, *Opere Mondo Saggio sulla forma epica dal Faust a Cent'anni di Solitudine* (Einaudi, 1994), Franco Moretti discusses *Moby-Dick* along with *Faust, Ulysses,* the *Cantos,* etc., to support his ideas on the modern epic. Roberto Birindelli surveys Italian criticism on Melville over recent years in his review of "Luca Briasco: La ricerca di Ishmael: *Moby-Dick* come avventura dell'interpretazione" (*RLMC* 48: 184–89). A one-day seminar on "The Italian translations of Melville" was organized in Venice this year. In "Melville in Italia" (*Nuovi Argomenti* 7: 12–13) Massimo Bacigalupo, a Melville translator himself, dwells on present and past translators. Among translations of other works, Bacigalupo deals with Eugenio Montale's rendering of *Billy Budd.* The 42-year-old Montale started to translate in order to make a living when he was dismissed in 1938 from his job at Gabinetto Viessieux because he was not a member of the Fascist Party. He had great difficulty in his efforts, as he often complained in his letters. However, translating *Billy Budd* was extremely important for him, as Silvia Zangrandi underscores in her "L'ultima alba di *Billy Budd* nella traduzione di Montale" (*Ling & L* 24–25: 169–75). Zangrandi discussed Montale's translation in 1992 (see *ALS 1993,* p. 373), and she now wants to investigate not so much its faithfulness, but the ways in which Montale confronted the original text. The Italian poet emphasized the musicality and the narrative dimension of the text, which he felt was in tune with his taste and his poetical sensibility. *Billy Budd, Marinaio* (Edisco) has been translated again by Alberto Lehmann. The book has a useful and competent introduction, ample notes, bibliography, working suggestions for students, and a guide for teachers. In "Nell'occhio tropicale di Melville," a chapter in *La Laguna di Venezia,* ed. Giovanni Caniato et al. (Cierre), Marilla Battilana expands on Melville's impressions of Venice.

Four new editions of Emily Dickinson appeared this year. The largest, *Poesie,* ed. Massimo Bacigalupo (Mondadori), contains 358 poems in English and Italian, an extensive bibliographical essay, and succinct notes on each poem, indicating meter, theme, allusions, etc. This is the first time that Dickinson has been so thoroughly annotated in Italy. The translation is accurate and literal, but poetically suggestive. A selection of Bacigalupo's translations, *51 Poesie* (Mondadori, 1996), made the Italian best-seller list for several weeks. Anthony L. Johnson provides an ample new introduction and notes to a new, two-volume edition of Margherita

Guidacci's classic translation *Poesie, Lettere* (Bompiani). A more personal selection of 100 poems is offered by Francesco Binni, with the suggestive title *Rime Imperfette* (Empiria). The poems are collected under headings—not traditional ones like Nature and Death, but "A Poet Without a Project?," "An Alphabet of the Self," etc. The translation is equally adventurous. Binni omits articles and prepositions leaving words naked, edgy, harsh, as Dickinson wrote them. Adriana Seri's anthology, *Mie forti madonne* (Mobydick, 1994), is more limited, with a risk of appearing minimalist, though it contains some unpublished poems. Marisa Bulgheroni begins her essay on "Tradurre Emily Dickinson" (*Acoma* 2: 9–15) with two quotations taken from an international conference on translating Dickinson held in Washington, D.C., in 1992 to affirm that the task needs a plurality of decodifying acts that challenge any theoretical plan. Bulgheroni then presents 12 poems translated by Italian writers. In the following issue of *Acoma* Mario Corona comments on his forthcoming translation of Walt Whitman's 1855 edition of *Leaves of Grass* (pp. 64–69). Corona was induced to translate the first edition because he wanted the Italian public to know the original text with its singular idiosyncracies and discontinuities, changes of tone, sudden enlightenments, as well as its unexpected and sometimes extravagant *décalages*.

This year Henry James is considered in only three articles. Donatella Izzo presents her essay on "Women, Portraits, and Painters: *The Madonna of the Future* and *The Sweetheart of M. Briseux*" (*RSAJ* 5: 5–28), which is part of a work in progress on feminine representation in James's tales. Izzo argues that these early tales can be read as powerful statements on the cultural and aesthetic construction of woman, although traditionally they have been interpreted as dealing with the problem of the artist. In "Tra Europa e America: tre donne jamesiane" (pp. 67–96), a chapter in *Verso la Sponda Invisibile* (ETS), Paolo Bertinetti analyzes the international theme through three feminine characters from *Daisy Miller, The Reverberator,* and *A London Life.* Michela Vanon Alliata's "A Caravan of Gypsies: James, Sargent, and the American Symptom" (*RSAJ* 5: 29–50) focuses on the affinities and differences between James and John Singer Sargent, James's favorite portrait painter. Though their expatriate lives may look similar, a closer examination reveals their diverging attitudes.

c. 20th-Century Prose   Edith Wharton continues to be popular in Italy. Cristina Giorcelli edited a fine bilingual translation by Emanuela Dal Fabbro of *Ethan Frome* (Marsilio) with biography, notes, and bibliography. In her ample and sound introduction, "Gusto del martirio ed espiazione: il vortice di Ethan Frome" (pp. 9–60), Giorcelli points out the various correspondences that link this text to a precise constellation of Hawthorne's works. However, Giorcelli has no wish to diminish Wharton's narrative power of invention and to make her not only James's but also Hawthorne's pupil. On the contrary, she wants to place Wharton with her disturbing creativity in the great tradition of the American novel. Gianfranca Balestra writes a perceptive introduction, "Il mercato delle lettere," to one of Wharton's early novels, *La Pietra di Paragone* (Tartaruga). As in Poe's *The Purloined Letter,* the letters sold in this novel are "the place of feminine sexuality and creativity," metaphors for writing itself and for the variety of readings. Balestra also publishes "What the Children Knew: The Manuscript of *Disintegration,* An Unfinished Novel" (*EWhR* 12: 7–11). Balestra underlines the importance of the unfinished manuscript on various grounds, but, above all, she thinks it offers one of Wharton's most cogent and moving representations of a little girl with her perceptions and feelings on the way to knowledge and maturity. Wharton's backward glance at her own life records facts and people with attention and amusement without organizing or judging, according to Luciano Morbiato in a review of *Uno sguardo indietro* (Riuniti, 1994) in *Ling & L* (24–25: 184–87). This special way of looking at reality was probably the result of Wharton's writing from the margin. Expatriation not only gave her a better perspective on American society, but it provided her with the artistic and professional stimuli she needed to become a writer. In "A Backward Glance Over Travelled Roads: Edith Wharton and Expatriation" (*RSAJ* 5: 5–28) Balestra explores the complexities of expatriation, both at biographical and literary levels. In the same issue in "A Reversal of Perspective: The Mother's Voice in Edith Wharton's *The Mother Recompense*" (pp. 29–51) Davida Gavioli argues that Wharton's *The Mother's Recompense* can be read as a text that suspends the cultural muteness of the mother, showing instead how disruptive a mother's voice can be. Luigino Biagioni devotes his contribution, "La forza animale in *Nightwood*" (*SCr* 78: 61–78), to the last chapter of Djuna Barnes's novel. Biagioni wants to show that this controversial part is the result of a particular process that runs through the novel: happiness may be reached only out of our practical and intellectual institutions.

Donata Banzato and Donatella Possamai examine Nabokov as translator in "Nabokov traduce se stesso" (*Testo a fronte* 13: 61–78). They compare the 1920 original Russian edition of *The Potato Egg* with Nabokov's 1973 translation. Though he professed to be in favor of a literal translation, Nabokov when put to the test was more interested in the final result. Bruno Cartosio confronts a similar problem, the transposition of Hemingway's *To Have and Have Not* into Howard Hawks's movie in "Modi di produzione: Hemingway e Hawks" (*Acoma* 3: 84–95). The poet Anna Cascella publishes a small, passionate book on *I Colori di Gatsby: Lettura di Fitzgerald* (Lithos). As Caterina Ricciardi writes in her introduction, the book "examines colour not only as a deliberate repetitious code, a manifestation of destiny and a place where evocative literary allusions (*Macbeth*'s dusty grey, *The Waste Land*'s wet lilac) converge, but also as a measure of the emotive and poetic tension of the text." In "Le Liste di Miller: Prole retorica di una famiglia surreale" (*Ling & L* 24–25: 115–24) Leonardo Terzo analyzes how Arthur Miller uses the list, which is the most elementary way to organize a subject. The enumerative form is also an escape from a painful situation, as Miller learned in his youth when he saw his sister ill-treated by their mother.

Daniela Daniele publishes *Città senza mappa* (Edizioni dell'Orso, 1994), the fruit of long and careful research. Daniele aims to compare the contemporary North American metropolis to the landscapes that emerge from the fiction of three authors of the postmodern generation: Thomas Pynchon, Donald Barthelme, and performance artist Laurie Anderson. Postmodern fiction imposes a pluri-linguistic, decentralized way of reading. Pynchon searches for improbable meaning in the disorder of metropolitan debris, Barthelme shows the anxious objects of urban art and architecture, and Anderson picks up the ambivalent messages of the technological city. A more optimistic view comes from Marge Piercy's fiction. In "Città alienate, città alternative: *Woman on the Edge of Time* di Marge Piercy" (pp. 249–66) in *La Città senza Confini,* ed. Carlo Pagetti (Bulzoni), Gianfranca Balestra points out that for Piercy the contemporary alienated city, though in danger of dramatic deterioration, can develop into an alternative city for which it is worthwhile to work, struggle, and write. In *Memoria Critica* (Empiria) Angela Giannitrapani argues that science fiction has become a predominantly feminine field (pp. 116–20). In the same book (pp. 25–40 and 131–54) Giannitrapani devotes four chapters to Ursula K. Le Guin's biography and works. Maria Vittoria D'Amico introduces Coleman Dowell's unpublished story, "Willow Sheridan Rode Voltaire" (*RSAJ* 5: 121–34). The story, probably part of a larger project, was chosen not only for its charm, but for the promise of an open work. Stefano Rosso's forthcoming book will concern American fiction on Vietnam. Meanwhile, in "Narrativa statunitense e guerra del Vietnam: un canone in formazione" (*Acoma* 4: 66–75) he discusses different kinds of narrative, the various periods into which such narrative can be divided, and the special nature of the Vietnam War. Anna Nadotti writes about another Vietnam War book, Robert Olen Butler's *I cento figli del drago* (Instar Libri), in her "Il profumo di zio Ho" (*Indice* 11: 21). Daniela Daniele interviews Mark Leyner and finds his *Mio Cugino, il mio gastroenterologo* (Frassinelli) more like a spot or a video clip than a narrative sequence (*Indice* 7: 11). In "Per nostra fortuna Raymond Federman" (*Il Ponte* 12: 170–71) Mario Materassi expresses thanks that sometimes Federman forgets his philosophical principles and gives us brilliant narrative passages in his *A tutti gli interessati* (Marsilio).

d. Ethnic Literature   The myth of Pocahontas has spread far and wide in Italy after this year's Disney movie, which generated three books. David Garnett's *Pocahontas* (Mondadori), translated by Salvatore Rosati in 1937, has been reprinted. Alide Cagidemetrio presents a bilingual translation of the work of another English writer, John Davis, *Il Capitano Smith e la principessa Pocahontas* (Marsilio). In her accurate introduction supplemented by many useful notes, Cagidemetrio discusses Davis's work in the context of the literary tradition of its period and then expands on the myth's treatment of Pocahontas in 19th- and 20th-century American literary works. A fine edition by Cinzia Biagiotti and Laura Coltelli, *Figlie di Pocahontas* (Giunti), has gathered a comprehensive collection of short stories and poems by contemporary Native American women. In the introduction to the short stories, "Il filo nelle perline: le storie delle donne indiane," Biagiotti comments on the placid tone of the language that tells of the resistance and survival of a whole nation. The women's words are similar to the threat that goes through the pearls, through the loom, the thread that stitches and mends the tears of the past. In "Donne fatte di parole" Laura Coltelli introduces the second part, an excellent selection of bilingual poems by 15 writers. Coltelli points out how Native American poetry and fiction turn around the feeling of communion and total identity that the writers have with a particular landscape. The book ends with biographies and bibliographies of single authors.

Laura Coltelli makes her interesting collection of interviews with 10 Native American writers, *Parole fatte d'alba: Gli scrittori indiani d'Amer-*

ica parlano (Castelvecchi), available to the Italian reader. These perceptive, accurate interviews, first published by the University of Nebraska
Press in 1990, help us discover the different voices of a culture that is
increasingly intriguing. Fedora Giordano's "The Anxiety of Discovery:
The Italian Interest in Native American Studies" (*RSAJ* 5: 81–110) outlines the various views on Native Americans held by Italian explorers,
missionaries, travelers, anthropologists, and writers over the past four
centuries. The position of the French Encyclopedists toward Native
Americans was ambivalent, as Franco Fido argues in his "I Philosophes,
l'America e gli Indiani" (*RLMC* 48: 47–56). Giorgio Mariani explores
the "Otherness" in Native American fiction in his stimulating essay,
"L'altrove nella narrativa indiano-americana, fra utopia e mimesi" (pp.
387–98) in *Per una topografia dell'Altrove,* ed. Maria Teresa Chialant and
Eleonora Rao (Liguori). While American heroes tend to search for their
self by escaping toward the frontier, Native American heroes search for a
collective self in a place where their kinspeople have lived. As it is
difficult to consider the Indian reservation as reassuring tribal country,
Native Americans must reconsider the reservation as a newly acquired
Indian land. In "Dai mondi sotteranei alla luce: l'universo nel racconto
degli Indiani d'America" (*Acoma* 2: 50–56) Daniele Fiorentino analyzes
the American Indian concept of the underground as a space where
natural things, whether plants, animals, or human beings, are generated
or regenerated. Both Mariani and Fiorentino review Sherman Alexie's
Lone Ranger fa a pugni in Paradiso (Frassinelli) in "Scheletri indiani" and
"Autostop da Spokane a Woodstock" (*Indice* 7: 10). They find the book
"extraordinary," though Mariani laments the lack of some useful notes in
the Italian translation. Leslie Marmon Silko speaks about her personal
experience of racism and the present situation in the United States in
"Steccati contro la libertà" (*Acoma* 4: 4–13). Daria Donnelly comments
on Silko's novel in *"Almanac of the Dead* di Leslie Silko: un intratteni-
mento rivoluzionario" (*Acoma* 5: 58–66). Silko's narrative style has become more rigorously Pueblo because she refuses to impose a hierarchy
on her more than 70 principal characters, and she will not close off
narrative strands.

Stefania Piccinato discusses an 18th-century African American autobiography in her perceptive essay, "Olaudah Equiano—Gustavus Vassa:
un uomo del '700 fra due culture" (pp. 237–45), in *Il senso del nonsenso,*
ed. Monique Streiff Moretti et al. (E.S.I., 1994). In his book Equiano, a
true son of his time, not only pleads for the abolition of slavery, but he

supports a clear economic program in which Africa and the United States would become equal commercial partners. A large part of *Acoma* 3 is taken up by contributions on African American women from 1761 to 1930. Cristina Mattiello's "I maschi non c'entrano per niente: predicatrici e profete nere nell'America dell'Ottocento" (pp. 24–28) and Elizabeth Vezzosi's "Donne nere, povertà, cittadinanza" (pp. 38–49) follow a more historical and sociological trend. Annalucia Accardo discusses women's autobiographies in "Resistenza, autorità e autorappresentazione nell'autobiografia delle donne nere prima della guerra civile" (pp. 14–23). Accardo argues that women's autobiographies resist the external definitions of identity imposed by dominant ideologies, and, while representing alternative models of women who have control over their lives and their narration, they revise the most popular modes of their time: the sentimental novel and the male slave narratives. In "La tradizione invisibile: le radici ottocentesche della narrativa femminile americana" (pp. 29–37) Giulia Fabi discusses some important issues of 19th-century African American women's fiction. Then she expands on Amelia E. Johnson's Sunday school novels, which reveal the author's conscious deployment of an aesthetic of invisibility.

In "Zora Neale Hurston: la mitologia e la storia" (*Acoma* 4: 76–87) Carla Cappetti shows how Hurston in *Their Eyes Were Watching God* was critical of bourgeois culture and institutions as well as of the ideologically and culturally subaltern position of the African American middle class. Toni Morrison's works, life, and ideas are the subject of various contributions. Alessandro Portelli compares the mother-daughter plot to the father-daughter subplot of *Beloved* in "Figlie e padri, scrittura e assenza in *Beloved* di Toni Morrison" (*Acoma* 5: 72–84). In the same issue Portelli and Bruno Cartosio publish a wide-ranging interview with Morrison, "La nostra amatissima: intervista con Toni Morrison" (pp. 67–71). Morrison discusses her political and social involvement in American society and her literary and teaching activity. In "Voglio una letteratura devastante" (*Indice* 2: 12–13) Chiara Spallino also interviews Morrison but on more specific problems of literary affiliation. Roberto Serrai presents Morrison's life and work in "La ricostruzione di una cultura: Toni Morrison" (*Il Ponte* 10: 163–66). Serrai appreciates Morrison's art of storytelling more than the cultural or political side of her writings. He maintains that Morrison won the Nobel Prize for Literature on her own merits and not as the result of a politically correct decision toward ethnic minorities. As Morrison writes, a number of key symbols and words reveal the "obscure, persistent, determinant African presence" in American society. Alessandro Portelli's "The Power of Blackness: gli afro-americani, le macchine, e l'energia del sottosuolo" (*Acoma* 2: 22–34) analyzes the dialectics of oppression and power in the work of authors such as Audre Lorde, Ralph Ellison, Hawthorne, and Richard Wright, as well as in oral history and folklore. Portelli's students interviewed Henry Louis Gates at the University of Rome. In "Identità e funzioni dell'intellettuale afroamericano" (*Acoma* 2: 64–68) Gates reconstructs his own experience and background to illustrate the encounter between African American literature and postmodernism and the writing of his *The Signifying Monkey.*

In her perceptive introduction to a bilingual selection of Leo Romero's poems, "Un poeta a Santa Fe" (*L'Ozio* 12: 79–97), Franca Bacchiega describes her fascination with the Southwest. Its peculiar atmosphere, its architecture, and its mixed population of Indian, Spanish, and English conquered many artists in the past, as Barbara Lanati writes in "L'orizzonte di Taos: la luce e l'arte di vedere" (*Acoma* 4: 44–55). Lanati follows the paths of the members of the American avant-garde in their "search for light" in the early decades of the 20th century. She focuses on Mabel Dodge Luhan and Georgia O'Keeffe. For Rudolfo Anaya, the roots of the literary imagination are always to be found in a sense of place. In his essay on "Lo spirito del luogo" (*Acoma* 4: 56–60) Anaya, one of the most important Chicano writers, finds that in a region like the Southwest, literature will register a diversity of interactions between culture and land as well as a constant crossing of the borders separating traditions, histories, and collective memories. Mario Materassi reviews Oscar Hijuelos's *Mambo Kings cantano canzoni d'amore* (*Ling & L* 24–25: 177–79). His review, which comes five years after the Italian translation, is the occasion for Materassi to write a provocative essay on the mechanisms of the publishing industry, which enable a trash book like *The Mambo Kings Sing Songs of Love* to win the Pulitzer Prize.

Elèna Mortara Di Veroli writes on "Travel and Metamorphosis in I. B. Singer's Fiction" (*Prospero* 2: 94–112). The article shows the surprising and imaginative way in which Singer conveyed the experience of traveling from the Old World to the New. Di Veroli examines *The Little Shoemakers* and *Love and Exile* to describe Singer's transition between two cultures and his metamorphosis in that process. Massimo Bacigalupo gives a vivid picture of Singer's last book, *Scum,* in his review of "Schiuma" (*Il verri* 1–2: 183–85). Reading *Scum* is like entering one of

Marc Chagall's paintings, with starry skies, charming Jewish women, rabbis, small donkeys. Saul Bellow's translation of essays, *I conti tornano: saggi 1948–1993* (Mondadori), is the subject of three reviews. In "Il bilancio di un dilettante" (*Indice* 9: 6) Guido Fink finds that in their variety the essays are in fact Bellow's indirect autobiography, a long monologue that the writer has with society, power, the market, the public. "In ossessivo ascolto del futuro" (*Indce* 9: 6) Marisa Bulgheroni ferrets out the alarm transmitted by the essays about the danger of mental annihilation and the loss of imagination. For Chiara Somaschini the essays are a lesson of depth in the confusion of contemporary superficiality (*Leggere* 76: 52). Luciana Pirè briefly introduces Susan Sontag's life and works in "Lo stile della volontà radicale" (*Indice* 7: 4) and in the same issue Vito Amoruso comments on Sontag's *L'amante del Vulcano* (Mondadori) in "Verità e mistero nel cratere del mondo." Amoruso thinks this novel is Sontag's most ambitious and best, blending an admirable narrative excellence and her typical intellectual passion. The first issue of *Acoma* opened with Grace Paley's poem, "It is the Responsibility," and ended with her *Midrash on Happiness*. Edward Lynch and Alessandro Portelli interview Paley on these subjects in "Responsabilità e felicità: Conversazioni con Grace Paley" (*Acoma* 5: 46–51). In the same issue (pp. 52–57) Annalucia Accardo writes on "Grace Paley: la difficoltà di ascoltare e l'impossibilità di tacere." The essay explores the different modes and connotations of speaking and silence in Paley's works. Is there a relation between a parrot in a cage and the innovative and revolutionary work of its owner-writer? In "Il pappagallo di Hugh Nissenson" (*Il Ponte* 10: 180–82) Mario Materassi thinks that Nissenson's parrot is involved in the making of the writer's latest novel, *The Song of the Earth*. Uncertainty about their own cultural identity is key to the works of Maxine Hong Kingston and of South African writer Zoe Wicomb, as Paola Splendore argues in her "Tra home e homeland: le patrie confuse di Maxine Hong Kingston e Zoe Wicomb," pp. 353–64 in *Per una topografia dell'Altrove.*

e. 20th-Century Poetry and Drama Many new books, editions, and articles have appeared this year. *La figlia che piange: Saggi su poesia e meta—poesia,* ed. Agostino Lombardo (Bulzoni), collects under the title of an early T. S. Eliot poem essays on English and American poetry by associates of Rome University La Sapienza. Valerio Massimo De Angelis offers an illuminating reading of Whitman's "By Blue Ontario's Shore" in its redactions (pp. 123–39). The other American contributions turn to the 20th century. Roberto Baronti Marchiò gives an excellent account of "Ezra Pound: the t(h)in artist" (pp. 193–212), showing the modernity of the early poetry. Gabriele Poole usefully compares Eliot's haunting "La Figlia che Piange" to Shelley's "To a Skylark" (pp. 213–22); Marco Nieli carefully reads Allen Ginsberg's "Death to Van Gogh's Ear," with interesting observations on the poet's development (pp. 281–300). A highly unusual and rewarding subject, discussed by Luca Briasco, is Vladimir Nabokov's pseudonymous poem at the center of *Pale Fire* (pp. 301–17). Chiara Midolo writes of Langston Hughes (pp. 319–28), Anna Scacchi of Anne Sexton (pp. 329–41), Riccardo Duranti of Raymond Carver (pp. 343–54), and the volume closes with Agostino Lombardo's fine general essay, "The American Dream of the American Artist" (pp. 355–72). Another book collecting many poets is Paola Zaccaria's *A Lettere Scarlatte: Poesia come Stregoneria: Emily Dickinson, H.D., Sylvia Plath, Anne Sexton, Robin Morgan, Adrienne Rich (e altre)* (Franco Angeli). Zaccaria's aim is to build a common space—a common house—where each poet has a special room but also a gathering place where she can talk with other poets. The poet as a witch, Allen Tate's definition of Emily Dickinson, is the figure Zaccaria tries to trace in this volume. Gender studies are also prominent in two books devoted to H.D. *H(ilda) D(oolittle) e il suo Mondo* (Palermo: Annali dell'Università), the proceedings of a conference, ed. Marina Camboni, collects articles and memoirs. Mary de Rachewiltz begins with an intimate insight into the Pound-H.D. relationship, while Perdita Schaffner rounds out the volume with childhood recollections of her mother. In other contributions Barbara Lanati expands on Amy Lowell and Imagist poetry; Marina Camboni enlightens the Ellenistic ideals of Imagists while discussing *Sea Garden;* Silvana Sciarrino writes on Dorothy Richardson and H.D.; Marina Sbisà and Patrizia Lendinara consider H.D.'s language; and Cinzia Leone and Alessandra Benanti examine the *Trilogy* and *Helen in Egypt.* A contributor to the Palermo symposium, Raffaella Baccolini, has published *Tradition Identity Desire: Revisionist Strategies in H.D.'s Late Poetry* (Pàtron), which has chapters on *By Avon River, Winter Love,* and *Hermetic Definition.* This major study of H.D. benefits from Baccolini's familiarity with the tradition of Dante's circle that inspired H.D. as well as Pound.

A welcome contribution to Pound studies is Giano Accame's *Ezra Pound economista: contro l'usura* (Settimo Sigillo). Accame, an economic journalist, offers a new consideration of Pound's apparently erratic economic (and political) writings. Accame claims that the monetary concerns that loom so large in the prose and the poetry, and which seemed less significant in Pound's time, have merged to become the main economic issue today. What Pound never tires of reiterating—that the control of money and finance is responsible for the world's poverty and wealth—is truer now than ever before. Accame places Pound firmly and interestingly in the American tradition of Andrew Jackson and Vernon L. Parrington. Animated by a genuine concern for economic equality, Pound wrote a typically American poem that is unique in world literature for the place it assigns to economics. Though not strictly a work of literary scholarship, Accame's study contains much new background material for the study of Pound's life and poetry and is written in precise, lively prose. Pound's politics are also prominently discussed in a special issue of *Futuro presente* (Winter 1995), in which Luca Gallesi has gathered together articles by Robert Richardson, Walter Baymann (on Canto 74), David A. Hill (on the Pre-Raphaelite Pound), William Pratt, Tim Redman, Giorgio Galli (Pound and the American esoteric tradition), and others. Luca Gallesi is also responsible for the reprint of Pound's *Jefferson e Mussolini* (Asefi), a revised Italian translation of *Jefferson and/or Mussolini* (1935), published by Pound in 1944 and unavailable since then. The Italian text is essential for the study of Pound's thought, besides being a brilliant piece of polemic in its own right. Marilla Battilana mentions this same book in her effort to find similarities in the lives, political ideas, spiritual closeness, interior dilemmas, and external circumstances of Dante and Pound in "Dante e Pound: Analogie biografiche e ideologiche" (*Ling & L* 24–25: 25–35). Pound loved Romagna, the birthplace of Mussolini but also of the principal Renaissance hero of *The Cantos,* as Massimo Bacigalupo remembers in "Pound incontra Sigismondo," pp. 139–55 in *Sui primi poeti del Novecento,* ed. Bacigalupo (Bulzoni). Bacigalupo shows that Malatesta provided Pound with both a subject and a method, for it was in the Malatesta Cantos that the definitive style of *The Cantos* was perfected. An unpublished Pound letter is presented by Luca Cesari and Anna Busetto Vicari in the small volume *Angolo sperso* (Raffaelli). A later work, *Elektra,* is sympathetically analyzed in detail by Marcello Gigante, "L'Elettra di Sofocle nell'interpretazione di Ezra Pound" (*Dioniso* 63, ii: 115–33). Richard Kidder's "The Archaic Future: Ezra Pound and the Sculpted Word," pp. 311–26 in *Per una topografia dell'Altrove,* is a thoughtful reading of Pound's modernism in the light of international primitivism (in painting and literature), with interesting observations on the "jungles" passage of Canto 20.

Sui primi poeti del Novecento also includes an article on "T. S. Eliot tra memoria e desiderio" (pp. 119–38) by Silvano Sabbadini, a fine scholar who died early in 1996. Romana Rutelli offers an appreciative close reading of Eliot's "The Death of Saint Narcissus" in "Sinestesie del visibile: la danza ossimorica del Santo Narciso" (*SCr* 10: 157–97); Narcissus is, for Rutelli, "all humanity." Two books on Eliot appeared in the course of the year. Andrea Carosso's *T. S. Eliot e i miti del moderno* (Edizioni dell'Orso) is largely devoted to a reading of "Praxis, Theory, and Ideology in the Critical and Philosophical Writings" and makes use of Eliot's Harvard papers (quoted in Italian). It is an ambitious study, which moves between history and theory. More modest in purpose is Andrew Thompson and Doug Thompson's *Transfiguration and Reconciliation in Eliot's* Four Quartets (Cideb). This commentary for students (with lexicon and index) provides many insights, especially on Eliot's borrowings from Dante. This year, a good one for Eliot, saw two new translations published. Massimo Bacigalupo's *Poesie 1905–1920* (Newton Compton) contains the poems of Eliot's first two volumes, including the long unavailable "Ode," with a detailed commentary (pp. 134–57), and an appendix of early work. This first new translation of *Prufrock* and *Poems* to appear in 30 years is more accurate than previous attempts. Bacigalupo discusses new developments in Eliot criticism in an article for *Poesia* (88: 2–6). Angelo Tonelli's *La terra desolata:* Quattro Quartetti (Feltrinelli) has no scholarly apparatus but offers a workmanlike poetic translation into modern Italian and includes Eliot's *Paris Review* interview. Tonelli has a way of speeding up the text by omitting punctuation, which makes Eliot sound more colloquial and contemporary.

Maria Anita Stefanelli has given us an original study with *Navigare la letteratura: Colombo e Caboto nel linguaggio di W. C. Williams e E. J. Pratt* (Associate). She considers Columbus in Williams's *In the American Grain* and Cabot in Pratt's long poem *The Witches' Brew* (1923), pointing out Williams's borrowings from Giacomo Leopardi's "Dialogue of Christopher Columbus and Peter Gutierrez." For students of Williams, this will be a helpful contribution, but its identification of sources less important than Stefanelli's argument on exploration, linguistic and oceanic, old and new. Two followers of Williams also received attention. Annalisa Goldoni and Marina Morbiducci have produced a fine Italian version of

Robert Creeley's "Helsinki Windows" and "Roman Sketchbook" in *Stanze* (Empiria). Creeley's seemingly linear poetry, always difficult to translate, has become even more so with its attention to the "half-tones of feelings and perceptions, steeped in that bundle of thoughts the poet succeeds in rendering through his concise language." James Laughlin has many friends and admirers in Italy, and his poems frequently appear in literary magazines. Two poems from his last collection to appear are introduced by Bacigalupo in "Scorciatoie" (*Nuovi Argomenti* 5: 31–33); Rita Severi presents and translates a choice of Laughlin's poems in "Poesie" (*Il verri* 3–4: 29–37). The monthly *Poesia* devoted ample space to New York, the city of poets, with poems by Pound, Whitman, Crane, Lowell, Ginsberg (introduced by Nicola Gardini in 79: 2–25), Adrienne Rich (Rosanna Vallarelli and Maria Luisa Vezzali in 85: 21–26), and Anne Sexton (Rosaria lo Russo and others in 90: 2–9). All articles are followed by new translations.

Finally, Mario Maffi's "Teatro americano contemporaneo" (*Acoma* 5: 40–45) outlines the development of American theater over the past 20 years, a disoriented, disillusioned, introspective period difficult to analyze. However, the chaotic and stimulating vitality of the American theater is living proof that it does not belong exclusively to American culture. Arthur Miller's plays are promptly presented to the Italian public by Masolino D'Amico, who cleverly translates and introduces *Vetri Rotti* (Einaudi).

University of Pisa

iv Japanese Contributions: Keiko Beppu

Japanese scholarship on American literature surveyed is impressive this year, so much so that it is a herculean task to cover all the achievements of Japanese Americanists. This survey, therefore, will necessarily be selective, but it also will represent both traditional and newer approaches to American literature and culture at the end of the 20th century.

Significant book-length studies this year are Akiko Miyake's *Taylor no Shi, Sono Kokoro [Edward Taylor: His Poetry and His Mind]* (Sugu Shobo); Kazuko Fukuoka's *Henbo Suru Tekusuto: Melville no Shosetsu [Transformation of the Texts: The Novels of Herman Melville]* (Eihosha); Takayuki Tatsumi's *E. A. Pou o Yomu [Disfiguration of Genres: A Reading in the Rhetoric of Edgar Allan Poe]* (Iwanami Shoten) and the interesting hybrid of literary and art criticism, *Nyu Yohku no Seikimatsu [New York*

Decadence] (Chikuma Shobo). *Hyakunen Mae no America: Seikitenkanki no America Shakai to Bunka [American Society and Culture at the Turn of the Century]* by Takashi Sasaki et al. (Kyoto: Shugakusha) rounds out the list.

Articles surveyed in this section are restricted, with a few exceptions, to those published in the academic journals *SALit, SELit,* and *EigoS*. Unless otherwise indicated, all books are published in Tokyo.

a. General/Topical Studies Since the publication of *The Columbia Literary History of the United States,* ed. Emory Elliott (1988), no discussion of American literature can overlook the issues of gender, race, or class. In 1991 that historical overview fathered *The Columbia History of the American Novel.* In response, *EigoS* featured a special forum on "Re-Writing a History of the American Novel" (141: 334–56), which both deconstructs and rereads American novels in the context of New Historicist discourses. "Ur-American Narrative" by Takayuki Tatsumi demonstrates that early American novels are an amalgam of existent narrative genres—sermons and sensational narratives of murder, rape, and Indian captivity (pp. 334–36). Such sensational narratives reappear in pop writings of today. In "No American Narrative Without American Indians Is American" Toshio Yagi presents a provocative rereading of Charles Brockden Brown's *Wieland* and James Fenimore Cooper's *The Last of the Mohicans* (pp. 337–39); Masashi Orishima's "American Naturalism Novel: A Square Beast as Symbol" (pp. 340–42) is a valid, though strained, reconsideration of American naturalism, which echoes Mark Seltzer's *Bodies and Machines* (1992); Yoichiro Miyamoto's "Hemingway's White America: Imperialism and Modernism" makes a good case for how—until recently—the Puritans were used to justify colonial expansionism. Miyamoto's thesis is that "The Snows of Kilimanjaro" and the popular film *Tarzan of the Apes* (1918) mirror imperialist geopolitics (pp. 343–45).

In "Recycling Thomas Jefferson: Mixed Blood and Nationality" (pp. 346–48) Michiko Shimokobe discusses "miscegenation and passing" in American history and literature by way of reading Barbara Chase-Riboud's *Sally Hemings* (1979) and *The President's Daughter* (1994). Yoshiaki Koshikawa's "Post Multiculturalism" (pp. 349–51) opens a debate on ethnonationalism in a postcolonial multicultural society.

EigoS this year also features a section called "Nature Writing: The New American Renaissance" (140: 554–61), with a contribution by Scott

Slovic and a brief commentary by Toshio Watanabe; also included is an informative reading list of "American nature writing," old and new. It is no surprise that Japanese scholars are attracted to this genre because of our own tradition of nature writing and our interest in Thoreau, Emerson, and Gary Snyder.

b. 17th-Century Poetry   Akiko Miyake's *Edward Taylor: His Poetry and His Mind* is the first book-length Japanese study of the 17th-century Puritan poet. Miyake, the author of *Ezra Pound and the Mysteries of Love* (see *ALS 1991*, pp. 454–55), employs her reading in Dante and in medieval religious writings to present Taylor as one of the greatest American poets, whose rivals in her eyes are Whitman and Pound. Miyake argues that Taylor's poetry is one continuous "meditation" that belongs to the tradition of Christian mysticism. That this mystical tradition constitutes the core of Taylor's religious belief that generates his poetry is clearly demonstrated by her translation of "Gods Determinations." The text of the original poem, with the translation and a detailed interpretation, constitute most of Miyake's 340-page book. *Edward Taylor: His Poetry and His Mind,* according to its author, offers two significant discoveries: first, medieval Christian mysticism as filtered through to 17th-century New England promised a hope for personal salvation by means of meditation in contrast to the grim message of damnation constructed during the following century; second, the poet's religious belief inspired his literary values, which Miyake contends are the basis for Taylor's greatness. Important discoveries, indeed, yet ones that need further research and exploration.

c. 19th-Century Fiction   Despite the shifting winds of critical reception, this year registered substantial scholarly responses to such canonical 19th-century writers as Poe, Hawthorne, Melville, and Twain: Takayuki Tatsumi's *Disfiguration of Genres: A Reading in the Rhetoric of Edgar Allan Poe,* Kazuko Fukuoka's *Transformation of the Texts: The Novels of Herman Melville;* a few original articles on Hawthorne and Twain; and Zenichiro Oshitani's monograph, *Stephen Crane no Me [The Eye of Stephen Crane]* (Osaka: Osaka Kyoikutosho).

   Disfiguration of Genres is a collection of essays and articles published in journals and magazines and now vigorously revised. The result is a book on Edgar Allan Poe and on the publishing business of his time that should interest both scholars and lay readers. *Disfiguration of Genres* consists of five chapters, each dealing with what have been considered marginal texts among Poe's works. Chapter 1 clarifies Poe's poetics of magazinism; he played with a variety of subgenres to cultivate his art of storytelling in order to write marketable fiction. The second chapter is a defense not only of Poe's twice-told review (in fact, thrice-written) of Hawthorne's "Twice-Told Tales," but also of Tatsumi's "twice-told/published scholarship"; chapter 3 on "The Masque of the Red Death" reads Poe's story as an allegory of reading; chapter 4 discusses Poe's interest in (pseudo)scientific discourse during the age of Jackson; and the final chapter traces the sea change made by Poe's acrobatic rhetoric in rewriting "Eleonora" into "The Domain of Arnheim," which relates in turn to his revivification stories, such as "Ligeia" and "Berenice," and his landscape narratives, "The Landscape Garden" or "Landor's Cottage." Tatsumi's analysis of Poe's review of Hawthorne's "Twice-Told Tales" satisfyingly explains Poe's principle of writing/reading literary criticism. The ultimate target of his critique turns out not to be Hawthorne alone but the American literary establishment that he and Longfellow epitomized. *Disfiguration of Genres* is an excellent study of how a writer may represent a certain ideology or spirit of the age.

Of related interest: Chitoshi Motoyama's chapter on Poe's *The Narrative of Arthur Gordon Pym* and "The Used Man" in *America Bungaku to Boryoku [Violence and the American Novel]* (Kenkyusha). Motoyama argues that violence in the United States is simply repressed do-goodism.

Kazuko Fukuoka's *Transformation of the Texts: Novels of Herman Melville* could be renamed "Disfiguration of Melville's Texts," because Fukuoka's concern, like Tatsumi's in his book on Poe, is the scrutinizing of Melville's texts to disclose the "rugged edges" that he left in rewriting/transforming them. But the book is traditional literary criticism in that it rests on close readings of Melville's major works in chronological order: *Typee, Redburn, White-Jacket, Moby-Dick, Pierre,* "Bartleby the Scrivener," *Israel Potter,* "I and My Chimney," and *The Confidence-Man.* Fukuoka demonstrates how Melville, in order to reach out to prospective readers, blended conventional literary genres, how he used popular genres and the rhetoric of sermons, travel sketches, adventure stories, and religious tracts to create his own fictional discourse, albeit with mixed success. Such reading of Melville's texts deconstructs the image of the proud alienated writer, very much like the protagonist of *Pierre* who prefers not to write to please the public.

The discussion of *Pierre* is the best, reading "the pastoral romance" as a revivalist novel. Fukuoka argues that Melville's interest in religious revivalism led him to write a fiction with an enthusiast—a key word in the novel—as its hero. Thus, Melville used revivalism much as Susan Warner did in *The Wide, Wide World.* The difference is that, whereas Melville started to write a story like Warner's, he diverged to expose the dangers inherent in evangelism.

Transformation of the Texts is a collection of articles written over 15 years but thoroughly revised. The book is elegantly written, supported by solid scholarship and familiarity with current critical theories. In all, it is a remarkable achievement worthy of the third Fukuhara prize, established in honor of Rintaro Fukuhara. An important contribution to Melville scholarship everywhere.

Significant articles published on Hawthorne are Naochika Takao's " 'A Strange Sympathy Betwixt Soul and Body!': Sadistic-Masochistic Sympathy in *The Scarlet Letter*" (*SALit* 32: 1–21) and Toshio Yagi's "American Family Game *SL-1850*" (*Review of American Literature* 15: 1–11). Using Gordon Hutner's idea of "sympathy," Takao contends that sympathy for Hawthorne opens up an impossible space of "presence," an interface between body and soul and between speaker and listener in the symbolic order of representation. Toshio Yagi's entertaining essay is different in tone and purpose. Yagi reads Hawthorne's masterpiece as a kind of software programmed "to de/construct the American family with the triangularity of adultery as its basic drive."

Mark Twain receives substantial critical attention this year, but no significant scholarship was published on Henry James. The most significant articles are Takaki Hiraishi's "American Literature as an Ideology: A Re-Reading of *Huckleberry Finn*" (*SALit* 32: 23–38); Takako Takeda's "Twinship: Relationship Between *Puddn'head Wilson* and 'Those Extraordinary Twins' " (*SELit* 72: 197–208); and Katsumi Satouchi's English-language "Invisible Center of *Roughing It:* A Reconsideration of the 'Flush Time' Sections" (*KALit* 32: 23–37). Hiraishi attempts to reread Mark Twain's works to expose what he tried to conceal beneath the surface of his ideal individualism and love of freedom. Takako Takeda's discussion of *Puddn'head Wilson,* a book that has received much critical attention in Japan in recent years, is a succinct textual study of the relationship between the novel and its ur-text; such textual twinship, Takeda argues, is heavily burdened with the author's socio/racial ambivalence concerning the inseparable identity—doubleness—of nature/nurture. Thus, Takeda joins in the controversy begun by Susan Gillman's *Mark Twain's Puddn'head Wilson: Race, Conflict, and Culture* (1991). In his essay on *Roughing It* Satouchi observes that the structural irregularity in Twain's works is often attributed to the failure of sustained narrative strategy on the author's part, but that the inclusion of the 'Flush Time' sections makes the book a historiography or a guide in the guise of a "personal narrative."

In *EigoS*'s feature, "Re-Writing a History of the American Novel," Masashi Orishima reconsiders American naturalism. Similarly, Zenichiro Oshitani's *The Eye of Stephen Crane* presents this American "naturalist" as a literary impressionist, a familiar thesis.

d. 20th-Century Fiction   Japanese studies on 20th-century American writers is comparatively meager this year. Original articles were published on no other 20th-century writers than Faulkner and Hemingway. Only Nobuaki Namiki's "The Image and the Text in *The Sound and the Fury*" (*SALit* 32: 39–55); Takeshi Morita's "Faulkner's Search for a New Family As It Ought to Be" (*Review of American Literature* 15: 53–61); and Kazuo Shimizu's chapter on Hemingway in *Violence and the American Novel* (pp. 153–211) are worth mentioning.

In "The Image and the Text in *The Sound and the Fury*" Namiki tries to clarify the reciprocal relationship between literature and painting that creates the unique textuality of Faulkner's novels. He examines how Faulkner succeeds in using the picture/image as narrative strategy in *The Sound and the Fury*, and he concludes that after some experimental struggles in *As I Lay Dying* and *Light in August* the writer found a form in *Absalom, Absalom!*, a narrative controlled by one image in the middle and the other at the end. A cleverly argued and clearly written essay. Takeshi Morita's discussion of "the American family" in Faulkner appears in the issue of *Review of American Literature* on "the cult of family." The family in Faulkner, with its absence and distortion, is portrayed and questioned in both its form and its nature. Morita concludes that Faulkner sought possibilities for a newer family as a basic unit in bettering humankind.

Shimizu's chapter in *Violence and the American Novel* is a traditional look at the nature of violence in such Hemingway texts as *Death in the Afternoon, Green Hills of Africa,* and *The Old Man and the Sea.* Clearly, Hemingway is one of the most significant American writers for Japanese scholars and readers.

e. Contemporary Fiction, Drama, and Poetry   Scholarship on contemporary American literature this year is also nominal, though varied. Yoshihiko Kihara's "Entropy, the Preterite, and the Tristero: Thomas Pynchon's *The Crying of Lot 49*" (*KALit* 32: 4–22) is an intelligent article analyzing one mystery in Pynchon's early novel; Kazushige Sagawa's chapter in *Violence and the American Novel* examines the meaning of the Holocaust in the works of Saul Bellow and Bernard Malamud.

More ambitious are the feminist discussions of contemporary drama: Eriko Hara's "Memory and Ethnicity in the Mother-Daughter Relationship: Asian American Women's Theatre" (*Review of American Literature* 15: 12–21); and Yuko Yaguchi's "Sam Shepard, *A Lie of the Mind:* Eve Sings a New Song" (*SALit* 32: 57–75). Hara introduces two Asian American women playwrights who demonstrate the significance of their theater in the context of gendered and racial ideologies. Yuko Yaguchi examines how the heroine, a victim of male violence in Shepard's *A Lie of the Mind,* manages to gain her voice.

Tomoyuki Iino's " 'This banality is most precious possession': John Ashbery" (*EigoS* 141: 294–96) is a perceptive analysis of a difficult yet important contemporary poet who was invited to speak this year by the English Literary Society of Japan. Iino points out the "banality" in Ashbery's allegedly difficult poetry.

f. American/Cultural Studies   Significant books on American culture published this year are Sadahide Kodama's *America no Japonizumu [The Japonism in America]* (Chuokoron Sha); Kenji Kobayashi's *America Bunka no Ima: Jinshu, Gender, Class [American Culture Now: Race, Gender, Class]* (Kyoto: Minerva); the aforementioned *American Society and Culture at the Turn of the Century* by Takashi Sasaki et al.; and Takayuki Tatsumi's *New York Decadence* and *Beibungaku Shisoshi no Monogatarigaku [New Americanist Poetics]* (Seido Sha).

Kodama's *The Japonism in America* surveys the influences of the Japonism on American culture from before the Civil War until the end of World War I. Kodama observes that the cultural impact of the Japonism are far-reaching, if short-lived, not only in literature and art, but in American domestic life: clothing, upholstery, interior decoration, architecture, and landscape gardening. Though the book is a thin general survey, it should stimulate further research in comparative cultural studies.

Kobayashi's *American Culture Now* is a rich resource for interdisciplinary studies of American literature and culture. The author's objective is primarily to read American literature, yet his discussions of 19th- and 20th-century writers (Twain, Fitzgerald, Hemingway) and more recently published writers (among them, Toni Morrison, Bobbie Ann Mason, Raymond Carver, Anne Beattie, Larry McCaffery) cross over to other disciplines. *American Culture Now* collects previously published essays like pieces of a quilt, opening possibilities for future study.

American Society and Culture at the Turn of the Century is the product of collaborative research conducted from 1988 to 1993 in the Department of American Studies at Doshisha University. Similar to Kobayashi's book, it is a traditional historical study containing 10 contributions written for this volume by scholars in literature, history, social welfare, and religion. A good overview is provided, breaking new ground.

Finally, Takayuki Tatsumi's *New York Decadence* is an interesting critical hybrid of both highbrow and lowbrow literature and art. The objects of Tatsumi's scholarly speculation include junk fiction, pop culture, serious literature, and literary criticism. *New York Decadence,* like Kobayashi's *American Culture Now,* discusses both contemporary and traditional American writers, although the author's interest is more in the avant-garde. The collapse of clear distinctions between genres is best illustrated in Tatsumi's highly urbane, creative criticism. The chapter "New York at the Fin de Siècle: Melville, Adams, and Duchamp" contains an entertaining and intelligent reading of Melville's "The Paradise of Bachelors and the Tartarus of Maids." The ultimate purpose of *New York Decadence* is to give voice to "the queer in the archive," to tell a new American narrative other than the one about "the city upon the hill." To question the tradition of this narrative is the subject of Tatsumi's *New Americanist Poetics.* This prolific scholar and critic is endowed with rich resourcefulness and agility of mind.

Kobe College

v Scandinavian Contributions: Jan Nordby Gretlund, Elisabeth Herion-Sarafidis, and Hans Skei

Scandinavian contributions to American literary scholarship this year must be deemed slight, although they are by no means without interest. Two book-length studies have appeared (both doctoral dissertations— one on William Styron, the other on John Gardner), but all other contributions are relatively brief articles. Most of the articles are collected in a Festschrift presented to Professor Orm Øverland at the University of

Bergen, Norway, on his 60th anniversary. The range of American literary scholarship in Scandinavia is in a sense reflected in this volume, *Performances in American Literature and Culture,* ed. Vidar Pedersen and Zeljka Svrljuga (Bergen), although most essays necessarily are limited by the format itself.

American literature is translated and then presented, reviewed, and discussed in newspapers and magazines in all Scandinavian countries. It is extremely difficult to keep track of all such presentations, and most of them, of course, are not printed in English. Few of these reviews and articles deserve to be called literary scholarship, but they are important in the sense that they demonstrate the ever-present and highly important influence that American culture exerts in Scandinavian countries.

a. 19th-Century Prose In "To Pray, to Think, to Act: Women as Abolitionists in Harriet Beecher Stowe's *Uncle Tom's Cabin*" (*Performances,* pp. 62–73) Inger Christensen suggests that Stowe, through her female characters, points to a solution to the problem of slavery; namely, that a change of heart was needed and that "women are the chief instrument by which this may be achieved." Before a political decision about slavery could be made, a change had to take place, and it had to begin with the inner person. Nevertheless, it may be worth discussing whether the enormous impact of *Uncle Tom's Cabin* had less to do with politics than with spirit.

In his humorous and instructive "Elements of Humanity in *Huck Finn:* A Pedagogue's Revised Notes—after Reminders from Novelist, Widow and Dogmatist" (*Performances,* pp. 119–32) Johannes Kjørven reminds us that teachers should be careful not to develop "a pet theory" about *Huckleberry Finn,* "or a distinctive interpretation of some particular aspect." Referring to Norman Mailer, to the Widow Douglas, and to the theologian Karl Barth, Kjørven establishes a distinction between Huck Finn as a fellow human being and as an individual. The human elements in the dual relation with Jim are considered to be the most important. Fellow humanity becomes "one of the determinations in the novel's anthropological vision of human existence as such, a constant and inviolable factor in it."

Zeljka Svrljuga's "Alice in Otherland: *The Diary of Alice James*" (*Performances,* pp. 280–93) reads James's diary in the light of her illness, scanning her discourse to find "knowledge beyond language" in an attempt to understand the repressed voice through the symptoms in the text. The only girl-child in the remarkable James family, and seriously ill, she was, as Svrljuga states, "marked by her otherness: femaleness and illness." So instead of being read as an account of Woman and hence of a Victim, Svrljuga presents a close reading of the diary and asks: "What did *she* want?" This brief article gives a number of interesting answers.

In "Pioneers on the Prairie: From Desert to Garden" (*Performances,* pp. 85–105) Øyunn Hestetun argues that despite numerous new critical perspectives, it still makes sense to talk about cultural primitivism and civilization and to use images of Garden and Desert when discussing books such as Cooper's *The Prairie* and Cather's *O Pioneers!* Hestetun accordingly bases her discussion of these two books on Henry Nash Smith's *Virgin Land* (1950), which, despite its shortcomings, remains a highly useful study. Hestetun discusses Cooper's and Cather's novels to show the ways in which they tell much of the story "of how the land of the interior was transformed in the course of the nineteenth century, framed by the Louisiana Purchase of 1803 and the official closing of the Frontier in 1890."

b. 20th-Century Prose   The determinism of naturalism is discussed by Helge Normann Nilsen in "Naturalism in Edith Wharton's 'Ethan Frome'" (*Performances,* pp. 179–87). Nilsen shows how natural, economic, and social forces dominate Wharton's characters, who have no hope of rising above their circumstances. Man is a helpless victim, yet Wharton is also saying, indirectly, that one must protest against the indifference of society and the universe.

Øyvind T. Gulliksen's article, "Ole E. Rølvaag, Thorstein Veblen, and the Independent Farmer" (*Performances,* pp. 74–84) merits comment because it includes discussions of the tragic fates of two great Norwegian-Americans—one who believed in keeping Norwegian culture and language within the larger community and one who clearly had become an American, a great sociologist, and an academic failure. Rølvaag's *Giants in the Earth* is discussed briefly in this narrative essay about a visit to Veblen's farm in Nerstrand, Minnesota.

In her essay "Saul Bellow's Moral Masochists" (*AmStScan* 27: 1–18) Lene Schøtt-Kristensen deals with four of Bellow's great sufferers. They are American Jews who apparently have lost their faith but still feel bound by their heritage. A conflict over the nature of suffering is seen as originating in Bellow's ambiguous attitude toward it. Is suffering ennobling, perhaps even redemptive, or is it just "neurotic and destructive"?

The essay shows that no answer is definite in Bellow's fiction. In the early novels, suffering often seems meaningful, but in the later novels it is mainly absurd. Schøtt-Kristensen ends by asking whether there is a real difference between "compulsive or neurotic suffering and submission to suffering by choice?" She believes that Bellow indicates a difference, but she argues that he is simply making a virtue of necessity.

Among Southern writers, William Styron has received well-earned attention in Scandinavia this year, but not primarily as a Southern writer. In *A Mode of Melancholy: A Study of William Styron's Novels* (Uppsala) Elisabeth Herion-Sarafidis suggests that critics have had an exaggerated interest in Styron's "Faulknerian imagination" and in the question of the Southernness of his fiction. Instead, she focuses on what is in Scandinavia considered a largely uncharted area of his work. She notes that the redemptive overtones of the (largely unconvincing and willed) endings of Styron's novels "seem subverted by states of psychomachy." The study suggests that Styron comes to affirmative resolutions only by skirting his actual subject. Herion-Sarafidis views his writings as an expedition toward "a psychological borderland." She sees an underworld of darkness in his work, which suggests to her that his aim was always, and even compulsively, "an exploration of consciousness." Whatever their variations, Herion-Sarafidis maintains, Styron's texts all express an earnest pursuit of the mechanisms of the psyche and reveal his attempts at mapping out "the landscape of depression." His purpose is to try to liberate the mind through the possibility of catharsis offered by the imagination and expressed in fiction. As a reaction to ruling trends in Styron criticism, Herion-Sarafidis downplays the writer's Southernness, if not to the point of denying it altogether, then certainly viewing it as of no importance. It is refreshing to see Southernness represented as diluting and confining, although the point is probably not necessary to make this fine study's valuable statement that Styron made "the mental processes of which we are unaware—the unquestionable matrix of his work." Herion-Sarafidis shows convincingly that it is in his acknowledgment of his despair and through his attempt to write himself whole that Styron manages to give expression to our life and time.

Bo G. Ekelund's dissertation *In the Pathless Forest: John Gardner's Literary Project* (Almqvist & Wiksell) is a substantial contribution to Gardner scholarship. Analyzing Gardner's field of production, Ekelund considers his literary career from the perspective of habitus and field, theories developed by sociologist Pierre Bourdieu. By applying Bourdieu's relational approach to the study of cultural phenomena, not only does a new picture of Gardner emerge, but also an alternative, complementary understanding of the field of fiction-writing during the 1960s and '70s. Staking out his territory, Ekelund explains that by "analyzing Gardner's career as a narrative which has emerged not from autonomous creative imagination seeking to embody itself in action, nor from the free play of social signifiers, nor from an absolutely determining social context, but from the interplay and exchanges between the habitus of the writer as it is geared towards his literary project and the dynamic structure of the literary field, we may proceed towards a sociological knowledge of both artist and field." Although it seems clear that Ekelund's interest has been primarily to put the Bourdieuan theories into practice, a purpose for which he might actually have chosen any writer, his efforts have resulted in a most illuminating portrayal, not only of Gardner, but also in some highly challenging interpretations of a few of Gardner's texts.

Ekelund's discussion is divided into two main parts. Interwoven with a most readable explanation and application of Bourdieu's ideas, Part I consists of a detailed delineation of the different social fields in which Gardner moved, the nature of his habitus, and the stages in his trajectory. In Part II Ekelund presents four readings of Gardner texts published in the 1970s-*Nickel Mountain, Grendel,* "The King's Indian," and *On Moral Fiction*—in which Gardner's choices, thematic as well as formal, are shown consistently to have been the result of compromises between his habitual schemes of perception and interpretation and various demands generated by the totality of the literary field. Two problems with the two-part structure selected by Ekelund: it is highly repetitive, and the two parts fail to mesh—the whole has no real unity.

In an interesting attempt to trace Harry Angstrom's life from beginning to end, Erik Kielland-Lund in "The Anatomy of Updike's Harry 'Rabbit' Angstrom: Thirty Years of American Life" (*Performances,* pp. 107–17) discusses each book of the Rabbit tetralogy, which he hails as "one of the most timebound and timeless literary masterpieces," on a par with Dos Passos's *U.S.A.* The parallels between Angstrom's steady decline and a general decline in American society are interpreted in some detail. The reassurance that Angstrom tries to present from time to time is shown to be a delusion.

The interest in black female writers, notably Toni Morrison and Alice Walker, is strong in Scandinavia. The only published article is Inger-

Anne Søfting's "Carnival and Black Music as Counterculture in Toni Morrison's *The Bluest Eye* and *Jazz*" (*AmStScan* 27: 81–102). Following a discussion of the ideology of carnival and African American music, which are both found to occupy a position between art and everyday life, Søfting discusses the relationship between blacks and whites in Morrison's first and her latest novels. Carnival and music are seen to erupt as signals of an alternative culture in *The Bluest Eye,* whereas *Jazz* is found to be much more of a polyphonic novel. Both novels are praised: *The Bluest Eye* for its diagnosis of the evil influence from the dominant culture; *Jazz* for its emphasis on "the mutually dependent and creative relationship between the reader and the text."

Sandra Lee Kleppe sends "Postcard from Raymond Carver's Northwest" (*Performances,* pp. 133–46), a meditation on the region where Carver was born, where he wrote and fished, and where he died in 1988. Much of his writing, even his late poetry in which observations and experiences from his younger years seem to reenter his writing, is closely linked to the Northwest. Kleppe shows how Carver's writing was always rooted in experience, and that the very life he led is indirectly but decisively responsible for his themes, his particular gift of seeing "more clearly." Kleppe's essay includes close readings of some of Carver's poetry, as well as clear observations about his storytelling method. More than anything else, the discussion of Carver's sense of place and the function of place in his fiction is at the center of this essay.

The pronounced Scandinavian interest in Paul Auster's fiction continues. Erik Østerud's "I skyggen af Babel" [In the Shadow of Babel] is subtitled "Intertextuality and Reduction in Paul Auster's *The New York Trilogy*" (*K&K* 22, i [1994]: 91–114). Østerud's point of departure is Auster's comment on *Don Quixote*—that Cervantes was possessed by books, and that was what made him a writer. Auster is preoccupied with the question of who the creating subject really is. Throughout the trilogy he plays with his own name, occupation, and identity. His own novels are the products of a constant awareness of other novels and of a conscious deconstruction of the tradition and genre conventions of the classic novel. His goal is to reduce his characters' superficial attributes so that he can confront them with the basics of living. The shadow of the tower of Babel is also cast by all the past literature with which Auster and the rest of us live in an intertextual symbiosis, but the signs of the old texts no longer signify. The awareness that meaning is read into texts is a liberating aspect in Auster's thinking, Østerud argues. The result, of course, is chaos, which creates a challenging situation in which anything may happen.

Inge Birgitte Siegumfeldt situates Auster's novels within the American and postmodern traditions in her essay "Paul Auster's Private 'I's" (*Anglofiles* December 1995: 62–68). Siegumfeldt discusses the idea of freedom in the light of Auster's *Leviathan,* and she focuses on the major postmodern elements in his fiction, primarily on his decentering of the subject. The essay concludes that Auster is not only a postmodern writer preoccupied with his role as a writer, but he is "very much an American writer concerned with the moral health of his country."

The Scandinavian interest in the fiction of Bret Easton Ellis seems not to abate. Britta Timm Knudsen's "Formen på grænsen" [The Shape of the Borderline] offers an interesting approach to Ellis's *American Psycho* (*K&K* 22, i [1994]: 115–31). Knudsen has a double vision of the novel. On one hand, it can be seen in the tradition of descriptive novels with an emphasis on vision as in Flaubert and Zola. On the other hand, it is a novel of excess, which seems to build on Georges Batailles's idea of exceeding as a possibility in our lives and thereby raises the question of meaning. Ellis deals in an obscene hyperreality that has no aesthetics but only a design. The reader will attempt to impose a homogenizing vision on the protagonist's universe, but his atrocities are attempts at producing something that does not fit the rest of the pattern. In subjectivity taken to the limit he even rebels against the novel's point of view, which is his own. Knudsen calls this conduct "destructive heroism." The space created in the novel has the surface structure of a painting. And it offers no alternative. It may be surrealistic in its technique, but not in its vision. The ritual battle between form and formlessness is both the surface and the whole of the novel. Knudsen concludes that *American Psycho* seems to mirror a familiar reality, but the familiar is revealed as monstrous.

Stephen King is the best-selling American author in Scandinavia today. To supply some basic information about the popular writer, Morten B. Christensen and Kristian Kristiansen have published *Bogen om Stephen King* [The Book About . . .] (Ultima, 1994), an interesting introduction and guide to his life and work. The emphasis is on King's work that has appeared in Danish. There is a detailed biography, which progresses by decades and tells us about his use of the pseudonym Richard Bachman, the young King's column in the university magazine the *Maine Campus,* the publication of *Carrie,* and the critics' reaction to it. The fate of King's novels in their film versions is discussed. The book's longest section is devoted to King's most popular novels, from the horror of *Carrie* to the mainstream *Dolores Claiborne.* Also listed are King's favorite movies and novels, taken from his nonfiction book *Dance Macabre,* and a bibliography. Christensen and Kristiansen conclude that King's popularity is less than mysterious. It is the result of his ability to tell a story well, and a good story is all that most readers ask for.

In his *Andre stemmer* [Other Voices] (Per Kofod) the novelist and poet Bo Green Jensen has collected 30 "workshop conversations," as he calls them, with some of the world's best contemporary authors. The interviews are mostly from the 1990s. Several American writers were among them and are placed by Jensen in their literary contexts. (The interview with Paul Auster was mentioned in *ALS 1992,* p. 335; for the meeting with John Ashbery, see *ALS 1994,* p. 461.) But there are conversations with the young novelist Allen Kurzweil, author of *A Case of Curiosities,* and three most welcome interviews with Douglas Coupland, William Gibson, and John Irving. Coupland feels that Bret Easton Ellis represents the '80s, while he himself is an expression of the '90s. The interviewer notes Coupland's optimism, his attacks on the spoiled-parent generation, and his interest in virtual reality. Coupland's neighbor, William Gibson, first wrote a trilogy about a frightening future in cyberspace. In *Virtual Light* (1993) Gibson breaks away from his usual genre of the future thriller and shows more interest in the human dimension of his characters. Jensen thinks Gibson will soon be ready to write a novel about today. Jensen's interview with John Irving, which marks their second meeting (see *ALS 1992,* p. 355), is mostly about *A Son of the Circus* (1994), supposed to be as labyrinthine and inscrutable as India itself, and about Irving's favorite writers, the realists of the 19th century, especially Charles Dickens.

c. 20th-Century Drama In "'If You Died Tonight, How Many People Would Come to Your Funeral?' Sociability and Anxiety in Miller, Carnegie and Riesman" (*Performances,* pp. 46–61), Fredrik Chr. Brøgger compares a success manual by Dale Carnegie, David Riesman's *The Lonely Crowd,* and Arthur Miller's *Death of a Salesman* to establish what appears to be a background for those American myths so obviously present in Miller's play. Brøgger's aim is to give an example of how the studies of literature and culture may be integrated, and although parallels

among the three texts undoubtedly are present, Miller's text far transcends the success manual and the sociological study.

Per Winther in "Robert Lowell's *The Old Glory:* Successful Integration
of Nineteenth-Century Sources with His Own Thematic Concerns?"
(*Performances,* pp. 294–308) draws interesting parallels between Hawthorne and Lowell before turning to Lowell's *The Old Glory,* for which
three Hawthorne texts and a novella by Melville are sources. Winther
investigates what he calls "Lowell's echoic method," which on the whole
he finds successful, but he is critical of some aspects of the dramatic form
that Lowell has chosen when reworking his "sources" into his own texts.
Lowell's sources are shown to have served him well, and he has succeeded
in establishing thematic symmetry between the texts and intertexts,
although the sources may also have reduced the artistic effectiveness of
the trilogy.

d. Theory and Criticism   In an attempt to take the temperature of the
contemporary scene in literary theory in American universities Claes-
Göran Holmberg went in search of a number of leading critics, publishing the interviews in *Texter och kontexter: Samtal med 15 amerikanska
litteraturforskare* (Absalon, 1994). In an introduction he briefly situates
the critics of his choice, identifying their present as well as past allegiances. The overall picture is interesting; while everyone seems to agree
that deconstruction is a thing of the past, such semioticians as Michael
Riffaterre and Frank Lentricchia, once involved in a project that Lentricchia termed "Marxist rhetoric," have different views on what the future
will bring in the field of theory. And while Hugh Kenner predicted the
rapid death of all theory, Jean Howard, the only female scholar included,
believes that poststructuralism, feminism, and Marxism together will
produce fruitful readings. A number of those interviewed agreed with
David Lloyd that feminism, New Historicism, cultural studies, and the
study of minority literatures will be the areas of greater interest for the
remainder of the '90s.

American New Criticism still exerts its influence on literary scholarship in Scandinavia, though perhaps more in the classroom than in
print. In Hans H. Skei's "American New Criticism and Reader Response
Theory; or, Never Quite Sure of Any of It" (*Performances,* pp. 252–61)
the imperceptible reader in New Criticism is discussed as a forerunner of
the very active and visible reader in reader-response theories. Skei dis-

cusses modern response theories as a reaction against New Criticism, but his major point is that interest in the reader has returned after a long period of neglect by formalist theories that insisted on the autonomy of the text.

Odense, Uppsala, Oslo Universities

vi Spanish Language Contributions: Antonio C. Márquez

Since the inception of the Foreign Contributions section in 1973, one entry has appeared on Spanish-language scholarship, which was limited to works published in Spain. What follows is an addendum to the 1988 entry and an update of significant tendencies and trends, followed by the initial appearance of the category, Spanish-language contributions from Latin America.

a. Spain: Fiction   José Antonio Gurpegui's claim that Hemingway has been a constant presence in the Spanish interest and valuation of American literature (see *ALS 1988*, p. 551) still holds. Cándido Pérez Gállego, the most renowned scholar of American literature in Spain, joined the critical bandwagon with "Hemingway y la guerra civil española," pp. 409–23 in *Estelas, laberintos, nuevas sendas,* ed. Angel G. Loureiro (Anthropos, 1988). Dismissing the canard that Hemingway had written a novel about Spain without Spaniards in *For Whom the Bell Tolls,* Pérez Gállego culls Nietzsche, Derrida, and Lacan in taking a postmodernist tack and stressing the novel's ambiguities, contradictions, paradoxes, and lack of resolution. Similar in method but less querulous, Beatriz Penas-Ibáñez's "El continuum modernista-postmodernista: *The Garden of Eden,* climax de un proceso de cambio literario (1946–1961)" (*Actas de I jornadas de lengua y literatura inglesa y norteamericana* [1990]: 41–61) places Hemingway's last novel under the purview of postmodernist theory and contributes to the reassessment of Hemingway's writings. The stream of biographical studies also continued unabated. Edward F. Stanton's paean to Hemingway and Iberia was translated, under the title *Hemingway en España* (Castalia, 1989); its popularity kindled affection for an American icon who said that he regretted not being born in Spain.

Only Faulkner can match Hemingway's currency and critical interest among Spanish scholars and critics, and a work appeared in the past decade that brought Faulkner criticism to an apex: María Elena Bravo's *Faulkner en España: Perspectivas de la narrativa de postguerra* (Península,

1985). Bravo's brilliant conspectus details the translation of Faulkner's work into Spanish, the initial criticism of his work (especially the historic role played by *La Revista de Occidente*), Faulkner's readership (emphasis is given to eminent writers such as Juan Benet and Camilo José Cela), and his influence on two generations of Spanish writers. Bravo reiterated her authoritative work in "Juan Benet desde la vanguardia: Buscando la palabra para Yoknapatawpha y region," pp. 245–253 in *Prosa hispanica de vanguardia,* ed. Fernando Burgos (Orígenes, 1986). In "Las muchas huellas de Faulkner" (*CHA* 442 [1987]: 126–32) Isabel de Armas likewise infers that Faulkner's exploration of "the burden of history" makes his work highly relevant to post-Franco Spain, and she sees Faulkner's influence extended to novels of the 1960s and 1970s. Federico Eguíluz Ortiz de Latierro contributed a valuable interpretive guide to a work that has bewildered and beguiled many Spanish readers in *"The Sound and the Fury:* Algunas claves para su lectura" (*Reden* 6 [1993]: 5–20). The belated translation of Joseph Blotner's *Faulkner: A Biography [Faulkner, una biografía]* (Destino, 1994), widely reviewed and acclaimed as a magnificent literary biography, capped a decade of vigorous Faulkner studies.

The interest in contemporary writers has steadily increased with wider circulation of texts and their introduction into university curriculums. Of special note, Pilar Alonso Rodríguez's *Tres aspectos de la frontera interior* (Salamanca: Ediciones Universidad Salamanca, 1987) was the most ambitious study of Jewish American literature published to date. A diligently researched literary history concentrating on the work of Saul Bellow, Bernard Malamud, and Philip Roth, it argues that Jewish American writers and their protagonists project the fundamental ambivalence and complexity of American society, and these circumstances have generated a vital, enriching literature. Among Jewish American writers, Bellow has received the most attention (in part because of his receiving the Nobel Prize and the wide translation of his books); his work has prompted spirited critical essays. To her impressive work on contemporary fiction, Pilar Alonso Rodríguez added "Entitades, relaciones y processos: Constituyentes basicos y recurrentes en la narrativa de Saul Bellow" (*Atlantis* 10, i–ii [1989]: 89–112), an overview of Bellow's major themes and narrative elements. In "Saul Bellow: Entre el modernismo y el postmodernismo" (*Actas de Las I jornadas de lengua y literatura inglesa y norteamericana* [1990]: 35–40) Francisco González-González bracketed Bellow between modernism and postmodernism and argued for the resiliency of his novels.

The multifaceted aspect of contemporary American fiction was reflected in an appealing range of essays. "La tradición afro-americana en *Beloved* de Toni Morrison" (*Revista Alicantina de estudios ingleses* [1989]: 31–41) by Isabel Duran Gimenez-Rico does pioneering work in exploring language bases and the fundamental role of the oral tradition in African American literature. Viorica Patea's "El camino iniciatico en *The Bell Jar*" (*Atlantis* 12: i [1990]: 129–48) offers a sharp examination of Sylvia Plath's autobiographical novel and its projection of the suicidal personality. Lesser-known writers were singled out as important contemporary literary figures worthy of study. María Eugenia Díaz Sánchez's " 'You Have Fallen into Art—Return of Life': *In the Heart of the Heart of the Country* de William Gass" (*Atlantis* 12, ii [1991]: 107–20) elucidates the esoteric and lyrical philosophical-literary terrain of Gass's fiction. María Antonia Alvarez is equally innovative in exploring new ground in "Reinventando el pasado: Tecnicas narrativas de la novela autobiográfica *Stop-Time* de Frank Conroy," pp. 77–86 in *Escritura autobiográfica: Actas del II seminario internacional del instituto de semiotica literaria y teatral,* ed. José Romera-Castillo (Visor, 1993); reading *Stop-Time* as an "autobiographical novel," she uses linguistic analysis to examine Conroy's narrative technique. Jesús Lerante De Castro brings Kurt Vonnegut into the postmodernist camp by applying Bakhtinian theory in *"The Sirens of Titan:* El universo post-modernista de Kurt Vonnegut" (*Reden* 8 [1994]: 61–79), and Esther Sánchez-Prado González lends a Lacanian psychoanalytic reading to Donald Barthelme's novel in *"The Dead Father:* Retrato de padre en la postmodernidad" (*Reden* 9 [1995]: 17–35). Less academic but serving a valuable purpose in introducing the reading public to American writers, *Quimera* has led the way with informed articles such as Jordi Lamarca's "Thomas Pynchon: Artista postmoderno" (1995: 34–38).

b. Spain: Poetry   American poetry has always been a distant cousin to prose fiction in its appeal to the Spanish reading public and as the subject of scholarship. Edgar Allan Poe, arguably the most popular 19th-century American writer in Spain, still holds some sway. Chiding American critics who have dismissed Poe as a crude sensationalist or cheapjack rhymester, critics such as Concha Zardoya in *Verdad, belleza y expresión (Letras Angloamericanas)* (1967) argue that Poe's aestheticism is a forerun-

ner of modernism. From another critical angle, in "El narcisismo es-
quizofrénico de Poe" (*Atlantis* 11, i–ii [1989]: 149–60) Fernando Montes-
Pazos loads up on psychoanalytical theory to examine Poe's aberrations
and poetic disequilibriums. More original and fetching, Francisco Manuel Marino's "Sobre la influencia de 'The Raven' de Poe en el 'Nouturnio'
de Curros Enriquez" (*Boletín del departamento de literatura española,
Valladolid* 15 [1990]: 121–34) offers a comparative study of Poe and the
Galician writer with engaging results. In "En torno a una concepción
unitaria: Los presupuestos teoricos de Edgar Allan Poe sobre el hecho
literario" (*Revista de filología de la universidad de La Laguna, Tenerife*
[1992]: 33–54) Francisco Javier Castillo gives Poe's literary theory and
poetics a turn with structural linguistic analysis.

The most recent criticism is notable for a surge of feminist studies and
the reading of American poets in a new light. In "Emily Dickinson o el
juego de la palabra esencial" (*Atlantis* 12, i [1990]: 115–28) Margarita
Ardanaz-Moran attributes the Belle of Amherst's genius to her ideological use of language. In the same vein in "El silencio femenino" (*Reden* 5
[1992]: 48–56) Mercedes Bengoechea Bartolomé offers a feminist reading
of poems by Marianne Moore, Elizabeth Bishop, and Adrienne Rich to
examine "women writers' identification with dominant sexist values, and
the need to alter man-made language."

c. Spain: General Work, Criticism, Bibliography   Ranging from bewilderment to tongue-in-cheek scoffing, the responses to currents in
contemporary American literary theory and criticism form the most
intriguing development in Spanish criticism. For instance, Dario Vil-
lanueva in *El polen de ideas: crítica, historia y literatura comparada* (Barcelona: Promociones y Publicaciones Universitarias, 1991) is vexed by
how literature departments in U.S. universities have been stampeded by
Foucault, Derrida, de Man, et al., but he is consoled that "the logomachy
of deconstruction luckily has not reached Spain." Undaunted, Cándido
Pérez Gállego engaged the hurly-burly of contemporary theory and
criticism in "Harold Bloom: Un 'superhombre' de la crítica Americana"
(*Reden* 5 [1992]: 1–10), placing Bloom over Derrida as a "visionary of
textuality" and proclaiming him the "superman of American literary
criticism." Bloom's visit in 1992 occasioned spirited interest and debate
over the crosscurrents of American criticism, exemplified by Fernando
Castañedo's "Harold Bloom: La agonía del lector fuerte" (*RO* 148 [1993]:

128–39). In keeping with the vigorous interest in the problematics of language and narratology, the critical banner of Bakhtin was unfurled to tent Henry James and Paul Bowles, respectively, in María Antonia Alvarez's "Relevancia de la tipología del discurso literario de Bajtín en Henry James," pp. 153–63, and Miguel Angel Muro's "El cronotopo de *El cielo protector,* de Paul Bowles," pp. 347–54, both signal essays in *Bajtín y la literatura,* ed. José Romera Castillo (Visor).

a. Latin America: The Beginnings The serious study of U.S. literature and the national culture that produced it can be traced to José Martí (1853–95), the Cuban revolutionary hero and one of the great men of letters of Latin America. Despite coining the phrase "en las entrañas del monstruo" ("in the belly of the monster") and passionately opposing U.S. imperialism, in the 1880s Martí wrote a series of erudite essays containing generous praise for Longfellow, Emerson, Whitman, and Twain which were collected in *Obra literaria* (Caracas: Biblioteca Ayacucho, 1987). Among other things, Martí started the lionization of Whitman, who remains to this day the most beloved of North American poets. Rubén Darío (1867–1916), the great Nicaraguan poet, novelist, critic, and essayist, similarly extolled the virtues of U.S. literature while at the same time condemning American expansionism. Darío started the long list of poetic homages to Whitman, among which the most famous are his and Neruda's. He affectionately called Poe "the sad swan who has best known dream and death," and his essays coupled Whitman and Twain as "sweet singers of the Yankee soul" (*Obras completas,* 1955).

The next generation marked a turning point in inter-American literary confluence and influence, with Lino Novás Calvo (1905–83) playing a signal role in the translation and dissemination of American writers. The Spanish-born Cuban novelist and critic initiated Hemingway and Faulkner studies in Latin America with "Dos Escritores Americanos" (1933) and "El demonio de Faulkner" (1933); he intrepidly translated Faulkner's *Sanctuary* [*Santuario* (1934)] and assimilated Faulknerian techniques into his own writing. Jorge Luis Borges (1899–1986), the redoubtable Argentinean poet, encyclopedist, and polyglot, emulated Novás Calvo in several remarkable ways; he translated Faulkner's *The Wild Palms* [*Las palmeras salvajes* (1941)], rendered the singular *Introducción a la literatura norteamericana* (1967), and masterfully translated *Leaves of Grass* [*Hojas de hierba*] (1969). Borges's critical survey of American literature, *Introducción a la literatura norteamericana* (1967), is an audacious work; terse, witty, and astute, Borges covers 300 years of American literary history in 92 pages.

b. Latin America: Fiction "The Boom," the phenomenonal literary explosion that occurred in Latin America in the 1960s, has an eclectic relation to American literature. The charter members and leading figures of "The Boom"—José Donoso, Gabriel García Márquez, Mario Vargas Llosa, and Carlos Fuentes—have all written literary criticism or personal accounts on the influence of American writers on their generation. The impact of American writers—Dos Passos, Hemingway, and Faulkner— on the Boom writers has been amply documented, most notably in García Márquez and Vargas Llosa's *La novela en América latina: Díalogo* (1968), Carlos Fuentes's *La nueva novela hispanoamericana* (1969) and *Casa con dos puertas* (1970), and Donoso's *Historia personal del Boom* (1972).

As in Spain, Hemingway and Faulkner form the axis of literary influence, with Faulkner taking the lion's share. In 1950 the eminent Uruguayan novelist and critic Mario Benedetti contributed to the foundation of Faulkner criticism with "Faulkner, novelista de la fatalidad," pp. 247–57 in *Crítica cómplice* (Alianza, 1988). Benedetti's scholarly essay, replete with exegetical footnotes and extrapolations of Sartre and Malraux, concluded that "Faulkner has written the most complex and intricately organized novels possibly in all of American literature." In 1957, the same year that it offered a translation of the famous interview between Faulkner and Jean Stein, the pioneering journal *Sur* published Emilio Sosa López's "El problema del mal en William Faulkner," a penetrating reading of *Absalom, Absalom!* in relation to Faulkner's Manichaean vision and exploration of "the problem of evil." Carlos E. Zavaleta, one of the most reputable Faulkner scholars, made a major contribution with his often cited *William Faulkner, novelista trágico* (1959), which judiciously praises Faulkner's epic novelistic vision while censuring his tortuous prolixity. Luis Domínguez's "Aproximación a William Faulkner" (*Atenea* 396 [1962]: 48–69) is a skillful exercise in literary history that places Faulkner in the first rank of 20th-century writers. Fuentes's *Casa con dos puertas* contains his superb "La novela como tragedia: William Faulkner"; Fuentes's survey of the Faulkner canon and his explanation for Faulkner's influence constitute a major critical work—the single most impressive Faulkner criticism to come out of Latin America.

Congruently, the nature and extent of Faulkner's influence on Latin American writers generated a welter of comparative studies such as Magalí Fernández's "Análisis comparativo de las obras de Agustín Yàñez y William Faulkner," pp. 296–317 in *Homenaje a Agustín Yáñez*, ed. Helmy R. Giacoman (Madrid: Las Américas, 1973); Corina Mathieu-Higginbotham's "Faulkner y Onetti: Una visión de la realidad a través de Jefferson y Santa María" (*Hispanófilia* 61 [1977]: 51–60); and Mercedes M. Robles's "La presencia de 'The Wild Palms,' de William Faulkner, en 'Punta de rieles,' de Manuel Rojas" (*RI* 45 [1979]: 563–71). As would be expected, the Faulkner-García Márquez literary connection has drawn the most attention. In "Faulkner and García Márquez: Una aproximación" (*Sur* 349 [1981]: 71–88) Octavio Corvalan does a workmanlike job of describing Faulknerian themes and narrative styles before examining the Faulknerian elements in García Márquez's *One Hundred Years of Solitude*. José Luis Ramos Escobar's "Desde Yoknapatawpha a Macondo: Un estudio comparado de William Faulkner y Gabriel García Márquez," pp. 287–313 in *En el punto de mira: Gabriel García Márquez*, ed. Ana María Hernández de López (Pliegos, 1985), is one of the best comparative studies. In it, Ramos Escobar demonstrates an excellent command of the Faulkner canon.

Hemingway takes second rank with a similar pattern of influence and critical reception. Carlos Fuentes's critical synopsis of Hemingway, pp. 105–11 in *Casa con dos puertas* and Mario Vargas Llosa's brilliantly succinct comparative study of Hemingway and García Márquez, pp. 150–56 in his massive critical biography, *García Márquez: Historia de un deicidio* (1971), led the way in establishing Hemingway's authority as a major influence. Critics and scholars offered confirmation in a bevy of appreciations and assessments: Mary Cruz's discerning *Cuba y Hemingway en el gran río azul* (1981) delivers the most comprehensive critique of Hemingway's Cuba-related novels. In his collection of essays applying Marxist analysis to U.S. literature and society, *Temas norteamericanos* (1985), José Rodríguez Feo includes "Ernest Hemingway: Una nota discrepante"; surprisingly caustic considering Hemingway's legendary fame and adulation in Cuba, Rodríguez Feo takes to task the American cult of individualism personified by Hemingway and centers on the macho heroics of solitary rebellion and alienation. A series of comparative studies on Hemingway and Latin American writers added to Hemingway's lasting reputation. Among these, Marie J. Peck's "José Pedro Díaz y Hemingway: Una mitología compartida" (*TCrit* 34–35 [1986]: 189–203) applies archetypal criticism in a comparison of *The Old Man and the Sea* and Díaz's *Los fuegos de San Telmo,* noting that both novels have a similar religious imagery and mythic patterns. Aden Hayes's "Hemingway y García Márquez: Tarde y temprano," pp. 53–62 in *Violencia y literatura en Colombia,* ed. Jonathan Tittler (Orígenes, 1989) focuses on the theme of violence to argue that García Márquez assiduously read Hemingway and adopted the "iceberg principle" in some of his short stories. The Colombian novelist-critic Manuel Zapata Olivella chimed in with *Hemingway, el cazador de la muerte* (Bogota: Editorial Arango, 1993); a hybrid narrative combining biography, criticism, and metafiction (Hemingway and the author are the central characters), it is a unique tribute to Hemingway "who inspired Zapata Olivella's life and work" and "who is everyday more and more admired by Latin-Americans."

c. Latin America: Poetry Faulkner and Hemingway joined Whitman to form a triumvirate of American writers. Beset by political strife and beleaguered by countless dictatorships throughout most of this century, Latin America has extended a long and lasting embrace to "the poet of democracy." Fernando Alegría, the most renowned *whitmanista,* contributed the most comprehensive study and caught the expanse and vitality of the Whitmanian legacy in *Walt Whitman en hispanoamérica* (1954), which contains a biography of Whitman, a critique of his philosophy and poetry, and a remarkable chapter on Whitman's influence on Hispanic American poetry. The next generation of readers and Whitman scholars burnished the poet's imposing reputation. Astrid Raby's "Whitman y los victorianos" (*Atenea* 433 [1976]: 33–48) reviews Victorian criticism of Whitman's poetry, his affront to bourgeois respectability, and his role as the apostle of freedom (including erotics and politics), which have never ceased to appeal to Latin American audiences. In "Friso de Whitman" (*Atenea* 435 [1977]: 17–29) Jorge Mendoza is similarly laudatory; building on Borges's and Neruda's estimation of Whitman, he celebrates Whitman as "one of the great voices of world literature." Fernando Alegría returned to the subject in "¿Cuál Whitman? Borges, Lorca, y Neruda" (*TCrit* 22–23 [1981]: 3–12). Alegría's piquant question—"Which Whitman?"—primes his argument that "three Whitmans," or three facets of his poetic vision, inspired and were refracted in three of the great Spanish-language poets of the 20th century. In *Temas norteamericanos* José Rodríguez Feo enfolds Whitman in a Marxist embrace; although the United States failed to follow his democratic humanism, Rodríguez Feo concludes, Whitman's *Leaves of Grass* "still represents one of the most beautiful testaments of love for humanity ever written." Frances R. Aparicio's "Borges y Whitman: Un abrazo panteista" (*Discurso Literario* 2 [1993]: 23–31) assembles a Pan-American transcendentalist trio (Emerson, Whitman, Borges), discusses Whitman's influence on Borges's poetics and offers provocative commentary on Borges's translation of *Leaves of Grass*.

The rest of the critical terrain is dotted by sundry investigations, with noteworthy contributions from critics and scholars who have endeavored to introduce American poets to Latin American audiences. The Venezuelan essayist-critic Ignacio Iribarren-Borges proffered an excellent collection of essays in *Escena y Lenguaje: Sobre teatro, poesía y narrativa* (1988) in which he surveys modern American poetry and evaluates the disparate talents and themes of Ezra Pound, Wallace Stevens, Carl Sandburg, Sylvia Plath, Robert Lowell, and Gwendolyn Brooks.

d. Latin America: General Work, Criticism, Bibliography   Irene Rostago Eytel in "Gestación y revisón canónica: El caso de la literatura norteamericana" (*RChL* 39 [1992]: 135–42) exemplifies scholars' keen interest in the changing definitions of American literature. Duly noting that Native American, African American, Asian American, and Chicano writers have vitalized and expanded the canon, Rostago Eytel sees the "revision and reformation of the canon and literary history of the United States" as a reflection of profound changes in the relations between literature and society. And in keeping with the shifting currents of U.S. literary production and scholarship, *Cuadernos Americanos,* beginning with the January–February 1996 issue, has initiated a series titled "La nueva américa," which is devoted to "the expression of the new America and the United States, multiracial and multicultural."

University of New Mexico

Even more than anthologies with their limited number of pages, the various reference books on the market register the yaw and pitch of the contemporary canon debate. Unfortunately, some of these books seem little more than crass attempts to ride the trade winds of literary fashion. If, as Arthur Schlesinger, Jr., has remarked, we have too much "pluribus" and not enough "unum" nowadays, some commercial publishers are poised to exploit the trend.

American Diversity, American Identity is a perfect case in point. A potpourri of 145 biographical sketches organized into overneat ethnic, regional, and gender classifications, the volume panders to its target audience of cutting-edge reference librarians. All "contributing reviewers" are listed in the front matter, though the specific authors of individual entries are nowhere indicated, presumably to forestall the charge that some contributors are colonizing their subjects. Such figures as Mark Twain, Whitman, Fitzgerald, Morrison, and Adrienne Rich are relegated to the epilogue because they apparently resist easy categorization. (Heaven forbid that Mark Twain is a mere "westerner," Fitzgerald a "midwesterner," Morrison a "bearer of the African American tradition," etc.). Some of the selections defy logic: Why are Lisa Alther and Larry Woiwode included, for example, and Charlotte Perkins Gilman and William Dean Howells omitted? A pair of CD-ROMs issued by Chadwyck-Healey seem vulnerable to a similar charge: *American Poetry Full-Text Database* ($8,995), an omnium-gatherum of more than 35,000 poems, most of them written before 1900, by more than 200 poets; and *Database of African-American Poetry, 1760–1900* ($3,995), containing the oeuvre of some 50 poets, from the familiar (Phillis Wheatley and Paul Laurence Dunbar) to the obscure and neglected (T. T. Purvis and Ann Plato). The publisher boasts that each poem on the first CD costs only about 26 cents. Surely libraries have more economical ways to budget their limited resources than to spend indiscriminately on such reference tools as these.

At the other extreme, the market niche filled by *A Reader's Guide to the Twentieth-Century Novel,* ed. Peter Parker (Oxford), is so slender it may not exist at all. The editor allows that the book "is primarily a work of enthusiasm" rather than "an academic guide to twentieth-century fiction"; that is, it does not presume to be a comprehensive guide. Still, its critical introductions to about 750 English-language novels published between 1900 and 1993 are often as entertaining as party conversation and betray no ideological bent.

Last year David Nordloh reviewed in this space (see *ALS 1994,* pp. 471–72) the first volume of the projected eight-volume edition of the new *Cambridge History of American Literature* under the general editorship of Sacvan Bercovitch. As though to close the frame, volume 8 ("Poetry and Criticism, 1940–1995") appears this year. (The other six volumes will be forthcoming.) Its two sections—"Poetry, Politics, and Intellectuals" by Robert von Hallberg and "Criticism Since 1940" by Evan Carton and Gerald Graff—chronicle the interactions between postwar aesthetic and critical narratives and probe the stress fractures in contemporary American literary study. In remarkably parallel ways, von Hallberg details the "academicization of poetry," and Carton and Graff record the rise of "a vast secular scholasticism" and the institutionalization of various critical establishments. In a breathtaking feat of self-reflection, Carton and Graff even discuss the very *Cambridge History* in which their essay appears. Theirs is a vigorous (if not trenchantly rigorous) defense of such New Americanists as Jane Tompkins and Michael Warner, in which they applaud dissent itself as a critical position. If the monumental(izing) *Literary History of the United States* (1948), ed. Robert Spiller, presumed to reinforce a liberal consensus view of the American canon, the *Cambridge History* works to destabilize that consensus and "teach the conflicts." Much as Emerson declared in "The American Scholar" that each age must write its own books, it is obvious by now that every generation of scholars will write its own American literary history. Despite its ambitious scope and design, however, the *Cambridge History* seems to be on as predictable if different a course as its distant ancestor.

Nearly a decade ago the subtitle ("A Diminished Thing") of a chapter on regionalism in the *Columbia Literary History of the United States* prompted a number of outraged responses by members of the Western Literature Association. However quaint or passé Western regional literature (not simply the western genre) as a field of literary inquiry may now seem, it continues to inspire solid, responsible research. The second, updated edition of *Bibliographical Guide to the Study of Western American Literature* contains 6,500 items on more than 500 western writers from Edward Abbey to Ann Zwinger. This volume is the standard reference tool in the field. The first volume of *Western American Novelists,* ed. Martin Kich (Garland), includes 2,900 items, most of them annotated, on seven mainstream Western writers, among them Walter Van Tilburg Clark, Vardis Fisher, and A. B. Guthrie, Jr. In many cases Kich's annotations are substantial and valuable assessments of published scholarship; too often, however, the bibliography merely lists articles, reviews of first editions, notices of film adaptations, or obituaries. A more specialized volume than the former compilation, it is less valuable precisely to the extent that its reach is limited.

Seventeen of the 22 figures covered in *American Novelists Since World War II* (DLB 152) are dealt with in earlier DLB volumes, in some cases (e.g., Bernard Malamud, Ernest J. Gaines, William Burroughs, Kurt Vonnegut) four or five times. The only five writers in this volume new to the DLB: Tom Wolfe, Robert Stone, Madison Jones, Donald Harington, and Louise Erdrich. Overall, I would say, economy of expression is not a series virtue. *Southern Women Writers,* vol. 12 in the DLB Documentary Series, ed. Mary Ann Wimsatt and Karen L. Rood, focuses on the careers of Flannery O'Connor, Katherine Anne Porter, and Eudora Welty and is a more substantial contribution to scholarship, though with generous excerpts from letters and interviews and distillations of contemporary reviews it seems designed to appeal to advanced undergraduate English majors. On the other hand, *The House of Scribner, 1846–1904,* ed. John Delaney, vol. 13 in the DLB Documentary Series, is a substantial contribution to American publishing history, putting literally hundreds of unpublished documents on the public record. The volume traces the growth of the distinguished New York publishing firm in detail, includes sketches of 36 writers in the Scribner stable, and profiles the various magazines issued by the firm. An exemplary documentary history.

A pair of servicable reference guides to American dramatic literature merit brief mention. *Guide to American Drama Explication,* ed. Rosalie Otero (Hall), is a solid listing of the most significant scholarship published since 1942 on American drama. Otero's compilation errs, if at all, on the side of inclusion. All of the major playwrights are represented, and not a few minor and neglected ones (e.g., George Washington Parke Custis and Douglas William Jerrold). Yvonne Shafer's *American Women Playwrights, 1900–1950* (Peter Lang) contains lengthy biographical sketches of 35 writers from the familiar (Susan Glaspell and Lillian Hellman) to the forgotten and obscure (Sophie Treadwell and Cornelia Otis Skinner). Many figures covered in the volume are admittedly better-known in genres other than theater (e.g., Gertrude Stein and Mae West), though Shafer wisely foregrounds their accomplishments as playwrights. Of related interest: *Oxford Companion to Women's Writing in the United States,* an encyclopedic project with some 800 entries on writers from Edith Abbott to Zitkala-Ša and on topics from abortion to Zionist writing by about 500 contributors.

A pair of useful guides to African American literature and culture also deserve praise. *Bibliographic Guide to Black Studies 1994* (Hall), the most recent in a series of annual subject bibliographies, lists some 20,000 items cataloged during the year by the Schomburg Collection of Negro Literature and History at the New York Public Library. And *The French Reception of African-American Literature: From the Beginnings to 1970,* ed. Michel Fabre (Greenwood), lists and annotates some 1,270 reviews and other published items, most of them in the mainstream French press. Admittedly incomplete, the volume nevertheless will prove indispensable to future researchers.

Contemporary Literary Criticism Yearbook 1994, ed. Christopher Giroux (Gale), features articles on new American authors (e.g., Albert French, Helen Elaine Lee, Anchee Min, and Lisa Shea) and prizewinners (e.g., Edward Albee, William Gaddis, and Ernest Gaines) as well as obituaries of Cleanth Brooks, Alice Childress, and Ralph Ellison. Two of the volume's essays this year are particularly valuable and timely: "Electronic 'Books': Hypertext and Hyperfiction" (pp. 367–404) and "Sylvia Plath and the Nature of Biography" (pp. 433–62).

The third edition of *Cloak and Dagger Fiction,* compiled by Myron J. Smith, Jr., and Terry White (Greenwood), will find a ready market among the aficionados of thrillers. Obviously a labor of love, the volume lists more than 5,800 texts (divided into pre- and post-1940 publications) with appendices devoted to author pseudonyms, recurring characters in series, and "spookspeak," the jargon of espionage. Among the authors represented are a couple of children of Democratic presidents (Margaret Truman, Elliott Roosevelt), a pair of presidential press secretaries (Ron

Nessen, Pierre Salinger), and a trio of Watergate conspirators (E. Howard Hunt, John Ehrlichman, G. Gordon Liddy). What can or should be said of an encyclopedia of literary esoterica that, in addition to Cooper's *The Spy*, Poe's "The Purloined Letter," and James's *The Princess Casamassima*, lists novels by the first sitting U.S. senator in space (Jake Garn), a Kennedy assassination conspiracy theorist (Jim Garrison), and a former Second Lady (Marilyn Quayle)? A glaring omission: former Vice President Spiro Agnew's novel *The Canfield Decision* (1976).

Finally, the late James D. Hart's venerable *Oxford Companion to American Literature* appears this year in its sixth incarnation. Revised and updated by Phillip W. Leininger, the new *Oxford Companion* contains more than 180 new and hundreds of revised entries (of a total of more than 5,000) reflecting recent trends in scholarship. May there ever remain a market for books like this one. It deserves a place on the shelf of every Americanist.

University of New Mexico

Author Index

Subject Index